OAK ISLAND

MYSTERY TREES

and other Forensic Answers

"Compendium"

Book Cover

The book cover was created by Designer and Illustrator Anna Orel. She also created several of the images within the book. Using a jigsaw puzzle motif, several of the photographs, illustrations, and images symbolically represent the varied forensic issues and artefacts analyzed within these two volumes. They include; an original photograph of the tall mystery canopied-trees of Oak Island, taken during the Bowdoin Expedition, circa 1909, an artistic illustration of the Oak Island trees with a Freemason temple by our co-author, Robert W. Cook, and a telescopic photograph of an existing stand of the same canopied-trees recently found on another island. On the back we find a box made of sycamore wood, filled with red clover, a chunk of rotted and decayed oak wood, a listing of the twenty questions asked and answered within these works, and all laying on a bed of coconut coir fiber. Held together by crime scene investigators tape with six black carpenter ants looking for more answers, the cover reflects the efforts to address and solve the Oak Island treasure story and the enigmatic puzzle it is.

San Antonio, Texas

Library of Congress Control Number: 2022905388

Ron & Stephanie –
Who coulda Known so
much about so little!
Love David

Robert W. Cook's 2022 watercolor painting of a Freemason Temple protected by those mysterious canopied trees on the shores of Oak Island. Can you make out Big Tancook island in the background – or, perhaps you can touch the red clover growing in abundance. Is not Oak Island a temple in and of itself?

Oak Island's fuzzy history.
The idea of fuzzy logic or fuzzy math came along not because people did not want accurate numbers or facts, but because they realized that there are few finite things in this world. A perfect example of this is water, which can be described as cold, warm, or hot. It would seem that one degree before freezing into ice would be as "cold" as water could get, and one degree before boiling into steam would be as "hot" as it could get. As for "warm," that's always been a subjective thing. Water actually boils sooner at higher elevation. Something similar is true for freezing water. So there is no exact point at which water freezes or boils everywhere, but there is a typical or average point at which it does, and this is generally accepted as the truth, even though it has been shown to be a fuzzy truth. Fuzzy truth, fuzzy logic, and fuzzy math were adopted in order to take into consideration the minute variables that can change an equation, or even a historical fact, if we could drill down to the absolute truth in the absolute moment, in the absolute point in the Universe, etc. Add "Time" and previous disruption (by Nature and by Man) into the equation and determining the exact history behind any artifact or structure, or anomaly, becomes extremely difficult. Assumptions can be made that are dramatically inaccurate, but they are the most obvious at the time. However, fuzzy history needs to be applied. The same is true with words written in books. Was the previous consulted author fully informed and can we take his or her words verbatim, or were those words based on assumptions made by others or even incorrectly entered information? All of this type of stuff has to be taken into consideration and a few "probablys," "might have beens," and "perhapes" need thrown in as fuzzy qualifiers, in our attempt to discover the "most likely" truth. It's just the way it is - for mathematicians, archeologists, historians, and treasure hunters.

- James A. McQuiston

Author of: *Oak Island Missing Links*; *Oak Island 1632*; *Oak Island Knights*; *Oak Island Endgame*; *Oak Island The Novel;* *Oak Island and the Mayflower*; *Oak Island and New Ross*; *Oak Island Curses, Codes and Secret Societies; and Oak Island Knights Templar and Freemasonry.*

OAK ISLAND, MYSTERY TREES

AND OTHER FORENSIC ANSWERS

VOLUME II,

COMPENDIUM

"What you thought you knew"
- Jackie Santos

BY
DAVID H. NEISEN

CO-AUTHORS
ROBERT W. COOK &
CHRISTOPHER L. BOZE

OCTOBER 2022

Acknowledgements

Though I in no way consider myself worthy of being included in the coterie of *Oak Island Experts* such as Doug Crowell, Les MacPhie, the Lagina Brothers, and authors like James Q. McQuiston, D`Arcy O`Connor, Hammerson Peters and more; surely Joy A. Steele and Gordon Fader are tenured members. In the first volume of *"Oak Island Mystery Trees and other Forensic Answers,"* I have given homage to those who came before this writing and made my research less cumbersome and hopefully, worthwhile.

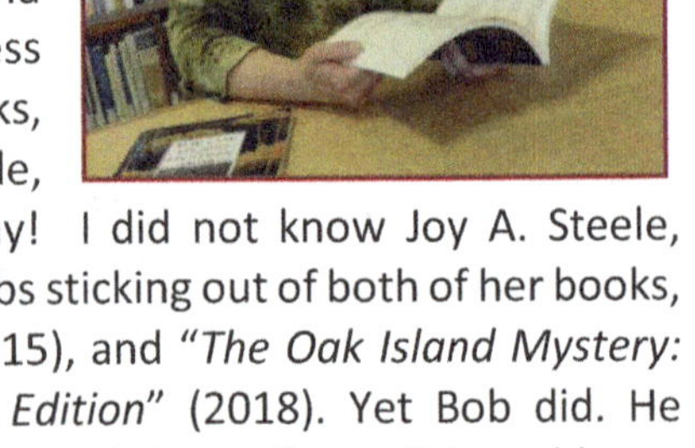

In conjunction with his co-authors, Robert W. Cook, a legend in his own realm of watercolor artistry and graphic expertise, has asked that we again honor Joy A. Steele, now deceased, and Gordon Fader, P.Geo. who's endless knowledge of the region and its rocks, has assisted in correcting this chronicle, while dabbling in botanical taxonomy! I did not know Joy A. Steele, though I own and have hundreds of tabs sticking out of both of her books, *"The Oak Island Mystery: Solved"* (2015), and *"The Oak Island Mystery: Solved, The Final Chapter – Second Edition"* (2018). Yet Bob did. He remembers her as *"one of my favorite people in our "sport."* I would very much liked to have discussed the issues in my book with her. R.I.P. Joy.

Gordon Fader, P.Geo was a name I frequently found in many a Nova Scotia science paper reference list. Remnants of his research are strewn in many chapters and appendices of this writing. Somehow Bob convinced Gordon to put away his rocks, grab a camera, and put on some botanist garb, and search the streets of Halifax to find the tree that does not exist! Truly a very talented man and I do appreciate using his previous work in my book, and especially those superb photos! So thank you both for your impact on us Couch Potatoes, as we attempt to answer our own questions about Oak Island; just as Gordon and Joy have done.

Dedication

Though they do not realize it until much older, we dedicate everything we do to our children. My kids, both adults, are the center of our lives while we become the periphery of theirs. It is how the circle of life goes.

My daughter, Halle, now finishing her graduate studies to become a Physician's Assistant, and her Chemical Engineer husband Kyle, have been more impactful on this product than they realize. She changed everything in her first read of my manuscript, causing me to separate the fun, light, airy exciting part of my writing, and put the boring technical stuff in a second volume. And here we are in Volume II. I am not sure how fun, light, and airy I made the topics of soil settlement, red clover migration, tree species, and coconut coir fiber in the *Book*, but here in the *Compendium* I infused the composition with quips of humor and my amateur perspective to the page, helping readers digest the technical stuff. Kyle corrected my 'old math.' Though honestly, none of his explanations of how to change volume and mass and weight into equations, permeated my brain. He simply offered me the corrections.

As for my son Joshua, a Satellite Engineer in the Army, he has provided the much needed soundboard to my frustration when chasing taxonomic characteristics, identification of Oak Island owners, and my babbling on about Swahili sewn boat variables and their historical use of coconut coir fiber. He seems to instinctively know when to listen and when to ground me in discussion of his mother and the furry family or bring me along with stories of his travels and travails, Army style; something I could reminisce with and completely relate to. I could now fully appreciate his and his sisters collegiate experience, as bibliographies, cited references, and literary styles became my own homework assignments. So it is clear to me if not to them, how much of them is in this effort and how proud I am when they complimented me on completing this goal - *and that I did it!*

Dedicating this effort to Halle and Joshua is part of everything Lisa and I do; and I hope in the future, as they recall the craziness of their dad, especially while researching for this book - they remember that.

Introduction

As you may recall from Volume 1 of "*Oak Island Mystery Trees and other Forensic Answers,*" Volume 2, "*The Compendium*" was to hold all that boring, technical research material our forensic investigation dug up. Shuffled to the website and now provided bound in color in this volume, the *Compendium* is home to the facts as the evidence has been laid out.

It is here where we wiggle into the weeds and prove how we wrangled our determinations. And where you can read and review to wrap your arms around these findings. From there, you can apply this knowledge to your favorite theorem of what went weird on Oak Island. I hope you find the evidence both compelling and cogent. More importantly, we hope you agree it is corroborated and complete.

If not convinced after reading the *Book*, we hope our forensic arguments and the evidence we present in the *Compendium*, can conclusively secure your consideration for your further thought and discussion.

The main thrust of ***this Compendium*** is to research, analyze, and forensically determine what is evidence and from that, what truth can be gleaned regarding these Oak Island specific topics, with the goal to provide the answers to the following questions:

- *What was the species of those unique, canopied trees of Oak Island?*
- *Why were they never felled for valuable timber during this entire saga?*
- *Did those towering, canopied trees cover Oak Island as the legend goes?*
- *Why were those trees on this one island and nowhere else in Nova Scotia?*
- *Did the trees die off one by one... or en masse by disease, ants, or old age?*
- *Why never any mention of the canopied-trees foliage in the autumn?*
- *How many trees did it take to build the platforms within the Money Pit?*
- *Can a timeline of the original depositors be created by studying the rate-of-compaction of soils on top and within the Money Pit?*

- *Can a timeline of the original depositors be created by studying the rate-of-rot of the oak logs making up the platforms within the Money Pit?*
- *When was the Money Pit on Oak Island, filled in?*
- *Why was red clover foreign to being on Oak Island and in Nova Scotia?*
- *Can red clover help determine who was on Oak Island when the Money Pit was filled in?*
- *How much coconut fiber was used in the constructs found on Oak Island?*
- *Where in the world did the coconut fiber come from?*
- *How did the coconut fiber get to Oak Island?*
- *What does the testing of those coconut fibers from Oak Island tell us about their true source and impact on the treasure story?*
- *How much dirt was dug out of the Money Pit and where did it go?*
- *What is true or not about the block and tackle, big oak trees, and the story of digging into the Money Pit in 1795?*
- *Using the forensic analysis from this research, can we postulate a When, a How, and a Who to the Oak Island saga? And will this lead us to a What?*

I introduce this non-fiction composition to answer these questions and follow their evidential trail to learn WHEN and HOW. This in turn, helps add to our deduction of the probable WHO, and the WHO leads us to the WHY. No doubt, the 20th question of WHAT, can ultimately be answered.

Additionally, this book was written not to outright *solve* the Oak Island Mystery, but to explain the impacts of determinable forensic findings which may lead to that final goal.

Perhaps you find the research missing certain aspects or approaches which you believe could have better impacted the outcome. Perhaps you have questions seeking answers through other engineering, botanical, or different disciplines. However you receive the efforts expressed in this two volume work, positively or negatively, we hope it promotes you taking the next steps in the research to answer your questions or correct the answers provided here. Each bit of evidence can piece together the puzzle, advancing the understanding of the image of what happened on Oak Island. So please join the fray, correct me whenever possible and ask yourself – *why not?*

NOTE

For those of you arborists, botanists, ecologists, and dendrochronologists – *warning!* I have bastardized the proper usage of Latin and common names for tree species throughout this book. In doing my research, I quickly ran into scenarios where the word "oak" was not only used as a species name, a group name, a product name, and a familial name for wood-type features – but as a descriptive name. I was getting confused. Likewise, their Latin names were presented in wide variation such as "Q. rubra," "Quercus rubra," and with other additional determiners such as "Quercus rubra L.," spanning over the hundreds of years of biological research literature. Hybrids confounded the confused. However, since they are not germane to our 1795 chronology, these descriptors are not used at all. Not wanting to confuse the general public more than I had become, I decided to follow the Latin name construct when it helped to distinguish the plethora of unique tree species being discussed. As with common name titles like black spruce, or fir, or burr oak, or bur oak... I decided to always capitalize both common names when discussing a species specifically. So within this book, you will see "Black Spruce," "Fir," or "Northern Red Oak" when those species are specifically discussed. Therefore, indulge me if you can and go for the *"heartwood"* of the issue and not *"shake like a leaf"* as I go *"against the grain."*

-REMINDER-

TEMPORARY
ONLINE REPOSITORY ACCESS
for
"OAK ISLAND: MYSTERY TREES"
BOOK OWNERS

The *Compendium* of sixteen APPENDICES, made of the assemblage of more than 514 textural pages, hundreds of original black/white and colored photographs, scientific illustrations and graphs, and an anthology of comments, conversations, calculations, and conclusions revolving around the creation and printing the book *"Oak Island, Mystery Trees and other Forensic Answers,"* is provided as a bonus and free to you the owner of this product. For access, go to the website,

"www.oakislandmysterytrees.com"

This is the repository of the material within this Volume II color print edition. It is available for you to read and review if you have legally purchased this product, allowing you access to the website, for however long it remains active.

Upon searching and locating the website, when prompted, enter the passcode

"COIR"

In CAPITAL letters to enter, peruse, read, and review all the materials and photographs which were used to base the forensic determinations discussed in the Book and presented here. The website has the same material as in the second volume of the two-volume complete set, and is called the...

"Oak Island, Mystery Trees and other Forensic Answers - Compendium."

This *Compendium* looks similar to this volume but its pages are in color, doing justice to all the colored images related to the forensic research summarized in this volume. The Compendium volume is available by retailers and wherever you purchased the first volume. We hope you enjoy both volumes and the website.

Glossary

ABACA: (Musa textilis) Species of Banana plant uniquely native to the Philippines. Used to make many items.

AMS: Acceleration Mass Spectrometry process.

ALKEBULAN: Ancient name for the African continent.

ANDESITE: Name of fine-grained rocks between granite and basalt.

ANGIOSPERM: Any of the flower-producing plants, producing seeds within "fruits."

ANHYDRITE: A soft, neutral, grayish, or light purple colored, rock which can evaporite when reacting to water, or saltwater. Most common with strata of gypsum sedimentary rock.

AUSTRONESIANS: Of or relating to Austronesia or its peoples, languages, or cultures. A member of any of the peoples speaking these languages. First people to invent oceangoing sailing technologies (catamarans, outrigger boats, lashed-lug-sewn boat building, and the crab claw sail), which enabled their islands of the Indo-Pacific.

AZORES: An archipelago of nine volcanic islands, located in the center of the Atlantic Ocean. An autonomous region of Portugal.

BATHYMETRIC: Bathymetry is the study of the "beds" or "floors" of water bodies, including the ocean, rivers, streams, and lakes.

BEACH RIDGE: Elevated formation of sand or other material running parallel to a shoreline.

BILGE: The bilge of a ship or boat is the part of the hull that would rest on the ground if the vessel were unsupported by water. The "turn of the bilge" is the transition from the bottom of a hull to the sides of a hull. Internally, the bilges is the lowest compartment on a ship.

BIOME: A uniquely identifiable ecology or natural area or habitat.

BOLE: The main stem of a tree; usually covered with bark; the bole is usually the part of that is commercially useful for lumber.

BLOCKHOUSE: A fortified building, jail, or meeting place made of squared timbers with a projecting upper story.

BLOWDOWN: Examples of Windthrow or Wind snap.

BRACKISH: Generally understood that brackish groundwater is water that has a greater dissolved-solids content than occurs in freshwater, but not as much as seawater.

BRECCIA: Rock/boulders composed of sharp-angled fragments embedded in a fine-grained matrix. A conglomerate in which the fragments, instead of being rounded or water-worn, are angular.

BRYOPHYTE: Bryophytes is the informal group name for mosses, liverworts, and hornworts. They are non-vascular plants, which means they have no roots or vascular tissue, but instead absorb water and nutrients from the air through their surface (e.g., their leaves).

BROWSER: Foraging animals which are picky and selective in what parts of a plant or which plant to eat.

BUTT LOG: A log cut from the bole immediately above the stump.

CANOPY: Cover of branches and foliage formed by the trees crown of foliage. Crown.

CAREENS: To deliberately list a vessel so that part of its bottom was exposed for caulking, cleaning, & repairing.

CAVINGS: Pertaining to small cave-ins within a tunnel or shaft. The collapse of smaller side walls or tops of tunnels that have not been cribbed effectively.

CENTRAL LEADER: The dominant upright branch which leads the trees growth height, while other branches appear secondary and grow at angles.

CLASTICS: Pertaining to rock or sediment composed mainly of fragments derived from preexisting rocks or minerals and moved from their place of origin. The term indicates sediment sources that are both within and outside the depositional basin.

CLAYEY: Any soil sample which contains at least 54% clay.

COCONUT CUPS: Were once also known as Treens (see definition). Often religious items in the possession of popes, cardinals, archbishops and bishops and the wealthier of society. Made from the shell of a coconut and most frequently adorned with jewels and precious metals. As in the procession of the Bishop of Durham in 1259 AD. Also sometimes called "coconut decanters with some found in Constantinople. These artefacts are now referred to as "Masers."

COFFERDAM: A cofferdam is a watertight, temporary, dam-like structure that is installed to enclose an area that is submerged under water to create dry conditions for workers to carry out their work. Also known as caissons, these temporary structures are used in trenchless technology where deep installations are involved or the soil is water bearing.

COIR: The outer protective husk and fibers or exocarp of the coconut, which shields the seed (nut) until time for germination. This does not include the nut (which we know as the coconut) but all the organic material outside the nut and within the exocarp (outer skin).

COIR FIBER: Also known as coco coir, coco fiber, and coir fiber. The end by-product fibers of retting coconut husks and used for manufacturing of cordage, netting, bedding, fabrics, plant medium and many more items. These fibers are chemically altered during the retting process to give the coir fibers their outstanding characteristics.

CONNATE: From the Latin *connatus* meaning 'born together', water that has remained trapped in a sedimentary rock since the original sediments were laid down in that water, prior to lithification. Connate water may be very old and saline.

CONTINENTAL SHELF: A shallow submarine plain of varying width forming a border to a continent and typically ending in a comparatively steep slope to the deep ocean floor.

COPRA: The meat or white edible internal flesh or mesocarp of the coconut seed (called the nut, or fruit).

CONIFERS: A tree that produces cones or certain berries. Most are evergreens with some exceptions. Soft resinous softwood. Any tree that produces seeds in cones.

CONIFEROUS TREE: Commonly called softwood or evergreen, trees that have cones and keep their needles throughout the winter, except for tamarack. Trees that are conifers.

COPSE: A thicket or grove of small trees, bushes.

CORDAGE: A general term for ropes and cables.

CRADLE HILL: Known also as "Cradle and knoll Topography." Currently called, "Tree Top Pit Mound Topography": The formation of pits when trees fall from windthrow or other causes and their root ball is torn or lifted from below ground, creating a pit or depression or hollow. Overtime, multiple occurrences cause a topography which appears to be multiple mounds and pits.

CRIBBING: A constructed frame, in this reference by lumber, used as a protective erect shell to allow miners access within a shaft or tunnel.

CROP ROTATION: The agricultural protocol to rotate various crop farming on a specific plot of land, and to include fallow or non-planting periods to maintain the health of the soil within that plot of land.

CULLING: Removing unwanted or undesirable plants from a landscape.

DAMASKS: Damask is a reversible figured fabric of silk, wool, linen, cotton, or synthetic fibers, with a pattern formed by weaving. Damasks are woven with one warp yarn and one weft yarn, usually with the pattern in warp-faced satin weave and the ground in weft-faced or sateen weave. Twill damasks include a twill-woven ground or pattern.

DEAD CARBON DIOXIDE: Volcanic eruptions release large quantities of CO2 which contain no C14, diluting the ratio of C12 to C14 in the atmosphere. This is called the "Dead carbon dioxide." This variance can alter the dating of radiocarbon-dating of vegetation where volcanic erupted debris is located as well as in the atmosphere.

DECIDUOUS TREE: Commonly referred to as hardwoods or broad leaf trees, in most cases, they lose their leaves in the fall.

DENDROLOGY: The science and study of wooded plants, specifically their taxonomic classifications.

DETRITUS: A collective term for rock and mineral coarse fragments occurring in sediments, which are detached or removed by mechanical means (e.g. disintegration, abrasion) and derived from pre-existing rocks and moved from their place of origin. Compare - clastic, epiclastic, pyroclastic.

DBH: Diameter of a tree measured at breast height (4.5 ' above ground).

DOLOMITE: A carbonate sedimentary rock consisting chiefly of (more than 50 percent by weight or by areal percentages under the microscope) the mineral dolomite.

DRIFTER: Individual buoys set afloat in water to track currents, salinity, speed and other datasets.

DRUMLIN: Piled overburden in an elongated or oval hill of glacial drift, creating hills, islands, or topographical relief above the normal terrain.

DRUPE: In botany, a stone-fruit; fruit in which the outer part of the pericarp becomes fleshy or softens like a berry, while the inner hardens like a nut, forming a stone with a kernel, as the plum, cherry, apricot, and peach. A fruit consisting of pulpy, coriaceous, or fibrous exocarp, without valves, containing a nut or stone with a kernel.

DUFF: The shallow layer of organic soil and litter of the forest floor which lies over the general mineral soil.

DUNNAGE: Loose or moveable material like boards, partitions, mats, blankets, planks or netting used to secure cargo from shifting, tipping, getting wet or damaged, while in a hold of a ship.

EDDY: A water current moving contrary to the direction of the main current, especially in a circular motion.

EEL GRASS: A member of the Zosteraceae family, which is spread worldwide. It exists only in saltwater environments. It is of little economic importance but was once used as packing and for cushion stuffing. A tidewater marine plant.

EMOLUMENTS: A payment for a job, employment, or grant of land; whereas the payment is made in cattle, livestock, harvested grains, or produce, and can include items made, milled, or woven.

EPICORMIC BRANCHING: Branches that grow out of the main stem of a tree from buds produced under the bark. Severe epicormic branching increases knottiness and reduces lumber quality.

ERRATICS: A rock fragment carried by glacial ice, or by floating ice (ice-rafting), and subsequently deposited at some distance from the outcrop from which it was derived, and generally, though not necessarily, resting on bedrock or sediments of different lithology. Coarse fragments range in size from a pebble to a house-size block.

EVAPORITE DEPOSITS: Are rocks or deposits precipitated from saturated surface or near-surface brines by hydrologies driven by solar evaporation.

EVERGREEN: (in reference to Oak species) Oaks which have evergreen growth habits, can be considered to be a type of oak tree, only as far as that they are in an evergreen type of oak class.

EXFILTRATION: Refers to a loss of water form a drainage system as the result of percolation, absorption, or reverse flow.

EXOCARP: The outermost layer of the pericarp of fruits; the skin or epicarp.

EXTIRPATED: Having reached a state of population, where the species is not growing in an area, close to extinction.

FELLING: The cutting of standing trees.

F.I.F.O.: An inventory method assuming the oldest products in a company's inventory are to be sold first. The costs associated with those older products are the ones used in calculating the cost to the buyer.

FILIPINO: People who are native to or citizens of the country the Philippines.

FISHERY: Either the enterprise of raising or harvesting fish, building where fish are processed for sail, or today, known as the site where fishing is performed. Fishing ground.

FLOATON: Floating islands of organic material, usually made of pumice and other sea-borne plants & debris.

FLOTSAM: Debris in the water that was not deliberately thrown overboard, often as a result from a shipwreck or accident.

FRENCH DRAIN: A construct to manage surface water and groundwater. With most French drains, the idea is to take water that could threaten a structure and move it to a place where it is no longer a threat. Usually a subterranean or trenched waterway, often filled with rocks or methods to keep soils from being eroded.

GEOENGINEER: The subfield of engineering concerned with designing and constructing tunnels, mines, and other human-designed geologic structures within and on earth. The artificial manipulation of the environments of the earth, especially as a means of counteracting global warming.

GEOPETAL: (geopedal) A feature in a rock that allows the observer to determine which direction was up in the past.

G.I.G.O.: Acronym for Garbage In, Garbage Out.

GIN SYSTEM: It was used at the head or a shaft or pit to raise coal, dirt, or spoils to the surface. Once excavated, dirt or material was hauled up by raising a container by a rope attached to a rope drum that was turned by the horses in the gin.

GLORYHOLE: A large hole, either at the surface or underground. When used to describe a surface feature the term is often derogative, thereby suggesting a large excavation made in an irresponsible and non-engineered fashion.

GRABENS: a portion of the earth's crust, bounded on at least two sides by faults, which has dropped downward in relation to adjacent portions.

GRAVING: The practice of cleaning a hull's bottom by burning barnacles, grass, and other foul material preparatory to recoating it with tar, Sulphur, etc. The vessel was careened or drydocked to perform this task.

GRAZZER: Foraging animals which are not selective when eating – cattle, sheep, horses.

GREATER ANTILLES: The Greater Antilles is a grouping of the larger islands in the Caribbean Sea, including Cuba, Hispaniola, Puerto Rico, Jamaica, and the Cayman Islands. Six island states share the region of the Greater Antilles in total, with Haiti and the Dominican Republic sharing the island of Hispaniola.

GREEN TIMBER: Also known as 'wet timber' is newly felled and is 50-60% of dry timber strength. Humid conditions underground promote decay. Timber from which the bark is removed has a longer life than the unpeeled variety.

GYPSUM: A widely distributed mineral consisting of hydrous calcium sulfate: $CaSO_4 \cdot H_2O$. It is the commonest sulfate mineral and is frequently associated with halite and anhydrite in evaporites, forming thick, extensive beds, especially in rocks of Permian and Triassic age.

GYRE: An endless, circular movement of water on the side of a stronger flow of water. Large water system of rotating ocean currents

HACKLE: To remove any unwanted fibers or material by using paddling, combing, or rubbing to further align the fibers into a continuous sliver for spinning.

HALIFAX GROUP: A slate-rich Acacia Brook Formation and overlying metasandstone-dominated Bear River Formation. Units in the overlying Halifax Group include the black slate-rich Cunard Formation and overlying grey slate-dominated Feltzen Formation. The upper part of the Government Point Formation farther east has yielded early Middle Cambrian trilobite fossils of Acado-Baltic affinity.

HAMMERGRAB: A device used on jobs where drilling has to be carried out free of vibrations or where partially cased or uncased drilled shafts are to be produced. The large dead weight in conjunction with the high closing force ensures maximum efficiency. The hydraulic turning device enables the grab to be turned ± 100 degrees to ensure calibration of the borehole. Device grabs loose material within shaft.

HANKS: A skein, as of threat or yarn. A definite length of thread or yarn looped onto a board, coiled into predetermined lengths, or knotted.

HARD MAST: Refers to hard coverings, like acorns, pinecones, hickory nuts, walnuts. See MAST.

HAWSER: A heavy rope or cable made of Manila hemp and used in mooring, warping, or kedging. Attaching a ship to a wharf bollard.

HOLOCENE HIGHSTAND: The maximum flooding surface and the overlying sequence boundary. Progradation results in basinward downlapping onto the maximum flooding surface. Basin centers may still be sediment starved if shelves are broad. Coastal depositional systems tend to be wave to fluvially dominated, thin, and widespread.

HYDROLOGY: A science dealing with the properties, distribution, and circulation of water on and below the earth's surface and in the atmosphere.

HYGRADING: Taking best quality trees, leaving the rest. Hygrading is the slow destruction of a forest via removing the higher quality trees and leaving the poorest quality trees. Hygrading is one of the main forest ailments that foresters fight against.

HYGROSCOPICITY: The capacity of a product or material to react to the moisture content of the air by absorbing or releasing water vapor. The significance of the absorption or release of water vapor is the water content. The water content is the percentage of the total mass of a product constituted by water.

INFLORESCENSE: The arrangement of flowers in a cluster on the stem of various plants. The arrangement helps to facilitate sexual reproduction in various ways.

IN SITU: "on site" or "in position." It can mean "locally", "on the premises", or "in place" to describe where an event takes place and is used in many different contexts. For example, in geology or biology, *in situ* may describe the way a measurement is taken, that is, in the same place the phenomenon is occurring without isolating it from other systems or altering the original conditions of the test.

IRON MONGER: A dealer in ironware or other hardware. Seller of products made my blacksmiths or foundries.

JAGGERY: A course, brown sugar made from the sap of palm trees or cane using evaporation, then often formed into bricks or cakes. From Portuguese *"jagara."*

JETSAM: Debris that was deliberately thrown overboard by a crew of a ship in distress, most often to lighten the ship's load.

KARST: A kind of topography formed in limestone, gypsum, or other soluble rocks by dissolution, and that is characterized by closed depressions, sinkholes, caves, and underground drainage. Various types of karst can be recognized depending upon the dominant surface features: karst dominated by closed depressions (sinkhole karst – temperate climates; cockpit karst – humid tropical climates), closed depressions and large rivers (fluviokarst), bare rock dominated by dissolution joints (pavement karst), tropical cone-, tower- or domed-hills (kegel karst), or karst thinly mantled with glacial drift (glaciokarst), etc.

KRUMMHOLZ: Trees severely stunted due to ice, severe winds and salt spray.

LAMBANOG: A traditional Filipino distilled palm liquor made from coconut palm sap. It is derived from tubâ that has been aged for at least 48 hours. It originates from Luzon island in the northern Philippines. It is commonly described as "coconut vodka" due to its clear to milky white color and high alcohol content.

LATERAL ROOT: Root system which emanate horizontally from the tree, not far below the soil level.

LEADER: The main shoot of a tree. Will form the trunk as the tree grows

LEOPOLDNIA: A mostly monoecious genus of flowering plant in the palm family from northern South America, where they are known as jará palm or pissava palm. The two known species are commercially important, especially L. piassaba, which yields sustenance and construction material. The genus is named for Maria Leopoldina, archduchess of Austria, and Brazilian empress.

LESSER ANTILLES: The Lesser Antilles are a group of islands in the Caribbean Sea. Most of them are part of a long, partially volcanic island arc between the Greater Antilles to the north-west and the continent of South America. The islands of the Lesser Antilles form the eastern boundary of the Caribbean Sea where it meets the Atlantic Ocean.

LIGNICOLOUS FUNGI: Types of fungi which destroy wood, Brown, White and Soft rot fungus.

LIMBERS: Watercourses or channels alongside or central to the keel or keelson, through which water could drain into the pump well.

LIMB SHEAR: The break or loss of a limb due to stress or force, like wind or snow.

LITHOLOGY: The study of the make-up of boulders

MACROPHYTE: An aquatic plant that grows in or near water and is either emergent, submergent, or floating. Floating, aquatic, hyperaccumulating plants absorb or accumulate contaminants by its roots, while the submerged plants accumulate metals by their whole body.

MANILLA GRASS: *(Zoysia matrella)* commonly known as Manila grass, is a species of mat-forming, perennial grass native to temperate coastal southeastern Asia and northern Australasia, from southern Japan, Taiwan, and southern China south through Thailand, Indonesia, Malaysia, and the Philippines to northern Australia, and west to the Cocos Islands in the eastern Indian Ocean.

MAPPILLA: A community of people who live in the Laccadive Islands off the southwestern coast of India, and part of the Indian State of Kerala. Term mappilla is a combination of two words: maha, which means great, and pilla, which is an endearing term that means child.

MAST: The reproductive bodies of plants and trees. Refers to the shell or covering of such.

MEANDERS: Water current in a winding path analogous to troughs and ridges in atmospheric jet streams.

MERLIGASH: Name of settlement which became Lunenburg.

MESOCARP: The edible part of the fruit with a pulp rich in fatty acids, amino acids, and vitamins. The middle layer of the pericarp of a fruit, between the endocarp and the exocarp. 'The fruit is a one-seeded drupe consisting of a fleshy exocarp and mesocarp and a hard endocarp that is united with the seed coat.

MESOSCALE ACTIVITY: Mesoscale is the study of phenomena with typical spatial scales between 10 and 1000 km. Examples of mesoscale phenomena include ocean currents, thunderstorms, gap winds, downslope windstorms, land-sea breezes, and squall lines. Many of the weather phenomena that most directly impact human activity occur on the mesoscale.

METAGRAYWACKE: A derived term of greywacke. A hard dark sandstone with poorly sorted angular grains of quartz, feldspar, and small rock fragments in a compact, clay-fine matrix.

METASILTSTONE: A metamorphosed sedimentary rock called siltstone. Since it has been metamorphosed, the prefix meta- is added to the rock name. The rock contains thin layers of clay and silt sized sediment.

MESTIZOS: (See Sangley)

MISSISSIPPIAN WINDSOR FORMATION: Vast marine evaporite deposits that currently have no modern analogues and remain of the most enigmatic of chemical sedimentary rocks. This group (ca 345 Ma), Maritimes Basin, Atlantic Canada is a saline giant that consists of two evaporite-rich sedimentary sequences that are subdivided into five subzones.

MUSHAMUSH: Is a lake and river aquatic region in the center of Lunenburg County. This area was an integral part of the Mi`kmaw territory. The area of today's Mahone Bay was called Mushamush because the river and lake system was known as Mushamush and empties into Mahone Bay Harbor.

MYRMECOLOGIST: A branch of entomology which specializes with ants.

NEAF: New England Acadian Forest ecoregion or biome.

OAK EVERGREEN: Live oak name given to different oak species have evergreen growth habits. Thus evergreen oaks (live oaks) can be considered to be a type of oak tree, only as far as that they are an evergreen type of oak.

O HORIZON: The upper layer of the topsoil which is mainly composed of organic materials such as dried leaves, grasses, dead leaves, small rocks, twigs, surface organisms, fallen trees, and other decomposed organic matter. This horizon of soil is often black, brown, or dark brown in color.

OROGENY: Process of mountain formation, especially by a folding and faulting of the earth's crust.

OVERBURDEN: Rock or soil overlying a mineral deposit, archaeological site, or other underground feature.

OVERSTORY: The higher foliage canopy of dominating trees in a stand of trees.

PACHYDERM: Any of various nonruminant mammals (such as an elephant, a rhinoceros, or a hippopotamus) of a former group (*Pachydermata*) that have hooves or nails resembling hooves and usually thick skin; especially : elephant.

PALYGORSKYTE: A type of Attapulgite clay, prized by Mayan culture.

PEDOLOGY: Study of soils formation, evolution, and theoretical frameworks through which to understand a soil body in context of the natural environment.

PHYTOGEOGRAPHY: The study of the geographic distribution of plants; correlated with zoogeography.

PHYTOPATHOLOGY: The science of plant diseases, an account of the diseases to which plants are liable; mycology.

PLANK: A piece of lumber (timber) rectangular in shape and thicker than a board, which is 1-1.5 inches thick and more than 4 inches wide.

PLASTICITY: The ability to be modified into a different shape or be shaped. The propensity of a solid material to undergo permanent deformation.

PLEISTOCENE DEPOSITS: The Pleistocene is the geological epoch that lasted from about 2,580,000 to 11,700 years ago, spanning the earth's most recent period of repeated glaciations.

POLE: Unit of measurement, 1 pole = 198", 300 poles = 1 mile. 5.5 yards. Equal to a perch. Not related to forestry.

POLE STAND: A stand of trees made up of pole timbers, which have 4 to 10 inches DBH growth.

POMOLOGY: The study of fruit, specifically the science of growing fruit and nuts.

PORPHERY: An igneous rock texture in which large crystals ae set within a very fine-grained matrix. Often a dark Swedish granite with an olive tinge, as described on OI.

PRIVATEER: A captain or commander or one of the crew of a privately owned vessel authorized by a government during wartime to attack and capture enemy vessels. This armed vessel was licensed to practice piracy for the betterment of the permitted government, and it carried Letters of marque showing authorization for such maritime behavior.

PUDDLED CLAY: Clay that is deliberately wetted and reworked by mechanical means to obtain a plasticity suitable form forming plugs, seals and caulking.

PUMP WELL: The cavity or compartment in the bottom of a hull, usually near amidships, where bilgewater collected and from which it was pumped out or bailed. Wells ranged from simple sumps between frames to watertight compartments extending the full height of the hold.

QUARTERNARY: The Quaternary is the current and most recent of the three periods of the Cenozoic Era in the geologic time scale of the International Commission on Stratigraphy. It follows the Neogene Period and spans from 2.588 ± 0.005 million years ago to the present.

QUERCUS: The genus Latin name for most "oak" tree classifications. Contains over 600 species within class.

RAISED BEACH: An area of land above the shore that is higher than the tideline.

RAN: In Norse mythology, Rán is a goddess and a personification of the sea. Rán and her husband Ægir, a jötunn who also personifies the sea, have nine daughters, who personify waves. The goddess is frequently associated with a net, which she uses to capture sea-goers.

RED OAK TREE: (Quercus rubra) is a member of the oak family that is deciduous. Known as Northern Red Oak.

RED OAK WOOD: Broad 'red oak group' (black oak, blackjack oak, pin oak, northern pin oak and shingle oak. This group is characterized by having bristles or points on the leaf lobes and acorns which mature in two growing seasons and sprout in the spring after maturity. Usually a lighter in weight, less hard than white oak wood.

RED CLOVER. *(Trifolium pretense)* A member of the Legumes family. Red flowers. Adds nitrogen, phosphorus, and potash back into the soil revitalizing it. Also a forage plant.

RESIN: Thick hydrocarbon liquids exuded by many members of the plant kingdom including a large number of the world's tree species. Tree resin plays an extremely important function in trees by rapidly sealing over wounds used as introductory pathways by invading insects and fungal disease agents. Also known as sap, pitch, rosin, amber or gum.

RESINOUS: Has or produces lots of resin, rosin, or sap. See RESIN.

RETTED: An old process whereby coconuts have the seed (nut removed) from the husk sack, and then soaked for +10 months in saltwater. Then beaten so it degrades into fibers. Which are dried and sorted for production.

RHIZOMES: In botany and dendrology, a rhizome is a modified subterranean plant stem that sends out roots and shoots from its nodes. Rhizomes are also called creeping rootstalks or just rootstalks. Rhizomes develop from axillary buds and grow horizontally. The rhizome also retains the ability to allow new shoots to grow upwards.

SANGLEY: Sangley and Mestizo de Sangley are archaic terms used in the Philippines to describe a person of pure overseas Chinese ancestry and mixed Chinese and native Filipino ancestry respectively during the Spanish Colonial Era in the Philippines.

SARGASSUM SUDS: Large, pelagic mats of *Sargassum* in the Sargasso Sea act as one of the only habitats available for ecosystem development; this is because the Sargasso Sea lacks any land boundaries. The Sargassum patches with a novel phosphodiesterase enzyme, produces suds which are used by bacteria to unstick themselves from seaweed. The bacteria release an enzyme which breaks down the sticky molecules (suds), naturally present on the seaweed surface act as a refuge for many species in different parts of their development, but also as a permanent residence for endemic species that can only be found living on and within the *Sargassum*.

SCOTIAN SHELF: A geological formation, part of the Continental shelf, located southwest of Nova Scotia, Canada. It covers an area of 120,000 square kilometers, is 700 kilometers long and ranges in width from 120 to 240 kilometers. It has an average depth of 90 meters.

SEA STEADING: Seasteading is the concept of creating permanent dwellings at sea, called seasteads, in international waters outside the territory claimed by any government. No one has yet created a structure on the high seas that has been recognized as a sovereign state.

SEA WRACK: Part of the common names of several species of seaweed in the family Fucaceae. It may also refer more generally to any seaweeds or seagrasses that wash up on beaches and may accumulate in the wrack zone.

SILVICULTURE: The art and science of controlling the establishment, growth, composition, health, and quality of forests and woodlands to meet the diverse needs and values of landowners and society such as wildlife habitat, timber, water resources, restoration, and recreation on a sustainable basis.

SINKHOLE: A hole that has been created by solution of water-soluble rock which overlaying soil has collapsed.

SISAL: The botanical name *Agave sisalana*, is a species of flowering plant native to southern Mexico but widely cultivated and naturalized in many other countries. It yields a stiff fibre used in making rope and various other products.

SLOOP: A single-masted, fore-and-aft-rigged sailing vessel, with or without a bowsprit, having a jib-headed or gaff mainsail, the latter sometimes with a gaff topsail, and one or more headsails.

SLUICE: Artificial channel for conducting water with a gate or valve to regulate flow.

SMACK: A smack was a traditional fishing boat used off the coast of Britain and the Atlantic coast of America for most of the 19th century.

SNAG: Standing dead trees.

SOFT MAST: Refers to soft coverings, like melons, apples, droops. See MAST.

SSSA: Soil Science Society of America.

STAND: A group of trees, with similarities in species composition, height/diameter distribution, and age composition.

STOWAGE: In nautical terminology, stowage is the amount of room available for stowing materials aboard a ship. The act of stowing cargo with cargo holds.

STULL: Platforms of timbers between levels for strengthening the mine by supporting the walls, and for storing ore and depositing wall rock and waste materials.

SUBAQUEOUS: Formed, living, or occurring under water.

SUPERFICIAL SOIL: Glacial clayey till of silty sand and clay.

SURFICIAL GEOLOGY: Refers to the study of landforms and the unconsolidated sediments that lie beneath them. The majority of the unconsolidated sediments found at the land surface were deposited during the late Wisconsin glaciation, 21,000 to 13,600 years ago.

SYNCLINES: In structural geology, a syncline is a fold with younger layers closer to the center of the structure, whereas an anticline is the inverse of a syncline.

TANNIN: Found commonly in the bark of trees, wood, leaves, buds, stems, fruits, seeds, roots, and plant galls. Tannins help to protect the individual plant species and is stored in the bark of trees and protect the tree from being infected by bacteria or fungi.

TAP ROOT: A deep root growing down into the ground which helps anchor the tree and maintain a water supply in dry soils.

TEPHROCHRONOLOGY: Is a geochronological technique that uses discrete layers of tephra — volcanic ash from a single eruption—to create a chronological framework in which paleoenvironmental or archaeological records can be placed.

THOR HEYERDAHL: a Norwegian adventurer and ethnographer with a background in zoology, botany, and geography. Heyerdahl is notable for his Kon-Tiki expedition in 1947, in which he sailed 8,000 km across the Pacific Ocean in a hand-built raft from South America to the Tuamotu Islands.

TODDY: A milky-white sour alcoholic drink made from fermented coconut milk.

TREE CROWN: See Canopy.

TREEN: The coconut shell was once known or referred to, when in the form of gold or silver mounted cups, drinking flasks and other objects which are called treen by antiquarians. Between 1250 and 1800 records show that these items were found in cathedrals and in castles from the Tyrol to Scotland. The term Treen is not a reference to handcrafted or homemade wooden house wares smaller than a spinning wheel. See Coconut Cups or Masers.

TRIASSIC PERIOD: The Triassic is a geologic period and system which spans 50.6 million years from the end of the Permian Period 251.902 million years ago, to the beginning of the Jurassic Period 201.36 Mya. The Triassic is the first and shortest period of the Mesozoic Era

TUBA: A Filipino alcoholic beverage created from the sap of coconut palm trees. During the Spanish colonial period, tubâ was introduced to Guam, the Marianas, and Mexico via the Manila Galleons.

TUCKAMORE: See 'Krummholz.' Specifically related to trees located in Newfoundland.

TURBUDITES: Sediments which are transported and deposited by density flow, not by tractional or frictional flow. The distinction is that, in a normal river or stream bed, particles of rock are carried along by frictional drag of water on the particle (known as tractional flow).The water must be travelling at a certain velocity in order to suspend the particle in the water and push it along.

UMBRELLA PINE: Known as Rome Pine, Italian Pine, or Stone Pine. Lives up to 180 years.

UNDERSTORY: The smaller trees, saplings, shrubs, and vegetation that grow beneath the large trees in woods or forests which make up the overstory or canopy.

VICTUALER: Someone or entity that provisions an army, a navy, or a ship with food, material or sundry goods as contracted or appointed.

VORTICITY: The measurement of the rate of rotational spin in a fluid. The state or condition of the rotating portions of a fluid in which vortex-motion occurs.

VUG: A small cavity in a rock or vein, often with a mineral lining of different composition from that of the surrounding rock. A hollow in a rock or in a lode. A geode. Small to medium-sized cavity inside rock that may be formed through a variety of processes.

WHITE OAK WOOD: A heavy, strong, fine-grained hard wood (burr oak, live oak, white oak, chinkapin oak). Rot resistant.

WHOI: Woods Hole Oceanic Institute. Prestigious research organization on ocean-related issues.

WINDSOR FORMATION: A geologic formation in Newfoundland and Labrador. It preserves fossils dating back to the Carboniferous period.

WINDTHROW: Uprooting a tree by wind.

WOLF TREE: A large older tree with a spreading crown and little or no timber value, but often great value for wildlife.

Table of Contents

(Continued form Volume I)

PROLOGUE

SECTION F: RESEARCHED MATERIAL

Prologue

This Volume II, *The Compendium*, is the repository of the appendices which discuss, research, examine, and calculate the myriad of issues affecting the answers to the twenty questions found in the Introduction. Less of a literary disquisition, the appendices provide a subset of the conducted research to summarize the reasoning for the answers to those twenty questions found in the Introduction.

Much of the research and review conducted were to prove negatives. Such as: no coconut coir fiber came from the Caribbean; coconut fiber was not used as dunnage on any sailing ship; or, the coconut fiber could not have floated as either flotsam or jetsam into Mahone Bay from ocean currents. Therefore, when researching, it was imperative to think and investigate any possible situation or historical scenario which may create a hole in the forensic answer given. Could a freak storm blown floating coconut fiber onto Oak Island?

As an example: Did the coconut coir fiber as an export item, transit any of the four main silk trade land routes? Was there evidence of its use along those tens of thousands of miles of mercantile maneuvering captured in historical records? Were they moved by camel, and which type of camel? What was the cost associated with moving such a large volume of worthless material? Who valued such a cargo to seek it? Or, was it the coconuts themselves as the cargo and was it retted at the receiving end? Would coconuts even survive such trips or rot along the route? History told us coconut cups called tureens, Treens, and mazers, were in fact cherished items carried by camel trains during the medieval period. Did the fiber find a ride along?

Like any researcher, complexities of the search topics took on a whole life of their own. After scouring history for coconut 'coir' fiber, you realize another word for the same subject exists – 'cayer,' frequently used by the Portuguese. As you dig deeper you find additional search words 'coco-fiber, 'Indie-nux,' 'Pharoahs nuts,' and even regional terms were used in very old documents, all names for the same thing. This comment is not to complain nor seek sympathy, but to alert the reader there were many more layers to this onion than simply using a Google search. And all of the peeling of that onion is not represented here but was performed in the examinations and reduced to the most pertinent pathway in answering the question, without limiting the scope of review.

We dealt with several timeframes when doing the historical examination. First we had the radiocarbon date period of the artifacts to investigate. We had to examine the immediate history of Canada, maritime travel, and what was happening wherever coconut coir fiber was available. Finally, close attention was given to natural weather and environmental conditions to ascertain if those events could cancel out or interrupt approaches to the island from those destinations, and time periods, such as massive flooding in Kerala, India, the effects of the Little Ice Age in Europe, or volcanic eruptions in the Icelandic region. Just because the coconut specimens were dated from 1130 to 1330 AD, did not give us the leisure to check between that period only, and call it quits. The point to be made is this *Compendium* only captures in these appendices, the subset of examinations which lead the reader to the conclusion the authors research led him too. An example: If a port within the Persian Gulf had a boatbuilder who repaired sewn boats with coir fiber but purchased the coir fiber from India and the climate forbade growing Coconut Palms, we felt it was not germane to recapture that historic observation for the sake of saying "we are aware of that." Instead, we limited our reportage to where shipbuilders had local access to coconut coir, Coconut Palms, and the retting process.

Sounds complicated, dense, and even nutty. But here you are expecting to understand why the *Book* gives the forensic answers it does. This drill was to just let you know, we went down many a rabbit hole to find the money hole. We hope as you wade through this mumbo-jumbo, those facts emerge as tried and true. If not - *think re-gifting!*

Appendix A
DISSECTING DUMBO DRUMLIN

All of the information provided within this Appendix is gleaned from other sources, reports, and publications including pertinent graphics and charts. This material is provided for the reader who is curious about the makeup of the island itself, and how the island has affected the hunt for treasure. I will credit the source of the reference information and thank those who have worked hard to give these scientific insights.

As mentioned earlier, Oak Island appears from above as a baby elephant. Using Isaac's Point as the trunk, the eastern drumlin as the head of the elephant, the western drumlin the body and the tail being the causeway, which connects our pachyderm permanently to its provincial home. Yet our Dumbo has more parts to it that are not as visible from the sky. So let's learn what this pachyderm is packing!

Preface: The entire submission between pencil graphics has been created by Steven Aitken, Ph.D., P.Geo (APEGA and APGNS) and was last modified January 14, 2021. ©Steven Aitken, 2021 |FBTOL. He authorizes its publication here.

"This text and illustrations provide a simplified overview of the geology of Oak Island and may help researchers solve some of the many mysteries surrounding the treasure allegedly buried at the Money Pit on the east side of the island. Most of the data used to generate this overview was derived from Les Macphie's comprehensive online database of historical reports and the online interactive maps provided by the Nova Scotia Department of Natural Resources: Geosciences and Mines Branch.[1,2] Imperial units are used throughout this overview (except where otherwise indicated) since most measurements from earlier investigations are imperial."

Surficial Geology

The inner islands of Mahone Bay, including Oak Island, are drumlins jutting above a stony till plain deposited during Pleistocene glacial events. They form part of the expansive Lunenburg Drumlin Field that extends from coastal areas seaward into Mahone Bay and are high enough to extend up to several meters above mean sea level, even during present Holocene highstand.[3] The long axes of drumlins are aligned northwest-southeast, and their sectional profiles indicate predominant southeastward ice flow during formation. Oak Island consists of two large drumlins and at least one smaller, submerged drumlin flanking the eastern margin of the island, which was identified on a multibeam bathymetric survey.[4] The maximum height above mean sea level of the western and eastern drumlins is about 33 and 52 ft, respectively. Both drumlins are characterized by distinct units of till, deposited during separate glacial events, and are themselves separated by periglacial sediments composed mostly of sand.[5] The drumlins are joined by a low saddle of stony till that is covered by organic-rich sediments deposited in a lagoon (swamp). The lagoon is separated from Mahone Bay by a curvate barrier bar that stretches about 1,150 ft between the two main drumlins. Similar barrier bars and related lagoons are common throughout Mahone Bay and adjacent coastal regions. How anyone could farm on Oak Island is hard to imagine since surficial deposits consist of stony till with abundant sand, gravel, cobbles, and boulders.

Surficial Geology

Elevation Map
Note: elevation grid generated using LiDAR data

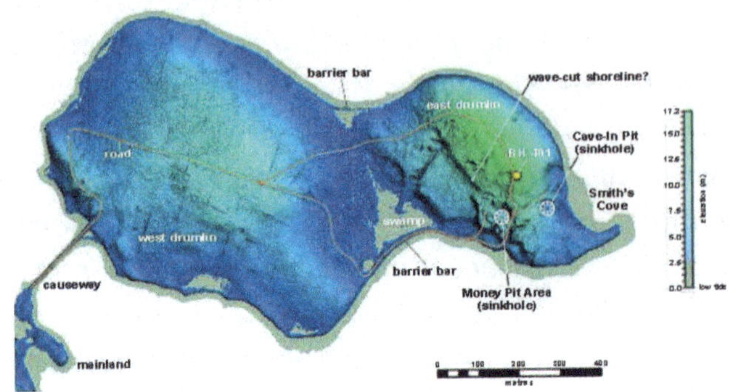

Contour Map with Cross Section Lines
Note: Feltzen outcrop locations are projected

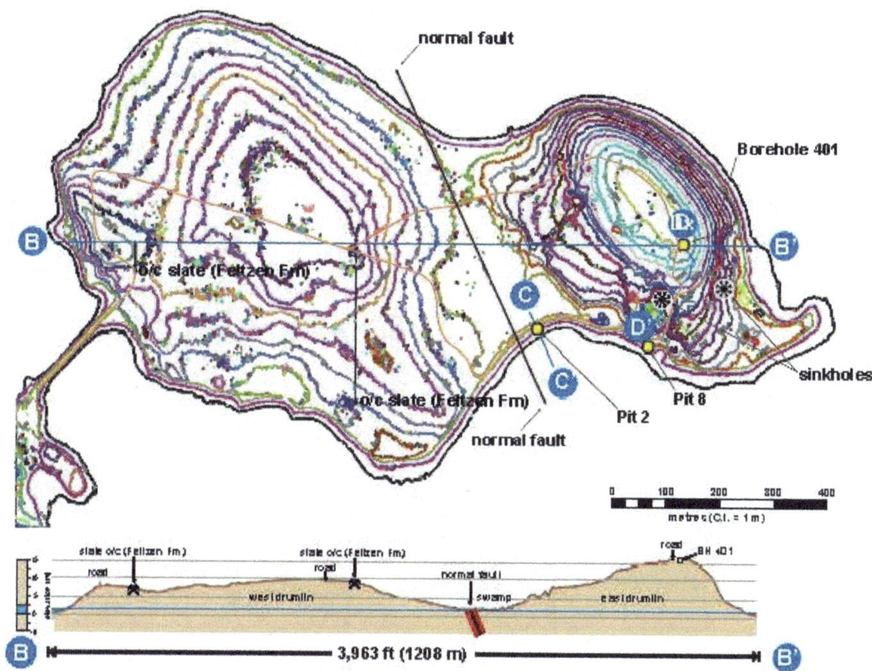

Bedrock Geology & Structure

Bedrock beneath Oak Island does consist of laminated slate (Feltzen Formation) exposed in places at surface on the west side of the island as well as bedded anhydrite (Windsor Group), which is buried by glacial till on the east side.

A normal fault separates the Feltzen Formation from the Windsor Group and the contact between them is unconformable (angular unconformity). The Feltzen Formation forms part of the Halifax Group (along with the Cunard Formation) and was deposited during the early Ordovician as silty turbidites in an oxygen-rich shelf or slope environment.[6] The Halifax and underlying Goldenville Group were folded during the Acadian orogeny (Devonian) and the Feltzen Formation occurs in the cores of upright northeast-trending synclines in the Mahone Bay area.[6,7]

In contrast, the Windsor Group was deposited during the Mississippian, possibly in fault-bounded grabens formed during extensional tectonism (late Devonian - early Mississippian) or preserved as fault-bounded remnants or outliers of regionally extensive carbonate deposits that once covered the Mahone Bay area.[8] The Windsor Group was later deformed and then exhumed by glacial erosion during the Quaternary (Pleistocene).[9] Only the lowermost part of the Windsor Group is preserved in the Mahone Bay area.

Bedrock Geology & Structure around Oak Island

Regional Structural Cross Section A-A

Note: no vertical exaggeration & Pleistocene deposits not shown

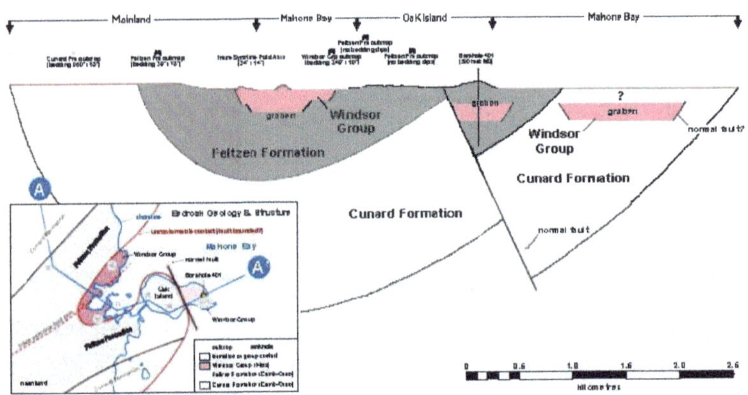

Sinkhole at the Money Pit

The Windsor Formation beneath Oak Island is riddled with fractures and dissolution cavities, especially within the upper 62 ft of the unit. Most cavities are floored with laminated geopetal sediment; others have collapsed due to extensive fracturing and loading, forming sinkholes filled with anhydrite breccia and sand. At least two sinkholes occur on Oak Island, and many have been identified on the mainland, especially on the north side of Mahone Bay where the Windsor Group was quarried.[10,11]

The Money Pit is a good example of a sinkhole. Collapse breccia covers the top of the Windsor Group (up to 10 ft thick) in boreholes W2, W5, W7 and W9. In addition, overlying deposits are overthickened by up 37 ft at the Money Pit, indicating infilling of a depression.

Sinkhole at the Money Pit

Note: measurements are from ground level to the top of the Windsor Group

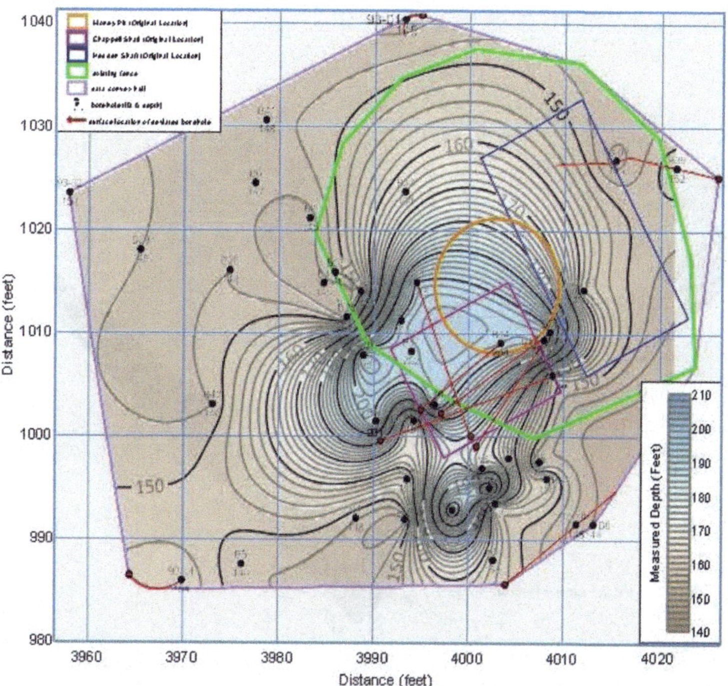

The depression under the oak tree with the block and tackle discovered by Daniel McGinnis in 1795 *could have been* the surface expression of this sinkhole. The upper part of the Windsor Group was probably subaerially exposed forming a karst terrain characterized by dissolution cavities and sinkholes, likely well before glacial sedimentation owing to the significant time gap between the Mississippian and Quaternary (about 340 Ma years). Alternatively, dissolution of carbonates particularly gypsum may have occurred in a subaqueous setting in the presence of undersaturated pore fluids such as brackish or connate waters, possibly during sea-level fluctuations (e.g., Pleistocene glacial-interglacial cycles). The Nova Scotia Department of Natural Resources characterized the area around Oak Island underlain by the Windsor Group as 'high risk' for the development of new sinkholes.[2]

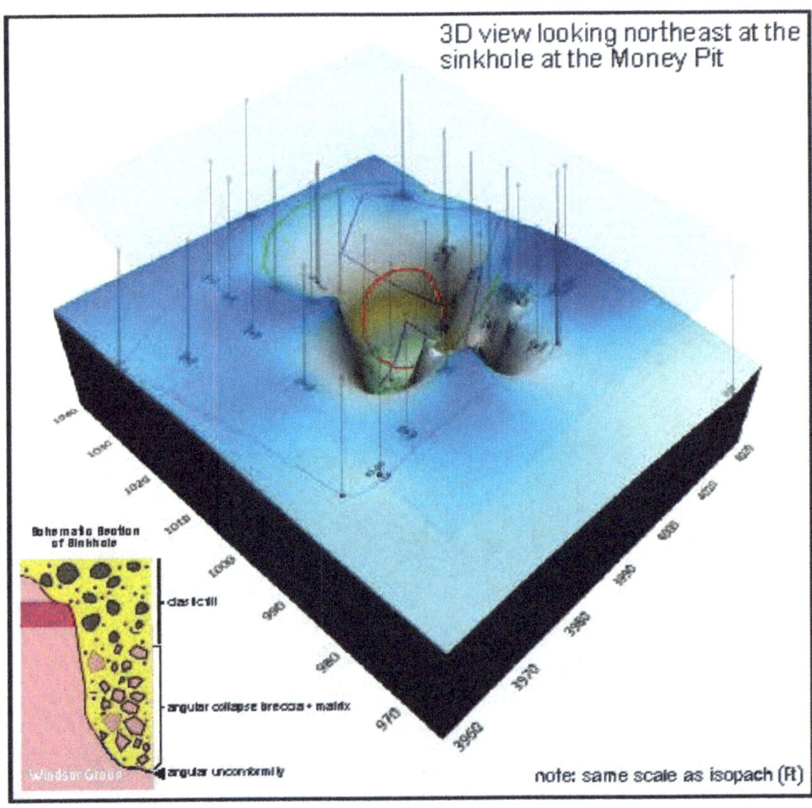

In addition, tidal gauges lowered into borehole 10X indicate that an extensive system of dissolution cavities and fractures in the Windsor Group are themselves interconnected and also connected to ocean water in Mahone Bay. The salinity of water at about -150 ft subsea depth in borehole 10X increased abruptly from near-zero to about 25 ppt, which compares closely to 30 ppt for ocean water in Mahone Bay.

Holocene Transgression

Much of Mahone Bay and its glacial deposits (e.g., stony till plain, drumlins) remained above sea level until about 6000 years BP [see end page] when a natural barrier (outer bedrock sill) was breached near the mouth of the bay during Holocene transgression (i.e., relative sea-level rise).[6,12] As sea water flooded the bay and mixed with proglacial lake water, smaller drumlins and till plains were drowned while larger drumlins became islands. The outermost sediments comprising these glacial deposits were winnowed resulting in transportation of fine-grained sediments (clay and silt) to deeper-water settings. Remaining coarse-grained sediments (sand, gravel, cobbles, and boulders) formed insitu veneers.[13]

Barrier bars often developed between closely spaced drumlins. Lagoons filled with organic material (e.g., stumps, twigs, branches, leafy debris, grasses, reeds) commonly formed behind them. These deposits, including the barrier bar and lagoon at Oak Island, are not manmade structures; they are products of natural geological processes. During transgression, growth of barrier bars was generated by up-drift erosion and sediment recycling of preexisting, submerged deposits (e.g., till, drumlins, bars) causing landward retreat (retrogradation) of new barrier bars and lagoons.[14] As this process continued, these deposits eventually became stacked (see Walther's Law of Facies). Lagoonal peat overlain by coarse-grained barrier bar deposits exposed near the base of beach pits No. 2 and 8 reported by the Woods Hole Oceanographic Institution (WHOI) are good examples of this scientific law.[13]

Radiometric dates and burial depths for the peat range from 2340 to 1940 years BP and 8 to 10 ft below mean sea-level. Relative sea-level has been on the rise in Mahone Bay at a near-constant rate of about 0.42 feet per century for the past 2300 years. Even during this short period of geological time, the geomorphology of Mahone Bay has changed dramatically.

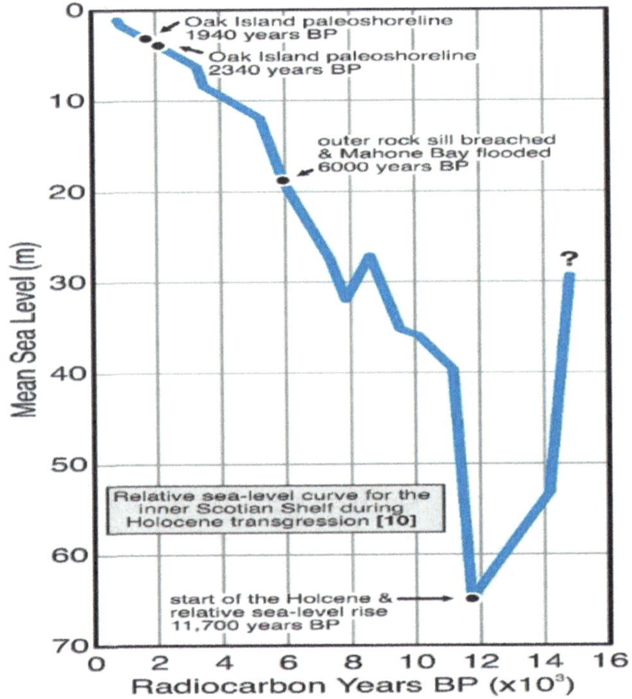

Stratigraphy in the Money Pit Area

Only strip logs from the Warnock-Hersey and Golder reports were used to define the stratigraphy.[15,16] Borehole spacing is tight, especially around the Money Pit, and the vast majority of these boreholes do not have deviation surveys. All boreholes are assumed to be vertical, but deviation is likely due to bit deflection and natural drift during the drilling process. Although measured depths are undoubtedly greater than true thickness, the isopach of glacial deposits at the Money Pit is valid, especially considering the high density of boreholes in the area. The isopach is not exact, but the depression (sinkhole) in the Windsor at the Money Pit is clearly defined.

Mississippian carbonates of the Windsor Group are unconformably overlain by Pleistocene glacial till and periglacial sediments. The Windsor Group is up to 180 ft thick and composed of bedded anhydrite with additional beds and nodules of dolomite, gypsum, limestone, sandstone, and andesite (volcanics). Dissolution cavities are common, especially in fractured areas near the top of the Windsor Group , and often floored by laminated geopetal sediment composed of fine-grained clastics (clay, silt, and sand). At the Money Pit, a depression (sinkhole) up to 47 ft deep in the Windsor is backfilled with breccia composed of angular fragments of anhydrite and periglacial and glacial deposits consisting mostly of sand.

Glacial deposits consist of three units of unconsolidated till with varying hardness, color, clast size and clast composition depending on source. Each unit is commonly separated by laminated or bedded periglacial deposits. Some of these periglacial deposits are composed of sand characterized by high porosity and permeability that locally caused significant water loss (up to 50%) and decreased pressure while drilling. These water-saturated conduits could have acted as 'flood tunnels' causing boreholes and shafts to flood. The three till units include:

1) brown to grey sandy till with variable amounts of clay, silt, gravel, cobbles, and boulders (Hartlen Till),
2) brown to grey sandy, clayey till with variable amounts of silt, gravel, cobbles, and boulders (Lawrencetown Till) and
3) dark brown clayey till with numerous boulders and variable amounts of sand, gravel, and cobbles (Stony Till). [17]

Together, the glacial and periglacial deposits are up to 212 ft thick where they partially fill and cover the depression (sinkhole) in the Windsor at the Money Pit.

NOTE: The preceding material and illustrations have been authorized by Steven Aitken, Ph.D., P.Geo (APEGA and APGNS) to be published within this book and was last modified January 14, 2021. ©Steven Aitken, 2021 |FBTOL. The author thanks Dr. Aitken for the privilege to share his information.

My Opinionated Opining

As I've admitted before, my background is in intelligence of foreign countries, not foreign rocks, boulders, sinkholes, and soils. The information that I have provided to you here is from experts in just those fields. So I have provided it to you the reader as this book is not about opinion, but about the facts as we know them or have deduced them to be. However, I do have that little voice in the back of my head, doubting some of what I've read in this appendix.

Nothing is finite and nothing is perfect in the analysis of such a messed up place as Oak Island. So with that caveat, I will simply say I do not believe the "depression" seen by McGinnis and company was formed by the processes of a sinkhole. The scientific conclusion in the "Sinkhole at the Money Pit" previously, states:

> *"The Money Pit is a good example of a sinkhole. Collapse breccia covers the top of the Windsor (up to 10 ft thick) in boreholes W2, W5, W7 and W9. In addition, overlying deposits are overthickened by up to 37 ft at the Money Pit, indicating infilling of a depression. The depression under the oak tree with the block and tackle discovered by Daniel McGinnis in 1795* ***could have been the surface expression of this sinkhole****."*

I have no doubt the Money Pit was dug within a prehistoric filled-in sinkhole. And that sinkhole was formed tens of thousands of years ago; then filled in with "breccia" and other glacial sediments and till composites which were washed into the unfilled sinkhole during the "barrier breach" 6000 years BP ago. *I get that too.* Perhaps I am taking these scientific comments too literally such that the implication is not "the depression seen by McGinnis was formed by a sinkhole;" rather, the sinkhole was filled in which 'could have' created a much larger depression (than just 13 ft diameter). And thousands of years later, McGinnis, Smith, and Vaughan happened to find a (smaller) depression formed by a previously filled-in pit that happened to have been dug in an ancient filled-in sinkhole!

Otherwise, I think the science here is attempting to whitewash the known historical facts as of 1795.

In concert with this issue, I also raise doubts about the *'requirement'* the islands were naturally formed together over thousands of years without any additional constructive support by man. I am not arguing that similar formations linking islands like Oak Island, do not exist with plenty of examples right in Mahone Bay. Perhaps my disagreement is tainted by the oft' spoken legend of a Spanish Galleon sunk in the space between the two islands with cofferdams entombing the burnt ship. And perhaps my opinion is additionally shaped by Dr. Spooner's determination the swamp was manmade circa 1200 years ago; also play into those 'laymen' beliefs. But this write-up above has too many "coulda's" or "possibly's" or other "inconclusive" phraseology to convince me this is hardcore scientific fact of this very peculiar island. - *Perhaps I've been compiling this book too long!*

Finally, I would offer an uneducated position based on assuming most of what the Woods Hole scientists and the Warnock-Hersey and Golder experts found and compiled with esteemed experts such as Gordon Fader and Les MacPhie. My view is based on an island whose insides have been dug up, drilled into, bulldozed, or exploded for decades and decades. The Money Pit had been excavated by ancient voyagers, who then, refilled the pit, most likely with soils (but not boulders) from that pit. The vast majority of the rocks, boulders, cobbles, and other detritus left strewn across the landscape. Then came the searchers! In the excellently written book by Graham Harris and Les MacPhie, titled "*Oak Island and Its Lost Treasure*," their Appendix on page 246 clearly proves the eastern drumlin has been tossed like a salad for crazed partygoers from *Weight Watchers*! They list more than two dozen shafts excavated and repeatedly re-excavated. Additionally, there were hundreds of drill holes, boreholes, and test holes penetrating the surface. And on top of all those disturbances were dozens of trenches, pits, tunnels, blasting, removals, wells, evulsions, and resurfacings to change completely the manifestation of the eastern end of Oak Island. Even Steve Guptill, member of the Fellowship and surveyor on The History Channel's, *"Curse of Oak Island,"* said in 2021 that since his arrival on the team they had drilled over 700 boreholes!

And as stated earlier in the scientific treatise herein by Dr. Aitken, the stratigraphic interpretation of the island is based *"Only strip logs from the Warnock-Hersey and Golder reports were used to define the stratigraphy."* [15,16] This was accomplished but forty years ago! So when someone looked at this reconstituted drumlin, what could one decipher from its chaotic history? I am just considering that doing a core sample(s) today to inform me of what the island's stratigraphic makeup was in 1795, a very pertinent point in this story, is meaningless after the abusive changes made to the island.

What little geology, soil sciences and understanding of the forest environment I may have absorbed while authoring this book, these three issues have not resolved themselves as they rattle around in my skull. Sinkholes are sinkholes and depressions are depressions. And I can understand a depression can be caused by a sinkhole. Why a refilled pit dug within a refilled sinkhole cannot in fact have a depression due to soil movement from the creation of that pit is a bit puzzling. Yet we are to believe the sinkhole created the depression only in a small subset area of its larger self in the exact spot where a hole was dug? I say - *Perhaps not.*

We will let the dueling dirt doctors duke it out on this dilemma!

* As discussed elsewhere in this book, the term BP, stands for **B**efore **P**resent. This acronym is used to represent a *specific historical referenced point.* The year '1950' is BP, or also known as YBP (*year before present*), or RCYBP (*radiocarbon year before present*). This specific year represents the "0" year from which to calculate the calendar year or range of years, of an artifacts *radiocarbon age*. So if an item has radiocarbon age of *843 years*, it means the item is 843 BP (1950). Therefore… BP (1950) – 843 = 1107 AD. This is a very basic example and can be much more complicated based on other factors.

Footnoted References

1. Macphie, L. (2019) Oak Island - Nova Scotia. Oak Island Tours Incorporated. https://www.oakislandtours.ca/les-macphieresearch.html.

2. Government of Nova Scotia, Department of Natural Resources, Geoscience and Mines Branch, Interactive Maps, SW Nova Scotia Bedrock Map and Karst Risk Map (2020). https://novascotia.ca/natr/meb/geoscience-online/maps-interactive.asp.

3. Stea, R. R. and Fowler, J. H. (1981) Pleistocene geology and till geochemistry of central Nova Scotia. Nova Scotia Department of Mines and Energy, Map 81-1, Sheet 4, 1981. https://searchworks.stanford.edu/view/2488697.

4. Fader, G. B. J. and Courtney, R. C. (1988) An interpretation of multibeam bathymetry off eastern Oak Island, Mahone Bay, Nova Scotia. Geological Survey of Canada (Atlantic), Bedford Institute of Oceanography, April 1998. https://geoscan.nrcan.gc.ca/starweb/geoscan/servlet.starweb?path=geoscan/fulle.web&search1=R=209918.

5. Stea, R. R. and Brown, Y. (1989) Variation in drumlin orientation, form and stratigraphy relating to successive ice flows in southern and central Nova Scotia, Sedimentary Geology, 62, 223-240. https://novascotia.ca/natr/meb/data/mg/map/pdf/map_1993-002_200_cln.pdf.

6. White, C. E. (2010) Stratigraphy of the Lower Paleozoic Goldenville and Halifax groups in the western part of southern Nova Scotia. Atlantic Geology, 46, 136-154. https://doi.org/10.4138/atlgeol.2010.008.

7. Waldron, J. W., Jamieson, R. A., Pothier, H. D., and White, C. E. (2015). Sedimentary and tectonic setting of a mass transport slope deposit in the Halifax Group, Halifax Peninsula, Nova Scotia, Canada. Atlantic Geology, 51, 84-104. https://doi.org/10.4138/atlgeol.2015.004.

8. Giles, P.S. (1981) The Windsor Group of the Mahone Bay area, Nova Scotia. Nova Scotia Department of Mines and Energy. Paper 81-3, 1981. https://novascotia.ca/natr/meb/data/pubs/81paper03/81paper03.pdf.

9. Barnes, N. E. and Piper, D. J. W. (1978) Late Quaternary geological history of Mahone Bay, Nova Scotia. Canadian Journal of Earth Sciences, 15, 586-593. https://www.nrcresearchpress.com/doi/pdfplus/10.1139/e78-063.

10. Giles, P. S. (1981) The Windsor Group of the Mahone Bay Area, Nova Scotia. Nova Scotia Department of Mines and Energy, Paper 81-3, 1981. https://novascotia.ca/natr/meb/pdf/81pap03.asp.

11. Calder, J. H. (1998) The Carboniferous evolution of Nova Scotia. Geological Society, London, Special Publications, 143, 261-302. https://doi.org/10.1144/GSL.SP.1998.143.01.19.

12. Fader, G. B. J. and Miller, R. O. (2008) Surficial geology, Halifax Harbour, Nova Scotia. Geological Survey of Canada, Bulletin 590; Natural Resources Canada; Geological Survey of Canada (Atlantic); Bedford Institute of Oceanography. https://doi.org/10.4095/224797.

13. Woods Hole Oceanographic Institution (1996) Oak Island hydrogeology, hydrography, and nearshore morphology. July- August 1995 Field Observations. Unpublished Draft Report by Aubrey, D. G, Spencer, W. D., Guiterez, B., Robertson V. W. and Gallo, D., April 8, 1996. https://www.oakislandtours.ca/les-macphie-research.html.

14. Carter, R. W. G., Orford, J. D., Forbes, D. L. and Taylor, R. B. (1987) Gravel barriers, headlands, and lagoons: an evolutionary model. Coastal Sediments '87, ASCE, New Orleans, LA, 1776-1792. https://www.jstor.org/stable/4298038?seq=1.

15. Warnock-Hersey International Limited (1969) Soils investigation, Oak Island, Nova Scotia. Report No. 530-110, received by Carr and Donald and Associates, Toronto, Ontario, July 31, 1969, and November 5, 1969. https://www.oakislandtours.ca/les-macphie-research.html.

16. Golder Associates, Subsurface Investigation, The Oak Island Exploration, Oak Island, Nova Scotia. Draft Report No. 69126, received by Triton Alliance Ltd., Montreal, Quebec, April 28, 1971. https://www.oakislandtours.ca/les-macphieresearch.html.

17. Stea, R. R. (2011) Appalachian Glacier Complex in Maritime Canada. In: Singh V.P., Singh P., Haritashya U.K. (eds) Encyclopedia of Snow, Ice and Glaciers. Encyclopedia of Earth Sciences Series. Springer, Dordrecht. https://doi.org/10.1007/978-90-481-2642-2_25.

Dr. Steven Aitken @ https://stevenaitken3.wixsite.com/scientific-facts.

Appendix B

THE TRUTH IN TIMBER AND TIMING

This appendix offers a deeper dive into the natural history and settlement period of Nova Scotia and the New England Acadian Forest (NEAF), as previously mentioned; and it is all relative to our area of interest - Oak Island. Not only does the history and ecology help us understand about those mystery canopied trees, but it frames our explanations of our forensic examinations, and gives a point of reference for WHO is behind all of this.

Interpretation of forest makeup and species identification by early explorers to the continent is subjective. They are offered as generalities and limited-value opinions. We note their observations of these trees for a fuller, but subjective picture of the area surrounding Oak Island. All of the comments and recollections by others revolving around any forensic element we are engaging in this book, are listed in Appendix C, *"On the Record."* This is the reportage of known "facts" to work with. Other historical records offer surmises and interpretations of the ecology and biology of Mahone Bay and immediate surroundings. Land ownership records of Oak Island provide scant record of human activities on the island prior to 1600 or clarity through 1795. The island was inhabited and being farmed. Photographic evidence does not extend earlier than 1887, toward the end of the second-phase chronology outlined below. However, what photography and film is available, does capture major changes to the forests and land usage on Oak Island. Yet really, together they fail to provide the absolute 'proof' of what tree species were on Oak Island. All images of the mystery canopied trees on Oak Island are in Appendix F, *"Guardians of the Keep"*.

On the following page are more photos of the mystery trees we are attempting to identify. The images capture those trees during their last few decades alive at the turn of the 18th Century and into first half of the 1900's. Carefully looking, in the first photo you can see three, perhaps four snags that have given up their role in mystifying and signaling the unique history of Oak Island.

Isaac's Point at Smith's Cove. Courtesy W.R. Macaskill, NS National Archives

"There is something in the trees awaiting discovery."
— Steve Magee

Isaac's Point from across South Shore Cove. Courtesy Nova Scotia Archives

New England Acadian Forest (NEAF)
Pre-European Settlement <1600 AD

Oak Island is located within a geographical area known as the New England Acadian Forest (NEAF) ecoregion, which encompasses 24 million hectares of the northeastern United States and eastern Canada. Specifically, the NEAF includes most of the New England area, the three Maritime Provinces of Canada with the exception of northernmost highlands of both New Brunswick and Nova Scotia, and portions of southeastern Quebec.[1] *See below.*

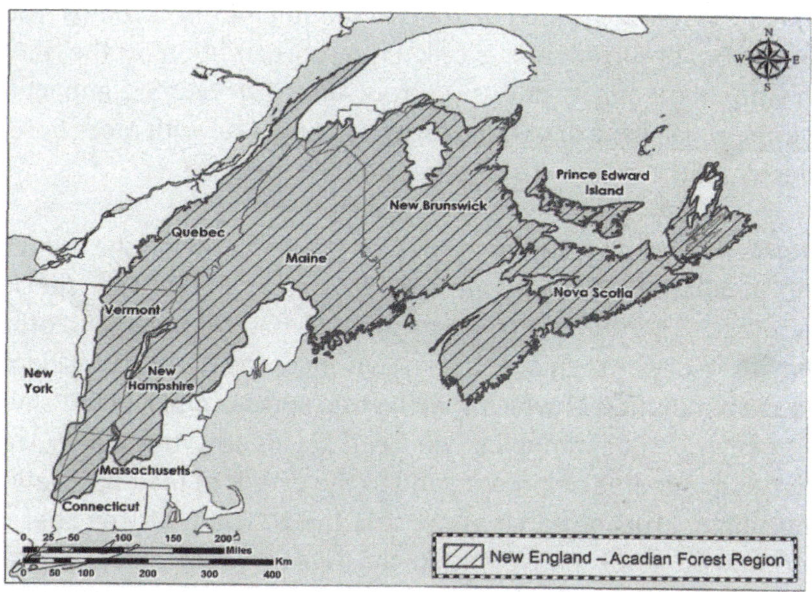

NEAF Ecoregion. Courtesy *Environmental Reviews*. **28**(3): 284-293. 2021.

The NEAF is a transitional forest composed of both northern boreal and southern temperate tree species.[1] Boreal forests are defined as forests growing in high-altitude environments where freezing temperatures occur for 6 to 8 months a year. They contain trees capable of reaching a minimum height of 5m, and a canopy cover of 10%.[2]

Conversely temperate forests are defined as being found south of the boreal forests and north of the tropics. Temperate forests have more moderate temperature variations.

Studies on forest composition have been performed to identify the species of trees, and their relative populations size and locations within the NEAF. Researchers divided ecoregion activity into three periods: 1) Dating back to the time of primeval forests - *pre-European Settlement (<1600)*; 2) How it has changed during *European Settlement (1600-1890)*; 3) Further impacts associated with *post-European Settlement (1890-2019).*[1] This forested region initially consisted of both boreal and temperate tree species. Their findings have concluded a transformation of the biomes' tree species has occurred. This is called the "borealization" of the NEAF. This phenomenon is due to current and historic land-impacting events, which have driven the forests to populate with more boreal species, at the expense of temperate tree species.[1]

More simply stated, research showed the reduction in the number and population of temperate tree species as boreal tree species increased. This was due to the impacts of man, weather, and other climatic issues as seen over the known life of the NEAF.[1] To validate my determination of which specific tree species graced Oak Island with such unique canopies, we need to identify the native tree species in our area of interest, and to the extent of their population and range. This research effort sets the baseline of tree species determined to be native within the NEAF. From there, we can investigate nonnative tree species and their candidacy as those Oak Island mystery trees.

So which tree species were around Oak Island prior to European Settlement in 1600?

Studies clearly illustrate the pre-settlement forest was dominated by <u>*temperate*</u> tree species.[1] Researchers estimate between 60% and 85% of those tree species in the NEAF persisted in a state of old growth (OG) (OG = >150 years old).[1] Of these tree species within the NEAF, Eastern Hemlock (*Tsuga canadensis*) and Red Spruce (*Picea rubens*) were identified as the 'signature' population species prior to pre-European settlement.[1] Other temperate tree species in the NEAF OG were American Beech (*Fafus grandifolia*), Sugar Maple (*Acer saccharum*), Eastern White Cedar (*Thuja occidentalis*), Yellow Birch (*Betula alleghaniensis*); and **to a lesser extent in population**, Eastern White Pine (*Pinus strobus*), White Ash (*Fraxinus americana*), and Red Oak (*Quercus rubra*).[1] Balsam Fir was also part of the NEAF but with higher proportions occurring only in the northern sectors of the ecoregion. Boreal "shade-tolerant" species such as Aspen (*Populus*), Red Pine (*Pinus resinosa*), Larch (*Larix laricina*), Pin Cherry (*Prunus*), Red Oak (*Quercus rubra*), and White Birch (*Betula papyrifera*), were **only minor components** of this historic forest composition.[1]

You may have noticed the species *Quercus rubra* (Northern Red Oak) was listed as both a temperate tree species and boreal "shade tolerant" tree species. This variant does have an impact on our story. Later in this book, we will discuss what this means regarding tree species morphology on Oak Island.

On the following page is a chart of the native tree species identified as living within the NEAF ecoregion during the pre-European settlement (<1600) period.[1] This chart further illustrates the percentage of general overlap of those specific native tree species' range within the NEAF as it would have been found had we walked those forests today. It also demonstrates the likelihood these native tree species would have been located in our area of interest. Information on all these native tree species is found in Appendix E. *"Known NEAF Neighbors"*.

Courtesy *Environmental Reviews*. **28**(3): 284-293. 2019.

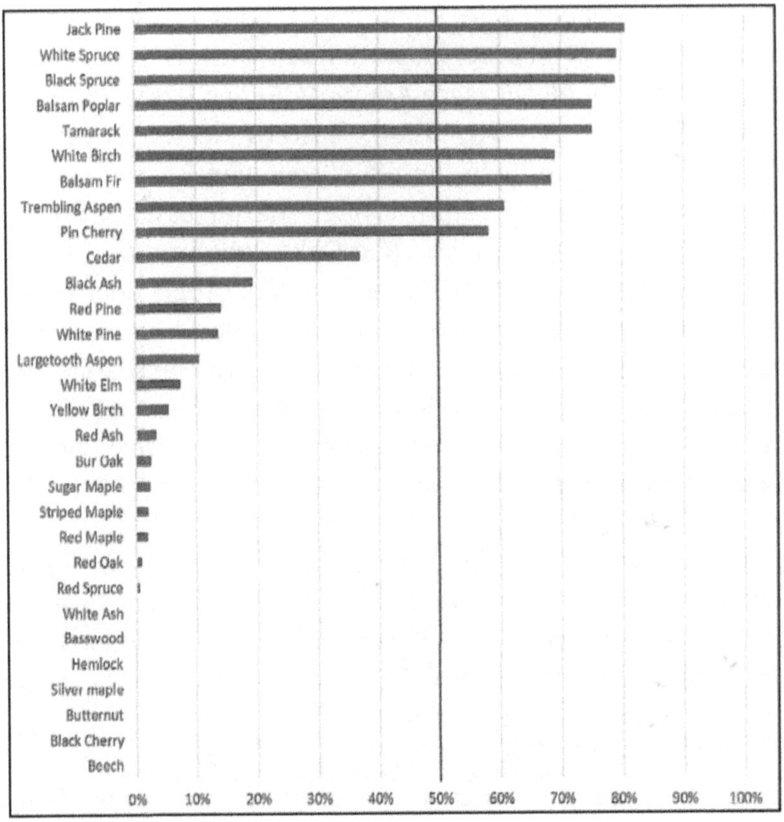

NEAF Native Tree Species and their percent of range within the NEAF.

Notice, Burr Oak encompassed only 3% of the NEAF, while (Northern) Red Oak was just under 1% respectively. This underlines how "rare" or uncommon it would be to see either tree species in our area of interest. However, the chart does not indicate stands or "groves" of a specific tree species which were not common throughout the NEAF but could have been or were within our area of interest. Yet, as we later reflect on the historical description and observations by those of the area and period, we see those commenters were also surprised to find these trees on Oak Island – *regardless of what they thought they were.* Therefore, they confirm by their remarking on the trees being nonnative, how rare in fact they were - *and found nowhere else within the NEAF.*

New England Acadian Forest (NEAF) European Settlement 1600-1890

During this second phase of the NEAF ecoregion transformation when borealization begins, researchers originally found the primeval Acadian forests were thick with a variety of softwoods and hardwoods in massive size and height. Nova Scotia was on the map as a destination primarily for the bounty of their fisheries. These well-stocked fisheries had become popular for harvesting by Vikings, Scots, Spanish, French, Portuguese, and English fishermen. So, the views of these thick OG forests with trees of unbelievable girth and length - crowding along the shoreline; brought a new purpose and way of life for those arriving to tame Nova Scotia.

England, though first to arrive (1497) ahead of Portugal (1498), Spain (1513), France (1524) and followed by the Dutch (1629), were the last to fully explore the New World lands in North America. Almost 100 years later In 1584, the preeminent geographer in Europe, Richard Hakluyt, the archdeacon of London's Westminster Abbey, wrote the manuscript *"A Discourse of Western Planting."* Hakluyt promoted the use of colonizing North America to find, develop, and harvest the natural resources for England's growing needs. The name of these resource-rich new lands included Acadia, New France, New England, and New Scotland – Nova Scotia. Yet Britain took roughly 175 years to embrace Hakluyt's concept, some 250 years after they first found such a cache of natural resources. Land clearing of the Province began as early as 1604-1605 with the first French settlements of Saint Croix Island in Maine and Port Royal in Nova Scotia.[2] The first sawmill was established in Annapolis (previously known as Port Royal), Nova Scotia, in 1612.[2] Timber was much sought after in Hakluyt's vision for European use. Oak was abundant for export for only 2 years before it was depleted in the Annapolis area.[2] Britain and France fought over New France - or New England, depending on distant world events and what month it was. French naval officer, Isaac de Razilly, was appointed as lieutenant governor in reclaiming New France from the English through The Treaty of St. Germain-en-Laye in 1632.[3] He came ashore at Le`Heve (20 miles from the Money Pit) on September 8, 1632 and built Fort Sainte-Marie-de-Grace. All vessels bringing provisions, men, and colonists in 1633, returned to France filled with felled lumber resources.[3]

In 1633, Nicolas Denys was the Governor of Cape Breton Island, Prince Edward Island, and the coastline from 'Canso to Gaspe' from 1654-1688. He surveyed these maritime landscapes to report lumber opportunities for the French government. These territories eventually included Mahone Bay and the regions along the eastern coasts of Nova Scotia. Denys wrote:

> *"some Oak, Pines, Firs of 3 sorts (Spruce, Fir & Hemlock), Birches (White Birch), Black Birches (Yellow Birch), Beeches, Aspens, Maples and Ashes were the predominant species. Those woods of the coast are as nothing in comparison with those which are inland and on the upper parts of the rivers. The trees [there] are very much more beautiful in height and thickness and stand more open and less confused. One could chase a Moose on horseback."* [4]

Early on, settler harvesting of rich hardwood forests eliminated 99% of the Burr Oak (*Quercus macrocarpa*), Silver Maple (*Acer saccharinum*), Basswood (*Tilia americana*), Ironwood (*Ostrya virginiana*) and Butternut (*Juglans cinerea*) species almost completely from the NEAF.[1] Felling of trees for ship masts started in Acadia just before the turn of the 17th century. Pine was milled for ship masts and exported to France, then England, and eventually to the new colonies and to the West Indies. The most important of these trees was *Pinus strobus* (Eastern White Pine).[5,6] In colonial days they were huge, straight, and found growing to heights of 230 ft.[5,6,7] They were lightweight, durable, and also the least resinous of all the pines. First English reference to Eastern White Pine was by John Josselyn writing about his trips to the New World in 1638 and 1663 in his book titled; "*Two Voyages to New England*." He wrote: "*The Pine Tree is a very large tree, very tall...*"[7]

The Eastern White Pine was twice the size and height of England's Scots Pine (*Pinus sylvestris*) and greatly impressed King George; for which the name "Kings Pines" soon ruled.[5,6,7]

The British Crown wanted to control and conserve its most pressing resource – massive timbers for use by the Royal Navy. Efforts to control the ownership of this newly found source started with the issuance of the Broad Arrow Policy. The act prohibited any Pine tree with a two ft or larger diameter... must be reserved for the Royal Navy and future ship mast use and not to be felled. In the colonies, England enforced the Broad Arrow program. This law became to be seen as the most disruptive of acts and is considered perhaps the most hated of all Crown directives against the colonies; a big step leading to eventual revolution.[6,7] Here it is inserted in governing documents, such as the 1691 Massachusetts Charter, wherein:

> *"... for better providing and furnishing of Masts for our Royal Navy we do hereby reserve to us ... ALL trees of the diameter of 24 inches and upward at 12 inches from the ground, growing upon any soils or tracts of land within our said Province or Territory not heretofore granted to any private person. We... forbid all persons whatsoever from felling, cutting, or destroying any such trees without the royal license from us."* [8]

Here, the Broad Arrow mark placed upon trees identified by surveyors as "Kings Pines." The mark onto the restricted trees by three axe or hatchet cuts, or similar markings, made the tree off-limits to landowners.[8]

Courtesy: Historical Society of New England

Commercial logging of Pine and Spruce was well established all along the Nova Scotia coast by 1696. As the lumber market spurred export, the Acadian forest supplied Red Spruce, Yellow Birch, Sugar Maple, Balsam Fir, White Spruce, Red

Maple, White Birch, Trembling Aspen, Eastern Hemlock, Beech, Pine and Cedar. Primarily, Oak was used to make an assortment of products like staves for barrels and specific ship parts, as it was nonporous. White Pine was for masts and boards, and Cedar for shingles.[7, 8]

White Spruce - ran in a band along the exposed Atlantic coast and was probably not very different in many areas than it is today as it is one of the few species able to withstand the constant drying effect of salt-laden sea winds. Mature and overmature forests were common.

Yellow Birch - with its close grain wood, was used in shipbuilding and found more durable than Oak especially for parts that would be underwater like planks and knees.

White Birch - (also called Canoe Birch) being fine-grained, and light was used to make wooden dishes, grain shovels, and wheels. Plus its bark functioned to cover the crevices of buildings problematic to shingling or clapboarding. One large White Birch would supply sufficient bark for the local Indians (Mi'kmaq) to make two canoes each capable of holding 10 people.

Sugar Maple - was used for furniture making, flooring, and fuel but was most useful left standing to spring tap its sap to make maple sugar and syrup – long used by the Mi`kmaq who showed the French how to tap trees.

Balsam Fir - was cut for poles, sawn into boards, and staves. Its balsam or resin was utilized for its medicinal properties.

White Ash – was desired from its ability to bend and retain its position afterwards. It was used for a great variety of purposes, including the construction of farming implements, as well as oars and staves.

White Cedar - (which was rare) and *Black Spruce*, grew in swamps. They were highly valued for their rot resistant qualities and used for fencepost and in the case of Cedar - as shingles.

Tamarack - also found growing in wet poorly drained areas, had very durable strong wood. Therefore, it was actively sought for shipbuilding and construction of such works that were exposed to alternate wet and dryness.

Black Spruce - one of the most lofty forest trees when not growing in a swamp, was highly valued for its strength and toughness and its squared timber and sawmill logs were used in all types of construction. The smaller White Spruce was similarly employed. Their small roots, typically very strong when kept moist, were used by the Mi`kmaq for cords.

Hemlock - not as strong as Spruce, had more limited utility. Yet when immersed in water, was durable and therefore was employed for wharves or fence posts and its bark was universally used in tanning leather.

White Pine - the monarch of the wilderness towering over all other trees. It was unrivalled as a staple of commerce and domestic use since its softwood was easy to work with the tools of the time. It supplied masts for large ships, square timber, deals, boards, shingles, and the wood used for the finishing of every kind of carpentry work. Mature White Pines frequently rose to heights of +200 feet with a four to six foot diameter. Easy targets to spot, their preferred habitats of dry, sandy ridges were actively sought out by colonists to homestead.[9]

To further control these timbers, in 1729 the Crown enacted "*An Act for the Better Preserving of his Majesty's Woods in America and for the Encouragement of the Importation of Naval Stores from Thence, and to Encourage the Importation of Masts, Yards and Bowsprits from that Part of Great Britain called New Scotland.*" [10]

With the act, England further angered colonists within the provinces of Nova Scotia, New Hampshire, Maine, Massachusetts Bay, Rhode Island, and Providence Plantation; as well as the Narragansett country of King's Province, Connecticut in New England, New York, and New Jersey... in America, by declaring:

> *"ye shall not cut, fell or destroy any white pine trees except those on private property, without a royal license for so doing."* [8]

Though the timber resources of Nova Scotia were imperfectly known as settlement was so sparse and scattered, some timber suitable for masts was indeed shipped from Halifax, between 1750 and 1775.[8] As colonization took off, so did the number of sawmills, growing from 565 in 1761 to 1,401 in 1861. In 1760, the naval storekeeper, Joseph Gerrish, informed the British Navy Board that on the La' Have (*previously Le Hève*) River, were available "*mast trees of considerable dimensions*."

In 1758, the Board of Admiralty ordered the first of twelve, new '*ships of the line,*' with the first of the 100-gun first-rate ships named the *HMS Victory*. The *Victory* required 6,000 fully mature Oak trees, a mixture of 8,000 Fir, Elm and Pine trees, 4 acres of fabric for its 23 sails, and 26 miles of flax and hemp rope, the thickest rope being 19" in circumference. Forty-seven years later, under the command of Sir Admiral Nelson, the *HMS Victory* would sail into British naval history just off the coast of Trafalgar. The timber, however, did not come from Nova Scotian forests, but from the remaining Ashdown Forest in the weald of Kent and Sussex.[11]

In 1763, Philip Peake, Foreman of Shipwrights, went to Chester and Mahone Bay in search for quality trees. He was seeking out Black Birch and trees suitable for oak and pine timber for capstan barrels, catheads, knees, standards, and cheeks as well as masts, spars, yards, and bowsprits. He returned with a rather discouraging report.

> *"having found only a few Black Birch fit for capstan barrels between thirty and thirty-three inches in diameter, some small oak, pine and spruce from sixteen inches and smaller, but very straight and tall. There was no oak timber for ships above 150 to 200 tons, some pine fit for masts of up to 20-gun ships, yards and topmasts for 40-gun and 50-gun ships, but at a great distance from the rivers, the ground being rough and rocky."*[10]

This is a report by someone who was keenly aware of tree species for the continued operation of their business, as well as size assessment of available trees. It is telling, as the report specifically addresses the forest, groves, and stands in our area of interest. 1763 is after The Shoreham Grant of 1759, which issued land grants for Oak Island and the town of Chester, as well as after the island was surveyed into available plots the year before, in 1762. Chester was but four years old and four miles away.[12] It was populated by 30 families on 30 acres, eking out its' existence.[12] Shipwright Peake could not have missed Oak Island in his review of timber sources within Mahone Bay due to its size, forest growth, and easy access within the bay. Other bay islands in his reconnoitering would have been quick to dismiss. The others most likely were covered by small conifer stands, barren rocky isles, or only offered dangerous access to their shores. Yet here we have an island renowned for its mighty and impressive Oaks, reportedly covering the island with their easily seen canopies! Would not those mighty 'oaks' offer resources for barrel staves, ship stems, posts, hawse pieces, planking, waterways, strings, framing timbers, tree nails, stern posts, catheads, knees, standards, cheeks, spars, bowsprits, or wing transoms - to any respectable Shipwright?

Soon, in 1774, Halifax itself was in dire need for lumber as a conflagration consumed a good part of the city and all the trees within a three to four mile radius around it. Wood had become scarce around settlements and by 1796 the high price of fuel would be a considerable concern during the six months of any Canadian winter. Woodcutters were venturing further and further into hostile Mi`kmaq territory to acquire the corded wood – at their peril!

Perhaps with firewood in mind, Daniel & Anthony Vaughan and James McLeod sought a Broad Arrow permit. The permit allowed the men to fell Pine trees on their Western Shore lots #1-6 on the mainland (900 acres).[9] You know them from their involvement in finding the Money Pit, just offshore! It said,

"Having caused the aforesaid lotts of land and the Pine Trees standing thereon to be inspected and surveyed, I do, incomformity to his Majesty's instructions, hereby grant lycense to the aforesaid David Vaughan, Anthony Vaughan and James McLeod to cut and take away the Pine Trees growing thereon; save and except thirty eight trees; being from sixteen inches and upwards in diameter and from twenty six feet' and upwards in length, which are marked (image) being fit and are to remain for his Majesty's service; and are therefore wholly excepted out of this lycense accordingly. Given under my hand at Halifax this 25th day of January 1788. (sgd) J.W. Wentworth"[9]

Most ecological change induced by colonization would take place in this period, beginning with the arrival of the majority of Loyalists in 1780. By 1801 the British Navy Board estimated they needed about 18,000 tons of timber, 13,000 tons of hemp to make about 15,260 tons of cordage, 1,400 tons of iron, 949 tons of copper, 200 tons of copper bolt staves, 18,000 barrels of tar, 5,500 barrels of pitch, 371,000 deals, 500 masts, and 111,000 wooden blocks. The cost was £2.9 million. Half of these masts would come from North America. It quickly became apparent the timber resources of Nova Scotia, in so far as they were known by 1783 or even by 1815, would not suffice. Those of New Brunswick and, after 1808, of Upper Canada and Lower Canada, came to dominate this supply source.[10]

"British North American timber, an insignificant English import commodity before 1800, became by 1808-1812 more than 60% of total British timber imports, and by 1830 more than 82%. By now the impact on the Ottawa, the Gatineau, the Saint John, and the Miramichi river valleys was especially important, it was no less so on select regions of Nova Scotia." [10]

Within one hundred years of commencement of commercial logging operations in Nova Scotia, commercial shipbuilding also *launched* in 1769.[2b] The industry grew as did its need for lumber. England saw shiploads of Fir increase from 565 in 1800, to 28,059 in 1861.[12]

It was not until the "golden age of sail" began its decline at the turn of the century, lumber exports would follow as well.[2b]

Courtesy: Library of Congress

By the latter 1800s, forest exploitation in Nova Scotia was on the decline from over harvesting, with White Pine being the only merchantable species.[2b] By 1847, reports mentioned Red Oak and Burr Oak were the only oak species still found in Nova Scotia.[13]

Logging and land clearing continued to expand across the NEAF as European settlements grew and new timber markets were exploited. Studies comparing pre- and post-European Settlement impacts to the forest indicate changes to forest composition were both widespread and severe.[1] Agricultural, livestock, and plantation clearing were initiated. This removed more than half of the Nova Scotian forest cover and cut over almost all of the rest.[1]

Although the Acadian Forest Region includes many thousands of miles of coastline, this region does not experience a typical maritime climate. The ocean does not temper the climate in eastern North America to the degree that it does in other areas, because the prevailing winds there are westerly, blowing off the continent.[2b] The Atlantic Ocean has a significant humidifying and moderating effect on both precipitation and temperature regimes. This causes milder winters and cooler summers than those in the center of Canada.[2b] What the Atlantic Ocean does wreak on the Maritimes - frequently, are thunderstorms, gales, and hurricanes which are extremely destructive as they cause fires, blowdowns, and destructive erosion.

Canada and its Atlantic waters are threatened by an average of six tropical storms a year, some at hurricane force.[14] Given the devastation caused by the gale-force winds and driving rain accompanying these extreme events, forests and habitats are affected in many ways, especially in coastal areas.

Nicolas Denys reported in 1672, thunderstorms often occurred, burning upwards of 10-15 league (30-45 mile) swaths in Nova Scotia.[2b] Large areas were charred by fires escaping attempts at land clearing. According to T.C. Haliburton, in the last 10 years of the 1700s,

> *"forest fires ran rampant over much of the province."*

The historical impact of severe weather on Nova Scotian forests is germane. The weather-induced morphology to tree species on Oak Island has played a role in the confusion to identify the mystery canopied trees. Storm blowdowns, which include windthrows and windsnaps, were so destructive, they frequently made historical journals of the area.[15] American meteorologist, I.R. Tannehill wrote in his book *"Hurricanes,"* about the storm of August 15, 1635, noting the 'widespread destruction of trees' throughout New England and Nova Scotia. Old growth stands in southern Nova Scotia, well over 300 years old, most likely originated as a result of this storm event. Likewise, in 1676 as E.R. Snow describes in his book *"The Vengeful Sea,"* a great hurricane tore into southwestern Nova Scotia, which destroyed OG Hemlock and Red Spruce stands aged at over 300 years. Titus Smith, Nova Scotia's first ecologist, reported in 1801 that *"trees were all blown down here* [an area in

Queens County] *by a hurricane about 80 years ago, which was followed by a fire next year, after which the young growth which now covers the ground, came up.*" This statement indicates that a hurricane occurred about 1721. E. R. Snow reports New England experienced storms in 1717 and in 1723. Studies of forest ages indicated many OG stands range about 250 years old, which suggest both storms severely affected Nova Scotia's forests.[15]

In 1798, The 'Great Storm' hit the province. This is the earliest well-documented storm to affect the forests of Nova Scotia. Thomas Chandler Haliburton in his "*Historical and Statistical Account of Nova Scotia, Vol. 2,*" published by Joseph Howe in 1829, states.

> *"on September 25, 1798, there was a dreadful storm and gale of wind at Halifax, by which shipping, wharves, and other property [was] completely destroyed. Most of the roads rendered impassible from the falling of the forest trees across them."*[16]

Titus Smith records his travels of 1801 and 1802 that in the area of Pollhook [*Ponhook*] Lake [*32 miles from Oak Island*], he was impeded by windfall and blowdown from the Great Storm. Smith noted in an area southwest of Windsor [*near Chester & New Ross*] he was "*...obliged to spend a half hour in going 100 yards because of the difficulty of traveling through forest blowdown.*"[14, 16]

More recent history better reveals the destructive power of wind against trees. 1954, Hurricane Edna destroyed 700 million board feet in Nova Scotia alone. In 2012, Hurricane Juan hit Halifax causing widespread blowdown of 100 million trees lost. Both storms represent greater timber destruction in single storms, than by all the annual felling by loggers.[14,17] The following chart chronicles the recognized storms which afflicted Mahone Bay, Nova Scotia prior to and around the start of our saga.

Major Nova Scotia storms within base timeline of Oak Island.[16]

8-15-1635	*Tannehill's Storm*	Also known as, The Great Colonial Hurricane
1676	*The '76 Storm*	
1717	*The '17 Storm*	
1723	*The '23 Storm*	
9-9-1775	*The Newfoundland Hurricane*	Deadliest Hurricane - 4,000 killed, storm surge 20-30 ft.
1798	*The Great Storm*	
9-3-1821	*The Long Island Hurricane*	Only major hurricane to directly hit NYC in 250 years
10-5-1869	*Saxby's Gale*	Prophesized 1 year earlier by British Navy Lt. S.M. Saxby
1873	*The Nova Scotia Storm*	Also known as "The Lord's Day Gale". #2 of 5 hurricanes
10-10-1885	*The Great Labrador Gale*	
1893		First Hurricane to directly hit Halifax
1900	*The Galveston Hurricane*	Remnants of Galveston's infamous storm slams Province
1924,26, 27	*The Great August Gales*	

Chart created by David Neisen

Robert Restall and his family began treasure hunting on Oak Island in 1959. They dealt with tremendous weather conditions, while actually living adjacent to the Money Pit, in small shack shelters. The winter of 1960-61 was such a calamity of temperatures below freezing, the bay froze over for three long months, and the wind whipping more than 35 mph on most days. This led Mildred Restall to write in her journal, *"The Reluctant Treasurer Hunter"* …*"you could walk through the woods and hear tree branches snap like a pistol shot."*[18] Then again in the fall of 1963, Hurricane Ginny reminded the Restalls of what torture Mother Nature could heave upon Oak Island. She wrote:

> *"In-rolling tide. The heavy seas played around the dock then lifted all 130 feet of it off the rocks and rocked it around as if undecided what to do with it, finally tired, dumped it 100 feet further down the beach… sixty feet of it in one piece, and the rest smashed and scattered all down the shoreline of the island."*[18]

At the end of that same year, the Restall family would be hunkering down to frozen mining equipment, four feet of snow, and with winds at 50 mph and gusting to 70 mph. One can only imagine the destructive force those storms battered Mahone Bay and Oak Island with and shaping the history for those mystery trees?

Oak Island itself has seen the same borealization of its' original forests over history as well. The tree species set has changed many times due to the felling of groves, clearing for agriculture and livestock, increased population, and a variety of industrial activities – mostly revolving around the search for treasure. By the time Daniel McGinnis roamed the eastern drumlins of Oak Island and was finding the Money Pit, we read and see evidence of those changes.

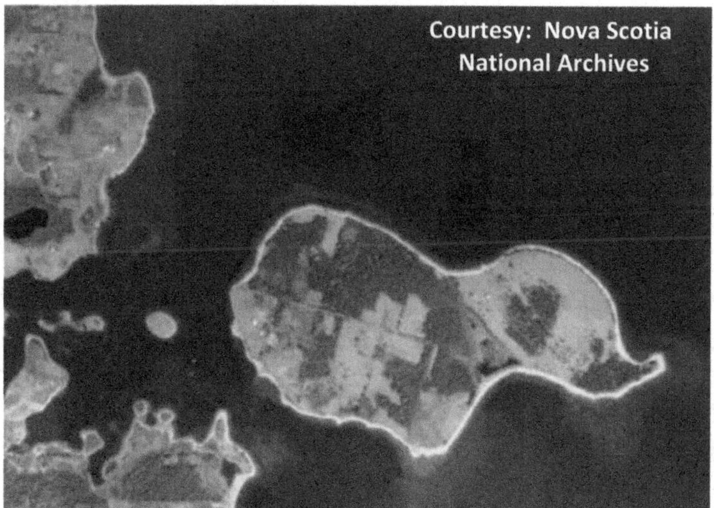

Though the above aerial photograph was taken in 1929, lot cultivation, tree harvesting, and population growth gives a clear testament to the constant regrowth of forest areas on the island. The forests of Oak Island today, have no direct relationship to the species growing in 1795.

New England Acadian Forest (NEAF) post-European Settlement 1890-2019

The latter majority of the third phase of the borealization of the New England Acadian Forest ecoregion is not part of our analysis. It "outdates" the forensic issues pursued within this book. However, some of this activity, primarily farming, timbering, livestock, and treasure mining on the island, will help inform us of what transpired back at the start of the 1800s.

Today, the Acadian forest bears more of a resemblance to a boreal forest than it used to, though it is still considered primarily a temperate ecoregion. These results were determined by reports of significant declines in Sugar Maple, Eastern Hemlock, Eastern White Pine, Burr Oak, and Northern Red Oak.[1, 2b] Past researchers and authors concluded: *the combination of abandoned farmland, clearcutting, conflagrations, introduced new tree species, storms, related insects' infestation and disease, as well as the considerable amount of boreal conifer plantation silviculture, all favored boreal tree species at the expense of temperate ones. Simply described, the opening up of a previously closed-canopy forest has allowed exposure-adapted boreal tree species to colonize and now approach domination of the NEAF ecoregion*.[1, 2b] There is little to remind Canadians or Nova Scotians of the primeval old growth forests which once covered the NEAF.[1]

To this point, we have identified the list of tree species "native" within the New England Acadian Forests (NEAF), during the pre-European Settlement period. On the following page is a graph contrasting changes in major tree species' range and population within the NEAF, from 1800 to 1993. The borealization of the NEAF is proven by the increase in number of boreal hardwood species from 22 to 27; while the number of temperate softwood species remains the same. The same cannot be said for oak species within our area of interest.

Change of Major Tree Species in NEAF, 1800-1993. [2b]

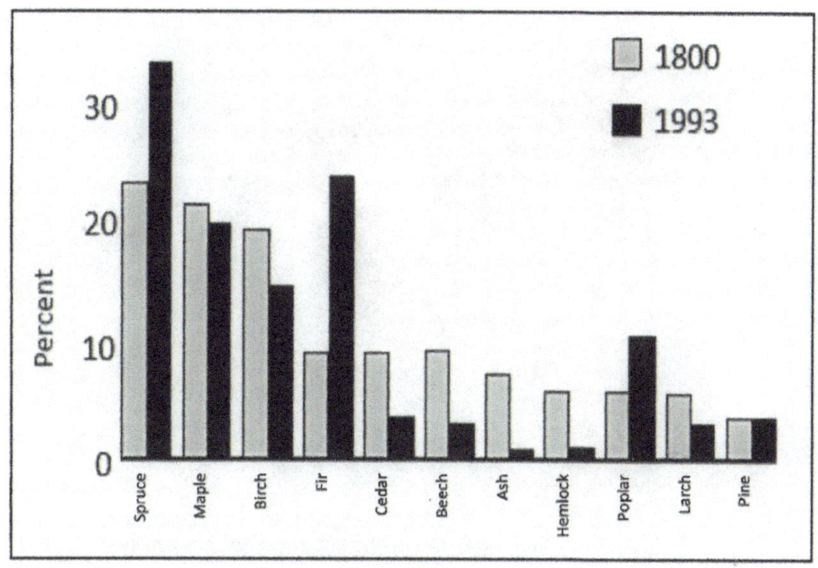

Courtesy: *The Forestry Chronicle*. V. 79, N. 3, P. 462-474. May/Jun 2003

The oak Genus *Quercus* is not represented in the above graphic, as the white oak tree species Burr Oak (*Q. macrocarpa*) was so completely sought out for harvesting. It is now extirpating as a native species of the NEAF.[19] Throughout sub-regions of the NEAF, Burr Oak has recently been categorized by the *Atlantic Canada Conservation Data Center's* "S" rankings, as an S-2.[19] This indicates the species is rare in the province, making it vulnerable to extirpation. New Brunswick also has listed Burr Oak as a "may be at risk" status.[19] This requires immediate intervention to stop the extinction and loss of valuable genetic variation. Similar species warnings are in effect in Maine, New Hampshire, and Maryland, while in both Nova Scotia and Prince Edward Island, natural Burr Oak occurrence outside ornamental plantings has never been documented![19] The Tamarack (*Larix larcinia*) was often used as a replacement for Burr Oak's wood characteristics. The Tamarack was also hunted to near protection status and represents 1.7% of the merchantable wood products in Nova Scotia today. The following map illustrates the range of the Burr Oak species today.

Burr Oak Species Range Today

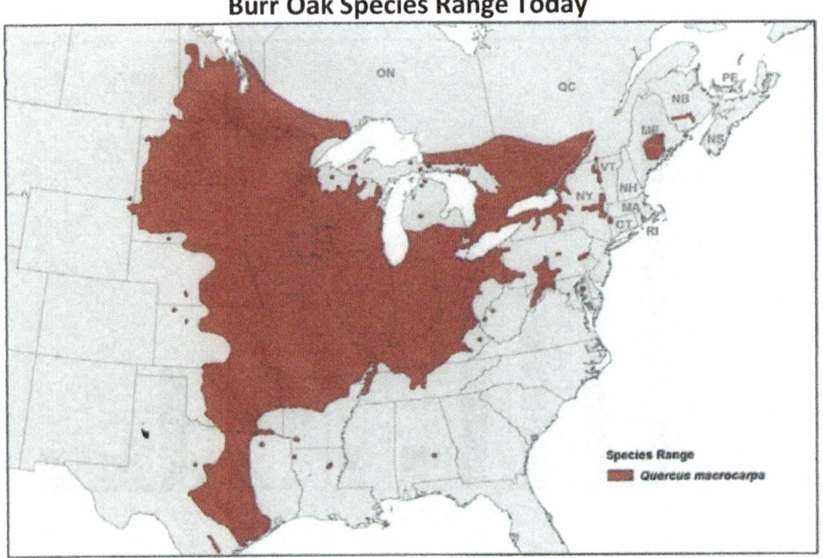

Courtesy: *Northeastern Naturalist*, 16(I):85-100. 2009

The only other *Quercus* species (*Quercus rubra*) - *Northern Red Oak*, remains the sole oak tree species identified as a surviving Canadian native. It represented less than 1% of the species population and range prior to the European settlement period discussed. It has survived and somewhat improved its standing amongst NEAF tree species since that time. This is primarily due to it being a "boreal shade-tolerant" tree as well. This species characteristic has helped the Red Oak find refuge throughout the NEAF and has assisted its survivability. The Northern Red Oak only represents .9% of today's merchantable wood products.[20] The existing indications point to us that 'native oaks' on Oak Island would have been a rare sight in *New Scotland* as late as 1795! Further taxonomic presentations in Appendix E, *"Known NEAF Neighbors"* provide the biological evidence on each of those species. It concludes none of the native species within the NEAF were related by species or twisted by a tropisms to be our canopied mystery trees.

Native NEAF tree species in 1600 compared to today. [1, 2b, 21]

NEAF Native Tree Species – 1600	NEAF Native Tree Species - 2021
Jack Pine *(Pinus banksiana)*	Jack Pine *(Pinus banksiana Lamb.)*
White Spruce *(Picea glauca)*	White Spruce *(Picea glauca (Moench)*
Black Spruce *(Picea mariana)*	Black Spruce *(Picea mariana (Mill) B.S.P.)*
Balsam Poplar *(Populus balsamifera)*	**Balsam Poplar** *(Populus balsamifera)*
Tamarack *(Larix laricina)* [Larch]	Tamarack *(Larix laricina K. Koch.)*
White Birch *(Betula papyrifera)*	**White Birch** *(Betula papyrifera Marshall)*
Balsam Fir *(Abies balsamea)*	Balsam Fir *(Abies balsamea)*
Trembling Aspen *(Populus tremuloides)*	**Trembling Aspen** *(Populus tremuloides)*
Pin Cherry *(Prunus pensylvanica)*	**Pin Cherry** *(Prunus pensylvanica)*
Cedar *(Fraxinus americana)*	Eastern White Cedar *(Thuga occidentalis)*
Black Ash *(Fraxinus nigra)*	**Black Ash** *(Fraxinus nigra)* *EXTIRPATING*
Red Pine *(Pinus resinosa)*	Red Pine *(Pinus resinosa Ait.)*
White Pine *(Pinus strobus)*	White Pine *(Pinus strobus L.)*
Largetooth Aspen*(Populus grandidentata)*	**Largetooth Aspen** *(Populus grandidentata)*
White Elm *(Ulmus americana)*	**White Elm** *(Ulmus americana)*
Yellow Birch *(Betula alleghaniensis)*	**Yellow Birch** *(Betula alleghaniensis Baitt.)*
Red Ash *(Fraxinus pennsylvanica)*	**Amer. Mountain Ash** *(Sorbus americana)*
Burr Oak *(Quercus macrocarpa)*	**Burr Oak** *(Quercus macrocarpa)* ***EXTIRP.***
Sugar Maple *(Acer saccharum)*	**Sugar Maple** *(Acer saccharum)*
Striped Maple *(Acer pensylvanicum)*	**Striped Maple** *(Acer pensylvanicum)*
Red Maple *(Acer rubrum)*	**Red Maple** *(Acer rubrum L.)*
Northern Red Oak *(Quercus rubra)*	**Northern Red Oak** *(Quercus rubra L.)*
Red Spruce *(Picea rubens)*	Red Spruce *(Picea rubens Sarg.)*
White Ash *(Fraxinus americana)*	**White Ash** *(Fraxinus americana L.)*
Basswood *(Tilia americana)*	**Basswood** *(Tilia americana)*
Hemlock (Tsuga canadensis)	Eastern Hemlock *(Tsuga canadensis (L.)*
Silver Maple *(Acer saccharinum)*	**Silver Maple** *(Acer saccharinum)*
Butternut *(Juglans cinerea)*	**Butternut** *(Juglans cinerea)*
Black Cherry *(Prunus serotina)*	**Black Cherry** *(Prunus serotina)*
***American* Beech** *(Fafus grandifolia)*	***American* Beech** *(Fafus grandifolia Ehrh.)*
Black Birch *(Betula nigra)*	**Grey Birch** *(Betula populifolia)*
Ironwood *(Ostrya virginiana)*	**Ironwood** *(Ostrya virginiana)*
	Chokecherry *(Prunus virginiana Ca. Red.)*
	Speckled Alder *(Alnus incana ssp. rugosa)*
	Staghorn Sumac *(Rhus typhina)*
	Serviceberry *(Anelanchier canadensis)*
	Black Willow *(Salix nigra)* ** tiny range*

Chart created by David Neisen

This represents the list of original native NEAF tree species with their common and Genus names, as compared to today's NEAF tree species and their Genus names. The list does not notate hybrid changes within some species family. Hardwoods species are shown in **bold** type.

If DNA testing were available of any fallen dead canopied tree or their remaining root systems, an answer could be final. Having talked to an Oak Island employed participant, they have confessed no remaining snags, logs, or root system remnants have been found of those canopied trees. However, our exploration of anecdotal historical records, commentary, and species taxonomy, will bring together the forensic evidence to ascertain the most likely tree species, and maybe even - *why on Oak Island?*

Footnoted References

1. "*Borealization of the New England Acadian Forest: a Review of the Evidence*." by Josh Noseworthy and Thomas M. Beckley. NRC Research Press. Global Conservation Solutions & Forestry and Environmental Management, University of New Brunswick. February 12, 2020. Environmental Reviews. 28(3): 284-293. https://doi.org/10.1139/er-2019-0068. © Canadian Science Publishing or its licensors. 12 pages.

2. "*Challenges for the Boreal Forest Zone and IBFRA*." by S. Nilsson, 2000. IIASA 16 pages, @ http://forestportal.efi.int/view.php?id=1087&c=I1. See website International Boreal Forest Research Association. http://ibfra.org/about-boreal-forests/.

2b. "*The Acadian forest: Historical condition and human impacts*." by J. Loo and N. Ives, Paper presented at the "Old-growth Forests in Canada: A Science Perspective" Conference, Oct. 14–19, 2001. Sault Ste. Marie, ON. MAI/JUIN 2003, VOL. 79, NO. 3, THE FORESTRY CHRONICLE.

3. "*Nova Scotian Biographies: Isaac Razilly 1587-1635*." by Peter Landry, 2012.

4. "*The Description and Natural History of the Coasts of North America*." by Nicolas Denys, 1632-1670. Pub. 1672, under title: "Description Geographique et Historique des Costes de L'Amerique Septentrionale: arec L'Histoire Naturelle du pais."

5. *"The King's Pines."* Nov. 10, 2015, Edition, Mountain Top Arboretum.

6. *"Eastern White Pine: Monarch of the Forest."* by Sheereen Othman, January 9, 2018 Edition, Arbor Day Foundation.

7. *"Two Voyages to the New World."* by John Josselyn, 1674.

[8]. "*New England masts and the King's Broad Arrow*." by Samuel F. Manning, 1979. Greenwich, London: Trustees of the National Maritime Museum. Inclusive of the 1691 Massachusetts Bay Colony Charter Act: *"An Act for the Preservation of White and other Pine-Trees growing in Her Majesties Colonies of New-Hampshire, The Massachusetts-Bay, and Province of Main, Rhode-Island, and Providence-Plantation, the Narraganset Country, or Kings-Province, and Connecticut in New-England, and New-York, and New-Jersey, in America, for the Masting her Majesties Navy."*

[9]. "*Changes in the Land: Indians, Colonists, and the Ecology of New England*." by William Cronon. 1983. (2010 current). See page 147. Farrar, Strauss and Giroux publishers. 288 pages. (Accessed 02-09-22).

[10]. "*The Halifax Naval Yard and Mast Contractors, 1775 – 1815*." by Julian Gwyn. Public Record Office, ADM106/1653, Wentworth to Navy Board, June 14, 1816. *The Northern Mariner/Le marin du nord,* XI, No. 4 (Oct. 2001), 1-25.

[11]. *"HMS Victory 100-gun First Ship-of-the-Line."* by JR Potts. AUS 173d AB, October 16, 2020. Naval Warfare Ships, Militaryfactory.com.

[12]. "*History of the County of Lunenburg – 2nd Edition*." by Mather Byles DeBrisay, Judge of County Courts and Member of the Historical Society of Nova Scotia. Harvard College Library, 4-7-1896, Cambridge, Mass. Second Edition, 1895. Originally written at Bridgewater & La Have, February 1870 . Pgs. 261-306.

[13]. *"Forests of Nova Scotia: A History."* by Ralph S. Johnson, 1986. Nova Scotia Department of Lands and Forests. Four East Publications, Halifax, Nova Scotia. Chapter The 19th century 1801-1852, pages 60-73. https://archive.org/details/forestsofnovasco0000john/page/n7/mode/2up.

[14]. *"Hurricanes and Tropical Storms."* Environment and Climate Change, Canada.ca. August 26, 2011. https://www.canada.ca/en/environment-climate-change/services/weather-general-tools-resources/hurricanes-tropical-storms.html.

[15]. *"Windthrow."* Ontario Department of Lands and Forests. 1953. Forest tree planting. 2d ed. Bull. No. R 1. Toronto, Canada: Ontario Department of Lands and Forests, Division of Reforestation. P. 68 [12130].

[16]. *"Woodlands shaped by past Hurricanes."* by David Dwyer, Forester. (originally published in Forest Times November 1979).

[17]. "*5 Worst Storms to Hit the East Coast*." by Paul Daly, Canadian Press, 2012. CBC News Posted: Sep 11, 2012. Last Updated: September 11, 2012. https://www.cbc.ca/news/canada/5-worst-storms-to-hit-the-east-coast-1.1138740.

[18]. *"The Restall Story – Oak Island Obsession."* Lee Lamb. Dundurn Press, Toronto, Ontario, Canada. Chapter 10, p. 160.

[19]. *"Past and Present Distribution of New Brunswick Bur Oak Populations: A Case for Conservation."* by Donnie A. McPhee and Jude A. Loo. Northeastern Naturalist, 16(1):85-100. 2009.

[20]. *"Module 1: Introduction to Silviculture, Lesson Three – Hardwood Tree Identification and Silvics/Quercus Rubra."* Woodlot, 2012. (Accessed 04-12-22). https://woodlot.novascotia.ca/book/export/html/84.

[21]. *"Early Survival and Growth of Planted Hardwoods in the Acadian Forest."* by Xu MA. Nanjing Forestry University, Introduction Section. The University of New Brunswick. January 2019. 48 pages.

Appendix C

ON THE RECORD

Within is a compilation of comments, quotes, records, publications, and conversations by owners, botanists, researchers, reporters, authors, scientists, treasure-seekers, and storytellers. This volume represent in many cases, the foundation of the forensic analysis being undertaken in this book. Without any tangible evidence to hold in ones' hand, this reportage is critical – although subject to human interpretation.

Opining About Oak Island. Courtesy IStock.com

Those chapters which explore specific topics such as coconut fiber, red clover and the depression, and description of the mystery canopied trees; will contain the appropriate opinions or subsets of opinions, reprinted in those related chapters. This appendix represents the entirety of worthwhile statements on these topics. Not every comment is captured. Many sources have repeated the same telling which is then again repeated elsewhere in the covering of this fascinating story. The goal of this appendix is to accumulate an assortment of statements, interpretations, reports, findings, or observations to add to the basis for forensic analysis. Some commentors are simply incorrect in their understanding. This includes scientific determinations and expert opinions. They still add value to understanding the evolution of the issues at hand. Some of the crazier opinions have stuck in the overall Oak Island legend like a poker in the eye. Examples mostly center around coconut fibers and the mystery canopied trees. This book has gone to great lengths to prove the factualness of those opinions and show why they are incorrect.

As you review this material, try to read what is a fib and what is a fact. Most of forensic examination is an attempt to extract lonely bits of truth from the heaps of cheap talk. Consider it the same as looking at a picture to see what is really being shown. Truths hide in plain sight. If you think you are good at it, go back to the previous page and look again at the illustration for what you can see.

Those Who Have Opined

Each entry is listed in chronological order. The assigned number will follow the quote, opinion or reportage, OR A PORTION THEREOF, with them should they be reposted in applicable chapters or other appendices. This allows the entry to be abbreviated for reposting yet allows the reader to find the entire text and context of the quotation, here in this appendix.

1. "Giovanni da Verrazzano Quotation." First European to leave a detailed account of his journey to North America, during his 1524 expedition to the Acadia region. Book by Rutkow,2012.

> *"the wooddes [were] so greate and thicke that an armye (where it never so greate) mighte have hydd it selfe therein. This land is Acadia (idyllic place)."*

2. "The Description and Natural History of the Coasts of North America," by Nicolas Denys, 1632-1670. Pub. 1672, under title: "Description Geographique et Historique des Costes de L'Amerique Septentrionale: arec L'Histoire Naturelle du pais."

> *In 1633, Nicolas Denys – the Governor of Cape Breton Island, Prince Edward Island, and the coastline from 'Canso to Gaspe' from 1654-1688; surveyed these maritime landscapes to report lumber opportunities to the French government. These territories included Mahone Bay and the regions along the eastern coasts of Nova Scotia. Denys wrote: "some Oak, Pines, Firs of 3 sorts (Spruce, Fir & Hemlock), Birches (White Birch), Black Birches (Yellow Birch), Beeches, Aspens, Maples and Ashes were the predominant species."*

3. "The Halifax Naval Yard and Mast Contractors, 1775-1815," by Julian Gwyn. www.cnrs-scrn.org/northern_mariner/Vol.11, said;

> *"In **1760** the naval storekeeper, Joseph Gerrish, informed the Navy Board that on the La Have River were available "mast trees of considerable dimensions." Three years later_**[1763]** Philip Peake, foreman of shipwrights, went to Chester and Mahone Bay in search of black birch, trees suitable for oak and pine timber for capstan barrels, catheads, knees, standards, and cheeks as well as masts, spars, yards, and bowsprits. He returned with a rather discouraging report, "having*

found only a few black birch fit for capstan barrels between thirty and thirty-three inches in diameter, some small oak, pine and spruce from sixteen inches and smaller, but very straight and tall. There was no oak timber for ships above 150 to 200 tons, some pine fit for masts of up to 20-gun ships, yards and topmasts for 40-gun and 50-gun ships, but at a great distance from the rivers, the ground being rough and rocky." Commodore Sir George Collier noted that the forest in the 1770s was still but two or three miles distant from the town of Halifax, while the rest of Nova Scotia was "one wild desert, thick wooded as possible with trees, which principally consists of what they call hemlock."

4. "Permit to Fell Timber at Western Shore," for Daniel & Anthony Vaughan," *1788*. Blockhouse Blog.

"Having caused the aforesaid lotts of land and the pine trees standing thereon to be inspected and surveyed, I do, incomformity to his Majesties instructions, hereby grant lycense to the aforesaid David Vaughan, Anthony Vaughan and James McLeod to cut and take away the pine trees growing thereon; save and except thirty eight trees; being from 16" and upwards in diameter and from 26' and upwards in length, which are marked (image) being fit and are to retain for his Majesty's service; and are therefore wholly excepted out of this lycense accordingly. Given under my hand at Halifax this 25th day of January 1788. J.W. Wentworth"

5. "Canadian Forestry Chronical," by Sidney Perley, 1847. Pubs-dif-ifc.org. 6-25-2020. Pgs. 72, 120, 141, 201.

Titus Smith, Ecologist to the Crown from 1801-02, reported *"Pine trees common between 125-175 feet tall."* In *1847*, Perley reported *"Red Pine from 70-80 feet tall, White Pine from 160 feet tall, and Butternut as much as 80 feet tall; while Red Oak and Bur Oak were the only Oak species found."*

6. "The Oak Island Folly - The Nova Scotian," September 30, 1861. Excerpts by Author "Patrick". Pgs. 1-4.

"The ground on the part of the island, where search is made for the treasure, is formed of compact clay, mixed with round lumps of stone to the depth of 110 feet, perfectly dry, excepting in one pit where the water comes in at 98 feet from the surface. Over 50 years ago, a company from Onslow took the earth from this pit, and found it was dug at some former period, and carefully filled in with earth, in which they found wood, charcoal, putty, & coconut fiber. At 93 feet from the surface they probed with a crowbar, and struck a platform of wood 5 feet beneath them; after which the water came in, and neither they, nor any company that followed them, ever again sent a shaft so far down...

... The following is a memorandum of one of several holes bored through this platform at 98 feet: 1) Six inches, spruce wood. 2) A space of 12 inches, through which the auger fell. 3) Four inches, oak wood. 4) Twenty inches of a material, which by its action upon, and the sound conveyed along the auger, resembled boring through small pieces of metal - coin, if you will - through which the auger passed by its own weight, in one turn. 5) Eight inches, oak wood. 6) Twenty inches, similar to the twenty above. 7) Four inches, oak wood; and then through spruce wood, into the clay below...

...At the shore there were drains laid most skillfully, and underneath, the sand covered with a kind of grass, which one of the best Botanists in the Province informed us grew nowhere in the British North American Provinces. This same grass was bored up from about the platforms in the old pit; it was also found in these drains - shewing the two works to be connected."

7. "Report to Inspector of Mines for the Province, John Rutherford," Employee Henry S. Poole, Esq. wrote about his observations of Oak Island, when visiting in 1861. He would in 1872, replace Rutherford as Inspector of Mines.

"I crossed to Oak Island and observed slate all the way along the main shore, but I could not see any, rock in situ on the island...

...I found the original shaft had caved in, and two others had been sunk alongside. One was open and said to be 120 feet deep, and in all that depth no rock had been struck. The excavated matter alongside was composed of sand and boulder rocks, and though the pit was some two hundred yards from the shore, the water in the shaft (which I measured to be within thirty eight feet of the top) rose and fell with the tide, showing a free communication between the sea and the shaft."

8. "The Oak Island Diggings," by Jotham Blanchard McCully, October 16, 1862. Published in "The Liverpool Transcript." Pgs. 3 & 8.

"Sometime after the arrival of these persons, a Mr. McGinnis went to Oak Island to make a farm, when he discovered the spot in question from its being sunken, and from the position of three oak trees, which stood in a triangular form round the pit. The bark had letters cut into it with a knife on each tree facing the pit, and one of the trees being so directly over the pit, that two large branches formed a crotch, were exactly perpendicular to the center, and had a hole bored through, and an oak treenail driven in, on which hung a tackle block...

...After going down ten feet they found a layer of oak timber, at twenty the same, and thirty the same...

...and we commenced where they first left off, and sunk the pit 93 feet, finding a mark every ten feet. Some of them were charcoal, some putty, and one at 80 feet was a stone cut square, two feet long and about a foot thick, with several characters on it. All the way down they were confined to a diameter of 16 feet, by the softness of the ground within that limit. The pick marks could be distinctly seen all around the sides of the pit. After they got down 93 feet, they forced a crowbar down and struck wood at five which appeared to be a platform from its being level, making in all to the supposed platform 98 feet...

...The second hole we bored struck the platform which the old diggers told us about - precisely at the depth they told us they had struck it with the crowbar, 98 feet. It proved to be spruce, six inches thick...

...then eight inches of oak, six inches spruce, and then seven feet worked clay, then hard clay which had never been disturbed...

...Work was evidently done by hands in both pits, and also at the beach, where we found flag stones made in the form of drains and covered with a kind of grass, not the growth of this country, and the outer rind of the coconut."

9. "Oak Island, The Reasons for Supposing Treasure is Buried There," by Paul Pry. For the Yarmouth Herald. 2-19-1863. Pgs. 1-6.

"It appears that about 64 years ago [1799]*, a man residing on the island first discovered indications of a pit having been dug. A circular piece of ground covered with clover, and oak trees growing by the side of it, a large bough of one of them extending over the spot, and a strong oak tree nail driven through the bough into the body of the tree, led the discoverer to suppose there was money buried there. Believing himself to be the first resident on the island, and having lived three years alone with his family, ...his surprise was very great on finding the circular clover field, where no clover was supposed to grow on the island. On making his discovery known to his neighbor on the mainland, a small company was formed. They found the earth where the clover grew, sunken below the level of the ground immediately around it. And on digging the earth, required only the shovel and spade, while the marks of a pick were clearly discernible all around the sides of the pit. The surrounding earth being of a hard bluish clay, so hard, that a strong man could only penetrate the soil two or three inches with the blow of a pick. At every ten feet a mark was discovered, some were of timber, one charcoal, one of putty, and the*

eighty feet mark was a stone about two feet long, cut square, which is yet to be seen in the chimney of an old house near the pit."

10. "History of the Oak Island Enterprise – Chapter 1," By James McNutt. Printed in "The Colonist" on 1-2-1864, Truro, Nova Scotia. Pgs. 1-4

"...At that time, this part of Nova Scotia was thinly settled, and few inroads had been made upon its primeval forests by the axes of former settlers. These men found the Island covered with a thick growth of wood, mostly oak; and very little of the mainland cleared...

...McGinnis, while roaming over the Island one day discovered a spot that gave unmistakable proof of having been visited by someone a good many years previously. He found that the first growth of wood had been cut down, and that another was springing up to supply its place. And some old stumps of oak trees that had been chopped down were visible. Near this place stood one of the original Oaks with a large, forked branch extending over the old clearing. To the forked part of this branch, by means of a wooden trunnel converting the fork into a small triangle, was attached an old tackle block. McGinnis immediately made known his discovery to those who had emigrated to the place with himself. ***All three were then living on terms of great intimacy...***

...The next day they visited the spot together, and on taking the block from the tree, it fell to the ground and tumbled to pieces. While investigating the place they found that the remains of a tolerably well-made road from it to the west shore of the Island, were still discernable...

...They found that the ground over which the block and tackle swung had settled and formed a hollow. They cleared the young timber from the sunken ground and removed the surface soil for about two feet, when they struck a tier of flag stones, evidently not formed there by nature. Afterwards they ascertained that these stones were not indigenous to the Island, but must have been taken from Gold River, about two miles distant. On removing the stones, they saw that they were entering the mouth of an old pit or shaft that had been filled up. The mouth was seven feet in diameter, and the sides of the pit were of tough, hard clay, but the earth with which it had been filled up was loose and easy to be removed. They dug ten feet lower down when they came across a tier of oak logs tightly attached to the sides, and the earth below the logs had settled nearly two feet. The outside of the logs was so rotten that they felt confident they must have been imbedded there for a great many years. On removing them they continued the work till they were fifteen feet further down...

...when they struck a second tier of oak logs, corresponding with the first. Ten feet lower down they found a tier of charcoal, and ten feet further a tier of putty. Further down was a flag stone about two feet long and one wide, with a number of rudely cut letters and figures upon it...

...After reaching a distance of ninety feet the earth in the center of the pit became softer and water began to show itself. At ninety-three feet it increased, and they had to take out one tub of water to two of earth."

11. "History of Oak Island Enterprise – Chapter II," by James McNutt. Printed in "The Colonist" on Dec. 1864. P. 4.

..."All they got instead was some more of the same description of grass already referred to - a small piece of wood, broken off the bilge of a cask and afterwards, a portion of the hoop that encased it...

...And from this bore they ascertained that the space containing the casks, between the upper and lower wooden obstructions, which they now called platforms, occupied six feet. Within this space no mud had protruded. Beneath the lower platform they continued the bore for a short distance without finding anything besides earth and mud. But from the way in which the auger penetrated this they judged that the earth had at one time been removed for at least eight feet below where they had encountered wood...

...They removed the covering as well as they could and found that the stones forming the arch of the drain were coated with a layer of the same kind of grass, they had found on the top of the upper platform in the old pit at a distance of ninety-eight feet from the surface. In investigating the drains further they found that they connected with one of larger dimensions, the stones forming which had been prepared with a hammer and were mechanically laid in such a way that the drain could not collapse. There were a number of tiers of stones strengthening the higher part of the drain, on the top of which was also found a coating of the same sort of grass as that already noticed. Over it came a layer of blue sand, such as before had not been seen on the Island. And over the sand was spread the gravel indigenous to the coast. Having laid bare the large drain for a short distance into the bank, they found that it had been so well made and protected that no earth had sifted through its arch to obstruct water passing through it."

12. "Account by James McNutt, Secretary of the Oak Island Eldorado Co.," known as the Halifax Co. Transcribed by Les MacPhie. Work carried out from Dec. 1866 - Jan. 1867. Pgs. 1-6.

".... to dig in the clover patch at the ten feet found a tier of wood and the pit to be 12 feet in diameter. At twenty another tier of wood, at 30 feet a tier of hued timber, and the pick marks was clearly to be seen on the hard sides. By this time, the work was too hard for ***four men*** *to carry on...*

...and resumed the work at 30 feet where the others left off. At 40 feet a tier of charcoal, at 50 feet a tier of smooth stones from the beach with figures and letters cut on them, at 60 feet a tier of manilla grass and the rind of a coconut, at 70 feet a tier of putty, at eighty feet a stone 3 feet long and 1 foot square with figures and letters cut on it, and it was free stone being different from any on that coast...

...Then, in boring the remaining holes, two oak planks were passed through of the thickness of 4 inches and about 3 feet apart. A sort of grass was brought up by the auger, the same as found in the pit at 60 feet and a substance white in color and much resembling putty."

... They then commenced between high and low water marks and, after clearing off the dirt and sand, found a pit covered with the same kind or grass and coconut rind as found at 60 feet in the pit. And also brought up with the auger underneath the grass. The pit was filled with broken stone nicely laid in arches running out below low water mark...

...also oak chips and manilla grass and two large smooth stones that had been taken off the surface of the earth...

...December 1866, boring through soft clay and blue mud, below 18 feet clay becomes more sandy and dry, at 20 feet water commenced to flow up the tube carrying up clay, gravel and stones as large as would come up through tube, also chips of wood and coconut fiber and a considerable amount of what appeared to be charcoal."

13. "John Brown Report on Boreholes I, II, and III." Transcript by Les MacPhie of report dated January 17, 1867, by John Brown of Walton Manganese Mines, to the Directors of The Oak Island Company and to W. J. Veith, J D Nash, John Selnes. Pg. 3.

..." I often at a depth of 150 ft threw money into the hole, of course it came up in the augur and I for one should not be in the least afraid to throw any amount in, and to bring up every piece...

...The original depression on the surface, as well as the old round pit, must be attributed to a natural caving having taken place from the layer of gravel upwards; such things are by no means uncommon ...

...At Oak Island at the present time, there is to be seen a depression on the surface, similar to the mouth of the old pit and probably caused by the same means. The cavings to Mr. Hill's tunnels show that it required but an excavation of 7 ft in height to cause a slip of 100 feet and what is still more curious, is, that these are round or nearly so, in shape. The old diggers assert, and subsequent investigation has proved that the so-called old Money Pit was not only round, but that it seemed to incline to the east. Now it would be impossible without very secure timbering, to sink through the clay that is found there, in any, but a perpendicular direction; the overhanging part not being able to support itself; no mention has I believe ever been made of any timber having been found. It seems also absolutely impossible that providing there had been a platform across the pit, that the two holes we put to the bottom should not have struck some portion of it."

...Should the ground have caved in (as I suppose) it would be broken up and very easy to remove. At a depth of 90 feet it may have become sufficiently consolidated to resist for a time the rising of the water, or until the diggers should have removed enough weight to allow the pressure of water to burst through and rise to tide level."

14. "Affidavit from S.C. Fraser to A.S. Lowden," copy by Frederick Blair. June 19, 1895.

"McNutt's boring after all other work on the island until last year was concluded; found disturbed earth, cocoanut fibre and pieces of wood down to 155 ft. Now there was tons and tons of that cocoanut fibre on the works at the shore and around the treasure in the pit. Pray what is it now doing 150 (? 50) feet below the former place of the treasure? ...I did not know that the earth of the island undisturbed, had cocoanut fibre and wood mixed with it. The pamphlet says, "East India grass," it is not; but cocoanut fibre nearly as well preserved as what I took off the cocoanut when examining and comparing them. ...The (pirates) had quite a road from the west of the Money Pit, quite visible to the oldest diggers of all, and easily traced when I was there and can yet if it is not plowed."

15. "History of the County of Lunenburg," by Mather Byles DeBrisay, Judge of County Courts and Member of the Historical Society of Nova Scotia. Harvard College Library, 4-7-1896, Cambridge, Mass. Second Edition, 1895. Originally written at Bridgewater and La Have, February 1870 . Pgs. 301-306

"Among the islands, none is more widely known than Oak Island, four miles from Chester, so called from the beautiful oak trees, some of which remain...

...The first settlers were John McMullen and Daniel McInnis, father of Mrs. Thomas Whitford [Mary], of Chester... "[Sam Ball]... The farm of thirty-six acres, on which he lived and which he cleared, is now occupied by Mr. Isaac Butler, who resided with him."... "He died there, December 14th, 1845, aged eighty -one years." The other occupants of the island are James McInnis, and Enos Jodrey. The pits hereinafter referred to were dug on the farm formerly owned by John Smith, who was born in Boston, Mass. August 20th, 1775, and died on the island, after a residence there of seventy one years, on September 29, 1857...

...Published December 20, 1863, and subsequently, by a member of the Oak Island Association... Three men — Smith, McInnis (grandfather of James McInnis) and Vaund [should be Vaughan] *emigrated from New England to Chester. Smith and McInnis took up land on Oak Island and Vaughan settled on the adjacent mainland...*

...McInnis one day discovered a spot that gave evidence of having been visited by someone a good many a year earlier. There had been cuttings away of the forest and oak stumps were visible. One of the original oaks was standing with a large, forked branch extending over the old clearing. To the forked part of this branch, by means of a treenail connecting the fork in a small triangle, was attached an old tackle block. The ground over which the block has been, had settled and formed a hollow. They cleared away the young trees and removed the surface soil for about two feet, when they struck a tier of flagstones , which they found differed from the island stones, and concluded they had been brought from the vicinity of Gold River. On removing these, they saw they were entering an old pit that had been filled up. The mouth was seven feet in diameter and the sides were of tough, hard clay; but the earth which had been used in filling was loose, and easy to be removed. Ten feet lower was a tier of oak logs, tightly attached to the sides, and the earth below them had settled nearly two feet. The logs were very much decayed on the outside. Removing these, they went fifteen feet farther down. They went on and struck a second tier of logs like those first found. Ten feet lower they came to charcoal, ten feet below it to putty, and farther down to a flagstone about two feet long and one foot wide, with rudely cut

letters and figures which they could not decipher. The engraved side was downwards. On reaching a depth of ninety feet, the earth in the center became softened, and water began to show itself. At ninety three feet, it increased, and they took out one tub of water to two of earth. Night coming on, they, as usual, probed the bottom with a crowbar, to see if they could strike anything. At the depth of ninety eight feet, five feet below where the bar entered, they met a hard impenetrable substance, bound by the sides of the pit."

16. "The Story of Oak Island – 1895," by Frederick L. Blair. Included in "Buried Treasure", part of Oak Island Treasure Company's Public Share Offering. "Additional" Information included.

"The Story in Detail: ...The island is about 1 mile in length and a half as broad. The formation is very hard, tough clay. The eastern end was originally covered with oak timber, several groves of which still remain...

...In 1795, three men – Smith, McGinnis, and Vaughn, visited the island and while rambling over the eastern part of it, came to a spot, of which the unusual and strange conditions at one engaged their attention. It had every appearance of having been cleared many years before. Red clover and other plants altogether foreign to the soil in its natural state were growing. Near the center stood a large oak tree with marks and figures on its trunk. One of the lower and larger branches of this, the outer end of which had been sawed off, projected directly over the center of a deep circular depression in the land about 13 feet in diameter. These and other "signs" shortly after led the three men named to commence work. After digging a few feet, they found that they were working in a well-defined shaft, the walls of which were hard and solid; and it is said that in some places old pick marks were plainly to be seen, while within these walls the earth was so loose that pics were not required. On reaching a depth of 10 feet they came to a covering of oak plank. They kept on digging until a dept of 30 feet was reached, finding marks at each 10 feet...

...Work was at once resumed by this company and the shaft was excavated to a depth of 95 feet. Marks were found every 10 feet, as before, and an iron bar was frequently used in taking soundings. The 90 foot mark was a flat stone about 3 feet long and 16 inches wide...

...Until the depth of 95 feet was reached no water had been encountered, neither had sand or gravel through which water could possibly percolate been met. It was Saturday evening when the depth above named had been reached, and it was at this point that a wooden platform was struck, extending over the entire surface of the shaft, as revealed by the soundings...

....The platform was struck at 98 ft., just as the old diggers, as before mentioned, found it when sounding with the iron bar. After going through this platform, which was five inches thick, and proved to be spruce...

...then 4 inches of oak and 6 inches of spruce; then into clay 7 ft. without striking anything else. In the next boring... On withdrawing the augur several splinters of oak, such as might come from the side of an oak stave, and a small quantity of brown fibrous substance, closely resembling the husk of a coconut, were brought up. The distance between the upper and lower platforms was found to be 6 feet...

...This evidently was not the case, (see the account of borings already given) as well as the fact that the shaft had been systematically filled up, with marks placed at every 10 ft., as previously stated. Smith's Cove, on the extreme eastern end of the island and about 30 rods from the Money Pit was first examined by reason of its many natural advantages as a starting point for work of this kind, and from the fact that at about the center of this cove it had always been noticed that at low tide, water was running out of the sand [bank]...

...After removing the sand and gravel covering the beach, they came to a covering or bed of a brown, fibrous plant, the fiber very much resembling the husk of a coconut, and when compared with the plant that was bored out of the Money Pit already mentioned, no difference in the two could be detected. However it was subsequently proved to be a tropical plant, in former times used as 'dunnage' in storing ship's cargo. The surface covered by this plant extended 145' along the shoreline, and from a little above low to high water mark, and about two inches in thickness. Underlying this and to the same extend was about 4-5" of decayed eelgrass, and under this was a compact mass of beach rocks free from sand or gravel...

...After removing the rocks nearest the low water, it was found that the clay (which with the sand and gravel originally formed the beach) had been dug out and removed and replaced by beach rocks. Resting on the bottom of this excavation were five well-constructed drains formed by having parallel lines of rocks about 8" apart and covering the same with "flat stones". These drains at the starting point were a considerable distance apart but converged towards a common center at the back of the excavation...

...Work went on until half of the rocks had been removed where the clay banks at the extreme sides showed a depth of 5 ft., at which depth a partially burned piece of oak wood was found."

ADDITIONAL: (P. 10)

"I spent some time, last summer and fall, on the island. While there, I lodged at the house of a Mr. Maginnis, who is a grandson of one of the discoverers. From him and Robert Creelman, who got his knowledge from Vaughn, another of the finders, I learned many more of the particulars of the discovery, having been connected with nearly every company from 1849 until now, he is thoroughly acquainted with the work described in this book and endorses the foregoing story in nearly every particular. Among the "other signs", which led the discoverers to dig, was the remains of a hoisting block, such as is used on sailing crafts, hanging to the limb of a tree, which over-hung the "Money Pit." Some accounts say this had fallen into the depression in the earth. It is not strange that at this late day there should be some variations in the story; but considering the nature of a hoisting fall, it is not improbable that both are correct. One of the ten feet marks found in the "Money Pit" was a layer of putty. This was used in glazing the windows for a house shortly after built on the Western Shore. Other layers were of charcoal. These articles are usually found among the stores of sea-going crafts. "The brown fibrous plant resembling the husk of a coconut" spoken of in the prospectus, which was found in such large quantities on the shore, and everywhere that the pirates' work was found, is called by some "Manilla Grass." It certainly is not the fiber used in manufacturing the manila rope, which is the fiber of a tree like the banana. S.C. Frazer writes, "The pamphlet says East India Grass." It is not; but is coconut fiber, nearly as well preserved as what I took off the coconut when examining and comparing them." Considerable of this was found among the sand, last summer, and carried away by visitors. Although it had been there perhaps 200 years, it is in a good state of preservation yet...

...The pirates had quite a road from the west of the Money Pit, quite visible to the oldest diggers of all, and easily traced when I was there, and could be yet if it has not been plowed."

17. "S.C. Fraser Letter to Mr. A.S. Lowden," Dated June 19, 1895. From Briggs Corner, Queens, N.B. Pgs. 1-5.

..."Second, a description of the tunnel that we cut off. It was made of round stones such as found abundantly on the beach and fields around the island. Where we found it was the mouth of it where it empties on to the treasure before it – the treasure – went down. Our base was 110 feet, our tunnel was four feet high, and the bottom of the pirate drain was near the top of our tunnel. We made no effort to stop the flow of water from the drain, first, we were at the wrong end...

...McNutt's boring after all other work on the island until last year was concluded; found disturbed earth, coconut fibre, and pieces of wood down to 155 feet. Now there was tons and tons of that coconut fiber on the works at the shore and around the treasure in the pit. Pray what is it doing 150' below the former place of the treasure?...

...I did not know that the earth of the island undisturbed, had coconut fibre and wood mixed with it. The pamphlet says, "East India Grass", it is not; but coconut fibre nearly as well preserved as what I took off the coconut when examining and comparing them...

...They (the pirates) had quite a road from the west of the money pit, quite visible to the oldest diggers of all, and easily traced when I was there and can yet if it is not plowed."

18. "Oak Island Mystery: The Kempton Variant," Summer 1909. Written by a hired schoolteacher by Reverend A. J. Kempton, for preparation for a book.

"Some 16 miles from the inner run of vessels sailing along the coast. The bay is studded with islands, and Oak Island is nicely sheltered from outside view. It is not a half mile from the mainland...

...Has still some fine oak trees on it and two good farms. About 1792 some German people settled on the mainland, near the island, and the beautiful island clothed with large oak trees soon attracted attention. In 1795 one of these old settlers sauntering about the island came to a spot among the oaks on the highest part of the island where the ground showed plain signs of having worked over for quite a space as all was level – no cradle hills, and in some places white clover was growing in profusion. Of course, this seemed strange to him and on his return to his home he mentioned to his family, and a neighbor and they made a special visit to the island to examine more closely. While looking the ground over, one of his sons, a lad of 15 looked up and to the surprise of all, there suspended from a large limb of one of the giant oaks was a heavy block, such as are used for hoisting, and boy like, he went up to examine...

...This block and the condition of the ground led the men to think that something must have been buried there, as the level ground and the white clover do not generally bear such acorns and what could be buried there unless it was 'some pirates money'. A large amount was spent in digging in different parts of the island to find the drain and after a long search two men found down under the stone and gravel and sand – the accumulated was of years some cocoa nut fiber, and west India grass. This removed, there were large slabs of blue slate stone as old farmers used in hearths to their fireplaces and were only

found away near the South west entrance to the bay 10 miles away. On raising some of these flat stone."

19. "History of Oak Island, Nova Scotia, and of the Work Done There at Different Time to Recover Buried Treasure," by Frederick L. Blair. 1926. known as Exhibit B. Pgs. 4-5.

"At its Eastern extremity lies a little crescent shaped bay, "Smith's Cove," whose shores were originally bordered with large oak trees. A number of these may still be seen. A century ago, in this portion of the country, settlers were few and far between, and Oak Island was without a single inhabitant. The space referred to have every appearance of having been cleared many years before. Red clover and other plants, foreign to the soil in its natural state, were growing. Near the center stood a large oak tree with marks and figures on its trunk. One of the lower and larger of its branches, the outer end of which had been sawed off, projected directly over the center of a deep circular depression in the land about thirteen feet in diameter...

...On reaching a depth of ten feet the workmen came to a covering or tier of logs, the ends embedded I the walls of the pit evidently for the purpose of carrying the weight of the earth above and thereby intending to prevent a subsidence at the surface. They kept on digging until a depth of thirty feet was reached, finding marks at each ten feet...

...Marks were found every 10 feet, as before, and an iron bar was frequently used in taking soundings. The 90-foot mark was a flat stone about three feet long and sixteen inches wide."

20. "Sworn Affidavit of J.W. Andrews, C.E.M.E Consult Engineer." As a boy, watched searcher operations in 1849 on Oak Island. Lives in Brooklyn, NY. N.S. Archives, MG1 Vol.383. Part of F. Blair report.

"First, the story as told by Messrs. Smith, Vaughan, and McGinnis of their discovery of the oak tree with block and tackle and chain in its crotch, and the circular cavity with grass grown over It, differing from the surrounding growth, was known to be a fact and firmly corroborated. Next, the digging a pit in this circular space which showed evidence of a previous excavation. Again, the sinking of the pit to a depth of (as memory serves) about 90 to 110 feet when water to the depth of 30 feet was found in this pit and morning when the workmen came to resume work...

...A covering of fiber over one of the plank platforms said to be coconut fiber – later said to be a vegetable growth from Japan or Mexico. I

have a sample of it that I have had for many years, which I obtained directly at the works."

21. "The Oak Island Treasure," by Charles B. Driscoll. The North American Review. June 1929 Edition.

"It was in the fall of 1795 that three young woodsmen, looking for adventure and game, beached their canoe on the Oak Island sands in a lonely little inlet shaded by towering evergreen oaks that stood a little back from the beach. Two or three live oaks still stand there, but in those days, there was a goodly grove of them. Book botanists will be tempted to quit my story right here, for they say live oak does not grow so far north and is seldom found north of Virginia. All I can say to that is, go to Oak Island and see, as I did. It is not difficult to get there."

22. "When the Last Live-Oak Dies," 3/13/2016, By Doug Crowell, Blockhouse Blog March 2016. Oak Island Mystery: Sub Section: Oak Island Mystery, 1934, By Frederick Griffin.

"Puzzle of the Live-Oaks – Illusion of the Spanish Main and the age when piracy was in flower comes from the presence of half a dozen live-oak trees. You'd swear they were palms on the sand spit. They are without branches or foliage low down and their spreading tops have a palm tree look. These oaks are a part of the island mystery. Where did they come from? How did they grow here? These lived-oaks, it is said, are southern trees, not found north of Texas or Louisiana. Yet here they are on Oak Island. None was ever found on the other 354 islands in Mahone Bay which are, in many cases, crested with the trees of the region, including many northern conifers. Fifty years ago [1884], old Chester people remember, there was a regular little grove of these lived-oaks on a spit at Smith's Cove. Most of them have died. Now a mere half dozen hoary and moribund old-timers remain with a kind of struggling majesty. He referred to the presence of live-oaks, foreign oaks he called them, on Oak Island. Why were they there? His father told him when he was a boy the island had been all oaks."

23. "To Nova Scotia: The Sunrise Province of Canada" by T. Morris Longstreth. Personal visit to Smith's Cove and Interview with anonymous Woman from Chester, Nova Scotia. 1935. P. 26.

"The shore curved like an old cutlass, making a sheltered cove for landing. The seawater had an uncanny clearness. Oak, very tall, and leafy only towards the tops like palms, were so dissimilar to any oaks I had ever seen that they lent the place an eerie air even in mid-morning. ...The island was uninhabited, of course, but they noticed

that some of the ground had been cleared years before, and red clover and other plants unusual to the soil were growing there. The young men were still more surprised to find a big oak in the clearing with one of its lower limbs sawn off. It looked as if this stump had accommodated a heavy block and tackle. Beneath was a circular depression some 13 feet across." "The three of them began digging, of course , as soon as they could fetch tools without stirring up suspicion, and they uncovered a sort of well. At ten feet down they came to a covering of oak plank. At twenty feet a second covering. And at thirty a third."

24. "Letter to R.V Harris by Hugh P. Bell," Head of Depart. Of Biology, Dalhousie University, July 22, 1937. MG1 Vol. 381, 1204

*"In reference to the fibrous material that you showed me this morning, I am not sufficiently familiar with all forms of fibrous to identify this with any degree of accuracy. My knowledge is limited to a few common forms. However it appeared to me to be angiosperm material probably from some member of the lower monocotyledons, but I do not wish you to take this as a definite statement on the matter. In view of the situation in which this material was found, I would suspect that it is a very old deposit of our common eel grass (**Zostera marina**). To get the accurate determination of this material it should be sent to the Bureau of Plant Industries, Washington. If it turns out to be eel grass it will be very interesting from a scientific standpoint for, as you know, this plant disappeared from the Coast a few years ago and is now coming back slowly. A noted English Botanist claims that the plant which is coming back is not the old form but a hybrid between that old form and another species. This if your material is identified as eel grass it could be determined from it whether the plant which grew on our coast a good many years ago was the same form with which we have been familiar. For this purpose samples of your material should be sent to the Oceanographic Institute, Woods Hole, Massachusetts and to both the Kew Garden and the British Museum, London, England. Of course this should not be done until after the people at the Bureau of Plant Industries have definitely identified it as eel grass."*

25. "Letter to Gilbert Hedden by R.V. Harris," August 27, 1937.

"I have a reply from the Gray Herbarium, Harvard University, about the oak leaves, which reads as follows; "<u>The specimen of oak which you sent, certainly belongs to the characteristics Red Oak of Nova Scotia. The leaves are small and shallowly lobed, but that is because, I take it, the trees grew in a somewhat exposed habitat. As for the fiber, I will hold it for opening of our college year, when some of our anatomists</u>

return to Cambridge, and ask then to examine it. Personally, I cannot speak with any authority of it. Very truly yours, RVH"

(Re: Oak leaves found underground)

26. "Letter to R.V Harris by Albert F. Hill," Research Assistant, Botanical Museum of Harvard University, October 22, 1937. MG1, Vol. 380.

*"As Professor Fernald has probably informed you the fiber samples which you sent to him were turned over to the Museum for Identification. The material has suffered somewhat from its burial in the ground, but even so it is readily distinguishable as **Manila hemp**. The external appearance is misleading, but typical Manila hemp fibers are to be noted in a microscopic examination of macerated material. It seems quite logical to surmise that the deposit on the shores of Oak Island in Mahone Bay represents the partly disintegrated remains of some ship's cables or hawsers."*

27. "Letter to Gilbert D. Hedden by R. V. Harris," Reporting findings from Harvard Universities letter from A.F. Hill above. October 26, 1937. MG1, Vol. 381, 1264.

*"I have just had a reply from the Botanical Museum of Harvard University, to whom I sent some of the cocoanut fibre. You will remember that this material was pronounced cocoanut fibre by the Smithsonian Institute. The Harvard Museum writes as follows; 1, The material has suffered somewhat from its burial in the ground, but even as it is readily distinguishable as **Manila hemp**, the external appearance is misleading, but typical Manila hemp fibers are to be noted in a microscopic examination of macerated material. 2, It seems quite logical to surmise that the deposit on the shores of Oak Island In Mahone Bay represents the partly disintegrated remains of some ship's cables or hawsers. I do not know whether this is a case of doctors differing. Possibly the two reports are not inconsistent."*

28. "Letter to R.V Harris by Fred L. Blair" November 5, 1937

*"Re: Cocoanut fibre; doctors differ. An expert at the Smithsonian Institution stated it was undoubtedly **cocoanut fibre** and under the conditions in which it was found, may have been there for hundreds of years. Other experts have before this, pronounced it **Manila hemp**. Considering the quantity found in former years, both at the shore and at the pit, I cannot see that it is of material importance whether it is one or the other. I prefer, however, to accept the Smithsonian opinion. Fraser, who superintended the work in the sixties [1860's], stated in a*

letter that were "tons and tons of cocoanut fibre on the shore and at the works" at the pit. A party told me in Chester in 1916, that he tramped over bushels of it at the pit mouth. That does not sound much like the remains of a ship's cable or hawser."

29. "Gilbert Hedden Interview with Capt. Anthony Vaughan (98)." Dated 1939.

"Born on the old Vaughn family farm, he was present on the island probably during the Truro Company digs. Apparently, he worked "the beach" at the age of 10 years old and recalled, "large quantities of fiber" being removed. Ultimately, he wasn't too impressed with life on the island and ran away at the age of 15 for a life on the sea. That the Vaughn's themselves did not put much stock in it (the Kidd Story) but did amass a great fortune in supplying lumber and other supplies to the various expeditions."

30. "Reply Letter to Mr. L. Elbert Smith of Dallas," by Gordon Blair, Traders Finance Corporation Limited, Saint John N.B., August 4, 1947.

"Replying in brief to your inquires, the shaft was originally circular in shape, 12 or 13 feet in diameter, and it was uniform in size as far as at least 90 feet. It was a very hard blue clay and was not shored or supported in any way by timber when opened. Some say it was cribbed when opened by the original workers, and that the cribbing was taken out as they refilled...

...No timber was encountered between ten feet below the surface and 95 feet, the latter being proved by drilling. There were marks every ten feet on the way down, such as a layer of charcoal, one of putty bladders, another of beach gravel, and one of coconut husks, etc."

31. "Oak Island Connection," by Kerrin Margiano, daughter of Jean McGinnis, and the descendants of the McGinnis Family. Story told by Grandfather George William McGinnis, who grew up on Oak Island as a child, recants his childhood and stories told by his previous relatives, circa 1950's. 2016. Chapters 1-7 & 15.

Grandpa Bill: "Over a century ago, when there were towering oak trees on the east end as thick as ten men around, Daniel arrived on the Isle of Oaks. The strange oak trees rose majestically above the sea of evergreens and the discoverers of the pit walked the island auld lang syne. Daniel and Mary were resourceful settlers and carved out a nice life for their family on the Isle of Oaks in New Alba...

...Grandpa Bill pointed out different paths that Daniel had made and had names for them. We walked along the shoreline to Smith's Cove,

and he said when he was young there was a perfectly straight line of fifteen oak trees along the point. There were no evergreens along the line, only large oaks...

...I have heard people talk of Oak Island and question what motivated Daniel/Donald and his friends to keep digging past layers of logs, without having any clue about the complex tunnel and flood system that lay below. I think I would be driven to dig by an arrow and a nicely laid floor of flagstone for a year or two, but they invested their lives into the pit."

"These men stood as strong as the towering Red Oak Trees, but they were planted in sandy soil... and just relay the facts as I heard them, but the oak trees are so unusual that I just cannot resist. The way the oak Trees grew were so very different from all the other oaks in the area. They shot straight up, with no branches along the trunk till the tree explodes in a wide canopy. These trees remind me of the trees drawn in the cartoons by Dr. Seuss, and they look out of place in Nova Scotia. The existence of these unusual trees inspired me to search for reasons why it would grow in this unique way. I found if oak trees are planted in sandy soil, they grow a very deep taproot, and they do this relatively quickly. Sandy soil allows the oak tree to shoot straight up and straight down. If you look at the straight line of trees that lined Smith's Cove you may wonder if they were planted with a purpose. It is my opinion that the oak trees we planted to reinforce the area underground. If the oak trees were planted for the strength of their root systems...

...As the trees were chopped down and the roots began to rot, I wonder if whatever they were planted to secure is now undermined and accessible...

...My red oak theory of the roots being used to reinforce the tunnels may be a reach. There is a simpler possibility, and that is someone wanted to have Gloucester Island stand out in Mahone Bay from the 360 other islands as Oak Island. A westbound ship would see the towering red canopy in September. I wondered how long a tree would have to grow to tower above evergreens. A formula was developed and used by the International Society of Arboriculture to predictand determine a tree's age. Applying this formula to a red oak tree of Oak Island, estimates the tree to be 171 years old [as of book publication in 2016]. The reference point for size came from two men standing next to the base of the tree in the picture above from 'oakislandcompendium.ca'...

...Grandpa Bill had many stories. According to him, it was a woman who was the first to notice the special area that became known as 'the money pit.' My grandfather Bill said that Mary, my great-great-great-great-

grandmother, was the person to discover the mark someone left in the area…

…One lovely afternoon the young married couple chased each other in the woods. Daniel caught Mary and lifted her high and swung her around till they were dizzy sand both fell to the ground laughing…

…She said she thought she was seeing things, but the arrow was still there even after she squinted a little harder. It looked odd how the line pointed straight down while following the natural curve of the bark. She was drawn closer, and Daniel asked Mary where she was going, but she did not say a word and just walked as if in a trance to the tree."

32. "Nova Scotia Bureau of Information: Oak Island," article published in 1953, by the defunct Nova Scotia Bureau of Information – now known as the Public Archives of Nova Scotia (MG1 Volume 1228). Bureau's "re-statement of all locally known circumstances" pertaining to Oak Island in Mahone Bay. (Blockhouse Blog, April 29, 2016).

"General Appearance: At one time the island was settled, and the numerous open spaces were covered with fine timothy hay, about knee deep. The blue waters of the Bay and the surrounding well-wooded islands, especially Apple Island, present a very pleasing picture, and Pirate Cove itself is very photogenic. Incidentally, the place ought to be called Rose Island, instead of Oak Island, as it is literally covered with handsome wild roses, while live oaks are far and few between." [written in 1951]

"The hourglass bulge next to the mainland is rather low, the outer one much higher with a fill shown on marine charts as 104 above sea level. There is a handsome stand of overgrown timber (Spruce) on the outer end of the island, and this shelters a former Tea Room now unoccupied. The bare branches of three large, dead oaks tower above the evergreens east of Pirate Cove [Smith's Cove today], and there are a few similar large dead oaks around the corner on the southern side [Isaac's Point]. There are a few other oaks in leaf, but all much smaller. The people along shore refer to the bare oaks as 'original' oaks, and the others as 'new' oaks."

33. "The Oak Island Enigma," by Thomas P. Leary. 1953. Pgs. 4-36.

"In 1795 the island was covered with a thick stand of trees, very similar to Red Oaks in bark and foliage. The origin of the Oaks has been the subject of much conjecture; they tower to 80 or 90 feet and sometimes live more than 250 years. The trunk flares out at the top into a

swaying umbrella shape, unlike other oaks on the mainland. A few stand today, like symbols of the mystery that shadows the ground on which they grew... Near the crest of the hill stood one of the Oaks...

...About 16 feet from the bottom of its trunk a heavy branch had been sawed off. The bark was scarred and cut on top of the limb. Looking down, he saw a slight depression in the ground under the tree; it was circular and about 13 feet in diameter. All signs seemed to indicate that someone had dug a pit beneath the tree and, using the branch as a support, had lowered something into the ground...

...The earth flew thick next day, and they found the dirt in the shallow depression much softer than the packed ground around it. They saw what they believed to be old tool marks on the sides of the pit as the loose earth crumbled away from it. At the ten foot level the shovels struck solid wood. After the dirt had been cleared away, they found themselves standing on a platform of oak planks three inches thick. There was some difficulty in tearing up these planks, for they were not simply laid into the soft dirt in the pit but solidly embedded in its sides... the digging went on to the twenty foot level. Here was another oak platform and more dirt under it. At thirty foot level, and a third oak platform...

...Lynd's company began in earnest and sank the shaft to ninety-five feet. Every ten feet was another layer of oak planks supporting the earth above it. At eighty foot point they uncovered a deep layer of charcoal. Beneath it was something stranger still – a thick bed of vegetable fiber had been stuffed into the hole. This fiber proved to be from the outer rind of the coconut, a material that will remain undecayed indefinitely when covered from the air. AT the ninety foot level was found a layer which was either ships putty or a sticky, light colored clay...

...We landed on the remains of Hedden's dock, partly destroyed by a hurricane in 1944. Most of the grim oaks were bare and dead, victims of the black ants, and a new crop of spruce growing thick around them. Out of curiosity I cut one down. It had seen some strange sights, for the tree-rings showed it was born in 1793. There are two left."

34. "Oak Island Obsession: The Restall Story," by Lee Lamb. 2006. Pgs.44-45. Passages include Mother Mildred Restall's personal journal entries entitled, "The Reluctant Treasure Hunter: Part One" 1955. Wife of treasure hunter Robert Restall, mother to Robby Restall Jr. and Ricky Restall, they lived on Oak Island from October 15, 1959, until Robert and Robby's death in a shaft, on August 17, 1965.

"...we have lots of Black Ants here and right now they are flying. Another week I am told, and their flying season is over. The natives

say they bite off all their wings. I sure hope they are right as the darned things are an inch and a quarter of an inch long. They claim these big black ants killed all the oak trees. How can that be? Give my regards to all. Will be seeing you soon, Bob". P. 83.

"... lying in bed you could look thru the window and see the tops of the tall spruce trees, their edges feathered with silver, standing solid & clear against the lighter sky." P. 98.

35. "Oak Island Plan of Pit Area Map", by Robert K. Restall Jr. 1964. Copyright.

Note: In the lower right corner of this map showing the easterly most end of Oak Island, Mr. Restall Jr. illustrates a tree labeled 'Twin Oak'. This tree is in the remaining 'woodland' on this part of the eastern and southern shore near Smith's Cove.

36. "Letter to R. V. Harris by William A. Rovertine," Dept. of Obstetrics and Gynecology, The Albany Medical College of Union University, Albany, NY. Dec. 22, 1965.

*"To date, the analyses have not been completed but I expect to have some results shortly. The carbon dating is being done by a nuclear instrumentation firm in Chicago as a public service for us. Since this firm does carbon dating on a paid service basis, samples submitted by paying customers much necessarily be processed first. The analysis of the **hair sample** is being done as a special favor by one of the foremost experts on human hair in the area. However, since this present position requires constant traveling, it took us some time to contact him. When I receive the results of the analysis, I will promptly forward them to you."*

37. "Letter to Robert Dunfield by R. V. Harris," reporting results from the Dept. of Obstetrics and Gynecology, The Albany Medical College of Union Univ., Albany, NY. January 31, 1966. MG1 Vol. 383.

*"Mr. Kirwan and the members of the Laboratory Staff, after spending considerable time in the examination of this hair sample, have found no evidence that would permit the scientific conclusion that it is **human hair**. In his opinion, it is an animal hair of unidentified origin."*

38. "Letter to Dr. C.G. L. Friedlander by R. V. Harris," Dalhousie University, Halifax, Nova Scotia. August 19, 1966. MG1 Vol. 385.

"At Oak Island there are huge quantities of coconut fibre buried below the surface of the shore in what is called Smith's Cove. The layer is approximately two feet thick and is covered by a deep layer of stone also about two feet thick. This fibre stretches for a length of 145 ft.

around the shore of the cove. In addition to finding the coconut fibre along the edge of the cove, there were smaller quantities found in excavating the so-called Money Pit; in which ten platforms of logs were found between the surface and a depth of 100 ft. On several of these platforms there was a quantity of coconut fibre. My assumption is that the fibre has been there at least for two hundred and fifty years and it is presumed that it came from the West Indies."

39. "Letter to R. V. Harris by K.J. McCallum," Professor of Chemistry, University of Saskatchewan, Saskatoon, Canada. September 15, 1966. MG1 Vol. 383, 2093M.

"It should also be appreciated that the measurement proports to give the age in terms of the time at which the particular organic material was growing." ... You indicate the presence of coconut fibre. I know little about this material, but I presume it is less likely that old coconut fibre would have been used."

40. "Report of Digging in Smith's Cove" by Daniel C. Blankenship, November 1969.

"Incidentally, large amounts of sticky blue clay was found in layers over the area near the log, as well as grass and some material that looks like coconut husks."

41. "Letter to The Oak Island Exploration c/o Jon Ergin by C.H. Schofield," National Research Council of Canada. October 7, 1970.

"As requested in our telephone conversation of September 14, 1970, and your letter of September 17, 1970, I forwarded four samples of fibrous material from the beach at Smith's Cove Oak Island to Dr. J.H. Soper, Chief Botanist, National Museum of Natural Sciences. ***Coconut fibers*** *were identified in three of the four samples."*

42. "Oak Island Money Pit New Expedition," by Al Masters. SAGA Magazine, Volume 43, Number 1, pg. 2-7. October 1971.

"...The islands name was derived from the beautiful grove of Red Oak trees on the islands Eastern end. The last fact was a curious one since the island was the only one in the Mahone group to bear oak trees."

43. "Initial letter on 'oak trees' to Chief Botanist, James H. Soper," at National Museums of Canada, Museum of Natural Sciences. Ottawa, Ontario K1A OM8 Canada. Letter sent by D`Arcy O'Connor, Dated March 26, 1975.

"Dear Dr., Soper; Thank you for your letter of March 21 and your assistance in helping me track down the data on the coconut fiber. At your suggestion I have written Dr. Paquin of the NRC's Technical Information Service and shall await his reply. At the risk of taxing your patience, I have something else on which I would like your opinion. The oak trees for which the island was named have very distinctive umbrella-like tops to them and were identified years ago by the Grey Herbarium of Harvard University as the Red Oak, which they said is common in Nova Scotia. But I have always been puzzled by the fact that among the approximately 350 islands in Mahone Bay, only Oak Island bears these trees. (Actually, most of them are dead now, there were many hundreds of them on the island in the 19th century and their presence was first noted in 1790. In addition, I have seen no evidence of these oaks on the mainland opposite oak island, which is only about 300 yards offshore. What I'd like to know is whether it would be possible by some fluke of nature for those oaks to have sprouted only in that one location, or is it more likely that the buds or acorns were transplanted from some other part of the mainland, having been purposely brought there by man? A related question concerns the legend, perhaps true, perhaps apocryphal, that when Oak Island's so-called money pit was first discovered in 1795, the discoverers noticed a large oak tree with a sawn off limb hanging over the pit. It was surmised that the limb had been used by the unknown designers of the oak island project to haul out excavated material with a block and tackle from the pit. If that story is indeed true, then I have always thought that it would be possible to make a very rough guess at the earliest period when the workings were designed, based on the maximum age that a Red Oak can live. (I have heard the figure 200 years, but I don't know whether that is correct). So what I am getting at, is say for argument's sake the tree in question was at or very near its maximum age in 1795. What is the earliest date at which that tree would have been large enough and the particular branch strong enough to have been used as a support for hoisting equipment? It has been claimed, by the way, that the branch was 15 feet up from the ground when discovered in 1795. I know that the selection of such a date may be a very approximate guess. However, it's relevant when one considers that some of the theories about who engineered Oak Island date the project as early as the mid-1500. Which, of course, would be impossible If, a) the story of the tree with its sawn-off branch is correct; and b) if Red Oaks live for no more than 200 years. I would be most interested in your opinion as to the maximum possible life span of this species of oak and then how many years prior to that maximum would it have been big enough (say with a trunk of 18 inches in diameter) for the use in question. Then again, there is no mention of the oak tree having been alive when it was seen in 1795. So, I'd also like to know approximately how many years after its death it could

remain standing where it was found. Since I have presumptuously dragged you into my research for the book, you may be interested in knowing something about the history of this baffling mystery. I am therefore enclosing a feature article I wrote on the subject while I was with the Wall Street Journal in 1975. I shall be greatly appreciating any information of thoughts you might have on my questions about the oak trees. Sincerely, D'Arcy O'Connor."

44. "Interview of Fred Nolan, Owner of Lots, 5,9,10,11,12,13,14." by D'Arcy O'Connor. May 18, 1975.

"...I have some coconut fiber. There's not much of that stuff left around. Restall gave me that. He found quite a bit of it on that beach in Smith's Cove."

45. "Interview of Charlotte Adams, who's family were caretakers on Oak Island from 1939-1945," April 27, 1976.

"...I remember when I was a very little girl there was a very old man that lived down the road, Mr. George Hiltz, grandfather to younger George Hiltz. And he told us about the oak tree with a cut limb sticking out and there was a ridge around where the limb was to lower the chests... There weren't too many oak trees on the island when we lived there. They were all dried up and dying. There was on big one we used to saw up for firewood. There was lots of spruce wood, apple trees, birch wood. It's mostly spruce trees now. When we were first there, there was a cleared areas people used to cut hay on and we used to grow gardens. We planted enough cabbage to make sauerkraut enough for the winter. We'd plant turnips in the spring and get them at the end of fall. There was a lot of rabbits and deer there too. The deer used to swim out from the mainland. The stone triangle, I saw it lots of times, was right down near where our cabin was in Smith's Cove."

46. "Interview of Claude C. Chappel, M.R. Chappell's cousin who also worked on Oak Island," by D'Arcy O'Connor. July 20, 1976.

"...I saw the parchment when Blair had it. And I saw the axe of course. I had a piece of oak (found underground) and I gave it to Dan. We dug up coconut fiber in 1931 too. Down on Smith's Cove."

47. "Interview of Claude C. Chappell, Son of Melbourne R. Chappell, who was believed owner of lots 6, 7, 8 , 15, 16, 17, 18, 19, 20, 23, 25, 26, 30, 31, 32." By D`Arcy O`Connor, July 20-21, 1976.

"...He (Restall) did an awful lot of digging around Smith's Cove by hand trying to locate drains. He found a lot of coconut fiber there too. In 1895 when father went to Oak Island for the first time, he told me that there was a pile of that coconut fiber that had been piled up on the sore by the searches in 1849 when they uncovered it. He said it was piled up on the shore and that it would fill a big truckload. And when I was there in 1931, I looked around and got several pieces of coconut fiber. Some of it was sent to the Smithsonian Institution for analysis; some of it was sent to Tobias for analysis in Montreal or Toronto. I don't know who did his (Tobias) analyzing. It wasn't dated, just authenticated as definitely coconut fiber; the fibers off the husks of coconut."

48. "Interview of Mildred Restall, wife of Robert Restall, treasure seeker," by D'Arcy O'Connor. August 10, 1976.

"...We used to find mats and mats of coconut fiber (in Smith's Cove). And do you know what we used to do? Dig it out and we had a shed down there with a little platform on it. We'd just leave it out there (to dry) and people would take pieces of it. We never realized the value of it at the time. Chappell had a hunk of it. I have none left, I know that. Now that coconut fiber; we called it coconut fiber. But that fellow (Erwin) Hamilton, he said that it was bark off spruce trees (scraped off by earlier searchers when they were making spruce timbers for their cribwork). He claims that's what it was. But it's been analyzed as coconut fiber. And when you pull bark off you take it off in long strips, not short pieces like that (which we found). We gave some of our fiber to people who had it analyzed, and they said it was the husk of coconuts. We had a fellow in the States who had it analyzed by some place in New York. We didn't have copies of the analysts' report, just in the letters... There were quite a few oak trees on the island when we were there. And down on that point of land at Smith's Cove there was still the remnants first year we were there of twin oak down there with just a few branches on it. (plainly visible in my 1931 air photo)."

49. "Interview of George T. Bates, who surveyed Oak Island with Mr. Roper," by D'Arcy O'Connor. August 16, 1976.

His Theory: "They go the water out of the dry dock, and all the coconut fiber that has been found in Smith's Cove beach was, I think, originally in that coffer dam to give the workmen dry footing the minute the water went out of the dry dock... They get the water down to the lower chamber. The vessel is high and dry. The coconut fiber is laid on the bottom (of the drydock for footing) to cover the slippery wood and slime."

50. "2 Page Letter from Robert R. Dunfield responding to questions," by D'Arcy O'Connor. October 21, 1976.

"...#3, Yes. The coconut fiber was analyzed to be "coir," a fibrous mass between the coconut shell and the outer husk, which was used as dunnage in the early days of primitive shipping. The so-called cement is nothing more than limestone."

51. "Interview of W. Lavern Johnson, Oak Island searcher from 1962 to 1965," by D'Arcy O'Connor. November 9, 1976.

"...The first indication of something unusual at Oak Island occurred in 1795 when McInnis, Vaughan, and Smith examined the old oak tree and the depression in the ground beneath the cut-off limb. Now in 1976, the Oak Island story has become such a mixture of fact, conjecture, and fantasy that in order to try to understand the problem of recovering the treasure one must try to look back to 1795 and decide what can be accepted as fact from that time to the present. The first fact was the oak tree which drew attention to the site in 1795. The second fact was the existence of the deep filled in shaft, established around 1805. When the deep shaft (which became known as the Money Pit) was opened in 1795 a layer of flat stones was found a short distance below the surface. Then as excavation continued timber platforms were found at intervals, the shaft being backfilled between the platforms... The Money Pit was un-cribbed so there was nothing to fasten climbing ladders to in the shaft. Therefore partial platforms set into the shaft walls at regular intervals for ladders to sit on would have been normal procedure in the excavation. Then when the shaft was being backfilled, the platforms would be completed to distribute the weight of the backfill. Had the depositor excavated on down to 150 feet he would have had to use the same system of partial platforms down to that depth, and he would have completed those platforms when backfilling to distribute the weight of the backfill."

January 13, 1977... #2), I have always contended that it could not have been buried before 1650 (they needed a big tree), and it could not have been buried after the middle 1700s when the area was becoming settled. # 14), The platforms were merely to distribute the weight of the 100+ feet of fill."

May 11, 1977... Our evidence, based on available records says that the first timber platform in the shaft was found about 10 feet down. Therefore there was only 10 feet of fill to settle and produce the depression that we are told existed near the base of the old oak tree. On the other hand if the treasure was retrieved it was retrieved at a date more recent than the date at which the shaft was filled. The probability would be that the retrieval shaft would be left open and unfilled. It follows that if the ten feet of fill at the top of the Money Pit settled enough to produce a noticeable depression, then the 20 or more feet of unfilled retrieval shaft would not be likely in fewer years fill in and have enough surrounding ground move over and flatten out to make the site not noticeable. There should actually be a much greater depression than was observable at the Money Pit site."

52. "Return letter 'about oak trees' from Chief Botanist, James H. Soper." National Museums of Canada, Museum of Natural Sciences. Ottawa, Ontario K1A OM8 Canada. #47 Dated April 4, 1977.

"Dear Mr. O'Connor, I have your letter of March 26th and found your 1975 article from the Wall Street Journal very interesting. Unfortunately, I cannot confirm any information on the possible origin of oak trees on Oak Island nor the growth rate and persistence of dead trees in that area. Perhaps a forester could tell you whether Red oak reaches a comparable age. You should write to the Director of the Harvard Forest at Petersham, Mass. Yours truly, James H. Soper"

53. "Telephonic interview with Craig Lorimer", Forester with Harvard Forest, Harvard University, Petersham, Mass. With D`Arcy O'Connor, April 18, 1977.

"The Red Oak in Nova Scotia usually lives to 250 years of age. 300 years would be 'Fairly common'; 350 years would be 'uncommon but still quite possible'. And 400 years would be 'very rare but possible in exceptional cases.' An 18-inch diameter tree would be about 60-90 years old and would be about 80 ft. tall. It would be strong enough to have a branch 15 feet up and supporting a block and tackle operation. That's a forest grown tree; if it was in a clearing or out in the open, the growth rate is even faster. A good estimate for Nova Scotia would be 70 years old for an 18-inch diameter tree. Red Oaks are fairly common in Nova Scotia (though there may be some white oak too). Red Oaks and other species commonly have an umbrella-shaped dome when they're grown in the open. To get a maximum earliest date for the deposit, assume the oak tree over the money pit was 350 years old when found in 1795; take off 70 years for time to reach 18 inches in trunk diameter. 1795-350=1445AD when oak was born. 1445 + 70 = 1515AD, earliest project could have been built and used that specific oak tree. A large oak tree would fall over within 10 or 20 years after it died. (also says there's no natural way oak buds could have gotten below ground – as Triton found below 160 feet)."

54. "Handbook for Biosolar Resources, Vol. II." by N.L. Taylor and R.P. Smith. 1981, Red Clover Trifolium pratense. P. 11-21. GaiaHerbs.com."

> *"Red clover is Native to; the Northern Atlantic and central Europe; the Mediterranean region; Balkans; Asia Minor, Iran, India, Himalayas; Russia from artic south to east Siberia and Caucuses and the Far East. It spread to England ca 1650 and was carried to America by British colonists."*

55. "Report on specimen "Beta-39897 to Richard C. Nieman," Drs. J.J. Stripp and M.A. Tamers, BETA Analytic Inc., Miami Florida. September 28, 1990.

> *"Please find enclosed the result on the fibers sample recently submitted for radiocarbon dating analysis on the Rush Priority basis. We hope this date will be useful in your research. A portion of the sample was saved for the possibility of a future AMS dating.*
> *Beta-39897 Oak Island Fibers 770 +/- 60 BP. 1950-770=**1180AD**.*
>
> *...However, Dr. Tamers stated that our previous carbon date of coconut fiber as provided by Dan Henske that was retrieved from Smith's Cove that dated 770 years old is scientifically reliable and can be depended upon within the 95% probability (2 standard deviations)."*

56. "Letter to "Oak Island Participants from Richard C. Nieman." 3 Pages. October 7, 1990.

> *"Subject: Carbon 14 analysis of coconut fiber. During our visit to Oak Island this summer, Dan Henske provided some samples of what is believed to be coconut fiber. Dan retrieved this material from Smith's (north) Cove after removing several feet of beach overburden. While I did not actually observe the removal of material from the beach, Dan informed me that this was the same material which had been removed in great quantity by earlier searches and the same material which had been identified by the Smithsonian as coconut fiber... My first step was to seek the counsel and advice of Mendel Peterson of the Smithsonian. In a telephone conversation Mendel advised that in this experience the only thing to be learned would be to date the material by the carbon-14 method... While Missouri Botanical was not prepared to identify the material, they did, however, suggest submitting the fibers to the Tropical Product Institute located in London, England. Since our fibers had already been identified as coconut fiber (or hemp) twice by the Smithsonian, once in 1919 and then again in 1930 and once by the Botanical Museum of Harvard University in 1937, I did not feel that much was to be gained by sending this sample to London for identification... I contacted Beta Analytical of Miami, Florida; who*

seemed quite prepared to perform the testing we were desirous to have done... In addition, we discussed the immersion in salt water over a long period of time and I learned that this condition should serve to preserve the sample when compared to material exposed to the atmosphere... The C-14 test was performed and I learned the result by telephone on October 4, 1990. Dr. Tamers informed me that the date translated to 1180 A.D. ± 60 years (1950-770=1180) and asked if I was shocked at the result. He assured me that since he was aware of the anticipated date, he checked and rechecked his procedures and found absolutely everything to have been performed correctly and had a high degree of confidence in the result... I can visualize no other reason for the presence of coconut fiber other than its incorporation as part of the original project and until evidence is present to the contrary, I can only believe that is was used as a filtration mechanism by the original constructors when the project was executed. It does not appear that the fiber could have been deposited by natural tidal action, a subject which has been dealt with at length by other authors. Also, since the last ice age concluded about 12,000 years ago, it does not appear that glacial till can explain a date of 1180 A.D. It appears modern science is trying to tell us something – I wonder what it is?"

57. "Report on specimen "Beta-66584 to Richard C. Nieman," Drs. J.J. Stripp and M.A. Tamers, BETA Analytic Inc., Miami Florida. October 6, 1993.

"As adjusted for dendro calibration, explained on attached sheet, date = 1229 AD. C-14 Age Years B.P.= 820, ± 70, organics."

58. "Letter by Dick Neiman forwarding Report on specimen "Beta-66584 to Oak Island Participant," BETA Analytic Inc., Miami Florida. October 6, 1993.

"...The date is 820 years before present ± 70 years. The before present refers to prior to 1950AD, thus dating the sample to 1950 – 820 = 1130AD, ± 70. This sample was physically obtained by David Tobias from Smith's Cove behind an old board wall (first section north side) and spent the last 20 years or so in the Island museum as sample 'S-2'. Beta Analytic, the C-14 lab that performed our test, indicated that coconut fiber is an ideal substance to date since the coconut is a growth that occurs annually. When compared to dating three material which can be grown over some considerable period of time, coconut material is much superior since a new harvest occurs every year and a comparatively accurate date may be determined. Wood from trees, on the other hand, is subject to considerable variance depending on the location of the sample... Beta also informs me that wood samples obtained from coastal areas are also subject to another potential inaccuracy. If the sample was obtained from a camp fire, or

any other application where driftwood could have been included, then the desired date could be significantly influenced. Finally, C-14 dates as modern as 300+ years are highly suspect from a scientific standpoint and are only to be used as confirmatory data and not the only source of dating. See Below."

Note: Dendro Adjustment Applied.

Beta-66584	Radiocarbon Age BP	820 ± 70
	Calibrated age(s)	cal AD 1228
	cal AD/BC age ranges obtained from intercepts (Method A):	
	one sigma**	cal AD 1168-1282
	two sigma**	cal AD 1036-1298

Summary of Above:

Minimum of cal age ranges (cal ages) maximum of cal age ranges:

Cal AD 1168	(1229)	1282
Cal AD 1036	(1229)	1298"

59. "Carbon Dating Results on specimens Beta-66107 and Beta-39897 to Dick Nieman," BETA Analytic Inc., Miami Florida. November 18, 1994. Only Beta-39897 (coconut fibers) is provided here.

"Beta-39897	Radiocarbon Age BP	770 ± 60
	Calibrated age(s)	cal AD 1278

Summary of Above:

Minimum of call age ranges (cal ages) maximum of cal age ranges:

cal AD 1225	(1278)	1290
cal AD 1168	(1278)	1374

Notation on page states: 95% confidence in range 1168-1374 AD."

60. "The Bones in the Pit – Who Built the Oak Island Money Pit and What's Hidden There," by Bill Thompson, Nov. 20, 2014. Historical Prelude. Pgs. 1-3.

"...The 150-acre island forty miles southwest of Halifax, Nova Scotia, is covered with the oak trees that gave the place its name."

...The following information is true. In the summer of 1795, a teenager named Daniel McGinnis took a rowboat to the uninhabited island, wandered around and saw a depression in the ground. A huge oak tree with an outstretched limb stood in a clearing. Hanging from the limb was an ancient block and tackle, some people say, the kind used on sailing ships. Directly below the end of the limb was the depression. The place looked to the boy as though someone had purposely cleared some trees and dug a hole, probably a long, long time ago...

...They began to dig in the saucer-like depression. The digging wasn't difficult; the ground was loosely packed, indicating someone had filled it in at a time in the past. As they dug the boys discovered other evidence that men had been here. Two feet down there was a layer of flat stones not indigenous to Oak Island. It soon became obvious they were clearing a round hole about twelve or thirteen feet in diameter. Pickaxes had been used to build it; their marks clearly became visible as the boys removed the fill dirt."

61. "The Oak Island Mystery – The World's Greatest Treasure Hunt," by Lionel & Patricia Fanthorpe. 2017. Chapter 1, p. 18 & 32. Second Edition.

"Having reached Oak Island, scarcely two hundred meters offshore, and he began to wonder through the huge red oaks that gave the island its name...The current name of Oak Island seems to be based on the presence of the red oaks with their characteristic umbrella domes. At one time they were far more numerous than they are today"

62. "The Curse of Oak Island – The Story of the World's Longest Treasure Hunt", by Randall Sullivan, 2018, 2nd Edition. Introduction p. 13-15.

"What most impressed the first Europeans to live in the Mahone Bay area, was that the island was covered with a magnificent forest of mature oak trees, with deep roots and stout trunks that supported massive spreading limbs, leaving most of the ground in the shadow of their canopy. It may have been the only island in Mahone Bay where oak trees grew, and certainly it was the only island covered with them. Those trees were what gave the island its eventual name...

...In 1776, a British cartographer named Des Barres attempted to name it Gloucester Isle, but it was overruled by the local's insistence on calling it Oak Island. *The islands' oaks, growing so close to the mainland...*

...Most of the trees on the other islands of Mahone Bay and on the mainland as well were evergreen softwoods – spruce and pine predominated – making the island a primary source of hardwood timber. That a single island among the dozens in Mahone Bays should be covered with oak trees was for a period of sixty years or so the principal mystery of the place. The first to describe the island in part and to remark on its impressive forest of oak trees was a French nobleman named Nicolys Denys, who had helped establish Le Have, the settlement at the entrance to Mahone Bay, in 1632. Denys could conceive of no explanation for how the oaks had gotten there...

...As the story is told, McGinnis was sixteen years old in the late spring of 1795 when he rowed to Oak Island one morning to explore it, all

alone. It was still early in the day, the story goes, when the teenager stumbled upon an unusual saucer-shaped depression in the earth, about 13 ft in diameter, on the elevated ground of the island's east drumlin. The forked limb of a giant oak extended over the clearing, cut off at a point where its two branches were still almost as thick as a man's thigh. Attached to the limb, about 15 feet above the ground, was a weather-worn wooden tackle block that was held in place with a wooden peg or "tree nail" of the type used in the construction of wooden ships...

...They went to work on the ground then, armed with pickaxes and shovels. They had reached a depth of only 2 feet, though, when they hit a tier of carefully laid flagstones. (They would later decide after some investigation that the rocks were not from Oak Island but instead had been moved there from Gold River, about two miles north on the mainland). Eagerly tossing the stones aside, McGinnis and his friends found themselves at the entrance to a large shaft. The sides were made of hard, packed clay, but the earth inside was loose and easy to shovel. Driven by the excitement of discovery, the three dug within a few days to a depth of 10 feet, where they struck solid wood. Assuming they had hit the top of a treasure chest, the teenagers shoveled feverishly, only to discover that what they had found was a level platforms of oak logs, all about 6 to 8 inches in diameter, the ends of which had been embedded in the walls of the shaft...

...What they had struck with their shovels, though, was another tier of oak logs, with their rotting ends embedded in the sides of the shaft exactly as the logs at 10 feet had been...

...made less of the oak stumps than the three remaining trees that grew in an equilateral triangle around the Money Pit. The articles make it clear that those here trees were what marked the ground between them. The Colonist articles also state that after observing the triangle of trees, McGinnis noticed that the bark of each trunk had letters and symbols carved into it...

...Among the many questions raised by these early accounts is this: just what kinds of oak trees were growing on Oak Island back in 1795? The original trees are long gone, mostly killed off by an infestation of black ants during the nineteenth century. R.V. Harris had noted that a number of his sources "apparently with a view to adding more mystery to their stories, have stated that this species of oak does not grow elsewhere in Nova Scotia, that they are southern trees found no farther north than Louisiana." Also, at least two historians who authored books on the subject of piracy and mentioned Oak Island in their works (Charles B. Driscoll whose "Doubloons" is regarded in Canada as a classic work) had written that the trees on the island were

the species known as live oak (Quercus virginiana), an evergreen oak found only in southern United States. Harris, though, asserted that the trees on the island were "undoubtedly" red oaks, which do grow on the Nova Scotia mainland...

...Those who insist the trees on Oak Island were brought north in wooden ships and planted there make much of the fact that the recovered fragment of the McNutt manuscript asserted that the first thing Daniel McGinnis had noticed that caused him to stop and consider the Money pit location was a circle of red clover growing in the spot, a variety of clover that was not native to Nova Scotia. This claim about the red clover and other nonnative plants growing around the Money Pit was repeated in T. M Longstreth's, "To Nova Scotia, published in 1935."

63. "The Oak Island Mystery, Solved: The Final Chapter," by Joy A. Steel and Gordon Fader. 2nd Edition, 2018, Pg. 2.

"According to tradition, the current name, Oak Island, likely reflects a grove of lofty red oaks that once grew on the island's eastern drumlin. These unique and impressive trees were not only a signature for the island but became part of its folklore as well. ...and the oaks are all gone; their sad disappearance reportedly due largely to plagues of black ants in the 1800s, with the last few trees dying about 1960. It seems to us, however, that regardless of the reasons given for the trees' disappearance, trees don't all die at once, but over time – one-by-one."

64. "The Secret Treasure of Oak Island, The Amazing True Story of a Centuries-old Treasure Hunt," by D`Arcy O`Connor. Updated Version. 2018.

"As he was wondering through the island's densely wooded eastern end, he came to an area that appeared to have been worked at some far earlier time. It was a small clearing in which rotted, moss-covered tree stumps were visible. In the center of the clearing stood a large oak tree with a thick limb about fifteen feet up that had been cut off several feet out from the trunk. Below the end of this branch the ground had settled into a shallow, saucer-shaped depression... They set to work digging in the center of the depression and found that their shovels could easily bite into the relatively loose soil. Two feet down they encountered the first of many pieces of evidence that someone had been there before. It was a layer of carefully laid flagstones – a type of rock that is not natural to Oak Island. (The stones were later found to have originated at Gold River, about two miles up the coast on the mainland). When they cleared away the earth and removed the flagstones, they found themselves working in what obviously was a refilled circular shaft, about thirteen feet in diameter. A section of

shaft, eventually dubbed the Money Pit, lay beneath the sawed-off limb, which presumably had been used by the original excavators to haul up earth. They noticed that the sides of the shaft were of tough clay and that pick marks were visible along its walls. At the ten-foot level they struck a tier of snugly fitted oak logs completely covering the pit and embedded into the clay walls. The pried the logs out and resumed digging, only to hit an identical wooden platform ten feet later... At a depth of thirty feet, another layer of oak logs was encountered. Below it, as was the case with the upper two layers, the ground had settled about two feet. The logs themselves were visibly rotten on their outer surfaces, indicating they had been there a long time."

65. "Oak Island and Its Lost Treasure" by Graham Harris & Les MacPhie, 2019. P. 26 & 27.

"...In the past, the island supported a dense growth of red oaks, but few remain. Legend tells that Oak Island was the only island in the bay to support such a growth...

..."We are told that McGinnis penetrated the growth of massive oaks that clothed the island and chanced upon a clearing where newer growth prevailed. There at the centre of the clearing stood an ancient oak tree from which dangled an old ship's tackle bloc suspended from a lopped-ff limb some sixteen feet above the ground. A bowl-shaped depression directly underneath suggested that the soil had sunk where someone had buried something in the distant past. According to some accounts the bark of the tree was heavily scored by rope marks. A bowl-shaped depression directly underneath suggested that the soil had sunk where someone had buried something in the distant past...

...It is reported that when they began to dig, they found themselves in a previously dug pit of circular shape, the diameter of which has been variously reported as between seven and sixteen feet, but he generally accepted dimension is thirteen feet. At a depth of two feet, they unearthed a layer of flagstones, which were later thought to have originated from Gold River a couple of miles to the north. The soil within the pit was loose, and the hard clay walls were indented by the marks of tools used by previous diggers. At ten feet they came across a platform of oak logs that extended across the pit, the ends of which were securely embedded in the walls. The logs were rotten on the outside, suggesting that they had been buried for many years. A two-foot gap was encountered below the oak log platform indicating that the logs still had enough strength and was sufficiently embedded in the hard natural ground to support the weight of ten feet of earth."

66. "The Oak Island Encyclopedia, Vol. 1." By Hammerson Peters. 2019. From Mysteries of Canada, Part 1, "The History". p. 18-22.

"There is a particular island off the coast of Nova Scotia – one of the 365 that pockmark Mahone Bay – called Oak Island. So named for the tall, broad-canopied oak trees which once dotted its surface, towering as they did over the shorter spruce trees which dominate the island today."

67. "Oak Islands Key Features and Landmarks" tab titled (Oak Trees), 2019. At www.oakislandmap.com/oak-islands-key-features-and-landmarks/ oak-trees-says.

"It is often quoted that Oak Island amongst all the islands (some 360 or so) in Mahone Bay was the only one to bear the mighty oak tree. The first question should therefore be… has anyone set out to prove or disprove this statement? It seems rather self-serving and somewhat suspect. Following that same line of enquiry, has anyone actually counted the Islands? Then there is the notion that the Oak trees that once occupied the Island's eastern shore are "different" or "not native" to Nova Scotia. Certainly, their appearance is different with long branchless trunks leading up to towering canopies. Google any species of Oak tree and it is difficult to find their equivalent. The explanation however may not be so clandestine as that of an alien species transplanted upon the shores of Oak Island. There is a website link below with a logical explanation and corresponding image to support just how the Oak trees on Oak Island may have obtained the shape shown in old photos. We quote the article here: "By growing up together, perhaps out of an abandoned pasture about eighty to a hundred years ago, these trees began growing upward and unfolding. They produced shade for each other, and the dominant growth direction was upward into the light-filled space. The lower branches, which never grew to great size, died off in the increasingly shady environment of the upward-shooting trees. In this way, the long, branchless trunk developed, and we need to imagine the seemingly meager crown of the individual trees as part of the larger, dense, green canopy of the whole forest." So, are the famous Oak Trees of Oak Island merely a product of their environment?

See *Attachment* of this book, for the entire referenced article by Craig Holdrege, entitled "*The Forming Tree*." @ http://natureinstitute.org/pub/ic/ic14/trees.pdf

68. "The Blockhouse Blog Column," by Doug Crowell. 2019. Blockhouse Investigations, at www.oakislandcompendium.ca.

"One piece of information that I found most interesting was their account of the 'original' oak trees. Though dead, I noted that they were referred to as 'Live Oak' trees. Driscoll, in much earlier account, almost three decades earlier in fact, also called them Live Oaks. Here we have two publications describing the trees as Live Oaks, and they had the benefit of seeing them in person. Perhaps we need to allow that the origin of the trees was less in doubt to those who saw them firsthand back then, than they are to us in the present day, who have no tangibles to work with. They were almost certainly not native to the area, but it seems that we have to give serious consideration to the idea that they were brought here from further down the North American continent."

69. "Curse of Oak Island, Season 7, Episode 21. Produced by Prometheus Production for The History Channel. Transcribed by Hammerson Peters in his *The Oak Island Encyclopedia*, 2019. Vol. II, p.233. Dr. Rodger C. Evans, Dir. Of the E.C. Smith Herbarium Biology Department and Plant Developmental Morphology & Systematics Laboratory at Acadia University; examine oak leaf and acorn clusters captured on Oct. 1959, by Robert Restall.

During this episode, Lee Lamb and Richard Restall, relatives of the Restall family, present the artefacts to Dr. Rogers for analysis. it was revealed Mr. Restall did not believe these specimens were from the mysterious canopy oak trees still remaining on the island, but rather came from the filtration system buried at Smith's Cove. Dr. Evans determines the oak leaf and acorns were not from a Red Oak, but possibly from a different oak species, possibly brought to the island by and planted long ago. Dr. Evans did not believe the acorns or leaf could have floated across the Atlantic Ocean from Europe or Africa due to their poor resistance to the effects of saltwater. Dr. Evans also did not believe any DNA material could be retrieved from the artefacts for further testing.

70. "Curse of Oak Island, Season 7, Episode 21 - *A Leaf of Faith*," Produced by Prometheus Production for The History Channel, Transcribed by Hammerson Peters in his *The Oak Island Encyclopedia*, 2019. Vol. II, p. 233. Scott Barlow, COOI Project Manager, said;

"I believe the mysterious trees which once grew on Oak Island were intentionally planted as a marker by the original treasure depositors."

71. "Oak Island Encyclopedia Vol. 1," by Hammerson Peters. Part One – The Discovery, June 2019. Pgs. 18-36.

"There is a particular island off the cost of Nova Scotia – one of the 365 that pockmark Mahone Bay – called Oak Island. So named for the tall, broad-canopied oak trees which once dotted it surface, towering as they did over the shorter spruce trees which dominate the island today."

"On the eastern end of the island, he came upon a clearing in the brush. In the middle of the clearing was a depression in the soil, and suspended directly above the depression from a sawed-off oak branch was a rusted and rotting block and tackle...

...Armed with picks and shovels, Daniel McGinnis, John Smith, and Anthony Vaughan rowed out to Oak Island and started digging in the depression on the eastern end of the island. They discovered that the soil in the clearing had indeed been previously worked and was relatively easy to dig through compared to the surrounding earth. Two feet from the surface, they uncovered a layer of flat flagstones which were not endemic to the island. Later, the young men learned that the stones had probably come from Gold River, a waterway which enters the Atlantic about two miles north, on the mainland ...

...After digging for some time, it became obvious to the three men that the hole in the clearing was really a circular shaft about 13 feet in diameter which had been filled in some time in the past. The shaft's clay walls were scored with pick marks made by the original excavators. At about ten feet below the surface, the young men came to a platform of tightly fitted oak logs which had been driven into the shaft walls. Certain that treasure lay beneath them, they eagerly tore the logs out, only to find a gap of about two feet followed by more dirt beneath. Like the one they had discovered 10 feet below the surface, this one also was followed by a gap of about two feet and more dirt. The trio kept digging to the 30-foot level, whereupon they unearthed yet another platform of oak logs..."

"A flagstone is a flat stone historically used for paving, flooring, fencing, and roofing. Many Oak Island researchers believe that, if a layer of flagstones was truly discovered in the Money Pit two feet below the surface, it was likely placed as a marker, and was gradually covered up by many years' worth of wind-blown dirt and detritus."

Oak Platforms: "According to many versions of the discovery legend, McGinnis, Smith, and Vaughan unearthed three platforms comprised of tightly fitted oak logs embedded into the clay walls of the shaft at 10, 20 & 30 feet below the surface. Some versions of the discovery story maintain that the oak logs were six to eight inches in diameter, and were rotten on the outside, indicating that they had been there for some time before discovery."

"The Company men dug through the first 30-feet the depth to which McGinnis, Smith, and Vaughan had dug in the summer of 1795 – without incident. At 30 feet, they came to the platform of tightly fitted oak logs which had caused the original three co-discoverers to abandon the dig. The diggers further excavated the Money Pit to a depth of 90 feet, finding oak log platforms solidly embedded into the clay walls of the shaft at regular ten-foot intervals. Some of the platforms were covered by a layer of charcoal, blue clay, or a brown straw-like materials they would later learn was coconut fibre."

The Money Pit: "...The Onslow Company excavations revealed that platforms of oak logs embedded in the pit's clay walls punctuated the circular shaft of the Money Pit to a depth of 90 feet. According to some accounts, some of the oak platforms were covered by layers of charcoal, beach stones, blue clay, and coconut fibers."

72. "Oak Island Resident statement," Robert S. Young, Current owner of Lot #5. On Oak Island, Nova Scotia. June 18, 2020. www.Oakislandlotfive.com, says:

"Lot Five has an inherently diverse mix of hardwoods and softwoods with a smattering of old growth oak, pine and maple trees, her forest floor playfully spongy to the step as per the innumerable unchecked cycles of decomposition and regeneration. I heartily espouse the practice of silviculture and today Lot Five stands as a testament to the many benefits of responsible forest management. With regard to the island's storied red oak trees many dodgy and spurious accounts keep circulating as to their current state; advanced by quasi-know-it-all's who postulate the false notion they're in a death spiral due to disease, insect infestation, deforestation or already long dead."

"Dr. R. V. Harris while researching his book "The Oak Island Mystery" studied the growth rate of red oaks on the island with results that determined a tree with a diameter of 16" was 200 years old."

"Today Lot Five is home to <u>28 healthy red oaks,</u> that best that mark including over a dozen bona fide old growth specimens boasting diameters from 22" to 36." Every oak on Lot Five has been identified, photographed, and tagged for long term study and although the largest of these are now nearing the end of life cycle, their progeny continue to populate the island and are well poised to vanguard the dynasty into perpetuity. They are a robust, handsome tree that will typically attain full height early in life to stake claim to the prized open

space above and then will bide the centuries to bulk out their girth. In old age they often end up resembling wonky umbrellas with a wide, flattish canopy atop a long, straightish trunk that through time tends to shed its lower branches. Multitudes of oaks abound around the island, of particular note is a spectacular grove that mirrors the western property line of Lot Nine running its length from the Centre Road down to the shoreline. The species of red oak found on Oak Island is ***Quercus rubra L****. Compared to the other lots on the island Lot Five is without peer; the proverbial odd one out that's never been ploughed, clear-cut, excavated or built upon and for posterity's sake it provides the very quintessential coup d'oeil of a once pristine, unsullied Oak Island."*

73. "Oak Island Resident statement," Robert S. Young, current owner of Lot #5. On Oak Island, Nova Scotia. June 22, 2020. www.Oakislandlotfive.com, responds to additional inquiry says:

"Thank you for your comment – the red oaks trees of Oak Island, especially those seen in the old pictures of Smith's Cove are in fact the same species as found elsewhere on the Island. The big difference that explains their umbrella appearance is that they were more openly exposed to the weather – it seems the high winds that are often found in storms and hurricanes cause these trees to go into a self-preservation mode and they shed the lower branches as a matter of survival. It's their unprotected location more than anything else that determines this unusual shape and not from being a special species of oak. In my opinion, the only species of red oak to have ever lived on the island is Quercus rubra L. I hope this answers your question and thanks for your inquiry."

74. "Email correspondence" July 3, 2020. from Botanist Howard Manning @ [redacted]. Comments:

"My area of plant recognition is mainly S. California. I do have one bit of conjecture regarding the transcript: here in SoCal 'Live oak' means an evergreen oak variety versus deciduous (losing leaves in the fall). Some evergreen varieties are 'coast live oak', 'inland live oak', 'canyon oak', and 'scrub oak'. Oakland, California was named for their 1600's forestation of coast live oak, now mostly gone. The tall trees in the photos don't ring a bell. None of the oaks I know grow in that pattern. Hope you solve it."

75. "Email correspondence" July 6, 2020. Cynthia Cohen, ISA Certified Botanist, UCLA, Simi Valley, California, comments:

"Sorry, but there's no easy answer for this one. There's insufficient information in the attached document (text and photos) to make any

kind of reasonable guess. I hadn't heard of this place before, and when I looked online, I discovered that many people have explored this question with only speculation as results... One small thing that may help with interpreting all that online speculation is to know that 'live oak' is a general term for any evergreen oak tree... A leading oak scholar with actual tree specimens showed that oak ID (to the species level) is difficult to impossible even when you have lots of info and know what you're doing. These days, much species ID is done with DNA analysis rather than by morphology (shape of things we see with the naked eye). From these photos in this document I'm not at all convinced that we're looking at oaks at all, but I know enough to say we could be, and there are lots of different trees in the photos submitted for analysis."

76. "Email correspondence" July 13, 2020. James Bridgland, Park Ecologist, Cape Breton Highlands National Park, Ingonish Beach, Nova Scotia, Canada, comments:

"I cannot offer informed comment on the trees at Mahone Bay [Oak Island], but the ones at Corney Brook, Nova Scotia, in the 1960's photo, are definitely White Birch. They may be slightly self-pruned from shading by the surrounding Spruce and Fir, but they look pretty typical of the species White Birch, and not at all unusual."

77. "Telephonic Conversation". With Mr. Robert (Bob) Brooster of RENTOKIL, Chester, Nova Scotia. August 2020. Reference: Black Carpenter Ants – Alates *(Lasius niger)* in the Mahone Bay area.

"Referencing Mildred Restall's book and Black flying ants: Mr. Brooster informed me that "Carpenter Ants do not attack, eat, or infest live wood, and they particularly avoid hardwood species (oak), unless they are dead and decaying. These ants cannot penetrate hardwood species and they prefer sap-producing softwoods like pines, firs, spruce, and maples. The main colonies live in the trees, usually pine trees and he recommended "Carpenter Ants in the House", by Destiny Malone, Adirondack.net 3-27-2013; for more information on the species." When we discussed the comments made by Mrs. Restall in her book, Mr. Brooster said; *"There are many more ants in the Maritimes as they like a high humidity environment, which often has lots of dead wood and detritus on the forest floor".* In referring to the story that the carpenter ants killed all the old oak trees on Oak Island, he said; *"that would require the oak trees to be severely injured or in advanced decay, as they would not attack a healthy oak. And it could take ants as much as 20 years to cause an oak tree to die. Ants cannot bring down trees*

themselves. Even an apple tree, which has a lot of sap – ants wouldn't touch it until it is more than 50% dead, he has seen."

78. "Open Social Media Comments" by Terry J. Deveau. 2021. Mi` kmaw Heritage Research and Restoration Association, Historian.

"My specialty is Acadian history, even more so than Oak Island research. I am Acadian and my family has lived here in Acadia since circa 1690. My family was part of the resistance that opposed the British expulsion, and when finally captured in 1761, were held as prisoners of war. Take it from me: we know very well where the Acadians lived in Nova Scotia throughout the 1600's and 1700's. The did live in a lot of places, but definitely not on Oak Island or near it. They were not building dikes on Oak Island, guaranteed. The nearest settlement was at Mirliqueche (which is today, Lunenburg). The Jesuit Priest, Abbe' LaLoutre forced almost all the Acadians to vacate Mirligueche in 1749-50 because he was concerned that they might become friendly with the British who were just then forming a settlement in Halifax, and he wanted to prevent any easing of tensions between the Catholic and Protestant populations. There never were any Acadians on Oak Island."

79. "Comments on Coconut Fiber as Dunnage," from J. Pennelope Goforth, Private National Archives Researcher. *Specialty:* Adventures in Alaska's Maritime History. 2021.

"I do a lot of research and writing on Alaska maritime history but never came across a reference to the use of coir (coconut fibers). I did a lot of poking around in the Alaska Commercial Company archives and the Alaska Steamship Company files but found nothing about their use as dunnage."

80. "Comments on Coconut Fiber as Dunnage," from Mike Constandy, Westmoreland Research, Private National Archives Research Co. *Specialty:* Naval and maritime research, admiralty, ships logs and plans, sea lane and terrestrial UXO, 2021.

"I have read thousands of 19th Century maritime documents, manifests, bills of lading, etc., over the last thirty years, but I do not recall seeing any information relating to coconut fibers (coir) used as dunnage."

81. "Conversations between arborists Michael Nentwich and Don Pylant," with David Vaughan, July 19, 2021. ISA certified Arborist.

"One of our earliest thoughts was the trees were Acacia because we felt the reason they would have not been harvested was they were

> *sacred. We considered the Free Masons and their sacred tree and also that they used oak leaves and acorns on their crest. We will give it* [photos submitted] *some serious thought."*

In July of 2021, I contacted Mr. John Giedraitis, Executive Officer of the Texas Chapter of International Society of Arboriculture, seeking help in identifying Oak Islands mysterious canopied trees. I was referred to David M. Vaughan a seasoned San Antonio arborist, who I engaged to assist in creating "field observations" for identifying trees and help in identifying the most likely species of those canopied trees on Oak Island. Along with his colleagues, arborists Michael Nentwich and Don Pylant, I provided them a photo portfolio along with past commentary as you've read here and included a set of questions about tree identification. These gentlemen have an impressive collective background to include San Antonio City Forester, Norfolk Manager of Parks and Urban Forestry, Norfolk City Forester, San Antonio Botanical Gardens, Kumanato, Japan En Sister City Gardens, Dallas Civic Center Garden Center, Fort Worth Botanical Gardens, and each own successful arboriculture businesses. Acacia, Black Locust, American Chestnut and Northern Red Oak were all considered as possible selectees.

Here are some more of their email conversations regarding candidate species which may be our mystery canopied trees from Oak Island...

> *"Looks like a fun read. I'm surprised American Chestnut is not mentioned. It northern range is into Maine and South Canada. It was the dominant lumber tree in its range until the blight." (June 7th)*
>
> *"As I recall, one of Don's crazy assumptions was Acacia. Guess crazy may now be genius." (July 19th)*
>
> *July 19th... "One of our earliest thoughts was the trees were Acacia because we felt the reason they would have not been harvested was they were sacred. We considered the Free Masons and their sacred tree and also that they used oak leaves and acorns on their crest. Will give it some serious thought."*
>
> *July 19th... "I'm not convinced they were true Acacia, but I could go with Black Locust (Robinia pseudoacacia). Black Locust is certainly cold hardy and has a broad growth habit."*

July 19th... "Vines says Black Locust prefers deep, well drained, calcareous soils. Native into New York, so certainly cold hardy. An aside (humor) what is a true Acacia anyway. They are all being renamed, reclassified. Scott Ogden in his talk stated that when this DVA reclassification is finished, there will not be any species of Acacia left in Texas. The entire Legume family is under attack. Look what they have already done to Tx Mt. Laurel and Eve's Necklace. I can't remember any of their new names and continue to struggle with Oak Wilt, Ganoderma, Kretzschmaria, and Hypoxylon Canker. Making matters worse, you need to know all of the old names to find reference into."

July 20th... "I think cold hardy is not an issue for Oak Island as they rarely dip below freezing. I also thought we had run the Sophora haters out on a rail – maybe not."

July 21st... "From the Acacia doc, the only thing that caught my eye was this paragraph: (Roof Timbers up to 12 cubits (17ft 9in/5.4m) long could be cut from the low-hanging, curved branches, and the wood was strong enough to form the main timbers of the hulls and ribs of small ships. Shorter pieces of wood were used to make the common Nile cargo barge. This boat was constructed from 2 ft (60 cm) long, fitted together like bricks. Acacia was also used for making furniture, chests, coffins and bows*). 1. Remembering the cut branch referenced, and the indication that strong timber was harvested from low-hanging branches. 2. Perhaps another 'reach' but the coffin was another common icon for Free Masons. The* [Robert] *Cook drawing was what first made me think Acacia. While there likely were not giraffes in Nova Scotia to lift the canopy, there may have been lower trees destroyed by the water table or harvested over time. I don't see a great deal of value in many of the traits listed in the tree ID doc. And some photos contradict the data shown. Ex: branches not at 90° – some photos show branches very near 90°. And we still don't have an explanation of the photos that seem to show a broader leaf."*

82. "Telephonic Conversation in August 2021" with BETA Analytic, Inc. President Ron E. Hatfield, Miami FL. The Scientific Lab which performs radiocarbon dating testing on submitted Oak Island artefacts since 1993.

"In a conversation with Ron Hatfield, we discussed in general the issue of possible specimen contamination. The conversation centered on the volcanic and petroleum-sourced ways organics could be altered in testing age. We discussed further how the old world process of retting coconut husks to acquire coir fibers was performed, and if it could be a source of contamination or alter in any way, testing of coconut coir

fibers. Mr. Hatfield indicated that if the retting process was as I described, it should have no bearing on organic material testing."

83. "Conversations with Botanist Dr. Stephen Bungard," Vice-County Recorder for the Botanical Society of Britain and Ireland. With David Neisen, December 12, 2021.

"I am afraid that you will be very disappointed to hear that the Raasay trees down by the shore are in fact Acer pseudoplatanus which here in the UK we call Sycamore. They certainly do not have the typical habit, but that is what they are. I was surprised by them when I first came here forty years ago. I now live less than a mile from them. I am the Vice- County Recorder for the area that covers Skye, Raasay and The Hebrides Small Isles. BSBI is the Botanical Society of Britain & Ireland. Yes, your Raasay image is the same group of trees I know. I attach some images from this morning. At the end of the day, I don't know whether their unusual growth form is down to genetic or environmental factors. They are in a very exposed position. If you want samples, I can get you some, though fresh leaves, flowers, or fruit will obviously not be available for some months. I cannot vouch for the canopied trees from Oak Island. Sycamore is native to central, eastern, and southern Europe. It is thought to have been introduced to the UK by the Romans. However, other reports suggest it was introduced to the UK from France in the Tudor era around the 1500s. More widespread planting occurred in the 1700s and the earliest reports of the species naturalising in the UK date from the mid-1800s. These trees were widely associated with the French connections of Mary Queen of Scots (1542-1587). A tree planted by Mary at Scone Palace stood till 1941, when it fell in a storm. I read that it was often planted to shelter and shade farmhouses as it can withstand salty winds. This group [trees] is certainly exposed to salty winds. It was 62 mph here last night from the southwest so they will have been blasted yet again.

The seed is extremely fertile, so sycamore has spread quickly across the UK and colonised many woodlands to the detriment of native species.

In 1773 Samuel Johnson and his amanuensis James Boswell came and stayed in [here] Raasay House. Boswell later published The Journal of a Tour to the Hebrides in which his entry for Friday 10th September 1773 includes this: "There are a number of trees near the house, which grow well; some of them of a pretty good size. They are mostly plane and ash." "Plane" is what Acer pseudoplatanus was originally called in Scotland and Plane or Scot's Plane is still used occasionally today.

This makes our trees likely to be in the region of 300 years old, if they were a "pretty good size" in 1773. The lifespan is said to be around 400 years and some of ours have died. Perhaps this group will all be gone after a few more decades. Coincidentally, there is a small patch of Quercus rubra (Northern Red Oak) in woodland about a kilometre away from the trees we are discussing, but these are the result of much more recent planting – probably mid-1900s.

84. "Machiasport, Maine: Cold Case for David Neisen." by Bryan G. Hopkins Ph.D., CPSS, Certified Professional Soils Scientist, 2021. C.E.O. Hopkins Scientific, LLC. Expert Witness Report, January 17, 2022. 8 pages.

"The parameters of our model have now been sufficiently outlined that we can provide a reasonable window of time in which these red oak logs could have been buried in the soil. We have set the decomposition mass ration to between 30% and 70%, We know that the cooler subsoil temperature (44 degrees F) increases the microbial growth rate by a factor of 3-4, we have set it at 3.5 for this model. We also know that the rate of decay for the sapwood and outer bark is roughly 16% annually while the rate of decay for the heartwood is approximately 1% annually. The diameter of the red oak logs is 7.5 inches, the total 2 dimensional surface area is calculated at approximately 139 cm2. It's also established that the composition of red oak logs is typically 10% sapwood and 90% heartwood (Brown 2019). 10% of the total surface area is 13.9 cm2 and 90% of the of total surface area is 125.8 cm2. When all the outlined variables are input into this rate of decay model, we can then calculate a window.

*Beginning with shorter end of the window, 70% original oak log mass remaining would take **175 years** to occur. For 50% of the original oak log mass to remain would take **273 years** to occur. For 30% of the original oak log mass to remain would take **420 years** to occur (Figure 1). While that range of 175 to 420 years is a significantly wide estimate of time, that is the best that can be derived given the information provided within the scenarios.*

The report cited here was for a blind study to scientifically analyze the rate of rot and decay as described in many Oak Island early writings. As you just read, the report does not base its determinations on what was said, as much as the impact of fungal digestion of wood fiber, over time, in the exact same environment that appeared in the depression and pit, now known as the Money Pit. Therefore, the forensic question is not based on accurate testimony or description of what searchers described of the condition of the oak logs of the platforms within the Money Pit, but the mycological processes over time, in such an environment. This eliminates the forensics based on subjective interpretations by witnesses.

85. "Curse of Oak Island," Season 3, Episode 11 – *Sword Play,"* Produced by Prometheus Production for The History Channel. Transcribed by Hammerson Peters in his *The Oak Island Encyclopedia*, 2019. Pages 353-355.

> *"...the vegetation Jack Begley, Dan Henskee, and Peter Fornetti dug up on Smith's Cove is indeed eelgrass, and that is was carbon dated to between 1470 and 1660, with a 95% degree of accuracy. The Eelgrass carbon dating does not match the carbon dating of coconut fiber dug up by Dan Henskee, Jack Begley, Alex Lagina, and Peter Fornetti in Season 1, Episode 2, which was carbon dated to between 1260 and 1400*AD. To make matters more bizarre, the layer of the much older coconut fiber, according to the Truro Company, lay overtop of the much younger eelgrass fiber. This seems to suggest that, if the carbon dates are to be believed, the Smith's Cove filter was constructed sometime after 1470 and the builders used relatively fresh eelgrass and 70-400 year old coconut fiber."

86. "Interview with British Academy Global Professor and Author Kathleen E. Kennedy, a.k.a. The Medieval Dr. K," by David H. Neisen. February 24-25, 2022.

Toward the end of February 2022 I came across an article written by Kathleen E. Kennedy, who at the time, was an adjunct professor at a Pennsylvania University. She had written an article which immediately caught my attention: *"Gripping it by the Husk: The Medieval English Coconut"* [see Arc Humanities Press, Vol. 3, Issue 1, 2017 pp 1-25 @ muse.jhu.edu]. After having read many books written about medieval trade routes and commodities it appeared someone finally had something to say about medieval coconuts! The article introduces the reader to "mazers," or as my research had called them – Tureens or Treens. And here she referred to them as Coconut Cups. She cleverly discusses how the coconut, thought to be rare, exotic, and only for the elitist of the Medieval times, had in fact, been quite available amongst much of England's society who fancied these handcrafted marvels of exotica. The pleasant discourse did not go as expected as I have spent quite some time, assuring my research has been accurate in its foundations. Below is the back and forth of our email conversation.

February 25, 2022 02:34 am, From David H. Neisen to K. E. Kennedy -

> *"I am researching why 1.54 metric tons of coconut coir fiber with ^{14}C dates pf 1130, 1180, 1185, 1278 and 1330AD were found in underground constructs in Nova Scotia in 1795. I am familiar with the history of sewn boats, Kerala India & Ceylon and other communities/societies who knew how to ret coconut husks to produce coir quality fibers. I've been traipsing thru Medieval history to find sources outside of those named locations, where Europeans could have acquired such an item in such quantity. Through other scientific means the underground constructs were closed or sealed between 173 and 470 years before that. You are the only one I keep running into that has the same cravings for coconut history. I would like to ask a few questions or get directed or even employ you in the production of a non-fiction, science-based book..."*

February 25, 2022 10:33 am, From K.E. Kennedy to David H. Neisen -

> *"Of course, coconuts were introduced into the Caribbean by Columbus in 1492 – that's quite well known and has been confirmed through peer-reviewed genetic testing. Thanks to its water mills and ports, by the 18th century New England was a center of coconut processing and manufacture, believe it or not, and this industry is well recorded in newspapers of the period. Coir was widely used by Europeans throughout the colonial period, thanks to its durability and resistance to salt water. So there's actually no surprise in finding coir, even substantial amounts of it, in 18th century Nova Scotia. Colonial economies enabled both copra and coir to become fully modern, mechanized industries by the 19th century in England and the US. Europeans enjoyed coconuts imported from India from Roman times until the colonial period, and then Europeans imported coconuts from India, Africa, and the Americas through the colonial period. That said, I know of no historical documentation for Europeans using copra or coir in bulk until the colonial period, and there was no financially practical way to transport it until then.*
>
> *I know this may not be what you want to hear, but it's how we do the work of history – it's like science in that way – sometimes new evidence conflicts with a hypothesis, or with old evidence, and then we have to decide which has the stronger claim to accuracy. Tricky, but as you are finding in your research, always interesting! Regards, Kathleen."*

I was quite surprised and taken aback by the learned professors comments; though very appreciative for her responding to me. This was my lengthy response to Professor Kennedy's initial comments,

February 25, 2022 02:34 am, From David H. Neisen to K. E. Kennedy -

> *"I had been under the impression from my research Vasco da Gamma was the first to bring the coconut into the Atlantic Ocean Basin in 1499, when he introduced them to both Cape Verde Islands off Africa and then Brazil.*
>
> *I know Columbus was looking for coconuts, but they would not have spread through the Caribbean as of yet. Or am I off here? My research says the first coconut palm found in the Caribbean was in Puerto Rico in 1549, and except for its growing migration in parts of the eastern coast of Brazil (1553) and then the outer Honduran islands (1610), its real introduction into the Caribbean was via slave ships emanating from the same areas and ports of the African coast, which now, 50 years later, had developed extensive coconut palm cultivation.*
>
> *Yet the knowledge or retting coconuts was neither part of the Portuguese adventures on the maritime silk/spice trade, nor during the slave trade industry. I am aware the coconut reached New Spain – Caribbean (port of Veracruz) from the African slave ships earlier in the same year, as were coconuts brought visa vie the Spanish Galleon trade convoys overland from the western coast of Mexico. Yet the knowledge and practice of retting was not brought along to Mexico via this route, nor had it been practiced in the Philippine archipelago.*
>
> *Both locations had access to better plant fibers with long cultural histories and were almost singularly used by them.* [Coconut] *husks were used as a fuel and as a fertilizer even back then. In Mexico, they were singularly used for sap production. Tapping for sap would prevent the tree from producing seeds (nuts) and therefore, it is my understanding, even coconuts for food were only of interest to the poor... But the coconut as a food/medicinal product is different than retting or buying retted coco coir fibers.*
>
> *Also, In your earlier statement, you said...*
>
> "Thanks to its water mills and ports, by the 18th century New England was a center of coconut processing and manufacture, believe it or not, and this industry is well recorded in newspapers of this period."
>
> My response was: *I have yet to be able to find any such reference within newspapers, county and trade records, and would love to learn more or be directed to such history.*

... Additionally, in your earlier statement, you said...

"Coir was widely used by Europeans throughout the colonial period, thanks to its durability and resistance to salt water. So there's actually no surprise in finding coir, even substantial amounts of it, in 18th century Nova Scotia."

My response was: *I am not surprised retted coco coir fiber in the form of cordage, mats, nets, etc., were available to the New England Colonies of which Nova Scotia was part of but to a lesser degree. What I would like clarification on, if you know or could steer me to it, was this an end product (cordage, etc.), shipped in to the ports from England or elsewhere, or was this the loose bulk or baled fibers extracted from coconut husks through retting... and is this the reference you make to processing and manufacture? And if you know, was the coconut husk actually processed in the colonies into coir fiber? Or, were finished coir twine, thread, or ropes brought into the colonies where this into rugs, carpet, drapes, textiles, etc.?*

...Again, you have been extremely supportive of my inquisition and I do thank you for support of veterans. Never can one be disappointed with an answer when seeking the truth. My book is full of conflicting facts, truths, and academic determinations. It is the readers opportunity to see the full picture and decide... or engage and further the research even more. [February 25, 2022, 7:03pm]

Below is her final contribution to our conversation.

February 25, 2022 1:35 pm, am, From K.E. Kennedy to David H. Neisen -

"Unfortunately, it sounds like you've got a lot of old information there about coconut history – which is understandable, but there's much better history available now. This looks very egotistical, but I'm going to paste in my own article citations below – not because my writing will be very useful, but for my footnotes – the citations to primary sources (like newspapers) and newer history not written by me WILL be useful to you I think. All my articles have been peer-reviewed, which doesn't mean that they're perfect, of course, but does mean that other experts have assessed them as quality. They're all published, so you don't need my permission to cite them and quote them in your own research. So – there's a lot of background reading for you to do if you follow up those footnotes, but it will set you on a stronger path I think. Now the bad news – I wish I could answer your smart questions about coir, but I honestly don't know the answers. I've done more work researching copra/oil and the whole nuts than coir, unfortunately, so I can't point you in useful directions on it. I hope this doesn't overwhelm you – asking

a historian for help can be like asking a firehose sometimes I fear – and again, apologies for not having the background to help you more specifically about coir. Regards, Kathleen." "See my writings...

- ***Naming the Coconut and (de)Colonizing the Middle Ages. (2022)***
  (This will be out this spring, and freely accessible at the link – it's not just medieval, but goes from Rome to the 17th century)

- ***The Coconut Cup as Material and Media: Extended Ecologies. (2021)***
  (This is about colonial Latin American coconuts)
  www.press.library.concordia.ca/projects/old-media-and-the-medieval-concept .

- ***The Forgotten New England Coconut Dipper in the 19th-Century American Landscape. (2019)***
  (This one will be available for free this year or next, and until then a library should be able to get a copy for you – it is based on 18th @ 19th century newspaper sources and will be useful to you – worth trying to get a library copy)

- ***Gripping it by the Husk: The Medieval English Coconut. (2017)***
  (General background for your purposes only, obviously not your period)
  www.muse.jhu.edu/article/758503 "

Holy Shamoly my dear researchers! Has history changed that much from last year to this year? Did Columbus "introduce' the coconut into the Caribbean after all? Was New England the center of coconut manufacture during the colonial period and recorded in all the newspapers I didn't read? And could it really be coconut coir fiber was widely used by Europeans throughout the colonial period and lots of it would be no Biggy in Nova Scotia? Is all this the "New History" along with the "new Math?"

Well it looks like it is time for some well-aged Tuba or a Toddy to start my research again. So how do you respond to statements like...

> *"Of course, coconuts were introduced into the Caribbean by Columbus in 1492 – that's quite well known and has been confirmed through peer-reviewed genetic testing."*
>
> *"Thanks to its water mills and ports, by the 18th century* **[1701 to 1800]** *New England was a center of coconut processing and manufacture, believe it or not, and this industry is well recorded in newspapers of the period."*
>
> *"So there's actually no surprise in finding coir, even substantial amounts of it, in 18th century* **[1701-1800]** *Nova Scotia."*

"Colonial economies enabled both copra and coir to become fully modern, mechanized industries by the 19th century **[1801 to 1900]** *in England and the US."*

"That said, I know of no historical documentation for Europeans using copra or coir in bulk until the colonial period, and there was no financially practical way to transport it until then."

So dutifully, I read her writings as well as investigated her references. Addressing her communications are found in Appendix I, *"Cuckoo for Coconuts."*

87. "Transport Information Service: COIR Shipping." International Shipping Container Handbook (CHB). Mar. 8, 2022. German Marine Insurers. https://www.tis-gdv.de/tis_e/ware/fasern/kokosfa/kokosfa-htm/

*"**Product name:** German/Kokosfasern, English/Coconut fiber, coir; French/Fibre de coco; Spanish/Fibra de coco; Scientific/Cocos nucifera.*

***Product description:** Coconut fiber belongs to the category fibers/fibrous materials, which are classified as Basketwork material (Coconut fiber, rattan cane, halfa, piassava, esparto). Coconut fiber is obtained from the fibrous husk (mesocarp) of the coconut (Cocos nucifera) from the coconut palm, which belongs to the palm family (Palmae). Coconut fiber has a high lignin content and thus a low cellulose content, as a result of which it is resilient, strong and highly durable. The remarkable lightness of the fibers is due to the cavities arising from the dried out sieve cells. Coconut fiber is the only fruit fiber usable in the textile industry. Coir is obtained by retting for up to 10 months in water followed by sun-drying. Once dry, the fiber is graded into "bristle" fiber (combed, approx. 20 – 40 cm long) and "mattress" fiber (random fibers, approx. 2 – 10 cm long). The best grade fibers are light in color, gold-yellow (fiber from not yet completely ripened nuts) or brown (fiber from ripe nuts). An excessively high water content within the bales results in self-heating and decay during long voyages. A moisture measurement must therefore be carried out before accepting the consignment and moisture-damaged bales must be rejected.*

***Intended use:** Coconut fiber is used to produce hawsers, ropes, cords, runners, mats, brooms, brushes, paintbrushes and as stuffing for mattresses and upholstered furniture.*

***Transporting:** Coconut fiber is transported in bales (compressed and uncompressed), in hanks and in rolls. The fibers are sometimes wrapped* *in jute or bamboo mats or are also shipped unpackaged. Steel strapping and coir cordage are used to ensure that packages hold together better.*

Handling: *In damp weather (rain, snow), the cargo must be protected from moisture since coconut fiber is strongly hygroscopic and readily absorbs moisture. This may lead to staining of the bales, decay and mold growth and to rusting of steel strapping. Rusty steel strapping contaminates the coconut fiber and reduces its value. Do not use hooks for cargo handling since they may lead to sparking when they come into contact with the strapping. In addition, smoking is absolutely prohibited during cargo handling.*

Cargo securing: *The cargo is to be secured in such a way that the bales/hanks or strapping are not damaged. Undamaged strapping is essential to maintain compression of the bales during transport. If the strapping is broken, compression is diminished, which at the same time results in an increased supply of oxygen to the inside of the bales. This in turn increases the risk of combustion or feeds a fire which has already started. Bursting or chafing of steel strapping may lead to sparking and external ignition.*

Risk factors and loss prevention: *Coconut fiber is strongly hygroscopic. It must be protected from sea, rain and condensation water and also from high levels of relative humidity, if decay, staining, self-heating, mold, attack by microorganisms and rusting of the steel strapping are to be avoided. It is advisable to carry out moisture measurements before accepting a consignment and, where seawater damage is suspected, to carry out a seawater test using the silver nitrate method. Moisture-damaged bales and hanks must not be accepted.*

Ventilation: *Since coconut fiber very readily absorbs oxygen, before anybody enters the hold, it must be ventilated and, if necessary, a gas measurement carried out, since a shortage of oxygen may endanger life.*

Biotic activity: *Coconut fiber belong to the class of goods in which respiration processes are suspended, but in which biochemical, microbial and other decomposition processes still proceed.*

Gasses: *Coconut fiber very readily absorbs oxygen. An oxygen shortage may therefore arise in closed holds and containers. Before anybody enters such holds, the holds must be ventilated and, if necessary, a gas measurement carried out. The increase in CO2 and CO content indicates a cargo fire.*

Self-heating / Spontaneous Combustion: *Coconut fiber has an oil content of 2-5% (coconut oil). Coconut fiber is assigned to Class 4.1 of the IMDG Code (Flammable solids). However, its specific characteristics and negative external influences (see below) may cause them to behave* *like a substance from Class 4.2 (substances liable to spontaneous combustion) of the IMDG Code. Its high cellulose content makes coconut fiber particularly liable to catch fire through external ignition. Therefore, protection from sparks, fire, naked lights and lit cigarettes must always be provided. Smoking is absolutely prohibited. Sparks may arise from bursting or chafing of the steel straps (and also as a result of inadequate cargo securing in the hold or container) and cause a cargo fire. Lightly compressed bales in particular ignite easily, while strongly hydraulically compressed bales rarely catch fire because they are so compact. In accordance with the IMDG Code, ventilation openings leading into the hold should be provided with spark-proof wire cloth. Spontaneous combustion may occur as a result of exposure to moisture, animal and vegetable fats/oils, oil-bearing seeds/fruits, copra and raw wool. This risk is further increased by the coconut oil present in coconut fiber. Coconut fiber is very highly susceptible to self-heating due to moisture. Bales compressed in an excessively moist condition are at risk of heating during extended voyages and storage, with the result being decay rather than spontaneous combustion. It is usually "mattress" fibers which are affected in this way, due to the vegetable flesh still adhering the fibers. Firefighting is best performed using CO_2 or foam. It is very difficult to extinguish a fire because of the excess of oxygen in the coconut fiber, which maintains the fire from the inside. When fighting a fire, do not break the steel straps or open the bales, since relieving the compression increases the oxygen supply and makes it impossible to fight the fire effectively. Water must not be used for firefighting, as this results in damage to the product.*

Odor: *Coconut fiber has a slight, unpleasant odor. A conspicuous musty odor indicates damage inside the bales. Since coconut fiber may easily cause odor-tainting, it must be stowed together with odor-sensitive products (e.g. foodstuffs). Coconut fiber itself, is sensitive to unpleasant or pungent odors.*

Contamination: *Coconut fiber causes contamination due to the coconut oil it contains and must therefore be stowed away from easily stained products. Coconut fiber is sensitive to contamination by dust, dirt, fats/oils and rust as well as oil-containing goods, such as oil-bearing seeds/fruits, copra, raw wool etc. since oil-impregnated fibers promote self-heating/cargo fire. Holds or containers must accordingly be clean and in a thoroughly hygienic condition. Rust contamination may be caused by rusty steel straps, among other things.*

Toxicity/hazard to health: *Since coconut fiber is highly oxygen-absorbent, a life-threatening shortage of oxygen may arise in the hold or container. Thus, before anybody enters the hold, it must be* *ventilated and, if necessary, a gas measurement carried out. The TLV for CO_2 concentration is 0.49 vol.%.*

Infestation/disease: *Insects, in particular ants and beetles, may damage the bales during storage ashore. Moisture results in attack by microorganisms: mildew stains: brownish to black spots with a musty odor caused by bacteria (Mesentericus, Subtilis and Proteus species). mold: green mold caused by Penicillium glaucum and Aspergillus glaucus. Red mold caused by Penicillium purpurgenum. Development of these microorganisms may go as far as to result in localized decay and complete breakdown of the fiber/fabric."*

88. "Conversations with Botanist Dr. Stephen Bungard," Vice-County Recorder for the Botanical Society of Britain and Ireland. With David Neisen, May 30, 2022. Regarding the Acer pseudoplatanus tree species alive on Raasay Island, Scotland; and thought to be parental stand of Oak Island trees.

"I have put some current images of the trees on the below link. Please feel free to use them however you wish. There are 11 trees in a partial ring of which two are dead and a third is dead from 2 m above ground.
Details:

Tree	Grid ref [1]	Circumference (m) [2]
1	NG54593639	1.4
2	NG54593643	1.6
3 (dead)	NG54603643	1.2*
4 (dead)	NG54603642	1.3*
5	NG54613640	1.6
6	NG54613639	1.2
7	NG54613639	1.4
8	NG54613639	1.0
9	NG54603639	1.4
10	NG54603639	1.2
11 (dead +2 m)	NG54593639	1.0

Notes:

1. The 10 metre square of the British National Grid (Ordnance Survey). These can be converted to latitude and longitude here: http://www.movable-type.co.uk/scripts/latlong-os-gridref.html
2. At cut 1.5 m above ground level
3. *Bark lost so diameter reduced

There are at least four stumps within the outer ring – perhaps more if one searched thoroughly. These four are not in the centre of the ring but rather, to one side.

Re: specimens, I can easily obtain leaf /shoot specimens, but I need to know how you would like them preserved. It might be possible to pay someone to fell one of the dead trees and take a cross-section for dendrochronology. No promises! Best wishes."

Footnoted References

1. "*American Canopy: Trees, Forests, and the Making of a Nation*." by Eric Rutkow, 2012. New York: Scribner, 2012. a Division of Simon & Schuster, Inc.

2. "*The Description and Natural History of the Coasts of North America*." by Nicolas Denys, 1632-1670. Pub. 1672, under title: "Description Geographique et Historique des Costes de L'Amerique Septentrionale: arec L'Histoire Naturelle du pais."

3. "*The Halifax Naval Yard and Mast Contractors, 1775-1815*." by Julian Gwyn. www.cnrs-scrn.org/northern_mariner/Vol.11.

4. "*Permit to Fell Timber at Western Shore*." for Daniel & Anthony Vaughan," *1788*. Blockhouse Blog.

5. "*Canadian Forestry Chronical*." by Sidney Perley, 1847. Pubs-dif-ifc.org. Jun. 25, 2020. Pgs. 72, 120, 141, 201.

6. "*The Oak Island Folly*." by 'Patrick,' 1861. Printed in *The Nova Scotian*, Sep. 30, 1861. Pgs. 1-4.

7. "*Report to Inspector of Mines for the Province, John Rutherford*." by Henry S. Poole, Esq. 1861. Printed by The Citizen Publishing Co. www.mininghistory.ns.ca.

8. "*The Oak Island Diggings*." by Jotham Blanchard McCully, Oct. 16, 1862. Published in *The Liverpool Transcript*. Pgs. 3 & 8.

9. "*Oak Island, The Reasons for Supposing Treasure is Buried There*." by Paul Pry. For the *Yarmouth Herald*. Feb. 18, 1863. Pgs. 1-6.

10. "*History of the Oak Island Enterprise – Chapter 1*." by James McNutt. Printed in *The Colonist* on Jan. 2, 1864, Truro, Nova Scotia. Pgs. 1-4.

11. "*History of Oak Island Enterprise – Chapter II*." by James McNutt. Printed in *The Colonist* on Dec. 1864. P. 4.

12. "*Account by James McNutt, Secretary of the Oak Island Eldorado Co*." Transcribed by Les MacPhie. Known as the Halifax Co. Diary of work carried out from Dec. 1866 - Jan. 1867. Pgs. 1-6.

13. "*John Brown Report on Boreholes I, II, and III*." by John Brown, Walton Manganese Mines, Jan. 17, 1867. to the Directors of The Oak Island Co. and to W. J. Veith, J D Nash, and John Selnes. Transcript by Les MacPhie. Pg. 3.

14. "*Affidavit from S.C. Fraser to A.S. Lowden*." copy by Frederick Blair. Jun. 19, 1895.

15. "*History of the County of Lunenburg*." by Mather Byles DeBrisay, Judge of County Courts and Member of the Historical Society of Nova Scotia. Harvard College Library, Apr. 7, 1896, Cambridge, Mass. Second Edition, 1895. Originally written at Bridgewater and La Have, Feb. 1870 . Pgs. 301-306

16. "*The Story of Oak Island – 1895*." by Frederick L. Blair. Included in *Buried Treasure*, part of Oak Island Treasure Company's Public Share Offering. "Additional" Information included section.

17. "*Fraser letter to Mr. A.S. Lowden*." by S.C. Fraser, Jun. 19, 1895. From Briggs Corner, Queens, N.B. Pgs. 1-5.

18. "*Oak Island Mystery: The Kempton Variant*." by Reverend A. J. Kempton, Summer 1909.

19. "*History of Oak Island, Nova Scotia, and of the Work Done There at Different Time to Recover Buried Treasure*." by Frederick L. Blair. 1926. known as Exhibit B. Pgs. 4-5.

20. "*Sworn Affidavit of J.W. Andrews, C.E.M.E Consult Engineer*." Brooklyn, NY. N.S. Archives, MG1 Vol.383. Part of F. Blair report.

21. "*The Oak Island Treasure*." by Charles B. Driscoll. *The North American Review*. Jun. 1929 Edition.

22. "*When the Last Live-Oak Dies*." by Doug Crowell, Mar. 13, 2016. *Blockhouse Blog*, Mar. 2016. Oak Island Mystery: Sub Section: Oak Island Mystery, 1934, By Frederick Griffin.

23. "*To Nova Scotia: The Sunrise Province of Canada*." by T. Morris Longstreth. Chester, Nova Scotia. 1935. Published by D. Appleton-Century Company, New York. 290 pages. P. 26.

24. "*Bell letter to R.V Harris*." by Hugh P. Bell, Head of Depart. Of Biology, Dalhousie University, Jul. 22, 1937. Nova Scotia National Archives, MG1 Vol. 381, 1204

25. "*Harris letter to Gilbert Hedden*." by R.V. Harris, Aug. 27, 1937.

26. "*Hill letter to R.V Harris*." by Albert F. Hill, Oct. 22, 1937. Research Assistant, Botanical Museum of Harvard University. Nova Scotia National Archives, MG1, Vol. 380.

27. "*Harris letter to Gilbert D. Hedden*." by R. V. Harris, Oct. 26, 1937. Reporting findings from Harvard Universities letter from A.F. Hill. Nova Scotia National Archives, MG1, Vol. 381, 1264.

28. "*Blair letter to R.V Harris*." by Fred L. Blair, Nov. 5, 1937.

29. "*Interview with Capt. Anthony Vaughan*." by Gilbert Hedden, dated 1939.

30. "*Blair reply Letter to Mr. L. Elbert Smith of Dallas*." by Gordon Blair, Aug. 4, 1947. Traders Finance Corporation Limited, Saint John N.B.

31. "*Oak Island Connection*," by Kerrin Margiano, 2016. Chapters 1-7 & 15.

32. "*Oak Island*." Published article by the Nova Scotia Bureau of Information, 1953. *Blockhouse Blog*, Apr. 29, 2016. Nova Scotia National Archives, MG1 Vol. 1228.

33. "*The Oak Island Enigma*." by Thomas P. Leary. 1953. Pgs. 4-36.

34. "*Oak Island obsession: The Restall Story*." by Lee Lamb. 2006. Excerpts of Mildred Restall's journal "*The Reluctant Treasure Hunter: Part One*" 1955. Pgs.44-45.

35. "*Oak Island Plan of Pit Area Map*." by Robert K. Restall Jr. 1964. Copyright.

36. "*Rovertine letter to R. V. Harris*." by William A. Rovertine, Dec. 22, 1965. Dept. of Obstetrics and Gynecology, The Albany Medical College of Union University, Albany, NY.

37. "*Harris letter to Robert Dunfield*." by R. V. Harris, Jan. 31, 1966. reporting results from the Dept. of Obstetrics and Gynecology, The Albany Medical College of Union Univ., Albany, NY. Nova Scotia National Archives. MG1 Vol. 383.

38. "*Harris letter to Dr. C.G. L. Friedlander*." by R. V. Harris, Aug. 19, 1966. Dalhousie University, Halifax, Nova Scotia. Nova Scotia National Archives, MG1 Vol. 385.

39. "*McCallum letter to R. V. Harris*." by K.J. McCallum, Sept. 15, 1966. Professor of Chemistry, University of Saskatchewan, Saskatoon, Canada. Nova Scotia National Archives, MG1 Vol. 383, 2093M.

40. "*Blankenship report of Digging in Smith's Cove*." by Daniel C. Blankenship, Nov. 1969.

41. "*Schofield letter to The Oak Island Exploration c/o Jon Ergin*." by C.H. Schofield, Oct. 7, 1970. National Research Council of Canada.

42. "*Oak Island Money Pit New Expedition.*" by Al Masters, Oct. 1971. *SAGA Magazine*, Volume 43, Number 1, pg. 2-7. Oct. 1971.

43. "*D`Arcy initial letter on 'oak trees' to Chief Botanist, James H. Soper*." by D`Arcy O`Connor, Mar. 26, 1975. National Museums of Canada, Museum of Natural Sciences. Ottawa, Ontario K1A OM8 Canada.

44. "*Interview of Fred Nolan, Owner of Lots, 5,9,10,11,12,13,14*." by D'Arcy O'Connor, May 18, 1975.

45. "*Interview of Charlotte Adams*." By D`Arcy O`Connor, Apr. 27, 1976.

46. "*Interview of Claude C. Chappel*." By D`Arcy O`Connor, Jul. 20, 1976.

47. "*Interview of M.R. Chappell, owner of lots 6, 7, 8 , 15, 16, 17, 18, 19, 20, 23, 25, 26, 30, 31, 32*." by D`Arcy O`Connor, Jul. 20-21, 1976.

48. "*Interview of Mildred Restall*." by D'Arcy O'Connor. Aug. 10, 1976.

49. "*Interview of George T. Bates*." by D'Arcy O'Connor. Aug. 16, 1976.

50. "*Interview question Written Responses to D`Arcy O`Connor*." by Robert R. Dunfield. Oct. 21, 1976.

51. "*Interview Responses of W. Lavern Johnson*." by D'Arcy O'Connor. Nov. 9, 1976.

52. "*Responding letter 'about oak trees' from Chief Botanist, James H. Soper*." to D`Arcy O`Connor, Apr. 4, 1977. National Museums of Canada, Museum of Natural Sciences. Ottawa, Ontario K1A OM8 Canada. #47.

53. "*Telephonic interview with Craig Lorimer*." with D`Arcy O'Connor, Apr. 18, 1977. Forester with Harvard Forest, Harvard University, Petersham, Mass.

54. "*Red Clover Trifolium pratense*." by N.L. Taylor and R.P. Smith, 1981. Handbook for Biosolar Resources, Vol. II, p. 11-21. www.GaiaHerbs.com.

55. "*Report on specimen "Beta-39897 to Richard C. Nieman*." by Drs. J.J. Stripp and M.A. Tamers, BETA Analytic Inc., Miami Florida. Sept. 28, 1990.

56. "*Nieman letter to 'Oak Island Participants*." by Richard C. Nieman, Oct. 7, 1990. 3 Pages.

57. "*Report on specimen "Beta-66584 to Richard C. Nieman*." by Drs. J.J. Stripp and M.A. Tamers, BETA Analytic Inc., Miami Florida. Oct. 6, 1993.

58. "*Nieman letter to 'Oak Island Participants #2*." by Dick Neiman, Oct. 6, 1993.

59. "*Report on ^{14}C on specimens Beta-66107 and Beta-39897 to Richard C. Nieman*." by BETA Analytic Inc., Miami Florida. Nov. 18, 1994.

60. "*The Bones in the Pit – Who Built the Oak Island Money Pit and What's Hidden There*." by Bill Thompson, Nov. 20, 2014. *Historical Prelude*. Pgs. 1-3.

61. "*The Oak Island Mystery – The World's Greatest Treasure Hunt*." by Lionel & Patricia Fanthorpe. 2017. Chapter 1, p. 18 & 32. Second Edition.

62. "*The Curse of Oak Island – The Story of the World's Longest Treasure Hunt*." by Randall Sullivan, 2018. 2nd Edition. Introduction p. 13-15.

63. "*The Oak Island Mystery, Solved: The Final Chapter*." by Joy A. Steel and Gordon Fader. 2018. 2nd Edition. Pg. 2.

64. "*The Secret Treasure of Oak Island, The Amazing True Story of a Centuries-old Treasure Hunt*." by D`Arcy O`Connor. 2018. Updated Version.

65. "*Oak Island and Its Lost Treasure*." by Graham Harris & Les MacPhie, 2019. P. 26 & 27.

66. "*The Oak Island Encyclopedia, Vol. 1*." by Hammerson Peters. 2019. From Mysteries of Canada, Part 1, "The History" p. 18-22.

67. "*Oak Islands Key Features and Landmarks*." tab titled (Oak Trees), 2019. At www.oakislandmap.com/oak-islands-key-features-and-landmarks/oak-trees-says.

68. "*The Blockhouse Blog Column Articles*." by Doug Crowell. 2019. Blockhouse Investigations, at www.oakislandcompendium.ca.

69. "*Comments by Dr. Rodger C. Evens, Dir. E.C. Smith Herbarium Biology Department and Plant Developmental Morphology & Systematics Laboratory at Acadia University*." Filmed on *Curse of Oak Island, Season 7, Episode #21*, by Prometheus Productions, 2019. On the History Channel or The Oak Island Encyclopedia, Vol. 2, p.233.

70. "*Comments by Scott Barlow, COOI Project manager*." filmed on Curse of Oak Island, Season 7, Episode #21, by Prometheus Productions, 2019. On the History Channel or The Oak Island Encyclopedia, Vol. 2, p. 233.

71. "*Part One – The Discovery*." by Hammerson Peters, Jun. 2019. Oak Island Encyclopedia Vol. 1, Pgs. 18-36.

72. "*Young Email Responses to David H. Neisen*." by Robert S. Young, Jun. 18, 2020. Current owner of Lot #5, on Oak Island, Nova Scotia. www.Oakislandlotfive.com.

73. "*Young Email Responses to David H. Neisen #2*." by Robert S. Young, Jun. 22, 2020. Current owner of Lot #5, on Oak Island, Nova Scotia. www.Oakislandlotfive.com.

74. "*Manning Email Response to Stuart Niesen*." by Botanist Howard Manning, Jul. 3, 2020.

75. "*Cohen Email Responses to David H. Neisen*." by Botanist Cynthia Cohen, Jul. 6, 2020.

76. "*Bridgland Email Responses to David H. Neisen*." by James Bridgland, Jul. 13, 2020. Park Ecologist, Cape Breton Highlands National Park, Ingonish Beach, Nova Scotia, Canada.

77. "*Brooster Telephonic Conversation with David H. Neisen*." with Mr. Robert (Bob) Brooster of RENTOKIL, Aug. 2020. Chester, Nova Scotia.

78. "*Open Social Media Comments*." by Terry J. Deveau, 2021. Mi`kmaw Heritage Research and Restoration Association, Historian.

79. "*Goforth Email Responses to David H. Neisen*." by J. Pennelope Goforth, 2021. National Archives Researcher. Specialty Alaskan Maritime History.

80. "*Constandy Email Responses to David H. Neisen*." by Mike Constandy, 2021. Westmoreland Research, National Archives Research Co. *Specialty:* Naval & maritime research, admiralty, ships logs & plans, sea lane & terrestrial UXO.

81. "*Group Email Responses between Arborists Michael Nentwich, Don Pylant and David Vaughan*." with David H. Neisen, Jul. 19, 2021.

82. "*Hatfield Telephonic Conversation with David H. Neisen*." by Ron E. Hatfield, Aug. 2021. BETA Analytic, Inc. President Ron E. Hatfield, Miami FL.

83. "*Neisen email Responses with Botanist Dr. Stephen Bungard*." With David H. Neisen, Dec. 12, 2021. Vice-County Recorder for the Botanical Society of Britain and Ireland.

84. "*Hopkins Reports to David H. Neisen*." by Bryan G. Hopkins Ph.D., CPSS, Certified Professional Soils Scientist, 2021. Turfgrass Producers International. National Association of Landscape Professionals. Golf Course Superintendents Association of America. Professor, Brigham Young University, Department of Plant and Wildlife Sciences. Officer, Soil Science Society of America – North American Proficiency Testing. C.E.O. Hopkins Scientific, LLC.

85. "*Transcription of Curse of Oak island, Season 3, Episode 11 – Sword Play,*" Produced by Prometheus Production for The History Channel. Transcribed by Hammerson Peters in his *The Oak Island Encyclopedia*, 2019. Pages 353-355.

86. "*Kennedy Email Responses with David H. Neisen*." by Kathleen E. Kennedy, Feb. 24, 2022. British Academy Global Professor, a.k.a. 'The Medieval Dr. K.'

87. "*Email Field Survey Report from BSBI Botanist Dr. Stephen Bungard*." With David Neisen, May 30, 2022. Vice-County Recorder for the Botanical Society of Britain and Island. Regarding the Acer pseudoplatanus tree species alive on Raasay Island, Scotland; and thought to be parental stand of Oak Island trees.

Appendix D

OBSCURE OWNERS OF OAK ISLAND

Of all the research and investigation performed for compiling such a book, this appendix was by far, the most exhausting and frustrating. Some investigations from afar, can provide a better view of the overall scope of things. Other examinations need close proximity and interaction with the topics searched. This effort required gobs of good luck, the written efforts by hundreds of others, and lots of meticulous sorting of nebulous documents which were illegible, penned with indecipherable script, and inevitably incomplete. One would think, cataloging the ownership of 32 lots on a small island over time, could not be so difficult. My book is way too long, and I would drop this appendix altogether, had not co-author Chris Boze handled the lions share from previous work he has researched and documents he has compiled.

This appendix is as complete as any other repository on Oak Island ownership that has been published. This book presents to you the year-to-year identification of ownership of each of the 32 lots on Oak Island. The period covers from 1751 with the very first owners, up to and including 2020. It is divided into three sections offering the linkage between owner, lot, and time.

> The first section is a 28-page ***Time Table*** providing a visual timeline with the transfer, sale, and death of lot owners.
>
> The second section is a collection of ***Owner Info Boxes*** providing personal background with biographical datasets.
>
> The third section is a ***Lot Listing*** showing all the related ownership milestones per lot, and the citations to prove them.

Throughout these sections, each owner is assigned a code number issued in numerical order (1 thru 68). Family members or relatives who purchased or were gifted lots, are assigned a sub-coded alphabet letter (a thru e) to help track legacy and ownership changes within families. The various ownerships by the McGinnis / McInnis / etc. member Lots, have been grouped and placed under a single code (32). Separate but related is "Daniel McKinnon" (32a) a.k.a. Daniel McKinnis, etc.. All other McInnis owners are placed within a single familial code. This protocol was used to counterbalance the enormity of crazy spellings of surnames and the repeated frequency of use of similar given name of identified owners. Frequently, names were recorded by others who seem oblivious to getting spelling correct.

A business relationship, such as with "M.R. Chappell" (10), John Whitney Lewis (10a), and Acadia Trust Company (10b) was similarly assigned and tracked together.

A *Legend* is provided to explain other markings and colorations used in the *Time Table*, the *Owner Info Boxes*, the L*ot List*, and carried through the endnote reference list. We expect many of you have heard or read other determinations of ownership differing from this presentation. In our research, we have reviewed many of those determinations made by other writers, authors, bloggers, and private hereditary family tree organizations. Some outside sources were used to complement our findings or finalize unique linkages. After review of the historical written records obtained, we are confident this compilation, to the degree it is finished, is the most accurate. However, should you have a document which you believe corrects this appendix or sheds additional light on ownership issues, we would very much like to invite you to log into our website and upload your information. Or, you may contact us via the website. You can help us create a complete archive of who lived on the Dumbo Drumlin over those past years. This may be of help to others in the future, and we thank you for helping us create the most accurate record available.

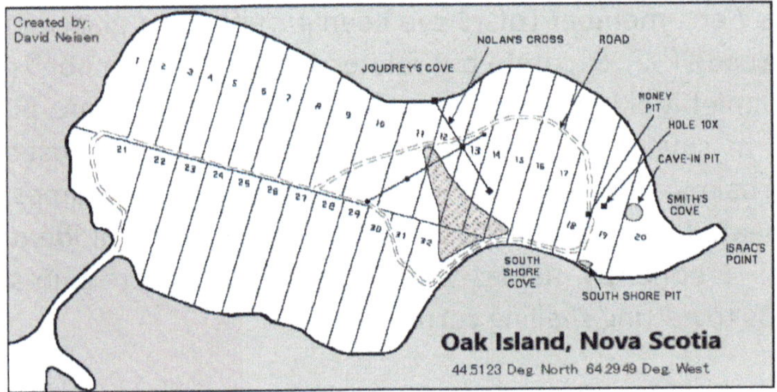

Oak Island Owner Legend

The following 28-page *Time Table* lists the island lots on the left side and the years across the top. The Oak Island Owners 'Codes" are shown in a chart at the end of the Legend. Within the body of the Table those codes are entered identifying who owned the lot on each given year. It is quite usual in that time period where 'holes' in the continuum of documented ownership did exist. Some of these were created when the Crown granted, escheated, and re-granted the same lots over a period of time. Other frequent occurrences found were when *Person **A*** owned *Lot **X*** and years later, *Person **B*** sold the same *Lot **X*** to *Person **C**.* What happened to *Person **A*** transferring *Lot **X*** to *Person **B**,* and when did that happen? - *Excellent question!*

Instead of guessing when such a transfer may have happened, we decided to enter the symbol [±] '*plus or minus*' to indicate why no ownership codes are entered for those years. This symbol identifies to you there is a break in documentation of the continuum of ownership, based on when the known transactions took place.

In a few instances, we have determined a source of lot ownership recordation is in error, such as with the *1818 Crandall Survey*. Therefore, in those instances, we have colored orange, those lots for the years we believe are in error or misleading.

We have placed the symbol [‽] *'Exclamation & Question Mark'* to warn viewers of the probable error in the historical record when found. Also, so you readily identify lot transfer milestones, as we have bolded and highlighted in light blue, the sellers' ownership code of the year before the sale, as well as the buyers' ownership code in the year of the sale or transfer. You will find in the Time Table several scenarios where *Person **A*** sold *Lot **X*** to *Person **B***, only for *Person **B*** to turn around in a short interval later (within the year), then having sold *Lot **X*** to *Person **C**.* We understand our legends convention may cause the dates of transfer to appear off by a year in a few circumstances. This may on occasion be due to the Tables construction of a year-to-year schedule. However the owners *Info Box* and *Lot List* will correctly list the Lots transfer date.

Furthermore, when an owner has died and the lot may be sold, given, kept by the family, or inherited, we mark the year of the death or probate year, in black highlight, with white lettering. Without record of immediate sale unless concurrently sold, we assume the family retains ownership at least through probate, and is so marked with the suffix code (**fam**) or (**heirs**).

As you know, Frederick Nolan successfully acquired several lots on Oak Island by finding errors in existing recorded deeds and historical documents. We have posted in this Time Table, the ownership of those lots as the Supreme Court of Nova Scotia had determined their ownership to be, including Mr. Nolan's successful acquisition. However, in the Lot List, we have meticulously notated the historical deed registrations which took place for those lots, through the myriad of inheritances, quit deeds, and share ownerships during this period; though many of those documents were later deemed by the Supreme Court, all for not. This cuts out the confusing back and forth and inheritance tracking in the Time Table, which would be extremely confusing in such a format. Yet again, the Lot List includes all those 'overturned' deeds, wills, and documents within the cited references for your tracking and review.

In the Time Table you will find the obvious term (**heirs**) indicating multiple parties have received 'shares' of a lot ownership or have signed over rights to property being transferred. Again, this is to make the Time Table usable and not clogged with too much info.

We hope you review the Time Table, Owner Info Boxes, and the Lot List to understand the additional complexities helping to make the Oak Island Treasure story a true conundrum. If you can, please help us to reflect the most true and accurate data for future researchers use. Private organizations providing access to family trees have shown not to be an accurate source for dates, names, and lot acquisitions in this quest. There are a plethora of family trees, both conflicting and others private and inaccessible. They may have some accurate data, but they may not with other datasets. So after finding so many variations, we have decided not to base any Table determinations on their postings. But it is very interesting to read!

A Late Update: The Table does not extend out past 2020 and since then, there have been some Lot ownership transfers. Lot #5 on Oak Island had been owned by Robert S. Young (**61**) until his death almost two years ago in 2020. His estate has sold the property to Rick and Marty Lagina, or to the Oak Island Tours, Inc. enterprise, or under another entity with which they control or own. Either way, now the Fellowship has more Oak Island to investigate.

Owner Codes

CODE	LOT OWNER	CODE	LOT OWNER
00	**CROWN OWNERSHIP**	35	**McMULLEN,** Neal
01	**ALLEN,** Ambrose	35a	**McMULLEN SMITH,** Neil
02	**ANDERSON,** James	37	**McNEIL,** Alexander
03	**BALL,** Samuel	38	**MELVIN,** Robert Sr.
03a	**BALL,** Isaac, "Butler"	38a	**MELVIN,** Nathaniel
04	**BEAMISH,** Clarence James	38b	**MELVIN,** David
04a	**GRAVES,** Edward	38c	**MELVIN,** Jacob
05	**BEARLSON,** John	38d	**MELVIN,** Robert Jr.
06a	**BEZANSON,** John	39	**MONRO,** John
06b	**BEZANSON,** George	39a	**MONROW,** James
06c	**BEZANSON,** Joseph	40	**NOLAN,** Frederick G.
07	**BLANKENSHIP,** Daniel C.	40a	**NOLAN,** Thomas J.
07a	**BLANKENSHIP,** Dave	41	**OAK ISLAND TOURS INC.**
08	**BOWIE,** William	42	**PATTILLO,** Alexander
09	**CHAPMAN,** Mary Ellen	42a	**PATILLO,** Fred
10	**CHAPPELL,** Melbourne R.	43	**PAYZANT,** Phillip
10a	**LEWIS,** John Whitney	44	**POWERS,** Erdie
10b	**ACADIA TRUST COMPANY**	45	**PRESCOTT,** Jonathan Dr.
11	**COCHRAN,** John P.	46	**PULSIFER,** John
12	**CONRAD,** Francis Arthur	47	**ROGERS,** Jeremiah
12a	**CONRAD,** Ingram Eli	48	**SECOMBE,** John Reverend
13	**CORKUM,** Burnell Stanley	49	**SHARP,** James
13a	**CORKUM,** All Corkum Relatives	50	**SHEPHARD,** Jacob
14	**CRANDALL,** Davie Wilbur	51	**SMITH,** Duncan
15	**DAUPHINEE,** Archibald C.	51a	**SMITH,** John
16	**ELLIS,** David	51b	**SMITH,** Joseph
17	**EMBREE,** Thomas	51c	**SMITH,** Thomas E.
18	**ERNST,** Abraham	52	**SMITH,** Edward
19	**GRAVES,** Anthony Thickpenny	53	**SMITH,** Richard & **GIFFORD,** John
19a	**SELLERS,** Henry	54	**STRACHAN, John**
19b	**SELLERS,** Sellyn	55	**TOBIAS,** David C.
20	**GRIMM,** George W. Jr.	56	**TRITON Alliance Syndicate**
21	**HATT,** Jacob & Mary Hovey	57	**VAUGHAN,** Anthony Sr.
21a	**HOVEY,** Thomas & Mary	57a	**VAUGHAN,** Anthony Jr.
22	**HEDDEN,** Gilbert D.	57b	**VAUGHAN,** Daniel
23	**HOPKINS,** George	57c	**VAUGHAN,** David & Sara
24	**JAMES,** Edward	57d	**VAUGHAN,** James – Sara & Family
25	**JOHNSTON,** John	58	**WOLLENHAUPT,** Casper
26	**KINGHORN,** John	59	**WALLS,** Wilbert & Genevieve
27	**KOSTRZEWA,** Alan	60	**WEBBER,** James
28	**LYNCH,** Timothy	61	**YOUNG,** Robert S.
29	**MALAY,** Mary & Joseph White	62	**YOUNG,** Thomas
30	**MARSHALL,** Martin	63	**YOUNG,** Wallace & Margaret
31	**MARTIN,** John	64	**ZINK,** Frederick
32	**McGINNIS,** Donald	65	**ZINK,** Timothy
32a	**McKINNON,** Daniel	66	**CUNNINGHAM,** Richard
34	**McLEAN,** Hector	67	**HOLT,** Moses
34a	**McLEAN,** Merton	68	**FORAS, Edward**

Time Table Section

Table 1. 1751 - 1760

LOTS	1751	1752	1753	1754	1755	1756	1757	1758	1759	1760
1	00	**00**	**53**	**00**	00	00	00	00	00	00
2	00	**00**	**53**	**00**	00	00	00	00	00	00
3	00	**00**	**53**	**00**	00	00	00	00	00	00
4	00	**00**	**53**	**00**	00	00	00	00	00	00
5	00	**00**	**53**	**00**	00	00	00	00	00	00
6	00	**00**	**53**	**00**	00	00	00	00	00	00
7	00	**00**	**53**	**00**	00	00	00	00	00	00
8	00	**00**	**53**	**00**	00	00	**00**	**45**	45	±
9	00	**00**	**53**	**00**	00	00	00	00	00	00
10	00	**00**	**53**	**00**	00	00	00	00	00	00
11	00	**00**	**53**	**00**	00	00	00	00	00	00
12	00	**00**	**53**	**00**	00	00	00	00	00	00
13	00	**00**	**53**	**00**	00	00	00	00	00	00
14	00	**00**	**53**	**00**	00	00	00	00	00	00
15	00	**00**	**53**	**00**	00	00	00	00	00	00
16	00	**00**	**53**	**00**	00	00	00	00	00	00
17	00	**00**	**53**	**00**	00	00	00	00	00	00
18	00	**00**	**53**	**00**	00	00	00	00	00	00
19	00	**00**	**53**	**00**	00	00	00	00	00	00
20	00	**00**	**53**	**00**	00	00	00	00	00	00
21	00	**00**	**53**	**00**	00	00	00	00	00	00
22	00	**00**	**53**	**00**	00	00	**00**	**45**	45	45
23	00	**00**	**53**	**00**	00	00	00	00	00	00
24	00	**00**	**53**	**00**	00	00	00	00	00	00
25	00	**00**	**53**	**00**	00	00	00	00	00	00
26	00	**00**	**53**	**00**	00	00	00	00	00	00
27	00	**00**	**53**	**00**	00	00	00	00	00	00
28	00	**00**	**53**	**00**	00	00	00	00	00	00
29	00	**00**	**53**	**00**	00	00	00	00	00	00
30	00	**00**	**53**	**00**	00	00	00	00	00	00
31	00	**00**	**53**	**00**	00	00	00	00	00	00
32	00	**00**	**53**	**00**	00	00	00	00	00	00

Table 2. 1761 - 1770

LOTS	1761	1762	1763	1764	1765	1766	1767	1768	1769	1770
1	00	00	00	00	00	00	00	00	00	00
2	00	00	00	00	**00**	**52**	52	52	52	52
3	00	00	00	00	00	00	00	00	00	00
4	00	00	00	00	00	00	00	00	00	00
5	00	00	00	00	00	00	00	00	00	00
6	00	00	00	00	**00**	**43**	**43**	**38**	38	38
7	00	00	00	00	**00**	**48**	**38**	38	38	38
8	±	±	±	±	±	±	±	±	±	±
9	00	00	00	00	±	±	±	±	±	±
10	00	00	00	00	±	±	±	±	±	±
11	00	00	00	00	±	±	±	±	±	±
12	00	00	00	**00**	**39**	39	39	39	39	39
13	00	00	00	00	±	±	±	±	±	±
14	00	00	00	00	±	±	±	±	±	±
15	00	00	00	00	00	00	00	00	00	00
16	00	00	00	00	00	00	**00**	**29**	29	29
17	00	00	00	00	±	±	±	±	±	±
18	00	00	00	00	±	±	±	±	±	±
19	00	00	00	00	**00**	**52**	**52**	**28**	28	28
20	00	00	00	00	±	±	±	±	±	±
21	00	00	00	00	±	±	±	±	±	±
22	45	45	45	45	45	45	45	45	45	45
23	00	00	00	00	±	±	±	±	±	±
24	00	00	00	00	00	00	00	00	00	00
25	00	00	00	00	±	±	±	±	±	±
26	00	00	00	00	00	00	00	00	00	00
27	00	00	00	00	00	00	00	00	00	00
28	00	00	00	00	00	00	00	00	00	00
29	00	00	00	**00**	**67**	67	67	67	±	±
30	00	00	00	00	±	±	±	±	±	±
31	00	00	00	00	**62**	00	00	00	00	00
32	00	00	00	00	00	00	00	00	00	00

Table 3. 1771 - 1780

LOTS	1771	1772	1773	1774	1775	1776	1777	1778	1779	1780
1	00	00	00	00	00	00	00	00	00	00
2	52	52	52	52	52	52	52	52	**52**	**38**
3	00	00	00	00	00	00	00	00	00	00
4	00	00	00	00	00	00	00	00	00	00
5	±	±	±	±	±	±	±	±	±	±
6	38	38	38	38	38	38	38	38	38	38
7	38	38	38	38	38	38	38	38	38	38
8	±	±	±	±	±	±	±	±	±	±
9	±	±	±	±	±	±	±	±	±	±
10	±	±	±	±	±	±	±	±	±	±
11	±	±	±	±	±	±	±	±	±	**60**
12	39	39	39	39	39	39	39	39	39	**39**
13	±	±	±	±	±	±	±	±	±	±
14	±	±	±	±	±	±	±	±	±	**60**
15	00	00	00	00	00	00	00	00	00	00
16	29	29	29	29	29	29	29	29	29	29
17	±	±	±	±	±	±	±	±	±	±
18	±	±	±	±	±	±	±	±	±	±
19	28	28	28	28	28	28	28	28	28	28
20	±	±	±	±	±	±	±	±	±	±
21	±	±	±	±	±	±	±	±	±	±
22	45	45	45	45	45	45	45	45	45	45
23	±	±	±	±	±	±	±	±	±	±
24	00	00	00	00	00	00	00	00	00	00
25	±	±	±	±	±	±	±	±	±	±
26	00	00	00	00	00	00	00	00	00	00
27	00	00	00	00	±	±	**47**	**16**	±	±
28	00	00	00	00	00	00	00	00	00	00
29	±	±	±	±	47	**47**	**47**	**16**	16	16
30	±	±	±	±	±	±	±	±	±	±
31	±	±	±	±	±	±	±	±	±	±
32	00	00	00	00	00	00	00	00	00	00

Table 4. 1781 - 1790

LOTS	1781	1782	1783	1784	1785	1786	1787	1788	1789	1790
1	00	00	**00**	**11**	**42**	42	42	42	42	42
2	38	38	38	38	38	38	**38**	38 fam	38 fam	38 fam
3	00	00	00	00	00	00	00	00	00	00
4	00	00	00	26	**26**	**37**	37	±	±	±
5	±	±	±	±	±	±	±	±	±	±
6	38	38	38	38	38	38	**38**	38 fam	**38 fam**	**50**
7	38	38	38	38	38	38	**38**	38 fam	**38 fam**	**50**
8	±	45	**45**	**38**	38	38	**38**	**38d**	38d	38d
9	57	57	57	57	57	57	**57**	**30**	30	30
10	57	57	57	57	57	57	**57**	**30**	30	30
11	**57b**	57b	57b	57b	57b	57b	57b	**57b**	**35**	35
12	**38**	38	38	38	38	38	**38**	38 fam	38 fam	38 fam
13	±	±	±	±	±	±	±	**57b**	**57b**	**38a**
14	**57b**	57b	57b	57b	57b	57b	57b	57b	**57b**	**38a**
15	00	00	00	00	00	00	00	00	00	00
16	29	29	29	29	29	29	29	29	29	29
17	±	±	±	±	57	57	57	57	**57**	**38a**
18	±	±	±	±	±	±	±	±	±	±
19	28	28	28	28	28	28	28	28	28	28
20	±	±	±	±	±	±	±	±	**37**	**37**
21	±	±	±	±	±	±	±	±	24	**37**
22	45	45	**45**	**38**	38	38	**38**	**38d**	38d	38d
23	±	±	**08**	**34**	34	34	**34**	**32**	32	32
24	00	00	**00**	**51**	**01**	01	01	01	01	**01**
25	±	±	±	±	±	**23**	**03**	03	03	03
26	00	00	00	**00**	**02**	02	**02**	**03**	03	03
27	±	±	±	±	**16**	**42**	42	42	42	**42**
28	00	00	**00**	**49**	49	49	**49**	**32**	32	32
29	16	16	16	16	16	16	?	?	?	?
30	±	±	±	±	±	±	±	±	±	±
31	±	±	±	±	±	±	±	±	±	±
32	00	00	**00**	**66**	**00**	00	00	00	00	00

Table 5. 1791 - 1800

LOTS	1791	1792	1793	1794	1795	1796	1797	1798	1799	1800
1	42	42	**42**	**32**	32	32	32	32	32	32
2	38 fam	38 fam	38 fam	38 fam	38 fam	38 fam	38 fam	38 fam	38 fam	38 fam
3	00	00	00	00	00	00	00	00	00	00
4	**31**	**31**	**57**	57	57	57	57	57	57	57
5	±	±	±	±	±	±	±	±	±	±
6	50	50	50	50	50	50	50	50	50	50
7	50	50	50	50	50	50	50	50	50	50
8	38d	38d	38d	38d	38d	38d	**38d**	**03**	03	03
9	30	**30**	**35**	35	35	35	35	35	35	35
10	30	**30**	**35**	35	35	35	35	35	35	35
11	35	35	35	35	35	35	35	35	35	35
12	38 fam	38 fam	38 fam	38 fam	38 fam	38 fam	38 fam	38 fam	38 fam	38 fam
13	38a	38a	38a	38a	38a	38a	38a	38a	38a	38a
14	38a	38a	38a	38a	38a	38a	38a	38a	38a	38a
15	00	00	00	00	00	00	00	00	00	00
16	29	29	29	29	29	29	**29**	**51a**	51a	51a
17	38a	38a	38a	38a	38a	38a	38a	38a	38a	38a
18	±	±	**58**	**58**	**51a**	51a	51a	51a	51a	51a
19	28	28	28	28	28	28	28	28	28	28
20	**24**	24	**24**	**06c**	06c	06c	06c	06c	06c	06c
21	**24**	**?**	**?**	**?**	**24**	**32**	32	32	32	32
22	38c	38c	38c	**38c**	**32a**	32a	32a	32a	32a	32a
23	32	32	32	32	32	32	32	32	32	32
24	**39**	39	39	39	39	39	39	**39**	**03**	03
25	03	03	03	03	03	03	03	03	03	03
26	03	03	03	03	03	03	03	03	03	03
27	**32**	32	32	32	32	32	32	32	32	32
28	32	32	32	32	32	32	32	32	32	32
29	?	?	?	**39**	**39**	**06a**	06a	06a	06a	06a
30	±	±	±	±	±	±	±	±	±	±
31	±	±	±	±	**21**	**21**	**06a**	06a	06a	06a
32	00	00	00	00	00	00	00	00	00	00

Table 6. 1801 - 1810

LOTS	1801	1802	1803	1804	1805	1806	1807	1808	1809	1810
1	32	32	32	32	32	32	32	32	32	32
2	38 fam	38 fam	57d	**57d**	57dfam	57dfam	57dfam	57dfam	57dfam	57dfam
3	±	±	57	**57d**	57dfam	57dfam	57dfam	57dfam	57dfam	57dfam
4	57	57	**57**	**17**	**17**	**06b**	**57**	57	57	57
5	±	±	**57d**	**57d**	57dfam	57dfam	57dfam	57dfam	57dfam	57dfam
6	50	50	50	50	50	50	50	50	50	**50**
7	50	50	50	50	50	50	50	50	50	**50**
8	03	03	03	03	03	03	03	03	03	03
9	35	35	35	35	35	35	35	35	35	35
10	35	35	35	35	35	35	35	35	35	35
11	35	35	35	35	35	35	35	35	35	35
12	38 fam	38 fam	38 fam	38 fam	38 fam	38 fam	38 fam	38 fam	38 fam	38 fam
13	38a	38a	38a	38a	**38a**	**35**	35	35	35	35
14	38a	38a	38a	38a	**38a**	**35**	35	35	35	35
15	00	00	00	00	00	00	00	00	00	00
16	51a	51a	51a	51a	51a	51a	51a	51a	51a	51a
17	38a	38a	38a	38a	**38a**	**51a**	51a	51a	51a	51a
18	51a	51a	51a	51a	51a	51a	51a	51a	51a	51a
19	±	±	**57d**	**57d**	57dfam	57dfam	57dfam	57dfam	57dfam	57dfam
20	06c	06c	06c	06c	06c	**06c**	**51a**	51a	51a	51a
21	32	32	32	32	32	32	32	32	32	32
22	32a	32a	32a	32a	32a	32a	32a	32a	32a	32a
23	32	32	32	32	32	32	32	32	32	32
24	03	03	03	03	03	03	03	03	03	03
25	03	03	03	03	03	03	03	03	03	03
26	03	03	03	03	03	03	03	03	03	03
27	32	32	32	32	32	32	32	32	32	32
28	32	32	32	32	32	32	32	32	32	32
29	06a	06a	06a	06a	06a	06a	06a	06a	**06a**	**32**
30	±	±	±	±	±	±	±	**46**	**46**	**03**
31	06a	06a	06a	06a	06a	**06a**	**03**	03	03	03
32	00	00	00	00	00	00	00	**00**	**03**	03

Table 7. 1811 - 1820

LOTS	1811	1812	1813	1814	1815	1816	1817	1818	1819	1820
1	32	32	32	32	32	32	32	32	32	32
2	57dfam	57dfam	57dfam	57dfam	57dfam	**57dfam**	**57c**	57c	57c	57c
3	57dfam	57dfam	57dfam	57dfam	57dfam	57dfam	57dfam	**57dfam**	**57c**	57c
4	57	57	57	57	57	57	57	57	57	57
5	57dfam	57dfam	57dfam	57dfam	57dfam	57dfam	57dfam	**57dfam**	**57c**	57c
6	**38a**	**03**	03	03	03	03	03	03	03	03
7	**38a**	**03**	03	03	03	03	03	03	03	03
8	03	03	03	03	03	03	03	03	03	03
9	35	35	35	35	35	35	35	35	35	35
10	35	35	35	35	35	35	35	35	35	35
11	35	35	35	35	35	35	35	35	35	35
12	38 fam	38 fam	38 fam	38 fam	38 fam	38 fam	38 fam	38 fam	38 fam	38 fam
13	35	35	35	35	35	35	35	35	35	35
14	35	35	35	35	35	35	35	35	35	35
15	00	00	00	00	00	00	**00**	**14**	**51a**	51a
16	51a	51a	51a	51a	51a	51a	51a	51a	51a	51a
17	51a	51a	51a	51a	51a	51a	51a	51a	51a	51a
18	51a	51a	51a	51a	51a	51a	51a	51a	51a	51a
19	57dfam	57dfam	57dfam	57dfam	57dfam	57dfam	57dfam	**57dfam**	**57c**	57c
20	51a	51a	51a	51a	51a	51a	51a	51a	51a	51a
21	32	32	32	32	32	32	32	32	32	32
22	32a	32a	32a	32a	32a	32a	32a	32a	32a	32a
23	32	32	32	32	32	32	32	32	32	32
24	03	03	03	03	03	03	03	03	03	03
25	03	03	03	03	03	03	03	03	03	03
26	03	03	03	03	03	03	03	03	03	03
27	32	32	32	32	32	32	32	32	32	32
28	32	32	32	32	32	32	32	32	32	32
29	32	32	32	32	32	32	32	32	32	32
30	03	03	03	03	03	03	03	03	03	03
31	03	03	03	03	03	03	03	03	03	03
32	03	03	03	03	03	03	03	03	03	03

Table 8. 1821 - 1830

LOTS	1821	1822	1823	1824	1825	1826	1827	1828	1829	1830
1	32	32	32	32	32	32	**32**	**32 fam**	32 fam	32 fam
2	57c	57c	57c	57c	57c	57c	57c	57c	57c	57c
3	57c	57c	57c	57c	57c	57c	57c	57c	57c	57c
4	57	57	57	57	57	57	57	57	57	57
5	57c	57c	57c	57c	57c	57c	57c	57c	57c	57c
6	03	03	03	03	03	03	03	03	03	03
7	03	03	03	03	03	03	03	03	03	03
8	03	03	03	03	03	03	03	03	03	03
9	35	35	35	35	35	**35**	**35a**	35a	35a	35a
10	35	35	35	35	35	**35**	**35a**	35a	35a	35a
11	35	35	35	35	35	**35**	**35a**	35a	35a	35a
12	±	±	±	±	**35**	**35**	**35a**	35a	35a	35a
13	35	35	35	35	35	**35**	**35a**	35a	35a	35a
14	35	35	35	35	35	**35**	**35a**	35a	35a	35a
15	51a	51a	51a	51a	51a	**51a**	51a	51a	51a	51a
16	51a	51a	51a	51a	51a	51a	51a	51a	51a	51a
17	51a	51a	51a	51a	51a	51a	51a	51a	51a	51a
18	51a	51a	51a	51a	51a	51a	51a	51a	51a	51a
19	57c	57c	57c	**57c**	**51a**	51a	51a	51a	51a	51a
20	51a	51a	51a	51a	51a	51a	51a	51a	51a	51a
21	32	32	32	32	32	32	**32**	**32 fam**	32 fam	32 fam
22	32a	32a	32a	32a	32a	32a	32a	32a	32a	32a
23	32	32	32	32	32	32	**32**	**32 fam**	32 fam	32 fam
24	03	03	03	03	03	03	03	03	03	03
25	03	03	03	03	03	03	03	03	03	03
26	03	03	03	03	03	03	03	03	03	03
27	32	32	32	32	32	32	**32**	**32 fam**	32 fam	32 fam
28	32	32	32	32	32	32	**32**	**32 fam**	32 fam	32 fam
29	32	32	32	32	32	32	**32**	**32 fam**	32 fam	32 fam
30	03	03	03	03	03	03	03	03	03	03
31	03	03	03	03	03	03	03	03	03	03
32	03	03	03	03	03	03	03	03	03	03

Table 9. 1831 - 1840

LOTS	1831	1832	1833	1834	1835	1836	1837	1838	1839	1840
1	32 fam	32 fam	32 fam	32 fam	32 fam	32 fam	32 fam	32 fam	32 fam	32 fam
2	**57c**	**32a**	32a	32a	32a	32a	32a	32a	32a	32a
3	**57c**	**32a**	32a	32a	32a	32a	32a	32a	32a	32a
4	57	57	57	57	57	57	57	57	57	57
5	**57c**	**19**	**19**	**68**	±	±	±	**19**	**64**	**19**
6	03	03	03	03	03	03	03	03	03	03
7	03	03	03	03	03	03	03	03	03	03
8	03	03	03	03	03	03	03	03	03	03
9	**35a**	**19**	**19**	**68**	**?**	**?**	**?**	**19**	**64**	**19**
10	**35a**	**19**	**19**	**68**	**?**	**?**	**?**	**19**	**64**	**19**
11	**35a**	**19**	**19**	**68**	**?**	**?**	**?**	**19**	**64**	**19**
12	**35a**	**19**	**19**	**68**	**?**	**?**	**?**	**19**	**64**	**19**
13	**35a**	**19**	**19**	**68**	**?**	**?**	**?**	**19**	**64**	**19**
14	**35a**	**19**	**19**	**68**	**?**	**?**	**?**	**19**	**64**	**19**
15	51a	51a	51a	51a	51a	51a	51a	51a	51a	51a
16	51a	51a	51a	51a	51a	51a	51a	51a	51a	51a
17	51a	51a	51a	51a	51a	51a	51a	51a	51a	51a
18	51a	51a	51a	51a	51a	51a	51a	51a	51a	51a
19	51a	51a	51a	51a	51a	51a	51a	51a	51a	51a
20	51a	51a	51a	51a	51a	51a	51a	51a	51a	51a
21	32 fam	32 fam	32 fam	32 fam	32 fam	32 fam	32 fam	32 fam	32 fam	32 fam
22	32a	32a	32a	32a	32a	32a	32a	32a	32a	32a
23	32 fam	32 fam	32 fam	32 fam	32 fam	32 fam	32 fam	32 fam	32 fam	32 fam
24	03	03	03	03	03	03	03	03	03	03
25	03	03	03	03	03	03	03	03	03	03
26	03	03	03	03	03	03	03	03	03	03
27	32 fam	32 fam	32 fam	32 fam	32 fam	32 fam	32 fam	32 fam	32 fam	32 fam
28	32 fam	32 fam	32 fam	32 fam	32 fam	32 fam	32 fam	32 fam	32 fam	32 fam
29	32 fam	32 fam	32 fam	32 fam	32 fam	32 fam	32 fam	32 fam	32 fam	32 fam
30	03	03	03	03	03	03	03	03	03	03
31	03	03	03	03	03	03	03	03	03	03
32	03	03	03	03	03	03	03	03	03	03

Table 10. 1841 - 1850

LOTS	1841	1842	1843	1844	1845	1846	1847	1848	1849	1850
1	32 fam	32 fam	32 fam	32 fam	32 fam	32 fam	32 fam	32 fam	32 fam	32 fam
2	32a	32a	32a	32a	32a	32a	32a	32a	32a	32a
3	32a	32a	32a	32a	32a	32a	32a	32a	32a	32a
4	57	57	57	57	57	57	57	57	57	**57**
5	**54**	54	54	54	54	54	54	54	54	54
6	03	03	03	03	03	**03**	**03a**	03a	03a	03a
7	03	03	03	03	03	**03**	**03a**	03a	03a	03a
8	03	03	03	03	03	**03**	**03a**	03a	03a	03a
9	**54**	54	54	54	54	54	54	54	54	54
10	**54**	54	54	54	54	54	54	54	54	54
11	**54**	54	54	54	54	54	54	54	54	54
12	**54**	54	54	54	54	54	54	54	54	54
13	**54**	54	54	54	54	54	54	54	54	54
14	**54**	54	54	54	54	54	54	54	54	54
15	51a	51a	51a	51a	51a	51a	51a	51a	51a	51a
16	51a	51a	51a	51a	51a	51a	51a	51a	51a	51a
17	51a	51a	51a	51a	51a	51a	51a	51a	51a	51a
18	51a	51a	51a	51a	51a	51a	51a	51a	51a	51a
19	51a	51a	51a	51a	51a	51a	51a	51a	51a	51a
20	51a	51a	51a	51a	51a	51a	51a	51a	51a	51a
21	32 fam	32 fam	32 fam	32 fam	32 fam	32 fam	32 fam	32 fam	32 fam	32 fam
22	32a	32a	32a	32a	32a	32a	32a	32a	32a	32a
23	32 fam	32 fam	32 fam	32 fam	32 fam	32 fam	32 fam	32 fam	32 fam	32 fam
24	03	03	03	03	03	**03**	03a	03a	03a	03a
25	03	03	03	03	03	**03**	03a	03a	03a	03a
26	03	03	03	03	03	**03**	03a	03a	03a	03a
27	32 fam	32 fam	32 fam	32 fam	32 fam	32 fam	32 fam	32 fam	32 fam	32 fam
28	32 fam	32 fam	32 fam	32 fam	32 fam	32 fam	32 fam	32 fam	32 fam	32 fam
29	32 fam	32 fam	32 fam	32 fam	32 fam	32 fam	32 fam	32 fam	32 fam	32 fam
30	03	03	03	03	03	**03**	03a	03a	03a	03a
31	03	03	03	03	03	**03**	03a	03a	03a	03a
32	03	03	03	03	03	**03**	03a	03a	03a	03a

Table 11. 1851 - 1860

LOTS	1851	1852	1853	1854	1855	1856	1857	1858	1859	1860
1	32 fam	32 fam	32 fam	32 fam	32 fam	32 fam	32 fam	32 fam	**32 fam**	**32 fam**
2	32a	32a	32a	32a	32a	32a	32a	32a	32a	32a
3	32a	32a	32a	32a	32a	32a	32a	32a	32a	32a
4	**32 fam**	32 fam	32 fam	32 fam	32 fam	32 fam	32 fam	32 fam	32 fam	**32 fam**
5	54	54	54	54	54	**54**	**19**	19	19	19
6	03a	03a	03a	03a	03a	03a	03a	03a	03a	03a
7	03a	03a	03a	03a	03a	03a	03a	03a	03a	03a
8	03a	03a	03a	03a	03a	03a	03a	03a	03a	03a
9	54	54	54	54	54	**54**	**19**	19	19	19
10	54	54	54	54	54	**54**	**19**	19	19	19
11	54	54	54	54	54	**54**	**19**	19	19	19
12	54	54	54	54	54	**54**	**19**	19	19	19
13	54	54	54	54	54	**54**	**19**	19	19	19
14	54	54	54	54	54	**54**	**19**	19	19	19
15	51a	**51a**	**51b,c**	51b,c	51b,c	**51b,c**	**19**	19	19	19
16	51a	**51a**	**51b,c**	51b,c	51b,c	**51b,c**	**19**	19	19	19
17	51a	**51a**	**51b,c**	51b,c	51b,c	**51b,c**	**19**	19	19	19
18	51a	**51a**	**51b,c**	51b,c	51b,c	**51b,c**	**19**	19	19	19
19	51a	**51a**	**51b,c**	51b,c	51b,c	**51b,c**	**19**	19	19	19
20	51a	**51a**	**51b,c**	51b,c	51b,c	**51b,c**	**19**	19	19	19
21	32 fam	32 fam	32 fam	32 fam	32 fam	32 fam	32 fam	**32 fam**	**32 fam**	**32 fam**
22	32a	32a	32a	32a	32a	32a	32a	32a	32a	32a
23	32 fam	32 fam	32 fam	32 fam	32 fam	32 fam	32 fam	32 fam	32 fam	**32 fam**
24	03a	03a	03a	03a	03a	03a	03a	03a	03a	03a
25	03a	03a	03a	03a	03a	03a	03a	03a	03a	03a
26	03a	03a	03a	03a	03a	03a	03a	03a	03a	03a
27	32 fam	32 fam	32 fam	32 fam	32 fam	32 fam	32 fam	32 fam	32 fam	**32 fam**
28	32 fam	32 fam	32 fam	32 fam	32 fam	32 fam	32 fam	32 fam	32 fam	**32 fam**
29	32 fam	32 fam	32 fam	32 fam	32 fam	32 fam	32 fam	32 fam	32 fam	**32 fam**
30	03a	03a	03a	03a	03a	03a	03a	03a	03a	03a
31	03a	03a	03a	03a	03a	03a	03a	03a	03a	03a
32	03a	03a	03a	03a	03a	03a	03a	03a	03a	03a

Table 12. 1861 - 1870

LOTS	1861	1862	1863	1864	1865	1866	1867	1868	1869	1870
1	32 fam	32 fam	32 fam	32 fam	32 fam	32 fam	32 fam	32 fam	32 fam	32 fam
2	32a	32a	32a	32a	32a	32a	32a	32a	32a	32a
3	32a	32a	32a	32a	32a	32a	32a	32a	32a	32a
4	32 fam	32 fam	32 fam	32 fam	32 fam	32 fam	32 fam	32 fam	32 fam	32 fam
5	19	19	19	19	19	19	19	19	19	19
6	03a	03a	03a	03a	03a	03a	03a	03a	03a	03a
7	03a	03a	03a	03a	03a	03a	03a	03a	03a	03a
8	03a	03a	03a	03a	03a	03a	03a	03a	03a	03a
9	19	19	19	19	19	19	19	19	19	19
10	19	19	19	19	19	19	19	19	19	19
11	19	19	19	19	19	19	19	19	19	19
12	19	19	19	19	19	19	19	19	19	19
13	19	19	19	19	19	19	19	19	19	19
14	19	19	19	19	19	19	19	19	19	19
15	19	19	19	19	19	19	19	19	19	19
16	19	19	19	19	19	19	19	19	19	19
17	19	19	19	19	19	19	19	19	19	19
18	19	19	19	19	19	19	19	19	19	19
19	19	19	19	19	19	19	19	19	19	19
20	19	19	19	19	19	19	19	19	19	19
21	32 fam	32 fam	32 fam	32 fam	32 fam	32 fam	32 fam	32 fam	32 fam	32 fam
22	32a	32a	32a	32a	32a	32a	32a	32a	32a	32a
23	32 fam	32 fam	32 fam	32 fam	32 fam	32 fam	32 fam	32 fam	32 fam	32 fam
24	03a	03a	03a	03a	03a	03a	03a	03a	03a	03a
25	03a	03a	03a	03a	03a	03a	03a	03a	03a	03a
26	03a	03a	03a	03a	03a	03a	03a	03a	03a	03a
27	32 fam	32 fam	32 fam	32 fam	32 fam	32 fam	32 fam	32 fam	32 fam	32 fam
28	32 fam	32 fam	32 fam	32 fam	32 fam	32 fam	32 fam	32 fam	32 fam	32 fam
29	32 fam	32 fam	32 fam	32 fam	32 fam	32 fam	32 fam	32 fam	32 fam	32 fam
30	03a	03a	03a	03a	03a	03a	03a	03a	03a	03a
31	03a	03a	03a	03a	03a	03a	03a	03a	03a	03a
32	03a	03a	03a	03a	03a	03a	03a	03a	03a	03a

Table 13. 1871 - 1880

LOTS	1871	1872	1873	1874	1875	1876	1877	1878	1879	1880
1	32 fam	32 fam	32 fam	32 fam	32 fam	32 fam	32 fam	32 fam	32 fam	32 fam
2	32 fam	32 fam	32 fam	32 fam	32 fam	32 fam	32 fam	32 fam	32 fam	32 fam
3	32 fam	32 fam	32 fam	32 fam	32 fam	32 fam	32 fam	32 fam	32 fam	32 fam
4	32 fam	32 fam	32 fam	32 fam	32 fam	32 fam	32 fam	32 fam	32 fam	32 fam
5	19	19	19	19	19	19	19	19	19	19
6	03a	03a	03a	03a	03a	03a	03a	03a	03a	03a
7	03a	03a	03a	03a	03a	03a	03a	03a	03a	03a
8	03a	03a	03a	03a	03a	03a	03a	03a	03a	03a
9	19	19	19	19	19	19	19	19	19	19
10	19	19	19	19	19	19	19	19	19	19
11	19	19	19	19	19	19	19	19	19	19
12	19	19	19	19	19	19	19	19	19	19
13	19	19	19	19	19	19	19	19	19	19
14	19	19	19	19	19	19	19	19	19	19
15	19	19	19	19	19	19	19	19	19	19
16	19	19	19	19	19	19	19	19	19	19
17	19	19	19	19	19	19	19	19	19	19
18	19	19	19	19	19	19	19	19	19	19
19	19	19	19	19	19	19	19	19	19	19
20	19	19	19	19	19	19	19	19	19	19
21	32 fam	32 fam	32 fam	32 fam	32 fam	32 fam	32 fam	32 fam	32 fam	32 fam
22	32 fam	32 fam	32 fam	32 fam	32 fam	32 fam	32 fam	32 fam	32 fam	32 fam
23	32 fam	32 fam	32 fam	32 fam	32 fam	32 fam	32 fam	32 fam	32 fam	32 fam
24	03a	03a	03a	03a	03a	03a	03a	03a	03a	03a
25	03a	03a	03a	03a	03a	03a	03a	03a	03a	03a
26	03a	03a	03a	03a	03a	03a	03a	03a	03a	03a
27	32 fam	32 fam	32 fam	32 fam	32 fam	32 fam	32 fam	32 fam	32 fam	32 fam
28	32 fam	32 fam	32 fam	32 fam	32 fam	32 fam	32 fam	32 fam	32 fam	32 fam
29	32 fam	32 fam	32 fam	32 fam	32 fam	32 fam	32 fam	32 fam	32 fam	32 fam
30	03a	03a	03a	03a	03a	03a	03a	03a	03a	03a
31	03a	03a	03a	03a	03a	03a	03a	03a	03a	03a
32	03a	03a	03a	03a	03a	03a	03a	03a	03a	03a

Table 14. 1881 - 1890

LOTS	1881	1882	1883	1884	1885	1886	1887	1888	1889	1890
1	32 fam	32 fam	32 fam	32 fam	32 fam	32 fam	32 fam	32 fam	32 fam	32 fam
2	32 fam	32 fam	32 fam	32 fam	32 fam	32 fam	32 fam	32 fam	32 fam	32 fam
3	32 fam	32 fam	32 fam	32 fam	32 fam	32 fam	32 fam	32 fam	32 fam	32 fam
4	32 fam	32 fam	32 fam	32 fam	32 fam	32 fam	32 fam	32 fam	32 fam	32 fam
5	19	19	19	19	19	19	19	19	19b	19b
6	03a	03a	03a	03a	03a	03a	03a	03a	03a	03a
7	03a	03a	03a	03a	03a	03a	03a	03a	03a	03a
8	03a	03a	03a	03a	03a	03a	03a	03a	03a	03a
9	19	19	19	19	19	19	19	19	19b	19b
10	19	19	19	19	19	19	19	19	19b	19b
11	19	19	19	19	19	19	19	19	19b	19b
12	19	19	19	19	19	19	19	19	19b	19b
13	19	19	19	19	19	19	19	19	19b	19b
14	19	19	19	19	19	19	19	19	19b	19b
15	19	19	19	19	19	19	19	19	19a	19a
16	19	19	19	19	19	19	19	19	19a	19a
17	19	19	19	19	19	19	19	19	19a	19a
18	19	19	19	19	19	19	19	19	19a	19a
19	19	19	19	19	19	19	19	19	19a	19a
20	19	19	19	19	19	19	19	19	19a	19a
21	32 fam	32 fam	32 fam	32 fam	32 fam	32 fam	32 fam	32 fam	32 fam	32 fam
22	32 fam	32 fam	32 fam	32 fam	32 fam	32 fam	32 fam	32 fam	32 fam	32 fam
23	32 fam	32 fam	32 fam	32 fam	32 fam	32 fam	32 fam	32 fam	32 fam	32 fam
24	03a	03a	03a	03a	03a	03a	03a	03a	03a	03a
25	03a	03a	03a	03a	03a	03a	03a	03a	03a	03a
26	03a	03a	03a	03a	03a	03a	03a	03a	03a	03a
27	32 fam	32 fam	32 fam	32 fam	32 fam	32 fam	32 fam	32 fam	32 fam	32 fam
28	32 fam	32 fam	32 fam	32 fam	32 fam	32 fam	32 fam	32 fam	32 fam	32 fam
29	32 fam	32 fam	32 fam	32 fam	32 fam	32 fam	32 fam	32 fam	32 fam	32 fam
30	03a	03a	03a	03a	03a	03a	03a	03a	03a	03a
31	03a	03a	03a	03a	03a	03a	03a	03a	03a	03a
32	03a	03a	03a	03a	03a	03a	03a	03a	03a	03a

Table 15. 1891 - 1900

LOTS	1891	1892	1893	1894	1895	1896	1897	1898	1899	1900
1	32 fam	32 fam	32 fam	32 fam	32 fam	**32 fam**	32 fam	32 fam	32 fam	32 fam
2	32 fam	32 fam	32 fam	32 fam	32 fam	**32 fam**	32 fam	32 fam	32 fam	32 fam
3	32 fam	32 fam	32 fam	32 fam	32 fam	**32 fam**	32 fam	32 fam	32 fam	32 fam
4	32 fam	32 fam	32 fam	32 fam	32 fam	**32 fam**	32 fam	32 fam	32 fam	32 fam
5	19b	19b	19b	19b	19b	19b	19b	19b	19b	19b
6	03a	03a	03a	03a	03a	03a	**03a**	**18,19a**	18,19a	18,19a
7	03a	03a	03a	03a	03a	03a	**03a**	**18,19a**	18,19a	18,19a
8	03a	03a	03a	03a	03a	03a	**03a**	**18,19a**	18,19a	18,19a
9	19b	19b	19b	19b	19b	19b	19b	19b	19b	19b
10	19b	19b	19b	19b	19b	19b	19b	19b	19b	19b
11	19b	19b	19b	19b	19b	19b	19b	19b	19b	19b
12	19b	19b	19b	19b	19b	19b	19b	19b	19b	19b
13	19b	19b	19b	19b	19b	19b	19b	19b	19b	19b
14	19b	19b	19b	19b	19b	19b	19b	19b	19b	19b
15	19a	19a	19a	19a	19a	19a	19a	19a	19a	19a
16	19a	19a	19a	19a	19a	19a	19a	19a	19a	19a
17	19a	19a	19a	19a	19a	19a	19a	19a	19a	19a
18	19a	19a	19a	19a	19a	19a	19a	19a	19a	19a
19	19a	19a	19a	19a	19a	19a	19a	19a	19a	19a
20	19a	19a	19a	19a	19a	19a	19a	19a	19a	19a
21	32 fam	32 fam	32 fam	32 fam	32 fam	**32 fam**	32 fam	32 fam	32 fam	32 fam
22	32 fam	32 fam	32 fam	32 fam	32 fam	**32 fam**	32 fam	32 fam	32 fam	32 fam
23	32 fam	32 fam	32 fam	32 fam	32 fam	**32 fam**	32 fam	32 fam	32 fam	32 fam
24	03a	03a	03a	03a	03a	03a	**03a**	**18,19a**	18,19a	18,19a
25	03a	03a	03a	03a	03a	03a	**03a**	**18,19a**	18,19a	18,19a
26	03a	03a	03a	03a	03a	03a	**03a**	**18,19a**	18,19a	18,19a
27	32 fam	32 fam	32 fam	32 fam	32 fam	**32 fam**	32 fam	32 fam	32 fam	32 fam
28	32 fam	32 fam	32 fam	32 fam	32 fam	**32 fam**	32 fam	32 fam	32 fam	32 fam
29	32 fam	32 fam	32 fam	32 fam	32 fam	**32 fam**	32 fam	32 fam	32 fam	32 fam
30	03a	03a	03a	03a	03a	03a	**03a**	**18,19a**	18,19a	18,19a
31	03a	03a	03a	03a	03a	03a	**03a**	**18,19a**	18,19a	18,19a
32	03a	03a	03a	03a	03a	03a	**03a**	**18,19a**	18,19a	18,19a

Table 16. 1901 - 1910

LOTS	1901	1902	1903	1904	1905	1906	1907	1908	1909	1910
1	32 fam	32 fam	32 fam	32 fam	32 fam	32 fam	32 fam	32 fam	32 fam	32 fam
2	32 fam	32 fam	32 fam	32 fam	32 fam	32 fam	32 fam	32 fam	32 fam	32 fam
3	32 fam	32 fam	32 fam	32 fam	32 fam	32 fam	32 fam	32 fam	32 fam	32 fam
4	32 fam	32 fam	32 fam	32 fam	32 fam	32 fam	32 fam	32 fam	32 fam	32 fam
5	19b	19b	19b	19b	19b	19b	19b	19b	19b	19b
6	18,19a	18,19a	18,19a	18,19a	18,19a	18,19a	18,19a	18,19a	18,19a	18,19a
7	18,19a	18,19a	18,19a	18,19a	18,19a	18,19a	18,19a	18,19a	18,19a	18,19a
8	18,19a	18,19a	18,19a	18,19a	18,19a	18,19a	18,19a	18,19a	18,19a	18,19a
9	19b	19b	19b	19b	19b	19b	19b	19b	19b	19b
10	19b	19b	19b	19b	19b	19b	19b	19b	19b	19b
11	19b	19b	19b	19b	19b	19b	19b	19b	19b	19b
12	19b	19b	19b	19b	19b	19b	19b	19b	19b	19b
13	19b	19b	19b	19b	19b	19b	19b	19b	19b	19b
14	19b	19b	19b	19b	19b	19b	19b	19b	19b	19b
15	19a	19a	19a	19a	19a	19a	19a	19a	19a	19a
16	19a	19a	19a	19a	19a	19a	19a	19a	19a	19a
17	19a	19a	19a	19a	19a	19a	19a	19a	19a	19a
18	19a	19a	19a	19a	19a	19a	19a	19a	19a	19a
19	19a	19a	19a	19a	19a	19a	19a	19a	19a	19a
20	19a	19a	19a	19a	19a	19a	19a	19a	19a	19a
21	32 fam	32 fam	32 fam	32 fam	32 fam	32 fam	32 fam	32 fam	32 fam	32 fam
22	32 fam	32 fam	32 fam	32 fam	32 fam	32 fam	32 fam	32 fam	32 fam	32 fam
23	32 fam	32 fam	32 fam	32 fam	32 fam	32 fam	32 fam	32 fam	32 fam	32 fam
24	18,19a	18,19a	18,19a	18,19a	18,19a	18,19a	18,19a	18,19a	18,19a	18,19a
25	18,19a	18,19a	18,19a	18,19a	18,19a	18,19a	18,19a	18,19a	18,19a	18,19a
26	18,19a	18,19a	18,19a	18,19a	18,19a	18,19a	18,19a	18,19a	18,19a	18,19a
27	32 fam	32 fam	32 fam	32 fam	32 fam	32 fam	32 fam	32 fam	32 fam	32 fam
28	32 fam	32 fam	32 fam	32 fam	32 fam	32 fam	32 fam	32 fam	32 fam	32 fam
29	32 fam	32 fam	32 fam	32 fam	32 fam	32 fam	32 fam	32 fam	32 fam	32 fam
30	18,19a	18,19a	18,19a	18,19a	18,19a	18,19a	18,19a	18,19a	18,19a	18,19a
31	18,19a	18,19a	18,19a	18,19a	18,19a	18,19a	18,19a	18,19a	18,19a	18,19a
32	18,19a	18,19a	18,19a	18,19a	18,19a	18,19a	18,19a	18,19a	18,19a	18,19a

Table 17. 1911 - 1920

LOTS	1911	1912	1913	1914	1915	1916	1917	1918	1919	1920
1	32 fam	32 fam	32 fam	32 fam	32 fam	32 fam	32 fam	32 fam	32 fam	32 fam
2	32 fam	32 fam	32 fam	32 fam	32 fam	32 fam	32 fam	32 fam	32 fam	32 fam
3	32 fam	32 fam	32 fam	32 fam	32 fam	32 fam	32 fam	32 fam	32 fam	32 fam
4	32 fam	32 fam	32 fam	32 fam	32 fam	32 fam	32 fam	32 fam	32 fam	32 fam
5	19b	19b	19b	19b	19b	19b	19b	19b	19b	19b
6	18	19a	All heirs	All heirs	All heirs	All heirs	All heirs	All heirs	All heirs	All heirs
7	18	19a	All heirs	All heirs	All heirs	All heirs	All heirs	All heirs	All heirs	All heirs
8	18	19a	All heirs	All heirs	All heirs	All heirs	All heirs	All heirs	All heirs	All heirs
9	19b	19b	19b	19b	19b	19b	19b	19b	19b	19b
10	19b	19b	19b	19b	19b	19b	19b	19b	19b	19b
11	19b	19b	19b	19b	19b	19b	19b	19b	19b	19b
12	19b	19b	19b	19b	19b	19b	19b	19b	19b	19b
13	19b	19b	19b	19b	19b	19b	19b	19b	19b	19b
14	19b	19b	19b	19b	19b	19b	19b	19b	19b	19b
15	19a	19a	All heirs	All heirs	All heirs	All heirs	All heirs	All heirs	All heirs	All heirs
16	19a	19a	All heirs	All heirs	All heirs	All heirs	All heirs	All heirs	All heirs	All heirs
17	19a	19a	All heirs	All heirs	All heirs	All heirs	All heirs	All heirs	All heirs	All heirs
18	19a	19a	All heirs	All heirs	All heirs	All heirs	All heirs	All heirs	All heirs	All heirs
19	19a	19a	All heirs	All heirs	All heirs	All heirs	All heirs	All heirs	All heirs	All heirs
20	19a	19a	All heirs	All heirs	All heirs	All heirs	All heirs	All heirs	All heirs	All heirs
21	32 fam	32 fam	32 fam	32 fam	32 fam	32 fam	32 fam	32 fam	32 fam	32 fam
22	32 fam	32 fam	32 fam	32 fam	32 fam	32 fam	32 fam	32 fam	32 fam	32 fam
23	32 fam	32 fam	32 fam	32 fam	32 fam	32 fam	32 fam	32 fam	32 fam	32 fam
24	18	19a	All heirs	All heirs	All heirs	All heirs	All heirs	All heirs	All heirs	All heirs
25	18	19a	All heirs	All heirs	All heirs	All heirs	All heirs	All heirs	All heirs	All heirs
26	18	19a	All heirs	All heirs	All heirs	All heirs	All heirs	All heirs	All heirs	All heirs
27	32 fam	32 fam	32 fam	32 fam	32 fam	32 fam	32 fam	32 fam	32 fam	32 fam
28	32 fam	32 fam	32 fam	32 fam	32 fam	32 fam	32 fam	32 fam	32 fam	32 fam
29	32 fam	32 fam	32 fam	32 fam	32 fam	32 fam	32 fam	32 fam	32 fam	32 fam
30	18	19a	All heirs	All heirs	All heirs	All heirs	All heirs	All heirs	All heirs	All heirs
31	18	19a	All heirs	All heirs	All heirs	All heirs	All heirs	All heirs	All heirs	All heirs
32	18	19a	All heirs	All heirs	All heirs	All heirs	All heirs	All heirs	All heirs	All heirs

Table 18. 1921 - 1930

LOTS	1921	1922	1923	1924	1925	1926	1927	1928	1929	1930
1	32 fam	32 fam	32 fam	32 fam	32 fam	32 fam	32 fam	32 fam	32 fam	63
2	32 fam	32 fam	32 fam	32 fam	32 fam	32 fam	32 fam	32 fam	32 fam	63
3	32 fam	32 fam	32 fam	32 fam	32 fam	32 fam	32 fam	32 fam	32 fam	63
4	32 fam	32 fam	32 fam	32 fam	32 fam	32 fam	32 fam	32 fam	32 fam	63
5	19b	19b	19b	19b	19b	19b	19b	19b	19b	19b
6	All heirs	All heirs	All heirs	All heirs	All heirs	All heirs	All heirs	All heirs	All heirs	All heirs
7	All heirs	All heirs	All heirs	All heirs	All heirs	All heirs	All heirs	All heirs	All heirs	All heirs
8	All heirs	All heirs	All heirs	All heirs	All heirs	All heirs	All heirs	All heirs	All heirs	All heirs
9	19b	19b	19b	19b	19b	19b	19b	19b	19b	19b
10	19b	19b	19b	19b	19b	19b	19b	19b	19b	19b
11	19b	19b	19b	19b	19b	19b	19b	19b	19b	19b
12	19b	19b	19b	19b	19b	19b	19b	19b	19b	19b
13	19b	19b	19b	19b	19b	19b	19b	19b	19b	19b
14	19b	19b	19b	19b	19b	19b	19b	19b	19b	19b
15	All heirs	All heirs	All heirs	All heirs	All heirs	All heirs	All heirs	All heirs	All heirs	All heirs
16	All heirs	All heirs	All heirs	All heirs	All heirs	All heirs	All heirs	All heirs	All heirs	All heirs
17	All heirs	All heirs	All heirs	All heirs	All heirs	All heirs	All heirs	All heirs	All heirs	All heirs
18	All heirs	All heirs	All heirs	All heirs	All heirs	All heirs	All heirs	All heirs	All heirs	All heirs
19	All heirs	All heirs	All heirs	All heirs	All heirs	All heirs	All heirs	All heirs	All heirs	All heirs
20	All heirs	All heirs	All heirs	All heirs	All heirs	All heirs	All heirs	All heirs	All heirs	All heirs
21	32 fam	32 fam	32 fam	32 fam	32 fam	32 fam	32 fam	32 fam	32 fam	63
22	32 fam	32 fam	32 fam	32 fam	32 fam	32 fam	32 fam	32 fam	32 fam	63
23	32 fam	32 fam	32 fam	32 fam	32 fam	32 fam	32 fam	32 fam	32 fam	63
24	All heirs	All heirs	All heirs	All heirs	All heirs	All heirs	All heirs	All heirs	All heirs	All heirs
25	All heirs	All heirs	All heirs	All heirs	All heirs	All heirs	All heirs	All heirs	All heirs	All heirs
26	All heirs	All heirs	All heirs	All heirs	All heirs	All heirs	All heirs	All heirs	All heirs	All heirs
27	32 fam	32 fam	32 fam	32 fam	32 fam	32 fam	32 fam	32 fam	32 fam	63
28	32 fam	32 fam	32 fam	32 fam	32 fam	32 fam	32 fam	32 fam	32 fam	63
29	32 fam	32 fam	32 fam	32 fam	32 fam	32 fam	32 fam	32 fam	32 fam	63
30	All heirs	All heirs	All heirs	All heirs	All heirs	All heirs	All heirs	All heirs	All heirs	All heirs
31	All heirs	All heirs	All heirs	All heirs	All heirs	All heirs	All heirs	All heirs	All heirs	All heirs
32	All heirs	All heirs	All heirs	All heirs	All heirs	All heirs	All heirs	All heirs	All heirs	All heirs

Table 19. 1931 - 1940

LOTS	1931	1932	1933	1934	1935	1936	1937	1938	1939	1940
1	**15**	15,63	15,63	15,63	15,63	15,63	15,63	15,63	15,63	15,63
2	**15**	15,63	15,63	15,63	15,63	15,63	15,63	15,63	15,63	15,63
3	**15**	15,63	15,63	15,63	15,63	15,63	15,63	15,63	15,63	15,63
4	**15**	15,63	15,63	15,63	15,63	15,63	15,63	15,63	15,63	15,63
5	19b	19b	19b	19b	19b	19b	19b	19b	19b	19b
6	All heirs	All heirs	All heirs	**All heirs**	**12,a**	**15**	**22**	22	22	22
7	All heirs	All heirs	All heirs	**All heirs**	**12,a**	**15**	**22**	22	22	22
8	All heirs	All heirs	All heirs	**All heirs**	**12,a**	**15**	**22**	22	22	22
9	19b	19b	19b	19b	19b	19b	19b	19b	19b	19b
10	19b	19b	19b	19b	19b	19b	19b	19b	19b	19b
11	19b	19b	19b	19b	19b	19b	19b	19b	19b	19b
12	19b	19b	19b	19b	19b	19b	19b	19b	19b	19b
13	19b	19b	19b	19b	19b	19b	19b	19b	19b	19b
14	19b	19b	19b	19b	19b	19b	19b	19b	19b	19b
15	All heirs	All heirs	**All heirs**	**All heirs**	**20**	20	20	20	20	20
16	All heirs	All heirs	**All heirs**	**All heirs**	**20**	20	20	20	20	20
17	All heirs	All heirs	**All heirs**	**All heirs**	**20**	20	20	20	20	20
18	All heirs	All heirs	**All heirs**	**All heirs**	**20**	20	20	20	20	20
19	All heirs	All heirs	**All heirs**	**All heirs**	**20**	20	20	20	20	20
20	All heirs	All heirs	**All heirs**	**All heirs**	**20**	20	20	20	20	20
21	**15**	15,63	15,63	15,63	15,63	15,63	15,63	15,63	15,63	15,63
22	**15**	15,63	15,63	15,63	15,63	15,63	15,63	15,63	15,63	15,63
23	**15**	15,63	15,63	15,63	15,63	15,63	15,63	15,63	15,63	15,63
24	All heirs	All heirs	All heirs	**All heirs**	**12,a**	**15**	**22**	22	22	22
25	All heirs	All heirs	All heirs	**All heirs**	**12,a**	**15**	**22**	22	22	22
26	All heirs	All heirs	All heirs	**All heirs**	**12,a**	**15**	**22**	22	22	22
27	**15**	15,63	15,63	15,63	15,63	15,63	15,63	15,63	15,63	15,63
28	**15**	15,63	15,63	15,63	15,63	15,63	15,63	15,63	15,63	15,63
29	**15**	15,63	15,63	15,63	15,63	15,63	15,63	15,63	15,63	15,63
30	All heirs	All heirs	All heirs	**All heirs**	**12,a**	**15**	**22**	22	22	22
31	All heirs	All heirs	All heirs	**All heirs**	**12,a**	**15**	**22**	22	22	22
32	All heirs	All heirs	All heirs	**All heirs**	**12,a**	**15**	**22**	22	22	22

Table 20. 1941 - 1950

LOTS	1941	1942	1943	1944	1945	1946	1947	1948	1949	1950
1	15,63	15,63	15,63	04	04	04	04	04	04	04
2	15,63	15,63	15,63	04	04	04	04	04	04	04
3	15,63	15,63	15,63	04	04	04	04	04	04	04
4	15,63	15,63	15,63	04	04	04	04	04	04	04
5	19b	19b	19b	19b	19b	19b	19b	19b	19b	All heirs
6	22	22	22	22	22	22	22	22	22	10a
7	22	22	22	22	22	22	22	22	22	10a
8	22	22	22	22	22	22	22	22	22	10a
9	19b	19b	19b	19b	19b	19b	19b	19b	19b	All heirs
10	19b	19b	19b	19b	19b	19b	19b	19b	19b	All heirs
11	19b	19b	19b	19b	19b	19b	19b	19b	19b	All heirs
12	19b	19b	19b	19b	19b	19b	19b	19b	19b	All heirs
13	19b	19b	19b	19b	19b	19b	19b	19b	19b	All heirs
14	19b	19b	19b	19b	19b	19b	19b	19b	19b	All heirs
15	20	20	20	20	20	20	20	20	22	10a
16	20	20	20	20	20	20	20	20	22	10a
17	20	20	20	20	20	20	20	20	22	10a
18	20	20	20	20	20	20	20	20	22	10a
19	20	20	20	20	20	20	20	20	22	10a
20	20	20	20	20	20	20	20	20	22	10a
21	15,63	15,63	15,63	04	04	04	04	04	04	04
22	15,63	15,63	15,63	04	04	04	04	04	04	04
23	15,63	15,63	15,63	04	04	04	04	04	04	04
24	22	22	22	22	22	22	22	22	22	10a
25	22	22	22	22	22	22	22	22	22	10a
26	22	22	22	22	22	22	22	22	22	10a
27	15,63	15,63	15,63	04	04	04	04	04	04	04
28	15,63	15,63	15,63	04	04	04	04	04	04	04
29	15,63	15,63	15,63	04	04	04	04	04	04	04
30	22	22	22	22	22	22	22	22	22	10a
31	22	22	22	22	22	22	22	22	22	10b
32	22	22	22	22	22	22	22	22	22	10a

Table 21. 1951 - 1960

LOTS	1951	1952	1953	1954	1955	1956	1957	1958	1959	1960
1	04	04	04	04	04	All heirs	10	10	10	10
2	04	04	04	04	04	All heirs	10	10	10	10
3	04	04	04	04	04	All heirs	10	10	10	10
4	04	04	04	04	04	All heirs	10	10	10	10
5	All heirs	All heirs	All heirs	All heirs	All heirs	All heirs	All heirs	All heirs	All heirs	All heirs
6	10b	10b	10b	10b	10b	10b	10	10	10	10
7	10b	10b	10b	10b	10b	10b	10	10	10	10
8	10b	10b	10b	10b	10b	10b	10	10	10	10
9	All heirs	All heirs	All heirs	All heirs	All heirs	All heirs	All heirs	All heirs	All heirs	All heirs
10	All heirs	All heirs	All heirs	All heirs	All heirs	All heirs	All heirs	All heirs	All heirs	All heirs
11	All heirs	All heirs	All heirs	All heirs	All heirs	All heirs	All heirs	All heirs	All heirs	All heirs
12	All heirs	All heirs	All heirs	All heirs	All heirs	All heirs	All heirs	All heirs	All heirs	All heirs
13	All heirs	All heirs	All heirs	All heirs	All heirs	All heirs	All heirs	All heirs	All heirs	All heirs
14	All heirs	All heirs	All heirs	All heirs	All heirs	All heirs	All heirs	All heirs	All heirs	All heirs
15	10b	10b	10b	10b	10b	10b	10	10	10	10
16	10b	10b	10b	10b	10b	10b	10	10	10	10
17	10b	10b	10b	10b	10b	10b	10	10	10	10
18	10b	10b	10b	10b	10b	10b	10	10	10	10
19	10b	10b	10b	10b	10b	10b	10	10	10	10
20	10b	10b	10b	10b	10b	10b	10	10	10	10
21	04	04	04	04	04	All heirs	10	10	10	All heirs
22	04	04	04	04	04	All heirs	10	10	10	All heirs
23	04	04	04	04	04	All heirs	10	10	10	All heirs
24	10b	10b	10b	10b	10b	10b	10	10	10	10
25	10b	10b	10b	10b	10b	10b	10	10	10	10
26	10b	10b	10b	10b	10b	10b	10	10	10	10
27	04	04	04	04	04	All heirs	10	10	10	All heirs
28	04	04	04	04	04	All heirs	10	10	10	All heirs
29	04	04	04	04	04	All heirs	10	10	10	All heirs
30	10b	10b	10b	10b	10b	10b	10	10	10	10
31	10b	10b	10b	10b	10b	10b	10	10	10	10
32	10b	10b	10b	10b	10b	10b	10	10	10	10

Table 22. 1961 - 1970

LOTS	1961	1962	1963	1964	1965	1966	1967	1968	1969	1970
1	10	10	10	10	10	±	±	±	±	±
2	10	10	10	10	10	±	±	±	±	±
3	10	10	10	10	10	±	±	±	±	±
4	10	10	10	10	10	±	±	±	±	±
5	19b	All heirs	**40**	40	40	40	40	40	40	40
6	All heirs	**10**	10	10	10	10	10	10	10	10
7	All heirs	**10**	10	10	10	10	10	10	10	10
8	All heirs	**10**	10	10	10	10	10	10	10	10
9	19b	All heirs	**40**	40	40	40	40	40	40	40
10	19b	All heirs	**40**	40	40	40	40	40	40	40
11	19b	All heirs	**40**	40	40	40	40	40	40	40
12	19b	All heirs	**40**	40	40	40	40	40	40	40
13	19b	All heirs	**40**	40	40	40	40	40	40	40
14	19b	All heirs	**40**	40	40	40	40	40	40	40
15	All heirs	**10**	10	10	10	10	10	10	10	10
16	All heirs	**10**	10	10	10	10	10	10	10	10
17	All heirs	**10**	10	10	10	10	10	10	10	10
18	All heirs	**10**	10	10	10	10	10	10	10	10
19	All heirs	**10**	10	10	10	10	10	10	10	10
20	All heirs	**10**	10	10	10	10	10	10	10	10
21	**10**	10	10	10	10	10	10	10	10	10
22	**10**	10	10	10	10	10	10	10	10	10
23	**10**	10	10	10	10	10	10	10	10	10
24	All heirs	**10**	10	10	10	10	10	10	10	10
25	All heirs	**10**	10	10	10	10	10	10	10	10
26	All heirs	**10**	10	10	10	10	10	10	10	10
27	**10**	10	10	10	10	10	10	10	10	10
28	**10**	10	10	10	10	10	10	10	10	10
29	**10**	10	10	10	10	10	10	10	10	10
30	All heirs	**10**	10	10	10	10	10	10	10	10
31	All heirs	**10**	10	10	10	10	10	10	10	10
32	All heirs	**10**	10	10	10	10	10	10	10	10

Table 23. 1971 - 1980

LOTS	1971	1972	1973	1974	1975	1976	1977	1978	1979	1980
1	±	±	±	10	10	**10**	**55**	55	55	55
2	±	±	±	10	10	**10**	**55**	55	55	55
3	±	±	±	10	10	**10**	**55**	55	55	55
4	±	±	±	10	10	**10**	**55**	55	55	55
5	40	40	40	40	40	40	40	40	40	40
6	10	10	10	10	10	**10**	**55**	55	55	55
7	10	10	10	10	10	**10**	**55**	55	55	55
8	10	10	10	10	10	**10**	**55**	55	55	55
9	40	40	40	40	40	40	40	40	40	40
10	40	40	40	40	40	40	40	40	40	40
11	40	40	40	40	40	40	40	40	40	40
12	40	40	40	40	40	40	40	40	40	40
13	40	40	40	40	40	40	40	40	40	40
14	40	40	40	40	40	40	40	40	40	40
15	10	10	10	10	10	**10**	**55**	55	55	55
16	10	10	10	10	10	**10**	**55**	55	55	55
17	10	10	10	10	10	**10**	**55**	55	55	55
18	10	10	10	10	10	**10**	**55**	55	55	55
19	10	10	10	10	10	**10**	**55**	55	55	55
20	10	10	10	10	10	**10**	**55**	55	55	55
21	10	10	10	10	10	**10**	**55**	55	55	55
22	10	10	10	10	10	**10**	**55**	55	55	55
23	10	10	10	**10**	**07**	07	07	07	07	07
24	10	10	10	10	10	**10**	**55**	55	55	55
25	10	10	10	10	10	**10**	**55**	55	55	55
26	10	10	10	10	10	**10**	**55**	55	55	55
27	10	10	10	10	10	**10**	**55**	55	55	55
28	10	10	10	10	10	**10**	**55**	55	55	55
29	10	10	10	10	10	**10**	**55**	55	55	55
30	10	10	10	10	10	**10**	**55**	55	55	55
31	10	10	10	10	10	**10**	**55**	55	55	55
32	10	10	10	10	10	**10**	**55**	55	55	55

Table 24. 1981 - 1990

LOTS	1981	1982	1983	1984	1985	1986	1987	1988	1989	1990
1	55	55	55	55	55	**55**	**41**	41	41	41
2	55	55	55	55	55	**55**	**41**	41	41	41
3	55	55	55	55	55	**55**	**41**	41	41	41
4	55	55	55	55	55	**55**	**41**	41	41	41
5	40	40	40	40	40	40	40	40	40	40
6	55	55	55	55	55	**55**	**41**	41	41	41
7	55	55	55	55	55	**55**	**41**	41	41	41
8	55	55	55	55	55	**55**	**41**	41	41	41
9	40	40	40	40	40	40	40	40	40	40
10	40	40	40	40	40	40	40	40	40	40
11	40	40	40	40	40	40	40	40	40	40
12	40	40	40	40	40	40	40	40	40	40
13	40	40	40	40	40	40	40	40	40	40
14	40	40	40	40	40	40	40	40	40	40
15	55	55	55	55	55	**55**	**41**	41	41	41
16	55	55	55	55	55	**55**	**41**	41	41	41
17	55	55	55	55	55	**55**	**41**	41	41	41
18	55	55	55	55	55	**55**	**41**	41	41	41
19	55	55	55	55	55	**55**	**41**	41	41	41
20	55	55	55	55	55	**55**	**41**	41	41	41
21	55	55	55	55	55	**55**	**41**	41	41	41
22	55	55	55	55	55	**55**	**41**	41	41	41
23	07	07	07	07	07	07	07	07	07	07
24	55	55	55	55	55	**55**	**41**	41	41	41
25	55	55	55	55	55	**55**	**41**	41	41	41
26	55	55	55	55	55	**55**	**41**	41	41	41
27	55	55	55	55	55	**55**	**41**	41	41	41
28	55	55	55	55	55	**55**	**41**	41	41	41
29	55	55	55	55	55	**55**	**41**	41	41	41
30	55	55	55	55	55	**55**	**41**	41	41	41
31	55	55	55	55	55	**55**	**41**	41	41	41
32	55	55	55	55	55	**55**	**41**	41	41	41

Table 25. 1991 - 2000

LOTS	1991	1992	1993	1994	1995	1996	1997	1998	1999	2000
1	41	41	41	41	41	41	41	41	41	41
2	41	41	41	41	41	41	41	41	41	41
3	41	41	41	41	41	41	41	41	41	41
4	41	41	41	41	41	41	41	41	41	41
5	40	40	40	40	**40**	**61**	61	61	61	61
6	41	41	41	41	41	41	41	41	41	41
7	41	41	41	41	41	41	41	41	41	41
8	41	41	41	41	41	41	41	41	41	41
9	40	40	40	40	40	40	40	40	40	40
10	40	40	40	40	40	40	40	40	40	40
11	40	40	40	40	40	40	40	40	40	40
12	40	40	40	40	40	40	40	40	40	40
13	40	40	40	40	40	40	40	40	40	40
14	40	40	40	40	40	40	40	40	40	40
15	41	41	41	41	41	41	41	41	41	41
16	41	41	41	41	41	41	41	41	41	41
17	41	41	41	41	41	41	41	41	41	41
18	41	41	41	41	41	41	41	41	41	41
19	41	41	41	41	41	41	41	41	41	41
20	41	41	41	41	41	41	41	41	41	41
21	41	41	41	41	41	41	41	41	41	41
22	41	41	41	41	41	41	41	41	41	41
23	07	07	07	07	07	07	07	07	07	07
24	41	41	41	41	41	41	41	41	41	41
25	41	41	41	41	41	41	41	41	41	41
26	41	41	41	41	41	41	41	41	41	41
27	41	41	41	41	41	41	41	41	41	41
28	41	41	41	41	41	41	41	41	41	41
29	41	41	41	41	41	41	41	41	41	41
30	41	41	41	41	41	41	41	41	41	41
31	41	41	41	41	41	41	41	41	41	41
32	41	41	41	41	41	41	41	41	41	41

Table 26. 2001 - 2010

LOTS	2001	2002	2003	2004	2005	2006	2007	2008	2009	2010
1	41	41	41	41	**41**	**55**	**41**	41	41	41
2	41	41	41	41	**41**	**55**	**41**	41	41	41
3	41	41	41	41	**41**	**55**	**41**	41	41	41
4	41	41	41	41	**41**	**55**	**41**	41	41	41
5	61	61	61	61	61	61	61	61	61	61
6	41	41	41	41	**41**	**55**	**41**	41	41	41
7	41	41	41	41	**41**	**55**	**41**	41	41	41
8	41	41	41	41	**41**	**55**	**41**	41	41	41
9	40	40	40	40	40	40	40	40	40	40
10	40	40	40	40	40	40	40	40	40	40
11	40	40	40	40	40	40	40	40	40	40
12	40	40	40	40	40	40	40	40	40	40
13	**40**	**25**	25	25	25	25	25	25	25	25
14	40	40	40	40	40	40	40	40	40	40
15	41	41	41	41	**41**	**55**	**41**	41	41	41
16	41	41	41	41	**41**	**55**	**41**	41	41	41
17	41	41	41	41	**41**	**55**	**41**	41	41	41
18	41	41	41	41	**41**	**55**	**41**	41	41	41
19	41	41	41	41	**41**	**55**	**41**	41	41	41
20	41	41	41	41	**41**	**55**	**41**	41	41	41
21	41	41	41	41	**41**	**55**	**41**	41	41	41
22	41	41	41	41	**41**	**55**	**41**	41	41	41
23	07	07	07	07	07	07	07	07	07	07
24	41	41	41	41	**41**	**55**	**41**	41	41	41
25	**41**	41	**41**	**55**	**27**	27	27	27	27	27
26	41	41	41	41	**41**	**55**	**41**	41	41	41
27	41	41	41	41	**41**	**55**	**41**	41	41	41
28	41	41	41	41	**41**	**55**	**41**	41	41	41
29	41	41	41	41	**41**	**55**	**41**	41	41	41
30	41	41	41	41	**41**	**55**	**41**	41	41	41
31	41	41	41	41	**41**	**55**	**41**	41	41	41
32	41	41	41	41	**41**	**55**	**41**	41	41	41

Table 27. 2011 - 2020

LOTS	2011	2012	2013	2014	2015	2016	2017	2018	2019	2020
1	41	41	41	41	41	41	41	41	**07**	41
2	41	41	41	41	41	41	41	41	**07**	41
3	41	41	41	41	41	41	41	41	**07**	41
4	41	41	41	41	41	41	41	41	**07**	41
5	61	61	61	61	61	61	61	61	61	**61**
6	41	41	41	41	41	41	41	41	**07**	41
7	41	41	41	41	41	41	41	41	**07**	41
8	41	41	41	41	41	41	41	41	**07**	41
9	40	40	40	40	**40**	**40a**	40a	40a	40a	40a
10	40	40	40	40	**40**	**40a**	40a	40a	40a	40a
11	40	40	40	40	**40**	**40a**	40a	40a	40a	40a
12	40	40	40	40	**40**	**40a**	40a	40a	40a	40a
13	25	25	25	25	25	25	25	25	25	25
14	40	40	40	40	**40**	**40a**	40a	40a	40a	40a
15	41	41	41	41	41	41	41	41	**07**	41
16	41	41	41	41	41	41	41	41	**07**	41
17	41	41	41	41	41	41	41	41	**07**	41
18	41	41	41	41	41	41	41	41	**07**	41
19	41	41	41	41	41	41	41	41	**07**	41
20	41	41	41	41	41	41	41	41	**07**	41
21	41	41	41	41	41	41	41	41	**07**	41
22	41	41	41	41	41	41	41	41	**07**	41
23	07	07	07	07	07	07	07	07	**07**	**07a**
24	41	41	41	41	41	41	41	41	**07**	41
25	27	27	27	27	27	27	27	27	27	27
26	41	41	41	41	41	41	41	41	**07**	41
27	41	41	41	41	41	41	41	41	**07**	41
28	41	41	41	41	41	41	41	41	**07**	41
29	41	41	41	41	41	41	41	41	**07**	41
30	41	41	41	41	41	41	41	41	**07**	41
31	41	41	41	41	41	41	41	41	**07**	41
32	41	41	41	41	41	41	41	41	**07**	41

Owner Info Box Section

The part of this appendix which contains the most subjective or unverifiable material is the *Owner Info Box* section. We guarantee none of these datasets as verified, whereas the ownership verification we are confident of. If we could not truly identify certain datasets, we left them blank. But if the dataset could be a year off, or parentage or even spouse names were close, we included what we had uncovered. Below is a simulation of what the empty Info Box datasets include. These titles will be removed should we have info entered in those fields.

Info Box Legend:

CODE	LOT OWNER NAME	SPOUSES NAME
DATE & PLACE OF BIRTH		DATE & PLACE OF DEATH
Lot #		
HISTORY OF BUYING, OWNING, SELLING OAK ISLAND LOT(S)		
ALIAS NAMES		
DATA ON CHILDREN & FAMILIAL RELATIONSHIPS		
REFERENCE CITATIONS		

00	English Crown Holdings / Escheats Reassignment
All Land on Oak Island and All Identified property lots	
Depends on which Granting Authority is given	

01	ALLEN, Ambrose	Elizabeth Church (1st) Mary Compton Vaughan (2nd)
1748		1840
Lot **24**		
Purchased lot 24 from Duncan Smith (51) on 02-24-95 for 10£. Sold lot 24 along with Plum and March Islands to John Monrowe (39) on 10-20-1791 for 10£.		
ALIASES		
Married 1st wife Elizabeth Church on 05-19-1789. 2nd wife Mary, granddaughter to Anthony Vaughan Sr.(57), and niece to Anthony Vaughan Jr (57A). Identified as "fisherman" on deed.		
2, 35, 39, 87, 99		

02	James Anderson	SPOUSES NAME
1748/1749		1796
Lot **26**		
Granted Lot 26 in Chester Township grant in 1784. Sold Lot 26 to Samuel Ball (03) in 1788 for 8£		
ALIAS NAMES		
Loyalist from Baltimore. Privateer, lived on a town lot in Chester. Granted 300 acres in Chester Township in 1784, escheats in 1813. Son was John Secomb Anderson.		
2, 24, 33, 34, 35, 42, 135		

03	**Samuel Ball**	Mary Catherine Wallace
South Carolina, 1761		Oak Island, 1846
Lots **6, 7, 8, 24, 25, 26, 30, 31, 32**		
Purchased Lot 25 from William Hopkins (23) on 09-22-1787 for 8£. Purchased Lot 26 from James Anderson (02) in 1788 for 8£. Purchased Lot 8 from Robert Melvin Jr. (38d) in 1798 for 6£. Purchased Lot 24 from John Munro (39) for 10£. Purchased Lot 31 from John Bezanson (06a) in 1807 for 11£. Granted Lot 32 by Crown (00) in 1809 for previous military loyalist service. Purchased Lot 30 from John Pulsifer (46) in 1810 for 10£. Purchased Lots 6 & 7 from Nathaniel Melvin (38a) in 1812 for 60£.		
NOTE: Never owned Lot 22 – 1807 record mistake. Lot 22 listed instead of 31. Corrected by Ball but listed incorrectly on the 1818 survey map.		
Married servant from Halifax, Mary Catherine Wallace in 1797 in Chester. 3 Children: Andrew B. (b. 1798/1808), Samuel Jr. (b./d. 1803) & Mary (b./d. 1804). Escaped slave from South Carolina who joined the King's Army under Gen. Clinton. Also fought under Major Ward as a wood cutter while in New Jersey. Evacuated to Shelburne in 1783.		
2, 9, 10, 11, 13, 17, 24, 25, 28, 29, 31, 33, 35, 72, 83, 88, 93, 108, 130a, 131, 132, 135,		

03a	**Isaac Ball (Butler)**	Sarah (b.1826)
1811		DATE & PLACE OF DEATH
Lots 6, 7, 8, 25, 26, 30, 31, 32		
Managed homestead owned by Samuel Ball (03). Then in 1898, deeded ½ ownership in same lots to Abraham Ernst (18) & Henry Sellers (19a).		
a.k.a. Isaac Butler		
Worked as Samuel Ball's assistant/butler. Children: Charles, seaman (b. 1845); Louisa (b.1847); Mary (b. 1849); Hannah (b. 1851), & Edward (b. 1853).		
9, 10, 13, 130a, 131, 132		

04	**Clarence James Beamish**	Mary Ellen Chapman
1893		07-25-1955
Lot **23**		
Beamish purchases Lot 23 & additional acreage from Archibald Dauphinee (15) and Margaret Young & (Wallace) (63) on 09-28-1944.		
ALIAS NAMES		
His daughter Ruth Beamish, marries Edward Graves (04a) who inherits part of Clarence James Beamish (04) property, along with wife, Mary Ellen Chapman (09) heirs.		
12, 16, 17, 18, 43, 170		

04a	**Edward Graves**	Ruth Graves
DATE & PLACE OF BIRTH		DATE & PLACE OF DEATH
Lot **23**		
Wife Ruth Graves inherits percentage of father, Clarence James Beamish (04) lot. Lot 23 is passed through to heirs of Ruth Graves & Edward Graves (Chapman group) see (09).		
Not related to Anthony T. Graves (19)		
Spouse is heir to land owned by Clarence James Beamish (04)		
1, 3, 12, 16, 17, 18, 170,		

05	**John Bearlson**	SPOUSES NAME
DATE & PLACE OF BIRTH		DATE & PLACE OF DEATH
Lot **22**		
Based on his name being on the list of 1765 Land Grant Participants, it is assumed he escheated or traded this lot to another (possibly Jonathan Prescott (45) before 1784, but this is strictly conjecture.		
ALIAS NAMES		
DATA ON CHILDREN & FAMILIAL RELATIONSHIPS		
39		

06a	**John J. Bezanson**	SPOUSES NAME
1754		DATE & PLACE OF DEATH
Lots **4, 29, 31**		
John J. Bezanson (06a) purchased Lot 29 and Plumb & Marsh Islands from John Monrow (39) on 11-16-1796 for 4£ 10s. Purchased Lot 31 from Jacob Hatt (21) on 06-28-1797 for 3£. Bezanson (06a) bought Lot 4 from Thomas Embree (17) on 04-01-1807 for 40£. He then sold Lot 4 to Anthony Vaughan Jr. (57) 19 days later on 04-19-1807, for 36£		
a.k.a. JJ Bezanon, John James Becanson, Jacques Bezanzon, John James Bexanson, John James Bissansa, J. Beyzanson, Joseph Bayzasar		
Arrived Chester from Lunenburg approx.1792, with wife, 8 children, settled around Middle River area. Purchased a sawmill and built a gristmill, became farmer and land speculator.		
31, 33, 35, 39, 44, 48, 63, 64, 65, 66, 98, 101, 105, 109		

06b	**George Bezanson**	SPOUSES NAME
DATE & PLACE OF BIRTH		DATE & PLACE OF DEATH
Lot **4**		
Purchased Lot 4 from Thomas Embree (17) on 03-24-1820, for 40£. Sold Lot 4 to Anthony Vaughan Jr. (57) on 04-19-1807 for 36£.		
a.k.a. George Beazanson.		
Related to JJ Bezanson.		
2, 31, 33, 35, 39, 44, 48, 63, 64, 65, 66, 98, 101, 105, 109		

06c	**Joseph Bezanson**	SPOUSES NAME
DATE & PLACE OF BIRTH		1822
Lot **20**		
Buys Lot 20 from Edward James (24) on 03-07-1794 5£ .		
ALIAS NAMES		
Related to JJ Bezanson.		
2, 35, 39, 44, 48, 63, 64, 65, 66, 98, 101, 105, 109		

07	Daniel C. Blankenship	SPOUSES NAME
1924		03-17-2019
Lot **23**		
Purchased Lot 23 from Melbourne R. Chappel (10) by quick deed on 09-19-1975 with a $15,000.00 mortgage. After his death, it was willed to his son Dave Blankenship (07a) and remains in the family today. Lot 23 is described as "The George McGinnis Property," as shown on Old Plan #1046, filed with the Department of Lands and Forests, Province of Nova Scotia. This plan is based on a survey done of Oak Island by William Nelson Dy Sr. and dated 07-06-1818.Oak Island Tours formed in 2006 with Dan Blankenship owning 50% and Rick & Marty Lagina owning 50%. See (41)		
a.k.a. Dan Blankenship		
Son is named Dave Blankenship (07a). Partners in Triton Alliance Syndicate (56), Triton Alliance LTD, Triton Alliance TLD/LTEE, Oak Island Tours and Island Tours, Inc. Initially worked for Robert Dunfield while the Restall family was excavating Smith's Cove area.		
19, 20, 23, 30, 36, 111, 112, 140,		

07a	Dave Blankenship	SPOUSES NAME
DATE & PLACE OF BIRTH		DATE & PLACE OF DEATH
Lot **23**		
Father Dan Blankenship (07) purchased the lot from Melbourne R. Chappel (10) on 09-19-1975, and he inherited it on his dad's passing in 2019.		
ALIAS NAMES		
Son to Dan C. Blankenship (07)		
30, 36, 111, 112, 140,		

08	William Bowie	SPOUSES NAME
1807		1877
Lot **23**		
Owns Lot 23 in 1784. Sold Lot 23 to Hector McLean (34) on 10-10-1784 for 22£ 6s 8pc.		
ALIAS NAMES		
Granted 150 acres in Chester Township in 1784, escheats in 1813.		
28, 34, 35, 61		

09	Mary Ellen Chapman (widower)	Basil Chapman
DATE & PLACE OF BIRTH		DATE & PLACE OF DEATH
Lot **23**		
Lot 23 was originally owned by William Bowie (08) who sold it to Hector McLean who sold it to Donald McInnis (32*) in 1788. Chapman sells her shares and those of all other Chapman heirs and of Clarence J. Beamish heirs (04) of land parcels which make up Lots 6, 7, 8, 15, 16, 17, 18, 19, 20, 23, 25, 26, 30, 31 & 32, to M.R. Chappell (10) 07-20-1961.		
a.k.a. Mary Ellen Beamish, deceased wife of Clarence James Beamish (04).		
Lot 23 is described in land deeds as "the George McGinnis (32*) Property" as shown on Old Plan #1046 filed with the Department of Lands & Forests. Plan based on survey done of Oak Island by William Nelson Dy Sr., dated 07-06-1818.Husband heir representing partial ownership of Kenneth Albert Chapman, Barbara Joan Chapman, Marjorie Ann Chapman, Judith Elizabeth Chapman, Carol Gladys Chapman, Robert Wayne Chapman, Linda Fay Chapman and minors.		
1, 3, 12, 16, 18, 20, 36, 170		

10	**Melbourne R. Chappell**	SPOUSES NAME
1887		1980
Lots **6, 7, 8, 15, 16, 17, 18, 19, 20, 23, 25, 26, 30, 31, 32**		
Through John Whitney Lewis (10b) and *Acadia Trust*, an intermediary, purchased lots from heirs of: Sellyn Sellers (19b), Henry Sellers (19a), McInnis members (32), Conrad brothers (12,12a), John Smith (51a), Samuel Ball (03), Abraham Ernst (18), Samuel Butler (03a), Thomas E. Smith (51c), Joseph Smith (51b), Anthony T. Graves (19), George W. Grimm Jr. (20), Erdie Powers (44), Burnell S. Corkum (13), Clarence James Beamish (04), Gilbert D. Hedden (22), Margaret Young (63), Archibald C. & Hannah Dauphinee (15), and Wilbert Walls (59), for Lots 6, 7, 8, 15, 16, 17, 18, 19, 20, 25, 26, 30, 31, 32, on 04-20-1957. Acquires inherited Lot shares by Mary Allen Chapmen and Clarence C. Beamish heirs to said lots on 07-20-1961. Chappell sells Lot 23 to Dan Blankenship (07 on 09-19-1975. Chappell sells Lots 6, 7, 8, 15, 16, 17, 18, 19, 20, 25, 26, 30, 31, 32, to David C. Tobias (55) on 06-15-1977.		
a.k.a. Mel Chappell		
Eventually goes into partnership with David Tobias (55 and Dan Blankenship (07) to form Triton Alliance (56). Some lots were not properly registered in court and Fred Nolan (40) was able through bitter court battle to acquire some Lots.		
14,15, 16, 17, 18, 19, 20, 36		

10a	**John Whitney Lewis**	Ann Lewis (New York)
DATE & PLACE OF BIRTH		DATE & PLACE OF DEATH
Lots **5, 6, 7, 8, 15, 16, 17, 18, 19, 20, 25, 26, 30, 31, 32**		
Purchased from Gilbert D. Hedden (22) on 05-26-1950, the above lots on behalf of Melbourne R. Chappell (10) to maintain secrecy. Sells said Lots to Acadia Trust Co. on 12-05-1950, as an intermediary, who then sells the same Lots to M.R. Chappell (10) on 04-20-1957.		
ALIAS NAMES		
DATA ON CHILDREN & FAMILIAL RELATIONSHIPS		
13, 14, 15		

10b	**ACADIA TRUST Co.**	SPOUSES NAME
		DATE & PLACE OF DEATH
Lots **7, 8, 15, 16, 17, 18, 19, 20, 25, 26, 30, (31), 32**		
Acadia Trust Co. (10b) purchase Lots 6, 7, 8, 15, 16, 17, 18, 19, 20, 25, 26, 30, 31, 32 from John Whitney & Ann Lewis (10a) on 11-27-1950.		
Lot 31 was missing from the list when lots were sold to John Whitney Lewis (10b) by Gilbert Hedden (22); and when sold by Lewis (10b) to Acadia Trust (10a), Lot 31 was shown, but Lot 26 was missing. Apparently both Lots 26 & 31 were considered transferred.		
13, 14, 15, 16		

11	**John P. Cochran**	SPOUSES NAME
1737		1785 in Royal Hospital in Chelsea
Lot **1**		
Received Lot 1 as part of Chester Township Land Grant in 1784. Sold Lot 1 to Alexander Pittillo (42) [Patillo] on 02-19-1785, for 5£, 16s 8p.		
ALIAS NAMES		
Received land as part of 1784 Chester township land grant.		
2, 34, 35, 67		

12	**Francis Arthur Conrad**	Eva Gertrude Dorey (1907-1987)
1905		1972
Lots **6, 7, 8, 25, 26, 30, 31, 32**		
Francis & Ingram Conrad sell Lots 6, 7, 8, 25, 26, 30, 31 & 32 to Archibald Dauphinee (15) on 09-14-1937.		
ALIAS NAMES		
Farmer. Brother to Ingram Eli Conrad (12a). Married wife in 1925.		
3, 9, 12, 16, 17, 36, 37		

12a	**Ingram Eli Conrad**	Quesetta May Swinamore (1902-1983)
1900		1979
Lots **6, 7, 8, 25, 26, 30, 31, 32**		
Francis & Ingram Conrad sell Lots 6, 7, 8, 25, 26, 30, 31 & 32 to Archibald Dauphinee (15) on 09-14-1937.		
ALIAS NAMES		
Married in 1921. Employed as a Cooper. Brother to Francis Arthur Conrad (12)		
3, 9, 16, 17, 36, 37		

13	**Burnell Stanley Corkum**	Hazel R. Freda (b. 1895-1965)
1897		1970
Lots **15, 16, 17, 18, 19, 20**		
Inherited percentage of shares in Lot ownership of Henry P. Sellers (19a) through his marriage to Elizabeth Bessie Anne Sellers. Sold percent share ownership in Lots 15, 16, 17, 18, 19, 20 to George W. Grimm Jr (20) in a number of land deeds transacted on 07-26-1935, representing multiple Corkum heirs.		
ALIAS NAMES		
Married 1923 to Hazel R. Freda. Merchant/shop owner. Burnell 'Stanley's' mother is Elizabeth Bessie Anne Sellers who's dad was Henry P. Sellers (19a), brother to Sellyn Sellers (19b). Familial ties with Flora Sophia S Corkum (13a), Henry Worrell Corkum (13b) Rose Elias Corkum (13c), Ruby Florence Corkum (13d) and Wilfred Whitney Corkum (13e).		
4, 5, 6, 7, 8, 13		

13a	**Flora Corkum**	SPOUSES NAME
1911		2012
Lots **15, 16, 17, 18, 19, 20**		
Inherited percentage of shares in Lot ownership of Henry P. Sellers (19a) through his marriage to Elizabeth Bessie Anne Sellers. Sold percent share ownership in Lots 15, 16, 17, 18, 19, 20 to George W. Grimm Jr (20) in a number of land deed transactions on 07-26-1935.		
a.k.a. Sophia Stolpestad		
Sibling. Mother is Elizabeth Bessie Anne Sellers, who's dad was Henry P. Sellers (19a).		
4, 5, 6, 13		

13b	**Henry Worrell Corkum**	Marry Sweet (b. 1917-2012)
1905		1977
Lots **15, 16, 17, 18, 19, 20**		
Inherited percentage of shares in Lot ownership of Henry P. Sellers (19a) through his marriage to Elizabeth Bessie Anne Sellers. Sold percent share ownership in Lots 15, 16, 17, 18, 19, 20 to George W. Grimm Jr (20) in a number of land deed transactions on 07-26-1935.		
ALIAS NAMES		
Sibling. Mother is Elizabeth Bessie Anne Sellers, who's dad was Henry P. Sellers (19a).		
4, 5, 6, 13		

13c	**Ross Elias**	Emma Corkum (b. 1906-1971)
1914		1968
Lots **15, 16, 17, 18, 19, 20**		
Inherited percentage of shares in Lot ownership of Henry P. Sellers (19a) through Henry's marriage to Elizabeth Bessie Anne Sellers and Ross's marriage to Emma Corkum above.. Sold percent share ownership in Lots 15, 16, 17, 18, 19, 20 to George W. Grimm Jr (20) in a number of land deed transactions on 07-26-1935.		
ALIAS NAMES		
Sibling. Mother is Elizabeth Bessie Anne Sellers, who's dad was Henry P. Sellers (19a).		
4, 5, 6, 13		

13d	**Ruby Florence**	Emerson Fenwick Greene (b. 1885-1963)
1899		1974
Lots **15, 16, 17, 18, 19, 20**		
Inherited percentage of shares in Lot ownership of Henry P. Sellers (19a) through Henry's his marriage to Elizabeth Bessie Anne Sellers and his marriage to Ruby Florence Corkum above. Sold percent share ownership in Lots 15, 16, 17, 18, 19, 20 to George W. Grimm Jr (20) in a number of land deed transactions on 07-26-1935.		
ALIAS NAMES		
Sibling. Mother is Elizabeth Bessie Anne Sellers, who's dad was Henry P. Sellers (19a).		
4, 5, 6, 13		

13e	**Wilfred Whitney**	Audrey Marcella Boutilier (b. 1909-1996)
1900		1982
Lots **15, 16, 17, 18, 19, 20**		
Inherited percentage of shares in Lot ownership of Henry P. Sellers (19a) through Henry's marriage to Elizabeth Bessie Anne Sellers, and Wilfred's marriage to Audrey Macella Boutiliier above. Sold percent share ownership in Lots 15, 16, 17, 18, 19, 20 to George W. Grimm Jr (20) in a number of land deed transactions on 07-26-1935.		
ALIAS NAMES		
Sibling. Mother is Elizabeth Bessie Anne Sellers, who's dad was Henry P. Sellers (19a).		
4, 5, 6, 13		

14	**Davie Wilbur Crandall**	Lucy Ellis (1780-1835)
1768		June 25, 1829 in Chester
Lot **15**		
Granted Lot 15 by 1818. Sells Lot 15 to John Smith (51a)on 06-10-1819.		
a.k.a. David Crandle		
David (Davie) Crandall was a lawyer, who married Lucy Ellis, the daughter of David Ellis (16) and Sarah Webber, daughter of James Webber (60), on 09-01-1796. David's mother was Mary Vaughan, sister of Anthony Vaughan Sr. (32).		
2, 25, 26, 31, 33, 35, 39, 103		

15	**Archibald C. Dauphinee**	Hannah McInnis (b. 1871)
1869		1952
Lots **6, 7, 8, 23, 25, 26, 30, 31, 32**		
Purchases Lot 23 from Margaret M. Young(63) on 10-01-1931. Purchases Lots 6, 7, 8, 25, 26, 30, 31 & 32 from Francis Conrad (12) on 09-14-1937. Dauphinee sells Lots 6, 7, 8, 25, 26, 30, 31 & 32 to Gilbert Hedden (22) on 09-14-1937. He sells Lot 23 to Clarence James Beamish (04) on 09-28-1944.		
ALIAS NAMES		
Married Hanna McInnis in Massachusetts in 1896.		
1, 3, 9, 10, 12, 36, 37		

16	**David Ellis**	Sarah Webber (b. 1762)
1748		1809
Lot **27, 29**		
Lot 27 ownership credit to Wroclawski. Ellis (16) purchased Lot 29 from Jeremiah Rogers (47) on 04-02-1778 for 5£.		
a.k.a. David Ells, Elles		
Fled Rhode Island in 1776 as a Loyalist and was granted 250 acres on the east side of Mahone Bay. 1791 Poll Tax shows as being a Blacksmith. 1793, 1794 & 1795 Poll Tax he is listed as a Farmer. Married Sarah Webber 11-12-1778. They had 9 children.		
28, 31, 32, 33, 35, 62, 89		

17	**Thomas Embree**	Deborah Hale (Bangs) widow
1758		1820
Lot **4**		
Purchased Lot 4 from Anthony Vaughan Sr. (57) on 06-01-1804 for 17£. Sold Lot 4 to JJ. Beazanson (06a) on 04-01-1807 for 40£.		
a.k.a. Thomas Embre, Thomas Embrey, Thomas Embry		
Evacuated Loyalist from New York. During revolution, served as Quartermaster for LTC Tarleton's "Legion of Green Devils" along with Neil McMullen (35). Captured at sea in a transport ship, Embree spent over a year as a POW. Married widow Deborah Hale (Bangs) on 03-14-1786. Gave birth to a daughter named Ann (1803-1880), who married Anthony Vaughan Jr. (57a). Embree listed as a Shopkeeper in Chester in 1791 Poll RZ.		
2, 27, 31, 35, 45, 65, 66, 70		

18	**Abraham Ernst**	Rachel Martha Graves (1855-1894)
1849		1911
Lots **6, 7, 8, 25, 26, 30, 31, 32**		
Received half ownership of above Lots by Samuel Ball's (03) will. Henry Sellers (19a) received the second half ownership of these lots.		
ALIAS NAMES		
Married Rachel in 1871. Abraham's parents were Jacob & Mary Ernst. Rachel's parents possibly Edward Graves (04a) and Ruth Graves. Children born were Mary, Edmond, Abraham, Urias & Sarah.		
9, 10, 13		

19	**Anthony Thickpenny Graves**	Anna Catherine Eliza Zinck (1823-1875)
1812		1888
Lots **5, 9, 10, 11, 12, 13, 14,** and **15, 16, 17, 18, 19, 20**		
Purchased lots 9-14 from Neil McMullen Smith (35a) on 06-18-1832 for 130£ which included a house and building. Purchased Lot 5 from David & Sara Vaughan (57c) (son of James Vaughan (57d), on 09-19-1832 for 20£ which included "houses, buildings, ways, privileges." Daughter Sophia Elizabeth Thickpenny marries Henry Sellers (19a) in 1865. Graves appears to be a land speculator and sells property, back and forth. Anthony Graves first sells lots 5, 9, 10, 11, 12, 13, 14 to Edward Foras (68) on 01-08-1834 for 200£; then sells the same lots to father-in-law Frederick Zinck (64) in 02-14-1839 for 35£. Frederick Zinck (64) then sells the same lots back to Graves on 03-29-1841 for 35£. The next day, Graves sells the same set of lots to John Strachan (54) on 03-30-1841 for 50£. Strachan (54) will later sell them back to Graves in 1857. Anthony Graves wills to his wife Anna Eliza Graves, his son-in-law Henry Sellers (19a) and his Daughter Sophia, as well as his other son-in-law Selvin Sellers (19b) and his wife Bessie, shares in ownership of the Lots 15, 16, 17, 18, 18, 19, 20, in his 07-14-1887 will.		
a.k.a. Anthony Thickpenny, Anthony Graves		
Spouse Eliza Elizabeth (Adelaide E. Publicover) a.k.a. Anna Eliza Graves. Their daughter Sophia Graves marries Henry Sellers (19a) in 1865 (her oxen fell into Cave-in-Pit).		
4, 5, 6, 7, 8, 13, 14, 34, 35, 38, 68, 69, 71		

19a	**Henry P. Sellers**	Sophia Sellers (1845-1931)
1839		1912
Lots **6, 7, 8, 25, 26, 30, 31, 32**		
Initially, John Smith (51a) [see 51a] owned the land up to 1825, where he deeded it to Thomas E. Smith (51c) & Joseph Smith (51b), his sons, in 1853. Both Smith brothers sold the lots to Anthony T. Graves (19) on 7-14-1887. Graves divides the lots into shares and gives half to Henry Sellers (19a) and his wife Sophia, and half to Henry's son Selvin Sellers (19b) and his wife Bessie in 1888 after Graves dies. Both Sellers parties, sell their interests in those Lots to George W. Grimm Jr. (20) on 07-27-1935,		
ALIAS NAMES		
Henry's wife, Sophia Sellers, who is the daughter of Anthony T. Graves (19), was plowing the field in1878 when her oxen fell into a pit and she became the discoverer of the Cave-in Pit." The daughter of Henry & Sophia is Erdie Powers (1869-1963) brother to Selvin.		
4, 5, 6, 7, 8, 9, 10, 11, 13, 14, 28		

19b	**Selwyn William Sellers**	Bessie Sellers (b.1881)
06-21-1873		07-23-19491949
Lots **15, 16, 17, 18, 19, 20**		
Initially, John Smith (51a) [see 51a] owned the land up to 1825, where he deeded it to Thomas E. Smith (51c) & Joseph Smith (51b), his sons, in 1853. Both Smith brothers sold the lots to Anthony T. Graves (19) on 7-14-1887. Graves divides the lots into shares and gives half to Henry Sellers (19a) and his wife Sophia, and half to Selvin Sellers (19b) and his wife Bessie in 1888 after Graves dies. Both Sellers parties, sell their interests in those Lots to George W. Grimm Jr. (20) on 07-27-1935,		
a.k.a. Sellyin, Sellyn, Selvyn Sellers		
Son of Henry Sellers (19a). Mining Lease issued in 09-09-1935. Married Bessie 12-07-1899.		
4, 5, 13, 14, 17, 25, 35, 36, 37, 132a, 170		

20	**George W. Grimm Jr.**	Marjorie Gifford (1899-1994)
1898		1971
Lots **6, 7, 8, 15, 16, 17, 18, 19, 20, 25, 26, 30, 31, 32**		
Purchases Lots 15, 16, 17, 18, 19, 20 from Selvin & Bessie Sellers (19b) (et. al.) on 07-27-1935. Purchases shares of said Lots owned by Erdie Powers (44) on 07-27-1935. Purchases shares of said Lots owned by Burnell Corkum (13) et. al., Wilbert Walls (59) et. al., on 07-27-1935. Purchases shares of said Lots owned by Genevieve Walls and heirs, on 07-27-1935. Acting on behalf of minor inheritors (Hope & Andrew), Burnell Corkum sells shares of said Lots on 07-27-1935 to George Grimm Jr. (20). Purchases Lots 6, 7, 8, 25, 26, 30, 31, 32 from Henry Sellers (19a) part of family. Grimm Jr. Sells Lots 15,16,17,18,19, 20 on 05-26-1950 to Gilbert D. Hedden (22). Then Hedden (22) sells them to John Whitney Lewis (10a) d.b.a. Acadian Trust Company (10a), who is a private buyer for Melbourne R. Chappell (10), who buys them as Acadia Trust Company on 04-12-1957.		
ALIAS NAMES		
Lawyer who processes deeds.		
3, 4, 6, 7, 8, 13, 14, 36, 37		

21	**Jacob Hatt**	Mary Hovey (21a) widowed
1759		DATE & PLACE OF DEATH
Lot **31**		
Inherited Lot 31 through his wife Mary Hovey (21/21a) in 1797. Sold Lot 31 to John J. Bezanson (06a) on 06-28-1797 for 3£.		
a.k.a. Jacob Hutt, Hat		
All siblings and father with the last name "Hatt." Often confused with Jacob Hutt. Identified as a ships carpenter. Married Mary Hovey in 1792.		
27, 31, 32, 33, 35, 63		

21a	**Cpt. Thomas Hovey**	Mary Hovey
DATE & PLACE OF BIRTH		1797
Lot **31**		
Owned Lot 31 prior to 1776. Lot 31 inherited by his wife Mary when Capt. Hovey (21a) dies the following year (1797). She then marries Jacob Hatt (21) in 1797 as well. He then also sells Lot 31 to John J. Bezanson (06a) in mid-1797.		
ALIAS NAMES		
Early settler of Chester & owned a town Lot 76 in 1764, Listed occupation as a cordwainer or one who makes new leather. Passed to his wife upon his death, who later married Jacob Hatt (21).		
2, 17, 40		

22	**Gilbert D. Hedden**	Marguerite C. Hedden
1903		1974
Lots **5, 6, 7, 8, (15), 16, 17, 18, 19, (20), 25, 26, 30, 31, 32**		
Hedden purchases Lots 6, 7, 8, 25, 26, 30, 31 & 32 from Archibald Dauphinee (15) on 09-14-1937. Hedden sells Lots 6, 7, 8, 15, 16, 17, 18, 19, 20, 25, 26, 30, 31, 32 to John Whitney Lewis (10a) on 05-26-1950.		
ALIAS NAMES		
DATA ON CHILDREN & FAMILIAL RELATIONSHIPS		
10, 13, 14, 36		

23	**William Hopkins**	SPOUSES NAME
DATE & PLACE OF BIRTH		DATE & PLACE OF DEATH
Lot **25**		
Sold Lot 25 to Samuel Ball (03) on 09-22-1787. Deed states Hopkins is a mariner, who lives in Chester. Possibly a loyalist granted land. (Lun. Land Deeds Vol. 6 pg. 24)		
CHILDREN OR FAMILIAL RELATIONSHIPS		
72		

24	**Edward James**	Sara Knaut
1757		1841
Lots **20, 21**		
Edward James (24) purchased Lot 20 from Alexander McNeil (37) on 01-19-1791 for 5£, 16s, 8pp, and purchased Lot 21 from Alexander McNeil (37) same time. Edward James (24) sold Lot 20 to Joseph Besanson (06c) on 03-07-1794 for 5£.		
ALIAS NAMES		
Served in the King's Orange Rangers as a Pay Officer. After Revolutionary War, became a merchant and then Representative for Lunenburg County, before becoming Sheriff of Lunenburg County. Married Sara Knaut, daughter to Lunenburg politician Phillip Knaut. Together Edward and Sara had 6 boys & 6 girls.		
2, 11, 25, 28, 35, 47, 48		

25	**John Johnston**	SPOUSES NAME
DATE & PLACE OF BIRTH		DATE & PLACE OF DEATH
Lot **13**		
Shown as owner of Lot 13 in 2007 map produced by Les MacPhie Archives. Frederick Nolan owned this lot previously. Likely purchased Lot 13 from David C. Tobias (55) 2005, when Tobias sold Lot 25 to Alan J. Kostrzewa (27).		
ALIAS NAMES		
DATA ON CHILDREN AND FAMILIAL RELATIONSHIPS		
30		

26 John Kinghorn	SPOUSES NAME
DATE & PLACE OF BIRTH	DATE & PLACE OF DEATH
Lot **4**	
Owns Lot 4 before 1786. Sold Lot 4 to Alexander McNeal (37) on 02-24-1786 for 18£ plus Town Lot #173.	
a.k.a. John Kinghorne	
Granted 500 acres in 1784 in Chester Township but escheats in 1813.	
2, 28, 34, 35, 39, 49	

27 Alan J. Kostrzewa	SPOUSES NAME
1957	DATE & PLACE OF DEATH
Lot **25**	
Purchased Lot 25 from David Tobias (55) in 2005.	
d.b.a. ***Center Road Ventures,*** *Partners Brian Urbach,* **Calla LLC**	
Partners with Rick & Marty Lagina and Craig Tester (Michigan Mafia) buying David Tobias (55) 50% ownership of Oak Island Tours. Owns and operates *Calla LLC* (1997) and is a producer on History Channels' Curse of Oak Island.	
30	

28 Timothy Lynch	SPOUSES NAME
1743	1812
Lot **19**	
Lynch/Zink (28) acquired Lot 19 from Edward Smith (52) on 03-28-1768. In 1791, Lot 19 was owned by Anthony Vaughan Sr. (57). There is no record of the sale from (28) to (57).	
a.k.a. Timothy Linch, Timothy Lynche, Timothy Zink	
Brought family of nine to Chester and established a Blacksmith Shop. Shown to own a Chester town lot in 1764. Yet in 1791, he listed his occupation as a ship's carpenter.	
22, 27, 29, 35, 40	

29 Mary Malay	Joseph (Jesse) White
DATE & PLACE OF BIRTH	DATE & PLACE OF DEATH
Lot **16**	
Drew Lot 16 in grant on 10-31-1768. Sold Lot 16 to John Smith (51a) on 01-25-1798 for 4£ 10s.	
ALIAS NAMES	
Widow from Halifax	
2, 13, 28, 74	

30 Martin Marshall	Ann Vaughan (b. 1777)
DATE & PLACE OF BIRTH	DATE & PLACE OF DEATH
Lots **9, 10**	
Purchased Lots 9 & 10 from Anthony Vaughan Sr. (57) on 12-22-1788. Sells both Lots 9 & 10 to Neal McMullen (35) in 1792.	
a.k.a. Mirten Marshall, Melvin Marshall	
Came to Nova Scotia in 1784 and first owned land in Shelburne, where he identified himself as a millwright. Married Ann Vaughan in 1788, she is the daughter of John Vaughan. John Vaughan was an older brother to Anthony Vaughan Sr. (57). In 1791 & 1793 he identifies as a wheelwright and was possibly employed by the Vaughan's. Martin Marshall is thought to have left for Georgia around 1792.	
2, 27, 30, 31, 32, 35, 39, 75, 76	

<table>
<tr><td>31</td><td>John Martin</td><td>Emily Compton</td></tr>
<tr><td colspan="2">DATE & PLACE OF BIRTH</td><td>DATE & PLACE OF DEATH</td></tr>
<tr><td colspan="3">Lot 4</td></tr>
<tr><td colspan="3">Owns Lot 4 in 1793. Sells Lot 4 to Anthony Vaughan Sr. (57) in 1793.</td></tr>
<tr><td colspan="3">ALIAS NAMES</td></tr>
<tr><td colspan="3">Part of Loyalist family arriving in Chester in 1784. Marries Emily Compton in 1811, who is the daughter of Mary Vaughan. Emily dies in 1797. Listed as farmer in 1791.</td></tr>
<tr><td colspan="3">27, 31, 32, 33. 35, 39</td></tr>
</table>

<table>
<tr><td>32</td><td>Donald McGinnis
(represents all McGinnis Clan)</td><td>Maria Barbara Saller (a.k.a. Sellers, Siler, Seiler, Zellers, Sawler)</td></tr>
<tr><td colspan="2">1758</td><td>1826</td></tr>
<tr><td colspan="3">Lots 1, 23, 27, 28, 29</td></tr>
<tr><td colspan="3">A "Donald MacGinnes" purchased Lot 28 from James Sharp (49) on 03-03-1788 for 7£. This is his 1st property in Chester. He purchased Lot 23 from Hector McLean (34) on 05-04-1790 for 7£. An erection and buildings are recorded on the deed. He purchased Lot 27 from Alexander Pattillo (42) in May 1791 for 6£. He purchased Lot 1 from Alexander Pattillo (42) on 09-09-1794 for 6£. He then purchased Lot 29 from the estate of J.J. Bezanson (06a) in 1810..</td></tr>
<tr><td colspan="3">a.k.a. Donald McKinnis, Dunagh McEnnis, Donald McInnis, Daniel Mcinnis Sr. Donald Daniel McInnis, Donald McKinnes, Donald McGennis, Donald Dunagh McGinnis, Donald McGinnas, Donald MacGinnis.</td></tr>
<tr><td colspan="3">Possibly Corporal Donald McInnis who was discharged from the 76th Regiment at Shelburne N.S. on 01-11-1784. On 02-04-1784 Donald McGinnas purchased a town lot in Shelburne. A Donagh McEnnis participated in the 1784 Chester Grand as well as the Port Hebert Grant. He married Maria Barbara Saller in 1795 and as of 1791 his occupation was listed as Farmer. His children were: John McKinnis (1797), Catherine McKinnis (1801), Mary McKinnis (1802), Donald McKinnis (1804), Henry McKinnis (1807). His will was probated by James Smith in 1827.</td></tr>
<tr><td colspan="3">2, 12, 16, 17, 18, 19, 27, 31, 32, 33, 34, 35, 38, 53, 79, 90, 91, 105, 169</td></tr>
</table>

<table>
<tr><td>33</td><td>Daniel McKinnis</td><td>SPOUSES NAME</td></tr>
<tr><td colspan="2">1804, Chester</td><td>DATE & PLACE OF DEATH</td></tr>
<tr><td colspan="3">Lot 2, 3, 22</td></tr>
<tr><td colspan="3">Recorded in the Chester Town Records is a son to Donald and Barbara and McKinnis known as Donald McKinnis, born in Chester on 8th of December in 1804. This son has been recorded in deeds as being Daniel McKinnon as well as Daniel McEnnis. He is also referred to as Donald McInnis in his father's 1827 will. On 3-14-1796, Daniel McKinnon bought Lot No. 22 from Jacob Melvin (38c), yeoman, of Chester for three pounds, ten shillings. (Lun Co. Deeds Vol. 4. pg. 140). On 11-2-1832 a Daniel McEnnis purchased lots 2 and 3 from David Vaughan (57c) for 28 pounds, which included all buildings and improvements. (Lun. Co Deeds Vol. 10 pg. 491)</td></tr>
<tr><td colspan="3">Aka Daniel Lacklan McKinnon, Donald McInnis Jr</td></tr>
<tr><td colspan="3">Occupation as yeoman. Joseph McKinnon (b. 1870). Florence (b.1880) Wife?</td></tr>
<tr><td colspan="3">39, 77, 169, 202</td></tr>
</table>

34	**Hector McLean**	SPOUSES NAME
DATE & PLACE OF BIRTH		DATE & PLACE OF DEATH
Lot **23**		
Purchased Lot 23 from William Bowie (08) on 10-10-1784 for 22£ 6s 8pp. Buildings were mentioned in sale. Sold Lot 23 to Donald McGinnis (32) on 05-04-1790 for 7£.		
ALIAS NAMES		
A lieutenant in the 84th Regiment during the Revolutionary War and later represented Hants County in the House of Assembly from 1793-1799. Brother-in-Law to Duncan Smith (51), who's sister is Margaret McLean (biological uncle to John Smith (51a).		
2, 39, 61, 79		

34a	**Merton McLean**	SPOUSES NAME
DATE & PLACE OF BIRTH		DATE & PLACE OF DEATH
Lot **23**		
HISTORY OF BUYING, OWNING, SELLING OAK ISLAND LOT(S)		
a.k.a. Hector McLean (34), Martin McLean		
DATA ON CHILDREN & FAMILIAL RELATIONSHIPS		
34, 39		

35	**Neal McMullen**	SPOUSES NAME
DATE & PLACE OF BIRTH		DATE & PLACE OF DEATH
Lots **9, 10, 11, (12), 13, 14**		
Neil McMullen was John Smith's(51a) stepfather and Neil McMullen Smith's(35a) non-biological grandfather. His first recorded property purchase in Chester was Lot 11 on 10-6-1789, bought from Daniel Vaughn(57b) for 8 pounds (Lun. Co. Records . Lots 9 and 10 were purchased together on 6-17-1793 for 22 pounds from Martin Marshall (30). Lots 13 and 14 were bought from Nathaniel Melvin (38a) in 1806 for 30 pounds.		
a.k.a. Neal, Neil, McMullen, McMullon, Mcmullen, Neil McMellon, Nill McMullen		
A Neil McMullen is on the muster records of the British Legion discharged in 1784 at Port Mouton. He may have served alongside Thomas Embry (17) under the command of Lt. Col. Tarleton's" Legion of Green Devils." The Ward Chapman papers record a Neil McMullen as a loyalist, discharged in Annapolis County during the summer of 1784 (along with one woman and three servants). McMullen married John Smith's mother on 7-22-1788 before settling on Oak Island. Ward Chapman Papers record Neil McMullen as a loyalist discharged in Annapolis County during summer of 1784 (along with one woman and 3 servants).		
2, 7, 17, 25, 26, 27, 31, 32, 35, 46, 76, 80, 81, 82		

35a	**Neal McMullen Smith**	Mary Elizabeth
1804 – Chester N.S.		DATE & PLACE OF DEATH
Lots **9, 10, 11, 12, 13, 14**		
1st child of John and Anne Smith, named after John Smith's (51a) stepfather Neil McMullen (35). Born on Oak Island. Bought Lots 9, 10, 11, 12, 13, 14, for 250 pounds on 12-21-1827 from non-biological grandfather Neil McMullen(35) (Vol 9. pg.53). Listed as a farmer on deed, whose wife was named Mary Elizabeth. A "house and building" was also mentioned. Sold all five lots to Anthony Graves (19) in 1832 for 130 pounds. (Lun Co. Land Deeds Vol. 10. pg. 56)		
a.k.a. Neil Smith, Neil McMullen Jr.		
DATA ON CHILDREN & FAMILIAL RELATIONSHIPS		
26, 68, 82		

37	**Alexander McNeil**	Susanna Beaty
DATE & PLACE OF BIRTH		DATE & PLACE OF DEATH
Lots **4, 20, 21**		
Purchased Lot 4 from John Kinghorn (26) on 02-24-1786 for 18£. How he acquired Lot 20 & 21 is unknown. Sells Lot 20 to Edward James (24) on 01-19-1791 for 5£ 16s 8pp. Also sells Lot 21 to Edward James (24) in 1791.		
ALIAS NAMES		
Occupation is listed as Joiner on Chester land deed for lot 4. On the Lot 20, McNeil is listed as a Carpenter from Lunenburg. Marries wife on 08-23-1788.		
25, 34, 35, 47, 49		

38	**Robert Melvin Sr.**	Sarah (1st wife), Phoebe Wilson (#2)
1716		1787
Lots **2, 6, 7, 8, 12, 22**		
Purchased Lot 7 from Rev. Secombe (48) on 11-17-1767 for 2£. He inherited Lot 6 as it was bequeathed to him from his good friend Phillip Payzant (43) on 06-12-1768. Purchased Lot 2 from Edward Smith (52) on 06-17-1780, by trading it for a town lot he had acquired earlier. Purchased Lot 12 from John Munro/Monroe (39) on 05-15-1781 for 3£. Purchased Lot 8 & 22 together from Jonathan Prescott (45) on 06-16-1784 for 15£. In 1788, Melvin Sr. (38) died, and his properties were distributed to some family members; Lot 22 went to Jacob Melvin (38c), Lot 8 went to Robert Melvin Jr (38d), Lot 2 & 12 stayed with family members until sold. Lots 6 & 7 were sold to Jacob Sheppard (50) in 1790.		
ALIAS NAMES		
Lt. Robert Melvin (38) arrived in Chester on 08-04-1761 with four motherless children as his 1st wife Sarah had died. Identified as one of Reverend John Secombe's (48) "First Class of Settlers to Chester" Melvin married 2nd wife Phebe Wilson in 1762 and had 8 more children. Upon his death in 1787 his lands were divided up amongst his surviving heirs or sold. Melvin was a land speculator and a carpenter. His oldest son from his first marriage, Eleazer Melvin was born in Concord in 1743, who became a Housewright or Joiner by trade.		
2, 17, 21, 25, 31, 33, 32, 35, 39, 50, 92, 94, 95, 96, 97		

38a	**Nathaniel Melvin**	Elizabeth - 1795
Chester, Nova Scotia, Jun. 24, 1765		1844
Lots **6, 7, 13, 14, 17**		
Born in Chester, he purchased Lot 17 from Anthony Vaughan Sr (57). on 6-25-1790 for 8 pounds (lun. Co. Deeds Vol.3. 450). Bought Lots 13 & 14 on 10-9-1790 for 8 pounds from Daniel Vaughan (57b) (Lun. Co. Vol.3. pg. 447.). Bought Lots 6 & 7 from stepfather Jacob Shepperd (50) possible dower on 11-14-1815 for 14 pounds. (Lun. Co. Land Deeds Vol.7. #188. 83.) Sold Lots 6-7 to Samuel Ball (03) and Lot 17 to John Smith (51a). Acquired his brother Robert Melvin Jr's (38d) 7th share of his father's estate. Possible ship builder, 1793 poll tax listed Nathaniel as master of a vessel. (Palmer Papers/Loyalist Melvins-H. Browne/ PW - Prop Own of OI to 1795 & Prop Owners Morris to Smith/Chester Town Book / Lun. Co. Land deeds available).		
ALIAS NAMES		
Robert Melvin's 1st son, from his second marriage (who died in 1787). Married Elizabeth in 1795. Occupation is shown as Master of a vessel in 1793. Possible shipbuilder.		
2, 17, 31, 32, 50, 81, 84, 85, 86, 102		

38b	**David Melvin**	Abigale Floyd (b. 1775)
Chester, Nova Scotia, April 9, 1770		DATE & PLACE OF DEATH
Lot **14**		
Assumed heir of Lot 14 from father, Robert Melvin Sr. (38). Continues to own Lot 14 in 1818.		
ALIAS NAMES		
Robert Melvin Sr's (38) 3rd son, from his 2nd marriage. Married Abigale Floyd, 11-05-1794. Abigale is sister to both Susannah and Mary Floyd, both of whom married brothers Robert Jr. (38d) and Jacob (38c).		
26, 32, 33, 50		

38C	**Jacob Melvin**	Mary Ann Floyd
Chester, Nova Scotia, 1774		1857
Lot **22**		
Assumed heir of Lot 22 from father, Robert Melvin Sr. (38). Sold Lot 22 to Daniel McKinnon aka (Daniel McInnis) (33) on 03-23-1796 for 3£ 10s.		
ALIAS NAMES		
Robert Melvin Sr's (38) fifth son, from his 2nd marriage. Married Mary Floyd, daughter to Thomas Floyd, in Chester on 07-03-1796. Mary is sister to both Susannah and Abigale Floyd, both of whom married Melvin brothers Robert Jr. (38d) and David (38b). Occupation listed as Mariner in his will, filed in Bedford Basin, Nova Scotia.		
2, 17, 50, 77		

38d	**Robert Melvin Jr.**	Susannah Floyd (b. 05-15-1778)
Chester, Nova Scotia, April 25, 1777		1862
Lot **8**		
Assumed heir of Lot 8 from father, Robert Melvin Sr. (38). Sold Lot 8 to Samuel Ball (03) on 05-23-1798 for 6£.		
ALIAS NAME		
Robert Melvin Jr. (38d) was born in Chester and was Robert Melvin Sr's (38) sixth son, from his 2nd marriage. Robert Jr. married Susannah Floyd, daughter of Thomas Floyd in 07-31-1800. Robert Jr. and Susannah had 10 children, born in Chester and St. Martins, Nova Scotia. Susannah is sister to both Mary and Abigale Floyd, both of whom married Melvin brothers Jacob (38c) and David (38b).		
2, 17, 50, 83		

39	**John Monro**	Mary Warters
DATE & PLACE OF BIRTH		DATE & PLACE OF DEATH
Lots **12, 24, 29**		
Purchased Lot 24 from Ambrose Allen (01) on 10-20-1791. Sold Lot 12 to Robert Melvin Sr. (38) on 05-15-1781 for 3£. Sold Lot 29 to JJ Bezanon (06a) on 11-16-1796. Sold Lot 24 to Samuel Ball (03) on 07-06-1799.		
a.k.a. Monroe, Munro, Monrow, Monrowe, John Monrow		
Married Mary Warters in 1773 by Rev. Secombe(48). Gave birth to a boy, Samuel Munro born 1777. Occupation listed as a Farmer.		
17, 27, 31, 33, 35, 64, 87, 88, 96		

39a	**James Monrow**	SPOUSES NAME
DATE & PLACE OF BIRTH		DATE & PLACE OF DEATH
Lot **12**		
HISTORY OF BUYING, OWNING, SELLING OAK ISLAND LOT(S)		
ALIAS NAMES		
DATA ON CHILDREN & FAMILIAL RELATIONSHIPS		
CITATION/REFERENCE SOURCES		

40	**Frederick G. Nolan**	SPOUSES NAME
1927		06-04-2016
Lots **5, 9, 10, 11, 12, 13, 14**		
In 1963, Nolan purchased lots 5, 9, 10, 11, 12, 13 & 14 from heirs of Sellyn Sellers (19b). Nolan determined the previous sale of these Lots were not properly court filed and therefore, still the property of Sellers heirs. Sold Lot 5 to Robert S. Young (61) June 1996		
a.k.a. Fred Nolan		
Occupation was as a Surveyor. Had one son, Thomas J. Nolan (40a), Longtime legal action against Dan Blankenship (07), David C. Tobias (55) and Triton Alliance Synd. (56), until Nova Scotia Supreme Court ruled in his favor to owning Lots he found were not properly listed in previous court filings. Prior to his passing, he was working with and part of the Lagina Fellowship Team.		
23, 30, 36, 129, 132a, 199, 700, 900, 901		

40a	**Thomas J. Nolan**	SPOUSES NAME
DATE & PLACE OF BIRTH		DATE & PLACE OF DEATH
Lots **9, 10, 11, 12, 13, 14**		
Inherited in 2016, Frederick Nolan's Lots 9, 10, 11, 12, 13, 14 and Frederick Nolan's home on the northern corner of the swamp, which he still owns.		
Tom Nolan		
Occupation Engineer. Company owner. Has joined the Lagina Fellowship and partnered in the Oak Island treasure hunt.		
51,900, 901		

41	**Oak Island Tours Inc.**
1987. Corporate entity started in 2006, operated in 2009.Registered in Traverse City, MI.	
Lots **1-32** except Lot **5** – Robert S. Young (61); Lot **23** – Dan Blankenship (07); Lots **9, 10, 11, 12, 13, 14** - Fred Nolan (40); and Lot **25** – Alan Kostrzewa (27).	
Partnership formed in 1987-2014 which included Daniel C. Blankenship (07) David C. Tobias (55) and Frederick G. Nolan (40) for a short period of time. David C. Tobias (55) sold to the "Michigan Mafia" members Craig Tester, Marty Lagina & Rick Lagina, his 50% ownership of the original company. Additionally, Dan Blankenship (07) owned the other 50%. Dave Blankenship (07a), Alan Kostrzewa (27) and Brian Urbach it is believed have joined forces by 2014 when the company refiled, revived and received the Canadian Treasure Trove License, which since has been restructured.	
A.k.a. Triton Alliances, Synd.; Triton Alliances Ltd.; Center Road Ventures;	
DATA ON CHILDREN & FAMILIAL RELATIONSHIPS	
23, 30, 112, 111, 700	

42	**Alexander Pattillo**	SPOUSES NAME
1748		1838
Lots **1, 27**		
Purchased Lot 27 from David Ellis (16) on 11-17-1786. Sold Lot 27 to Donald McGinnis (32) on 05-03-1791 for 6£. Purchased Lot 1 from John Cochran (11) on 02-19-1785. Sold Lot 1 to Donald McGinnis (32) on 09-09-1794.		
a.k.a. Alex Pattelo, Alexander Patilo, Pittillio		
From Aberdeen Scotland and came to Chester in 1783. Occupation included lime burning, operating a brick factory in Chester supplying Halifax and Shelborne and owned a coastal vessel. Son - Capt. James Pittillo who died in 1887.		
2, 27, 29, 32, ,33 ,35, 39, 67, 89, 90, 91		

42a	**Fred Patillo**	SPOUSES NAME
DATE & PLACE OF BIRTH		DATE & PLACE OF DEATH
Lot **27**		
HISTORY OF BUYING, OWNING, SELLING OAK ISLAND LOT(S)		
ALIAS NAMES		
DATA ON CHILDREN & FAMILIAL RELATIONSHIPS		
39		

43	**Phillip Payzant**	SPOUSES NAME
1746		1795?
Lot **6**		
Acquired Lot 6 through a drawing on 08-20-1766. Signed over Lot 6 to Robert Melvin Sr. (38) on 06-22-1768.		
ALIAS NAMES		
Survivor of the "Payzant Massacre" on Covey's Island, 1756. Gave Lot 6 to his good friend Robert Melvin Sr.(38) for being a good friend. Melvin helped Payzant escape to Concord after he killed one of the men responsible for the massacre of his family back 1756.		
2, 11, 21, 35, 39		

44	**Erdie Powers** (widow)	? Powers
Western Shore, 07-19-1870		1963
Lots **15, 17, 18, 19, 20**		
Through inheritance, sold shares in ownership of Lots 15, 17, 18, 19, 20 to George W. Grimm Jr. (20) on 07-27-1935.		
Erdie Sellers, Mary Sellers, Estella "Erdie" Mary Sellers.		
Daughter of Henry & Sophia Sellers (19a), brother to Selvyn Sellers (19b).		
5, 13		

45	**Dr. Jonathan Prescott**	Mary Vessie (1st), Ann Blagden (2nd)
1725		1807
Lots **8, 22**		
Granted land in the Chester area before 1758. Sells Lot 8 & Lot 22 to Robert Melvin Sr. (38) on 06-15-1784 for 15£.		
ALIAS NAMES		
One of the founders of Chester and Justice of the Peace, Prescott was a surgeon, merchant, distiller and political figure as well as maintained a schooner and a fishing fleet. Jonathan Prescott was Captain of Engineers during the 1745 Siege of Louisburg. First wife died in 1757.		
2, 27, 29, 32, 35, 92		

46	**John Pulsifer**	Mary Vaughan (b. 1760)
1750		DATE & PLACE OF DEATH
Lot **30**		
Owns Lot 30 in 1810. Sold Lot 30 for 10£ to Samuel Ball (03) on 04-02-1810.		
a.k.a. John Poulsifer, John Pousler		
Marries Mary Vaughan, daughter to Daniel Vaughan (57b) (1733-1811)		
27, 31, 32, 33, 35, 93		

47	**Jeremiah Rogers**	SPOUSES NAME
DATE & PLACE OF BIRTH		DATE & PLACE OF DEATH
Lots **27, 29**		
Wroclawski believed Rogers owned Lots 27 & 29 prior to 1771 and that Rogers sold Lot 27 to J. Bezanson (06a) in 1782, but there is no record. Rogers did sell Lot 29 to David Ellis (16) on 04-02-1778 for 5£.		
ALIAS NAMES		
Rogers was Master of the armed sloop "Ulysses under Gov. Cornwallis in 1753, which carried a contingent of Rangers. He participated in establishment of Halifax and Lunenburg as well as the "Expulsion of Acadians" in 1755. His marriage was the 1st marriage performed by Rev. Secombe in Chester. One of the "1st Class of Settlers. He came from "Hannover" with a wife and 7 children. Roger's son, also known as Jeremiah Rogers, served in the British Legion Calvary in 1782 as a Farrier.		
2, 11, 28, 35, 39, 41, 52, 62, 98		

48	**Reverend John Seccombe**	Mercy Williams
1708		1792
Lot **7**		
Drew Lot 7 from a grant in 1767. Sells Lot 7 to Robert Melvin Sr. (38) on 11-17-1767.		
a.k.a. Seecombe, Seccombe, Secomb, Seccomb, Secombe.		
Was a Harvard educated Congregational Minister and spiritual leader who helped establish the township of Chester after arriving with founder Capt. Timothy Houghton and 30 other settlers. Married Mercy Williams in 1736. Had a daughter who was also named Mercy.		
11, 21, 29, 41, 94		

49	**James Sharp**	SPOUSES NAME
DATE & PLACE OF BIRTH		DATE & PLACE OF DEATH
Lot **28**		
Lot 28 granted to James Sharpe (49) by Governor Parr possibly in 1785. Sold Lot 28 to "Donald MacInnis" (32) on 03-03-1788 for 7£ 15s.		
a.k.a. James Sharpe		
Deed of Sale of Lot 28 reflected James Sharpe occupation as Mason. Lot 28 granted by Governor Parr possibly in 1785 as part of 12,400 general land grants to settlers.		
35, 39, 53		

50	**Jacob Shephard**	Phoebe Melvin, widow of Robert Melvin Sr. (38)
1716		1787
Lots **6, 7**		
Acquired Lots 6 & 7 through marriage to Phoebe Melvin on 08-02-1790, who was previously married to deceased Robert Melvin Sr. (38), his 2nd wife. Sells Lots 6 & 7 to Nathaniel Melvin (38a), son of Robert Melvin Sr. (38) 11-14-1815.		
a.k.a. Jacob Sheppard		
Occupation in 1793 is listed as Farmer.		
31, 32, 33, 35, 39, 50, 86		

51	**Duncan Smith**	Margaret (McLean)
1749		1788
Lot **24**		
Granted Lot 24 in 1784 and sold Lot 24 to Allen Ambrose (01) on 02-24-1785 for 10£.		
ALIAS NAMES		
A Blacksmith from Dumbarton, Scotland and was in the Scottish Regiment of the 74th, during the Revolutionary War. Moved to Halifax in 1784, where Smith (according to Family Lore), made handcuffs for the military and received threats while living in Halifax. Wife Margaret McLean is sister to Hector McLean (34). Duncan is father to John Smith (51a).		
26, 99		

51a	**John Smith**	Anne Floyd (1783-1852)
1775		1857
Lots **15, 16, 17, 18, 19, 20**		
Yeoman John Smith purchases Lot 18 from Casper Wollenhaupt (58) on 06-26-1795, for 7£ 15s. Then John Smith (51a) purchased Lot 16 from Mary Malay (29) on 01-25-1798. Purchases Lot 17 from Nathaniel Melvin (38a) in 1808. Lot 20 Smith buys from Joseph Bezanson (06c) on 02-07-1807. He purchased Lot 15 from David Crandell (14) on 06-10-1819. John Smith (51a) purchased Lot 19 from David Vaughan (57c) in July 1825.		
John Smith (51a) was born in Boston to Duncan Smith (51) and Mother Margaret McLean (sister to Hector McLean (34)). After Duncan's death, John Smith's mother marries Neil McMullen (35) in 1788 and the family moves to Oak Island. Now older, John Smith (51a) marries Anne in 1799, and they produce 11 kids, 7 of which die on the island and are buried on Oak Island with John Smith (51a). **His 1st born son was named Neil McMullen Smith**. Occupation in Chester Township 1793 Poll Tax is as Farmer and then Laborer in 1794 Poll Tax. **NOTE: There are 3 John Smiths living in Chester in the 1790's. John Smith Sr. and John Smith Jr. are unrelated to John Smith (51a) of Oak Island. Our Oak Island John Smith marries Anne Floyd (1783-1852) in 1799.**		
2, 4, 5, 6, 7. 8, 13, 14, 17, 25, 26, 31, 32, 33, 35, 39, 100, 101, 102, 103, 104		

51b	**Joseph Smith**	SPOUSES NAME
DATE & PLACE OF BIRTH		DATE & PLACE OF DEATH
Lots **15, 16, 17, 18, 19, 20**		
Inherited Lots 15, 16, 17, 18, 19, 20 with ¼ % ownership, in 1853.		
ALIAS NAMES		
Son of John Smith (51a).		
4, 5, 6, 7, 8, 13, 14		

51c	**Thomas E. Smith**	SPOUSES NAME
DATE & PLACE OF BIRTH		DATE & PLACE OF DEATH
Lot **4**		
ALIAS NAMES		
Son of John Smith (51a).		
4, 5, 6, 7, 8, 13, 14		

52	**Edward Smith**	SPOUSES NAME
1784		1813
Lots **2, 19**		
Drew Lots 2 & 19 in Grant on 08-20-1766. Traded Lot 2 to Robert Melvin Sr. (38) for a town lot on 06-07-1780. Sold Lot 19 to Timothy Zink (65) on 03-28-1768 for 5£		
ALIAS NAMES		
No relationship to other Smith island owners. First town Clerk of Chester.		
2, 22, 35, 95		

53	**Richard Smith** & **John Gifford** (Co-owners/Partners)	
DATE & PLACE OF BIRTH		DATE & PLACE OF DEATH
Island #28 (Oak Island)		
Granted 3 island in Mahone Bay, one being Island #28 (Oak Island) in December of 1753, by Governor Lawrence.		
ALIAS NAMES		
Both partners were "fishing merchants" from New York prior to arriving at Island #28.		
See: Chapter Two, "Fishy Business."		

55	**David C. Tobias**	SPOUSES NAME
DATE & PLACE OF BIRTH		05-04-2012
Lots **6, 7, 8, 15, 16, 17, 18, 19, 20, 25, 26, 27, 28, 29, 30, 31, 32**		
Purchased Lots 6, 7, 8, 15, 16, 17, 18, 19, 20, 25, 26, 27, 28, 29, 30, 31, 32 from M.R. Chappell (10) on 06-15-1977. Approached and established partnership with Mel Chappell (10) and Dan Blankenship (07) to form Triton Alliance (56). Corporate converted to Oak Island Tours, Inc.(41) which excluded Fred Nolan who was entangled with Triton Alliance. Entity gained ownership of all Oak Island Lots except the lot Dan Blankenship lived on.		
Triton Alliance		
DATA ON CHILDREN & FAMILIAL RELATIONSHIPS		
20, 23, 36		

56	**Triton Alliance**	
1967		2011
Lots **6, 7, 8, 15, 16, 17, 18, 19, 20, 25, 26, 27, 28, 29, 30, 31, 32**		
Entity changed names over extended period with different shareholders, yet with David C. Tobias (55) remaining in control until Oak Island Tours, Inc. (41) was formed.		
1. (1967-1969) Triton Alliance Syndicate, 2. (1969-1987) Triton Alliance Ltd., 3. (2009-2011) Triton Alliance LTD/LTEE.		
Principals are Daniel C. Blankenship (07), David C. Tobias (55), Robert Dunfield, Fred G. Nolan (40). Second version of company had Principles Dan Blankenship (07) and David C. Tobias (55) with Melbourne R. Chappel (10) as a shareholder. Third version of company had Principles Dan Blankenship (07), Rick Lagina and Rick Neiman, dissolved in 2014.		
23, 36, 111, 112, 700		

<table>
<tr><td>57</td><td>Anthony Vaughan Sr.</td><td>Annie Armstrong (1753-1830)</td></tr>
<tr><td colspan="2">1751, Rhode Island</td><td>1835</td></tr>
<tr><td colspan="3">Lots 2, 4, 5, 9, 10, 15, 17, 19</td></tr>
<tr><td colspan="3">Unknown when Anthony Vaughan Sr. acquired Lots 9, 10, 17 or 19. Vaughan sells Lots 9 & 10 to Martin Marshall (30) on 12-22-1788. Vaughan sold Lot 17 to Nathaniel Melvin (38a) on 06-25-1790 for 8£. Sold Lot 4 to Thomas Embree (17) on 06-06-1804 for 17£. NOTE: As per his will, lots 2, 5, 15 & 19 were to be divided up and split between sons.</td></tr>
<tr><td colspan="3">ALIAS NAMES</td></tr>
<tr><td colspan="3">Born in Rhode Island he came to Chester in 1772 and granted 900 acres of land on the Western Shore area of Mahone Bay. Given permit to harvest pine timber in 1778 at Western Shore with brother Daniel Vaughan and James McLeod. Also operated a saw mill and grist mill on the Vaughan Stream adjacent to their acreage. Listed as Farmer in both Chester Township 1793 & 1794 Poll Tax. Married Annie Armstrong in 1803/1777. Sons Anthony Vaughan Jr. (57a) (b. 1782-1860), and James Jackson Vaughan (57d) (b.1777-1804), David Vaughan Jr. (57c) (b.1770-1791), John Armstrong Vaughan (1780-1860).</td></tr>
<tr><td colspan="3">2, 27, 29, 31, 32, 54, 70, 75, 84</td></tr>
</table>

<table>
<tr><td>57a</td><td>Anthony Vaughan Jr.</td><td>Elizabeth Nelson (1785 deceased)</td></tr>
<tr><td colspan="2">Chester N.S. 1782</td><td>1860</td></tr>
<tr><td colspan="3">Lot See Anthony Vaughan Sr.</td></tr>
<tr><td colspan="3">Born on the mainland across from Oak Island, Anthony Jr. has played a major role in the Oak Island treasure legend.</td></tr>
<tr><td colspan="3">ALIAS NAMES</td></tr>
<tr><td colspan="3">Son of Anthony Vaughan Sr. (57). Sons: James Leander Vaughan (b. 1805), Nelson Harris Vaughan (1808-1879), David Harris Vaughan (1817-1900), George Vaughan (1810-1878), Jacob Vaughan (1815-1894).</td></tr>
<tr><td colspan="3">65, 66</td></tr>
</table>

<table>
<tr><td>57b</td><td>Daniel Vaughan</td><td>Lydia Elidia Harrington (1749-1814)</td></tr>
<tr><td colspan="2">Rhode Island, 1746 / 7</td><td>1808 / 10</td></tr>
<tr><td colspan="3">Lots 11, 13, 14</td></tr>
<tr><td colspan="3">Purchased Lots 13 & 14 from James Webber (60) on 10-08-1781. Sold Lots 13 & 14 to Nathaniel Melvin (38) on 10-09-1790 for 8£. Unrecorded when Daniel Vaughan came into possession of Lot 11, but he sold Lot 11 to Neil McMullen Sr. (35) on 10-06-1789 for 8£.</td></tr>
<tr><td colspan="3">ALIAS NAMES</td></tr>
<tr><td colspan="3">Operated as a Privateer during French/Indian War. Came to Chester approx.. 1772 and was granted License Jan. 1788, to harvest pine timber at Western Shore with brother Anthony Vaughan Sr. (57) and James McLeod. Also operated a saw mill and grist mill on Vaughan Stream along Vaughan 900-acre property. Married Lydia Harrington in 1768 at St. John's Church in Lunenburg. Daniel received many land grants between 1791 and 1793, and by 1796 he moved his family to New Brunswick where he began a shipbuilding business with his sons.</td></tr>
<tr><td colspan="3">2, 29, 34, 56, 57, 58, 80, 85</td></tr>
</table>

57c	**David Vaughan**	Sarah Bezanson
Chester N.S. 1795		1888
Lot **2, 3, 5, 19**		
David Vaughan was the oldest son of James Jackson Vaughan (57d), son of Anthony Vaughan Sr. (57). It is unknown how he came to own his Oak Island lots. After James (57d) early death, his estate fell to his wife Sarah Bezanson and their small children. It is possible that lots owned on Oak Island were divided into shares upon James Vaughan's (57d) death in 1804 and left to his children as an inheritance. Along with **David**, lot shares were held by siblings **Mary Compton-Allen** (1798-1883), **Annie Kiser** (1800-1880) and **James Vaughan** (1804). It is unknown how David acquires lot 3 but he begins purchasing his sibling's shares in Oak Island lots 2, 5 & 19. He buys shares in lots 2, 5 & 19 from brother James Vaughan (57d) in 1817. Again David buys share lots 2, 5 & 19 from sister Mary Vaughan in 1819 (L. Deed Vol. 8 page 343). Finally gets share lots 2, 5 & 19 sold by Peter Kiser (husband of sister Annie Vaughan) to David Vaughan (57c) in 1821. (L. Deed Vol. 8 page 343). After consolidation of all lot shares David Vaughan (57c) sells Lot 5 to Anthony T. Graves (19) on 09-19-1832. Vaughan sells Lots 2 & 3 to Daniel McEnnis (33) on 11-02-1832. David Vaughan (57c) sells Lot 19 to John Smith (51a) on 06-10-1819.		
ALIAS NAMES		
CHILDREN OR FAMILIAL RELATIONSHIPS		
69, 78, 104, 106		

57d	**James Vaughan**	Mary Millet (1775-1844)
1777 Chester N.S.		1804
Lots **2, 3, 5, 19**		
See son, DAVID VAUGHAN (57c)		
James Jackson Vaughan was the oldest child to Anthony Vaughan Sr. (57). When or how he received these lots is unknown, but lot possession transferred to his family upon his death in 1804. He married Mary in 1796. His young children were **David Vaughan (57c)** (1795-1888), **Mary Compton-Allen** (1798-1883), **Annie Vaughan Kiser** (1800-1880) and **James Vaughan** (1805-1892). Around 1819 the siblings began selling their Oak Island lot shares to brother David Vaughan (57c), who consolidates the lots.		
See VAUGHAN Citations.		

58	**Casper Wollenhaupt**	Ann Mary Jacob
1755		1809
Lot **18** (Money Pit site)		
Unknown how or when Lot 18 was acquired. Questionable paperwork not properly filed, no owner in 1785. Sold Lot 18 to John Smith (51a) on 06-26-1795 for 7£ 15s.		
ALIAS NAMES		
Father came to Halifax as a Weaver but died when Casper was a child. Possibly his mother was from or married into the Wolfe Family. Married Ann Mary Jacob in 1778. Became a wealthy merchant and powerful political figure in Lunenburg.		
11, 34, 39, 100		

59	**Wilbert Walls**	Genevieve Walls
DATE & PLACE OF BIRTH		DATE & PLACE OF DEATH
Lot **15, 16, 17, 18, 19 & 20**		
Wilbert Walls and Genevieve Walls sell their share of ownership in Lots 15, 16, 17, 18, 19, 20 to George W. Grimm Jr (20) on 07-27-1935.		
ALIAS NAMES		
Genevieve is Daughter to Abraham Ernst (18) (1880-1922)		
7		

60	**James Webber**	Sarah Fowle (b. 1736)
1728		1804
Lots **11**, **13, 14**		
Unknown how he acquired Lots 11, 13, 14. Sold Lots 11 & 14 to Daniel Vaughan (57b) on 10-08-1781 for 9£ 10s.Also recorded as owner of Lot 13 by Wroclawski, selling the lot to Daniel Vaughan. No recorded deed.		
ALIAS NAMES		
Webber arrived in Chester in 1760, with a 500 acre Grant on Windsor Road. Webber's Hill is the namesake. Listed as Owner of a Chester Town Lot in 1764. Occupation as Farmer in Chester 1793 Poll Tax. Father to Sarah Webber who married David Ellis (16)		
2, 26, 29, 39, 58		

61	**Robert S. Young**	SPOUSES NAME
May 27, 1955		Oct. 28, 2020
Lot **5**		
Purchased Lot 5 from Fred Nolan (40) in 1996.		
ALIAS NAMES		
See: www.oakislandlotfive.com for more information.		
23, 30, 31		

62	**Thomas Young**	SPOUSES NAME
DATE & PLACE OF BIRTH		DATE & PLACE OF DEATH
Lot **31**		
Drew lot 31 on 8-24-1765 – Wroclawski		
ALIAS NAM		
DATA ON CHILDREN & FAMILIAL RELATIONSHIPS		
12		

63	**Wallace Young**	Margaret M. Young
DATE & PLACE OF BIRTH		DATE & PLACE OF DEATH
Acquires Lot **23** and other acreage, thought in 1765 but unclear.		
Margaret M. Young borrows money (50% value) against Lot 23, through Archibald Dauphinee (15) on 10-01-1931/05-27-1935. Possibly to finance Wallace Young's mercantile business. Along with Archibald D. Dauphinee (15), Wallace Young's wife Margaret Young (63) sells Lot 23 to Clarence James Beamish (04) on 09-28-1944.		
ALIAS NAMES		
Merchant		
1, 2, 3, 12		

64	**"George" Frederick Zink**	Catherine Conrad (1797-1869)
1808		1864
Lots **5, 9, 10, 11, 12, 13. 14**		
Anthony Graves (19) sells Lots 5, 9, 10, 11, 12, 13, 14 to Frederick Zinck (64) on 02-14-1839 for 35£. Frederick Zinck (64) then sells the same lots back to Graves on 03-29-1841 for 35£. This set of transactions occur between periods when Graves (19) sells the property to others, such as E. Foras (68) and J. Strachan (54) for a profit, with payment to F. Zinck (64). F. Zinck is son to George Casper Zinck (1764-1849) who was married to Sophia Dorothea Elisabeth Conrad. said to be the father-in-law to Graves, whose second wife was Anna (Catherine) Eliza Zinck.		
George Zinck, Zink		
Merchant. Lived in Blandford (east side of Mahone Bay / East Chester area.		
1, 2, 3, 12		

65	**Timothy Zink**	SPOUSES NAME
1743		1812
Lot **19**		
Purchased Lot 19 from Edward Smith (52) on 03-28-1768 for 5£. Lot 19 is found to be owned by John Monro (39) in 1780 who sells it to Robert Melvin Sr. (38) until he dies in 1787. There is no record of Zink/Lynch (65) selling to John Monro (39).		
a.k.a. Zinck, Zink, Timothy Lynch, Linch.		
Unclear background... William Zink is 39 in 1871 census. A Benjamin Zink (b. 1842). Andrew Zink (b. 1802) in 1871 census of Lunenburg. See Casper Zink Sr.		
2, 22, 29, 59		

66	**Richard Cunningham**	Elisabeth Day
1748, Ireland		1823
Lot **32**		
Acquired Lot 32 prior to 1784. He received 200 acres with brother Joseph Pernette's 1765 Grant on the Le Have River.		
ALIAS NAMES		
Arrived from Ireland with brothers John Cunningham and Michael Cunningham in 1769. A farmer and land speculator. Was father to future political figure and local official John Cunningham. Married Elisabeth in 1775.		
2, 11, 60		

67	**Moses Holt**	
Lot **29 or 31 ?**		
Listed as owner of Lot 31 by Wroclawski before 1771. (PW – Property Owners Morris to Smith) ????		
ALIAS NAMES		
CHILDREN OR FAMILIAL RELATIONSHIPS		
2		

68	**John Strachan**	SPOUSES NAME
DATE & PLACE OF BIRTH		DATE & PLACE OF DEATH
Lots **5, 9, 10, 11, 12, 13, 14**		
Strachan purchases Lots 5, 9, 10, 11, 12, 13, 14 from Anthony T. Graves (19) on 03-30-1841 for 50£. Strachan is said to have sold Lots 9, 10, 11, 12, 13, 14 back to Anthony Graves (19) in 1857.		
ALIAS NAMES		
Listed as a merchant from Halifax.		
128		

Lot List Section

The *Lot List* chronologically displays the ownership milestones of each Lot in numerical order. Entries show: **year**, (actual date), **Owner transfer info with** (Owner codes), **Lot #**, **Citation #** with document, and source description and location. These ownership milestones track with the *Time Table* and the citation numbers are listed in the Owners Info Boxes section of this appendix.

Lot 1.

1753 - (12-27-1753) **Governor Charles Lawrence, to Capt. John Gifford (53) and Richard Smith (53) – ALL LOTS**

#123 Source - NS Archives and Record Management "Allotment" Book, P. 137, Reel #13044; "Old Book" #1, P. 44. Granted Gifford Island #12, Young Island #13, and Smith Island #28, to establish a fishery. Escheated.

1784 - The Crown (00), issues Chester Land Grants, to John Cochran (11) – Lot 1

#34 Source – "*Nova Scotia Land Papers: 1795-1800, Green James and Others*." 1784 – Lunenburg County. 37,950 acres granted in Chester, including License to Occupy, Memorial, Warrant to Survey, Surveyor's Report & Surveyor's Certificate. See citation.

1785 - (02-19-1785) **John Cochran (11), to Alexander Pitillo (42) – Lot 1**

#67 Source – Lunenburg Co. Land Deeds, recorded 03-02-1786, Vol. 3, P. 226, No. #370. 11>42 – **Lot 1**

#35 Source - "*Habitation on Oak Island*." Beaton Institute, Cape Breton University. Created by Surveyor William Dy Sr., called 'The Old Plan' No. 1046. Department of Lands & Forests, n.d. MG 12, 75 NSNA. Also Published in Joy Steele/Gordon Fader's book "*Oak Island Mystery Solved-Final Chapter*." P. 10. 2nd Ed. 2016.

1794 - (09-1794) **Alexander Pattillo (42), to Donald McInnis (32) – Lot 1**

#91 Source – Lunenburg Co. Land Deeds, recorded 10-27-1781, Vol. 4, P. 192, No. #232. 42>32 – **Lot 1**

#35 Source - "*Habitation on Oak Island*." Beaton Institute, Cape Breton University. Created by Surveyor William Dy Sr., called 'The Old Plan' No. 1046. Department of Lands & Forests, n.d. MG 12, 75 NSNA. Also Published in Joy Steele/Gordon Fader's book "*Oak Island Mystery Solved-Final Chapter*." P. 10. 2nd Ed. 2016.

1827 - Donald McGinnis (32) dies, in late 1826 and his will is probated in 1827 – Lot 1

#2 Source - Paul Wroclawski Research & Property Owners Charles Morris to John Smith; collected through 02-06-2008.

#17 Source – "*Chester Township Records, 1762-1830*." Births, Marriages, and Deaths. NSNA MG9, B 9-3.

1859 - James McInnis (McInnis Family) (32fam) – Lot 1

#35 Source - "*Habitation on Oak Island*." Beaton Institute, Cape Breton University. Created by Surveyor William Dy Sr., called 'The Old Plan' No. 1046. Department of Lands & Forests, n.d. MG 12, 75 NSNA. Also Published in Joy Steele/Gordon Fader's book "*Oak Island Mystery Solved-Final Chapter*." P. 10. 2nd Ed. 2016.

1896 - James Henry McInnis (32fam) dies, passes to Arthur Curran McInnis (32fam) – Lot 1

#1 Source – N.S. Supreme Court, Book No. 368, recorded 10-01-1931, Book 20, P. 423, No. #368. (originally Book No. 20, P. 74, No.69) – **Lot 1**

#17 Source – "*Chester Township Records, 1762-1830*." Births, Marriages, and Deaths. NSNA MG9, B 9-3.

1915 - Arthur Curran Mcinnis (32fam) dies, passes to John Mcinnis Family (32fam) – Lot 1

#1 Source – N.S. Supreme Court, Book No. 368, recorded 10-01-1931, Book 20, P. 423, No. #368. (originally Book No. 20, P. 74, No.69) – **Lot 1**

#17 Source – "*Chester Township Records, 1762-1830*." Births, Marriages, and Deaths. NSNA MG9, B 9-3.

1930 - John McInnis Family (32fam), pass to inheritors Wallace and Margaret Young, et. al. (63) – Lot 1

#169 Source – Lunenburg Co. Land Deed, recorded 06-21-1930, Book 20, P. 74, No. #69. Deeded on 06-09-1930. **- Lot 1**

#1 Source – N.S. Supreme Court, Book No. 368, recorded 10-01-1931, Book 20, P. 423, No. #368. (originally Book No. 20, P. 74, No.69) **– Lot 1**

#3 Source – City & County of San Francisco, Calif. Records; & NSNA, recorded 05-27-1935, Book No. 21. P. 96, No. #148. **- Lot 1**

1931 - (09-22-1931) **Wallace & Margaret Young (63), sell 50% of prop. Val. & share, to Archibald C. Dauphinee (15) – Lot 1**

#1 Source – N.S. Supreme Court, Book No. 368, recorded 10-01-1931, Book 20, P. 423, No. #368. (originally Book No. 20, P. 74, No.69) 63>15 **– Lot 1**

1944 - (09-28-1944) **Archibald Dauphinee (15) & Margaret Young (63), to Clarence James Beamish (04) – Lot 1**

#12 Source – Lunenburg Co. Land Deeds, recorded 10-25-1955, Deed #1142 on 10-25-1944. NSNA. 15,63>04 **- Lot 1**

1955 - (07-25-1955) **Clarence Beamish (04) dies, property probated with minor heirs – Lot 1**

#999 Source – "*Death Registrations: 1864-1877; 1908—1960*." Vital Statistics Division of Service Nova Scotia and Municipal Relations, compiler. See citation.

1955 - Heirs of Clarence Beamish (04) & deceased wife Mary Ellen Chapman (09), to M.R. Chappell (10) – Lot 1

#18 Source - Halifax Office of Registrar of Deeds, Book 907 P. 605, dated 12-23-1946 with the Canada Permanent Trust Company, and filed on 02-22-1961. 04,09>10 **- Lot 1**

1977 - (06-15-1977) **M.R. Chappell (10), to David C. Tobias (55)** for all shares regarding Lots, **1, 2, 3, 4, 6, 7, 8, 15, 16, 17, 18, 19, 20, 21, 22, 24, 25, 26, 27, 28, 29, 30, 31, 32. – Lot 1**

#20 Source – Filed in Halifax Co. Land Deeds, recorded on 06-29-1977, No. #582. NSNA. 10>55 **- Lots 6, 7, 8, 15, 16, 17, 18, 19, 20, 25, 26, 30, 31, 32**

1987 - (12-09-1987) **David Tobias (55) and his lots, join Dan Blankenship (07) to form Oak Island Tours Inc (41) – Lot 1**

#111 Source – "*The Open Database of the Corporate World. Oak Island Tours Inc. Company Number 2272393*." Incorporated Date, 12-09-1987. Opencorporates.

#112 Source – "*The Curse of Oak Island, The Story of the World's Longest Treasure Hunt*." By Randall Sullivan, 2018. Page 422.

2007 - David Tobias (55), sells his Lots to Rick & Marty Lagina who become equal partners with Dan Blankenship (07) in Oak Island Tours (41) which own/control Lots 1, 2, 3, 4, 6, 7, 8, 15, 16, 17, 18, 19, 20, 21, 22, 24, 26, 27, 28, 29, 30, 31, 32. – Lot 1

#111 Source – "*The Open Database of the Corporate World. Oak Island Tours Inc. Company Number 2272393*." Incorporated Date, 12-09-1987. Opencorporates.

#112 Source – "*The Curse of Oak Island, The Story of the World's Longest Treasure Hunt*." By Randall Sullivan, 2018. Page 422.

2007 - **MacPhie Archives "*Oak Island Lot Distribution Map, 2007*."** Lots ***1, 2, 3, 4, 6, 7, 8, 15, 16, 17, 18, 19, 20, 21, 22, 24, 26, 27, 28, 29, 30, 31, 32*** - Oak Island Tours (41); Lot ***5*** – Robert S. Young (61); Lots ***9, 10, 11, 12, 14*** – Fred Nolan (40); Lot ***13*** – John Johnston (25); Lot ***23*** – Dan/Dave Blankenship (07); and Lot ***25*** – Alan Kostrzewe (27). **– All Lots**

#30 Source - "*Oak Island Lot Ownership Map, 2007*," By MacPhie Archives. **All Lots**

Lot 2.

1753 - (12-27-1753) **Governor Charles Lawrence, to Capt. John Gifford (53) and Richard Smith (53) – ALL LOTS**

#123 Source - NS Archives and Record Management "Allotment" Book, P. 137, Reel #13044; "Old Book" #1, P. 44. Granted Gifford Island #12, Young Island #13, and Smith Island #28, to establish a fishery. Escheated.

1766 - (08-20-1766) **Crown (00), to Edward Smith (52), drew lot – Lot 2**

#124 Source – "*Nova Scotia Land Papers: 1795-1800, Green James and Others*." 1784 – Lunenburg County. 37,950 acres granted in Chester, including License to Occupy,

Memorial, Warrant to Survey, Surveyor's Report & Surveyor's Certificate. See citation. Drew Lot 00>52 **- Lot 2**

1780 - (06-17-1780) **Edward Smith (52), to Robert Melvin (38) - Lot 2**

#95 Source – Lunenburg Co. Land Deeds, recorded 08-08-1785, Vol. 3, P. 180-181, No. #295. 52>38 **– Lot 2**

#35 Source - "*Habitation on Oak Island*." Beaton Institute, Cape Breton University. Created by Surveyor William Dy Sr., called 'The Old Plan' No. 1046. Department of Lands & Forests, n.d. MG 12, 75 NSNA. Also Published in Joy Steele/Gordon Fader's book "*Oak Island Mystery Solved-Final Chapter*." P. 10. 2nd Ed. 2016.

1787 - **Robert Melvin (38) dies, his properties will be dispersed amongst his sons – Lot 2**

#17 Source – "*Chester Township Records, 1762-1830*." Births, Marriages, and Deaths. NSNA MG9, B 9-3.

1803 - **James Vaughan (57d) – Lot 2**

#17 Source – "*Chester Township Records, 1762-1830*." Births, Marriages, and Deaths. NSNA MG9, B 9-3..

1804 - **James Vaughan (57d) dies,** probated to **James Vaughan Family (57d) – Lot 2**

#17 Source – "*Chester Township Records, 1762-1830*." Births, Marriages, and Deaths. NSNA MG9, B 9-3.

1817 - **Vaughan/Vaughan/Kiser (Keyser) (57d), to David Vaughan (57c) – Lot 2**

#106 Source – Lunenburg Co. Land Deeds, recorded 06-26-1823, Vol. 8, P. 323, 343, 344, No. #513. 57d>57c **– Lots 2, 5, 17**

#35 Source - "*Habitation on Oak Island*." Beaton Institute, Cape Breton University. Created by Surveyor William Dy Sr., called 'The Old Plan' No. 1046. Department of Lands & Forests, n.d. MG 12, 75 NSNA. Also Published in Joy Steele/Gordon Fader's book "*Oak Island Mystery Solved-Final Chapter*." P. 10. 2nd Ed. 2016.

1832 - (11-02-1832) **David Vaughan (57c), to Daniel McEnnis (32a) – Lot 2**

#78 Source – Lunenburg Co. Land Deeds, recorded 04-16-1835, Vol. 10, P. 495, No. #495. 57c>32a **– Lot 2 & 3**

#35 Source - "*Habitation on Oak Island*." Beaton Institute, Cape Breton University. Created by Surveyor William Dy Sr., called 'The Old Plan' No. 1046. Department of Lands & Forests, n.d. MG 12, 75 NSNA. Also Published in Joy Steele/Gordon Fader's book "*Oak Island Mystery Solved-Final Chapter*." P. 10. 2nd Ed. 2016.

1870 - (01-05-1870) **Daniel McKinnon/ Daniel McInnis (yeoman) (32a) dies, property passed to family (32fam) – Lot 2**

#202 Source – Last Will and Testament Extractions, Lunenburg County, Mf:0558683.

1930 - **John McInnis Family (32fam), pass to inheritors Wallace and Margaret Young, et. al. (63) – Lot 2**

#169 Source – Lunenburg Co. Land Deed, recorded 06-21-1930, Book 20, P. 74, No. #69. Deeded on 06-09-1930. **- Lot 2**

#1 Source – N.S. Supreme Court, Book No. 368, recorded 10-01-1931, Book 20, P. 423, No. #368. (originally Book No. 20, P. 74, No.69) **– Lot 2**

#3 Source – City & County of San Francisco, Calif. Records; & NSNA, recorded 05-27-1935, Book No. 21. P. 96, No. #148. **- Lot 2**

1931 - (09-22-1931) **Wallace & Margaret Young (63), sell 50% of prop. Val. & share, to Archibald C. Dauphinee (15) – Lot 2**

#1 Source – N.S. Supreme Court, Book No. 368, recorded 10-01-1931, Book 20, P. 423, No. #368. (originally Book No. 20, P. 74, No.69) 63>15 **– Lot 2**

1944 - (09-28-1944) **Archibald Dauphinee (15) & Margaret Young (63), to Clarence James Beamish (04) – Lot 2**

#12 Source – Lunenburg Co. Land Deeds, recorded 10-25-1955, Deed #1142 on 10-25-1944. NSNA. 15,63>04 **- Lot 2**

1955 - (07-25-1955) **Heirs of Clarence Beamish (04) & wife Mary Ellen Chapman (09), to M.R. Chappell (10) – Lot 2**

#18 Source - Halifax Office of Registrar of Deeds, Book 907 P. 605, dated 12-23-1946 with the Canada Permanent Trust Company, and filed on 02-22-1961. 04,09>10 **- Lot 23**

1977 - (06-15-1977) **M.R. Chappell (10), to David C. Tobias (55)** for all shares regarding Lots, **1, 2, 3, 4, 6, 7, 8, 15, 16, 17, 18, 19, 20, 21, 22, 24, 25, 26, 27, 28, 29, 30, 31, 32. – Lot 2**

#20 Source – Filed in Halifax Co. Land Deeds, recorded on 06-29-1977, No. #582. NSNA. 10>55 **- Lots 6, 7, 8, 15, 16, 17, 18, 19, 20, 25, 26, 30, 31, 32**

1987 - (12-09-1987) **David Tobias (55) and his lots, join Dan Blankenship (07) to form Oak Island Tours Inc (41) – Lot 2**

#111 Source – "*The Open Database of the Corporate World. Oak Island Tours Inc. Company Number 2272393*." Incorporated Date, 12-09-1987. Opencorporates.

#112 Source – "*The Curse of Oak Island, The Story of the World's Longest Treasure Hunt*." By Randall Sullivan, 2018. Page 422.

2007 - David Tobias (55), sells his Lots to Rick & Marty Lagina who become equal partners with Dan Blankenship (07) in Oak Island Tours (41) which own/control Lots 1, 2, 3, 4, 6, 7, 8, 15, 16, 17, 18, 19, 20, 21, 22, 24, 26, 27, 28, 29, 30, 31, 32. – Lot 2

#111 Source – "*The Open Database of the Corporate World. Oak Island Tours Inc. Company Number 2272393*." Incorporated Date, 12-09-1987. Opencorporates.

#112 Source – "*The Curse of Oak Island, The Story of the World's Longest Treasure Hunt*." By Randall Sullivan, 2018. Page 422.

2007 - MacPhie Archives "*Oak Island Lot Distribution Map, 2007*." Lots ***1, 2, 3, 4, 6, 7, 8, 15, 16, 17, 18, 19, 20, 21, 22, 24, 26, 27, 28, 29, 30, 31, 32*** - Oak Island Tours (41); Lot ***5*** – Robert S. Young (61); Lots ***9, 10, 11, 12, 14*** – Fred Nolan (40); Lot ***13*** – John Johnston (25); Lot ***23*** – Dan/Dave Blankenship (07); and Lot ***25*** – Alan Kostrzewe (27). **– All Lots**

#30 Source - "*Oak Island Lot Ownership Map, 2007*," By MacPhie Archives. **All Lots**

Lot 3.

1753 - (12-27-1753) **Governor Charles Lawrence, to Capt. John Gifford (53) and Richard Smith (53) – ALL LOTS**

#123 Source - NS Archives and Record Management "Allotment" Book, P. 137, Reel #13044; "Old Book" #1, P. 44. Granted Gifford Island #12, Young Island #13, and Smith Island #28, to establish a fishery. Escheated.

1803 - James Vaughan (57d) – Lot 3

#17 Source – "*Chester Township Records, 1762-1830*." Births, Marriages, and Deaths. NSNA MG9, B 9-3.

1804 - James Vaughan (57d) dies, Probated to James Vaughan Family (57d) – Lot 3

#17 Source – "*Chester Township Records, 1762-1830*." Births, Marriages, and Deaths. NSNA MG9, B 9-3.

1819 - Vaughan/Vaughan/Kiser (Keyser) (57d), to David Vaughan (57c) – Lot 3

#106 Source – Lunenburg Co. Land Deeds, recorded 06-26-1823, Vol. 8, P. 323, 343, 344, No. #513. 57d>57c – **Lots 2, 5, 17**

1832 - (11-02-1832) **David Vaughan (57c), to Daniel McEnnis (32a) – Lot 3**

#78 Source – Lunenburg Co. Land Deeds, recorded 04-16-1835, Vol. 10, P. 495, No. #495. 57c>32a **– Lot 2 & 3**

#35 Source - "*Habitation on Oak Island*." Beaton Institute, Cape Breton University. Created by Surveyor William Dy Sr., called 'The Old Plan' No. 1046. Department of Lands & Forests, n.d. MG 12, 75 NSNA. Also Published in Joy Steele/Gordon Fader's book "*Oak Island Mystery Solved-Final Chapter*." P. 10. 2nd Ed. 2016.

1870 - (01-05-1870) **Daniel McKinnon/ Daniel McInnis (yeoman) (32a) dies, property passed to family (32fam) – Lot 3**

#202 Source – Last Will and Testament Extractions, Lunenburg County, Mf:0558683.

1915 - Arthur Curran Mcinnis (32fam) dies, passes to John Mcinnis Family (32fam) – Lot 3

#1 Source – N.S. Supreme Court, Book No. 368, recorded 10-01-1931, Book 20, P. 423, No. #368. (originally Book No. 20, P. 74, No.69) **– Lot 3**

1930 - John McInnis Family (32fam), pass to inheritors Wallace and Margaret Young (63), et. al., – Lot 3

#169 Source – Lunenburg Co. Land Deed, recorded 06-21-1930, Book 20, P. 74, No. #69. Deeded on 06-09-1930. **- Lot 3**

#1 Source – N.S. Supreme Court, Book No. 368, recorded 10-01-1931, Book 20, P. 423, No. #368. (originally Book No. 20, P. 74, No.69) – **Lot 3**

#3 Source – City & County of San Francisco, Calif. Records; & NSNA, recorded 05-27-1935, Book No. 21. P. 96, No. #148. **- Lot 3**

1931 - (09-22-1931) **Wallace & Margaret Young (63), sell 50% of prop. Val. & share, to Archibald C. Dauphinee (15) – Lot 3**

#1 Source – N.S. Supreme Court, Book No. 368, recorded 10-01-1931, Book 20, P. 423, No. #368. (originally Book No. 20, P. 74, No.69) 63>15 – **Lot 3**

1944 - (09-28-1944) **Archibald Dauphinee (15) & Margaret Young (63), to Clarence James Beamish (04) – Lot 3**

#12 Source – Lunenburg Co. Land Deeds, recorded 10-25-1955, Deed #1142 on 10-25-1944. NSNA. 15,63>04 **- Lot 3**

1955 - (07-25-1955) **Clarence James Beamish (04) dies, his Lots 1, 2, 3, 4, 21, 22, 23, 27, 28, 29 passed to his wife, Ellen Chapman (09) – Lot 3**

#16 Source - Nova Scotia Supreme Court Book 27, P. 339, No. #638. NSNA. Represent heirs shares of "South & West part Oak Island," "George McInnis Property," and "James McInnis Property." 07-20-1961. 04,09>10 **- Lot 6, 7, 8, 15, 16, 17, 18, 19, 20, 23, 25, 26, 30, 31, 32**

#18 Source - Halifax Office of Registrar of Deeds, Book 907 P. 605, dated 12-23-1946 with the Canada Permanent Trust Company, and filed on 02-22-1961. 04,09>10 **- Lot 3**

1955 - (07-25-1955) **Heirs of Clarence Beamish (04) & wife Mary Ellen Chapman (09), to M.R. Chappell (10) – Lot 3**

#16 Source - Nova Scotia Supreme Court Book 27, P. 339, No. #638. NSNA. Represent heirs shares of "South & West part Oak Island," "George McInnis Property," and "James McInnis Property." 07-20-1961. 04,09>10 **- Lot 6, 7, 8, 15, 16, 17, 18, 19, 20, 23, 25, 26, 30, 31, 32**

#18 Source - Halifax Office of Registrar of Deeds, Book 907 P. 605, dated 12-23-1946 with the Canada Permanent Trust Company, and filed on 02-22-1961. 04,09>10 **- Lot 3**

1977 - (06-15-1977) **M.R. Chappell (10), to David C. Tobias (55)** for all shares regarding Lots **1, 2, 3, 4, 6, 7, 8, 15, 16, 17, 18, 19, 20, 21, 22,24, 25, 26, 27, 28, 29, 30, 31, 32. – Lot 3**

#20 Source – Filed in Halifax Co. Land Deeds, recorded on 06-29-1977, No. #582. NSNA. 10>55 **- Lots 6, 7, 8, 15, 16, 17, 18, 19, 20, 25, 26, 30, 31, 32**

1987 - (12-09-1987) **David Tobias (55) and his lots, join Dan Blankenship (07) to form Oak Island Tours Inc (41) – Lot 3**

#111 Source – "*The Open Database of the Corporate World. Oak Island Tours Inc. Company Number 2272393*." Incorporated Date, 12-09-1987. Opencorporates.

#112 Source – "*The Curse of Oak Island, The Story of the World's Longest Treasure Hunt*." By Randall Sullivan, 2018. Page 422.

2007 - **David Tobias (55), sells his Lots to Rick & Marty Lagina who become equal partners with Dan Blankenship (07) in Oak Island Tours (41) which own/control Lots 1, 2, 3, 4, 6, 7, 8, 15, 16, 17, 18, 19, 20, 21, 22, 24, 26, 27, 28, 29, 30, 31, 32. – Lot 3**

#111 Source – "*The Open Database of the Corporate World. Oak Island Tours Inc. Company Number 2272393*." Incorporated Date, 12-09-1987. Opencorporates.

#112 Source – "*The Curse of Oak Island, The Story of the World's Longest Treasure Hunt*." By Randall Sullivan, 2018. Page 422.

2007 - **MacPhie Archives "*Oak Island Lot Distribution Map, 2007*."** Lots ***1, 2, 3, 4, 6, 7, 8, 15, 16, 17, 18, 19, 20, 21, 22, 24, 26, 27, 28, 29, 30, 31, 32*** - Oak Island Tours (41); Lot ***5*** – Robert S. Young (61); Lots ***9, 10, 11, 12, 14*** – Fred Nolan (40); Lot ***13*** – John Johnston (25); Lot ***23*** – Dan/Dave Blankenship (07); and Lot ***25*** – Alan Kostrzewe (27). **– All Lots**

#30 Source - "*Oak Island Lot Ownership Map, 2007*," By MacPhie Archives. **All Lots**

Lot 4.

1753 - (12-27-1753) **Governor Charles Lawrence, to Capt. John Gifford (53) and Richard Smith (53) – ALL LOTS**

#123 Source - NS Archives and Record Management "Allotment" Book, P. 137, Reel #13044; "Old Book" #1, P. 44. Granted Gifford Island #12, Young Island #13, and Smith Island #28, to establish a fishery. Escheated.

1786 - (02-24-1786) **John Kinghorn (26), to Alexander McNeil (37) – Lot 4**

#49 Source – Lunenburg Co. Land Deeds, recorded 09-11-1788, Vol. 3, P. 355, No. #583. 26>37 – **Lot 4**

#35 Source - "*Habitation on Oak Island*." Beaton Institute, Cape Breton University. Created by Surveyor William Dy Sr., called 'The Old Plan' No. 1046. Department of Lands & Forests, n.d. MG 12, 75 NSNA. Also Published in Joy Steele/Gordon Fader's book "*Oak Island Mystery Solved-Final Chapter*." P. 10. 2nd Ed. 2016.

1793 - (07-16-1793) **John Martin (31), to Anthony Vaughan (57) – Lot 4**

#203 Source - Lunenburg Co. Land Deeds, recorded 05-10-1809, Vol. 6, P. 117, No. #252. 31>57 - **Lot 4**

#35 Source - "*Habitation on Oak Island*." Beaton Institute, Cape Breton University. Created by Surveyor William Dy Sr., called 'The Old Plan' No. 1046. Department of Lands & Forests, n.d. MG 12, 75 NSNA. Also Published in Joy Steele/Gordon Fader's book "*Oak Island Mystery Solved-Final Chapter*." P. 10. 2nd Ed. 2016.

#57 Source – "*Daniel Vaughan, 1747-1808*." The Free Family Tree. See citation.

1804 - (06-01-1804) **Anthony Vaughan Sr. (57), to Thomas Embree (17) – Lot 4**

#70 Source – Lunenburg Co. Land Deeds, recorded 03-10-1807, Vol. 6, P. 730, No. #750. 57>17 – **Lot 4**

#35 Source - "*Habitation on Oak Island*." Beaton Institute, Cape Breton University. Created by Surveyor William Dy Sr., called 'The Old Plan' No. 1046. Department of Lands & Forests, n.d. MG 12, 75 NSNA. Also Published in Joy Steele/Gordon Fader's book "*Oak Island Mystery Solved-Final Chapter*." P. 10. 2nd Ed. 2016.

1807 - (04-01-1807) **Thomas Embree (17), to George Bezanson (06b) – Lot 4**

#65 Source – Lunenburg Co. Land Deeds, recorded 03-24-1808, Vol. 6, P. 64, No. #139. 17>06b – **Lot 4**

#35 Source - "*Habitation on Oak Island*." Beaton Institute, Cape Breton University. Created by Surveyor William Dy Sr., called 'The Old Plan' No. 1046. Department of Lands & Forests, n.d. MG 12, 75 NSNA. Also Published in Joy Steele/Gordon Fader's book "*Oak Island Mystery Solved-Final Chapter*." P. 10. 2nd Ed. 2016.

1807 - (04-20-1807) **George Bezanson (06b), to Anthony Vaughan (57) – Lot 4**

#66 Source – Lunenburg Co. Land Deeds, recorded 10-03-1807, Vol. 6, P. 30, No. #65. 06b>57 – **Lot 4**

#35 Source - "*Habitation on Oak Island*." Beaton Institute, Cape Breton University. Created by Surveyor William Dy Sr., called 'The Old Plan' No. 1046. Department of Lands & Forests, n.d. MG 12, 75 NSNA. Also Published in Joy Steele/Gordon Fader's book "*Oak Island Mystery Solved-Final Chapter*." P. 10. 2nd Ed. 2016.

1851 - **Anthony Vaughan (57), to James McInnis (32fam) – McInnis Family – Lot 4**

#35 Source - "*Habitation on Oak Island*." Beaton Institute, Cape Breton University. Created by Surveyor William Dy Sr., called 'The Old Plan' No. 1046. Department of Lands & Forests, n.d. MG 12, 75 NSNA. Also Published in Joy Steele/Gordon Fader's book "*Oak Island Mystery Solved-Final Chapter*." P. 10. 2nd Ed. 2016.

1896 - James Henry McInnis (32fam) dies, passes to Arthur Curran McInnis (32fam) – Lot 4

#1 Source – N.S. Supreme Court, Book No. 368, recorded 10-01-1931, Book 20, P. 423, No. #368. (originally Book No. 20, P. 74, No.69) – **Lot 4**

1915 - Arthur Curran Mcinnis (32fam) dies, passes to John Mcinnis Family (32fam) – Lot 4

#1 Source – N.S. Supreme Court, Book No. 368, recorded 10-01-1931, Book 20, P. 423, No. #368. (originally Book No. 20, P. 74, No.69) – **Lot 4**

1930 - John McInnis Family (32fam), pass to inheritors Wallace and Margaret Young (63) et. al., – Lot 4

#169 Source – Lunenburg Co. Land Deed, recorded 06-21-1930, Book 20, P. 74, No. #69. Deeded on 06-09-1930. **- Lot 4**

#1 Source – N.S. Supreme Court, Book No. 368, recorded 10-01-1931, Book 20, P. 423, No. #368. (originally Book No. 20, P. 74, No.69) – **Lot 4**

#3 Source – City & County of San Francisco, Calif. Records; & NSNA, recorded 05-27-1935, Book No. 21. P. 96, No. #148. **- Lot 4**

1931 - (09-22-1931) **Wallace & Margaret Young (63), sell 50% of prop. Val. & share, to Archibald C. Dauphinee (15) – Lot 4**

#1 Source – N.S. Supreme Court, Book No. 368, recorded 10-01-1931, Book 20, P. 423, No. #368. (originally Book No. 20, P. 74, No.69) 63>15 – **Lot 4**

1944 - (09-28-1944) **Archibald Dauphinee (15) & Margaret Young (63), to Clarence James Beamish (04) – Lot 4**

#12 Source – Lunenburg Co. Land Deeds, recorded 10-25-1955, Deed #1142 on 10-25-1944. NSNA. 15,63>04 **- Lot 4**

1955 - (07-25-1955) **Clarence James Beamish (04) dies, his Lots 1, 2, 3, 4, 21, 22, 23, 27, 28, 29 passed to his wife, Ellen Chapman (09) – Lot 4**

#16 Source - Nova Scotia Supreme Court Book 27, P. 339, No. #638. NSNA. Represent heirs shares of "South & West part Oak Island," "George McInnis Property," and "James McInnis Property." 07-20-1961. 04,09>10 **- Lot 6, 7, 8, 15, 16, 17, 18, 19, 20, 23, 25, 26, 30, 31, 32**

#18 Source - Halifax Office of Registrar of Deeds, Book 907 P. 605, dated 12-23-1946 with the Canada Permanent Trust Company, and filed on 02-22-1961. 04,09>10 **- Lot 4**

1955 - (07-25-1955) **Heirs of Clarence Beamish (04) & wife Mary Ellen Chapman (09), to M.R. Chappell (10) – Lot 4**

#18 Source - Halifax Office of Registrar of Deeds, Book 907 P. 605, dated 12-23-1946 with the Canada Permanent Trust Company, and filed on 02-22-1961. 04,09>10 **- Lot 4**

1977 - (06-15-1977) **M.R. Chappell (10), to David C. Tobias (55)** for all shares regarding Lots **1, 2, 3, 4, 6, 7, 8, 15, 16, 17, 18, 19, 20, 21, 22,24, 25, 26, 27, 28, 29, 30, 31, 32. – Lot 4**

#20 Source – Filed in Halifax Co. Land Deeds, recorded on 06-29-1977, No. #582. NSNA. 10>55 **- Lots 6, 7, 8, 15, 16, 17, 18, 19, 20, 25, 26, 30, 31, 32**

1987 - (12-09-1987) **David Tobias (55) and his lots, join Dan Blankenship (07) to form Oak Island Tours Inc (41) – Lot 4**

#111 Source – "*The Open Database of the Corporate World. Oak Island Tours Inc. Company Number 2272393*." Incorporated Date, 12-09-1987. Opencorporates.

#112 Source – "*The Curse of Oak Island, The Story of the World's Longest Treasure Hunt*." By Randall Sullivan, 2018. Page 422.

2007 - David Tobias (55), sells his Lots to Rick & Marty Lagina who become equal partners with Dan Blankenship (07) in Oak Island Tours (41) which own/control Lots 1, 2, 3, 4, 6, 7, 8, 15, 16, 17, 18, 19, 20, 21, 22, 24, 26, 27, 28, 29, 30, 31, 32. – Lot 4

#111 Source – "*The Open Database of the Corporate World. Oak Island Tours Inc. Company Number 2272393*." Incorporated Date, 12-09-1987. Opencorporates.

#112 Source – "*The Curse of Oak Island, The Story of the World's Longest Treasure Hunt*." By Randall Sullivan, 2018. Page 422.

2007 - MacPhie Archives "*Oak Island Lot Distribution Map, 2007*." Lots ***1, 2, 3, 4, 6, 7, 8, 15, 16, 17, 18, 19, 20, 21, 22, 24, 26, 27, 28, 29, 30, 31, 32*** - Oak Island Tours (41); Lot ***5*** – Robert S. Young (61); Lots ***9, 10, 11, 12, 14*** – Fred Nolan (40); Lot ***13*** – John Johnston (25); Lot ***23*** – Dan/Dave Blankenship (07); and Lot ***25*** – Alan Kostrzewe (27). **– All Lots**

#30 Source - "*Oak Island Lot Ownership Map, 2007*," By MacPhie Archives. **All Lots**

Lot 5.

1753 - (12-27-1753) **Governor Charles Lawrence, to Capt. John Gifford (53) and Richard Smith (53) – ALL LOTS**

#123 Source - NS Archives and Record Management "Allotment" Book, P. 137, Reel #13044; "Old Book" #1, P. 44. Granted Gifford Island #12, Young Island #13, and Smith Island #28, to establish a fishery. Escheated.

1803 - James Vaughan (57d) – Lot 5

#17 Source – "*Chester Township Records, 1762-1830*." Births, Marriages, and Deaths. NSNA MG9, B 9-3.

1804 - James Vaughan (57d) dies, – Probated to James Vaughan Family (57d) – Lot 5

#17 Source – "*Chester Township Records, 1762-1830*." Births, Marriages, and Deaths. NSNA MG9, B 9-3.

1819 - **Vaughan/Vaughan/Kiser (Keyser) (57fam), to David Vaughan (57c) – Lot 5**
#106 Source – Lunenburg Co. Land Deeds, recorded 06-26-1823, Vol. 8, P. 323, 343, 344, No. #513. 57d>57c – **Lots 2, 5, 17**

1832 - (09-29-1832) **David Vaughan (57c), to Anthony T. Graves (19), includes Lots 5, 9, 10, 11, 12, 13, 14 – Lot 5**
#69 Source – Lunenburg Co. Land Deeds, recorded 03-37-1834, Vol. 10, P. 348. 57c>19 – **Lot 5**
#35 Source - "*Habitation on Oak Island*." Beaton Institute, Cape Breton University. Created by Surveyor William Dy Sr., called 'The Old Plan' No. 1046. Department of Lands & Forests, n.d. MG 12, 75 NSNA. Also Published in Joy Steele/Gordon Fader's book "*Oak Island Mystery Solved-Final Chapter*." P. 10. 2nd Ed. 2016.

1834 - (01-08-1834) **Anthony T. Graves (19), to Edward Foras (68) includes Lots 5, 9, 10, 11, 12, 13, 14 – Lot 5**
#125 Source – Chester Township Land Deeds, recorded 02-12-1834, Vol. 10, P. 323, No. #425. 19>68 **- Lots 5, 9, 10, 11, 12, 13, 14**

1839 - (02-14-1839) **Anthony T. Graves (19), to Frederick Zink (64) includes Lots 5, 9, 10, 11, 12, 13, 14 – Lot 5**
#71 Source – Paul Wroclawski Research & Property Owners Charles Morris to John Smith; collected through 02-06-2008.
#126 Source – Lunenburg Co. Land Deeds, Vol. 12, P. 21, No. #36. 19>64 **- Lots 5, 9, 10, 11, 12, 13, 14**

1841 - (03-29-1841) **Frederick Zink (64), to Anthony T. Graves (19) includes Lots 5, 9, 10, 11, 12, 13, 14 – Lot 5**
#127 Source - Lunenburg Co. Land Deeds, recorded 03-29-1841, Vol. 12, P. 210, No. #377. 64>19 **- Lots 5, 9,10, 11, 12, 13, 14**

1841 - (03-30-1841) **Anthony T. Graves (19), to John Strachan (54) includes Lots 5, 9, 10, 11, 12, 13, 14 – Lot 5**
#128 Source – Lunenburg Co. Land Deeds, recorded 04-07-1841, Vol. 12 P. 210, No. #378. 19>54 **- Lots 5, 9, 10, 11, 12, 13, 14**

1857 - John Strachan (54), back to Anthony T. Graves (19) includes Lots 5, 9, 10, 11, 12, 13, 14 – Lot 5

1888 - Anthony t. Graves (19) dies, and Lots 5, 9, 10, 11, 12, 13, 14 15, 16, 17, 18, 19, 20 are inherited by Henry Sellers (19a) of which, 5, 9, 10, 11, 12, 13, 14 go to Selwyn William Sellers (19b), Henry's son. – Lot 5
#36 Source - "Notes on the Triton/Nolan Pact & Lawsuit, RE Ownership of Oak Island Lots." Unknown Source, 1971. 3 pages. **Lots 5, 9, 10, 11,12, 13, 14**
#37 Source - "*Oak Island Plan of Property Owned by Sellyn Sellers*." by wildlife artist, S. Edgar March. Chester Township Land Deeds, recorded 09-05-1935, Book 24, P.368. NSNA. **All Lots**
#170 Source – "*Selwyn William Sellers, 1873-1949*." FamilySearch, See citation.

1949 - (07-23-1949) **Selvyn Sellers (19b) dies, and Lots 5, 9, 10, 11, 12, 13, 14 disbursed amongst his heirs (all heirs) – Lot 5**
#36 Source - "Notes on the Triton/Nolan Pact & Lawsuit, RE Ownership of Oak Island Lots." Unknown Source, 1971. 3 pages. **Lots 5, 9, 10, 11,12, 13, 14**

1963 - Frederick Nolan (40) purchases Lots, of Sellers (19a,b), Conrad (12,12a), & Corkum heirs (13a) – Lot 5
#36 Source - "Notes on the Triton/Nolan Pact & Lawsuit, RE Ownership of Oak Island Lots." Unknown Source, 1971. 3 pages. **Lots 5, 9, 10, 11,12, 13, 14**

1985 - (12-17-1985) **N.S. Supreme Court rules Lots 5, 9, 10, 11, 12, 13, 14 are owned by Fred G. Nolan (40) – Lot 5**
#132a Source - Nova Scotia Supreme Court ruling, recorded 04-07-1986 at Bridgewater, N.S. 55,56><40 **- Lots 5, 9, 10, 11, 12, 13, 14**

1996 - (06-1996) **Fred Nolan (40), to Robert S., Young (61) – Lot 5**
#129 Source – "*Robert S. Young (1996-2020)*." (61), Wikipedia. See citation.. **– Lot 5**

2007 - **MacPhie Archives "*Oak Island Lot Distribution Map, 2007*."** Lots ***1, 2, 3, 4, 6, 7, 8, 15, 16, 17, 18, 19, 20, 21, 22, 24, 26, 27, 28, 29, 30, 31, 32*** - Oak Island Tours (41); Lot ***5*** – Robert S. Young (61); Lots ***9, 10, 11, 12, 14*** – Fred Nolan (40); Lot ***13*** – John Johnston (25); Lot ***23*** – Dan/Dave Blankenship (07); and Lot ***25*** – Alan Kostrzewe (27). **– All Lots**

#30 Source - "*Oak Island Lot Ownership Map, 2007*," By MacPhie Archives. **All Lots**

2020 - (10-28-2020) **Robert S. Young (61) dies, heirs sell property – Lot 5**

#129 Source – "*Robert S. Young (1996-2020)*." (61), Wikipedia. See citation.. **– Lot 5**

2022 - **Robert Young (61) heirs, to Cerca Trova Ltd, a Rick & Marty Lagina controlled entity. - Lot 5**

#130 Source – PROPERTYOnline, Lunenburg Country, AAN #08219605. Robert Young (61) **– Lot 5**

Lot 6.

1753 - (12-27-1753) **Governor Charles Lawrence, to Capt. John Gifford (53) and Richard Smith (53) – ALL LOTS**

#123 Source - NS Archives and Record Management "Allotment" Book, P. 137, Reel #13044; "Old Book" #1, P. 44. Granted Gifford Island #12, Young Island #13, and Smith Island #28, to establish a fishery. Escheated.

1766 - (08-20-1766) **Crown (00), to Phillip Payzant (43), drew lot – Lot 6**

#34 Source – "*Nova Scotia Land Papers: 1795-1800, Green James and Others*." 1784 – Lunenburg County. 37,950 acres granted in Chester, including License to Occupy, Memorial, Warrant to Survey, Surveyor's Report & Surveyor's Certificate. See citation. 00>42 **- Lot 6**

1768 - (06-22-1768) **Phillip Payzant (43) dies, signed over by Payzant (43) for friendship, to Robert Melvin (38) – Lot 6**

#2 Source - Paul Wroclawski Research & Property Owners Charles Morris to John Smith; collected through 02-06-2008.

#21 Source – Lunenburg Co. Land Deeds, recorded 06-18-1782, Vol. 2, P. 493, No. #646. NSNA. 43>38 **- Lot 6**

1787 - **Robert Melvin Sr. (38) dies,** in 1788 probated and willed to wife **Phebe Melvin (38fam) – Lot 6**

#17 Source – "*Chester Township Records, 1762-1830*." Births, Marriages, and Deaths. NSNA MG9, B 9-3.

1790 - (05-23-1790) **Widow Phebe Melvin (38),** by marriage to **Jacob Sheppard (50) – Lot 6**

#17 Source – "*Chester Township Records, 1762-1830*." Births, Marriages, and Deaths. NSNA MG9, B 9-3.

1811 - (11-14-1811) **Widow Melvin/Jacob Sheppard (50), to Nathaniel Melvin (38) – Lot 6**

#86 Source – Lunenburg Co. Land Deeds, recorded 04-22-1815, Vol. 7, P. 188, No. #188. 50>38a **- Lot 6 & 7**

1812 - (12-07-1812) **Nathaniel Melvin (38a), to Samuel Ball (03) – Lot 6**

#24 Source – "*Bee Stanton's Samuel Ball Map 1787 - 1812*." @ www.creative@beestanton website. **Lots 6, 7, 8, 24, 25, 26, 30, 31, 32**

#35 Source - "*Habitation on Oak Island*." Beaton Institute, Cape Breton University. Created by Surveyor William Dy Sr., called 'The Old Plan' No. 1046. Department of Lands & Forests, n.d. MG 12, 75 NSNA. Also Published in Joy Steele/Gordon Fader's book "*Oak Island Mystery Solved-Final Chapter*." P. 10. 2nd Ed. 2016.

#107 Source – Lunenburg Co. Land Deeds, recorded 04-13-1815, Vol. 6, P. 83, No. #189. 38a>03 **- Lot 6**

1819 - **Samuel Ball (03) – Lot 6**

#17 Source – "*Chester Township Records, 1762-1830*." Births, Marriages, and Deaths. NSNA MG9, B 9-3.

#131 Source -"*The Black Settlers of 'Treasure Oak Island' The Primary Generation – Samuel Ball (03)*." See citation. **– Lots 6, 7, 8, 24, 25, 26, 30, 31, 32**

#132 Source - "*Who Was Samuel Ball*," Published by Deb Minter 07-06-2021. Facebook online, "*Oak Island: History not Myth*." Posted 06-23-2021. **– Lots 6, 7, 8, 24, 25, 26, 30, 31, 32**

1846 - Samuel Ball (03) dies, property transfers to Isaac Butler (Ball) (03a) – Lot 6

- **#17** Source – "*Chester Township Records, 1762-1830*." Births, Marriages, and Deaths. NSNA MG9, B 9-3.
- **#108** Source – "*Samuel Ball Will, Lunenburg, N.S.*" Will Extracts – See citation.
- **#130a** Source – Lunenburg Co. Registrar, Book 1, P. 37, dated 10-01-1841, recorded 01-05-1846. Last Will & Testament of Samuel Ball (03). **– Lots 6, 7, 8, 24, 25, 26, 30, 31, 32**

1898 - (01-17-1898) **Isaac Butler (Ball) (03a), deeds ½ lot to Abraham Ernst (18) & ½ lot Henry Sellers (19a) – Lot 6**

- **#13** Source – Dominion of Canada Book No. #693, NSNA. **- Lots 6, 7, 8, 15, 16, 17, 18, 19, 20, 25, 26, 30, 32 [**Lot 31 missing**]**
- **#108** Source – "*Samuel Ball Will, Lunenburg, N.S.*" Will Extracts – See citation.

1912 - Abraham Ernst (18) dies 1911, Henry Sellers (19a) dies 1912, & his wife (Sophia Elizabeth Graves Sellers) dies 1931; leaving inherited lots to future heirs. **– Lot 6**

- **#199** Source – "*Letter from Blair to Harris 02-16-1035*." on purchasing remaining lots 1–14. **Lots 1, 2, 3, 4, 5, 6, 7, 8, 9, 10, 11, 12, 13, 14**

1937 - (09-14-1937) **Francis & Eva G. Conrad (12) and Ingram & Quesetta M. Conrad (12a), to Archibald D. Dauphinee (15) – Lot 6**

- **#9** Source - Dominion of Canada Book No. 8, P. 218-219, No. #655. (originally in Book 8, P. 218-219, No. #132) NSNA. 12,12a**>**15 **- Lot 6, 7, 8, 25, 26, 30, 31, 32**

1937 - (09-13-1937) **Archibald D. & Hannah Dauphinee (15), to Gilbert Hedden (22) – Lot 6**

- **#10** Source - Dominion of Canada Book No. 21, P. 402-403, No. #656. (originally in Book 21, P.218-219, No. #132) NSNA. 15**>**22 **– Lot 6, 7, 8, 25, 26, 30, 31, 32**

1950 - (05-26-1950) **Gilbert & Margarite Hedden (22), to John Whitney Lewis (10a) – Lot 6**

- **#13** Source – Dominion of Canada Book No. #693, NSNA. 22**>**10a **- Lots 6, 7, 8, 15, 16, 17, 18, 19, 20, 25, 26, 30, 32 [**Lot 31 missing**]**

1950 - (12-05-1950) **Ann & John Whitney Lewis (10a), to Acadia Trust Co. (10b) – Lot 6**

- **#14** Source - Dominion of Canada, NSNA #880. (original filings list – see citation). 10a**>**10b **- Lot 6, 7, 8, 15, 16, 17, 18, 19, 20, 25, 30, 31, 32 [**Lot 26 missing**]**

1957 - (04-20-1957) **Acadia Trust Company (10b), to M.R. Chappell (10) – Lot 6**

- **#15** Source - Registry of Deeds at Bridgewater and Registry of Probate, Book 26, P. 195, Quit Claim No. 374, NSNA. 10b**>**10 **- Lot 6, 7, 8, 15, 16, 17, 18, 19, 20, 25, 26, 30, 31, 32**

1961 - (07-21-1961) **Mary Ellen Chapman (09) & heirs of Clarence J. Beamish (04), to M.R. Chappell, Lots 5, 6, 7, 8, 15, 16, 17, 18, 19, 20, 23, 25, 26, 30, 31, 32 (10) – Lot 6**

- **#16** Source - Nova Scotia Supreme Court Book 27, P. 339, No. #638. NSNA. Represent heirs shares of "South & West part Oak Island," "George McInnis Property," and "James McInnis Property." 07-20-1961. 09,04**>**10 **- Lot 6, 7, 8, 15, 16, 17, 18, 19, 20, 23, 25, 26, 30, 31, 32**

1977 - (06-15-1977) **M.R. Chappell (10), to David C. Tobias (55)** for all shares regarding **Lots, 1, 2, 3, 4, 6, 7, 8, 15, 16, 17, 18, 19, 20, 21, 22, 24, 25, 26, 27, 28, 29, 30, 31, 32. – Lot 6**

- **#20** Source – Filed in Halifax Co. Land Deeds, recorded on 06-29-1977, No. #582. NSNA. 10**>**55 **- Lots 6, 7, 8, 15, 16, 17, 18, 19, 20, 25, 26, 30, 31, 32**

1987 - (12-09-1987) **David Tobias (55) and his lots, join Dan Blankenship (07) to form Oak Island Tours Inc (41) – Lot 6**

- **#111** Source – "*The Open Database of the Corporate World. Oak Island Tours Inc. Company Number 2272393*." Incorporated Date, 12-09-1987. Opencorporates.
- **#112** Source – "*The Curse of Oak Island, The Story of the World's Longest Treasure Hunt*." By Randall Sullivan, 2018. Page 422.

2007 - David Tobias (55), sells his Lots to Rick & Marty Lagina who become equal partners with Dan Blankenship (07) in Oak Island Tours (41) which own/control Lots 1, 2, 3, 4, 6, 7, 8, 15, 16, 17, 18, 19, 20, 21, 22, 24, 26, 27, 28, 29, 30, 31, 32. – Lot 6

- **#111** Source – "*The Open Database of the Corporate World. Oak Island Tours Inc. Company Number 2272393*." Incorporated Date, 12-09-1987. Opencorporates.
- **#112** Source – "*The Curse of Oak Island, The Story of the World's Longest Treasure Hunt*." By Randall Sullivan, 2018. Page 422.

2007 - MacPhie Archives "*Oak Island Lot Distribution Map, 2007*." Lots ***1, 2, 3, 4, 6, 7, 8, 15, 16, 17, 18, 19, 20, 21, 22, 24, 26, 27, 28, 29, 30, 31, 32*** - Oak Island Tours (41); Lot ***5*** – Robert S. Young (61); Lots ***9, 10, 11, 12, 14*** – Fred Nolan (40); Lot ***13*** – John Johnston (25); Lot ***23*** – Dan/Dave Blankenship (07); and Lot ***25*** – Alan Kostrzewe (27). – **All Lots**

#30 Source - "*Oak Island Lot Ownership Map, 2007*," By MacPhie Archives. **All Lots**

Lot 7.

1753 - (12-27-1753) **Governor Charles Lawrence, to Capt. John Gifford (53) and Richard Smith (53) – ALL LOTS**

#123 Source - NS Archives and Record Management "Allotment" Book, P. 137, Reel #13044; "Old Book" #1, P. 44. Granted Gifford Island #12, Young Island #13, and Smith Island #28, to establish a fishery. Escheated.

1767 - Crown (00), to Rev. John Secombe (48) – Lot 7

#34 Source – "*Nova Scotia Land Papers: 1795-1800, Green James and Others*." 1784 – Lunenburg County. 37,950 acres granted in Chester, including License to Occupy, Memorial, Warrant to Survey, Surveyor's Report & Surveyor's Certificate. See citation. 00>48 **- Lot 7**

1767 - (11-17-67) **Rev. John Secombe (48), to Robert Melvin Sr. (38) – Lot 7**

#94 Source - Lunenburg Co. Land Deeds, Vol. 1, P. 1770, No. #336. 48>38 **- Lot 7**

1787 - Robert Melvin Sr. (38) dies, in 1788 probated and willed to wife **Phebe Melvin (38fam) – Lot 7**

#17 Source – "*Chester Township Records, 1762-1830*." Births, Marriages, and Deaths. NSNA MG9, B 9-3.

1790 - (05-23-1790) **Widow Phebe Melvin (38),** transfer ownership thru marriage to **Jacob Sheppard (50) – Lot 7**

#17 Source – "*Chester Township Records, 1762-1830*." Births, Marriages, and Deaths. NSNA MG9, B 9-3.

1811 - (11-14-1811) **Widow Melvin/Jacob Sheppard (50), to Nathaniel Melvin (38a) – Lot 7**

#86 Source – Lunenburg Co. Land Deeds, recorded 04-22-1815, Vol. 7, P. 188, No. #188. 50>38a **- Lot 6 & 7**

1812 - (12-07-1812) **Nathaniel Melvin(38a), to Samuel Ball (03) – Lot 7**

#24 Source – "*Bee Stanton's Samuel Ball Map 1787 - 1812*." @ www.creative@beestanton website. **Lots 6, 7, 8, 24, 25, 26, 30, 31, 32**

#35 Source - "*Habitation on Oak Island*." Beaton Institute, Cape Breton University. Created by Surveyor William Dy Sr., called 'The Old Plan' No. 1046. Department of Lands & Forests, n.d. MG 12, 75 NSNA. Also Published in Joy Steele/Gordon Fader's book "*Oak Island Mystery Solved-Final Chapter*." P. 10. 2nd Ed. 2016.

#107 Source – Lunenburg Co. Land Deeds, recorded 04-13-1815, Vol. 6, P. 83, No. #189. 38a>03 **- Lot 7**

1819 - Samuel Ball (03) – Lot 7

#17 Source – "*Chester Township Records, 1762-1830*." Births, Marriages, and Deaths. NSNA MG9, B 9-3.

#131 Source -"*The Black Settlers of 'Treasure Oak Island' The Primary Generation – Samuel Ball (03)*." See citation. **– Lots 6, 7, 8, 24, 25, 26, 30, 31, 32**

#132 Source - "*Who Was Samuel Ball*," Published by Deb Minter 07-06-2021. Facebook online, "*Oak Island: History not Myth*." Posted 06-23-2021. **– Lots 6, 7, 8, 24, 25, 26, 30, 31, 32**

1846 - Samuel Ball (03) dies, property transfers to Isaac Butler (Ball) (03a) – Lot 7

#17 Source – "*Chester Township Records, 1762-1830*." Births, Marriages, and Deaths. NSNA MG9, B 9-3.

#108 Source – "*Samuel Ball Will, Lunenburg, N.S.*" Will Extracts – See citation.

#130a Source – Lunenburg Co. Registrar, Book 1, P. 37, dated 10-01-1841, recorded 01-05-1846. Last Will & Testament of Samuel Ball (03). **– Lots 6, 7, 8, 24, 25, 26, 30, 31, 32**

1898 - (01-17-1898) **Isaac Butler (Ball) (03a), deeds ½ lot to Abraham Ernst (18) & ½ lot Henry Sellers (19a) – Lot 7**

#13 Source – Dominion of Canada Book No. #693, NSNA. **- Lots 6, 7, 8, 15, 16, 17, 18, 19, 20, 25, 26, 30, 32** [Lot 31 missing]

#108 Source – "*Samuel Ball Will, Lunenburg, N.S.*" Will Extracts – See citation.

1912 - Abraham Ernst (18) dies 1911, Henry Sellers (19a) dies 1912, & his wife (Sophia Elizabeth Graves Sellers) dies 1931; leaving inherited lots to future heirs. **– Lot 7**

#199 Source – "*Letter from Blair to Harris 02-16-1035.*" on purchasing remaining lots 1–14. – **Lots 1, 2, 3, 4, 5, 6, 7, 8, 9, 10, 11, 12, 13, 14**

1937 - (09-14-1937) **Francis & Eva G. Conrad (12) and Ingram & Quesetta M. Conrad (12a), to Archibald D. Dauphinee (15) – Lot 7**

#9 Source - Dominion of Canada Book No. 8, P. 218-219, No. #655. (originally in Book 8, P. 218-219, No. #132) NSNA. 12,12a>15 **- Lot 6, 7, 8, 25, 26, 30, 31, 32**

1937 - (09-13-1937) **Archibald D. & Hannah Dauphinee (15), to Gilbert Hedden (22) – Lot 7**

#10 Source - Dominion of Canada Book No. 21, P. 402-403, No. #656. (originally in Book 21, P.218-219, No. #132) NSNA. 15>22 **– Lot 6, 7, 8, 25, 26, 30, 31, 32**

1950 - (05-26-1950) **Gilbert D. Hedden & Margarite C. Hedden (22), to John Whitney Lewis (10a) – Lot 7**

#13 Source – Dominion of Canada Book No. #693, NSNA. 22>10a **- Lots 6, 7, 8, 15, 16, 17, 18, 19, 20, 25, 26, 30, 32** [Lot 31 missing]

1950 - (12-05-1950) **Ann & John Whitney Lewis (10a), to Acadia Trust Co. (10b) – Lot 7**

#14 Source - Dominion of Canada, NSNA #880. (original filings list – see citation). 10a>10b **- Lot 6, 7, 8, 15, 16, 17, 18, 19, 20, 25, 30, 31, 32** [Lot 26 missing]

1957 - (04-20-1957) **Acadia Trust Company (10b), to M.R. Chappell (10) – Lot 7**

#15 Source - Registry of Deeds at Bridgewater and Registry of Probate, Book 26, P. 195, Quit Claim No. 374, NSNA. 10b>10 **- Lot 6, 7, 8, 15, 16, 17, 18, 19, 20, 25, 26, 30, 31, 32**

1961 - (07-21-1961) **Mary Ellen Chapman (09) & heirs of Clarence J. Beamish (04), to M.R. Chappell, Lots 5, 6, 7, 8, 15, 16, 17, 18, 19, 20, 23, 25, 26, 30, 31, 32 (10) – Lot 7**

#16 Source - Nova Scotia Supreme Court Book 27, P. 339, No. #638. NSNA. Represent heirs shares of "South & West part Oak Island," "George McInnis Property," and "James McInnis Property." 07-20-1961. 09,04>10 **- Lot 6, 7, 8, 15, 16, 17, 18, 19, 20, 23, 25, 26, 30, 31, 32**

1977 - (06-15-1977) **M.R. Chappell (10), to David C. Tobias (55)** for all shares regarding Lots, **1, 2, 3, 4, 6, 7, 8, 15, 16, 17, 18, 19, 20, 21, 22, 24, 25, 26, 27, 28, 29, 30, 31, 32. – Lot 7**

#20 Source – Filed in Halifax Co. Land Deeds, recorded on 06-29-1977, No. #582. NSNA. 10>55 **- Lots 6, 7, 8, 15, 16, 17, 18, 19, 20, 25, 26, 30, 31, 32**

1987 - (12-09-1987) **David Tobias (55) and his lots, join Dan Blankenship (07) to form Oak Island Tours Inc (41) – Lot 7**

#111 Source – "*The Open Database of the Corporate World. Oak Island Tours Inc. Company Number 2272393.*" Incorporated Date, 12-09-1987. Opencorporates.

#112 Source – "*The Curse of Oak Island, The Story of the World's Longest Treasure Hunt.*" By Randall Sullivan, 2018. Page 422.

2007 - David Tobias (55), sells his Lots to Rick & Marty Lagina who become equal partners with Dan Blankenship (07) in Oak Island Tours (41) which own/control Lots 1, 2, 3, 4, 6, 7, 8, 15, 16, 17, 18, 19, 20, 21, 22, 24, 26, 27, 28, 29, 30, 31, 32. – Lot 7

#111 Source – "*The Open Database of the Corporate World. Oak Island Tours Inc. Company Number 2272393.*" Incorporated Date, 12-09-1987. Opencorporates.

#112 Source – "*The Curse of Oak Island, The Story of the World's Longest Treasure Hunt.*" By Randall Sullivan, 2018. Page 422.

2007 - MacPhie Archives "*Oak Island Lot Distribution Map, 2007.*" Lots ***1, 2, 3, 4, 6, 7, 8, 15, 16, 17, 18, 19, 20, 21, 22, 24, 26, 27, 28, 29, 30, 31, 32*** - Oak Island Tours (41); Lot ***5*** – Robert S. Young (61); Lots ***9, 10, 11, 12, 14*** – Fred Nolan (40); Lot ***13*** – John Johnston (25); Lot ***23*** – Dan/Dave Blankenship (07); and Lot ***25*** – Alan Kostrzewe (27). **– All Lots**

#30 Source - "*Oak Island Lot Ownership Map, 2007,*" By MacPhie Archives. **All Lots**

Lot 8.

1753 - (12-27-1753) **Governor Charles Lawrence, to Capt. John Gifford (53) and Richard Smith (53) – ALL LOTS**

#123 Source - NS Archives and Record Management "Allotment" Book, P. 137, Reel #13044; "Old Book" #1, P. 44. Granted Gifford Island #12, Young Island #13, and Smith Island #28, to establish a fishery. Escheated.

1758 - Crown (00) grants or Jonathan Prescott (45) trades granted land sometime prior between 1754-1783. - **Lot 8**

#2 Source - Paul Wroclawski Research & Property Owners Charles Morris to John Smith; collected through 02-06-2008.

1784 - (06-16-1784) **Jonathan Prescott (45), to Robert Melvin Sr. (38) – Lot 8**

#92 Source – Lunenburg Co. Land Deeds, recorded 09-27-1790, Vol. 3, P. 429-30, No. #709. 45>38 **- Lot 8 & 22**

1787 - Robert Melvin Sr. (38) dies,1788 probate & willed to **Robert Melvin Jr. (38d) – Lot 8**

#17 Source – "*Chester Township Records, 1762-1830*." Births, Marriages, and Deaths. NSNA MG9, B 9-3.

1798 - (05-23-1798) **Robert Melvin Jr. (38d), to Samuel Ball (03) – Lot 8**

#24 Source – "*Bee Stanton's Samuel Ball Map 1787 - 1812*." @ www.creative@beestanton website. **Lots 6, 7, 8, 24, 25, 26, 30, 31, 32**

#35 Source - "*Habitation on Oak Island*." Beaton Institute, Cape Breton University. Created by Surveyor William Dy Sr., called 'The Old Plan' No. 1046. Department of Lands & Forests, n.d. MG 12, 75 NSNA. Also Published in Joy Steele/Gordon Fader's book "*Oak Island Mystery Solved-Final Chapter*." P. 10. 2nd Ed. 2016.

#83 Source – "*Loyalist Melvins-H*." By Palmer Papers. Browne & Chester Township Books citations, Vol. 6, P. 26, No. #51. 38d>03 **- Lot 8**

1812 - Oak Island Samuel Ball (03) "*Ownership Map, Lots 6, 7, 8, 24, 25, 26, 30, 31, 32, Hook Island, Mainland Farm, 2007*" **– Lot 8**

#24 Source – "*Bee Stanton's Samuel Ball Map 1787 - 1812*." @ www.creative@beestanton website. **Lots 6, 7, 8, 24, 25, 26, 30, 31, 32**

#35 Source - "*Habitation on Oak Island*." Beaton Institute, Cape Breton University. Created by Surveyor William Dy Sr., called 'The Old Plan' No. 1046. Department of Lands & Forests, n.d. MG 12, 75 NSNA. Also Published in Joy Steele/Gordon Fader's book "*Oak Island Mystery Solved-Final Chapter*." P. 10. 2nd Ed. 2016.

#131 Source -"*The Black Settlers of 'Treasure Oak Island' The Primary Generation – Samuel Ball (03)*." See citation. **– Lots 6, 7, 8, 24, 25, 26, 30, 31, 32**

#132 Source - "*Who Was Samuel Ball*," Published by Deb Minter 07-06-2021. Facebook online, "*Oak Island: History not Myth*." Posted 06-23-2021. **– Lots 6, 7, 8, 24, 25, 26, 30, 31, 32**

1846 - Samuel Ball (03) dies, property transfers to Isaac Butler (Ball) (03a) – Lot 8

#17 Source – "*Chester Township Records (births, marriages, & deaths), 1762-1830*." Nova Scotia Archives MG9, B 9-3.

#108 Source – "*Samuel Ball Will, Lunenburg, N.S.*" Will Extracts – See citation.

#130a Source – Lunenburg Co. Registrar, Book 1, P. 37, dated 10-01-1841, recorded 01-05-1846. Last Will & Testament of Samuel Ball (03). **– Lots 6, 7, 8, 24, 25, 26, 30, 31, 32**

1898 - (01-17-1898) **Isaac Butler (Ball) (03a), deeds ½ lot to Abraham Ernst (18) & ½ lot Henry Sellers (19a) – Lot 8**

#13 Source – Dominion of Canada Book No. #693, NSNA. 22>10a **- Lots 6, 7, 8, 15, 16, 17, 18, 19, 20, 25, 26, 30, 32** [Lot 31 missing]

#108 Source – "*Samuel Ball Will, Lunenburg, N.S.*" Will Extracts – See citation.

1912 - Abraham Ernst (18) dies 1911, Henry Sellers (19a) dies 1912, & his wife (Sophia Elizabeth Graves Sellers) dies 1931; leaving inherited lots to future heirs. **– Lot 8**

#199 Source – "*Letter from Blair to Harris 02-16-1035*." on purchasing remaining lots 1–14. – **Lots 1, 2, 3, 4, 5, 6, 7, 8, 9, 10, 11, 12, 13, 14**

1937 - (09-14-1937) **Francis & Eva G. Conrad (12) and Ingram & Quesetta M. Conrad (12a), to Archibald D. Dauphinee (15) – Lot 8**

#9 Source - Dominion of Canada Book No. 8, P. 218-219, No. #655. (originally in Book 8, P. 218-219, No. #132) NSNA. 12,12a>15 **- Lot 6, 7, 8, 25, 26, 30, 31, 32**

1937 - (09-13-1937) **Archibald D. & Hannah Dauphinee (15), to Gilbert Hedden (22) – Lot 8**
#10 Source - Dominion of Canada Book No. 21, P. 402-403, No. #656. (originally in Book 21, P.218-219, No. #132) NSNA. 15>22 **– Lot 6, 7, 8, 25, 26, 30, 31, 32**

1950 - (05-26-1950) **Gilbert & Margarite Hedden (22), to John Whitney Lewis (10a) – Lot 8**
#13 Source – Dominion of Canada Book No. #693, NSNA. 22>10a **- Lots 6, 7, 8, 15, 16, 17, 18, 19, 20, 25, 26, 30, 32** [Lot 31 missing]

1951 - (12-05-1950) **Ann & John Whitney Lewis (10a), to Acadia Trust Co. (10b) – Lot 8**
#14 Source - Dominion of Canada, NSNA #880. (original filings list – see citation). 10a>10b **- Lot 6, 7, 8, 15, 16, 17, 18, 19, 20, 25, 30, 31, 32** [Lot 26 missing]

1957 - (04-20-1957) **Acadia Trust Company (10b), to M.R. Chappell (10) – Lot 8**
#15 Source - Registry of Deeds at Bridgewater and Registry of Probate, Book 26, P. 195, Quit Claim No. 374, NSNA. 10b>10 **- Lot 6, 7, 8, 15, 16, 17, 18, 19, 20, 25, 26, 30, 31, 32**

1961 - (07-21-1961) **Mary Ellen Chapman (09) & heirs of Clarence J. Beamish (04), to M.R. Chappell, Lots 5, 6, 7, 8, 15, 16, 17, 18, 19, 20, 23, 25, 26, 30, 31, 32 (10) – Lot 8**
#16 Source - Nova Scotia Supreme Court Book 27, P. 339, No. #638. NSNA. Represent heirs shares of "South & West part Oak Island," "George McInnis Property," and "James McInnis Property." 07-20-1961. 09,04>10 **- Lot 6, 7, 8, 15, 16, 17, 18, 19, 20, 23, 25, 26, 30, 31, 32**

1977 - (06-15-1977) **M.R. Chappell (10), to David C. Tobias (55)** for all shares regarding Lots, **1, 2, 3, 4, 6, 7, 8, 15, 16, 17, 18, 19, 20, 21, 22, 24, 25, 26, 27, 28, 29, 30, 31, 32. – Lot 8**
#20 Source – Filed in Halifax Co. Land Deeds, recorded on 06-29-1977, No. #582. NSNA. 10>55 **- Lots 6, 7, 8, 15, 16, 17, 18, 19, 20, 25, 26, 30, 31, 32**

1987 - (12-09-1987) **David Tobias (55) and his lots, join Dan Blankenship (07) to form Oak Island Tours Inc (41) – Lot 8**
#111 Source – "*The Open Database of the Corporate World. Oak Island Tours Inc. Company Number 2272393*." Incorporated Date, 12-09-1987. Opencorporates.
#112 Source – "*The Curse of Oak Island, The Story of the World's Longest Treasure Hunt*." By Randall Sullivan, 2018. Page 422.

2007 - David Tobias (55), sells his Lots to Rick & Marty Lagina who become equal partners with Dan Blankenship (07) in Oak Island Tours (41) which own/control Lots 1, 2, 3, 4, 6, 7, 8, 15, 16, 17, 18, 19, 20, 21, 22, 24, 26, 27, 28, 29, 30, 31, 32. – Lot 8
#111 Source – "*The Open Database of the Corporate World. Oak Island Tours Inc. Company Number 2272393*." Incorporated Date, 12-09-1987. Opencorporates.
#112 Source – "*The Curse of Oak Island, The Story of the World's Longest Treasure Hunt*." By Randall Sullivan, 2018. Page 422.

2007 - MacPhie Archives "*Oak Island Lot Distribution Map, 2007*." Lots ***1, 2, 3, 4, 6, 7, 8, 15, 16, 17, 18, 19, 20, 21, 22, 24, 26, 27, 28, 29, 30, 31, 32*** - Oak Island Tours (41); Lot ***5*** – Robert S. Young (61); Lots ***9, 10, 11, 12, 14*** – Fred Nolan (40); Lot ***13*** – John Johnston (25); Lot ***23*** – Dan/Dave Blankenship (07); and Lot ***25*** – Alan Kostrzewe (27). **– All Lots**
#30 Source - "*Oak Island Lot Ownership Map, 2007*," By MacPhie Archives. **All Lots**

Lot 9.

1753 - (12-27-1753) **Governor Charles Lawrence, to Capt. John Gifford (53) and Richard Smith (53) – ALL LOTS**
#123 Source - NS Archives and Record Management "Allotment" Book, P. 137, Reel #13044; "Old Book" #1, P. 44. Granted Gifford Island #12, Young Island #13, and Smith Island #28, to establish a fishery. Escheated.

1788 - (12-22-1788) **Anthony Vaughan Sr. (57), to Martin Marshall (30) – Lot 9**
#75 Source - Paul Wroclawski Research & Property Owners Charles Morris to John Smith; collected through 02-06-2008. 57>30 **– Lot 9 & 10**

1793 - (06-17-1793) **Martin Marshall (30), to Neil McMullen (35) – Lot 9**
#76 Source – Lunenburg Co. Land Deeds, recorded 07-15-1795, Vol. 4, P. 99, No. #123. **– Lot 9 & 10**
#35 Source - "*Habitation on Oak Island*." Beaton Institute, Cape Breton University. Created by Surveyor William Dy Sr., called 'The Old Plan' No. 1046. Department of Lands & Forests, n.d. MG 12, 75 NSNA. Also Published in Joy Steele/Gordon Fader's book "*Oak Island Mystery Solved-Final Chapter*." P. 10. 2nd Ed. 2016.

1827 - (12-21-1827) **Neil McMullen (35), to Neil McMullen Smith (35a) – Lot 9**
#82 Source – Lunenburg Co. Land Deeds, recorded 12-27-1827, Vol. 9, P. 53. 35>35a **- Lot 9, 10, 11, 12, 13, 14**

1832 - (06-18-1832) **Neil McMullen Smith (35a), to Anthony T. Graves (19) – Lot 9**
#68 Source – Lunenburg Co. Land Deeds, recorded 10-11-1832, Vol. 10, P. 76, No. #101. 35a>19 **- Lots 9, 10, 11, 12, 13, 14**

1834 - (01-08-1834) **Anthony T. Graves (19), to Edward Foras (68) – Lot 9**
#125 Source – Chester Township Land Deeds, recorded 02-12-1834, Vol. 10, P. 323, No. #425. 19>68 **- Lots 5, 9, 10, 11, 12, 13, 14**

1839 - (02-14-1839) **Anthony T. Graves (19), to Frederick Zink (64) – Lot 9**
#71 Source - Paul Wroclawski Research & Property Owners Charles Morris to John Smith; collected through 02-06-2008.
#126 Source – Lunenburg Co. Land Deeds, Vol. 12, P. 21, No. #36. 19>64 **- Lots 5,9,10,11,12,13,14**

1841 - (03-29-1841) **Frederick Zink (64), to Anthony T. Graves (19) – Lot 9**
#127 Source - Lunenburg Co. Land Deeds, recorded 03-29-1841, Vol. 12, P. 210, No. #377. 64>19 **- Lots 5, 9,10, 11, 12, 13, 14**

1841 - (03-30-1841) **Anthony T. Graves (19), to John Strachan (54) – Lot 9**
#128 Source – Lunenburg Co. Land Deeds, recorded 04-07-1841, Vol. 12 P. 210, No. #378. 19>54 **- Lots 5, 9, 10, 11, 12, 13, 14**

1857 - **John Strachan (54), to Anthony T. Graves (19) – Lot 9**

1888 - **Anthony T. Graves (19) dies, and Lots 5, 9, 10, 11, 12, 13, 14 15, 16, 17, 18, 19, 20 are inherited by Henry Sellers (19a) of which, 5, 9, 10, 11, 12, 13, 14 go to Selwyn William Sellers (19b), Henry's son. – Lot 9**
#36 Source - "Notes on the Triton/Nolan Pact & Lawsuit, RE Ownership of Oak Island Lots." Unknown Source, 1971. 3 pages. **Lots 5, 9, 10, 11,12, 13, 14**
#37 Source - "*Oak Island Plan of Property Owned by Sellyn Sellers*." by wildlife artist, S. Edgar March. Chester Township Land Deeds, recorded 09-05-1935, Book 24, P.368. NSNA. **All Lots**
#170 Source – "*Selwyn William Sellers, 1873-1949*." FamilySearch, See citation.

1949 - (07-23-1949) **Selvyn Sellers (19b) dies, and Lots 5, 9, 10, 11, 12, 13, 14 disbursed amongst his heirs (all heirs) – Lot 9**
#36 Source - "Notes on the Triton/Nolan Pact & Lawsuit, RE Ownership of Oak Island Lots." Unknown Source, 1971. 3 pages. **Lots 5, 9, 10, 11,12, 13, 14**

1963 - **Frederick Nolan (40), purchases Lots owned by Sellers (19a,b), Conrad (12,12a), & Corkum heirs (13a) Lots, 5, 9, 10, 11, 12, 13, 14 – Lot 9**
#36 Source - "Notes on the Triton/Nolan Pact & Lawsuit, RE Ownership of Oak Island Lots." Unknown Source, 1971. 3 pages. **Lots 5, 9, 10, 11,12, 13, 14**

1985 - (12-17-1985) **N.S. Supreme Court rules the Lots 5, 9, 10, 11, 12, 13, 14 are owned by Fred Nolan (40) – Lot 9**
#132a Source - Nova Scotia Supreme Court ruling, recorded 04-07-1986 at Bridgewater, N.S. 55,56><40 **- Lots 5, 9, 10, 11, 12, 13, 14**

2015 - **Fred Nolan (40) dies, & property is transferred to son, Thomas J. Nolan (40a) –Lot 9**
#900 Source – "*Frederick Gerald Nolan: 1927-2016*." Find-a-Grave. See citation.
#901 Source – "*Obituary for Frederick G. Nolan*." Halifax Funeral Home. See citation.

2007 - **MacPhie Archives "*Oak Island Lot Distribution Map, 2007*."** Lots ***1, 2, 3, 4, 6, 7, 8, 15, 16, 17, 18, 19, 20, 21, 22, 24, 26, 27, 28, 29, 30, 31, 32*** - Oak Island Tours (41); Lot ***5*** – Robert S. Young (61); Lots ***9, 10, 11, 12, 14*** – Fred Nolan (40); Lot ***13*** – John Johnston (25); Lot ***23*** – Dan/Dave Blankenship (07); and Lot ***25*** – Alan Kostrzewe (27). **– All Lots**
#30 Source - "*Oak Island Lot Ownership Map, 2007*," By MacPhie Archives. **All Lots**

Lot 10.

1753 - (12-27-1753) **Governor Charles Lawrence, to Capt. John Gifford (53) and Richard Smith (53) – ALL LOTS**
#123 Source - NS Archives and Record Management "Allotment" Book, P. 137, Reel #13044; "Old Book" #1, P. 44. Granted Gifford Island #12, Young Island #13, and Smith Island #28, to establish a fishery. Escheated.

1788 - (12-22-1788) **Anthony Vaughan (57), to Martin Marshall (30) – Lot 10**

#75 Source - Paul Wroclawski Research & Property Owners Charles Morris to John Smith; collected through 02-06-2008. 57>30 **– Lot 9 & 10**

1793 - (06-17-1793) **Martin Marshall (30), to Neil McMullen (35) – Lot 10**

#76 Source – Lunenburg Co. Land Deeds, recorded 07-15-1795, Vol. 4, P. 99, No. #123. 30>35 **– Lot 9 & 10**

#35 Source - "*Habitation on Oak Island*." Beaton Institute, Cape Breton University. Created by Surveyor William Dy Sr., called 'The Old Plan' No. 1046. Department of Lands & Forests, n.d. MG 12, 75 NSNA. Also Published in Joy Steele/Gordon Fader's book "*Oak Island Mystery Solved-Final Chapter*." P. 10. 2nd Ed. 2016.

1827 - (12-21-1827) **Neil McMullen (35), to Neil McMullen Smith (35a) – Lot 10**

#82 Source – Lunenburg Co. Land Deeds, recorded 12-27-1827, Vol. 9, P. 53. 35>35a **- Lot 9, 10, 11, 12, 13, 14**

1832 - (06-18-1832) **Neil McMullen Smith (35a), to Anthony T. Graves (19) – Lot 10**

#68 Source – Lunenburg Co. Land Deeds, recorded 10-11-1832, Vol. 10, P. 76, No. #101. 35a>19 **- Lots 9, 10, 11, 12, 13, 14**

1834 - (01-08-1834) **Anthony T. Graves (19), to Edward Foras (68) – Lot 10**

#125 Source – Chester Township Land Deeds, recorded 02-12-1834, Vol. 10, P. 323, No. #425. 19>68 **- Lots 5, 9, 10, 11, 12, 13, 14**

1839 - (02-14-1839) **Anthony T. Graves (19), to Frederick Zink (64) – Lot 10**

#71 Source - Paul Wroclawski Research & Property Owners Charles Morris to John Smith; collected through 02-06-2008.

#126 Source – Lunenburg Co. Land Deeds, Vol. 12, P. 21, No. #36. 19>64 **- Lots 5,9,10,11,12,13,14**

1841 - (03-29-1841) **Frederick Zink (64), to Anthony T. Graves (19) – Lot 10**

#127 Source - Lunenburg Co. Land Deeds, recorded 03-29-1841, Vol. 12, P. 210, No. #377. 64>19 **- Lots 5, 9,10, 11, 12, 13, 14**

1841 - (03-30-1841) **Anthony T. Graves (19), to John Strachan (54) – Lot 10**

#128 Source – Lunenburg Co. Land Deeds, recorded 04-07-1841, Vol. 12 P. 210, No. #378. 19>54 **- Lots 5, 9, 10, 11, 12, 13, 14**

1857 - John Strachan (54), to Anthony T. Graves (19) – Lot 10

1888 - Anthony T. Graves (19) dies, and Lots 5, 9, 10, 11, 12, 13, 14 15, 16, 17, 18, 19, 20 are inherited by Henry Sellers (19a) of which, 5, 9, 10, 11, 12, 13, 14 go to Selwyn William Sellers (19b), Henry's son. – Lot 10

#36 Source - "Notes on the Triton/Nolan Pact & Lawsuit, RE Ownership of Oak Island Lots." Unknown Source, 1971. 3 pages. **Lots 5, 9, 10, 11,12, 13, 14**

#37 Source - "*Oak Island Plan of Property Owned by Sellyn Sellers*." by wildlife artist, S. Edgar March. Chester Township Land Deeds, recorded 09-05-1935, Book 24, P.368. NSNA. **All Lots**

#170 Source – "*Selwyn William Sellers, 1873-1949*." FamilySearch, See citation.

1949 - (07-23-1949) **Selvyn Sellers (19b) dies, and Lots 5, 9, 10, 11, 12, 13, 14 disbursed amongst his heirs (all heirs) – Lot 10**

#36 Source - "Notes on the Triton/Nolan Pact & Lawsuit, RE Ownership of Oak Island Lots." Unknown Source, 1971. 3 pages. **Lots 5, 9, 10, 11,12, 13, 14**

1963 - Frederick Nolan (40), purchases Lots owned by Sellers (19a,b), Conrad (12,12a), & Corkum heirs (13a) – Lot 10

#36 Source - "Notes on the Triton/Nolan Pact & Lawsuit, RE Ownership of Oak Island Lots." Unknown Source, 1971. 3 pages. **Lots 5, 9, 10, 11,12, 13, 14**

1985 - (12-17-1985) **N.S. Supreme Court rules the Lots 5, 9, 10, 11, 12, 13, 14 are owned by Fred Nolan (40) – Lot 10**

#132a Source - Nova Scotia Supreme Court ruling, recorded 04-07-1986 at Bridgewater, N.S. 55,56><40 **- Lots 5, 9, 10, 11, 12, 13, 14**

2015 - Fred Nolan (40) dies, & property is transferred to son, Thomas Nolan (40a) –Lot 10

#900 Source – "*Frederick Gerald Nolan: 1927-2016*." Find-a-Grave. See citation.

#901 Source – "*Obituary for Frederick G. Nolan*." Halifax Funeral Home. See citation.

2007 - MacPhie Archives "*Oak Island Lot Distribution Map, 2007*." Lots ***1, 2, 3, 4, 6, 7, 8, 15, 16, 17, 18, 19, 20, 21, 22, 24, 26, 27, 28, 29, 30, 31, 32*** - Oak Island Tours (41); Lot ***5*** – Robert S. Young (61); Lots ***9, 10, 11, 12, 14*** – Fred Nolan (40); Lot ***13*** – John Johnston (25); Lot ***23*** – Dan/Dave Blankenship (07); and Lot ***25*** – Alan Kostrzewe (27). – **All Lots**

#30 Source - "*Oak Island Lot Ownership Map, 2007*," By MacPhie Archives. **All Lots**

Lot 11.

1753 - (12-27-1753) **Governor Charles Lawrence, to Capt. John Gifford (53) and Richard Smith (53) – ALL LOTS**

#123 Source - NS Archives and Record Management "Allotment" Book, P. 137, Reel #13044; "Old Book" #1, P. 44. Granted Gifford Island #12, Young Island #13, and Smith Island #28, to establish a fishery. Escheated.

1781 - James Webber (60), to Daniel Vaughan (57b) – Lot 11

#58 Source – Lunenburg Co. Land Deeds, recorded 10-27-1781, Vol. 2, P. 16, No. #25. 60>57b **- Lot 11**

#2 Source - Paul Wroclawski Research & Property Owners Charles Morris to John Smith; collected through 02-06-2008.

#57 Source – "*Daniel Vaughan, 1747-1808*." The Free Family Tree. See citation.

1789 - (10-26-1789) **Daniel Vaughan (57b), to Neil McMullen (35) – Lot 11**

#80 Source – Lunenburg Co. Land Deeds, recorded 05-25-1797, Vol. 4, P. 230, No. #374. 57b>35 **- Lot 11**

#35 Source - "*Habitation on Oak Island*." Beaton Institute, Cape Breton University. Created by Surveyor William Dy Sr., called 'The Old Plan' No. 1046. Department of Lands & Forests, n.d. MG 12, 75 NSNA. Also Published in Joy Steele/Gordon Fader's book "*Oak Island Mystery Solved-Final Chapter*." P. 10. 2nd Ed. 2016.

1827 - (12-21-1827) **Neil McMullen (35), to Neil McMullen Smith (35a) – Lot 11**

#82 Source – Lunenburg Co. Land Deeds, recorded 12-27-1827, Vol. 9, P. 53. 35>35a **- Lot 9, 10, 11, 12, 13, 14**

1832 - (06-18-1832) **Neil McMullen Smith (35a), to Anthony T. Graves (19) – Lot 11**

#68 Source – Lunenburg Co. Land Deeds, recorded 10-11-1832, Vol. 10, P. 76, No. #101. 35a>19 **- Lots 9, 10, 11, 12, 13, 14**

1834 - (01-08-1834) **Anthony T. Graves (19), to Edward Foras (68) – Lot 11**

#125 Source – Chester Township Land Deeds, recorded 02-12-1834, Vol. 10, P. 323, No. #425. 19>68 **- Lots 5, 9, 10, 11, 12, 13, 14**

1839 - (02-14-1839) **Anthony T. Graves (19), to Frederick Zink (64) – Lot 11**

#71 Source - Paul Wroclawski Research & Property Owners Charles Morris to John Smith; collected through 02-06-2008.

#126 Source – Lunenburg Co. Land Deeds, Vol. 12, P. 21, No. #36. 19>64 **- Lots 5,9,10,11,12,13,14**

1841 - (03-29-1841) **Frederick Zink (64), to Anthony T. Graves (19) – Lot 11**

#127 Source - Lunenburg Co. Land Deeds, recorded 03-29-1841, Vol. 12, P. 210, No. #377. 64>19 **- Lots 5, 9,10, 11, 12, 13, 14**

1841 - (03-30-1841) **Anthony T. Graves (19), to John Strachan (54) – Lot 11**

#128 Source – Lunenburg Co. Land Deeds, recorded 04-07-1841, Vol. 12 P. 210, No. #378. 19>54 **- Lots 5, 9, 10, 11, 12, 13, 14**

1857 - John Strachan (54), to Anthony T. Graves (19) – Lot 11

1888 - Anthony T. Graves (19) dies, and Lots 5, 9, 10, 11, 12, 13, 14 15, 16, 17, 18, 19, 20 are inherited by Henry Sellers (19a) of which, 5, 9, 10, 11, 12, 13, 14 go to Selwyn William Sellers (19b), Henry's son. – Lot 11

#36 Source - "Notes on the Triton/Nolan Pact & Lawsuit, RE Ownership of Oak Island Lots." Unknown Source, 1971. 3 pages. **Lots 5, 9, 10, 11,12, 13, 14**

#37 Source - "*Oak Island Plan of Property Owned by Sellyn Sellers*." by wildlife artist, S. Edgar March. Chester Township Land Deeds, recorded 09-05-1935, Book 24, P.368. NSNA. **All Lots**

#170 Source – "*Selwyn William Sellers, 1873-1949*." FamilySearch, See citation.

1949 - (07-23-1949) **Selvyn Sellers (19b) dies, and Lots 5, 9, 10, 11, 12, 13, 14 disbursed amongst his heirs (all heirs) – Lot 11**
#36 Source - "Notes on the Triton/Nolan Pact & Lawsuit, RE Ownership of Oak Island Lots." Unknown Source, 1971. 3 pages. **Lots 5, 9, 10, 11,12, 13, 14**

1963 - Frederick Nolan (40), purchases Lots owned by Sellers (19a,b), Conrad (12,12a), & Corkum heirs (13a) – Lot 11
#36 Source - "Notes on the Triton/Nolan Pact & Lawsuit, RE Ownership of Oak Island Lots." Unknown Source, 1971. 3 pages. **Lots 5, 9, 10, 11,12, 13, 14**

1985 - (12-17-1985) **N.S. Supreme Court rules the Lots 5, 9, 10, 11, 12, 13, 14 are owned by Fred Nolan (40) – Lot 11**
#132a Source - Nova Scotia Supreme Court ruling, recorded 04-07-1986 at Bridgewater, N.S. 55,56><40 **- Lots 5, 9, 10, 11, 12, 13, 14**

2015 - Fred Nolan (40) dies, & property transferred to son, Thomas J. Nolan (40a) –Lot 11
#900 Source – "*Frederick Gerald Nolan: 1927-2016*." Find-a-Grave. See citation.
#901 Source – "Obituary for Frederick G. Nolan." Halifax Funeral Home. See citation.

2007 - MacPhie Archives "*Oak Island Lot Distribution Map, 2007*." Lots ***1, 2, 3, 4, 6, 7, 8, 15, 16, 17, 18, 19, 20, 21, 22, 24, 26, 27, 28, 29, 30, 31, 32*** - Oak Island Tours (41); Lot ***5*** – Robert S. Young (61); Lots ***9, 10, 11, 12, 14*** – Fred Nolan (40); Lot ***13*** – John Johnston (25); Lot ***23*** – Dan/Dave Blankenship (07); and Lot ***25*** – Alan Kostrzewe (27). **– All Lots**
#30 Source - "Oak Island Lot Ownership Map, 2007," By MacPhie Archives. **All Lots**

Lot 12

1753 - (12-27-1753) **Governor Charles Lawrence, to Capt. John Gifford (53) and Richard Smith (53) – ALL LOTS**
#123 Source - NS Archives and Record Management "Allotment" Book, P. 137, Reel #13044; "Old Book" #1, P. 44. Granted Gifford Island #12, Young Island #13, and Smith Island #28, to establish a fishery. Escheated.

1780 - John Munro/Monrowe/Monro/etc. (39) – Lot 12 owns Lot in 1781 but unknown how.

1781 - (05-15-1781) **John Munro (39), to Robert Melvin Sr. (38) – Lot 12**
#96 Source – Lunenburg Co. Land Deeds, recorded 08-10-1790, Vol. 3, P. 425, No. #702. 39>38 **- Lot 12**
#35 Source - "*Habitation on Oak Island*." Beaton Institute, Cape Breton University. Created by Surveyor William Dy Sr., called 'The Old Plan' No. 1046. Department of Lands & Forests, n.d. MG 12, 75 NSNA. Also Published in Joy Steele/Gordon Fader's book "Oak Island Mystery Solved-Final Chapter." P. 10. 2nd Ed. 2016.

1787 - Robert Melvin Sr. (38) dies, lots transfer to family (38fam) – Lot 12

1827 - (12-21-1827) **Neil McMullen (35), to Neil McMullen Smith (35a) – Lot 12**
#82 Source – Lunenburg Co. Land Deeds, recorded 12-27-1827, Vol. 9, P. 53. 35>35a **- Lot 9, 10, 11, 12, 13, 14**

1832 - (06-18-1832) **Neil McMullen Smith (35a), to Anthony T. Graves (19) – Lot 12**
#68 Source – Lunenburg Co. Land Deeds, recorded 10-11-1832, Vol. 10, P. 76, No. #101. 35a>19 **- Lots 9, 10, 11, 12, 13, 14**

1834 - (01-08-1834) **Anthony T. Graves (19), to Edward Foras (68) – Lot 12**
#125 Source – Chester Township Land Deeds, recorded 02-12-1834, Vol. 10, P. 323, No. #425. 19>68 **- Lots 5, 9, 10, 11, 12, 13, 14**

1839 - (02-14-1839) **Anthony T. Graves (19), to Frederick Zink (64) – Lot 12**
#71 Source - Paul Wroclawski Research & Property Owners Charles Morris to John Smith; collected through 02-06-2008.
#126 Source – Lunenburg Co. Land Deeds, Vol. 12, P. 21, No. #36. 19>64 **- Lots 5,9,10,11,12,13,14**

1841 - (03-29-1841) **Frederick Zink (64), to Anthony T. Graves (19) – Lot 12**
#127 Source - Lunenburg Co. Land Deeds, recorded 03-29-1841, Vol. 12, P. 210, No. #377. 64>19 **- Lots 5, 9,10, 11, 12, 13, 14**

1841 - (03-30-1841) **Anthony T. Graves (19), to John Strachan (54) – Lot 12**
#128 Source – Lunenburg Co. Land Deeds, recorded 04-07-1841, Vol. 12 P. 210, No. #378. 19>54 **- Lots 5, 9, 10, 11, 12, 13, 14**

1857 - John Strachan (54), to Anthony T. Graves (19) – Lot 12

1888 - Anthony T. Graves (19) dies, and Lots 5, 9, 10, 11, 12, 13, 14 15, 16, 17, 18, 19, 20 are inherited by Henry Sellers (19a) of which, 5, 9, 10, 11, 12, 13, 14 go to Selwyn William Sellers (19b), Henry's son. – Lot 12

#36 Source - "Notes on the Triton/Nolan Pact & Lawsuit, RE Ownership of Oak Island Lots." Unknown Source, 1971. 3 pages. **Lots 5, 9, 10, 11,12, 13, 14**

#37 Source - "*Oak Island Plan of Property Owned by Sellyn Sellers*." by wildlife artist, S. Edgar March. Chester Township Land Deeds, recorded 09-05-1935, Book 24, P.368. NSNA. **All Lots**

#170 Source – "*Selwyn William Sellers, 1873-1949*." FamilySearch, See citation.

1949 - (07-23-1949) **Selvyn Sellers (19b) dies, and Lots 5, 9, 10, 11, 12, 13, 14 disbursed amongst his heirs (all heirs) – Lot 12**

#36 Source - "Notes on the Triton/Nolan Pact & Lawsuit, RE Ownership of Oak Island Lots." Unknown Source, 1971. 3 pages. **Lots 5, 9, 10, 11,12, 13, 14**

1963 - Frederick Nolan (40), purchases Lots owned by Sellers (19a,b), Conrad (12,12a), & Corkum heirs (13a) – Lot 12

#36 Source - "Notes on the Triton/Nolan Pact & Lawsuit, RE Ownership of Oak Island Lots." Unknown Source, 1971. 3 pages. **Lots 5, 9, 10, 11,12, 13, 14**

1985 - (12-17-1985) **N.S. Supreme Court rules the Lots 5, 9, 10, 11, 12, 13, 14 are owned by Fred Nolan (40) – Lot 12**

#132a Source - Nova Scotia Supreme Court ruling, recorded 04-07-1986 at Bridgewater, N.S. 55,56><40 **- Lots 5, 9, 10, 11, 12, 13, 14**

2007 - MacPhie Archives "*Oak Island Lot Distribution Map, 2007*." Lots ***1, 2, 3, 4, 6, 7, 8, 15, 16, 17, 18, 19, 20, 21, 22, 24, 26, 27, 28, 29, 30, 31, 32*** - Oak Island Tours (41); Lot ***5*** – Robert S. Young (61); Lots ***9, 10, 11, 12, 14*** – Fred Nolan (40); Lot ***13*** – John Johnston (25); Lot ***23*** – Dan/Dave Blankenship (07); and Lot ***25*** – Alan Kostrzewe (27). **– All Lots**

#30 Source - "*Oak Island Lot Ownership Map, 2007*," By MacPhie Archives. **All Lots**

2015 - Fred Nolan (40) dies, & property transferred to son, Thomas J. Nolan (40a) –Lot 12

#900 Source – "*Frederick Gerald Nolan: 1927-2016*." Find-a-Grave. See citation.

#901 Source – "*Obituary for Frederick G. Nolan*." Halifax Funeral Home. See citation.

Lot 13.

1753 - (12-27-1753) **Governor Charles Lawrence, to Capt. John Gifford (53) and Richard Smith (53) – ALL LOTS**

#123 Source - NS Archives and Record Management "Allotment" Book, P. 137, Reel #13044; "Old Book" #1, P. 44. Granted Gifford Island #12, Young Island #13, and Smith Island #28, to establish a fishery. Escheated.

1764 - "1765 Land Grant Participants (not on OI)." Received a Chester town Lot in 1764. No Records of OI Lot Ownership **– Lot 13**

#29 Source – "*History of Chester, 1759-1767*." W.I.N.S. Chester Branch.

1790 - (10-09-1790) **Daniel Vaughan (57b), to Nathaniel Melvin (38a) – Lot 13**

#85 Source – Lunenburg Co. Land Deeds, recorded 09-27-1790. Vol. 3, P. 447, No. #736. 57b>38a **Lot 13 & 14**

1806 - (07-15-1806) **Nathaniel Melvin (38a), to Neil McMullen (35) – Lot 13**

#81 Source – Lunenburg Co. Land Deeds, recorded 07-15-1806, Vol. 6, P. 675, No. #690. 38a>35 **- Lot 13 & 14**

#25/26 Source – "*2-Page Oak Island Lot Ownership Map, Jul. 6, 1818*." And "*Old Plan Map of Oak Island 1818*." By David W. Crandell Survey Map. NSNA. **Lots 13, 14, 15, 16, 17, 18**

#35 Source - "*Habitation on Oak Island*." Beaton Institute, Cape Breton University. Created by Surveyor William Dy Sr., called 'The Old Plan' No. 1046. Department of Lands & Forests, n.d. MG 12, 75 NSNA. Also Published in Joy Steele/Gordon Fader's book "*Oak Island Mystery Solved-Final Chapter*." P. 10. 2nd Ed. 2016.

1827 - (12-21-1827) **Neil McMullen (35), to Neil McMullen Smith (35a) – Lot 13**

#82 Source – Lunenburg Co. Land Deeds, recorded 12-27-1827, Vol. 9, P. 53. 35>35a **- Lot 9, 10, 11, 12, 13, 14**

1832 - (06-18-1832) **Neil McMullen Smith (35a), to Anthony T. Graves (19) – Lot 13**
#68 Source – Lunenburg Co. Land Deeds, recorded 10-11-1832, Vol. 10, P. 76, No. #101. 35a>19 **- Lots 9, 10, 11, 12, 13, 14**

1834 - (01-08-1834) **Anthony T. Graves (19), to Edward Foras (68) – Lot 13**
#125 Source – Chester Township Land Deeds, recorded 02-12-1834, Vol. 10, P. 323, No. #425. 19>68 **- Lots 5, 9, 10, 11, 12, 13, 14**

1839 - (02-14-1839) **Anthony T. Graves (19), to Frederick Zink (64) includes Lots 5, 9, 10, 11, 12, 13, 14 – Lot 13**
#71 Source – Paul Wroclawski Research & Property Owners Charles Morris to John Smith; collected through 02-06-2008.
#126 Source – Lunenburg Co. Land Deeds, Vol. 12, P. 21, No. #36. 19>64 **- Lots 5,9,10,11,12,13,14**

1841 - (03-29-1841) **Frederick Zink (64), to Anthony T. Graves (19) – Lot 13**
#127 Source - Lunenburg Co. Land Deeds, recorded 03-29-1841, Vol. 12, P. 210, No. #377. 64>19 **- Lots 5, 9,10, 11, 12, 13, 14**

1841 - (03-30-1841) **Anthony T. Graves (19), to John Strachan (54) – Lot 13**
#128 Source – Lunenburg Co. Land Deeds, recorded 04-07-1841, Vol. 12 P. 210, No. #378. 19>54 **- Lots 5, 9, 10, 11, 12, 13, 14**

1857 - John Strachan (54), to Anthony T. Graves (19) – Lot 13

1888 - Anthony T. Graves (19) dies, and Lots 5, 9, 10, 11, 12, 13, 14 15, 16, 17, 18, 19, 20 are inherited by Henry Sellers (19a) of which, 5, 9, 10, 11, 12, 13, 14 go to Selwyn William Sellers (19b), Henry's son. – Lot 13
#36 Source - "Notes on the Triton/Nolan Pact & Lawsuit, RE Ownership of Oak Island Lots." Unknown Source, 1971. 3 pages. **Lots 5, 9, 10, 11,12, 13, 14**
#37 Source - "*Oak Island Plan of Property Owned by Sellyn Sellers*." by wildlife artist, S. Edgar March. Chester Township Land Deeds, recorded 09-05-1935, Book 24, P.368. NSNA. **All Lots**
#170 Source – "*Selwyn William Sellers, 1873-1949*." FamilySearch, See citation.

1949 - (07-23-1949) **Selvyn Sellers (19b) dies, and Lots 5, 9, 10, 11, 12, 13, 14 disbursed amongst his heirs (all heirs) – Lot 13**
#36 Source - "Notes on the Triton/Nolan Pact & Lawsuit, RE Ownership of Oak Island Lots." Unknown Source, 1971. 3 pages. **Lots 5, 9, 10, 11,12, 13, 14**

1963 - Frederick Nolan (40), purchases Lots owned by Sellers (19a,b), Conrad (12,12a), & Corkum heirs (13a) – Lot 13
#36 Source - "Notes on the Triton/Nolan Pact & Lawsuit, RE Ownership of Oak Island Lots." Unknown Source, 1971. 3 pages. **Lots 5, 9, 10, 11,12, 13, 14**

1985 - (12-17-1985) **N.S. Supreme Court rules the Lots 5, 9, 10, 11, 12, 13, 14 are owned by Fred Nolan (40) – Lot 13**
#132a Source - Nova Scotia Supreme Court ruling, recorded 04-07-1986 at Bridgewater, N.S. 55,56><40 **- Lots 5, 9, 10, 11, 12, 13, 14**

2007 - **MacPhie Archives "*Oak Island Lot Distribution Map, 2007*."** Lots ***1, 2, 3, 4, 6, 7, 8, 15, 16, 17, 18, 19, 20, 21, 22, 24, 26, 27, 28, 29, 30, 31, 32*** - Oak Island Tours (41); Lot ***5*** – Robert S. Young (61); Lots ***9, 10, 11, 12, 14*** – Fred Nolan (40); Lot ***13*** – John Johnston (25); Lot ***23*** – Dan/Dave Blankenship (07); and Lot ***25*** – Alan Kostrzewe (27). **– All Lots**
#30 Source - "*Oak Island Lot Ownership Map, 2007*," By MacPhie Archives. **All Lots**

2015 - Fred Nolan (40) dies, & property transferred to son, Thomas J. Nolan (40a) –Lot 13
#900 Source – "*Frederick Gerald Nolan: 1927-2016*." Find-a-Grave. See citation.
#901 Source – "*Obituary for Frederick G. Nolan*." Halifax Funeral Home. See citation.

Lot 14.

1753 - (12-27-1753) **Governor Charles Lawrence, to Capt. John Gifford (53) and Richard Smith (53) – ALL LOTS**
#123 Source - "*The Life and Administration of Governor Charles Lawrence 1749-1760*." Granted Smith Island [#28 – Oak Island] to establish a fishery. Escheated.

1781 - **James Webber (60), to Daniel Vaughan (57b) – Lot 14**
#58 Source – Lunenburg Co. Land Deeds, recorded 10-27-1781, Vol. 2, P. 16, No. #25. **- Lot 14**

1790 - (10-09-1790) **Daniel Vaughan (57b), to Nathaniel Melvin (38a) – Lot 14**
#85 Source – Lunenburg Co. Land Deeds, recorded 09-27-1790. Vol. 3, P. 447, No. #736. 57b>38a **Lot 13 & 14**

1806 - (07-05-1806) **Nathaniel Melvin (38a), to Neil McMullen (35) – Lot 14**
#81 Source – Lunenburg Co. Land Deeds, recorded 07-15-1806, Vol. 6, P. 675, No. #690. 38a>35 **- Lot 13 & 14**
#2 Source - Paul Wroclawski Research & Property Owners Charles Morris to John Smith; collected through 02-06-2008.

1827 - (12-21-1827) **Neil McMullen (35), to Neil McMullen Smith (35a) – Lot 14**
#82 Source – Lunenburg Co. Land Deeds, recorded 12-27-1827, Vol. 9, P. 53. 35>35a **- Lot 9, 10, 11, 12, 13, 14**

1832 - (06-18-1832) **Neil McMullen Smith (35a), to Anthony T. Graves (19) – Lot 14**
#68 Source – Lunenburg Co. Land Deeds, recorded 10-11-1832, Vol. 10, P. 76, No. #101. 35a>19 **- Lots 9, 10, 11, 12, 13, 14**

1834 - (01-08-1834) **Anthony T. Graves (19), to Edward Foras (68) – Lot 14**
#125 Source – Chester Township Land Deeds, recorded 02-12-1834, Vol. 10, P. 323, No. #425. 19>68 **- Lots 5, 9, 10, 11, 12, 13, 14**

1839 - (02-14-1839) **Anthony T. Graves (19), to Frederick Zink (64) – Lot 14**
#71 Source - Paul Wroclawski Research & Property Owners Charles Morris to John Smith; collected through 02-06-2008.
#126 Source – Lunenburg Co. Land Deeds, Vol. 12, P. 21, No. #36. 19>64 **- Lots 5,9,10,11,12,13,14**

1841 - (03-29-1841) **Frederick Zink (64), to Anthony T. Graves (19) – Lot 14**
#127 Source - Lunenburg Co. Land Deeds, recorded 03-29-1841, Vol. 12, P. 210, No. #377. 64>19 **- Lots 5, 9,10, 11, 12, 13, 14**

1841 - (03-30-1841) **Anthony T. Graves (19), to John Strachan (54) – Lot 14**
#128 Source – Lunenburg Co. Land Deeds, recorded 04-07-1841, Vol. 12 P. 210, No. #378. 19>54 **- Lots 5, 9, 10, 11, 12, 13, 14**

1857 - **John Strachan (54), to Anthony T. Graves (19) – Lot 14**

1888 - **Anthony T. Graves (19) dies, and Lots 5, 9, 10, 11, 12, 13, 14 15, 16, 17, 18, 19, 20 are inherited by Henry Sellers (19a) of which, 5, 9, 10, 11, 12, 13, 14 go to Selwyn William Sellers (19b), Henry's son. – Lot 14**
#36 Source - "Notes on the Triton/Nolan Pact & Lawsuit, RE Ownership of Oak Island Lots." Unknown Source, 1971. 3 pages. **Lots 5, 9, 10, 11,12, 13, 14**
#37 Source - "*Oak Island Plan of Property Owned by Sellyn Sellers*." by wildlife artist, S. Edgar March. Chester Township Land Deeds, recorded 09-05-1935, Book 24, P.368. NSNA. **All Lots**
#170 Source – "*Selwyn William Sellers, 1873-1949*." FamilySearch, See citation.

1949 - (07-23-1949) **Selvyn Sellers (19b) dies, and Lots 5, 9, 10, 11, 12, 13, 14 disbursed amongst his heirs (all heirs) – Lot 14**
#36 Source - "Notes on the Triton/Nolan Pact & Lawsuit, RE Ownership of Oak Island Lots." Unknown Source, 1971. 3 pages. **Lots 5, 9, 10, 11,12, 13, 14**

1963 - **Frederick Nolan (40), purchases Lots owned by Sellers (19a,b), Conrad (12,12a), & Corkum heirs (13a) – Lot 14**
#36 Source - "Notes on the Triton/Nolan Pact & Lawsuit, RE Ownership of Oak Island Lots." Unknown Source, 1971. 3 pages. **Lots 5, 9, 10, 11,12, 13, 14**

1985 - (12-17-1985) **N.S. Supreme Court rules the Lots 5, 9, 10, 11, 12, 13, 14 are owned by Fred Nolan (40) – Lot 14**
#132a Source - Nova Scotia Supreme Court ruling, recorded 04-07-1986 at Bridgewater, N.S. 55,56><40 **- Lots 5, 9, 10, 11, 12, 13, 14**

2007 - **MacPhie Archives "*Oak Island Lot Distribution Map, 2007*."** Lots ***1, 2, 3, 4, 6, 7, 8, 15, 16, 17, 18, 19, 20, 21, 22, 24, 26, 27, 28, 29, 30, 31, 32*** - Oak Island Tours (41); Lot ***5*** – Robert S. Young (61); Lots ***9, 10, 11, 12, 14*** – Fred Nolan (40); Lot ***13*** – John Johnston (25); Lot ***23*** – Dan/Dave Blankenship (07); and Lot ***25*** – Alan Kostrzewe (27). **– All Lots**
#30 Source - "*Oak Island Lot Ownership Map, 2007*," By MacPhie Archives. **All Lots**

2015 - Fred Nolan (40) dies, & property transferred to son, Thomas J. Nolan (40a) –Lot 14
#900 Source – "*Frederick Gerald Nolan: 1927-2016*." Find-a-Grave. See citation.
#901 Source – "*Obituary for Frederick G. Nolan*." Halifax Funeral Home. See citation.

Lot 15.

1753 - (12-27-1753) **Governor Charles Lawrence, to Capt. John Gifford (53) and Richard Smith (53) – ALL LOTS**
#123 Source - NS Archives and Record Management "Allotment" Book, P. 137, Reel #13044; "Old Book" #1, P. 44. Granted Gifford Island #12, Young Island #13, and Smith Island #28, to establish a fishery. Escheated.

1818 - Granted by Crown (00), to David Crandell (14) – Lot 15
#25/26 Source – "*2-Page Oak Island Lot Ownership Map, Jul. 6, 1818*." And "*Old Plan Map of Oak Island 1818*." By David W. Crandell Survey Map. NSNA. **Lots 13, 14, 15, 16, 17, 18**
#34 Source – "*Nova Scotia Land Papers: 1795-1800, Green James and Others*." 1784 – Lunenburg County. 37,950 acres granted in Chester, including License to Occupy, Memorial, Warrant to Survey, Surveyor's Report & Surveyor's Certificate. See citation.
00>14 **- Lot 15**

1819 - (06-10-1819) **David Crandell (14), to John Smith (51a) – Lot 15**
#103 Source – Lunenburg Co. Land Deeds, recorded 1820, Vol. 7, P. 413-414. 14>51a **- Lot 15**
#25/26 Source – "*2-Page Oak Island Lot Ownership Map, Jul. 6, 1818*." And "*Old Plan Map of Oak Island 1818*." By David W. Crandell Survey Map. NSNA. **Lots 13, 14, 15, 16, 17, 18**
#35 Source - "*Habitation on Oak Island*." Beaton Institute, Cape Breton University. Created by Surveyor William Dy Sr., called 'The Old Plan' No. 1046. Department of Lands & Forests, n.d. MG 12, 75 NSNA. Also Published in Joy Steele/Gordon Fader's book "*Oak Island Mystery Solved-Final Chapter*." P. 10. 2nd Ed. 2016.

1852 - John Smith (51a) dies. Lots 15, 16, 17, 18, 19, 20 willed to Joseph Smith (51b) and Thomas E. Smith (51c) – Lot 15
#4 Source - Probate Registry at Lunenburg & Registrar of Deeds in Bridgewater, Book, 16, P. 485; Book 21, P. 114, No. #173. **– Lots 15, 16, 17, 18, 19, 20**

1853 - (03-29-1853) **Heirs Joseph Smith (51b) & Thomas E. Smith (51c), sell Lots 15, 16, 17, 18, 19, 20 to Anthony Graves (19) – Lot 15**
#4 Source - Probate Registry at Lunenburg & Registrar of Deeds in Bridgewater, Book, 16, P. 485; Book 21, P. 114, No. #173. **– Lots 15, 16, 17, 18, 19, 20**

1887 - (07-14-1887) **Anthony Graves (19) dies, Estate property of Lots 5, 9, 10, 11, 12, 13, 14, 15, 16, 17, 18, 19, 20 split, with 15, 16, 17, 18, 19, 20 staying with Henry Sellers (19a) – Lot 15**
#4 Source - Probate Registry at Lunenburg & Registrar of Deeds in Bridgewater, Book, 16, P. 485; Book 21, P. 114, No. #173. **– Lots 15, 16, 17, 18, 19, 20**

1912 - Henry Sellers (19a) dies, his Lots 6, 7, 8, 15, 16, 17, 18, 19, 20, 25, 26, 30, 31, 32 divided into shares with inheritors. See following deeds/court probates – Lot 15
#4 Source - Probate Registry at Lunenburg & Registrar of Deeds in Bridgewater, Book, 16, P. 485; Book 21, P. 114, No. #173. **– Lots 15, 16, 17, 18, 19, 20**
#5 Source - Dominion Canada and Lunenburg Co. Land Deeds, Book No. 21, P. 114-115, No. #174. (originally filed at Bridgewater N.S. Book No. 16, P. 485). NSNA. **– Lots 15, 16, 17, 18, 19, 20**
#6 Source - Dominion Canada and Lunenburg Co. Land Deeds, Book No. 21, P. 115-116, No. #175. Selling party includes Ruby E. Corkum, Wilfred & Audrey W. Corkum, Henry & Mary L. Corkum, and single adults Flora Corkum & Ross Corkum. NSNA. **– Lots 15, 16, 17, 18, 19, 20**
#7 Source - Dominion Canada and Lunenburg Co. Land Deeds, Book No. 21, P. 184, No. #295. (originally filed at Bridgewater, N.S., Book No. 16, P. 485) NSNA. **– Lots 15, 16, 17, 18, 19, 20**
#8 Source - Prothonotary of Nova Scotia Supreme Court in Lunenburg, file No. #3196, recorded on 02-03-1936, Book No. 21, P. 185-186, No. #297. NSNA. **– Lot 15, 16, 17, 18, 19, 20**

1935 - (07-27-1935) **Selvyn & Bessie Sellers heirs (19b), to George Grimm Jr. (20) – Lot 15**
#4 Source - Probate Registry at Lunenburg & Registrar of Deeds in Bridgewater, Book, 16, *P. 485; Book 21, P. 114, No. #173.* 19b>20 ***– Lots 15, 16, 17, 18, 19, 20***

1935 - (07-27-1935) **Erdie Powers (44), to George W. Grimm Jr. (20) – Lot 15**
#5 Source - Dominion Canada and Lunenburg Co. Land Deeds, Book No. 21, P. 114-115, No. #174. (originally filed at Bridgewater N.S. Book No. 16, P. 485). NSNA. 44>20 – **Lots 15, 16, 17, 18, 19, 20**

1935 - (07-27-1935) **Burnell & Hazel Corkum, et. al (13), to George Grimm Jr. (20) – Lot 15**
#6 Source - Dominion Canada and Lunenburg Co. Land Deeds, Book No. 21, P. 115-116, No. #175. Selling party includes Ruby E. Corkum, Wilfred & Audrey W. Corkum, Henry & Mary L. Corkum, and single adults Flora Corkum & Ross Corkum. NSNA. 13>20 – **Lots 15, 16, 17, 18, 19, 20**

1935 - (07-27-1935) **Genevieve & Wilbert Walls (59), to George W. Grimm Jr. (20) – Lot 15**
#7 Source - Dominion Canada and Lunenburg Co. Land Deeds, Book No. 21, P. 184, No. #295. (originally filed at Bridgewater, N.S., Book No. 16, P. 485) NSNA. 59>20 – **Lots 15, 16, 17, 18, 19, 20**

1935 - (07-27-1935) **Burnell Corkum, Guardian of Andrew & Hope Corkum (13), to George Grimm Jr. (20) – Lot 15**
#8 Source - Prothonotary of Nova Scotia Supreme Court in Lunenburg, file No. #3196, recorded on 02-03-1936, Book No. 21, P. 185-186, No. #297. NSNA. 13a>20 – **Lot 15, 16, 17, 18, 19, 20**

1949 - George W. Grimm Jr. (20), to Gilbert D. Hedden (22) lots 15, 16, 17, 18, 19, 20, - Lot 15
#13 Source – Dominion of Canada Book No. #693, NSNA. **- Lots 6, 7, 8, 15, 16, 17, 18, 19, 20, 25, 26, 30, 32** [Lot 31 missing]

1950 - (05-26-1950) **Gilbert D. Hedden & Margarite C. Hedden (22), Lots 6, 7, 8, 25, 26, 30, 31*, 32, & 15, 16, 17, 18, 19, 20 to John Whitney Lewis (10a) – Lot 15**
#13 Source – Dominion of Canada Book No. #693, NSNA. 22>10a **- Lots 6, 7, 8, 15, 16, 17, 18, 19, 20, 25, 26, 30, 32** [Lot 31 missing]

1950 - (12-05-1950) **John Whitney Lewis & Ann Lewis (10a), Lots 6, 7, 8, 15, 16, 17, 18, 19, 20, 25, 26*, 30, 31, 32 to Acadia Trust Company (10b) – Lot 15**
#14 Source - Dominion of Canada, NSNA #880. (original filings list – see citation). 10a>10b **- Lot 6, 7, 8, 15, 16, 17, 18, 19, 20, 25, 30, 31, 32** [Lot 26 missing]

1957 - (04-20-1957) **Acadia Trust Company (10b), Lots 6, 7, 8, 15, 16, 17, 18, 19, 20, 25, 26, 30, 31, 32 to M.R. Chappell (10) – Lot 15**
#15 Source - Registry of Deeds at Bridgewater and Registry of Probate, Book 26, P. 195, Quit Claim No. 374, NSNA. 10b>10 **- Lot 6, 7, 8, 15, 16, 17, 18, 19, 20, 25, 26, 30, 31, 32**

1961 - (07-21-1961) **Mary Ellen Chapman (09) & heirs of Clarence J. Beamish (04), to M.R. Chappell, Lots 5, 6, 7, 8, 15, 16, 17, 18, 19, 20, 23, 25, 26, 30, 31, 32 (10) – Lot 15**
#16 Source - Nova Scotia Supreme Court Book 27, P. 339, No. #638. NSNA. Represent heirs shares of "South & West part Oak Island," "George McInnis Property," and "James McInnis Property." 07-20-1961. 09,04>10 **- Lot 6, 7, 8, 15, 16, 17, 18, 19, 20, 23, 25, 26, 30, 31, 32**

1977 - (06-15-1977) **Melbourne R. Chappell (10), to David C. Tobias (55) – Lot 15**
#20 Source – Filed in Halifax Co. Land Deeds, recorded on 06-29-1977, No. #582. NSNA. 10>55 **- Lots 6, 7, 8, 15, 16, 17, 18, 19, 20, 25, 26, 30, 31, 32**

1987 - (12-09-1987) **David Tobias (55) and his lots, join Dan Blankenship (07) to form Oak Island Tours Inc (41) – Lot 15**
#111 Source – "*The Open Database of the Corporate World. Oak Island Tours Inc. Company Number 2272393*." Incorporated Date, 12-09-1987. Opencorporates.
#112 Source – "*The Curse of Oak Island, The Story of the World's Longest Treasure Hunt*." By Randall Sullivan, 2018. Page 422.

2007 - David Tobias (55), sells his Lots to Rick & Marty Lagina who become equal partners with Dan Blankenship (07) in Oak Island Tours (41) which own/control Lots 1, 2, 3, 4, 6, 7, 8, 15, 16, 17, 18, 19, 20, 21, 22, 24, 26, 27, 28, 29, 30, 31, 32. – Lot 15
#111 Source – "*The Open Database of the Corporate World. Oak Island Tours Inc. Company Number 2272393*." Incorporated Date, 12-09-1987. Opencorporates.
#112 Source – "*The Curse of Oak Island, The Story of the World's Longest Treasure Hunt*." By Randall Sullivan, 2018. Page 422.

2007 - MacPhie Archives "*Oak Island Lot Distribution Map, 2007*." Lots ***1, 2, 3, 4, 6, 7, 8, 15, 16, 17, 18, 19, 20, 21, 22, 24, 26, 27, 28, 29, 30, 31, 32*** - Oak Island Tours (41); Lot ***5*** – Robert S. Young (61); Lots ***9, 10, 11, 12, 14*** – Fred Nolan (40); Lot ***13*** – John Johnston (25); Lot ***23*** – Dan/Dave Blankenship (07); and Lot ***25*** – Alan Kostrzewe (27). **– All Lots**

#30 Source - "*Oak Island Lot Ownership Map, 2007*," By MacPhie Archives. **All Lots**

Lot 16.

1753 - (12-27-1753) **Governor Charles Lawrence, to Capt. John Gifford (53) and Richard Smith (53) – ALL LOTS**

#123 Source - NS Archives and Record Management "Allotment" Book, P. 137, Reel #13044; "Old Book" #1, P. 44. Granted Gifford Island #12, Young Island #13, and Smith Island #28, to establish a fishery. Escheated.

1768 - (10-31-1768) **Mary Malay / Jesse (Joseph) White (29) drew lot – Lot 16**

#2 Source - Paul Wroclawski Research & Property Owners Charles Morris to John Smith; collected through 02-06-2008.

#34 Source – "*Nova Scotia Land Papers: 1795-1800, Green James and Others*." 1784 – Lunenburg County. 37,950 acres granted in Chester, including License to Occupy, Memorial, Warrant to Survey, Surveyor's Report & Surveyor's Certificate. See citation. 00>29 **- Lot 16**

1798 - (01-20-1798) **Mary Malay (29), to John Smith (51a) – Lot 16**

#74 Source – Lunenburg Co. Land Deeds, recorded 03-09-1799, Vol. 4, P. 369, No. #539. 29>51a **- Lot 16**

#25/26 Source – "*2-Page Oak Island Lot Ownership Map, Jul. 6, 1818*." And "*Old Plan Map of Oak Island 1818*." By David W. Crandell Survey Map. NSNA. **Lots 13, 14, 15, 16, 17, 18**

#35 Source - "*Habitation on Oak Island*." Beaton Institute, Cape Breton University. Created by Surveyor William Dy Sr., called 'The Old Plan' No. 1046. Department of Lands & Forests, n.d. MG 12, 75 NSNA. Also Published in Joy Steele/Gordon Fader's book "*Oak Island Mystery Solved-Final Chapter*." P. 10. 2nd Ed. 2016.

1852 - John Smith (51a) dies. Lots 15, 16, 17, 18, 19, 20 willed to Joseph Smith (51b) and Thomas E. Smith (51c) – Lot 16

#4 Source - Probate Registry at Lunenburg & Registrar of Deeds in Bridgewater, Book, 16, P. 485; Book 21, P. 114, No. #173. **– Lots 15, 16, 17, 18, 19, 20**

1853 - (03-29-1853) **Heirs Joseph Smith (51b) & Thomas E. Smith (51c), sell Lots 15, 16, 17, 18, 19, 20 to Anthony Graves (19) – Lot 16**

#4 Source - Probate Registry at Lunenburg & Registrar of Deeds in Bridgewater, Book, 16, P. 485; Book 21, P. 114, No. #173. **– Lots 15, 16, 17, 18, 19, 20**

1887 - (07-14-1887) **Anthony Graves (19) dies, Estate property of Lots 5, 9, 10, 11, 12, 13, 14, 15, 16, 17, 18, 19, 20 split, with 15, 16, 17, 18, 19, 20 staying with Henry Sellers (19a) – Lot 16**

#4 Source - Probate Registry at Lunenburg & Registrar of Deeds in Bridgewater, Book, 16, P. 485; Book 21, P. 114, No. #173. **– Lots 15, 16, 17, 18, 19, 20**

1912 - Henry Sellers (19a) dies, his Lots 6, 7, 8, 15, 16, 17, 18, 19, 20, 25, 26, 30, 31, 32 divided into shares with inheritors. See following deeds/court probates – Lot 16

#4 Source - Probate Registry at Lunenburg & Registrar of Deeds in Bridgewater, Book, 16, P. 485; Book 21, P. 114, No. #173. **– Lots 15, 16, 17, 18, 19, 20**

#5 Source - Dominion Canada and Lunenburg Co. Land Deeds, Book No. 21, P. 114-115, No. #174. (originally filed at Bridgewater N.S. Book No. 16, P. 485). NSNA. **– Lots 15, 16, 17, 18, 19, 20**

#6 Source - Dominion Canada and Lunenburg Co. Land Deeds, Book No. 21, P. 115-116, No. #175. Selling party includes Ruby E. Corkum, Wilfred & Audrey W. Corkum, Henry & Mary L. Corkum, and single adults Flora Corkum & Ross Corkum. NSNA. **– Lots 15, 16, 17, 18, 19, 20**

#7 Source - Dominion Canada and Lunenburg Co. Land Deeds, Book No. 21, P. 184, No. #295. (originally filed at Bridgewater, N.S., Book No. 16, P. 485) NSNA. **– Lots 15, 16, 17, 18, 19, 20**

#8 Source - Prothonotary of Nova Scotia Supreme Court in Lunenburg, file No. #3196, recorded on 02-03-1936, Book No. 21, P. 185-186, No. #297. NSNA. **– Lot 15, 16, 17, 18, 19, 20**

1935 - (07-27-1935) **Selvyn & Bessie Sellers heirs (19b), to George Grimm Jr. (20) – Lot 16**
#4 Source - Probate Registry at Lunenburg & Registrar of Deeds in Bridgewater, Book, 16, *P. 485; Book 21, P. 114, No. #173. 19b>20 – **Lots 15, 16, 17, 18, 19, 20***

1935 - (07-27-1935) **Erdie Powers (44), to George W. Grimm Jr. (20) – Lot 16**
#5 Source - Dominion Canada and Lunenburg Co. Land Deeds, Book No. 21, P. 114-115, No. #174. (originally filed at Bridgewater N.S. Book No. 16, P. 485). NSNA. 44>20 – **Lots 15, 16, 17, 18, 19, 20**

1935 - (07-27-1935) **Burnell & Hazel Corkum, et. al (13), to George Grimm Jr. (20) – Lot 16**
#6 Source - Dominion Canada and Lunenburg Co. Land Deeds, Book No. 21, P. 115-116, No. #175. Selling party includes Ruby E. Corkum, Wilfred & Audrey W. Corkum, Henry & Mary L. Corkum, and single adults Flora Corkum & Ross Corkum. NSNA. 13>20 – **Lots 15, 16, 17, 18, 19, 20**

1935 - (07-27-1935) **Genevieve & Wilbert Walls (59), to George W. Grimm Jr. (20) – Lot 16**
#7 Source - Dominion Canada and Lunenburg Co. Land Deeds, Book No. 21, P. 184, No. #295. (originally filed at Bridgewater, N.S., Book No. 16, P. 485) NSNA. 59>20 – **Lots 15, 16, 17, 18, 19, 20**

1935 - (07-27-1935) **Burnell Corkum, Guardian of Andrew & Hope Corkum (13), to George Grimm Jr. (20) – Lot 16**
#8 Source - Prothonotary of Nova Scotia Supreme Court in Lunenburg, file No. #3196, recorded on 02-03-1936, Book No. 21, P. 185-186, No. #297. NSNA. 13>20 – **Lot 15, 16, 17, 18, 19, 20**

1949 - George W. Grimm Jr. (20), to Gilbert D. Hedden (22) lots 15, 16, 17, 18, 19, 20, - Lot 16
#13 Source – Dominion of Canada Book No. #693, NSNA. - **Lots 6, 7, 8, 15, 16, 17, 18, 19, 20, 25, 26, 30, 32** [Lot 31 missing]

1950 - (05-26-1950) **Gilbert D. Hedden & Margarite C. Hedden (22), Lots 6, 7, 8, 25, 26, 30, 31*, 32, & 15, 16, 17, 18, 19, 20 to John Whitney Lewis (10a) – Lot 16**
#13 Source – Dominion of Canada Book No. #693, NSNA. 22>10a - **Lots 6, 7, 8, 15, 16, 17, 18, 19, 20, 25, 26, 30, 32** [Lot 31 missing]

1950 - (12-05-1950) **John Whitney Lewis & Ann Lewis (10a), Lots 6, 7, 8, 15, 16, 17, 18, 19, 20, 25, 26*, 30, 31, 32 to Acadia Trust Company (10b) – Lot 16**
#14 Source - Dominion of Canada, NSNA #880. (original filings list – see citation). 10a>10b - **Lot 6, 7, 8, 15, 16, 17, 18, 19, 20, 25, 30, 31, 32** [Lot 26 missing]

1957 - (04-20-1957) **Acadia Trust Company (10b), Lots 6, 7, 8, 15, 16, 17, 18, 19, 20, 25, 26, 30, 31, 32 to M.R. Chappell (10) – Lot 16**
#15 Source - Registry of Deeds at Bridgewater and Registry of Probate, Book 26, P. 195, Quit Claim No. 374, NSNA. 10b>10 - **Lot 6, 7, 8, 15, 16, 17, 18, 19, 20, 25, 26, 30, 31, 32**

1961 - (07-21-1961) **Mary Ellen Chapman (09) & heirs of Clarence J. Beamish (04), to M.R. Chappell, Lots 5, 6, 7, 8, 15, 16, 17, 18, 19, 20, 23, 25, 26, 30, 31, 32 (10) – Lot 16**
#16 Source - Nova Scotia Supreme Court Book 27, P. 339, No. #638. NSNA. Represent heirs shares of "South & West part Oak Island," "George McInnis Property," and "James McInnis Property." 07-20-1961. 09, 04>10 - **Lot 6, 7, 8, 15, 16, 17, 18, 19, 20, 23, 25, 26, 30, 31, 32**

1977 - (06-15-1977) **Melbourne R. Chappell (10), to David C. Tobias (55) – Lot 16**
#20 Source – Filed in Halifax Co. Land Deeds, recorded on 06-29-1977, No. #582. NSNA. 10>55 - **Lots 6, 7, 8, 15, 16, 17, 18, 19, 20, 25, 26, 30, 31, 32**

1987 - (12-09-1987) **David Tobias (55) and his lots, join Dan Blankenship (07) to form Oak Island Tours Inc (41) – Lot 16**
#111 Source – "*The Open Database of the Corporate World. Oak Island Tours Inc. Company Number 2272393*." Incorporated Date, 12-09-1987. Opencorporates.
#112 Source – "*The Curse of Oak Island, The Story of the World's Longest Treasure Hunt*." By Randall Sullivan, 2018. Page 422.

2007 - David Tobias (55), sells his Lots to Rick & Marty Lagina who become equal partners with Dan Blankenship (07) in Oak Island Tours (41) which own/control Lots 1, 2, 3, 4, 6, 7, 8, 15, 16, 17, 18, 19, 20, 21, 22, 24, 26, 27, 28, 29, 30, 31, 32. – Lot 16
#111 Source – "*The Open Database of the Corporate World. Oak Island Tours Inc. Company Number 2272393*." Incorporated Date, 12-09-1987. Opencorporates.
#112 Source – "*The Curse of Oak Island, The Story of the World's Longest Treasure Hunt*." By Randall Sullivan, 2018. Page 422.

2007 - MacPhie Archives "*Oak Island Lot Distribution Map, 2007*." Lots ***1, 2, 3, 4, 6, 7, 8, 15, 16, 17, 18, 19, 20, 21, 22, 24, 26, 27, 28, 29, 30, 31, 32*** - Oak Island Tours (41); Lot ***5*** – Robert S. Young (61); Lots ***9, 10, 11, 12, 14*** – Fred Nolan (40); Lot ***13*** – John Johnston (25); Lot ***23*** – Dan/Dave Blankenship (07); and Lot ***25*** – Alan Kostrzewe (27). – **All Lots**

#30 Source - "*Oak Island Lot Ownership Map, 2007*," By MacPhie Archives. **All Lots**

Lot 17.

1753 - (12-27-1753) **Governor Charles Lawrence, to Capt. John Gifford (53) and Richard Smith (53) – ALL LOTS**

#123 Source - NS Archives and Record Management "Allotment" Book, P. 137, Reel #13044; "Old Book" #1, P. 44. Granted Gifford Island #12, Young Island #13, and Smith Island #28, to establish a fishery. Escheated.

1790 - (06-25-1790) **Anthony Vaughan (57), to Nathaniel Melvin (38a) – Lot 17**

#84 Source – Lunenburg Co. Land Deeds, recorded 04-14-1791, Vol. 3, P. 450, No. #741. 57>38a **- Lot 17**

#35 Source - "*Habitation on Oak Island*." Beaton Institute, Cape Breton University. Created by Surveyor William Dy Sr., called 'The Old Plan' No. 1046. Department of Lands & Forests, n.d. MG 12, 75 NSNA. Also Published in Joy Steele/Gordon Fader's book "*Oak Island Mystery Solved-Final Chapter*." P. 10. 2nd Ed. 2016.

1808 - (03-21-1808) **Nathaniel Melvin (38a), to John Smith (51a) – Lot 17**

#102 Source – Lunenburg Co. Land Deeds, recorded 03-21-1808, Vol. 6, P. 63-64, No. #138.

#25/26 Source – "*2-Page Oak Island Lot Ownership Map, Jul. 6, 1818*." And "*Old Plan Map of Oak Island 1818*." By David W. Crandell Survey Map. NSNA. **Lots 13, 14, 15, 16, 17, 18**

#35 Source - "*Habitation on Oak Island*." Beaton Institute, Cape Breton University. Created by Surveyor William Dy Sr., called 'The Old Plan' No. 1046. Department of Lands & Forests, n.d. MG 12, 75 NSNA. Also Published in Joy Steele/Gordon Fader's book "*Oak Island Mystery Solved-Final Chapter*." P. 10. 2nd Ed. 2016.

1852 - John Smith (51a) dies. Lots 15, 16, 17, 18, 19, 20 willed to Joseph Smith (51b) and Thomas E. Smith (51c) – Lot 17

#4 Source - Probate Registry at Lunenburg & Registrar of Deeds in Bridgewater, Book, 16, P. 485; Book 21, P. 114, No. #173. **– Lots 15, 16, 17, 18, 19, 20**

1853 - (03-29-1853) **Heirs Joseph Smith (51b) & Thomas E. Smith (51c), sell Lots 15, 16, 17, 18, 19, 20 to Anthony Graves (19) – Lot 17**

#4 Source - Probate Registry at Lunenburg & Registrar of Deeds in Bridgewater, Book, 16, P. 485; Book 21, P. 114, No. #173. **– Lots 15, 16, 17, 18, 19, 20**

1887 - (07-14-1887) **Anthony Graves (19) dies, Estate property of Lots 5, 9, 10, 11, 12, 13, 14, 15, 16, 17, 18, 19, 20 split, with 15, 16, 17, 18, 19, 20 staying with Henry Sellers (19a) – Lot 17**

#4 Source - Probate Registry at Lunenburg & Registrar of Deeds in Bridgewater, Book, 16, P. 485; Book 21, P. 114, No. #173. **– Lots 15, 16, 17, 18, 19, 20**

1912 - Henry Sellers (19a) dies, his Lots 6, 7, 8, 15, 16, 17, 18, 19, 20, 25, 26, 30, 31, 32 divided into shares with inheritors. See following deeds/court probates – Lot 17

#4 Source - Probate Registry at Lunenburg & Registrar of Deeds in Bridgewater, Book, 16, P. 485; Book 21, P. 114, No. #173. **– Lots 15, 16, 17, 18, 19, 20**

#5 Source - Dominion Canada and Lunenburg Co. Land Deeds, Book No. 21, P. 114-115, No. #174. (originally filed at Bridgewater N.S. Book No. 16, P. 485). NSNA. **– Lots 15, 16, 17, 18, 19, 20**

#6 Source - Dominion Canada and Lunenburg Co. Land Deeds, Book No. 21, P. 115-116, No. #175. Selling party includes Ruby E. Corkum, Wilfred & Audrey W. Corkum, Henry & Mary L. Corkum, and single adults Flora Corkum & Ross Corkum. NSNA. **– Lots 15, 16, 17, 18, 19, 20**

#7 Source - Dominion Canada and Lunenburg Co. Land Deeds, Book No. 21, P. 184, No. #295. (originally filed at Bridgewater, N.S., Book No. 16, P. 485) NSNA. **– Lots 15, 16, 17, 18, 19, 20**

#8 Source - Prothonotary of Nova Scotia Supreme Court in Lunenburg, file No. #3196, recorded on 02-03-1936, Book No. 21, P. 185-186, No. #297. NSNA. **– Lot 15, 16, 17, 18, 19, 20**

1935 - (07-27-1935) **Selvyn & Bessie Sellers heirs (19b), to George Grimm Jr. (20) – Lot 17**

#4 Source - Probate Registry at Lunenburg & Registrar of Deeds in Bridgewater, Book, 16, P. 485; Book 21, P. 114, No. #173. 19b>20 – **Lots 15, 16, 17, 18, 19, 20**

1935 - (07-27-1935) **Erdie Powers (44), to George W. Grimm Jr. (20) – Lot 17**

#5 Source - Dominion Canada and Lunenburg Co. Land Deeds, Book No. 21, P. 114-115, No. #174. (originally filed at Bridgewater N.S. Book No. 16, P. 485). NSNA. 44>20 – **Lots 15, 16, 17, 18, 19, 20**

1935 - (07-27-1935) **Burnell & Hazel Corkum, et. al (13), to George Grimm Jr. (20) – Lot 17**

#6 Source - Dominion Canada and Lunenburg Co. Land Deeds, Book No. 21, P. 115-116, No. #175. Selling party includes Ruby E. Corkum, Wilfred & Audrey W. Corkum, Henry & Mary L. Corkum, and single adults Flora Corkum & Ross Corkum. NSNA. 13>20 – **Lots 15, 16, 17, 18, 19, 20**

1935 - (07-27-1935) **Genevieve & Wilbert Walls (59), to George W. Grimm Jr. (20) – Lot 17**

#7 Source - Dominion Canada and Lunenburg Co. Land Deeds, Book No. 21, P. 184, No. #295. (originally filed at Bridgewater, N.S., Book No. 16, P. 485) NSNA. 59>20 – **Lots 15, 16, 17, 18, 19, 20**

1935 - (07-27-1935) **Burnell Corkum, Guardian of Andrew & Hope Corkum (13), to George Grimm Jr. (20) – Lot 17**

#8 Source - Prothonotary of Nova Scotia Supreme Court in Lunenburg, file No. #3196, recorded on 02-03-1936, Book No. 21, P. 185-186, No. #297. NSNA. 13>20 – **Lot 15, 16, 17, 18, 19, 20**

1949 - George W. Grimm Jr. (20), to Gilbert D. Hedden (22) lots 15, 16, 17, 18, 19, 20, - Lot 17

#13 Source – Dominion of Canada Book No. #693, NSNA. **- Lots 6, 7, 8, 15, 16, 17, 18, 19, 20, 25, 26, 30, 32 [Lot 31 missing]**

1950 - (05-26-1950) **Gilbert D. Hedden & Margarite C. Hedden (22), Lots 6, 7, 8, 25, 26, 30, 31*, 32, & 15, 16, 17, 18, 19, 20 to John Whitney Lewis (10a) – Lot 17**

#13 Source – Dominion of Canada Book No. #693, NSNA. 22>10a **- Lots 6, 7, 8, 15, 16, 17, 18, 19, 20, 25, 26, 30, 32 [Lot 31 missing]**

1950 - (12-05-1950) **John Whitney Lewis & Ann Lewis (10a), Lots 6, 7, 8, 15, 16, 17, 18, 19, 20, 25, 26*, 30, 31, 32 to Acadia Trust Company (10b) – Lot 17**

#14 Source - Dominion of Canada, NSNA #880. (original filings list – see citation). 10a>10b **- Lot 6, 7, 8, 15, 16, 17, 18, 19, 20, 25, 30, 31, 32 [Lot 26 missing]**

1957 - (04-20-1957) **Acadia Trust Company (10b), Lots 6, 7, 8, 15, 16, 17, 18, 19, 20, 25, 26, 30, 31, 32 to M.R. Chappell (10) – Lot 17**

#15 Source - Registry of Deeds at Bridgewater and Registry of Probate, Book 26, P. 195, Quit Claim No. 374, NSNA. 10b>10 **- Lot 6, 7, 8, 15, 16, 17, 18, 19, 20, 25, 26, 30, 31, 32**

1961 - (07-21-1961) **Mary Ellen Chapman (09) & heirs of Clarence J. Beamish (04), to M.R. Chappell, Lots 5, 6, 7, 8, 15, 16, 17, 18, 19, 20, 23, 25, 26, 30, 31, 32 (10) – Lot 17**

#16 Source - Nova Scotia Supreme Court Book 27, P. 339, No. #638. NSNA. Represent heirs shares of "South & West part Oak Island," "George McInnis Property," and "James McInnis Property." 07-20-1961. 09,04>10 **- Lot 6, 7, 8, 15, 16, 17, 18, 19, 20, 23, 25, 26, 30, 31, 32**

1977 - (06-15-1977) **Melbourne R. Chappell (10), to David C. Tobias (55) – Lot 17**

#20 Source – Filed in Halifax Co. Land Deeds, recorded on 06-29-1977, No. #582. NSNA. 10>55 **- Lots 6, 7, 8, 15, 16, 17, 18, 19, 20, 25, 26, 30, 31, 32**

1987 - (12-09-1987) **David Tobias (55) and his lots, join Dan Blankenship (07) to form Oak Island Tours Inc (41) – Lot 17**

#111 Source – "*The Open Database of the Corporate World. Oak Island Tours Inc. Company Number 2272393*." Incorporated Date, 12-09-1987. Opencorporates.

#112 Source – "*The Curse of Oak Island, The Story of the World's Longest Treasure Hunt*." By Randall Sullivan, 2018. Page 422.

2007 - David Tobias (55), sells his Lots to Rick & Marty Lagina who become equal partners with Dan Blankenship (07) in Oak Island Tours (41) which own/control Lots 1, 2, 3, 4, 6, 7, 8, 15, 16, 17, 18, 19, 20, 21, 22, 24, 26, 27, 28, 29, 30, 31, 32. – Lot 17

#111 Source – "*The Open Database of the Corporate World. Oak Island Tours Inc. Company Number 2272393*." Incorporated Date, 12-09-1987. Opencorporates.

#112 Source – "*The Curse of Oak Island, The Story of the World's Longest Treasure Hunt*." By Randall Sullivan, 2018. Page 422.

2007 - **MacPhie Archives "*Oak Island Lot Distribution Map, 2007*."** Lots ***1, 2, 3, 4, 6, 7, 8, 15, 16, 17, 18, 19, 20, 21, 22, 24, 26, 27, 28, 29, 30, 31, 32*** - Oak Island Tours (41); Lot ***5*** – Robert S. Young (61); Lots ***9, 10, 11, 12, 14*** – Fred Nolan (40); Lot ***13*** – John Johnston (25); Lot ***23*** – Dan/Dave Blankenship (07); and Lot ***25*** – Alan Kostrzewe (27). **– All Lots**

#30 Source - "*Oak Island Lot Ownership Map, 2007*," By MacPhie Archives. **All Lots**

Lot 18.

1753 - (12-27-1753) **Governor Charles Lawrence, to Capt. John Gifford (53) and Richard Smith (53) – ALL LOTS**

#123 Source - NS Archives and Record Management "Allotment" Book, P. 137, Reel #13044; "Old Book" #1, P. 44. Granted Gifford Island #12, Young Island #13, and Smith Island #28, to establish a fishery. Escheated.

1785 - **Island Shares document shows no owner of Lot 18 in 1785 – Lot 18**

1795 - (06-26-1795) - **Casper Wollenhaupt (58), to John Smith (51a) – Lot 18**

#100 Source – Lunenburg Co. Land Deeds, recorded 07-16-1795, Vol. 4, P. 101, No. #24. 58>51a **- Lot 18**

#25/26 Source – "*2-Page Oak Island Lot Ownership Map, Jul. 6, 1818*." And "*Old Plan Map of Oak Island 1818*." By David W. Crandell Survey Map. NSNA. **Lots 13, 14, 15, 16, 17, 18**

#35 Source - "*Habitation on Oak Island*." Beaton Institute, Cape Breton University. Created by Surveyor William Dy Sr., called 'The Old Plan' No. 1046. Department of Lands & Forests, n.d. MG 12, 75 NSNA. Also Published in Joy Steele/Gordon Fader's book "*Oak Island Mystery Solved-Final Chapter*." P. 10. 2nd Ed. 2016.

1818 - **John Smith (51a) – Lot 18**

#25/26 Source – "*2-Page Oak Island Lot Ownership Map, Jul. 6, 1818*." And "*Old Plan Map of Oak Island 1818*." By David W. Crandell Survey Map. NSNA. **Lots 13, 14, 15, 16, 17, 18**

1852 - **John Smith (51a) dies. Lots 15, 16, 17, 18, 19, 20 willed to Joseph Smith (51b) and Thomas E. Smith (51c) – Lot 18**

#4 Source - Probate Registry at Lunenburg & Registrar of Deeds in Bridgewater, Book, 16, P. 485; Book 21, P. 114, No. #173. **– Lots 15, 16, 17, 18, 19, 20**

1853 - (03-29-1853) **Heirs Joseph Smith (51b) & Thomas E. Smith (51c), sell Lots 15, 16, 17, 18, 19, 20 to Anthony Graves (19) – Lot 18**

#4 Source - Probate Registry at Lunenburg & Registrar of Deeds in Bridgewater, Book, 16, *P. 485; Book 21, P. 114, No. #173. 19b>20* ***– Lots 15, 16, 17, 18, 19, 20***

1887 - (07-14-1887) **Anthony Graves (19) dies, Estate property of Lots 5, 9, 10, 11, 12, 13, 14, 15, 16, 17, 18, 19, 20 split, with 15, 16, 17, 18, 19, 20 staying with Henry Sellers (19a) – Lot 18**

#4 Source - Probate Registry at Lunenburg & Registrar of Deeds in Bridgewater, Book, 16, P. 485; Book 21, P. 114, No. #173. **– Lots 15, 16, 17, 18, 19, 20**

1912 - **Henry Sellers (19a) dies, his Lots 6, 7, 8, 15, 16, 17, 18, 19, 20, 25, 26, 30, 31, 32 divided into shares with inheritors. See following deeds/court probates – Lot 18**

#4 Source - Probate Registry at Lunenburg & Registrar of Deeds in Bridgewater, Book, 16, P. 485; Book 21, P. 114, No. #173. **– Lots 15, 16, 17, 18, 19, 20**

#5 Source - Dominion Canada and Lunenburg Co. Land Deeds, Book No. 21, P. 114-115, No. #174. (originally filed at Bridgewater N.S. Book No. 16, P. 485). NSNA. 44>20 **– Lots 15, 16, 17, 18, 19, 20**

#6 Source - Dominion Canada and Lunenburg Co. Land Deeds, Book No. 21, P. 115-116, No. #175. Selling party includes Ruby E. Corkum, Wilfred & Audrey W. Corkum, Henry & Mary L. Corkum, and single adults Flora Corkum & Ross Corkum. NSNA. **– Lots 15, 16, 17, 18, 19, 20**

#7 Source - Dominion Canada and Lunenburg Co. Land Deeds, Book No. 21, P. 184, No. #295. (originally filed at Bridgewater, N.S., Book No. 16, P. 485) NSNA. **– Lots 15, 16, 17, 18, 19, 20**

#8 Source - Prothonotary of Nova Scotia Supreme Court in Lunenburg, file No. #3196, recorded on 02-03-1936, Book No. 21, P. 185-186, No. #297. NSNA. **– Lot 15, 16, 17, 18, 19, 20**

1935 - (07-27-1935) **Selvyn & Bessie Sellers heirs (19b), to George Grimm Jr. (20) – Lot 18**

#4 Source - Probate Registry at Lunenburg & Registrar of Deeds in Bridgewater, Book, 16, P. 485; Book 21, P. 114, No. #173. 19b>20 **– Lots 15, 16, 17, 18, 19, 20**

1935 - (07-27-1935) **Erdie Powers (44), to George W. Grimm Jr. (20) – Lot 18**
#5 Source - Dominion Canada and Lunenburg Co. Land Deeds, Book No. 21, P. 114-115, No. #174. (originally filed at Bridgewater N.S. Book No. 16, P. 485). NSNA. 44>20 – **Lots 15, 16, 17, 18, 19, 20**

1935 - (07-27-1935) **Burnell & Hazel Corkum, et. al (13), to George Grimm Jr. (20) – Lot 18**
#6 Source - Dominion Canada and Lunenburg Co. Land Deeds, Book No. 21, P. 115-116, No. #175. Selling party includes Ruby E. Corkum, Wilfred & Audrey W. Corkum, Henry & Mary L. Corkum, and single adults Flora Corkum & Ross Corkum. NSNA. 13>20 – **Lots 15, 16, 17, 18, 19, 20**

1935 - (07-27-1935) **Genevieve & Wilbert Walls (59), to George W. Grimm Jr. (20) – Lot 18**
#7 Source - Dominion Canada and Lunenburg Co. Land Deeds, Book No. 21, P. 184, No. #295. (originally filed at Bridgewater, N.S., Book No. 16, P. 485) NSNA. 59>20 – **Lots 15, 16, 17, 18, 19, 20**

1935 - (07-27-1935) **Burnell Corkum, Guardian of Andrew & Hope Corkum (13), to George Grimm Jr. (20) – Lot 18**
#8 Source - Prothonotary of Nova Scotia Supreme Court in Lunenburg, file No. #3196, recorded on 02-03-1936, Book No. 21, P. 185-186, No. #297. NSNA. 13>20 – **Lot 15, 16, 17, 18, 19, 20**

1949 - **George W. Grimm Jr. (20), to Gilbert D. Hedden (22) lots 15, 16, 17, 18, 19, 20, - Lot 18**
#13 Source – Dominion of Canada Book No. #693, NSNA. **- Lots 6, 7, 8, 15, 16, 17, 18, 19, 20, 25, 26, 30, 32** [Lot 31 missing]

1950 - (05-26-1950) **Gilbert D. Hedden & Margarite C. Hedden (22), Lots 6, 7, 8, 25, 26, 30, 31*, 32, & 15, 16, 17, 18, 19, 20 to John Whitney Lewis (10a) – Lot 18**
#13 Source – Dominion of Canada Book No. #693, NSNA. 22>10a **- Lots 6, 7, 8, 15, 16, 17, 18, 19, 20, 25, 26, 30, 32** [Lot 31 missing]

1950 - (12-05-1950) **John Whitney Lewis & Ann Lewis (10a), Lots 6, 7, 8, 15, 16, 17, 18, 19, 20, 25, 26*, 30, 31, 32 to Acadia Trust Company (10b) – Lot 18**
#14 Source - Dominion of Canada, NSNA #880. (original filings list – see citation). 10a>10b **- Lot 6, 7, 8, 15, 16, 17, 18, 19, 20, 25, 30, 31, 32** [Lot 26 missing]

1957 - (04-20-1957) **Acadia Trust Company (10b), Lots 6, 7, 8, 15, 16, 17, 18, 19, 20, 25, 26, 30, 31, 32 to M.R. Chappell (10) – Lot 18**
#15 Source - Registry of Deeds at Bridgewater and Registry of Probate, Book 26, P. 195, Quit Claim No. 374, NSNA. 10b>10 **- Lot 6, 7, 8, 15, 16, 17, 18, 19, 20, 25, 26, 30, 31, 32**

1961 - (07-21-1961) **Mary Ellen Chapman (09) & heirs of Clarence J. Beamish (04), to M.R. Chappell, Lots 5, 6, 7, 8, 15, 16, 17, 18, 19, 20, 23, 25, 26, 30, 31, 32 (10) – Lot 18**
#16 Source - Nova Scotia Supreme Court Book 27, P. 339, No. #638. NSNA. Represent heirs shares of "South & West part Oak Island," "George McInnis Property," and "James McInnis Property." 07-20-1961. 09,04>10 **- Lot 6, 7, 8, 15, 16, 17, 18, 19, 20, 23, 25, 26, 30, 31, 32**

1977 - (06-15-1977) **Melbourne R. Chappell (10), to David C. Tobias (55) – Lot 18**
#20 Source – Filed in Halifax Co. Land Deeds, recorded on 06-29-1977, No. #582. NSNA. 10>55 **- Lots 6, 7, 8, 15, 16, 17, 18, 19, 20, 25, 26, 30, 31, 32**

1987 - (12-09-1987) **David Tobias (55) and his lots, join Dan Blankenship (07) to form Oak Island Tours Inc (41) – Lot 18**
#111 Source – "*The Open Database of the Corporate World. Oak Island Tours Inc. Company Number 2272393*." Incorporated Date, 12-09-1987. Opencorporates.
#112 Source – "*The Curse of Oak Island, The Story of the World's Longest Treasure Hunt*." By Randall Sullivan, 2018. Page 422.

2007 - **David Tobias (55), sells his Lots to Rick & Marty Lagina who become equal partners with Dan Blankenship (07) in Oak Island Tours (41) which own/control Lots 1, 2, 3, 4,**
#111 Source – "*The Open Database of the Corporate World. Oak Island Tours Inc. Company Number 2272393*." Incorporated Date, 12-09-1987. Opencorporates.
#112 Source – "*The Curse of Oak Island, The Story of the World's Longest Treasure Hunt*." By Randall Sullivan, 2018. Page 422.

2007 - **MacPhie Archives "*Oak Island Lot Distribution Map, 2007*."** Lots ***1, 2, 3, 4, 6, 7, 8, 15, 16, 17, 18, 19, 20, 21, 22, 24, 26, 27, 28, 29, 30, 31, 32*** - Oak Island Tours (41); Lot ***5*** – Robert S. Young (61); Lots ***9, 10, 11, 12, 14*** – Fred Nolan (40); Lot ***13*** – John Johnston (25); Lot ***23*** – Dan/Dave Blankenship (07); and Lot ***25*** – Alan Kostrzewe (27). **– All Lots**
#30 Source - "*Oak Island Lot Ownership Map, 2007*," By MacPhie Archives. **All Lots**

Lot 19.

1753 - (12-27-1753) **Governor Charles Lawrence, to Capt. John Gifford (53) and Richard Smith (53) – ALL LOTS**

#123 Source - NS Archives and Record Management "Allotment" Book, P. 137, Reel #13044; "Old Book" #1, P. 44. Granted Gifford Island #12, Young Island #13, and Smith Island #28, to establish a fishery. Escheated.

1766 - (08-20-1766) **Crown (00), to Edward Smith (52) drew lot – Lot 19**

#117 Source - Paul Wroclawski Research & Property Owners Charles Morris to John Smith; collected through 02-06-2008. 00>52 **- Lot 19**

1768 - (03-28-1768) **Edward Smith (52), to Timothy Lynch (28) – Lot 19**

#22 Source - Recorded MG1, Vol. 384 NSNA. (originally recorded on 08-25-1770, Book 1, P. 347, No. #913). NSNA. 52>28/65 **- Lot 19**

#35 Source - "*Habitation on Oak Island*." Beaton Institute, Cape Breton University. Created by Surveyor William Dy Sr., called 'The Old Plan' No. 1046. Department of Lands & Forests, n.d. MG 12, 75 NSNA. Also Published in Joy Steele/Gordon Fader's book "*Oak Island Mystery Solved-Final Chapter*." P. 10. 2nd Ed. 2016.

1803 - James Vaughan (57d) – Lot 19

#17 Source – "*Chester Township Records, 1762-1830*." Births, Marriages, & Deaths. NSNA MG9, B 9-3

1804 - James Vaughan (57d) dies, Probated to **James Vaughan Family (57dfam) - Lot 19**

#17 Source – "*Chester Township Records, 1762-1830*." Births, Marriages, & Deaths. NSNA MG9, B 9-3

1819 James Vaughan/Vaughan/Kiser (Keyser) (57dfam), to David Vaughan (57c) – Lot 19

#106 Source – Lunenburg Co. Land Deeds, recorded 06-26-1823, Vol. 8, P. 323, 343, 344, No. #513. 57d>57c **– Lots 2, 5, 17**

#35 Source - "*Habitation on Oak Island*." Beaton Institute, Cape Breton University. Created by Surveyor William Dy Sr., called 'The Old Plan' No. 1046. Department of Lands & Forests, n.d. MG 12, 75 NSNA. Also Published in Joy Steele/Gordon Fader's book "*Oak Island Mystery Solved-Final Chapter*." P. 10. 2nd Ed. 2016.

1825- (07-1825) **David Vaughan (57c), to John Smith (51a) – Lot 19**

#104 Source – Lunenburg Co. Land Deeds, recorded 04-20-1827, Vol. 8, P. 514, No. #843. 57c>51a **- Lot 19**

#25/26 Source – "*2-Page Oak Island Lot Ownership Map, Jul. 6, 1818*." And "*Old Plan Map of Oak Island 1818*." By David W. Crandell Survey Map. NSNA. **Lots 13, 14, 15, 16, 17, 18**

#35 Source - "*Habitation on Oak Island*." Beaton Institute, Cape Breton University. Created by Surveyor William Dy Sr., called 'The Old Plan' No. 1046. Department of Lands & Forests, n.d. MG 12, 75 NSNA. Also Published in Joy Steele/Gordon Fader's book "*Oak Island Mystery Solved-Final Chapter*." P. 10. 2nd Ed. 2016.

1852 - John Smith (51a) dies. Lots 15, 16, 17, 18, 19, 20 willed to Joseph Smith (51b) and Thomas E. Smith (51c) – Lot 19

#4 Source - Probate Registry at Lunenburg & Registrar of Deeds in Bridgewater, Book, 16, P. 485; Book 21, P. 114, No. #173. **– Lots 15, 16, 17, 18, 19, 20**

1853 - (03-29-1853) **Heirs Joseph Smith (51b) & Thomas E. Smith (51c), sell Lots 15, 16, 17, 18, 19, 20 to Anthony Graves (19) – Lot 19**

#4 Source - Probate Registry at Lunenburg & Registrar of Deeds in Bridgewater, Book, 16, P. 485; Book 21, P. 114, No. #173. **– Lots 15, 16, 17, 18, 19, 20**

1887 - (07-14-1887) **Anthony Graves (19) dies, Estate property of Lots 5, 9, 10, 11, 12, 13, 14, 15, 16, 17, 18, 19, 20 split, with 15, 16, 17, 18, 19, 20 staying with Henry Sellers (19a) – Lot 19**

#4 Source - Probate Registry at Lunenburg & Registrar of Deeds in Bridgewater, Book, 16, P. 485; Book 21, P. 114, No. #173. **– Lots 15, 16, 17, 18, 19, 20**

1912 - Henry Sellers (19a) dies, his Lots 6, 7, 8, 15, 16, 17, 18, 19, 20, 25, 26, 30, 31, 32 divided into shares with inheritors. See following deeds/court probates – Lot 19

#4 Source - Probate Registry at Lunenburg & Registrar of Deeds in Bridgewater, Book, 16, *P. 485; Book 21, P. 114, No. #173.* ***– Lots 15, 16, 17, 18, 19, 20***

#5 Source - Dominion Canada and Lunenburg Co. Land Deeds, Book No. 21, P. 114-115, No. #174. (originally filed at Bridgewater N.S. Book No. 16, P. 485). NSNA. **– Lots 15, 16, 17, 18, 19, 20**

#6 Source - Dominion Canada and Lunenburg Co. Land Deeds, Book No. 21, P. 115-116, No. #175. Selling party includes Ruby E. Corkum, Wilfred & Audrey W. Corkum, Henry & Mary L. Corkum, and single adults Flora Corkum & Ross Corkum. NSNA. – **Lots 15, 16, 17, 18, 19, 20**

#7 Source - Dominion Canada and Lunenburg Co. Land Deeds, Book No. 21, P. 184, No. #295. (originally filed at Bridgewater, N.S., Book No. 16, P. 485) NSNA. – **Lots 15, 16, 17, 18, 19, 20**

#8 Source - Prothonotary of Nova Scotia Supreme Court in Lunenburg, file No. #3196, recorded on 02-03-1936, Book No. 21, P. 185-186, No. #297. NSNA. – **Lot 15, 16, 17, 18, 19, 20**

1935 - (07-27-1935) **Selvyn & Bessie Sellers heirs (19b), to George Grimm Jr. (20) – Lot 19**

#4 Source - Probate Registry at Lunenburg & Registrar of Deeds in Bridgewater, Book, 16, *P. 485; Book 21, P. 114, No. #173. 19b> 20 – **Lots 15, 16, 17, 18, 19, 20***

1935 - (07-27-1935) **Erdie Powers (44), to George W. Grimm Jr. (20) – Lot 19**

#5 Source - Dominion Canada and Lunenburg Co. Land Deeds, Book No. 21, P. 114-115, No. #174. (originally filed at Bridgewater N.S. Book No. 16, P. 485). NSNA. 44>20 – **Lots 15, 16, 17, 18, 19, 20**

1935 - (07-27-1935) **Burnell & Hazel Corkum, et. al (13), to George Grimm Jr. (20) – Lot 19**

#6 Source - Dominion Canada and Lunenburg Co. Land Deeds, Book No. 21, P. 115-116, No. #175. Selling party includes Ruby E. Corkum, Wilfred & Audrey W. Corkum, Henry & Mary L. Corkum, and single adults Flora Corkum & Ross Corkum. NSNA. 13>20 – **Lots 15, 16, 17, 18, 19, 20**

1935 - (07-27-1935) **Genevieve & Wilbert Walls (59), to George W. Grimm Jr. (20) – Lot 19**

#7 Source - Dominion Canada and Lunenburg Co. Land Deeds, Book No. 21, P. 184, No. #295. (originally filed at Bridgewater, N.S., Book No. 16, P. 485) NSNA. 59>20 – **Lots 15, 16, 17, 18, 19, 20**

1935 - (07-27-1935) **Burnell Corkum, Guardian of Andrew & Hope Corkum (13), to George Grimm Jr. (20) – Lot 19**

#8 Source - Prothonotary of Nova Scotia Supreme Court in Lunenburg, file No. #3196, recorded on 02-03-1936, Book No. 21, P. 185-186, No. #297. NSNA. 13>20 – **Lot 15, 16, 17, 18, 19, 20**

1949 - George W. Grimm Jr. (20), to Gilbert D. Hedden (22) lots 15, 16, 17, 18, 19, 20, - Lot 19

#13 Source – Dominion of Canada Book No. #693, NSNA. **- Lots 6, 7, 8, 15, 16, 17, 18, 19, 20, 25, 26, 30, 32** [Lot 31 missing]

1950 - (05-26-1950) **Gilbert D. Hedden & Margarite C. Hedden (22), Lots 6, 7, 8, 25, 26, 30, 31*, 32, & 15, 16, 17, 18, 19, 20 to John Whitney Lewis (10a) – Lot 19**

#13 Source – Dominion of Canada Book No. #693, NSNA. 22>10a **- Lots 6, 7, 8, 15, 16, 17, 18, 19, 20, 25, 26, 30, 32** [Lot 31 missing]

1950 - (12-05-1950) **John Whitney Lewis & Ann Lewis (10a), Lots 6, 7, 8, 15, 16, 17, 18, 19, 20, 25, 26*, 30, 31, 32 to Acadia Trust Company (10b) – Lot 19**

#14 Source - Dominion of Canada, NSNA #880. (original filings list – see citation). 10a>10b **- Lot 6, 7, 8, 15, 16, 17, 18, 19, 20, 25, 30, 31, 32** [Lot 26 missing]

1957 - (04-20-1957) **Acadia Trust Company (10b), Lots 6, 7, 8, 15, 16, 17, 18, 19, 20, 25, 26, 30, 31, 32 to M.R. Chappell (10) – Lot 19**

#15 Source - Registry of Deeds at Bridgewater and Registry of Probate, Book 26, P. 195, Quit Claim No. 374, NSNA. 10b>10 **- Lot 6, 7, 8, 15, 16, 17, 18, 19, 20, 25, 26, 30, 31, 32**

1961 - (07-21-1961) **Mary Ellen Chapman (09) & heirs of Clarence J. Beamish (04), to M.R. Chappell, Lots 5, 6, 7, 8, 15, 16, 17, 18, 19, 20, 23, 25, 26, 30, 31, 32 (10) – Lot 19**

#16 Source - Nova Scotia Supreme Court Book 27, P. 339, No. #638. NSNA. Represent heirs shares of "South & West part Oak Island," "George McInnis Property," and "James McInnis Property." 07-20-1961. 09,04>10 **- Lot 6, 7, 8, 15, 16, 17, 18, 19, 20, 23, 25, 26, 30, 31, 32**

1977 - (06-15-1977) **Melbourne R. Chappell (10), to David C. Tobias (55) – Lot 19**

#20 Source – Filed in Halifax Co. Land Deeds, recorded on 06-29-1977, No. #582. NSNA. 10>55 **- Lots 6, 7, 8, 15, 16, 17, 18, 19, 20, 25, 26, 30, 31, 32**

1987 - (12-09-1987) **David Tobias (55) and his lots, join Dan Blankenship (07) to form Oak Island Tours Inc (41) – Lot 19**

#111 Source – "*The Open Database of the Corporate World. Oak Island Tours Inc. Company Number 2272393*." Incorporated Date, 12-09-1987. Opencorporates.

#112 Source – "*The Curse of Oak Island, The Story of the World's Longest Treasure Hunt*." By Randall Sullivan, 2018. Page 422.

2007 - **David Tobias (55), sells his Lots to Rick & Marty Lagina who become equal partners with Dan Blankenship (07) in Oak Island Tours (41) which own/control Lots 1, 2, 3, 4, 6, 7, 8, 15, 16, 17, 18, 19, 20, 21, 22, 24, 26, 27, 28, 29, 30, 31, 32. – Lot 19**

#111 Source – "The Open Database of the Corporate World. Oak Island Tours Inc. Company Number 2272393." Incorporated Date, 12-09-1987. Opencorporates.

#112 Source – "The Curse of Oak Island, The Story of the World's Longest Treasure Hunt." By Randall Sullivan, 2018. Page 422.

2007 - **MacPhie Archives "*Oak Island Lot Distribution Map, 2007*."** Lots ***1, 2, 3, 4, 6, 7, 8, 15, 16, 17, 18, 19, 20, 21, 22, 24, 26, 27, 28, 29, 30, 31, 32*** - Oak Island Tours (41); Lot ***5*** – Robert S. Young (61); Lots ***9, 10, 11, 12, 14*** – Fred Nolan (40); Lot ***13*** – John Johnston (25); Lot ***23*** – Dan/Dave Blankenship (07); and Lot ***25*** – Alan Kostrzewe (27). **– All Lots**

#30 Source - "Oak Island Lot Ownership Map, 2007," By MacPhie Archives. **All Lots**

Lot 20.

1753 - (12-27-1753) **Governor Charles Lawrence, to Capt. John Gifford (53) and Richard Smith (53) – ALL LOTS**

#123 Source - NS Archives and Record Management "Allotment" Book, P. 137, Reel #13044; "Old Book" #1, P. 44. Granted Gifford Island #12, Young Island #13, and Smith Island #28, to establish a fishery. Escheated.

1791 - (01-19-1791) **Alexander McNeil (37), to Edward James (24) – Lot 20**

#47 Source – Lunenburg Co. Land Deeds, recorded 03-12-1791, Vol. 3, P. 12, No. #16. 37>24 **– Lot 20**

#35 Source - "*Habitation on Oak Island*." Beaton Institute, Cape Breton University. Created by Surveyor William Dy Sr., called 'The Old Plan' No. 1046. Department of Lands & Forests, n.d. MG 12, 75 NSNA. Also Published in Joy Steele/Gordon Fader's book "*Oak Island Mystery Solved-Final Chapter*." P. 10. 2nd Ed. 2016.

1794 - (03-07-1794) **Edward James (24), to Joseph Bezanson (06c) – Lot 20**

#48 Source – Lunenburg Co. Land Deeds, recorded 10-09-1800, Vol. 5, P. 140, No. #167. 24>06c **– Lot 20**

#35 Source - "*Habitation on Oak Island*." Beaton Institute, Cape Breton University. Created by Surveyor William Dy Sr., called 'The Old Plan' No. 1046. Department of Lands & Forests, n.d. MG 12, 75 NSNA. Also Published in Joy Steele/Gordon Fader's book "*Oak Island Mystery Solved-Final Chapter*." P. 10. 2nd Ed. 2016.

1807 - (02-07-1807) **Joseph Bezanson (06c), to John Smith (51a) – Lot 20**

#101 Source – Lunenburg Co. Land Deeds, recorded 03-02-1810, Vol. 6, P. 150-51, No. #333. 06c>51a **- Lot 20**

#25/26 Source – "2-Page Oak Island Lot Ownership Map, Jul. 6, 1818." And "Old Plan Map of Oak Island 1818." By David W. Crandell Survey Map. NSNA. **Lots 13, 14, 15, 16, 17, 18**

#35 Source - "*Habitation on Oak Island*." Beaton Institute, Cape Breton University. Created by Surveyor William Dy Sr., called 'The Old Plan' No. 1046. Department of Lands & Forests, n.d. MG 12, 75 NSNA. Also Published in Joy Steele/Gordon Fader's book "*Oak Island Mystery Solved-Final Chapter*." P. 10. 2nd Ed. 2016.

1852 - **John Smith (51a) dies. Lots 15, 16, 17, 18, 19, 20 willed to Joseph Smith (51b) and Thomas E. Smith (51c) – Lot 20**

#4 Source - Probate Registry at Lunenburg & Registrar of Deeds in Bridgewater, Book, 16, P. 485; Book 21, P. 114, No. #173. **– Lots 15, 16, 17, 18, 19, 20**

1853 - (03-29-1853) **Heirs Joseph Smith (51b) & Thomas E. Smith (51c), sell Lots 15, 16, 17, 18, 19, 20 to Anthony Graves (19) – Lot 20**

#4 Source - Probate Registry at Lunenburg & Registrar of Deeds in Bridgewater, Book, 16, P. 485; Book 21, P. 114, No. #173. **– Lots 15, 16, 17, 18, 19, 20**

1887 - (07-14-1887) **Anthony Graves (19) dies, Estate property of Lots 5, 9, 10, 11, 12, 13, 14, 15, 16, 17, 18, 19, 20 split, with 15, 16, 17, 18, 19, 20 staying with Henry Sellers (19a) – Lot 20**

#4 Source - Probate Registry at Lunenburg & Registrar of Deeds in Bridgewater, Book, 16, P. 485; Book 21, P. 114, No. #173. **– Lots 15, 16, 17, 18, 19, 20**

1912 - Henry Sellers (19a) dies, his Lots 6, 7, 8, 15, 16, 17, 18, 19, 20, 25, 26, 30, 31, 32 divided into shares with inheritors. See following deeds/court probates – Lot 20

- #4 Source - Probate Registry at Lunenburg & Registrar of Deeds in Bridgewater, Book, 16, P. 485; Book 21, P. 114, No. #173. **– Lots 15, 16, 17, 18, 19, 20**
- #5 Source - Dominion Canada and Lunenburg Co. Land Deeds, Book No. 21, P. 114-115, No. #174. (originally filed at Bridgewater N.S. Book No. 16, P. 485). NSNA. 44>20 **– Lots 15, 16, 17, 18, 19, 20**
- #6 Source - Dominion Canada and Lunenburg Co. Land Deeds, Book No. 21, P. 115-116, No. #175. Selling party includes Ruby E. Corkum, Wilfred & Audrey W. Corkum, Henry & Mary L. Corkum, and single adults Flora Corkum & Ross Corkum. NSNA. **– Lots 15, 16, 17, 18, 19, 20**
- #7 Source - Dominion Canada and Lunenburg Co. Land Deeds, Book No. 21, P. 184, No. #295. (originally filed at Bridgewater, N.S., Book No. 16, P. 485) NSNA. **– Lots 15, 16, 17, 18, 19, 20**
- #8 Source - Prothonotary of Nova Scotia Supreme Court in Lunenburg, file No. #3196, recorded on 02-03-1936, Book No. 21, P. 185-186, No. #297. NSNA. **– Lot 15, 16, 17, 18, 19, 20**

1935 - (07-27-1935) **Selvyn & Bessie Sellers heirs (19b), to George Grimm Jr. (20) – Lot 20**

- #4 Source - Probate Registry at Lunenburg & Registrar of Deeds in Bridgewater, Book, 16,

1935 - (07-27-1935) **Erdie Powers (44), to George W. Grimm Jr. (20) – Lot 20**

- #5 Source - Dominion Canada and Lunenburg Co. Land Deeds, Book No. 21, P. 114-115, No. #174. (originally filed at Bridgewater N.S. Book No. 16, P. 485). NSNA. 44>20 **– Lots 15, 16, 17, 18, 19, 20**

1935 - (07-27-1935) **Burnell & Hazel Corkum, et. al (13), to George Grimm Jr. (20) – Lot 20**

- #6 Source - Dominion Canada and Lunenburg Co. Land Deeds, Book No. 21, P. 115-116, No. #175. Selling party includes Ruby E. Corkum, Wilfred & Audrey W. Corkum, Henry & Mary L. Corkum, and single adults Flora Corkum & Ross Corkum. NSNA. 13>20 **– Lots 15, 16, 17, 18, 19, 20**

1935 - (07-27-1935) **Genevieve & Wilbert Walls (59), to George W. Grimm Jr. (20) – Lot 20**

- #7 Source - Dominion Canada and Lunenburg Co. Land Deeds, Book No. 21, P. 184, No. #295. (originally filed at Bridgewater, N.S., Book No. 16, P. 485) NSNA. 59>20 **– Lots 15, 16, 17, 18, 19, 20**

1935 - (07-27-1935) **Burnell Corkum, Guardian of Andrew & Hope Corkum (13), to George Grimm Jr. (20) – Lot 20**

- #8 Source - Prothonotary of Nova Scotia Supreme Court in Lunenburg, file No. #3196, recorded on 02-03-1936, Book No. 21, P. 185-186, No. #297. NSNA. 13>20 **– Lot 15, 16, 17, 18, 19, 20**

1949 - George W. Grimm Jr. (20), to Gilbert D. Hedden (22) lots 15, 16, 17, 18, 19, 20, - Lot 20

- #13 Source – Dominion of Canada Book No. #693, NSNA. **- Lots 6, 7, 8, 15, 16, 17, 18, 19, 20, 25, 26, 30, 32** [Lot 31 missing]

1950 - (05-26-1950) **Gilbert D. Hedden & Margarite C. Hedden (22), Lots 6, 7, 8, 25, 26, 30, 31*, 32, & 15, 16, 17, 18, 19, 20 to John Whitney Lewis (10a) – Lot 20**

- #13 Source – Dominion of Canada Book No. #693, NSNA. 22>10a **- Lots 6, 7, 8, 15, 16, 17, 18, 19, 20, 25, 26, 30, 32** [Lot 31 missing]

1950 - (12-05-1950) **John Whitney Lewis & Ann Lewis (10a), Lots 6, 7, 8, 15, 16, 17, 18, 19, 20, 25, 26*, 30, 31, 32 to Acadia Trust Company (10b) – Lot 20**

- #14 Source - Dominion of Canada, NSNA #880. (original filings list – see citation). 10a>10b **- Lot 6, 7, 8, 15, 16, 17, 18, 19, 20, 25, 30, 31, 32** [Lot 26 missing]

1957 - (04-20-1957) **Acadia Trust Company (10b), Lots 6, 7, 8, 15, 16, 17, 18, 19, 20, 25, 26, 30, 31, 32 to M.R. Chappell (10) – Lot 20**

- #15 Source - Registry of Deeds at Bridgewater and Registry of Probate, Book 26, P. 195, Quit Claim No. 374, NSNA. 10b>10 **- Lot 6, 7, 8, 15, 16, 17, 18, 19, 20, 25, 26, 30, 31, 32**

1961 - (07-21-1961) **Mary Ellen Chapman (09) & heirs of Clarence J. Beamish (04), to M.R. Chappell, Lots 5, 6, 7, 8, 15, 16, 17, 18, 19, 20, 23, 25, 26, 30, 31, 32 (10) – Lot 20**

- #16 Source - Nova Scotia Supreme Court Book 27, P. 339, No. #638. NSNA. Represent heirs shares of "South & West part Oak Island," "George McInnis Property," and "James McInnis Property." 07-20-1961. 09,04>10 **- Lot 6, 7, 8, 15, 16, 17, 18, 19, 20, 23, 25, 26, 30, 31, 32**

1977 - (06-15-1977) **M.R. Chappell (10), to David C. Tobias (55)** for all shares regarding Lots, **1, 2, 3, 4, 6, 7, 8, 15, 16, 17, 18, 19, 20, 21, 22, 24, 25, 26, 27, 28, 29, 30, 31, 32. – Lot 20**

- #20 Source – Filed in Halifax Co. Land Deeds, recorded on 06-29-1977, No. #582. NSNA. 10>55 **- Lots 6, 7, 8, 15, 16, 17, 18, 19, 20, 25, 26, 30, 31, 32**

1987 - (12-09-1987) **David Tobias (55) and his lots, join Dan Blankenship (07) to form Oak Island Tours Inc (41) – Lot 20**

#111 Source – "*The Open Database of the Corporate World. Oak Island Tours Inc. Company Number 2272393*." Incorporated Date, 12-09-1987. Opencorporates.

#112 Source – "*The Curse of Oak Island, The Story of the World's Longest Treasure Hunt*." By Randall Sullivan, 2018. Page 422.

2007 - David Tobias (55), sells his Lots to Rick & Marty Lagina who become equal partners with Dan Blankenship (07) in Oak Island Tours (41) which own/control Lots 1, 2, 3, 4, 6, 7, 8, 15, 16, 17, 18, 19, 20, 21, 22, 24, 26, 27, 28, 29, 30, 31, 32. – Lot 20

#111 Source – "*The Open Database of the Corporate World. Oak Island Tours Inc. Company Number 2272393*." Incorporated Date, 12-09-1987. Opencorporates.

#112 Source – "*The Curse of Oak Island, The Story of the World's Longest Treasure Hunt*." By Randall Sullivan, 2018. Page 422.

2007 - MacPhie Archives "*Oak Island Lot Distribution Map, 2007*." Lots ***1, 2, 3, 4, 6, 7, 8, 15, 16, 17, 18, 19, 20, 21, 22, 24, 26, 27, 28, 29, 30, 31, 32*** - Oak Island Tours (41); Lot ***5*** – Robert S. Young (61); Lots ***9, 10, 11, 12, 14*** – Fred Nolan (40); Lot ***13*** – John Johnston (25); Lot ***23*** – Dan/Dave Blankenship (07); and Lot ***25*** – Alan Kostrzewe (27). **– All Lots**

#30 Source - "*Oak Island Lot Ownership Map, 2007*," By MacPhie Archives. **All Lots**

Lot 21.

1753 - (12-27-1753) **Governor Charles Lawrence, to Capt. John Gifford (53) and Richard Smith (53) – ALL LOTS**

#123 Source - NS Archives and Record Management "Allotment" Book, P. 137, Reel #13044; "Old Book" #1, P. 44. Granted Gifford Island #12, Young Island #13, and Smith Island #28, to establish a fishery. Escheated.

1791 - Alexander McNeil (37), to Edward James (24) No Deed Found – Lot 21

#25/26 Source – "*2-Page Oak Island Lot Ownership Map, Jul. 6, 1818*." And "*Old Plan Map of Oak Island 1818*." By David W. Crandell Survey Map. NSNA. **Lots 13, 14, 15, 16, 17, 18**

#35 Source - "*Habitation on Oak Island*." Beaton Institute, Cape Breton University. Created by Surveyor William Dy Sr., called 'The Old Plan' No. 1046. Department of Lands & Forests, n.d. MG 12, 75 NSNA. Also Published in Joy Steele/Gordon Fader's book "*Oak Island Mystery Solved-Final Chapter*." P. 10. 2nd Ed. 2016.

#47a Source – Lunenburg Co. Land Deeds, recorded 03-12-1791, Vol. 3, P. 12, No. #16. 37>24 **– Lot 21** [Crandell Survey only]

1796 - Edward James (24), to Donald McGinnis (32) No Deed Found – Lot 21

1827 - Donald McGinnis (32) dies, in late 1826 and his will is probated in 1827 – Lot 21

#2 Source - Paul Wroclawski Research & Property Owners Charles Morris to John Smith; collected through 02-06-2008.

#17 Source – "*Chester Township Records, 1762-1830*." Births, Marriages, & Deaths. NSNA MG9, B 9-3

1859 - Daniel McInnis (32a), to James McInnis / Donald McGinnis & coded as family (32fam) – Lot 21

#25/26 Source – "*2-Page Oak Island Lot Ownership Map, Jul. 6, 1818*." And "*Old Plan Map of Oak Island 1818*." By David W. Crandell Survey Map. NSNA. **Lots 13, 14, 15, 16, 17, 18**

#35 Source - "*Habitation on Oak Island*." Beaton Institute, Cape Breton University. Created by Surveyor William Dy Sr., called 'The Old Plan' No. 1046. Department of Lands & Forests, n.d. MG 12, 75 NSNA. Also Published in Joy Steele/Gordon Fader's book "*Oak Island Mystery Solved-Final Chapter*." P. 10. 2nd Ed. 2016.

1896 - James Henry McInnis (32fam) dies, passes to Arthur Curran McInnis (32fam) – Lot 21

#1 Source – N.S. Supreme Court, Book No. 368, recorded 10-01-1931, Book 20, P. 423, No. #368. (originally Book No. 20, P. 74, No.69) **– Lot 21**

1915 - Arthur Curran Mcinnis (32fam) dies, passes to John Mcinnis Family (32fam) – Lot 21

#1 Source – N.S. Supreme Court, Book No. 368, recorded 10-01-1931, Book 20, P. 423, No. #368. (originally Book No. 20, P. 74, No.69) **– Lot 21**

1930 - John McInnis Family (32fam), pass to inheritors Wallace and Margaret Young, (63) et. al. – Lot 21

#169 Source – Lunenburg Co. Land Deed, recorded 06-21-1930, Book 20, P. 74, No. #69. Deeded on 06-09-1930. **- Lot 1**

#1 Source – N.S. Supreme Court, Book No. 368, recorded 10-01-1931, Book 20, P. 423, No. #368. (originally Book No. 20, P. 74, No.69) **– Lot 21**

#3 Source – City & County of San Francisco, Calif. Records; & NSNA, recorded 05-27-1935, Book No. 21. P. 96, No. #148. **- Lot 21**

1931 - (09-22-1931) **Wallace & Margaret Young (63), sell 50% of prop. Val. & share, to Archibald C. Dauphinee (15) – Lot 21**

#1 Source – N.S. Supreme Court, Book No. 368, recorded 10-01-1931, Book 20, P. 423, No. #368. (originally Book No. 20, P. 74, No.69) 63>15 **– Lot 21**

1935 - (09-05-1935) **Oak Island Plan of Prop. Owned by S. Sellers (19a), shows Dauphinee (15) owner – Lot 21**

#37 Source - "*Oak Island Plan of Property Owned by Sellyn Sellers*." by wildlife artist, S. Edgar March. Chester Township Land Deeds, recorded 09-05-1935, Book 24, P.368. NSNA. **All Lots**

1944 - (09-28-1944) **Archibald Dauphinee (15) & Margaret Young (63), to Clarence James Beamish (04) – Lot 21**

#12 Source – Lunenburg Co. Land Deeds, recorded 10-25-1955, Deed #1142 on 10-25-1944. NSNA. 15,63>04 **- Lot 21**

1955 - (07-25-1955) **Clarence James Beamish (04) dies, his wife already deceased passes property inheritance to Mary Ellen Chapman (09) and heirs – Lot 21**

#18 Source - Halifax Office of Registrar of Deeds, Book 907 P. 605, dated 12-23-1946 with the Canada Permanent Trust Company, and filed on 02-22-1961. 09,04>10 **- Lot 23**

#16 Source - Nova Scotia Supreme Court Book 27, P. 339, No. #638. NSNA. Represent heirs shares of "South & West part Oak Island," "George McInnis Property," and "James McInnis Property." 07-20-1961. 09,04>10 **- Lot 6, 7, 8, 15, 16, 17, 18, 19, 20, 23, 25, 26, 30, 31, 32**

#170 Source – "*Selwyn William Sellers, 1873-1949*." FamilySearch, See citation.

1961 - (02-22-1961) **Heirs of Mary Ellen Chapman (09) & heirs of Clarence Beamish (04), to M.R. Chappell (10) – Lot 21**

#170 Source – "*Selwyn William Sellers, 1873-1949*." FamilySearch, See citation.

#18 Source - Halifax Office of Registrar of Deeds, Book 907 P. 605, dated 12-23-1946 with the Canada Permanent Trust Company, and filed on 02-22-1961. 09,04>11 **- Lot 23**

#16 Source - Nova Scotia Supreme Court Book 27, P. 339, No. #638. NSNA. Represent heirs shares of "South & West part Oak Island," "George McInnis Property," and "James McInnis Property." 07-20-1961. 09,04>10 **- Lot 6, 7, 8, 15, 16, 17, 18, 19, 20, 23, 25, 26, 30, 31, 32**

1977 - (06-15-1977) **M.R. Chappell (10), to David C. Tobias (55)** for all shares regarding Lots, **1, 2, 3, 4, 6, 7, 8, 15, 16, 17, 18, 19, 20, 21, 22, 24, 25, 26, 27, 28, 29, 30, 31, 32. – Lot 21**

#20 Source – Filed in Halifax Co. Land Deeds, recorded on 06-29-1977, No. #582. NSNA. 10>55 **- Lots 6, 7, 8, 15, 16, 17, 18, 19, 20, 25, 26, 30, 31, 32**

1987 - (12-09-1987) **David Tobias (55) and his lots, join Dan Blankenship (07) to form Oak Island Tours Inc (41) – Lot 21**

#111 Source – "*The Open Database of the Corporate World. Oak Island Tours Inc. Company Number 2272393*." Incorporated Date, 12-09-1987. Opencorporates.

#112 Source – "*The Curse of Oak Island, The Story of the World's Longest Treasure Hunt*." By Randall Sullivan, 2018. Page 422.

2007 - David Tobias (55), sells his Lots to Rick & Marty Lagina who become equal partners with Dan Blankenship (07) in Oak Island Tours (41) which own/control Lots 1, 2, 3, 4, 6, 7, 8, 15, 16, 17, 18, 19, 20, 21, 22, 24, 26, 27, 28, 29, 30, 31, 32. – Lot 21

#111 Source – "*The Open Database of the Corporate World. Oak Island Tours Inc. Company Number 2272393*." Incorporated Date, 12-09-1987. Opencorporates.

#112 Source – "*The Curse of Oak Island, The Story of the World's Longest Treasure Hunt*." By Randall Sullivan, 2018. Page 422.

2007 - **MacPhie Archives "*Oak Island Lot Distribution Map, 2007*."** Lots ***1, 2, 3, 4, 6, 7, 8, 15, 16, 17, 18, 19, 20, 21, 22, 24, 26, 27, 28, 29, 30, 31, 32*** - Oak Island Tours (41); Lot ***5*** – Robert S. Young (61); Lots ***9, 10, 11, 12, 14*** – Fred Nolan (40); Lot ***13*** – John Johnston (25); Lot ***23*** – Dan/Dave Blankenship (07); and Lot ***25*** – Alan Kostrzewe (27). – **All Lots**

#30 Source - "*Oak Island Lot Ownership Map, 2007*," By MacPhie Archives. **All Lots**

Lot 22.

1753 - (12-27-1753) **Governor Charles Lawrence, to Capt. John Gifford (53) and Richard Smith (53) – ALL LOTS**

#123 Source - NS Archives and Record Management "Allotment" Book, P. 137, Reel #13044; "Old Book" #1, P. 44. Granted Gifford Island #12, Young Island #13, and Smith Island #28, to establish a fishery. Escheated.

1784 - (06-16-1784) **Jonathan Prescott (45), to Robert Melvin (38) – Lot 22**

#92 Source – Lunenburg Co. Land Deeds, recorded 09-27-1790, Vol. 3, P. 429-30, No. #709. 45>38 **- Lot 8 & 22**

#35 Source - "*Habitation on Oak Island*." Beaton Institute, Cape Breton University. Created by Surveyor William Dy Sr., called 'The Old Plan' No. 1046. Department of Lands & Forests, n.d. MG 12, 75 NSNA. Also Published in Joy Steele/Gordon Fader's book "*Oak Island Mystery Solved-Final Chapter*." P. 10. 2nd Ed. 2016.

1788 - Probate – **Robert Melvin Sr (38) dies, 1787 willed to Robert Melvin Jr. (38d) – Lot 22**

#83 Source – "*Loyalist Melvins-H*." By Palmer Papers. Browne & Chester Township Books citations, Vol. 6, P. 26, No. #51. - **Lot 22**

1796 - (03-14-1796) **Jacob Melvin (38c), to Daniel McKinnon (32a) – Lot 22**

#77 Source – Lunenburg Co. Land Deeds, recorded 04-14-1796, Vol. 4, P. 140, No. #170. 38c>32a **- Lot 22**

#83 Source – "*Loyalist Melvins-H*." By Palmer Papers. Browne & Chester Township Books citations, Vol. 6, P. 26, No. #51.

#35 Source - "*Habitation on Oak Island*." Beaton Institute, Cape Breton University. Created by Surveyor William Dy Sr., called 'The Old Plan' No. 1046. Department of Lands & Forests, n.d. MG 12, 75 NSNA. Also Published in Joy Steele/Gordon Fader's book "*Oak Island Mystery Solved-Final Chapter*." P. 10. 2nd Ed. 2016.

1870 - (01-05-1870) **Daniel McKinnon/ Daniel McInnis (yeoman) (32a) dies, property passed to family (32fam) – Lot 22**

#202 Source – Last Will and Testament Extractions, Lunenburg County, Mf:0558683.

1896 - **James Henry McInnis (32fam) dies, passes to Arthur Curran McInnis (32fam) – Lot 22**

#1 Source – N.S. Supreme Court, Book No. 368, recorded 10-01-1931, Book 20, P. 423, No. #368. (originally Book No. 20, P. 74, No. #368. – **Lot 22**

1915 - **Arthur Curran Mcinnis (32fam) dies, passes to John Mcinnis Family (32fam) – Lot 22**

#1 Source – N.S. Supreme Court, Book No. 368, recorded 10-01-1931, Book 20, P. 423, No. #368. (originally Book No. 20, P. 74, No.69) – **Lot 22**

1930 - **John McInnis Family (32fam), pass to inheritors Wallace and Margaret Young (63) et. al. – Lot 22**

#169 Source – Lunenburg Co. Land Deed, recorded 06-21-1930, Book 20, P. 74, No. #69. Deeded on 06-09-1930. 32>32 **- Lot 22**

#1 Source – N.S. Supreme Court, Book No. 368, recorded 10-01-1931, Book 20, P. 423, No. #368. (originally Book No. 20, P. 74, No.69) – **Lot 22**

#3 Source – City & County of San Francisco, Calif. Records; & NSNA, recorded 05-27-1935, Book No. 21. P. 96, No. #148. **- Lot 22**

1931 - (09-22-1931) **Wallace & Margaret Young (63), sell 50% of prop. Val. & share, to Archibald C. Dauphinee (15) – Lot 22**

#1 Source – N.S. Supreme Court, Book No. 368, recorded 10-01-1931, Book 20, P. 423, No. #368. (originally Book No. 20, P. 74, No.69) 63>15 – **Lot 22**

1944 - (09-28-1944) **Archibald Dauphinee (15) & Margaret Young (63), to Clarence James Beamish (04) – Lot 22**

#12 Source – Lunenburg Co. Land Deeds, recorded 10-25-1955, Deed #1142 on 10-25-1944. NSNA.

1955 - (07-25-1955) **Clarence James Beamish (04) dies, his wife already deceased passes property inheritance to Mary Ellen Chapman (09) and heirs – Lot 22**

- #18 Source - Halifax Office of Registrar of Deeds, Book 907 P. 605, dated 12-23-1946 with the Canada Permanent Trust Company, and filed on 02-22-1961. 09,04>10 **- Lot 22**
- #16 Source - Nova Scotia Supreme Court Book 27, P. 339, No. #638. NSNA. Represent heirs shares of "South & West part Oak Island," "George McInnis Property," and "James McInnis Property." 07-20-1961. 09,04>10 **- Lot 6, 7, 8, 15, 16, 17, 18, 19, 20, 23, 25, 26, 30, 31, 32**
- #170 Source – "*Selwyn William Sellers, 1873-1949*." FamilySearch, See citation.

1961 - (02-22-1961) **Heirs of Mary Ellen Chapman (09) & heirs of Clarence Beamish (04), to M.R. Chappell (10) – Lot 22**

- #170 Source – "*Selwyn William Sellers, 1873-1949*." FamilySearch, See citation.
- #18 Source - Halifax Office of Registrar of Deeds, Book 907 P. 605, dated 12-23-1946 with the Canada Permanent Trust Company, and filed on 02-22-1961. 09,04>10 **- Lot 22**
- #16 Source - Nova Scotia Supreme Court Book 27, P. 339, No. #638. NSNA. Represent heirs shares of "South & West part Oak Island," "George McInnis Property," and "James McInnis Property." 07-20-1961. 09,04>10 **- Lot 6, 7, 8, 15, 16, 17, 18, 19, 20, 23, 25, 26, 30, 31, 32**

1977 - (06-15-1977) **M.R. Chappell (10), to David C. Tobias (55)** for all shares regarding Lots, **1, 2, 3, 4, 6, 7, 8, 15, 16, 17, 18, 19, 20, 21, 22, 24, 25, 26, 27, 28, 29, 30, 31, 32. – Lot 22**

- #20 Source – Filed in Halifax Co. Land Deeds, recorded on 06-29-1977, No. #582. NSNA. 10>55 **- Lots 6, 7, 8, 15, 16, 17, 18, 19, 20, 25, 26, 30, 31, 32**

1987 - (12-09-1987) **David Tobias (55) and his lots, join Dan Blankenship (07) to form Oak Island Tours Inc (41) – Lot 22**

- #111 Source – "*The Open Database of the Corporate World. Oak Island Tours Inc. Company Number 2272393*." Incorporated Date, 12-09-1987. Opencorporates.
- #112 Source – "*The Curse of Oak Island, The Story of the World's Longest Treasure Hunt*." By Randall Sullivan, 2018. Page 422.

2007 - **David Tobias (55), sells his Lots to Rick & Marty Lagina who become equal partners with Dan Blankenship (07) in Oak Island Tours (41) which own/control Lots 1, 2, 3, 4, 6, 7, 8, 15, 16, 17, 18, 19, 20, 21, 22, 24, 26, 27, 28, 29, 30, 31, 32. – Lot 22**

- #111 Source – "*The Open Database of the Corporate World. Oak Island Tours Inc. Company Number 2272393*." Incorporated Date, 12-09-1987. Opencorporates.
- #112 Source – "*The Curse of Oak Island, The Story of the World's Longest Treasure Hunt*." By Randall Sullivan, 2018. Page 422.

2007 - **MacPhie Archives "*Oak Island Lot Distribution Map, 2007*."** Lots ***1, 2, 3, 4, 6, 7, 8, 15, 16, 17, 18, 19, 20, 21, 22, 24, 26, 27, 28, 29, 30, 31, 32*** - Oak Island Tours (41); Lot **5** – Robert S. Young (61); Lots ***9, 10, 11, 12, 14*** – Fred Nolan (40); Lot ***13*** – John Johnston (25); Lot ***23*** – Dan/Dave Blankenship (07); and Lot **25** – Alan Kostrzewe (27). **– All Lots**

- #30 Source - "*Oak Island Lot Ownership Map, 2007*," By MacPhie Archives. **All Lots**

Lot 23.

1753 - (12-27-1753) **Governor Charles Lawrence, to Capt. John Gifford (53) and Richard Smith (53) – ALL LOTS**

- #123 Source - NS Archives and Record Management "Allotment" Book, P. 137, Reel #13044; "Old Book" #1, P. 44. Granted Gifford Island #12, Young Island #13, and Smith Island #28, to establish a fishery. Escheated.

1784 - (10-10-1784) **William Bowie (08), to Hector McLean (34) – Lot 23**

- #61 Source – Lunenburg Co. Land Deeds, recorded 04-08-1788, Vol. 3, P. 340, No. #554. 08>34 **– Lot 23**
- #35 Source - "*Habitation on Oak Island*." Beaton Institute, Cape Breton University. Created by Surveyor William Dy Sr., called 'The Old Plan' No. 1046. Department of Lands & Forests, n.d. MG 12, 75 NSNA. Also Published in Joy Steele/Gordon Fader's book "*Oak Island Mystery Solved-Final Chapter*." P. 10. 2nd Ed. 2016.

1788 - (01-05-1788) **Hector McLean (34), to Donald McInnis (32) – Lot 23**

#79 Source – Lunenburg Co. Land Deeds, recorded Vol. 3, P. 418-19, No. #690. 34>32 **- Lot 23**

#35 Source - "*Habitation on Oak Island*." Beaton Institute, Cape Breton University. Created by Surveyor William Dy Sr., called 'The Old Plan' No. 1046. Department of Lands & Forests, n.d. MG 12, 75 NSNA. Also Published in Joy Steele/Gordon Fader's book "*Oak Island Mystery Solved-Final Chapter*." P. 10. 2nd Ed. 2016.

1827 - Donald McGinnis (32) dies, in late 1826 and his will is probated and property remains in the family, coded as (32fam) in 1827 – Lot 23

#2 Source - Paul Wroclawski Research & Property Owners Charles Morris to John Smith; collected through 02-06-2008.

#17 Source – "*Chester Township Records, 1762-1830*." Births, Marriages &Deaths. NSNA MG9, B 9-3

1896 - James Henry McInnis (32fam) dies, his property passes to Arthur Curran McInnis (32fam) which stays in the McInnis family – Lot 23

#1 Source – N.S. Supreme Court, Book No. 368, recorded 10-01-1931, Book 20, P. 423, No. #368. (originally Book No. 20, P. 74, No.69) **– Lot 23.**

1915 - Arthur Curran Mcinnis (32fam) dies, passes to John Mcinnis Family (32fam) which stays in the McInnis family – Lot 23

#1 Source – N.S. Supreme Court, Book No. 368, recorded 10-01-1931, Book 20, P. 423, No. #368. (originally Book No. 20, P. 74, No.69) **– Lot 23**

1930 - John McInnis Family (32fam), deeded properties by Salome Esther, widow of Arthur C. Mcinnis. pass to inheritors Wallace and Margaret Young, et. al. (63) – Lot 23

#169 Source – Lunenburg Co. Land Deed, recorded 06-21-1930, Book 20, P. 74, No. #69. Deeded on 06-09-1930. **- Lot 23**

#1 Source – N.S. Supreme Court, Book No. 368, recorded 10-01-1931, Book 20, P. 423, No. #368. (originally Book No. 20, P. 74, No.69) **– Lot 23**

#3 Source – City & County of San Francisco, Calif. Records; & NSNA, recorded 05-27-1935, Book No. 21. P. 96, No. #148. **- Lot 23**

1931 - (10-01-1931) **Margaret M. Young (63), to Archibald & Hannah Dauphinee (15) – Lot 23**

#1 Source – N.S. Supreme Court, Book No. 368, recorded 10-01-1931, Book 20, P. 423, No. #368. (originally Book No. 20, P. 74, No.69) 63>15 **– Lot 23**

1935 - (05-27-1935) **Mary Young, Margaret & Wallace Young (63), to Hannah & Archibald A. Dauphinee (15) – Lot 23**

#3 Source – City & County of San Francisco, Calif. Records; & NSNA, recorded 05-27-1935, Book No. 21. P. 96, No. #148. 63>15 **- Lot 23**

1944 - (09-28-1944) **Archibald & Hannah Dauphinee (15) and Margaret Young (63), to Clarence Beamish (04) – Lot 23**

#12 Source – Lunenburg Co. Land Deeds, recorded 10-25-1955, Deed #1142 on 10-25-1944. NSNA. 15,63>04 **- Lot 23**

1955 - (07-25-1955) **Clarence James Beamish (04) dies, his wife already deceased passes property inheritance to Mary Ellen Chapman (09) and heirs – Lot 23**

#18 Source - Halifax Office of Registrar of Deeds, Book 907 P. 605, dated 12-23-1946 with the Canada Permanent Trust Company, and filed on 02-22-1961. 09,04>10 **- Lot 23**

#16 Source - Nova Scotia Supreme Court Book 27, P. 339, No. #638. NSNA. Represent heirs shares of "South & West part Oak Island," "George McInnis Property," and "James McInnis Property." 07-20-1961. 09,04>10 **- Lot 6, 7, 8, 15, 16, 17, 18, 19, 20, 23, 25, 26, 30, 31, 32**

#170 Source – "*Selwyn William Sellers, 1873-1949*." FamilySearch, See citation.

1961 - (02-22-1961) **Heirs of Mary Ellen Chapman (09) & heirs of Clarence Beamish (04), to M.R. Chappell (10) – Lot 23**

#170 Source – "*Selwyn William Sellers, 1873-1949*." FamilySearch, See citation.

#18 Source - Halifax Office of Registrar of Deeds, Book 907 P. 605, dated 12-23-1946 with the Canada Permanent Trust Company, and filed on 02-22-1961. 09,04>10 **- Lot 23**

#16 Source - Nova Scotia Supreme Court Book 27, P. 339, No. #638. NSNA. Represent heirs shares of "South & West part Oak Island," "George McInnis Property," and "James McInnis Property." 07-20-1961. 09,04>10 **- Lot 6, 7, 8, 15, 16, 17, 18, 19, 20, 23, 25, 26, 30, 31, 32**

1975 - (09-19-1976) **M.R. Chappell (10), to Dan Blankenship (07) – Lot 23**

#19 Source - Owner transfer by Quit Claim Deed from M.R. Chappell (10) to Dan Blankenship (07) on 09-19-1975, filed in Chester Deed Office, Book 54, P. 161. 10>07 **– Lot 23**

2007 - **MacPhie Archives "*Oak Island Lot Distribution Map, 2007*."** Lots ***1, 2, 3, 4, 6, 7, 8, 15, 16, 17, 18, 19, 20, 21, 22, 24, 26, 27, 28, 29, 30, 31, 32*** - Oak Island Tours (41); Lot ***5*** – Robert S. Young (61); Lots ***9, 10, 11, 12, 14*** – Fred Nolan (40); Lot ***13*** – John Johnston (25); Lot ***23*** – Dan/Dave Blankenship (07); and Lot ***25*** – Alan Kostrzewe (27). **– All Lots**

#30 Source - "*Oak Island Lot Ownership Map, 2007*," By MacPhie Archives. **All Lots**

2019 - (03-17-2019) **Dan Blankenship (07) dies, and property is transferred to his son, Dave Blankenship (07a) – Lot 23**

#140 Source – "*Daniel C. Blankenship Obituary*. " Published obituary, See citation. **– Lot 23.**

Lot 24.

1753 - (12-27-1753) **Governor Charles Lawrence, to Capt. John Gifford (53) and Richard Smith (53) – ALL LOTS**

#123 Source - NS Archives and Record Management "Allotment" Book, P. 137, Reel #13044; "Old Book" #1, P. 44. Granted Gifford Island #12, Young Island #13, and Smith Island #28, to establish a fishery. Escheated.

1784 - **Crown (00)** granted lot to **Duncan Smith (51),** father of **John Smith (51a)** –

1785 - (02-24-1785) **Duncan Smith (51), to Allen Ambrose (01) – Lot 24**

#99 Source – Lunenburg Co. Land Deeds, recorded 02-28-1785, Vol. 3, P. 154, No. #248. 51>01 **- Lot 24**

#2 Source - Paul Wroclawski Research & Property Owners Charles Morris to John Smith; collected through 02-06-2008.

#35 Source - "*Habitation on Oak Island*." Beaton Institute, Cape Breton University. Created by Surveyor William Dy Sr., called 'The Old Plan' No. 1046. Department of Lands & Forests, n.d. MG 12, 75 NSNA. Also Published in Joy Steele/Gordon Fader's book "*Oak Island Mystery Solved-Final Chapter*." P. 10. 2nd Ed. 2016.

1791 - (10-20-1791) **Allen Ambrose (01), sells lot w/ Plum & March Islands, to John Monrowe/Monro (39) – Lot 24**

#87 Source – Lunenburg Co. Land Deeds, recorded 07-04-1794, Vol. 4, P. 39, No. #52. 01>39 **- Lot 24**

#35 Source - "*Habitation on Oak Island*." Beaton Institute, Cape Breton University. Created by Surveyor William Dy Sr., called 'The Old Plan' No. 1046. Department of Lands & Forests, n.d. MG 12, 75 NSNA. Also Published in Joy Steele/Gordon Fader's book "*Oak Island Mystery Solved-Final Chapter*." P. 10. 2nd Ed. 2016.

1799 - (07-06-1799) **John Munro (39), to Samuel Ball (03) – Lot 24**

#88 Source – Lunenburg Co. Land Deeds, recorded 10-11-1832, Vol. 6, P. 26, No. #55. 39>03 **- Lot 24**

#24 Source – "*Bee Stanton's Samuel Ball Map 1787 - 1812*." @ www.creative@beestanton website. **Lots 6, 7, 8, 24, 25, 26, 30, 31, 32**

#35 Source - "*Habitation on Oak Island*." Beaton Institute, Cape Breton University. Created by Surveyor William Dy Sr., called 'The Old Plan' No. 1046. Department of Lands & Forests, n.d. MG 12, 75 NSNA. Also Published in Joy Steele/Gordon Fader's book "*Oak Island Mystery Solved-Final Chapter*." P. 10. 2nd Ed. 2016.

1812 - **Oak Island Samuel Ball (03) – Lot 24**

#24 Source – "*Bee Stanton's Samuel Ball Map 1787 - 1812*." @ www.creative@beestanton website. **Lots 6, 7, 8, 24, 25, 26, 30, 31, 32**

#131 Source -"*The Black Settlers of 'Treasure Oak Island' The Primary Generation – Samuel Ball (03)*." See citation. **– Lots 6, 7, 8, 24, 25, 26, 30, 31, 32**

#132 Source - "*Who Was Samuel Ball*," Published by Deb Minter 07-06-2021. Facebook online, "*Oak Island: History not Myth*." Posted 06-23-2021. **– Lots 6, 7, 8, 24, 25, 26, 30, 31, 32**

1845 - (12-14-1845) **Samuel Ball (03) dies, Isaac Butler (Ball) (03a)** inherits Balls **Lots 6, 7, 8, 24, 25, 26, 30, 31, 32. – Lot 24**

#17 Source – "*Chester Township Records, 1762-1830*." Births, Marriages, and Deaths. NSNA MG9, B 9-3.

#130a Source – Lunenburg Co. Registrar, Book 1, P. 37, dated 10-01-1841, recorded 01-05-1846. Last Will & Testament of Samuel Ball (03). **– Lots 6, 7, 8, 24, 25, 26, 30, 31, 32**

#108 Source – "*Samuel Ball Will, Lunenburg, N.S.*" Will Extracts – See citation.

1846 - **Isaac Butler (Ball) (03a)** with new wife Sarah Hannah, Simeon Ball & Elizabeth Best continue to live on Oak Island. **– Lot 24**

#131 Source -"*The Black Settlers of 'Treasure Oak Island' The Primary Generation – Samuel Ball (03)*." See citation. **– Lots 6, 7, 8, 24, 25, 26, 30, 31, 32**

#132 Source - "*Who Was Samuel Ball*," Published by Deb Minter 07-06-2021. Facebook online, "*Oak Island: History not Myth*." Posted 06-23-2021. **– Lots 6, 7, 8, 24, 25, 26, 30, 31, 32**

1898 - (01-17-1898) **Isaac Butler (Ball) (03a), deeds ½ lot to Abraham Ernst (18) & ½ lot Henry Sellers (19a) – Lot 24**

#13 Source – Dominion of Canada Book No. #693, NSNA. **- Lots 6, 7, 8, 15, 16, 17, 18, 19, 20, 25, 26, 30, 32** [Lot 31 missing]

#108 Source – "*Samuel Ball Will, Lunenburg, N.S.*" Will Extracts – See citation.

1912 - **Abraham Ernst (18) dies 1911, Henry Sellers (19a) dies 1912, & his wife (Sophia Elizabeth Graves Sellers) dies 1931;** leaving inherited lots to future heirs. **– Lot 24**

#199 Source – "*Letter from Blair to Harris 02-16-1035*." on purchasing remaining lots 1–14. – **Lots 1, 2, 3, 4, 5, 6, 7, 8, 9, 10, 11, 12, 13, 14**

1937 - (09-14-1937) **Francis & Eva G. Conrad (12) and Ingram & Quesetta M. Conrad (12a), to Archibald D. Dauphinee (15) – Lot 24**

#9 Source - Dominion of Canada Book No. 8, P. 218-219, No. #655. (originally in Book 8, P. 218-219, No. #132) NSNA. 12,12a>15 **- Lot 6, 7, 8, 25, 26, 30, 31, 32**

1937 - (09-13-1937) **Archibald D. & Hannah Dauphinee (15), to Gilbert Hedden (22) – Lot 24**

#10 Source - Dominion of Canada Book No. 21, P. 402-403, No. #656. (originally in Book 21, P.218-219, No. #132) NSNA. 15>22 **– Lot 6, 7, 8, 25, 26, 30, 31, 32**

1950 - (05-26-1950) **Gilbert D. Hedden & Margarite C. Hedden (22), to John Whitney Lewis (10a) – Lot 24**

#13 Source – Dominion of Canada Book No. #693, NSNA. 22>10a **- Lots 6, 7, 8, 15, 16, 17, 18, 19, 20, 25, 26, 30, 32** [Lot 31 missing]

1951 - (12-05-1950) **John Whitney Lewis & Ann Lewis (10a), to Acadia Trust Company (10b) – Lot 24**

#14 Source - Dominion of Canada, NSNA #880. (original filings list – see citation). 10a>10b **- Lot 6, 7, 8, 15, 16, 17, 18, 19, 20, 25, 30, 31, 32** [Lot 26 missing]

1957 - (04-20-1957) **Acadia Trust Company (10b), to M.R. Chappell (10) – Lot 24**

#15 Source - Registry of Deeds at Bridgewater and Registry of Probate, Book 26, P. 195, Quit Claim No. 374, NSNA. 10b>10 **- Lot 6, 7, 8, 15, 16, 17, 18, 19, 20, 25, 26, 30, 31, 32**

1961 - (07-21-1961) **Mary Ellen Chapman (09) & heirs of Clarence J. Beamish (04), to M.R. Chappell, Lots 5, 6, 7, 8, 15, 16, 17, 18, 19, 20, 23, 25, 26, 30, 31, 32 (10) – Lot 24**

#16 Source - Nova Scotia Supreme Court Book 27, P. 339, No. #638. NSNA. Represent heirs shares of "South & West part Oak Island," "George McInnis Property," and "James McInnis Property." 07-20-1961. 09,04>10 **- Lot 6, 7, 8, 15, 16, 17, 18, 19, 20, 23, 25, 26, 30, 31, 32**

1977 - (06-15-1977) **M.R. Chappell (10), to David C. Tobias (55)** for all shares regarding Lots, **1, 2, 3, 4, 6, 7, 8, 15, 16, 17, 18, 19, 20, 21, 22, 24, 25, 26, 27, 28, 29, 30, 31, 32. – Lot 24**

#20 Source – Filed in Halifax Co. Land Deeds, recorded on 06-29-1977, No. #582. NSNA. 10>55 **- Lots 6, 7, 8, 15, 16, 17, 18, 19, 20, 25, 26, 30, 31, 32**

1987 - (12-09-1987) **David Tobias (55) and his lots, join Dan Blankenship (07) to form Oak Island Tours Inc (41) – Lot 24**

#111 Source – "*The Open Database of the Corporate World. Oak Island Tours Inc. Company Number 2272393*." Incorporated Date, 12-09-1987. Opencorporates.

#112 Source – "*The Curse of Oak Island, The Story of the World's Longest Treasure Hunt*." By Randall Sullivan, 2018. Page 422.

2007 - **David Tobias (55), sells his Lots to Rick & Marty Lagina who become equal partners with Dan Blankenship (07) in Oak Island Tours (41) which include Lots 1, 2, 3, 4, 6, 7, 8, 15, 16, 17, 18, 19, 20, 21, 22, 24, 26, 27, 28, 29, 30, 31, 32 – Lot 24**

#111 Source – "*The Open Database of the Corporate World. Oak Island Tours Inc. Company Number 2272393*." Incorporated Date, 12-09-1987. Opencorporates.

#112 Source – "*The Curse of Oak Island, The Story of the World's Longest Treasure Hunt*." By Randall Sullivan, 2018. Page 422.

2007 - MacPhie Archives "*Oak Island Lot Distribution Map, 2007*." Lots ***1, 2, 3, 4, 6, 7, 8, 15, 16, 17, 18, 19, 20, 21, 22, 24, 26, 27, 28, 29, 30, 31, 32*** - Oak Island Tours (41); Lot ***5*** – Robert S. Young (61); Lots ***9, 10, 11, 12, 14*** – Fred Nolan (40); Lot ***13*** – John Johnston (25); Lot ***23*** – Dan/Dave Blankenship (07); and Lot ***25*** – Alan Kostrzewe (27). – **All Lots**

#30 Source - "*Oak Island Lot Ownership Map, 2007*," By MacPhie Archives. **All Lots**

Lot 25.

1753 - (12-27-1753) **Governor Charles Lawrence, to Capt. John Gifford (53) and Richard Smith (53) – ALL LOTS**

#123 Source - NS Archives and Record Management "Allotment" Book, P. 137, Reel #13044; "Old Book" #1, P. 44. Granted Gifford Island #12, Young Island #13, and Smith Island #28, to establish a fishery. Escheated.

1787 - (09-22-1787) **William Hopkins (23), to Samuel Ball (03) – Lot 25**

#72 Source – Lunenburg Co. Land Deeds, recorded 08-24-1807, Vol. 6, P. 24, No. #51. 23>03 **- Lot 25**

#24 Source – "*Bee Stanton's Samuel Ball Map 1787 - 1812*." @ www.creative@beestanton website. **Lots 6, 7, 8, 24, 25, 26, 30, 31, 32**

#35 Source - "*Habitation on Oak Island*." Beaton Institute, Cape Breton University. Created by Surveyor William Dy Sr., called 'The Old Plan' No. 1046. Department of Lands & Forests, n.d. MG 12, 75 NSNA. Also Published in Joy Steele/Gordon Fader's book "*Oak Island Mystery Solved-Final Chapter*." P. 10. 2nd Ed. 2016.

1812 - Oak Island Samuel Ball (03) – Lot 25

#24 Source – "*Bee Stanton's Samuel Ball Map 1787 - 1812*." @ www.creative@beestanton website. **Lots 6, 7, 8, 24, 25, 26, 30, 31, 32**

#131 Source -"*The Black Settlers of 'Treasure Oak Island' The Primary Generation – Samuel Ball (03)*." See citation. **– Lots 6, 7, 8, 24, 25, 26, 30, 31, 32**

#132 Source - "*Who Was Samuel Ball*," Published by Deb Minter 07-06-2021. Facebook online, "*Oak Island: History not Myth*." Posted 06-23-2021. **– Lots 6, 7, 8, 24, 25, 26, 30, 31, 32**

1845 - (12-14-1845) **Samuel Ball (03) dies, Isaac Butler (Ball) (03a)** handles property **- Lot 25**

#17 Source – "*Chester Township Records, 1762-1830*." Births, Marriages & Deaths. NSNA MG9, B 9-3

#130a Source – Lunenburg Co. Registrar, Book 1, P. 37, dated 10-01-1841, recorded 01-05-1846. Last Will & Testament of Samuel Ball (03). **– Lots 6, 7, 8, 24, 25, 26, 30, 31, 32**

#108 Source – "*Samuel Ball Will, Lunenburg, N.S.*" Will Extracts – See citation.

1845 - Isaac Butler (Ball) (03a) with new wife Sarah Hannah, Simeon Ball & Elizabeth Best continue to live on Oak Island. **– Lot 25**

#131 Source -"*The Black Settlers of 'Treasure Oak Island' The Primary Generation – Samuel Ball (03)*." See citation. **– Lots 6, 7, 8, 24, 25, 26, 30, 31, 32**

#132 Source - "*Who Was Samuel Ball*," Published by Deb Minter 07-06-2021. Facebook online, "*Oak Island: History not Myth*." Posted 06-23-2021. **– Lots 6, 7, 8, 24, 25, 26, 30, 31, 32**

1898 - (01-17-1898) **Isaac Butler (Ball) (03a), deeds ½ lot to Abraham Ernst (18) & ½ lot Henry Sellers (19a) – Lot 25**

#13 Source – Dominion of Canada Book No. #693, NSNA. 22>10a **- Lots 6, 7, 8, 15, 16, 17, 18, 19, 20, 25, 26, 30, 32** [Lot 31 missing]

#108 Source – "*Samuel Ball Will, Lunenburg, N.S.*" Will Extracts – See citation.

1912 - Abraham Ernst (18) dies 1911, Henry Sellers (19a) dies 1912, & his wife (Sophia Elizabeth Graves Sellers) dies 1931; leaving inherited lots to future heirs. **– Lot 25**

#199 Source – "*Letter from Blair to Harris 02-16-1035*." on purchasing remaining lots 1–14. – **Lots 1, 2, 3, 4, 5, 6, 7, 8, 9, 10, 11, 12, 13, 14**

1937 - (09-14-1937) **Francis & Eva G. Conrad (12) and Ingram & Quesetta M. Conrad (12a), to Archibald D. Dauphinee (15) – Lot 25**

#9 Source - Dominion of Canada Book No. 8, P. 218-219, No. #655. (originally in Book 8, P. 218-219, No. #132) NSNA. 12,12a>15 **- Lot 6, 7, 8, 25, 26, 30, 31, 32**

1937 - (09-13-1937) **Archibald & Hannah Dauphinee (15), to Gilbert Hedden (22) – Lot 25**

#10 Source - Dominion of Canada Book No. 21, P. 402-403, No. #656. (originally in Book 21, P.218-219, No. #132) NSNA. 15>22 **– Lot 6, 7, 8, 25, 26, 30, 31, 32**

1950 - (05-26-1950) **Gilbert D. Hedden & Margarite C. Hedden (22), to John Whitney Lewis (10a) – Lot 25**

#13 Source – Dominion of Canada Book No. #693, NSNA. 22>10a **- Lots 6, 7, 8, 15, 16, 17, 18, 19, 20, 25, 26, 30, 32** [Lot 31 missing]

1950 - (12-05-1950) **John Whitney Lewis & Ann Lewis (10a), to Acadia Trust Company (10b) – Lot 25**

#14 Source - Dominion of Canada, NSNA #880. (original filings list – see citation). 10a>10b **- Lot 6, 7, 8, 15, 16, 17, 18, 19, 20, 25, 30, 31, 32** [Lot 26 missing]

1957 - (04-20-1957) **Acadia Trust Company (10b), to M.R. Chappell (10) – Lot 25**

#15 Source - Registry of Deeds at Bridgewater and Registry of Probate, Book 26, P. 195, Quit Claim No. 374, NSNA. 10b>10 **- Lot 6, 7, 8, 15, 16, 17, 18, 19, 20, 25, 26, 30, 31, 32**

1961 - (07-21-1961) **Mary Ellen Chapman (09) & heirs of Clarence J. Beamish (04), to M.R. Chappell, Lots 5, 6, 7, 8, 15, 16, 17, 18, 19, 20, 23, 25, 26, 30, 31, 32 (10) – Lot 25**

#16 Source - Nova Scotia Supreme Court Book 27, P. 339, No. #638. NSNA. Represent heirs shares of "South & West part Oak Island," "George McInnis Property," and "James McInnis Property." 07-20-1961. 09,04>10 **- Lot 6, 7, 8, 15, 16, 17, 18, 19, 20, 23, 25, 26, 30, 31, 32**

1977 - (06-15-1977) **M.R. Chappell (10), to David C. Tobias (55)** for all shares regarding Lots, **1, 2, 3, 4, 6, 7, 8, 15, 16, 17, 18, 19, 20, 21, 22, 24, 25, 26, 27, 28, 29, 30, 31, 32. – Lot 25**

#20 Source – Filed in Halifax Co. Land Deeds, recorded on 06-29-1977, No. #582. NSNA. 10>55 **- Lots 6, 7, 8, 15, 16, 17, 18, 19, 20, 25, 26, 30, 31, 32**

1987 - (12-09-1987) **David Tobias (55) and his lots, join Dan Blankenship (07) to form Oak Island Tours Inc (41) – Lot 25**

#111 Source – "*The Open Database of the Corporate World. Oak Island Tours Inc. Company Number 2272393*." Incorporated Date, 12-09-1987. Opencorporates.

#112 Source – "*The Curse of Oak Island, The Story of the World's Longest Treasure Hunt*." By Randall Sullivan, 2018. Page 422.

2005 - David Tobias (55), to Center Road Developments, Alan Kostrzewa (27) and Brian Urbach, - Lot 25

#700 Source – "*Oak Island Mystery*." Wikipedia, *Oak Island Mystery*. See citation.

2007 - MacPhie Archives "*Oak Island Lot Distribution Map, 2007*." Lots ***1, 2, 3, 4, 6, 7, 8, 15, 16, 17, 18, 19, 20, 21, 22, 24, 26, 27, 28, 29, 30, 31, 32*** - Oak Island Tours (41); Lot ***5*** – Robert S. Young (61); Lots ***9, 10, 11, 12, 14*** – Fred Nolan (40); Lot ***13*** – John Johnston (25); Lot ***23*** – Dan/Dave Blankenship (07); and Lot ***25*** – Alan Kostrzewe (27). **– All Lots**

#30 Source - "*Oak Island Lot Ownership Map, 2007*," By MacPhie Archives. **All Lots**

Lot 26.

1753 - (12-27-1753) **Governor Charles Lawrence, to Capt. John Gifford (53) and Richard Smith (53) – ALL LOTS**

#123 Source - NS Archives and Record Management "Allotment" Book, P. 137, Reel #13044; "Old Book" #1, P. 44. Granted Gifford Island #12, Young Island #13, and Smith Island #28, to establish a fishery. Escheated.

1784 - Crown (00) granted lot to James Anderson (02) – Lot 26

#2 Source - Paul Wroclawski Research & Property Owners Charles Morris to John Smith; collected through 02-06-2008.

1788 - (11-10-1788) **James Anderson (02), to Samuel Ball (03) – Lot 26**

#135 Source – Lunenburg Co. Land Deeds, recorded 08-25-1807, Vol. 6, P. 25, No. #52. 02>03 **- Lot 26**

#24 Source – "*Bee Stanton's Samuel Ball Map 1787 - 1812*." @ www.creative@beestanton website. **Lots 6, 7, 8, 24, 25, 26, 30, 31, 32**

#35 Source - "*Habitation on Oak Island*." Beaton Institute, Cape Breton University. Created by Surveyor William Dy Sr., called 'The Old Plan' No. 1046. Department of Lands & Forests, n.d. MG 12, 75 NSNA. Also Published in Joy Steele/Gordon Fader's book "*Oak Island Mystery Solved-Final Chapter*." P. 10. 2nd Ed. 2016.

1812 - Oak Island Samuel Ball (03) – Lot 26

#24 Source – "*Bee Stanton's Samuel Ball Map 1787 - 1812*."

#131 Source -"*The Black Settlers of 'Treasure Oak Island' The Primary Generation – Samuel Ball (03)*." See citation. **– Lots 6, 7, 8, 24, 25, 26, 30, 31, 32**

#132 Source - "*Who Was Samuel Ball*," Published by Deb Minter 07-06-2021. Facebook online, "*Oak Island: History not Myth*." Posted 06-23-2021. **– Lots 6, 7, 8, 24, 25, 26, 30, 31, 32**

1845 - (12-14-1845) **Samuel Ball (03) dies, Isaac Butler (Ball) (03a) handles property - Lot 26**

#17 Source – "*Chester Township Records, 1762-1830*." Births, Marriages, and Deaths. NSNA MG9, B 9-3.

#130a Source – Lunenburg Co. Registrar, Book 1, P. 37, dated 10-01-1841, recorded 01-05-1846. Last Will & Testament of Samuel Ball (03). **– Lots 6, 7, 8, 24, 25, 26, 30, 31, 32**

1845 - Isaac Butler (Ball) (03a) with new wife Sarah Hannah, Simeon Ball & Elizabeth Best continue to live on Oak Island. **– Lot 26**

#131 Source -"*The Black Settlers of 'Treasure Oak Island' The Primary Generation – Samuel Ball (03)*." See citation. **– Lots 6, 7, 8, 24, 25, 26, 30, 31, 32**

#132 Source - "*Who Was Samuel Ball*," Published by Deb Minter 07-06-2021. Facebook online, "*Oak Island: History not Myth*." Posted 06-23-2021. **– Lots 6, 7, 8, 24, 25, 26, 30, 31, 32**

1898 - (01-17-1898) **Isaac Butler (Ball) (03a), deeds ½ lot to Abraham Ernst (18) & ½ lot Henry Sellers (19a) – Lot 26**

#13 Source – Dominion of Canada Book No. #693, NSNA. **- Lots 6, 7, 8, 15, 16, 17, 18, 19, 20, 25, 26, 30, 32** [Lot 31 missing]

#108 Source – "*Samuel Ball Will, Lunenburg, N.S.*" Will Extracts – See citation.

1912 - Abraham Ernst (18) dies 1911, Henry Sellers (19a) dies 1912, & his wife (Sophia Elizabeth Graves Sellers) **dies 1931;** leaving inherited lots to future heirs. **– Lot 26**

#199 Source – "*Letter from Blair to Harris 02-16-1035*." on purchasing remaining lots 1–14. – **Lots 1, 2, 3, 4, 5, 6, 7, 8, 9, 10, 11, 12, 13, 14**

1937 - (09-14-1937) **Francis & Eva G. Conrad (12) and Ingram & Quesetta M. Conrad (12a), to Archibald D. Dauphinee (15) – Lot 26**

#9 Source - Dominion of Canada Book No. 8, P. 218-219, No. #655. (originally in Book 8, P. 218-219, No. #132) NSNA. 12,12a>15 **- Lot 6, 7, 8, 25, 26, 30, 31, 32**

1937 - (09-13-1937) **Archibald & Hannah Dauphinee (15), to Gilbert Hedden (22) – Lot 26**

#10 Source - Dominion of Canada Book No. 21, P. 402-403, No. #656. (originally in Book 21, P.218-219, No. #132) NSNA. 15>22 **– Lot 6, 7, 8, 25, 26, 30, 31, 32**

1950 - (05-26-1950) **Gilbert D. Hedden & Margarite C. Hedden (22), to John Whitney Lewis (10a) – Lot 26**

#13 Source – Dominion of Canada Book No. #693, NSNA. 22>10a **- Lots 6, 7, 8, 15, 16, 17, 18, 19, 20, 25, 26, 30, 32** [Lot 31 missing]

1950 - (12-05-1950) **John Whitney & Ann Lewis (10a), to Acadia Trust Company (10b) – Lot 26**

#14 Source - Dominion of Canada, NSNA #880. (original filings list – see citation). 10a>10b - **Lot 6, 7, 8, 15, 16, 17, 18, 19, 20, 25, 30, 31, 32** [Lot 26 missing]

1957 - (04-20-1957) **Acadia Trust Company (10b), to M.R. Chappell (10) –Lot 26**

#15 Source - Registry of Deeds at Bridgewater and Registry of Probate, Book 26, P. 195, Quit Claim No. 374, NSNA. 10b>10 **- Lot 6, 7, 8, 15, 16, 17, 18, 19, 20, 25, 26, 30, 31, 32**

1961 - (07-21-1961) **Mary Ellen Chapman (09) & heirs of Clarence J. Beamish (04), to M.R. Chappell, Lots 5, 6, 7, 8, 15, 16, 17, 18, 19, 20, 23, 25, 26, 30, 31, 32 (10) – Lot 26**

#16 Source - Nova Scotia Supreme Court Book 27, P. 339, No. #638. NSNA. Represent heirs shares of "South & West part Oak Island," "George McInnis Property," and "James McInnis Property." 07-20-1961. 09,04>10 **- Lot 6, 7, 8, 15, 16, 17, 18, 19, 20, 23, 25, 26, 30, 31, 32**

1977 - (06-15-1977) **M.R. Chappell (10), to David C. Tobias (55)** for all shares regarding Lots, **1, 2, 3, 4, 6, 7, 8, 15, 16, 17, 18, 19, 20, 21, 22, 24, 25, 26, 27, 28, 29, 30, 31, 32. – Lot 26**

#20 Source – Filed in Halifax Co. Land Deeds, recorded on 06-29-1977, No. #582. NSNA. 10>55 **- Lots 6, 7, 8, 15, 16, 17, 18, 19, 20, 25, 26, 30, 31, 32**

1987 - (12-09-1987) **David Tobias (55) and his lots, join Dan Blankenship (07) to form Oak Island Tours Inc (41) – Lot 26**

#111 Source – "*The Open Database of the Corporate World. Oak Island Tours Inc. Company Number 2272393*." Incorporated Date, 12-09-1987. Opencorporates.

#112 Source – "*The Curse of Oak Island, The Story of the World's Longest Treasure Hunt*." By Randall Sullivan, 2018. Page 422.

2007 - David Tobias (55), sells his Lots to Rick & Marty Lagina who become equal partners with Dan Blankenship (07) in Oak Island Tours (41) which own/control Lots 1, 2, 3, 4, 6, 7, 8, 15, 16, 17, 18, 19, 20, 21, 22, 24, 26, 27, 28, 29, 30, 31, 32. – Lot 26

#111 Source – "*The Open Database of the Corporate World. Oak Island Tours Inc. Company Number 2272393*." Incorporated Date, 12-09-1987. Opencorporates.

#112 Source – "*The Curse of Oak Island, The Story of the World's Longest Treasure Hunt*." By Randall Sullivan, 2018. Page 422.

2007 - MacPhie Archives "***Oak Island Lot Distribution Map, 2007***." Lots ***1, 2, 3, 4, 6, 7, 8, 15, 16, 17, 18, 19, 20, 21, 22, 24, 26, 27, 28, 29, 30, 31, 32*** - Oak Island Tours (41); Lot ***5*** – Robert S. Young (61); Lots ***9, 10, 11, 12, 14*** – Fred Nolan (40); Lot ***13*** – John Johnston (25); Lot ***23*** – Dan/Dave Blankenship (07); and Lot ***25*** – Alan Kostrzewe (27). **– All Lots**

#30 Source - "*Oak Island Lot Ownership Map, 2007*," By MacPhie Archives. **All Lots**

Lot 27.

1753 - (12-27-1753) **Governor Charles Lawrence, to Capt. John Gifford (53) and Richard Smith (53) – ALL LOTS**

#123 Source - NS Archives and Record Management "Allotment" Book, P. 137, Reel #13044; "Old Book" #1, P. 44. Granted Gifford Island #12, Young Island #13, and Smith Island #28, to establish a fishery. Escheated.

1778 - Jeremiah Rogers (47), to David Ellis (16) – Lot 27 [No records Found**]**

#25/26 Source – "*2-Page Oak Island Lot Ownership Map, Jul. 6, 1818*." And "*Old Plan Map of Oak Island 1818*." By David W. Crandell Survey Map. NSNA. **Lots 13, 14, 15, 16, 17, 18**

#136 Source – Crandall 1818 Survey. 47>16 **- Lot 27**

#41 Source – "*Reverend John Seccomb's Diary*." NSNA, MG 1, Vol.797c, No. #5.

#52 Source - "Foreign Protestants & Settlements of Nova Scotia." By Winthrop Bell.

1786 - (11-27-1786) **David Ellis (16), TO Alexander Pattillo (42) – Lot 27**

#89 Source - Paul Wroclawski Research & Property Owners Charles Morris to John Smith; collected through 02-06-2008. 16>42 **- Lot 27**

#35 Source - "*Habitation on Oak Island*." Beaton Institute, Cape Breton University. Created by Surveyor William Dy Sr., called 'The Old Plan' No. 1046. Department of Lands & Forests, n.d. MG 12, 75 NSNA. Also Published in Joy Steele/Gordon Fader's book "*Oak Island Mystery Solved-Final Chapter*." P. 10. 2nd Ed. 2016.

1791 - (05-03-1788) **Alexander Pattillo (42), to Donald McGinnis (32) – Lot 27**

#90 Source – Lunenburg Co. Land Deeds, recorded 03-09-1807, Vol. 3, P. 730, No. #749. **- Lot 27**

#35 Source - "*Habitation on Oak Island*." Beaton Institute, Cape Breton University. Created by Surveyor William Dy Sr., called 'The Old Plan' No. 1046. Department of Lands & Forests, n.d. MG 12, 75 NSNA. Also Published in Joy Steele/Gordon Fader's book "*Oak Island Mystery Solved-Final Chapter*." P. 10. 2nd Ed. 2016.

1827 - Donald McGinnis (32) dies, in late 1826 and his will is probated in 1827 with the family (32fam) maintaining ownership, - Lot 27

#2 Source - Paul Wroclawski Research & Property Owners Charles Morris to John Smith; collected through 02-06-2008.

1896 - James Henry McInnis (32fam) dies, his property passes to Arthur Curran McInnis (32fam) which stays in the McInnis family – Lot 27

#1 Source – N.S. Supreme Court, Book No. 368, recorded 10-01-1931, Book 20, P. 423, No. #368. (originally Book No. 20, P. 74, No.69) **– Lot 27**

1915 - Arthur Curran Mcinnis (32fam) dies, passes to John Mcinnis Family (32fam) which stays in the McInnis family – Lot 27

#1 Source – N.S. Supreme Court, Book No. 368, recorded 10-01-1931, Book 20, P. 423, No. #368. (originally Book No. 20, P. 74, No.69) **– Lot 27**

1930 - John McInnis Family (32fam), deeded properties by Salome Esther, widow of Arthur C. Mcinnis. pass to inheritors Wallace and Margaret M. Young, et. al. (63) – Lot 27

#169 Source – Lunenburg Co. Land Deed, recorded 06-21-1930, Book 20, P. 74, No. #69. Deeded on 06-09-1930. **- Lot 27**

#1 Source – N.S. Supreme Court, Book No. 368, recorded 10-01-1931, Book 20, P. 423, No. #368. (originally Book No. 20, P. 74, No.69) – **Lot 27**

#1 Source – N.S. Supreme Court, Book No. 368, recorded 10-01-1931, Book 20, P. 423, No. #368. (originally Book No. 20, P. 74, No.69) – **Lot 27**

1931 - (09-22-1931) **Margaret M. Young (63), to Archibald & Hannah Dauphinee (15) –Lot 27**

#1 Source – N.S. Supreme Court, Book No. 368, recorded 10-01-1931, Book 20, P. 423, No. #368. (originally Book No. 20, P. 74, No.69) 63>15 – **Lot 27**

1935 - (05-27-1935) **Mary Young & Margaret M. Young (63), to Hannah & Archibald A. Dauphinee (15) – Lot 27**

#3 Source – City & County of San Francisco, Calif. Records; & NSNA, recorded 05-27-1935, Book No. 21. P. 96, No. #148. 63>15 - **Lot 27**

1944 - (09-28-1944) **Archibald & Hannah Dauphinee (15) and Margaret M. Young (63), to Clarence Beamish (04) – Lot 27**

#12 Source – Lunenburg Co. Land Deeds, recorded 10-25-1955, Deed #1142 on 10-25-1944. NSNA. 15,63>04 - **Lot 27**

1955 - (07-25-1955) **Clarence James Beamish (04) dies, his wife already deceased passes property inheritance to Mary Ellen Chapman (all heirs) and heirs – Lot 27**

#18 Source - Halifax Office of Registrar of Deeds, Book 907 P. 605, dated 12-23-1946 with the Canada Permanent Trust Company, and filed on 02-22-1961. 09,04>10 - **Lot 27**

#16 Source - Nova Scotia Supreme Court Book 27, P. 339, No. #638. NSNA. Represent heirs shares of "South & West part Oak Island," "George McInnis Property," and "James McInnis Property." 07-20-1961. 09,04>10 - **Lot 6, 7, 8, 15, 16, 17, 18, 19, 20, 23, 25, 26, 30, 31, 32**

#170 Source – "*Selwyn William Sellers, 1873-1949*." FamilySearch, See citation.

1961 - (02-22-1961) **Heirs of Mary Ellen Chapman & of Clarence Beamish (all heirs), to M.R. Chappell (10) – Lot 27**

#170 Source – "*Selwyn William Sellers, 1873-1949*." FamilySearch, See citation.

#18 Source - Halifax Office of Registrar of Deeds, Book 907 P. 605, dated 12-23-1946 with the Canada Permanent Trust Company, and filed on 02-22-1961. 09,04>10 - **Lot 27**

#16 Source - Nova Scotia Supreme Court Book 27, P. 339, No. #638. NSNA. Represent heirs shares of "South & West part Oak Island," "George McInnis Property," and "James McInnis Property." 07-20-1961. 09,04>10 - **Lot 6, 7, 8, 15, 16, 17, 18, 19, 20, 23, 25, 26, 30, 31, 32**

1977 - (06-15-1977) **M.R. Chappell (10), to David C. Tobias (55) for shares regarding Lots, 1, 2, 3, 4, 6, 7, 8, 15, 16, 17, 18, 19, 20, 21, 22, 24, 25, 26, 27, 28, 29, 30, 31, 32. – Lot 27**

#20 Source – Filed in Halifax Co. Land Deeds, recorded on 06-29-1977, No. #582. NSNA. 10>55 - **Lots 6, 7, 8, 15, 16, 17, 18, 19, 20, 25, 26, 30, 31, 32**

1987 - (12-09-1987) **David Tobias (55) and his lots, join Dan Blankenship (07) to form Oak Island Tours Inc (41) – Lot 27**

#111 Source – "*The Open Database of the Corporate World. Oak Island Tours Inc. Company Number 2272393*." Incorporated Date, 12-09-1987. Opencorporates.

#112 Source – "*The Curse of Oak Island, The Story of the World's Longest Treasure Hunt*." By Randall Sullivan, 2018. Page 422.

2007 - David Tobias (55), sells his Lots to Rick & Marty Lagina who become equal partners with Dan Blankenship (07) in Oak Island Tours (41) which own/control Lots 1, 2, 3, 4, 6, 7, 8, 15, 16, 17, 18, 19, 20, 21, 22, 24, 26, 27, 28, 29, 30, 31, 32. – Lot 27

#111 Source – "*The Open Database of the Corporate World. Oak Island Tours Inc. Company Number 2272393*." Incorporated Date, 12-09-1987. Opencorporates.

#112 Source – "*The Curse of Oak Island, The Story of the World's Longest Treasure Hunt*." By Randall Sullivan, 2018. Page 422.

2007 - MacPhie Archives "*Oak Island Lot Distribution Map, 2007*." Lots ***1, 2, 3, 4, 6, 7, 8, 15, 16, 17, 18, 19, 20, 21, 22, 24, 26, 27, 28, 29, 30, 31, 32*** - Oak Island Tours (41); Lot ***5*** – Robert S. Young (61); Lots ***9, 10, 11, 12, 14*** – Fred Nolan (40); Lot ***13*** – John Johnston (25); Lot ***23*** – Dan/Dave Blankenship (07); and Lot ***25*** – Alan Kostrzewe (27). – **All Lots**

#30 Source - "*Oak Island Lot Ownership Map, 2007*," By MacPhie Archives. **All Lots**

Lot 28.

1753 - (12-27-1753) **Governor Charles Lawrence, to Capt. John Gifford (53) and Richard Smith (53) – ALL LOTS**

#123 Source - NS Archives and Record Management "Allotment" Book, P. 137, Reel #13044; "Old Book" #1, P. 44. Granted Gifford Island #12, Young Island #13, and Smith Island #28, to establish a fishery. Escheated.

1784 - Governor Parr (00) James Sharp (49) – Lot 28

#53 Source – Lunenburg Co. Land Deeds, recorded 05-25-1790, Vol. 3, P. 418, No. #689. **– Lot 28**

#34 Source – "Nova Scotia Land Papers: 1795-1800, Green James and Others." 1784 – Lunenburg County. 37,950 acres granted in Chester, including License to Occupy, Memorial, Warrant to Survey, Surveyor's Report & Surveyor's Certificate. See citation. Granted by Gov. Parr. 00>49 **- Lot 28**

1788 - (03-03-1788) **James Sharp (49), to Donald McGinnis (32) – Lot 28**

#53 Source – Lunenburg Co. Land Deeds, recorded 05-25-1790, Vol. 3, P. 418, No. #689. **– Lot 28**

#35 Source - "Habitation on Oak Island." Beaton Institute, Cape Breton University. Created by Surveyor William Dy Sr., called 'The Old Plan' No. 1046. Department of Lands & Forests, n.d. MG 12, 75 NSNA. Also Published in Joy Steele/Gordon Fader's book "Oak Island Mystery Solved-Final Chapter." P. 10. 2nd Ed. 2016.

1827 - Donald McGinnis (32) dies, in late 1826 and his will is probated in 1827 with the family (32fam) maintaining ownership, - Lot 28

#2 Source - Paul Wroclawski Research & Property Owners Charles Morris to John Smith; collected through 02-06-2008.

1896 - James Henry McInnis (32fam) dies, his property passes to Arthur Curran McInnis (32fam) which stays in the McInnis family – Lot 28

#1 Source – N.S. Supreme Court, Book No. 368, recorded 10-01-1931, Book 20, P. 423, No. #368. (originally Book No. 20, P. 74, No.69) **– Lot 28.**

1915 - Arthur Curran Mcinnis (32fam) dies, passes to John Mcinnis Family (32fam) which stays in the McInnis family – Lot 28

#1 Source – N.S. Supreme Court, Book No. 368, recorded 10-01-1931, Book 20, P. 423, No. #368. (originally Book No. 20, P. 74, No.69) **– Lot 28**

1930 - John McInnis Family (32fam), deeded properties by Salome Esther, widow of Arthur C. Mcinnis. pass to inheritors Wallace and Margaret Young, et. al. (63) – Lot 28

#169 Source – Lunenburg Co. Land Deed, recorded 06-21-1930, Book 20, P. 74, No. #69. Deeded on 06-09-1930. **- Lot 28**

#1 Source – N.S. Supreme Court, Book No. 368, recorded 10-01-1931, Book 20, P. 423, No. #368. (originally Book No. 20, P. 74, No.69) 63>15 **– Lot 28**

#3 Source – City & County of San Francisco, Calif. Records; & NSNA, recorded 05-27-1935, Book No. 21. P. 96, No. #148. 63>15 **- Lot 28**

1931 - (10-01-1931) **Margaret M. Young (63), to Archibald & Hannah Dauphinee (15) –Lot 28**

#1 Source – N.S. Supreme Court, Book No. 368, recorded 10-01-1931, Book 20, P. 423, No. #368. (originally Book No. 20, P. 74, No.69) 63>15 **– Lot 28**

1935 - (05-27-1935) **Mary Young & Margaret Wallace Young (63), to Hannah & Archibald A. Dauphinee (15) – Lot 28**

#3 Source – City & County of San Francisco, Calif. Records; & NSNA, recorded 05-27-1935, Book No. 21. P. 96, No. #148. 63>15 **- Lot 28**

1944 - (09-28-1944) **Archibald & Hannah Dauphinee (15) and Margaret Young (63), to Clarence Beamish (04) – Lot 28**

#12 Source – Lunenburg Co. Land Deeds, recorded 10-25-1955, Deed #1142 on 10-25-1944. NSNA. 15,63>04 **- Lot 28**

1955 - (07-25-1955) **Clarence James Beamish (04) dies, his wife already deceased passes property inheritance to Mary Ellen Chapman (09) and heirs – Lot 28**

#18 Source - Halifax Office of Registrar of Deeds, Book 907 P. 605, dated 12-23-1946 with the Canada Permanent Trust Company, and filed on 02-22-1961. 04,09>10 **- Lot 28**

#16 Source - Nova Scotia Supreme Court Book 27, P. 339, No. #638. NSNA. Represent heirs shares of "South & West part Oak Island," "George McInnis Property," and "James McInnis Property." 07-20-1961. 04,09>10 **- Lot 6, 7, 8, 15, 16, 17, 18, 19, 20, 23, 25, 26, 30, 31, 32**

#170 Source – "*Selwyn William Sellers, 1873-1949*." FamilySearch, See citation.

1961 - (02-22-1961) **Heirs of Mary Ellen Chapman & of Clarence Beamish (allheirs), to M.R. Chappell (10) – Lot 28**

#170 Source – "*Selwyn William Sellers, 1873-1949*." FamilySearch, See citation.

#18 Source - Halifax Office of Registrar of Deeds, Book 907 P. 605, dated 12-23-1946 with the Canada Permanent Trust Company, and filed on 02-22-1961. 04,09>10 **- Lot 28**

#16 Source - Nova Scotia Supreme Court Book 27, P. 339, No. #638. NSNA. Represent heirs shares of "South & West part Oak Island," "George McInnis Property," and "James McInnis Property." 07-20-1961. 04,09>10 **- Lot 6, 7, 8, 15, 16, 17, 18, 19, 20, 23, 25, 26, 30, 31, 32**

1975 - (09-19-1976) **M.R. Chappell (10), to Dan Blankenship (07) – Lot 28**

#19 Source - Owner transfer by Quit Claim Deed from M.R. Chappell (10) to Dan Blankenship (07) on 09-19-1975, filed in Chester Deed Office, Book 54, P. 161. 10>07 **– Lot 28**

1977 - (06-15-1977) **M.R. Chappell (10), to David C. Tobias (55)** for all shares regarding Lots, **1, 2, 3, 4, 6, 7, 8, 15, 16, 17, 18, 19, 20, 21, 22, 24, 25, 26, 27, 28, 29, 30, 31, 32. – Lot 28**

#20 Source – Filed in Halifax Co. Land Deeds, recorded on 06-29-1977, No. #582. NSNA. 10>55 **- Lots 6, 7, 8, 15, 16, 17, 18, 19, 20, 25, 26, 30, 31, 32**

1987 - (12-09-1987) **David Tobias (55) and his lots, join Dan Blankenship (07) to form Oak Island Tours Inc (41) – Lot 28**

#111 Source – "*The Open Database of the Corporate World. Oak Island Tours Inc. Company Number 2272393*." Incorporated Date, 12-09-1987. Opencorporates.

#112 Source – "*The Curse of Oak Island, The Story of the World's Longest Treasure Hunt*." By Randall Sullivan, 2018. Page 422.

2007 - **David Tobias (55), sells his Lots to Rick & Marty Lagina who become equal partners with Dan Blankenship (07) in Oak Island Tours (41) which now own/control Lots 1, 2, 3, 4, 6, 7, 8, 15, 16, 17, 18, 19, 20, 21, 22, 24, 26, 27, 28, 29, 30, 31, 32. – Lot 28**

#111 Source – "*The Open Database of the Corporate World. Oak Island Tours Inc. Company Number 2272393*." Incorporated Date, 12-09-1987. Opencorporates.

#112 Source – "*The Curse of Oak Island, The Story of the World's Longest Treasure Hunt*." By Randall Sullivan, 2018. Page 422.

2007 - **MacPhie Archives "*Oak Island Lot Distribution Map, 2007*."** Lots ***1, 2, 3, 4, 6, 7, 8, 15, 16, 17, 18, 19, 20, 21, 22, 24, 26, 27, 28, 29, 30, 31, 32*** - Oak Island Tours (41); Lot ***5*** – Robert S. Young (61); Lots ***9, 10, 11, 12, 14*** – Fred Nolan (40); Lot ***13*** – John Johnston (25); Lot ***23*** – Dan/Dave Blankenship (07); and Lot ***25*** – Alan Kostrzewe (27). **– All Lots**

#30 Source - "*Oak Island Lot Ownership Map, 2007*," By MacPhie Archives. **All Lots**

Lot 29.

1753 - (12-27-1753) **Governor Charles Lawrence, to Capt. John Gifford (53) and Richard Smith (53) – ALL LOTS**

#123 Source - NS Archives and Record Management "Allotment" Book, P. 137, Reel #13044; "Old Book" #1, P. 44. Granted Gifford Island #12, Young Island #13, and Smith Island #28, to establish a fishery. Escheated.

1765 - **Crown (00), to Moses Holt (67) – Lot 29**

#34 Source – "*Nova Scotia Land Papers: 1795-1800, Green James and Others*." 1784 – Lunenburg County. 37,950 acres granted in Chester, including License to Occupy, Memorial, Warrant to Survey, Surveyor's Report & Surveyor's Certificate. See citation. Drawn by Holt. **- Lot 29**

#2 Source - Paul Wroclawski Research & Property Owners Charles Morris to John Smith; collected through 02-06-2008.

1778 - (04-02-1778) **Jerimiah Rogers (47), to David Ellis (16) – Lot 29**

#62 Source – Lunenburg Co. Land Deeds, recorded 10-13-1778, Vol. 2, P. 208-209, No. #301. 47>16 **– Lot 29**

1796 - (11-16-1796) **John Monrow (39), to John J. Bezanson (06a) – Lot 29**

#65 Source – Lunenburg Co. Land Deeds, recorded 03-24-1808, Vol. 5, P. 278, No. #330. 39>06a **- Lot 29**

#35 Source - "*Habitation on Oak Island*." Beaton Institute, Cape Breton University. Created by Surveyor William Dy Sr., called 'The Old Plan' No. 1046. Department of Lands & Forests, n.d. MG 12, 75 NSNA. Also Published in Joy Steele/Gordon Fader's book "*Oak Island Mystery Solved-Final Chapter*." P. 10. 2nd Ed. 2016.

1810 - John J. Bezanson (06a) estate, to Donald McInnis (32) – Lot 29

#105 Source – Lunenburg Co. Land Deeds, recorded 1810, Vol. 6, P. 151, No. #335. 06a>32 **- Lot 29**

#35 Source - "*Habitation on Oak Island*." Beaton Institute, Cape Breton University. Created by Surveyor William Dy Sr., called 'The Old Plan' No. 1046. Department of Lands & Forests, n.d. MG 12, 75 NSNA. Also Published in Joy Steele/Gordon Fader's book "*Oak Island Mystery Solved-Final Chapter*." P. 10. 2nd Ed. 2016.

1827 - Donald McGinnis (32) dies, in late 1826 and his will is probated in 1827 with the family (32fam) maintaining ownership, - Lot 29

#2 Source - Paul Wroclawski Research & Property Owners Charles Morris to John Smith; collected through 02-06-2008.

1896 - James Henry McInnis (32fam) dies, his property passes to Arthur Curran McInnis (32fam) which stays in the McInnis family – Lot 29

#1 Source – N.S. Supreme Court, Book No. 368, recorded 10-01-1931, Book 20, P. 423, No. #368. (originally Book No. 20, P. 74, No.69) – **Lot 29**

1915 - Arthur Curran Mcinnis (32fam) dies, passes to John Mcinnis Family (32fam) which stays in the McInnis family – Lot 29

#1 Source – N.S. Supreme Court, Book No. 368, recorded 10-01-1931, Book 20, P. 423, No. #368. (originally Book No. 20, P. 74, No.69) – **Lot 29**

1930 - John McInnis Family (32fam), deeded properties by Salome Esther, widow of Arthur C. Mcinnis. pass to inheritors Wallace and Margaret Young, et. al. (63) – Lot 29

#169 Source – Lunenburg Co. Land Deed, recorded 06-21-1930, Book 20, P. 74, No. #69. Deeded on 06-09-1930. **- Lot 29**

#1 Source – N.S. Supreme Court, Book No. 368, recorded 10-01-1931, Book 20, P. 423, No. #368. (originally Book No. 20, P. 74, No.69) – **Lot 29**

#3 Source – City & County of San Francisco, Calif. Records; & NSNA, recorded 05-27-1935, Book No. 21. P. 96, No. #148. **- Lot 29**

1931 - (10-01-1931) **Margaret M. Young (63), to Archibald & Hannah Dauphinee (15) – Lot 29**

#1 Source – N.S. Supreme Court, Book No. 368, recorded 10-01-1931, Book 20, P. 423, No. #368. (originally Book No. 20, P. 74, No.69) 63>15 – **Lot 29**

1935 - (05-27-1935) **Mary Young & Margaret Wallace Young (63), to Hannah & Archibald A. Dauphinee (15) – Lot 29**

#3 Source – City & County of San Francisco, Calif. Records; & NSNA, recorded 05-27-1935, Book No. 21. P. 96, No. #148. 63>15 **- Lot 29**

1944 - (09-28-1944) **Archibald & Hannah Dauphinee (15) and Margaret M. Young (63), to Clarence Beamish (04) – Lot 29**

#12 Source – Lunenburg Co. Land Deeds, recorded 10-25-1955, Deed #1142 on 10-25-1944. NSNA. 15,63>04 **- Lot 29**

1955 - (07-25-1955) **Clarence James Beamish (04) dies, his wife already deceased passes property inheritance to Mary Ellen Chapman (09) and heirs – Lot 29**

#18 Source - Halifax Office of Registrar of Deeds, Book 907 P. 605, dated 12-23-1946 with the Canada Permanent Trust Company, and filed on 02-22-1961. 04,09>10 **- Lot 29**

#16 Source - Nova Scotia Supreme Court Book 27, P. 339, No. #638. NSNA. Represent heirs shares of "South & West part Oak Island," "George McInnis Property," and "James McInnis Property." 07-20-1961. 04,09>10 **- Lot 6, 7, 8, 15, 16, 17, 18, 19, 20, 23, 25, 26, 30, 31, 32**

#170 Source – "*Selwyn William Sellers, 1873-1949*." FamilySearch, See citation.

1961 - (02-22-1961) **Heirs of Mary Ellen Chapman & of Clarence Beamish (allheirs), to M.R. Chappell (10) – Lot 29**

#170 Source – "*Selwyn William Sellers, 1873-1949*." FamilySearch, See citation.

#18 Source - Halifax Office of Registrar of Deeds, Book 907 P. 605, dated 12-23-1946 with the Canada Permanent Trust Company, and filed on 02-22-1961. 09,04>10 **- Lot 29**

#16 Source - Nova Scotia Supreme Court Book 27, P. 339, No. #638. NSNA. Represent heirs shares of "South & West part Oak Island," "George McInnis Property," and "James McInnis Property." 07-20-1961. 04,09>10 **- Lot 6, 7, 8, 15, 16, 17, 18, 19, 20, 23, 25, 26, 30, 31, 32**

1975 - (09-19-1976) **M.R. Chappell (10), to Dan Blankenship (07) – Lot 29**

#19 Source - Owner transfer by Quit Claim Deed from M.R. Chappell (10) to Dan Blankenship (07) on 09-19-1975, filed in Chester Deed Office, Book 54, P. 161. 10>07 **– Lot 29**

1977 - (06-15-1977) **M.R. Chappell (10), to David C. Tobias (55)** for all shares regarding Lots, **1, 2, 3, 4, 6, 7, 8, 15, 16, 17, 18, 19, 20, 21, 22, 24, 25, 26, 27, 28, 29, 30, 31, 32. – Lot 29**

#20 Source – Filed in Halifax Co. Land Deeds, recorded on 06-29-1977, No. #582. NSNA. 10>55 **- Lots 6, 7, 8, 15, 16, 17, 18, 19, 20, 25, 26, 30, 31, 32**

1987 - (12-09-1987) **David Tobias (55) and his lots, join Dan Blankenship (07) to form Oak Island Tours Inc (41) – Lot 29**

#111 Source – "*The Open Database of the Corporate World. Oak Island Tours Inc. Company Number 2272393*." Incorporated Date, 12-09-1987. Opencorporates.

#112 Source – "*The Curse of Oak Island, The Story of the World's Longest Treasure Hunt*." By Randall Sullivan, 2018. Page 422.

2007 - David Tobias (55), sells his Lots to Rick & Marty Lagina who become equal partners with Dan Blankenship (07) in Oak Island Tours (41) which own/control Lots 1, 2, 3, 4, 6, 7, 8, 15, 16, 17, 18, 19, 20, 21, 22, 24, 26, 27, 28, 29, 30, 31, 32. – Lot 29

#111 Source – "*The Open Database of the Corporate World. Oak Island Tours Inc. Company Number 2272393*." Incorporated Date, 12-09-1987. Opencorporates.

#112 Source – "*The Curse of Oak Island, The Story of the World's Longest Treasure Hunt*." By Randall Sullivan, 2018. Page 422.

2007 - MacPhie Archives "*Oak Island Lot Distribution Map, 2007*." Lots ***1, 2, 3, 4, 6, 7, 8, 15, 16, 17, 18, 19, 20, 21, 22, 24, 26, 27, 28, 29, 30, 31, 32*** - Oak Island Tours (41); Lot ***5*** – Robert S. Young (61); Lots ***9, 10, 11, 12, 14*** – Fred Nolan (40); Lot ***13*** – John Johnston (25); Lot ***23*** – Dan/Dave Blankenship (07); and Lot ***25*** – Alan Kostrzewe (27). **– All Lots**

#30 Source - "*Oak Island Lot Ownership Map, 2007*," By MacPhie Archives. **All Lots**

Lot 30.

1753 - (12-27-1753) **Governor Charles Lawrence, to Capt. John Gifford (53) and Richard Smith (53) – ALL LOTS**

#123 Source - NS Archives and Record Management "Allotment" Book, P. 137, Reel #13044; "Old Book" #1, P. 44. Granted Gifford Island #12, Young Island #13, and Smith Island #28, to establish a fishery. Escheated.

1810 - (04-02-1810) **John Pulsifier (46), to Samuel Ball (03) – Lot 30**

#93 Source - Lunenburg Co. Land Deeds, filed 09-20-1810, Vol. 6, P. 175, No. #389. **- Lot 30**

1812 - Oak Island Samuel Ball (03) "*Ownership Map, Lots 6, 7, 8, 24, 25, 26, 30, 31, 31, Hook Island, Mainland Farm, 2007*" **– Lot 30**

#24 Source – "*Bee Stanton's Samuel Ball Map 1787 - 1812*." @ www.creative@beestanton website. **Lots 6, 7, 8, 24, 25, 26, 30, 31, 32**

#35 Source - "*Habitation on Oak Island*." Beaton Institute, Cape Breton University. Created by Surveyor William Dy Sr., called 'The Old Plan' No. 1046. Department of Lands & Forests, n.d. MG 12, 75 NSNA. Also Published in Joy Steele/Gordon Fader's book "*Oak Island Mystery Solved-Final Chapter*." P. 10. 2nd Ed. 2016.

#131 Source -"*The Black Settlers of 'Treasure Oak Island' The Primary Generation – Samuel Ball (03)*." See citation. **– Lots 6, 7, 8, 24, 25, 26, 30, 31, 32**

#132 Source - "*Who Was Samuel Ball*," Published by Deb Minter 07-06-2021. Facebook online, "*Oak Island: History not Myth*." Posted 06-23-2021. **– Lots 6, 7, 8, 24, 25, 26, 30, 31, 32**

1846 - Samuel Ball (03) dies, property transfers to Isaac Butler (Ball) (03a) – Lot 30

#17 Source – "*Chester Township Records, 1762-1830*." Births, Marriages & Deaths. NSNA MG9, B 9-3

#108 Source – "*Samuel Ball Will, Lunenburg, N.S.*" Will Extracts – See citation.

#130a Source – Lunenburg Co. Registrar, Book 1, P. 37, dated 10-01-1841, recorded 01-05-1846. Last Will & Testament of Samuel Ball (03). **– Lots 6, 7, 8, 24, 25, 26, 30, 31, 32**

1898 - (01-17-1898) **Isaac Butler (Ball) (03a), deeds ½ lot to Abraham Ernst (18) & ½ lot Henry Sellers (19a) – Lot 30**

#13 Source – Dominion of Canada Book No. #693, NSNA. **- Lots 6, 7, 8, 15, 16, 17, 18, 19, 20, 25, 26, 30, 32** [Lot 31 missing]

#108 Source – "*Samuel Ball Will, Lunenburg, N.S.*" Will Extracts – See citation.

1912 - Abraham Ernst (18) dies 1911, Henry Sellers (19a) dies 1912, & his wife (Sophia Elizabeth Graves Sellers) dies 1931; leaving inherited lots to future heirs. **– Lot 30**

#199 Source – "*Letter from Blair to Harris 02-16-1035.*" on purchasing remaining lots 1–14. – **Lots 1, 2, 3, 4, 5, 6, 7, 8, 9, 10, 11, 12, 13, 14**

1937 - (09-14-1937) **Francis & Eva G. Conrad (12) and Ingram & Quesetta M. Conrad (12a), to Archibald D. Dauphinee (15) – Lot 30**

#9 Source - Dominion of Canada Book No. 8, P. 218-219, No. #655. (originally in Book 8, P. 218-219, No. #132) NSNA. 12,12a>15 **- Lot 6, 7, 8, 25, 26, 30, 31, 32**

1937 - (09-13-1937) **Archibald D. & Hannah Dauphinee (15), to Gilbert Hedden (22) – Lot 30**

#10 Source - Dominion of Canada Book No. 21, P. 402-403, No. #656. (originally in Book 21, P.218-219, No. #132) NSNA. 15>22 **– Lot 6, 7, 8, 25, 26, 30, 31, 32**

1950 - (05-26-1950) **Gilbert & Margarite Hedden (22), to John Whitney Lewis (10a) – Lot 30**

#13 Source – Dominion of Canada Book No. #693, NSNA. 22>10a **- Lots 6, 7, 8, 15, 16, 17, 18, 19, 20, 25, 26, 30, 32** [Lot 31 missing]

1951 - (12-05-1950) **Ann & John Whitney Lewis (10a), to Acadia Trust Co. (10b) – Lot 30**

#14 Source - Dominion of Canada, NSNA #880. (original filings list – see citation). 10a>10b **- Lot 6, 7, 8, 15, 16, 17, 18, 19, 20, 25, 30, 31, 32** [Lot 26 missing]

1957 - (04-20-1957) **Acadia Trust Company (10b), to M.R. Chappell (10) – Lot 30**

#15 Source - Registry of Deeds at Bridgewater and Registry of Probate, Book 26, P. 195, Quit Claim No. 374, NSNA. 10b>10 **- Lot 6, 7, 8, 15, 16, 17, 18, 19, 20, 25, 26, 30, 31, 32**

1961 - (07-21-1961) **Mary Ellen Chapman (09) & heirs of Clarence J. Beamish (04), to M.R. Chappell, Lots 5, 6, 7, 8, 15, 16, 17, 18, 19, 20, 23, 25, 26, 30, 31, 32 (10) – Lot 30**

#16 Source - Nova Scotia Supreme Court Book 27, P. 339, No. #638. NSNA. Represent heirs shares of "South & West part Oak Island," "George McInnis Property," and "James McInnis Property." 07-20-1961. 04,09>10 **- Lot 6, 7, 8, 15, 16, 17, 18, 19, 20, 23, 25, 26, 30, 31, 32**

1977 - (06-15-1977) **M.R. Chappell (10), to David C. Tobias (55)** for all shares regarding Lots, **1, 2, 3, 4, 6, 7, 8, 15, 16, 17, 18, 19, 20, 21, 22, 24, 25, 26, 27, 28, 29, 30, 31, 32. – Lot 30**

#20 Source – Filed in Halifax Co. Land Deeds, recorded on 06-29-1977, No. #582. NSNA. 10>55 **- Lots 6, 7, 8, 15, 16, 17, 18, 19, 20, 25, 26, 30, 31, 32**

1987 - (12-09-1987) **David Tobias (55) and his lots, join Dan Blankenship (07) to form Oak Island Tours Inc (41) – Lot 30**

#111 Source – "*The Open Database of the Corporate World. Oak Island Tours Inc. Company Number 2272393.*" Incorporated Date, 12-09-1987. Opencorporates.

#112 Source – "*The Curse of Oak Island, The Story of the World's Longest Treasure Hunt.*" By Randall Sullivan, 2018. Page 422.

2007 - David Tobias (55), sells his Lots to Rick & Marty Lagina who become equal partners with Dan Blankenship (07) in Oak Island Tours (41) which own/control Lots 1, 2, 3, 4, 6, 7, 8, 15, 16, 17, 18, 19, 20, 21, 22, 24, 26, 27, 28, 29, 30, 31, 32. – Lot 30

#111 Source – "*The Open Database of the Corporate World. Oak Island Tours Inc. Company Number 2272393.*" Incorporated Date, 12-09-1987. Opencorporates.

#112 Source – "*The Curse of Oak Island, The Story of the World's Longest Treasure Hunt.*" By Randall Sullivan, 2018. Page 422.

2007 - MacPhie Archives "*Oak Island Lot Distribution Map, 2007.*" Lots ***1, 2, 3, 4, 6, 7, 8, 15, 16, 17, 18, 19, 20, 21, 22, 24, 26, 27, 28, 29, 30, 31, 32*** - Oak Island Tours (41); Lot ***5*** – Robert S. Young (61); Lots ***9, 10, 11, 12, 14*** – Fred Nolan (40); Lot ***13*** – John Johnston (25); Lot ***23*** – Dan/Dave Blankenship (07); and Lot ***25*** – Alan Kostrzewe (27). **– All Lots**

#30 Source - "*Oak Island Lot Ownership Map, 2007,*" By MacPhie Archives. **All Lots**

Lot 31.

1753 - (12-27-1753) **Governor Charles Lawrence, to Capt. John Gifford (53) and Richard Smith (53) – ALL LOTS**

#123 Source - NS Archives and Record Management "Allotment" Book, P. 137, Reel #13044; "Old Book" #1, P. 44. Granted Gifford Island #12, Young Island #13, and Smith Island #28, to establish a fishery. Escheated.

1765 - Crown (00) Granted to **Thomas Young (62)** No such document or person in Chester **– Lot 31**

#2 Source - Paul Wroclawski Research & Property Owners Charles Morris to John Smith; collected through 02-06-2008.

#40 Source – "A True Copy of "James J. Thompson, Provincial Land Surveyors List of First Settlers and their Lots."

#34 Source – "*Nova Scotia Land Papers: 1795-1800, Green James and Others*." 1784 – Lunenburg County. 37,950 acres granted in Chester, including License to Occupy, Memorial, Warrant to Survey, Surveyor's Report & Surveyor's Certificate. See citation. See citation #2. 00>62 **- Lot 31**

1797 - (06-28-1797) **Jacob Hatt (21), to John J. Bezanson (06a) – Lot 31**

#63 Source - Lunenburg Co. Land Deeds, recorded 09-28-1802, Vol. 5, P. 275-76, No. #327. 21>06a **- Lot 31**

#35 Source - "*Habitation on Oak Island*." Beaton Institute, Cape Breton University. Created by Surveyor William Dy Sr., called 'The Old Plan' No. 1046. Department of Lands & Forests, n.d. MG 12, 75 NSNA. Also Published in Joy Steele/Gordon Fader's book "*Oak Island Mystery Solved-Final Chapter*." P. 10. 2nd Ed. 2016.

1807 - (08-28-1807) **John J. Bezanson (06a), to Samuel Ball (03) – Lot 31**

#109 Source – Lunenburg Co. Land Deeds, recorded 02-07-1808, Vol. 6, P. 26, No. #56. 06a>03 **- Lot 31**

#24 Source – "*Bee Stanton's Samuel Ball Map 1787 - 1812*." @ www.creative@beestanton website. **Lots 6, 7, 8, 24, 25, 26, 30, 31, 32**

#35 Source - "*Habitation on Oak Island*." Beaton Institute, Cape Breton University. Created by Surveyor William Dy Sr., called 'The Old Plan' No. 1046. Department of Lands & Forests, n.d. MG 12, 75 NSNA. Also Published in Joy Steele/Gordon Fader's book "*Oak Island Mystery Solved-Final Chapter*." P. 10. 2nd Ed. 2016.

1812 - Oak Island Samuel Ball (03) "*Ownership Map, Lots 6, 7, 8, 24, 25, 26, 30, 31, 31, Hook Island, Mainland Farm, 2007*" **– Lot 31**

#24 Source – "*Bee Stanton's Samuel Ball Map 1787 - 1812*." @ www.creative@beestanton website. **Lots 6, 7, 8, 24, 25, 26, 30, 31, 32**

#35 Source - "*Habitation on Oak Island*." Beaton Institute, Cape Breton University. Created by Surveyor William Dy Sr., called 'The Old Plan' No. 1046. Department of Lands & Forests, n.d. MG 12, 75 NSNA. Also Published in Joy Steele/Gordon Fader's book "*Oak Island Mystery Solved-Final Chapter*." P. 10. 2nd Ed. 2016.

#131 Source -"*The Black Settlers of 'Treasure Oak Island' The Primary Generation – Samuel Ball (03)*." See citation. **– Lots 6, 7, 8, 24, 25, 26, 30, 31, 32**

#132 Source - "*Who Was Samuel Ball*," Published by Deb Minter 07-06-2021. Facebook online, "Oak Island: History not Myth." Posted 06-23-2021. **– Lots 6, 7, 8, 24, 25, 26, 30, 31, 32**

1846 - Samuel Ball (03) dies, property transfers to Isaac Butler (Ball) (03a) – Lot 31

#17 Source – "*Chester Township Records, 1762-1830*." Births, Marriages, and Deaths. NSNA MG9, B 9-3.

#108 Source – "*Samuel Ball Will, Lunenburg, N.S*." Will Extracts – See citation.

#130a Source – Lunenburg Co. Registrar, Book 1, P. 37, dated 10-01-1841, recorded 01-05-1846. Last Will & Testament of Samuel Ball (03). **– Lots 6, 7, 8, 24, 25, 26, 30, 31, 32**

1898 - (01-17-1898) **Isaac Butler (Ball) (03a), deeds ½ lot to Abraham Ernst (18) & ½ lot Henry Sellers (19a) – Lot 31**

#13 Source – Dominion of Canada Book No. #693, NSNA. **- Lots 6, 7, 8, 15, 16, 17, 18, 19, 20, 25, 26, 30, 32** [Lot 31 missing]

#108 Source – "*Samuel Ball Will, Lunenburg, N.S*." Will Extracts – See citation.

1912 - Abraham Ernst (18) dies 1911, Henry Sellers (19a) dies 1912, & his wife (Sophia Elizabeth Graves Sellers) dies 1931; leaving inherited lots to future heirs. **– Lot 31**

#199 Source – "*Letter from Blair to Harris 02-16-1035*." on purchasing remaining lots 1–14. – **Lots 1, 2, 3, 4, 5, 6, 7, 8, 9, 10, 11, 12, 13, 14**

1937 - (09-14-1937) **Francis & Eva G. Conrad (12) and Ingram & Quesetta M. Conrad (12a), to Archibald D. Dauphinee (15) – Lot 31**

#9 Source - Dominion of Canada Book No. 8, P. 218-219, No. #655. (originally in Book 8, P. 218-219, No. #132) NSNA. 12,12a>15 **- Lot 6, 7, 8, 25, 26, 30, 31, 32**

1937 - (09-13-1937) **Archibald D. & Hannah Dauphinee (15), to Gilbert Hedden (22) – Lot 31**
#10 Source - Dominion of Canada Book No. 21, P. 402-403, No. #656. (originally in Book 21, P.218-219, No. #132) NSNA. 15>22 **- Lot 6, 7, 8, 25, 26, 30, 31, 32**

1950 - (05-26-1950) **Gilbert & Margarite Hedden (22), to John Whitney Lewis (10a) – Lot 31**
#13 Source – Dominion of Canada Book No. #693, NSNA. 22>10a **- Lots 6, 7, 8, 15, 16, 17, 18, 19, 20, 25, 26, 30, 32** [Lot 31 missing]

1951 - (12-05-1950) **Ann & John Whitney Lewis (10a), to Acadia Trust Co. (10b) – Lot 31**
#14 Source - Dominion of Canada, NSNA #880. (original filings list – see citation). 10a>10b **- Lot 6, 7, 8, 15, 16, 17, 18, 19, 20, 25, 30, 31, 32** [Lot 26 missing]

1957 - (04-20-1957) **Acadia Trust Company (10b), to M.R. Chappell (10) – Lot 31**
#15 Source - Registry of Deeds at Bridgewater and Registry of Probate, Book 26, P. 195, Quit Claim No. 374, NSNA. 10b>10 **- Lot 6, 7, 8, 15, 16, 17, 18, 19, 20, 25, 26, 30, 31, 32**

961 - (07-21-1961) **Mary Ellen Chapman (09) & heirs of Clarence J. Beamish (04), to M.R. Chappell, Lots 5, 6, 7, 8, 15, 16, 17, 18, 19, 20, 23, 25, 26, 30, 31, 32 (10) – Lot 31**
#16 Source - Nova Scotia Supreme Court Book 27, P. 339, No. #638. NSNA. Represent heirs shares of "South & West part Oak Island," "George McInnis Property," and "James McInnis Property." 07-20-1961. 09,04>10 **- Lot 6, 7, 8, 15, 16, 17, 18, 19, 20, 23, 25, 26, 30, 31, 32**

1977 - (06-15-1977) **M.R. Chappell (10), to David C. Tobias (55)** for all shares regarding Lots, **1, 2, 3, 4, 6, 7, 8, 15, 16, 17, 18, 19, 20, 21, 22,24, 25, 26, 27, 28, 29, 30, 31, 32. – Lot 31**
#20 Source – Filed in Halifax Co. Land Deeds, recorded on 06-29-1977, No. #582. NSNA. 10>55 **- Lots 6, 7, 8, 15, 16, 17, 18, 19, 20, 25, 26, 30, 31, 32**

1987 - (12-09-1987) **David Tobias (55) and his lots, join Dan Blankenship (07) to form Oak Island Tours Inc (41) – Lot 31**
#111 Source – "*The Open Database of the Corporate World. Oak Island Tours Inc. Company Number 2272393*." Incorporated Date, 12-09-1987. Opencorporates.
#112 Source – "*The Curse of Oak Island, The Story of the World's Longest Treasure Hunt*." By Randall Sullivan, 2018. Page 422.

2007 - David Tobias (55), sells his Lots to Rick & Marty Lagina who become equal partners with Dan Blankenship (07) in Oak Island Tours (41) which own/control Lots 1, 2, 3, 4, 6, 7, 8, 15, 16, 17, 18, 19, 20, 21, 22, 24, 26, 27, 28, 29, 30, 31, 32. – Lot 31
#111 Source – "*The Open Database of the Corporate World. Oak Island Tours Inc. Company Number 2272393*." Incorporated Date, 12-09-1987. Opencorporates.
#112 Source – "*The Curse of Oak Island, The Story of the World's Longest Treasure Hunt*." By Randall Sullivan, 2018. Page 422.

2007 - MacPhie Archives "*Oak Island Lot Distribution Map, 2007*." Lots ***1, 2, 3, 4, 6, 7, 8, 15, 16, 17, 18, 19, 20, 21, 22, 24, 26, 27, 28, 29, 30, 31, 32*** - Oak Island Tours (41); Lot ***5*** – Robert S. Young (61); Lots ***9, 10, 11, 12, 14*** – Fred Nolan (40); Lot ***13*** – John Johnston (25); Lot ***23*** – Dan/Dave Blankenship (07); and Lot ***25*** – Alan Kostrzewe (27). **– All Lots**
#30 Source - "*Oak Island Lot Ownership Map, 2007*," By MacPhie Archives. **All Lots**

Lot 32.

1753 - (12-27-1753) **Governor Charles Lawrence, to Capt. John Gifford (53) and Richard Smith (53) – ALL LOTS**
#123 Source - NS Archives and Record Management "Allotment" Book, P. 137, Reel #13044; "Old Book" #1, P. 44. Granted Gifford Island #12, Young Island #13, and Smith Island #28, to establish a fishery. Escheated.

1784 - Crown (00) granted to **Richard Cunningham (66) Escheated – Lot 32**
#11 Source – "*History of Lunenburg Co. / Richard Cunningham – 1748-1823*." www.wikitree.com/wiki/Cunningham-13844

1809 - Crown (00) granted to **Samuel Ball (03) – Lot 32**
#34 Source – "*Nova Scotia Land Papers: 1795-1800, Green James and Others*." 1784 – Lunenburg County. 37,950 acres granted in Chester, including License to Occupy, Memorial, Warrant to Survey, Surveyor's Report & Surveyor's Certificate. See citation. 00>03 **- Lot 32**

#24 Source – "*Bee Stanton's Samuel Ball Map 1787 - 1812*." @ www.creative@beestanton website. **Lots 6, 7, 8, 24, 25, 26, 30, 31, 32**

#25/26 Source – "*2-Page Oak Island Lot Ownership Map, Jul. 6, 1818*." And "*Old Plan Map of Oak Island 1818*." By David W. Crandell Survey Map. NSNA. **Lots 13, 14, 15, 16, 17, 18**

1812 - Oak Island Samuel Ball (03) "*Ownership Map, Lots 6, 7, 8, 24, 25, 26, 30, 31, 31, Hook Island, Mainland Farm, 2007*" **– Lot 32**

#24 Source – "*Bee Stanton's Samuel Ball Map 1787 - 1812*." @ www.creative@beestanton website. **Lots 6, 7, 8, 24, 25, 26, 30, 31, 32**

#35 Source - "*Habitation on Oak Island*." Beaton Institute, Cape Breton University. Created by Surveyor William Dy Sr., called 'The Old Plan' No. 1046. Department of Lands & Forests, n.d. MG 12, 75 NSNA. Also Published in Joy Steele/Gordon Fader's book "*Oak Island Mystery Solved-Final Chapter*." P. 10. 2nd Ed. 2016.

#131 Source -"*The Black Settlers of 'Treasure Oak Island' The Primary Generation – Samuel Ball (03)*." See citation. **– Lots 6, 7, 8, 24, 25, 26, 30, 31, 32**

#132 Source - "*Who Was Samuel Ball*," Published by Deb Minter 07-06-2021. Facebook online, "*Oak Island: History not Myth*." Posted 06-23-2021. **– Lots 6, 7, 8, 24, 25, 26, 30, 31, 32**

1846 - Samuel Ball (03) dies, property transfers to Isaac Butler (Ball) (03a) – Lot 32

#17 Source – "*Chester Township Records, 1762-1830*." Births, Marriages, and Deaths. NSNA MG9, B 9-3.

#108 Source – "*Samuel Ball Will, Lunenburg, N.S*." Will Extracts – See citation.

#130a Source – Lunenburg Co. Registrar, Book 1, P. 37, dated 10-01-1841, recorded 01-05-1846. Last Will & Testament of Samuel Ball (03). **– Lots 6, 7, 8, 24, 25, 26, 30, 31, 32**

1898 - (01-17-1898) **Isaac Butler (Ball) (03a), deeds ½ lot to Abraham Ernst (18) & ½ lot Henry Sellers (19a) – Lot 32**

#13 Source – Dominion of Canada Book No. #693, NSNA. **- Lots 6, 7, 8, 15, 16, 17, 18, 19, 20, 25, 26, 30, 32** [Lot 31 missing]

#108 Source – "*Samuel Ball Will, Lunenburg, N.S*." Will Extracts – See citation.

1912 - Abraham Ernst (18) dies 1911, Henry Sellers (19a) dies 1912, & his wife (Sophia Elizabeth Graves Sellers) dies 1931; leaving inherited lots to future heirs. **– Lot 32**

#199 Source – "*Letter from Blair to Harris 02-16-1035*." on purchasing remaining lots 1–14. – **Lots 1, 2, 3, 4, 5, 6, 7, 8, 9, 10, 11, 12, 13, 14**

1937 - (09-14-1937) **Francis & Eva G. Conrad (12) and Ingram & Quesetta M. Conrad (12a), to Archibald D. Dauphinee (15) – Lot 32**

#9 Source - Dominion of Canada Book No. 8, P. 218-219, No. #655. (originally in Book 8, P. 218-219, No. #132) NSNA. 12,12a>15 **- Lot 6, 7, 8, 25, 26, 30, 31, 32**

1937 - (09-13-1937) **Archibald D. & Hannah Dauphinee (15), to Gilbert Hedden (22) – Lot 32**

#10 Source - Dominion of Canada Book No. 21, P. 402-403, No. #656. (originally in Book 21, P.218-219, No. #132) NSNA. 15>22 **– Lot 6, 7, 8, 25, 26, 30, 31, 32**

1950 - (05-26-1950) **Gilbert & Margarite Hedden (22), to John Whitney Lewis (10a) – Lot 32**

#13 Source – Dominion of Canada Book No. #693, NSNA. 22>10a **- Lots 6, 7, 8, 15, 16, 17, 18, 19, 20, 25, 26, 30, 32** [Lot 31 missing]

1951 - (12-05-1950) **Ann & John Whitney Lewis (10a), to Acadia Trust Co. (10b) – Lot 32**

#14 Source - Dominion of Canada, NSNA #880. (original filings list – see citation). 10a>10b **- Lot 6, 7, 8, 15, 16, 17, 18, 19, 20, 25, 30, 31, 32** [Lot 26 missing]

1957 - (04-20-1957) **Acadia Trust Company (10b), to M.R. Chappell (10) – Lot 32**

#15 Source - Registry of Deeds at Bridgewater and Registry of Probate, Book 26, P. 195, Quit Claim No. 374, NSNA. 10b>10 **- Lot 6, 7, 8, 15, 16, 17, 18, 19, 20, 25, 26, 30, 31, 32**

1961 - (07-21-1961) **Mary Ellen Chapman (09) & heirs of Clarence J. Beamish (04), to M.R. Chappell, Lots 5, 6, 7, 8, 15, 16, 17, 18, 19, 20, 23, 25, 26, 30, 31, 32 (10) – Lot 32**

#16 Source - Nova Scotia Supreme Court Book 27, P. 339, No. #638. NSNA. Represent heirs shares of "South & West part Oak Island," "George McInnis Property," and "James McInnis Property." 07-20-1961. 09,04>10 **- Lot 6, 7, 8, 15, 16, 17, 18, 19, 20, 23, 25, 26, 30, 31, 32**

1977 - (06-15-1977) **M.R. Chappell (10), to David C. Tobias (55)** for all shares regarding Lots, **1, 2, 3, 4, 6, 7, 8, 15, 16, 17, 18, 19, 20, 21, 22, 24, 25, 26, 27, 28, 29, 30, 31, 32. – Lot 32**

#20 Source – Filed in Halifax Co. Land Deeds, recorded on 06-29-1977, No. #582. NSNA. 10>55 **- Lots 6, 7, 8, 15, 16, 17, 18, 19, 20, 25, 26, 30, 31, 32**

1987 - (12-09-1987) **David Tobias (55) and his lots, join Dan Blankenship (07) to form Oak Island Tours Inc (41) – Lot 32**

#111 Source – "*The Open Database of the Corporate World. Oak Island Tours Inc. Company Number 2272393*." Incorporated Date, 12-09-1987. Opencorporates.

#112 Source – "*The Curse of Oak Island, The Story of the World's Longest Treasure Hunt*." By Randall Sullivan, 2018. Page 422.

2007 - David Tobias (55), sells his Lots to Rick & Marty Lagina who become equal partners with Dan Blankenship (07) in Oak Island Tours (41) which own/control Lots 1, 2, 3, 4, 6, 7, 8, 15, 16, 17, 18, 19, 20, 21, 22, 24, 26, 27, 28, 29, 30, 31, 32. – Lot 32

#111 Source – "*The Open Database of the Corporate World. Oak Island Tours Inc. Company Number 2272393*." Incorporated Date, 12-09-1987. Opencorporates.

#112 Source – "*The Curse of Oak Island, The Story of the World's Longest Treasure Hunt*." By Randall Sullivan, 2018. Page 422.

2007 - **MacPhie Archives "*Oak Island Lot Distribution Map, 2007*."** Lots ***1, 2, 3, 4, 6, 7, 8, 15, 16, 17, 18, 19, 20, 21, 22, 24, 26, 27, 28, 29, 30, 31, 32*** - Oak Island Tours (41); Lot ***5*** – Robert S. Young (61); Lots ***9, 10, 11, 12, 14*** – Fred Nolan (40); Lot ***13*** – John Johnston (25); Lot ***23*** – Dan/Dave Blankenship (07); and Lot ***25*** – Alan Kostrzewe (27). **– All Lots**

#30 Source - "*Oak Island Lot Ownership Map, 2007*," By MacPhie Archives. **All Lots**

Footnoted References

1 "*Margaret M. Young (63), **TO** Archibald A. & Hannah Dauphinee (15) – Lots **23**, Oct. 1, 1931*." Filed with Commissioner of the Supreme Court of Nova Scotia. Book No. 368, Deeded on 09-22-1931. Originally Book No. 20, P.74, No.69. NSNA. **Lot 23**

2 "*Research Through Paul Wroclawski's website, Oakislandtheories.com*." Includes Oak Island Lot Ownership to 1795 and Lot Ownership research from Charles Morris through John Smith (51a). Collected material as of Feb. 6, 2008.

3 "*Mary Young & Margaret Wallace Young (62), **TO** Hannah Dauphinee & Archibald A. Dauphinee (15) – Lots **23 and additional acreage**, May 27, 1935*." Filed with the City & Co. of San Francisco, State of Calif. Book No. 21, P. 96, No. #148. NSNA. **Lot 23**

4 "*Selvin & Bessie Sellers (19b), **TO** George W. Grimm Jr. (20) – Lots **15, 16, 17, 18, 19, 20**, Jul. 27, 1935*." Filed with Dominion of Canada. Book No. #21, P. 114, No. #173. (originally filed at Bridgewater, N.S., Book No. 16, P. 485) NSNA. **Lots 15, 16, 17, 18, 19, 20**

5 "*Erdie Powers (44) , **TO** George W. Grimm Jr. (20) – Lots **15, 16, 17, 18, 19, 20**, Jul. 27, 1935*." Filed with Dominion of Canada. Book No. 21, P. 114-115, No. 174. (originally filed at Bridgewater, N.S., Book No. 16, P. 485). NSNA. **Lots 15, 16, 17, 18, 19, 20**

6 "*Burnell S. & Hazel R. Corkum et. al (13a), **TO** George W. Grimm Jr. (20) – Lots **15, 16, 17, 18, 19, 20**, Jul. 27, 1935*." Filed by Dominion of Canada. Book No. 21, P. 115-116, No. #175. Selling party includes: Hazel R. Corkum, Ruby E. Corkum, Wilfred & Audrey W. Corkum, Henry & Mary L. Corkum, and single adults Flora Corkum & Ross Corkum. NSNA. **Lots 15, 16, 17, 18, 19, 20.**

7 "*Genevieve Walls et. al. (59), **TO** George W. Grimm Jr. (20) – Lots **15, 16, 17, 18, 19, 20**, Jul. 27, 1935*." Filed with the Dominion of Canada, Book No. 21, P. 184, No. #295. (originally filed at Bridgewater, N.S., Book No. 16, P. 485). NSNA. **Lots 15, 16, 17, 18, 19, 20.**

8 "*Burnell Corkum, Guardian of Andrew & Hope Gorkum (13a), **TO** George W. Grimm Jr. (20) – Lots **15, 16, 17, 18, 19, 20**, Jul. 27, 1935*." Filed with Supreme Court of Nova Scotia. SCONS File #3196. Book No. 21, P. 185-186, No. #297. NSNA. **Lots 15, 16, 17, 18, 19, 20.**

9 "*Francis Conrad et al. (12), **TO** Archibald D. Dauphinee (15) – Lots **6, 7, 8, 25, 26, 30, 31, 32**,*

Sep. 14, 1937." Filed with the Dominion of Canada. Deed included joint ownership with Francis & Eva Gertrude Conrad (12) and Ingram & Quesetta May Conrad (12a). Book No. 8, P. 218-219, No. 132 (now No. 655). NSNA. **Lots 6, 7, 8, 25, 26, 30, 31, 32**

10 "*Archibald D. & Hannah Dauphinee (15). **TO** Gilbert Hedden (22) – Lots **6, 7, 8, 25, 26, 30, 31, 32**, Sep. 13, 1937.*" Filed with the Dominion of Canada. Book No. 21, P. 402-403, No. #656. (originally in Book 8, P. 218-219, No. 132). Lots **6, 7, 8, 25, 26, 30, 31, 32**.

11 "*History of the County of Lunenburg – 2nd Edition.*" by Mather Byles DeBrisay, Judge of County Courts and Member of the Historical Society of Nova Scotia. Harvard College Library, Apr. 7, 1896, Cambridge, Mass. Second Edition, 1895. Originally written at Bridgewater and La Have, February 1870 .

12 "*Archibald D. & Hannah Dauphinee (15) and Margaret Young (63). **TO** Clarence James Beamish (04) – Lot **23 and additional island acreage**, Sep. 28, 1944.*" Filed with the Dominion of Canada. No. #1142. NSNA. See description of Lots and parcels. **Lot 23**

13 "*Gilbert D. Hedden & Margarite C. Hedden (22). **TO** John Whitney Lewis (10a) – Lots **6, 7, 8, 15, 16, 17, 18, 19, 20, 25, 26, 30, 32** , May. 26, 1950.*" Filed Dominion of Canada Book No. #693 NSNA. (originally in Book 8, P. 218-219, No 132; Book 16, P. 485; Book 21, P. 114, No. 173; Book 21, P. 114-115, No 174; Book 21, P. 115-116, No. 175; Book 21, P. 184, No. 295; Book 21, P. 185-186, No. 297. **Lots *6, 7, 8, 25, 26, 30, 32***, & **Lots *15, 16, 17, 18, 19, 20*.** [Lot 31 missing]

14 "*John Whitney Lewis & Ann Lewis (10a). **TO** Acadia Trust Co. (10b) – Lots **6, 7, 8, 15, 16, 17, 18, 19, 20, 25, 30, 31, 32**, Dec. 5, 1950.*" Filed with the Dominion of Canada, NSNA No. #880. (originally in Book 8, P. 218-219, No #132; Book 16, P. 485; Book 21, P. 114, No. #173; Book 21, P. 114-115, No #174; Book 21, P. 115-116, No. #175; Book 21, P. 184, No. #295; Book 21, P. 185-186, No. #297; Book 22, P. 493, No. #891; Book 21, P. 402-403, No. #656. **Lots *6, 7, 8, 15, 16, 17, 18, 19, 20, 25, 30, 31, and 32*.** [Lot 26 missing]

15 "*Acadia Trust Company (10b). **TO** M. R. Chappell (10). Recorded – Lots **6, 7, 8, 15, 16, 17, 18, 19, 20, 25, 26, 30, 31, 32**, Apr. 20, 1957.*" Filed with the Registry of Deeds at Bridgewater and Registry of Probate, Book 26, P. 195, Quick Claim No. #374. NSNA. **Lots *6, 7, 8, 15, 16, 17, 18, 19, 20, 25, 26, 30, 31 and 32*.**

16 "*Mary Allen Chapman (09) & all heirs of Clarence J. Beamish (04). **TO** M. R. Chappell (10) – land parcels which make up Lots **6, 7, 8, 15, 16, 17, 18, 19, 20, 23, 25, 26, 30, 31, 32**, Jul. 20, 1961.*" Filed Nova Scotia Supreme Court, Book 27, P. 339, No. #638. NSNA. Representing inheritance of shares for Kenneth Albert Chapman, Barbara Joan Chapman, Marjorie Ann Chapman, Judith Elizabeth Chapman, Carol Gladys Chapman, Robert Wayne Chapman, and Linda Fay Chapman in selling shares of ownership in the parcel of land lots on Oak Island known as "*south and west part of the island,*" "*George McInnis Property,*" and the "*James McInnis Property,*" making up **Lots *6, 7, 8, 15, 16, 17, 18, 19, 20, 23, 25, 26, 30, 31, 32*.**

17 "*Chester Township Records, 1762 – 1830.*" Records kept by Town Clerk of 'Births, Marriages and Deaths.' NSNA, MG9, B 9-3. See specific records cited.

18 "*Heirs of Mary Ellen Chapman (09) & Clarence James Beamish (04). **TO** M. R. Chappell (10) – Lot **23**, Jul. 25, 1955.*" Filed by the Canada Permanent Trust Company on 02-22-1961, and Book 907, P. 605. On 02-02-1961, NSNA. Lot #23 is described as "*The George McGinnis Property*" as shown on Old Plan #1046, filed with the Department of Lands & Forests, based on survey taken by William Nelson Dy, Sr., dated 07-06-1818. This represents the final transfer of heir ownerships of Lot **23** to M.R. Chappell. **Lot 23**

19 "*M.R. Chappell (10). **TO** Dan Blankenship (07) – Lot **23**, Sep. 19, 1975.*" Filed Quit Claim Deed in Chester Deed Office, recorded on 09-26-1975, Book 54, P. 161. **Lot 23**

20 "*Melbourne R. Chappell (10). **TO** David C. Tobias (55) – Lots **6, 7, 8, 15, 16, 17, 18, 19, 20, 25, 26, 30, 31, 32**, Jun. 15, 1977.*" Filed in Halifax Co. Land Deeds, Nova Scotia, recorded on 06-29-1977, No. #582. **Lots *6, 7, 8, 15, 16, 17, 18, 19, 20, 25, 26, 30, 31, 32***

21 "*Philip Payzant (43), **TO** Robert Melvin Sr. (38), – Lot **6**, Jun. 22, 1768*." Chester Township Public Notice of Will & Testament of land transfer of Lot 6, Oak Island, by Philip Paysant (43) to Robert Melvin (38). Witnessed by John Seecombe (48) and Thomas Floyd. 1 Page. See Citation #2. **Lot 6**

22 "*Edward Smith (52), **TO** Timothy Linch/Zink (28/65) – Lot **19**, Mar. 28, 1768*." Recorded MG1, Vol. 384, NSNA. (originally Filed in Chester Township recorded on 08-25-1770, Book 1, No. 913, P. 347. NSNA. **Lot 19.**

24 "*Oak Island, Samuel Ball (03) Lot Ownership Map – Lots **6, 7, 8, 24, 25, 26, 30, 31, 32**, Hook Island, Mainland Farm, 2004*." Reflects Lot ownership changes between the years 1787 through 1812. Provided by Bee Stanton, 2004. www.creative@beestanton website.

25 "*2-page Oak Island Lot Ownership Map, Jul. 6, 1818*." Map from D.W. Crandall (14) Made by Surveyor Nelson Dy Sr. Signed by Robert Smith and labeled "Old Plan." NSNA. [Considered in error]

26 "*Old Plan Map of Oak Island 1818*." Only showing eastern end of Oak Island and provided by David W. Crandell (14) and shows ownership of the following: Lot ***13*** – Neal McMullen (35), Lot ***14*** – David Melvin (38b), Lot ***15*** – David W. Crandell (14), Lot ***16, 17, 18*** – John Smith (51a).

27 "*Chester Township Poll Tax Roll, 1791*." Chester/Lunenburg county – 1791. NSNA. RG 1, Vol. 444. No. 4.

28 "*Lunenburg County, Nova Scotia Land Deeds*." Land Deed Index Vol. 1, 1759-1850; Vol. 2-13, 1775-1849 - Lunenburg, Nova Scotia, Canada Records, FamilySearch and Land Deeds. Image 8 of 540. (https://www.familysearch.org/ark:/61903/3:1:3Q9M-CSV5-G97C-P: may27,2022).

28a Source - Lunenburg Co. Land Deeds: Index Vol. 1, 1759-1850; Vol. 2-13, 1775 -1849; Lunenburg, Nova Scotia, Canada Record, Registrar of Deeds & FamilySearch. See citation.

28b Source – Lunenburg Co. Land Deed: Index Vol. 1, 1759-1850. Recorded 08-25-1807 Lunenburg Co. Land Deeds, Vol. 6, P. 25, No. #52.

28c Source - Lunenburg Co. Land Deeds, Index Vol. 1, 1759-1850; Vol. 2-13, 1775-1849; Lunenburg, Nova Scotia, Canada Record, FamilySearch (htpps://www.familysearch.org/ark:/61903/3:1:3Q9M-CSV5 G97C-P:may27,2022); Image 8 0f 540, Lunenburg District, NS, Registrar of Deeds.

29 "*W.I.N.S. Chester Branch, History of Chester 1759-1767*." Progress-Enterprise Co. 1967.

30 "*Oak Island Lot Distribution Map, 2007*." Provided by MacPhie Archives. P. 5. Identifies Lots ***1, 2, 3, 4, 6, 7, 8, 15, 16, 17, 18, 19, 20, 21, 22, 24, 26, 27, 28, 29, 30, 31, 32*** - Oak Island Tours (41); Lot ***5*** – Robert S. Young (61); Lots ***9, 10, 11, 12, 14*** – Fred Nolan (40); Lot ***13*** – John Johnston (25); Lot ***23*** – Dan/Dave Blankenship (07); and Lot ***25*** – Alan Kostrzewe (27). **– All Lots**

31 "*Chester Township Poll Tax Roll, 1793*." Chester/Lunenburg County – 1793. NSNA, RG1, Vol. 444, No. #62.

32 "*Chester Township Poll Tax Roll, 1794*." Chester/Lunenburg County – 1794. NSNA, RG1, Vol. 444½, No. #24.

33 "*Chester Township Poll Tax Roll, 1795*." Chester/Lunenburg County – 1795. NSNA, RG1, Vol. 444½, No. #59.

34 "*Nova Scotia Land Papers: 1795-1800, Green, James and Others – 1784 – Lunenburg County*." 37,950 acres granted in Chester. Includes: License to Occupy, Memorial, Warrant to Survey, Surveyor's Report and Surveyor's Certificate. @ https://archives.novascotia.ca/land-papers/archives/?ID=313&Doc=document&Page=201101417.

35 "*Oak Island Lot Ownership Map, 1781*." Created by William Nelson Dy Sr., Jul. 6, 1818. Old Plan No. 1046, Dept. of Lands and Fisheries. Beaton Institute, Cape Breton University. Also published in Joy Steel/Gordon Fader's *Oak Island Mystery Solved – Final Chapter*, P. 10, 2nd Edition, 2016.

36 "*Notes on the Triton/Nolan Pact & Lawsuit, RE Ownership of Oak Island Lots*." Unknown source. 3 Pages. 1971. Lots ***5, 9, 10, 11, 12, 13***, & ***14***. Pursuant court case voids improperly registered Land deeds & transfers, heretofore listed as Citations 4, 9, 10, 13, 14, 15, and 20. **Lots 5, 9, 10, 11, 12, 13, 14**

37 "*Oak Island Plan of Property Owned by Sellyn Sellers (19b), Sep. 5, 1935*." by Wildlife Artist, S. Edgar March (1870-1967). Registered Chester Township Land Deeds, Book 24, p. 368. Shows Lots ***1, 2, 3, 4, 21, 22, 23, 27, 28, 29*** - Archibald Dauphinee (15); Lots ***6, 7, 8, 24, 25, 26, 30, 31, 32*** – Sam Ball (03) (Ingram & Francis Conrad (12,12a)); Lots ***9, 10, 11, 12, 13, 14, 15, 16, 17, 18, 19, 20*** – George W. Grimm Jr. (04) (Sellyn Sellers (19b)). **All Lots**

38 "*Old Church Map of Early Western Shore & Mahone Bay Island Owners*." Unknown origin. Five Property Owners identified on Oak Island: *J. Mcinnes* (Northwest); *G. Mcinnes* (West Central); *T. Graves* (Isaacs Point); *J. Boutiller* (South Central).

39 "*1765 Land Grant Participants*." Includes: Jacques Boutilier, 1767. James Pernette, 1757. George Boehner. Casper Wollenhaupt (930 ac.), 1765. Joseph Pernette (810 ac.), 1765. George Boehner Sr. (160 ac.), 1765. John James Bissansa (445 ac.), 1765. John Smith (330 ac.), 1765. McKinnon, 1791. John Bearlson, 1897. Merton McLean, 1764. Ambrose Allen, 1785. William Hopkins, 1787. Jeremiah Rogers, 1778. Fred Patillo, 1791. James Sharp, 1776. John J. Beassion. James Becanson. Alexander Patillo. Robert Melvin. John Kinghorn. John Martin. Phillip Payzant. Jacob Shephard. Melvin Marshall. James Webber. Davie Crandall. Joseph Bazasar. NSNA.

40 "*A True Copy of, James J. Thompson, Provincial Land Surveyors List of First Settlers and their Lots*." 1764 List is an earlier version than the 1784 List copied by Judge Debrisay's The History of Lunenburg County, 1st Edition. This 1764 Thompson List was fist included in the booklet, "*Some Historical Events of Chester, Nova Scotia*," by Cottnam T. Smith, 1945. Publisher unknown.

41 "*Reverend John Seccomb's (48) Diary*." Nova Scotia National Archives, MG 1, Vol. 797C, No. #5.

42 "*1871 Census*."

43 "*Halifax County Records*."

44 "*Nova Scotia National Archives, #201109808*."

45 "*Thomas Embree (17), 1758-1820*." The Free Family Tree @ www.wikitree.com/wiki/Embree897.

46 "*Muster Roll – Neil McMullen (35), 1884*." Nova Scotia National Archives, RG-8, C Series, Vol. 1884, P. 1-2.

47 "*Alexander McNeil (37), **TO** Edward James (24) - Lot **20** & **21**, Jan. 19, 1791*." Lunenburg Co. Land Deeds, Vol. 3, P. 12, No. #16. **– Lot 20 & 21**

48 "*Edward James (24), **TO** Joseph Bezanson (06c) - Lot **20**, Mar. 7, 1794*." Lunenburg Co. Land Deeds, Vol. 5, P. 140, No. #167. **Lot 20**

49 "*John Kinghorn (26), **TO** Alexander McNeil (37) - Lot **4**, Feb. 24, 1786*." Lunenburg Co. Land Deeds, Vol. 3, P. 355, No. #583. **Lot 4**

50 "*The Loyalist Melvins (38) of Charleston, Massachusetts, and Nova Scotia*." by Howard Storm Browne, UE. Williamsburg, Virginia. 18 pages.

51 "*History Channel's, Curse of Oak Island, Cable Show*."

52 "*Foreign Protestants & Settlements of Nova Scotia*." by Winthrop Bell.

53 "*James Sharp (49) **TO** Donald MacGinnes (32) – Lot **28**, Mar. 3, 1788.*" Lunenburg Co. Land Deeds, Vol. 3, P. 419. No. #689. **Lot 28**

54 "*Anthony Vaughan (57), 1751-1835*." The Free Family Tree @ www.wikitree.com/wiki/vaughan-4730.

55 "*Newport Township 1817 Census*."

56 "*Hants County Nova Scotia Census – Daniel Vaughan (57b)*."

57 "*Daniel Vaughan (57b), 1747-1808*." The Free Family Tree @ www.wikitree.com/wiki/vaughan-2098.

58 "*James Webber (60), **TO** Daniel Vaughan **(57b)** – Lots **14**, Oct. 8, 1781*." Lunenburg County Land Deeds, Vol. 2, P. 16, No. #25. **Lot 14**

59 "*Lunenburg Census, 1784 – Timothy Zink (65)*."

60 "*Richard Cunningham, 1748-1823*." The Free Family Tree @ www.wikitree.com/wiki/cunningham-13844.

61 "*William Bowie, **TO** Hector McLean (34) – Lot **23**, Oct. 10, 1784*." Lunenburg Co. Land Deeds, Vol. 3, P. 340. No. #554. **Lot 23**

62 "*Jeremiah Rogers (47), **TO** David Ellis (16) – Lot **29**, Apr. 2, 1778*." Lunenburg Co. Land Deeds, Vol. 2, P. 208, No. #301. **Lot 29**

63 "*Jacob Hatt (21), **TO** John J. Bezanson (06a) – Lot **31**, Jun. 28, 1797*." Lunenburg Co. Land Deeds, Vol. 5, P. 275-76, No. #377. **Lot 31**

64 "*John Monrow (39), **TO** John J. Bezanson (06a) – Lot **29**, Plumb & Marsh Islands, Nov. 16, 1796*." Lunenburg Co. Land Deeds, Vol. 5, P. 278, No. #330. **Lot 29**

65 "*Thomas Embree (17), **TO** George Beazanson (06b) – Lot **4**, Apr. 01, 1807*." Lunenburg Co. Land Deeds, Vol. 6, P. 64, No. #139. **Lot 4**

66 "*George Bezanson (06b), **TO** Anthony Vaughan Jr. (57a) - Lot **4**, Apr. 19, 1807*." Lunenburg Co. Land Deeds, Vol. 5, P. 30, No. #64. **Lot 4**

67 "*John Cochran (11), **TO** Alexander Pittillo (42) – Lot **1**, Feb. 19, 1785*." Lunenburg Co. Land Deeds, Vol. 3, P. 226. **Lot 1**

68 "*Neil McMullen Smith (35a), **TO** Anthony T. Graves (19) – Lots **9, 10, 11, 12, 13, 14**, Jun. 18, 1832*." Lunenburg Co. Land Deeds, Vol. 10, #76, P. 56. **Lot 9, 10, 11, 12, 13, 14**

69 "*David Vaughan (57c), **TO** Anthony T. Graves (19) – Lot **5**, Sep. 19, 1832*." Lunenburg Co. Land Deeds, Vol. 10, #348. **Lot 5**

70 "*Anthony Vaughan Sr. (57), **TO** Thomas Embree (17) – Lot **4**, Jun 1, 1804*." Lunenburg Co. Land Deeds, Vol. 6, P. 730, No. #750. **Lot 4**

71 "*Anthony T. Graves (19), **TO** Frederick Zink (64) – Lots **5, 9, 10, 11, 12, 13, 14**, Feb. 14, 1839*." See Citation #2. **Lots 5, 9, 10, 11, 12, 13, 14**

72 "*William Hopkins (23), **TO** Samuel Ball (03) – Lot **25**, Sep. 22, 1787*." Lunenburg Co. Land Deeds, Vol. 6, P. 24. No. #51. **Lot 25**

73 "*Frederick Joudrey, 1743-1812*." The Free Family Tree @ www.wikitree.com/wiki/joudrey-156.

74 "*Mary Malay (29), **TO** John Smith (51a) – Lot **16**, Jan. 20, 1798*." Lunenburg Co. Land Deeds, Vol.4, P. 369, No. #539. **Lot 16**

75. "*Anthony Vaughan Sr. (57), **TO** Martin Marshall (30) – Lots **9** & **10**, Dec. 22, 1788*." See Citation #2. **Lot 9 & 10**

76 "*Martin Marshall (30), **TO** Neal McMullen (35) – Lots **9** & **10**, Jun. 17, 1793*." Lunenburg Co. Land Deeds, recorded 07-15-1795, Vol. 4, P. 99, No. #123. **Lot 9 & 10**

77 "*Jacob Melvin (38c), **TO** Daniel McKinnon (32a) – Lot **22**, Mar. 14, 1795*." Lunenburg Co. Land Deeds, Vol. 4, P. 140, No. #170. **Lot 22**

78 "*David Vaughan (57c), **TO** Daniel McEnnis (32a) – Lot **2** & **3**, Nov. 2, 1832*." Lunenburg Co. Land Deeds, Vol. 10, P. 491. **Lot 2 & 3**

79 "*Hector McLean (34), **TO** Donald McGinnis (32) – Lot **23**, May 4, 1790*." Lunenburg Co. Land Deeds, Vol. 3, P. 418-19; No. #690 & Vol. 3, P. 340, No. #555. **Lot 23**

80 "*Daniel Vaughn (57b), **TO** Neal McMullen Sr. (35) – Lot **11**, Oct. 6, 1789*." Lunenburg Co. Land Deeds, recorded 05-25-1797, Vol. 4, P. 230, No. #374. **Lot 11**

81 "*Nathaniel Melvin (38a), **TO** Neal McMullen Sr. (35) – Lots **13** & **14**, 1806*." Lunenburg Co. Land Deeds, recorded 07-15-1806, Vol. 6, P. 675, No. #690. **Lots 13 & 14**

82 "*Neal McMullen Sr. (35), **TO** Neal McMullen Smith (35a) – Lots **9, 10, 11, 12, 13, 14**, Dec. 21, 1827*." Lunenburg Co. Land Deeds, Vol. 9, P. 53. **Lots 9, 10, 11, 12, 13, 14**

83 "*Robert Melvin Jr. (38d), **TO** Samuel Ball (03) – Lot **8**, May 23, 1798*." See Palmer Papers, Loyalist Melvins-H., Browne/Chester Town Book, Citations, Vol. 6, P. 26, No. #51. **Lot 8**

84 "*Anthony Vaughan Sr. (57), **TO** Nathaniel Melvin (38a) – Lot **17**, Jun. 25, 1790*." Lunenburg Co. Land Deeds, Vol. 3, 450. **Lot 17**

85 "*Daniel Vaughan (57b), **TO** Nathaniel Melvin (38a) – Lots **13** & **14**, Oct. 9, 1790*." Lunenburg Co. Land Deeds, Vol. 3, P. 447, No. #736. **Lots 13 & 14**

86 "*Jacob Sheppard (50), **TO** Nathaniel Melvin (38a) – Lots **6** & **7**, Nov. 14, 1815*." Lunenburg Co. Land Deeds, Vol. 7, #188.83. **Lots 6 & 7**

87 "*Ambrose Allen (01), **TO** John Monroe (39) – Lot **24**, Oct. 20, 1791*." Lunenburg Co. Land Deeds, Vol. 4, P. 39, No. #52. **Lot 24**

88 "*John Monroe (39), **TO** Samuel Ball (03) – Lot **24**, Jul. 6, 1799*." Lunenburg Co, Land Deeds, recorded 10-11-1832. Vol. 6, P. 26, No. #55. **Lot 24**

89 "*David Ellis (16), **TO** Alexander Pattillo (42) – Lot **27**, Nov. 17, 1786*." See Citation #2. **Lot 27**

90 "*Alexander Pattillo (42), **TO** Donald McGinnis (32) – Lot **27**, May 3, 1791*." Lunenburg Co. Land Deeds, recorded 03-09-1807, Vol. 3, P. 730, No. #749. **Lot 27**

91 "*Alexander Pattillo (42), **TO** Donald McGinnis (32) – Lot **1**, Sep. 9, 1794*." Lunenburg Co. Land Deeds, Vol. 4, P. 192, No. #232. **Lot 1**

92 "*Dr. Jonathan Prescott (45), **TO** Robert Melvin Sr. (38) – Lot **8** & **22**, Jun. 16, 1784*." Lunenburg Co. Land Deeds, recorded 09-27-1790, Vol. 3, P. 429-30, No. #709. **Lot 8 & 22**

93 "*John Pulsifer (46), **TO** Samuel Ball (03) – Lot **30**, Apr. 2, 1810*." Lunenburg Co. Land Deeds, recorded 09-20-1810, Vol. 6, P. 175, No. #389. **Lot 30**

94 "*Rev. John Seccombe (48), **TO** Robert Melvin Sr. (38) – Lot **7**, Nov. 17, 1767*." Lunenburg Co. Land Deeds, Vol. 1, P. 1770, No. #336. **Lot 7**

95 "*Edward Smith (52), **TO** Robert Melvin Sr. (38) – Lot **2**, Jun. 17, 1780*." Lunenburg Co. Land Deeds, recorded 08-08-1785, Vol. 3, P. 180-181, No. #295. **Lot 2**

96 "*John Munroe (39), **TO** Robert Melvin Sr. (38) – Lot **12**, May 15, 1781*." Lunenburg Co. Land Deeds, recorded 08-10-1790, Vol. 3, P. 425, No. #702. **Lot 12**

97 "*Unknown Source, **TO** Robert Melvin Sr. (38) – Lot **19**, 1784*." See Citation #2. **Lot 19**

98 "*Jeremiah Rogers (47), **TO** J. Bexanson (06c) – Lot **27**, 1782*." See Citation #2. **Lot 27**

99 "*Duncan Smith (51), **TO** Allen Ambrose (01) – Lot **24**, Feb. 24, 1785*." Lunenburg Co. Land Deeds, recorded 02-28-1785, Vol. 3, P. 154, No. #248. **Lot 24**

100 "*Casper Wollenhaupt (58), **TO** John Smith (51a) – Lot **18**, Jun. 26, 1795*." Lunenburg Co. Land Deeds, recorded 07-16-1795, Vol. 4, P. 101, No. #24. **Lot 18**

101 "*Joseph Bezanson (06c), **TO** John Smith (51a) – Lot **20**, Feb. 7, 1807*." Lunenburg Co. Land Deeds, recorded 03-02-1810, Vol. 6, P. 150-51, No. #333. **Lot 20**

102 "*Nathaniel Melvin (38a), **TO** John Smith (51a) – Lot **17**, Mar. 21, 1808*." Lunenburg Co. Land Deeds, recorded 03-21-1808, Vol. 6, P. 63-64, No. #138. **Lot 17**

103 "*David Crandell (14), **TO** John Smith (51a) – Lot **15**, Jun. 10, 1819*." Lunenburg Co. Land Deeds, recorded 1820, Vol. 7, P. 413-414. **Lot 15**

104 "*David Vaughan (57c), **TO** John Smith (51a) – Lot **19**, Jul. 1827*." Lunenburg Co. Land Deeds, recorded 04-20-1827, Vol. 8, P. 514, No. #843. **Lot 19**

105 "*J.J. Beasanson (06a) Estate, **TO** Donald McGinnis (32) - Lot **29**, 1810*." Lunenburg Co. Land Deeds, recorded 1810, Vol. 6, P. 151, No. #335. **Lot 29**

106 "*James Columbus Vaughan (57d), **TO** David Vaughan (57c) – Lots **2**, **5**, **17**, Jun. 26, 1823*." Lunenburg Co. Land Deeds, Vols. 8, #513, P. 323, 343, 344, No. #513. **Lots 2, 5, 17**

107 "*Nathaniel Melvin (38a), **TO** Samuel Ball (03) – Lot **6**, Dec. 7, 1812*." Lunenburg Co. Land Deeds, Vol. 6 P.83, No. #189. **Lot 6**

108 "*Samuel Ball (03) Will, Lunenburg, N.S*." Will Extracts www.occities.org/heartland/meadows/5699/lunwilla.html.

109 "*John J. Bezanson (06a), **TO** Samuel Ball (03) – Lot **31**, Aug. 28, 1807*." Lunenburg Co. Land Deeds, Vol. 6, P. 26, No. #56. **Lot 31**

110 "*Crown (00), **TO** Richard Cunningham (66) – Lot **32**, 1784*." **Lot 32**

111 "*The Open Database of the Corporate World. Oak Island Tours Inc*." Opencorporates, Company Number 2272393. Incorporated Date, 12-09-1987, Corporate Officers: Craig Tester, George Monroe, Martin Lagina, Richard Lagina, Dan Blankenship. **Lot 20**

112 "*The Curse of Oak Island, The Story of the World's Longest Treasure Hunt*." By Randall Sullivan, 2018. P. 422.

113 "*Crown (00), **TO** Samuel Ball (03) – Lot **32**, 1809*." **Lot 32**

114 "*Crown (00), **TO** Thomas Young (62) – Lot **31**, 1765*." **Lot 31**

115 "*Crown (00), **TO** Moses Holt (67)* **– *Lot 29*,** *1765*." **Drew Lot. Lot 29**

116 "*Crown (00), **TO** James Sharp (49) – Lot **28**, 1784*." Granted by Gov. Parr. **Lot 28**

117 "*Crown (00), **TO** Edward Smith (52) – Lot **19**, Aug. 20, 1766*." Drew Lot. **Lot 19**

118 "*Crown (00), **TO** David Crandell (14) – Lot **15**, 1818*." **Lot 15**

119 "*Crown (00), **TO** Mary Malay / Jesse White (29) – Lot **16**, 1768*." **Lot 16**

120 "*Anthony Vaughan Sr. (57), **TO** Martin Marshall (30) – Lot **10**, 1784*." **Lot 10**

121 "*Crown (00), **TO** Phillip Payzant (43) – Lot **6**, Aug. 20, 1766*." **Lot 6**

122 "*Crown (00), **TO** Rev. John Secombe (48) – Lot **7**, 1767*." **Lot 7**

123 NS Archives and Record Management "Allotment" Book, P. 137, Reel #13044; "Old Book" #1, P. 44. Granted Gifford Island #12, Young Island #13, and Smith Island #28, to establish a fishery. Escheated.

124 "*Crown (00), **TO** Edward Smith (52) – Lot **2**, Aug. 20, 1766*." Drew Lot. **Lot 2**

125 "*Anthony T. Graves (19), **TO** Edward Foras (68) – Lots **5, 9, 10, 11, 12, 13, 14**, Jan. 8, 1834*." Chester Township Land Deeds, recorded 02-12-1834, Vol. 10, P. 323, No. #425. **Lots 5, 9, 10, 11, 12, 13, 14**

127 "*Frederick Zink (64), **TO** Anthony T. Graves (19), Lots **5, 9, 10, 11, 12, 13, 14**, Mar. 29, 1841*." Lunenburg Co. Land Deeds, recorded 03-29-1841, Vol. 12, P. 210, No. #377. **Lots 5, 9, 10, 11, 12, 13, 14**

128 "*Anthony T. Graves (19), **TO** John Strachan (54) – Lots **5, 9, 10, 11, 12, 13, 14**, Mar. 30, 1841*." Lunenburg Co. Land Deeds, recorded 04-07-1841, Vol. 12 P. 210, 378. Witnesses E. Pike & A. Primrose. **Lots 5, 9, 10, 11, 12, 13, 14**

129 "*Robert S. Young (61) (1996-2020)*." en.wikipedia.org/wiki/Oak_Island. **Lot 5**

130 "*PROPERTYOnline, Lunenburg County, AAN #08219605*." Robert S. Young (61). Reported by FaceBook Social Group, "*Oak Island From the Other Side of the Causeway*," pub. 07-20-2022. **Lot 5**

130a "*Samuel Ball (03) Last Will & Testament*." Last Will & Testament, Lunenburg Co. Registrar, Book 1, P. 37, Dated 10-01-1841, Probated 01-05-184. **Lots 6, 7, 8, 24, 25, 26, 30, 31, 32**

131 "*The Black Settlers of 'Treasure Oak Island' The Primary Generation – Samuel Ball*." See,www.wsog.blogspot.com/2006/05/black-settlers-of-treasure-oak-island_07.html. **Lots 6, 7, 8, 24, 25, 26, 30, 31, 32**

132 "*Who Was Samuel Ball (03)*." Published by Deb Minter 07-06-2021. Facebook site, "*Oak Island: History not Myth*." Posted 06-23-2021. **Lots 6, 7, 8, 24, 25, 26, 30, 31, 32**

132a "*Nova Scotia Supreme Court Final Order after Ruling*." Triton/Tobias v. F. Nolan. N.S. Supreme Court No. 0802, recorded 04-07-1986. Bridgewater, N.S. **Lots 5, 9, 10, 11, 12, 13, 14**

135 "*James Anderson (02), **TO** Samuel Ball (03), Lot **26**, Nov. 10, 1788*." Lunenburg Co. Land Deeds, recorded 08-25-1807, Vol. 6, P. 25, No. #52. **Lot 26**

136 "*Jerimiah Rogers (47), to David Ellis (16), Lot **27**, 1778*." Crandall 1818 Survey, **Lot 27**

140 "*Obituary of Daniel Blankenship (07)*." https://www.echovita.com/ca/obituaries/ns/mahone-bay/daniel-christian-blankenship-8948996. **Lot 23**

169 "*Salome Esther McInnis (widow) (32), **TO** John McInnis (32) – Lot **1**, June 09, 1930*." Lunenburg Co. Land Deeds, Book 20, P. 74, No. #69. **Lot 1**

170 "*FamilySearch: Selwyn William Sellers (19b), 1873-1949*." https://ancestors.familysearch.org/en/LTDN-XC3/selwyn-william-sellers-1873-1949.

199 "*Letter to Reginald V. Harris regarding Lots **1, 2, 3, 4, 5, 6, 7, 8, 9, 10, 11, 12, 13, 14** Oak Island*." By Fred L. Blair, dated 02-16-1035 **Lots 1, 2, 3, 4, 5, 6, 7, 8, 9, 10, 11, 12, 13, 14**

200 "*Edward Smith (52), to Timothy Lynch (28), Lot **19**, Mar. 28, 1768*." Paul Wroclawski. **Lot 19**

202 "*Last Will and Testament of Daniel McKinnon (32a)*." Extractions, Lunenburg County, Mf:0558683.

203 "*John Martin (31), **TO** Anthony Vaughan (57) – Lot **4**, Jul. 16, 1793*." Lunenburg Co. Land Deeds, Vol. 6, P. 64, No. #139. **Lot 4**

700 "*Oak Island Tours & The Michigan Group (2005-present)*." Wikipedia, *Oak Island Mystery*. https://en.wikipedia.org/wiki/Oak_Island_mystery **Lots**

900 "*Find-a-Grave: Frederick Gerald Nolan (40)*." https://www.findagrave.com/memorial/173079240/frederick-gerald-nolan **Lot 9, 10, 11, 12, 13, 14**

901 "*Obituary of Frederick G. Nolan (40) at Halifax Funeral Home*." https://atlanticfuneralhomeshalifax.sharingmemories.ca/site/FrederickGNolan.html **Lot 9, 10, 11, 12, 13, 14**

999 "*Death Registrations: 1864-1877; 1908-1960*." Vital Statistics Division of Service Nova Scotia and Municipal Relations, Compiler. @ https;//www.novascotiagenealogy.com/Deaths.aspx. **Lot 1**

Appendix E

KNOWN NEAF NEIGHBORS

In this appendix is a chart of tree species identified as having inhabited the New England Acadia Forest (NEAF) pre-settlement period (<1600AD). These species represent all the *native* trees known to have grown in Nova Scotia up through 1795 and were probably living within our area of interest.

These species are not considered as possible contenders to be the species of canopied trees in photographs taken of Oak Island. Their full taxonomical information can be found online explaining why.

The chart ONLY contains some of the specific taxonomical identifiers of those native species, which may show the tree to be incompatible to contend as our mystery tree. These listed species would not, through environmental conditions or other tropisms, morph into those canopied trees. Nor do these species shown in this chart, whether growing within a forest or growing individually, exhibit the appearance or growth characteristics seen of those Oak Island mystery trees.

Some of the taxonomical identifiers of the species listed which would not make them a contender, include production of pinecones, catkins, berries, flower stalks, nuts, flowers, or other conspicuous fruits or growths. Nor species which grow needle-like leaves, frond-like leaves, or very small leaves. Nor do species which grow thick, heavily fissured, ridged, papery, striped, or peeling bark, or distinguishable colored bark fit their description. Nor species which have boles that are straight, short, stout, or thick. Nor species which are intolerant to salt mist, flooding, shade, salty soils, or prohibit growth of understory plants. Nor species susceptible to windthrow, limb shear, ice shear, ice damage, snow load, or have small, shallow root systems and known to topple. Nor species which are poisonous to livestock, eaten by animals. Nor species who are short-lived, short in stature, or are finely branched, have hairs on branches, branch tips, leaves or twigs. Nor species with drooping branches, right-angle branching, spoke branching or grow primary branches on bottom half of tree. And those species which produce colorful autumn foliage, whether evergreen or deciduous, would most likely, not be a contender to be named the species of those canopied trees. None of these "traits" were identified or observed with being similar to our mystery canopied trees

Though Burr Oak, Northern Red Oak, White Birch, and Butternut are native trees found within the NEAF prior to 1795; they are not listed here. Many people have voiced strong opinions that these specific species of tree, are, or could have been, those canopied trees. Due to the insistence of many people, these four species were forensically examined, along with others from around the world, in much greater depth. Therefore, these and those certain foreign trees receive additional scrutiny and are examined in Appendix G, "*Dendro Disguised.*"

The following chart provides for each specific named tree, a photograph and a drawing or line-art representation of the full grown mature tree. Both images represent species examples 'outside' a forest or standing alone. The specimen line art depict the species unencumbered of any morphologies or tropisms. Considerations should be made of images with fall coloring, unique fruit or sexual organs, and crown shape. If visible, bark coloring and patterns, branch formations, and bole shape and size, can capture other important determinants for elimination of consideration. Many of these characteristics alone would negate these species as candidates. Finally, some images used have been pixelated to remove shadows, people, or objects which may make the examples characteristics harder to see. The trees were never enhanced or modified, other than in removing conflicting images within the photographs frame.

The reasoning behind disqualifying a species without using dendrochronology or DNA analysis, is simply because we have no specimens with which to compare. The comparison of species characteristics and hereditary behavior from the observed growth history, can be enough to rule on a tree species. It can be deduced certain species are unable, incapable, or not likely to grow or exhibit the tendencies observed against examining those mystery canopy trees. Likewise, trees which exhibit growth patterns, shapes or unique characteristics which are similar to those mystery trees, are further examined later in this book.

I am neither an arborist, a botanist, an ecologist nor a tree whisperer, so there is a chance we are surprised with the final findings. I am however, using the literature and expert opinions of arborists, botanists, and ecologists, in making the final decision. So perhaps, we are all wrong.

Additionally, Chapters #3, *"Wooden You Know,"* Chapter #4, *"Barking up the Wrong Tree,"* and Appendices G, *"Dendro Disguised,"* and F, *"Guardians of the Keep,"* will present the evidence and forensic arguments to persuade you in our identification of those mystery trees of Oak Island; which is spelled out in Chapter #6, "*Mirror Images*."

For NEAF native tree species of the day, see the Chart on the following pages...

NAME, SPECIES	DISQUALIFING CHARACTERISTIC	PHOTO / IMAGE
Jack Pine *(Pinus banksiana)* *Ref. #1a,b*	CONIFEROUS EVERGREEN: Med. Size 70 ft. Produces pinecones. Most shade intolerant pine. Stem breaks from common wind, ice, and snow loads. Stands deteriorates after 70 years.	
White Spruce *(Picea glauca)* *Ref. #2a,b*	CONIFEROUS EVERGREEN: Lg. 50-110 ft. Produces pinecones, colored pink, red or green. Tree is glabrous, has needle-like leaves. Bark is thin and scaly, flaking off in small circular patches.	
Black Spruce *(Picea mariana)* *Ref. #3a,b*	CONIFEROUS EVERGREEN: Small upright tree, 15-50 ft. Narrow pointed crown with drooping branches, upturned tips. Needle-like four-sided. Dense cover small hairs on bark of young branch tips. Small pinecones in bunches. Susceptible to windthrow.	
Balsam Poplar *(Populus balsamifera)* *Ref. #4a,b*	DECIDUOUS: 50-80 Ft. trees, with leaves 3-6", shiny dark green out-side, whitish underside. Sweet fragrance from sticky red resin of large pointy buds. Branches subject to limb shear. Seed disbursed on cottony tusks of hair.	
Tamarack *(Larix laricina)* *[Larch]* *Ref. #5a,b*	CONIFEROUS & DECIDUOUS: 30-60 Ft. Needle-like leaves light blue/green then turn bright yellow before falling off. Bark is tight, flaky, and pink in color and produces small cones, bright red in color, turning brown.	
Balsam Fir *(Abies balsamea)* *Ref. #6a,b*	CONIFEROUS EVERGREEN: 20-30 Ft. Narrow pyramidal to conical with spire-like crown. Pinecones appear upright on branches in brown/copper color. Thick dense needles directed upward and forward. Does not tolerate clay soils.	

NAME, SPECIES	DISQUALIFING CHARACTERISTIC	PHOTO / IMAGE
Trembling Aspen *(Populus tremuloides)* *Ref. #7a,b*	DECIDUOUS: Max height, 50ft. Max age, 90 yrs. Commonly uprooted from wind. Yellow fall foliage. Pyramidal or rounded crown. Bark thin, produces catkins. Intolerant of standing water, flooding, shade. Eaten by animals.	
Pin Cherry *(Prunus pensylvanica)* *Ref. #8a,b*	DECIDUOUS: Max height, 25ft. Max age 30yrs. Very shade intolerant. Grouped berries in fall. Toxic to livestock. White flowers in spring, requires much light & moisture to survive. Shallow root system. Attracts bugs.	
Red Cedar *(Juniperus virginiana)* *Ref. #9a,b*	CONIFEROUS EVERGREEN: 20-50′ Ft, up to 850 years old. Very aromatic. Leaves are lace-like fronds which turn brown with age. Shredded reddish-brown bark easily strips from trunk. Grows pale blue/green hard berries holding seeds.	
Black Ash *(Fraxinus nigra)* *Ref. #10a,b*	DECIDUOUS: Produces long single-seed samaras. Fall foliage is yellow and quickly lose their leaves. Maximum height of 50ft. Highly susceptible to ice damage.	
Red Pine *(Pinus resinosa)* *Ref. #11a,b*	CONIFEROUS EVERGREEN: Grows a straight, tall bole, with a conical crown. Thin flaky bright orange-red bark in upper crown. Self-trimming of branches below crown. Produces purple pinecones turning blue.	
E. White Pine *(Pinus strobus)* *Ref. #12a,b*	CONIFEROUS: (DECIDUOUS NEEDLES abscise every 18 months) Produce pinecones every 3-5 years. Branches are spaced every 18 inches on the trunk with 5-6 branches appearing 'spoke-like' on a wheel, Tall.	

NAME, SPECIES	DISQUALIFING CHARACTERISTIC	PHOTO / IMAGE
Largetooth Aspen *(Populus grandidentata)* *Ref. #13a,b*	DECIDUOUS: Produces catkins. Straight trunks with ascending branches. Very shade intolerant, lower limbs die off. Rapid growth of suckers. 60ft tall. Max age, 60 yrs. Not wind firm.	
White Elm *(Ulmus americana)* *Ref. #14a,b*	DECIDUOUS: Produces a flat samara with papery wings. Vase-shaped crown. Foliage turns bright yellow in fall. Shorter tree height.	
Yellow Birch *(Betula alleghaniensis)* *Ref. #15a,b*	DECIDUOUS: Single stemmed, produces catkins in spring, thin, papery, and shiny yellow-bronze bark, with flaky golden curls as it separates from bole. Leaves in autumn are a bright yellow.	
Red Ash *(Fraxinus pennsylvanica)* *Ref. #16a,b*	DECIDUOUS: Hairy leaves and twigs produce samaras. Trunk is straight & upright, forming thick layer of gray bark with interlaced ridges forming diamond pattern. Yellowish leaves in fall.	
Sugar Maple *(Acer saccharum)* *Ref. #17a,b*	DECIDUOUS: Fall foliage ranges from bright yellow, orange, to fluorescent red orange. Produces samaras.	
Striped Maple *(Acer pensylvanicum)* *Ref. #18a,b*	DECIDUOUS: Grows less than 30ft. An Understory tree. Intensive yellow autumn foliage. Trunk red brown. Needs shading. Moderate wind resistance.	

NAME, SPECIES	DISQUALIFING CHARACTERISTIC	PHOTO / IMAGE
Red Maple *(Acer rubrum)* *Ref. #19a,b*	DECIDUOUS: Intolerant to salt spray, salty soils. Various crown shapes. Rich red (or yellow) foliage in autumn. Produces 2" winged samaras in spring. Max height 60ft tall. Has red tinge on twigs, flowers.	
Red Spruce *(Picea rubens)* *Ref. #20a,b*	CONFIFEROUS: 60-130 ft tall. Tall trunk, narrow conical crown. Leaves are needle-like yellow green, with cones.	
White Ash *(Fraxinus americana)* *Ref. #21a,b*	DECIDUOUS: Rounded, open-grown crown produces samaras, Spectacular red/ maroon to purple fall foliage. Valuable hard wood now vary rare in Nova Scotia. Finely branched with 35° angle from vertical. Shade Intolerant	
Basswood *(Tilia americana)* *Ref. #22a,b*	DECIDUOUS: Straight trunk, tall domed crown, with bract set of cymes flowers – fragrant & showy. Fall foliage is yellow-pale. Leaves up to 10" long. Very rare to find pure stand. Shallow roots, no taproot.	
Eastern Hemlock *(Tsuga canadensis)* *Ref. #23a,b*	CONNIFEROUS: Straight trunk, pyramidal shape with long pendulous limbs, often drooping down. Evergreen needles. 60-100 ft. Tall.	
Silver Maple *(Acer saccharinum)* *Ref. #24a,b*	DECIDUOUS: Short bole, medium size tree. Produces samaras. Cannot compete with overstory. Shallow roots & highly susceptible to ice damage & brittle wood, leading to windthrow. Frequent root rot.	

NAME, SPECIES	DISQUALIFING CHARACTERISTIC	PHOTO / IMAGE
Black Cherry *(Prunus serotina)* *Ref. #25a,b*	DECIDUOUS: Max 60 ft, pyramidal crown. Showy white flowers in clusters with fruit. Dark scaly bark. Prone to storm damage. Highly susceptible to ice damage. Poisonous to livestock.	
American Beech *(Fafus grandifolia)* *Ref. #26a,b*	DECIDUOUS: (retains leaves in fall and winter) 50-75ft tall. Imposing tree. Smooth, tight gray bark, rounded crown, heavy dense growth. Shallow wide spread roots, moderate windfirmness. Small shiny triangular brown nuts. Maximum age, 80 years.	
Black Birch *(Betula nigra)* *Ref. #27a,b*	DECIDUOUS: Short bole. Yellow fall foliage. Many small samaras. Heavy pollen producer. Bark is red/brown to brown/gay and peels off horizontally while pressed into thick plates. Produces catkins.	
Ironwood *(Ostrya virginiana)* *Ref. #28a,b*	DECIDUOUS: Grows less than 40ft tall. An Understory tree. Produces catkins. Vibrant fall colors range from yellowish to orange or red.	

One thing that I have learned in writing this book is - *never be absolute in your determinations!* When dealing with nature, no one has the riddle solved nor the answers pegged. Go with what you learn and observe and be ready and understanding when your entire premise is flipped on its head. If not with that thinking, one would never have been able to solve the question about those mystery canopied trees. Everyone involved in this search was found to be wrong in their initial assumptions!

Footnoted References

[1]. "*Borealization of the New England – Acadian Forest: a review of the evidence*," by Josh Noseworthy and Thomas M. Beckley. Environmental Reviews. 28(3): 284-293. https://doi.org/10.1139/er-2019-0068. © Canadian Science Publishing or its licensors.

[1a]. "*Jack Pine/Pinus banksiana L.*" by T.D. Rudolph and P.R. Laidly. US Forest Service, US Department of Agriculture. *https://www.srs.fs.usda.gov/pubs/misc/ag_654/volume_1/pinus/banksiana.ht*

[1b]. "*Jack Pine Silhouette*." Natural Resources Canada. Last modified on Apr. 8, 2015. https://tidcf.nrcan.gc.ca/en/trees/factsheet/43.

[2a]. "*White Spruce/Picea mariana.*" Last modified on Feb. 23, 2022. https://en.wikipedia.org/wiki/Picea_glauca.

[2b]. "*White Spruce Silhouette*." Plants Database, Natural Resources Conservation Services. US Department of Agriculture. https://plants.usda.gov/.

[3a]. "*Black Spruce/Picea mariana.*" Last modified on Feb. 23, 2022. https://en.wikipedia.org/wiki/Picea_mariana.

[3b]. "*Black Spruce Silhouette*." Monado. Science Notes. Last modified on Aug. 9, 2007. https://sciencenotes.wordpress.com/2007/08/09/tree-silhouettes/.

[4a]. "*Balsam poplar/Populus balsamifera*." Editor Maureen Rogers. HERBALPEDIA, The Herb Growing & Marketing Network, Silver Spring, PA. https://www.herbworld.com/learningherbs/POPLAR,%20BALSAM.pdf.

[4b]. "*Balsam Poplar Silhouette*." Top Tree Species for Calgary. Official web site of the City of Calgary, Alberta, Canada. https://www.calgary.ca/csps/parks/planning-and-operations/tree-management/top-tree-species-for-calgary.html.

[5a]. "*Tamarack/Larix larcinia.*" American Conifer Society. *CONIFER Quality Magazine*. www.confiersociety.org/conifers/larix-larcina/.

[5b]. "*Tamarack Silhouette*." Natural Resources Canada. Last modified Apr. 8, 2015. https://tidcf.nrcan.gc.ca/en/trees/factsheet/34.

[6a]. "*Balsam fir/Abies balsamea.*" North Carolina Extension Service Tool Box. https://plants.ces.ncsu.edu/plants/abies-balsamea/.

[6b]. "*Balsam fir Silhouette*." Natural Resources Canada. Last modified Apr. 8, 2015. https://tidcf.nrcan.gc.ca/en/trees/factsheet/80.

[7a]. "*Trembling Aspen/Populus tremuloides.*" by Janet L. Howard. 1996. Populus tremuloides. In: Fire Effects Information System, [Online]. U.S. Department of Agriculture, Forest Service, Rocky Mountain Research Station, Fire Sciences Laboratory (Producer). https://www.fs.fed.us/database/feis/plants/tree/poptre/all.html [04-04-2022].

[7b]. "*Trembling Aspen Silhouette*." Natural Resources Canada. Last modified Apr. 8, 2015. https://tidcf.nrcan.gc.ca/en/trees/factsheet/58.

[8a]. "*Pin Cherry/Prunus pensylvanica.*" by G.W. Wendel. U.S. Department of Agriculture, Forest Service. www.srs.fs.usda.gov/pubs/misc/ag_654/volume_2/prunus/pensylvanica.htm.

[8b]. "*Pin Cherry Silhouette*." Natural Resources Canada. Last modified Apr. 8, 2015. https://tidcf.nrcan.gc.ca/en/trees/factsheet/59.

[9a]. "*Red Cedar/Juniperus virginiana.*" by Sandra McLean Cutler, Author of "Dwarf & Unusual Conifers Coming of Age. https://www.conifersociety.org/conifers/juniperus-virginiana/.

[9b]. "*Red Cedar Silhouette*." Natural Resources Canada. Last modified Apr. 8, 2015. https://tidcf.nrcan.gc.ca/en/trees/factsheet/133.

[10a]. "*Black Ash/Fraxinus nigra.*" Classic Landscape Plant Finder. http://plants.classiclandscapes.com/11050016/Plant/157/Black_Ash.

[10b]. "*Black Ash Silhouette*." Natural Resources Canada. Last modified Apr. 8, 2015. https://tidcf.nrcan.gc.ca/en/trees/factsheet/27.

[11a]. "*Red Pine/Pinus resinosa.*" "*Lessons from the Red Pine,*" By J.S. Esposito, Nov. 20, 2013. https://jsesposito.wordpress.com/2013/11/20/lessons-from-the-red-pine/.

[11b]. "*Red Pine Silhouette*." Natural Resources Canada. Last modified Apr. 8, 2015. https://tidcf.nrcan.gc.ca/en/trees/factsheet/49.

[12a]. "*Eastern White Pine/Pinus strobus.*" Native Plant Trust – Go Botany. https://gobotany.newenglandwild.org/species/pinus/strobus/.

[12b]. "*Eastern White Pine Silhouette*." Natural Resources Canada. Last modified on 04-08-2015. https://tidcf.nrcan.gc.ca/en/trees/factsheet/50.

[13a]. "*Largetooth Aspen/Populus grandidentata.*" Plant Images. http://www.psn3.com/Peuplier,a,grandes,dents/fiche.html.

[13b]. "*Largetooth Aspen Silhouette*." Natural Resources Canada. Last modified on Apr. 8, 2015. https://tidcf.nrcan.gc.ca/en/trees/factsheet/55.

14a. "*White Elm/Ulmus americana.*" by Calvin F. Bey. U.S. Department of Agriculture, Forest Service. https://www.srs.fs.usda.gov/pubs/misc/ag_654/volume_2/ulmus/americana.

14b. "*White Elm Silhouette*." Natural Resources Canada. Last modified on Apr. 8, 2015. https://tidcf.nrcan.gc.ca/en/trees/factsheet/76.

15a. "*Yellow Birch/Betula alleghaniensis.*" Tree Plantation – Yellow Birch Trees. https://www.treeplantation.com/yellow-birch.html.

15b. "*Yellow Birch Silhouette*." Natural Resources Canada. Last modified on Apr. 8, . https://tidcf.nrcan.gc.ca/en/trees/factsheet/15.

16a. "*Red Ash/Fraxinus pennsylvanica,*" by Richard Webb, Bugwood.org. https://www.forestryimages.org/browse/detail.cfm?imgnum=1480634.

16b. "*Red Ash Silhouette*." Natural Resources Canada. Last modified on Apr. 8, 2015. https://tidcf.nrcan.gc.ca/en/trees/factsheet/28.

17a. "*Sugar Maple/Acer saccharum.*" Moon Nurseries Inc. Maryland. https://moonnurseries.com/product/acer-saccharum-commemoration/.

17b. "*Sugar Maple Silhouette*." Natural Resources Canada. Last modified on Apr. 8, 2015. https://tidcf.nrcan.gc.ca/en/trees/factsheet/86.

18a. "*Striped Maple/Acer pensylvanicum.*" by Susan McDougall. The Trees of North America. https://northamericantrees.com/acer-pensylvanicum.html.

18b. "*Striped Maple Silhouette*." Natural Resources Canada. Last modified on 04-08-2015. https://tidcf.nrcan.gc.ca/en/trees/factsheet/83.

19a. "*Red Maple/Acer rubrum.*" Nature Hills online Nursery. Plant photos. https://www.naturehills.com/red-maple.

19b. "*Red Maple Silhouette*." Natural Resources Canada. Last modified on Apr. 8,2015. https://tidcf.nrcan.gc.ca/en/trees/factsheet/84.

20a. "*Red Spruce/Picea rubens.*" Natural Resources Canada. Last modified on Apr. 8, 2015. https://treecanada.ca/resources/canadas-arboreal-emblems/red-spruce/.

20b. "*Red Spruce Silhouette*." Natural Resources Canada. Last modified on Apr. 8, 2015. https://tidcf.nrcan.gc.ca/en/trees/factsheet/41.

21a. "White Ash/Fraxinus americana." By Richard C. Schlesinger. U.S. Department of Agriculture, Forest Service. https://www.srs.fs.usda.gov/pubs/misc/ag_654/volume_2/fraxinus/americana.

[21b]. "*White Ash Silhouette*." Natural Resources Canada. Last modified on Apr. 8, 2015. https://tidcf.nrcan.gc.ca/en/trees/factsheet/26.

[22a]. "*Basswood/Tilia americana*." by Dr. Jeff Kirwan, et. al. A program of Montgomery County, Maryland Government. Dec. 7, 2018. Landowner Factsheets © 2004 Virginia Tech Forestry Department, all rights reserved. https://treemontgomery.org/wp-content/uploads/2018/12/american-basswood-fall-color.png.

[22b]. "*Basswood Silhouette*." BritannicaKIDS. American Forestry Institute. https://kids.britannica.com/students/assembly/view/126778.

[23a]. "*Eastern Hemlock/Tsuga canadensis.*" Published by Supidpto Chakrabarti on Jun. 7, 2016 in *Hemlock*. Coniferous Forest Online. Article was last reviewed on 26th December 2019. https://www.coniferousforest.com/eastern-hemlock-canadian-hemlock.htm.

[23b]. "*Eastern Hemlock Silhouette*." (Tsuga Canadensis: Canadian Hemlock) by Edward F. Gilman and Dennis G. Watson. University of Florida IFAS Extension Service. Environmental Horticulture Department Document ENH-803, 1993. https://edis.ifas.ufl.edu/publication/ST646.

[24a]. "*Silver Maple/Acer saccharinum.*" by Dr. Jeff Kirwan, et. al. A program of Montgomery County, Maryland Government. Dec. 7, 2018. Landowner Factsheets © 2004 Virginia Tech Forestry Department, all rights reserved. https://treemontgomery.org/wp-content/uploads/2018/12/silver-maple-fall.png.

[24b]. "*Silver Maple Silhouette*." Natural Resources Canada. Last modified on Apr. 8, 2015. https://tidcf.nrcan.gc.ca/en/trees/factsheet/85.

[25a]. "*Black Cherry/Prunus serotina*." Ontario Ministry of Northern Development, Mines, Natural Resources and Forestry. Published Jul. 18, 2019. Last modified Oct. 6, 2021. https://www.ontario.ca/page/black-cherry.

[25b]. "*Black Cherry Silhouette*." Natural Resources Canada. Last modified on Apr. 8, 2015. https://tidcf.nrcan.gc.ca/en/trees/factsheet/60.

[26a]. "*American Beech/Fafus grandifolia.*" by Jim King, King Nursery, Oswego, Illinois. https://www.kingnurseryil.com/product/american-beech-7-gal-18-42/.

[26b]. "*American Beech Silhouette*." Natural Resources Canada. Last modified on Apr. 8, 2015. https://tidcf.nrcan.gc.ca/en/trees/factsheet/25.

[27a]. "*Black Birch/Betula nigra.*" by H.E. Grelan. Southern Research Station, U.S. Department of Agriculture, Forest Service. https://www.srs.fs.usda.gov/pubs/misc/ag_654/volume_2/betula/nigra.htm.

27b. "*Black Birch Silhouette*." www.iStock.com.

28a. "*Ironwood/Ostrya virginiana*." Jim Whiting Nursery & Garden Center. Rochester, MN. https://plants.jimwhitingnursery.com/Plant-Name/Ostrya-virginiana-Hop-Hornbeam-or-Ironwood.

28b. "*Ironwood Silhouette*." Natural Resources Canada. Last modified on Apr. 8, 2015. https://tidcf.nrcan.gc.ca/en/trees/factsheet/36.

Appendix F

GUARDIANS OF THE KEEP

This Appendix provides images of Oak Island from the past which I've gathered over the period of writing this book. The emphasis on the collection was to acquire images of those mystery canopied trees at different times, seasons, and settings. Many of these images came from the generous contributions of both co-authors, Christopher L. Boze and Robert W. Cook. A great deal more came from the Nova Scotia National Information Services fond, and Nova Scotia National Archives as well as other photographs passed around on social media. The dates and descriptions assigned to each image is as correct as I was able to run them down. These photographs span less than half a century and include images of the island for comparison sake. Some have been identified with different dates and I haven't been able to confirm one over the other. As you look at these old photographs please attempt to gleam identifying traits which all of these trees share, when they were heralded as the namesake of "Oak" Island.

The first TWELVE images listed were used by arborists, botanists, ecologists, foresters, and pest control specialists to opine on the identification of those mystery canopied trees. Some of those observations were captured in Chapter 3, "*Wooden You Know*," are all posted in Appendix C, "*On the Record*," and Appendix G, "*Dendro Disguised*," and referred to throughout this book.

Image 1. (Above) Famous mystery canopied trees of Oak Island, Nova Scotia. Courtesy: Robert W. Cook.[1]

Courtesy: Nova Scotia Archives

Image 2. (Above) View from mainland of Eastern Drumlin of Oak Island. Looking carefully, you can see Frog Island in the background. Note the view of those "oaks" towering over the 'entire' island.[2] The can be seen growing above the darker forest canopy seen along the shoreline.

Courtesy: Harold Reid, Nova Scotia National Archives, circa 1933.

Image 3. (Above) Oak Island aerial view from southeast looking west. Lower right corner is Isaac's Point with the remaining 7 or more, canopied trees growing within the conifer groves. Trees circled.[3]

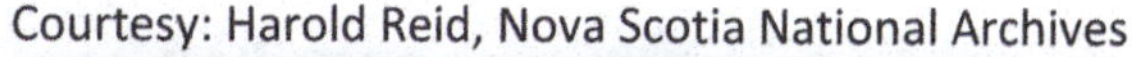

Courtesy: Harold Reid, Nova Scotia National Archives

Image 4. (Right) Another aerial shot of Smith's Cove and Isaac's Point looking west with the swamp in the background.[4]

Several tall snags can be seen in the center of the photo near the building with another tree clearly seen just off the beach.

All five following photographs, courtesy Bowdin Expedition, Nova Scotia Archives

Image 5. (Below) Note the upward branching of limbs and the thin, sinuous +80 Ft. height of the tree trunks climbing to the sky. Circa 1909.[5]

5

6

Image 6. (1909) Above image from the higher elevation atop the eastern drumlin and near the shaft, with Frog Island in the background. Four canopied trees can be seen, the larger in the background, growing from below the high ridge.[6] Note the barkless appearance and upward branching. Small spruce trees litter the understory, with a shrub or clover in the forefront.

Image 7. (Left) Also on top of the eastern drumlin, several canopied trees in early succession, with clearly viewable upwardly vase shaped crowns. No limbs at 90° angles, nor heavy trunks with deep ridged, fissured & dark bark. All seen in open growth stand with a few much smaller shrub-like saplings on right in background. No catkins, nuts, acorns, samaras, needles, fruit, samaras, pinecones, or flowers seen. Circa 1909.[7]

Image 8. (Above) View from Isaac's Point to Smith's Cove at low tide.[8] Circa 1909. Shows mining camp with more than a dozen canopied trees. Largest on left appears to have trunk split from ground level. All with same taxonomic characteristics discussed within this book.

Image 9. (Below) Closeup of mining camp with the closest view of the leaves, bark and branching of a possible canopied tree. Tree leans left and outward, giving one branch a false 90° angle look. All branches appear to be sacrificed by the tree as it grows taller. Photo taken same day Franklin Roosevelt visited Oak Island, in background.[9]

Courtesy Bowdin Expedition, Nova Scotia Archives. Circa 1909-12.

Image 10. (Next page) Enlarged closeup of bole on canopied tree from above photo. Note lighter colored bark which appears spotted with a growth, such as lichens, are not uncommon in maritime stands.[10]

"The shedding of lateral twigs, stems, and branches is frequently observed phenomenon of woody plants, with many species of angiosperm and gymnosperm having the capacity to shed such laterals. Among gymnosperms however, only the species of *Coniferales* (conifers and *Gnetales*, are able to 'practice' **cladoptosis** – to expand, only 2 of the 9 genera of Pinaceae (pines) possess such an ability). In these species, Millington & Chaney (1973) outline two distinct mechanisms by which a branch may be shed: (1) an interaction of biotic and mechanical agents ('self-cleaning' or 'natural pruning'), (2) physiological processes (cladoptosis). [11]

Most often, both mechanisms deal with access to light to produce energy to sustain the tree. Clearly, these trees are not in any need for light as they grow extremely tall on a very exposed south-east exposure.

Image 12. (below) Here is an enlargement of the foliage seen in Image 9, on the previous page. Leaves appear to be small, perhaps growing in small groups or small bunches on twigs emanating from limbs – *or seasonal early regrowth.*

Both images are magnifications of Image 9.

Above images courtesy Bowdin Expedition, Nova Scotia Archives.

Courtesy NS Information Services, Nova Scotia National Archives. Circa 1947.

Image 13. (Above) Both photos are of snags (standing dead timber) of those canopied trees once on Oak Island. The Osprey nest was visible in one of these snags as recently as within the last half century. They are provided for the viewer to notice the branching at the top of the long sinuous trunk which once held the umbrella-shaped foliage which create the interesting canopy tops. There are no trees, logs, stump, nor roots which remain of those mystery canopy trees on Oak Island. Circa 1947.[13]

Image of Osprey Nest courtesy: Robert Young, oakislandlotfive.ca

With the exception of one pine on the right side, the vase-shaped trees with umbrella canopies paint the background of this group posing for history.[14]

Courtesy Bowdin Expedition, Nova Scotia Archives.

Below is a colored B&W, possibly for making into a postcard. The widespread stand of these exposed towering trees, continue to maintain their iconic canopy and upward-reaching branching. Foliage appears to be small, but dense. The famed apple tree is in the far left background, making this view, a south easterly one.[15]

Colored photo called "Dodge Photo," courtesy Robert Young Collection.

All four photos on page, Courtesy Nova Scotia Archives

(Above) View of Isaac's Point in background with Smith's Cove in foreground. No existing understory as the area was used for livestock foraging during this time period. Fence meanders around the dig operations. Approximately 28 live canopied trees seen in this photo. Two or three appear to be twin trunked. A dead snag appears to have been growing from within the beach on the far side. No 90° branching, all canopies similar at the top five feet of the crown. All trunks thin and sinuous in growth and appearing to have light-colored bark. All trees seem to be well dispersed over this terrain.[16]

1897[20]

1945[21]

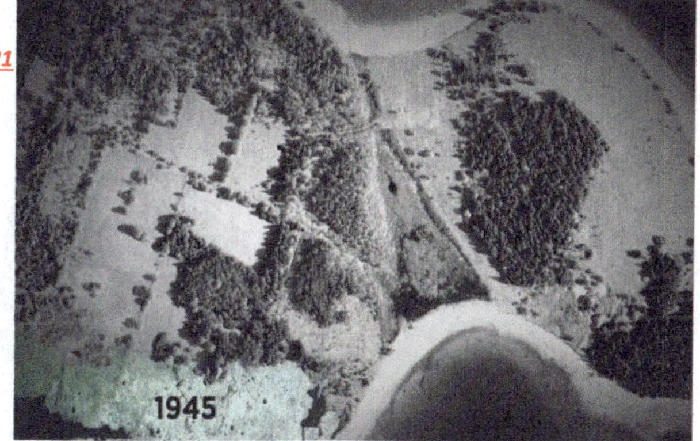

Courtesy:
Nova Scotia
Information
Service Fond
Nova Scotia
National
Archives

Courtesy: Clara Dennis, NS National Archives

1981[22]

Closely examine the photograph below with the Oak Island banner in red, in the upper left corner. Oak Island is in the background and is not the mainland in the foreground. Round Island and the sand bar or shoal can be seen on the right and both are the same two small islands found on the western end of Oak Island today. Please note the very distant background of Oak Island, where you can make out our tall, canopied trees above the forest canopy on the center area of the island. They can be made out immediately above the building on the left in the center-right of the island. They continue to be seen left of that building in the distant background.

Photo courtesy Nova Scotia National Archives. Altered by David Neisen.[22]

Here are a few more photographs which show how the mystery canopied trees on Oak Island would have appeared to cover the entire island, yet they were only home to lots #18, #19, and #20 on the far end of the eastern drumlin.

View From South Shore cove. Courtesy Bowdin Expedition, NS Archives.[23]

View from Western Shores, mainland. Courtesy Nova Scotia Archives.[24]

View from Chester today. Courtesy tourismchester.ca.[25]

Note: Oak Island has Northern Red Oaks on the western drumlin (right side) today, yet they maintain canopy uniformity and not peak over in an "emergent layer" or above the forest overstory, like those mystery canopied trees on the eastern drumlin did!

Footnoted References

[1]. "*Smith's Cove with boat watercolor*." by Robert W. Cook. 2018. www.bobcookartistry.com.

[2]. "*View of Oak Island from mainland*." B/W photo. Courtesy Nova Scotia National Archives.

[3]. "*Aerial view of Eastern Drumlin*." Circa 1933. B/W photo. Courtesy Harold Reid, Nova Scotia National Archives.

[4]. "*Aerial view of Eastern Drumlin – 2*." Circa 1933. B/W photo. Courtesy Harold Reid, Nova Scotia National Archives.

[5]. "*Isaac's Point Trees w Boat on beach*." Circa 1909. B/W photo. Courtesy Henry Livingston Bowdin Expedition, The Old Gold Salvage and Wrecking Company. Nova Scotia National Archives.

[6]. "*Trees atop Crest with Frog Island in Back*." Circa 1909. B/W photo. Courtesy Henry Livingston Bowdin Expedition, The Old Gold Salvage and Wrecking Company. Nova Scotia National Archives.

[7]. "*Canopied Tree stand on bluff over Smiths Cove*." Circa 1909. B/W photo. Courtesy Henry Livingston Bowdin Expedition, The Old Gold Salvage and Wrecking Company. Nova Scotia National Archives.

[8]. "*Early Bowdin Camp at Smiths Cove*." Circa 1909. B/W photo. Courtesy Henry Livingston Bowdin Expedition, The Old Gold Salvage and Wrecking Company. Nova Scotia National Archives.

[9]. "*Roosevelt Arrives at Camp*." Circa 1910-12. B/W photo. PUBLIC DOMAIN / WIKIMEDIA COMMONS.

[10]. "*Cladoptosis: An Interesting phenomenon*." Plantclinic.tamu.edu/2013/11/15/cladoptosis-an-interesting-phenonmenon/.

[12]. "*Dead Snags of Oak Island*." Circa 1947. B/W photo. Courtesy NS Information Services No. 6219. Nova Scotia National Archives.

[13]. "*Dead Tree Osprey Nest*." B/W photo. Courtesy Robert Young, owner www.oakislandlotfive.ca.

[14]. "*Drilling Crew on Oak Island*." Circa 1909-11. B/W photo. Courtesy Henry Livingston Bowdin Expedition, The Old Gold Salvage and Wrecking Company. Nova Scotia National Archives.

15. "*Dodge Photo*." Colored photo. Courtesy Robert Young Collection, Nova Scotia National Archives.

16. "*Smith's Cove Image – Early Dig*." Circa 1909-1911. B/W photo. Courtesy Henry Livingston Bowdin Expedition, The Old Gold Salvage and Wrecking Company. Nova Scotia National. Archives.

17. "*Smith's Cove Image – Logs*." Circa 1909. B/W photo. Courtesy Henry Livingston Bowdin Expedition, The Old Gold Salvage and Wrecking Company. Nova Scotia National Archives.

18. "*Smith's Cove Image – Boiler*." Circa 1909 B/W photo. Courtesy Henry Livingston Bowdin Expedition, The Old Gold Salvage and Wrecking Company. Nova Scotia National Archives.

19. "*Smith's Cove Image – Closeup*." Circa 1909. B/W photo. Courtesy Henry Livingston Bowdin Expedition, The Old Gold Salvage and Wrecking Company. Nova Scotia National Archives.

20. "*Smith's Cove w/ Fence*." B/W photo. Courtesy Nova Scotia National Archives.

21. "*1945 Aerial of OI western drumlin*." B/W photo. Courtesy of Information Services Fond, Nova Scotia National Archives.

22. "*View of Smith's Cove through the Trees*." 1981. B/W photo. Courtesy of Clara Dennis Fond, 541 No. 96. Nova Scotia National Archives.

23. "*View from South Shore*." Circa 1909. B/W photo. Courtesy Henry Livingston Bowdin Expedition, The Old Gold Salvage and Wrecking Company. Nova Scotia National Archives..

24. "*View of Oak Island from mainland*." B/W photo. Courtesy of Nova Scotia National Archives.

25. "*View of Oak Island from Chester*." Colored photo. Courtesy of the Municipality of Chester. Last Modified 09-30-2020. https://t.co/hE46SzPa3I. www.tourismchester.ca.

Appendix G

DENDRO DISGUISED

Each tree species being reviewed is illustrated with a line drawing showing no leaves, and as a standalone specimen. Since our mystery canopied trees were far enough apart to have been considered 'outside a forest,' we want the best "apples to apples" images for comparison. The selected images best depict branch angulation, bole straightness, and crown shape. Additionally, each tree is shown in a photograph by itself or within a small group to demonstrate the species morphology when grown in an open setting. Later in this section, some photographs of multiple trees attempt to offer images which help interpret the species as possible look-alikes for those Oak Island mystery canopied trees.

Tree species have listed information on particular aspects like hardiness and range, height and crown type, longevity, and intolerance levels; are all part of the jigsaw puzzle pieces required to fit our known image. Some anecdotes are more esoteric and may only be important in determining 'why' the tree may have been chosen. Perhaps the tree was edible, did the tree provide a valuable wood type, was it revered for a historical or biblical reason, or did it have valuable chemical compounds?

I used multiple sources to list the characteristics of the species in the following pages. This allowed for a variety of taxonomic characteristics claimed for these individual species. Some contenders may involve hybridized or variant types of these trees.

Our selected contender identified as the species of those mystery canopied trees of Oak Island is among the trees shown here in this Appendix. It is further explained in Chapter 6, "*Mirror Images.*"

Worldly Wood Contenders

You may have seen or heard of trees which resemble those on Oak Island. Again, we tend to use sight recognition of a tree species characteristic and heritable crown shapes to make those linkages. Further analysis is needed to see "which" species could survive in our area of interest. Looks are not everything! *Can they survive the weather? Can they tolerate the impact from the ocean? Can they live in the extreme temperatures? Do they speak Canadian?*

The New England Acadian Forest did not provide a viable 'native' tree species to pass the candidacy test to be those trees from Oak Island. Therefore, we turn to other candidates from around North America and the world. Wherever we find them, we will review their 'resumes' to see their chance of being identified as a qualified candidate for selection. Up at bat are: *Albizia, Acacia, Aleppo Pine, Butternut, Umbrella Pine, Maritime Pine, White Birch, Cork Oak and a last minute entrant – European Sycamore*. These tree species and some of their relatives, all bear a remarkable resemblance to those canopied trees on Oak Island. Some of these species represent a challenge in proper identification. Some of the 'species' have been reassigned botanical family relationships; others are dramatically different in appearance from one native country to another native country. All appear to escape a perfect match to our canopied trees. But one of them is the candidate for further examination?

The Butternut, White Birch, and Cork Oak species were added to this mix, as they have been popularly theorized on social media, as '*the*' Oak Island tree. Therefore, they needed to be scrutinized. I hope as we trailblaze through this forensic forest, none of you have gone too far out on a limb.

Those "worldly contenders" competing to be identified as the tree species from Oak Island, are shown on the following pages.

Albizia (*Falcataria moluccana*)
Moluccan Albizia

Common Name: **Albiza, Batai Wood, Peacock's Plume, Moluccan Albizia.**
Tree Type: **Broadleaf Perennial, deciduous.**
Max Height: **50m (150 feet).**
Longevity: **Often dies early from windthrow.**
Hardiness: **Max. north range – 30N Latitude Lowest Temp. 5 C. prefers tropical rain forests.**
Native Locale: **Papua New Guinea, Solomon Islands.**
Description: **Fast-growing tree (7m first year) cultivated for timber and animal fodder. Has large trunk. Bole is branchless to 20m, alone it opens up a large umbrella-like canopy.[2]**

Courtesy [1]

Source:
***Falcataria moluccana* / Albizia Moluccan. https://hawaii-forest.com/albizia-moluccana/.** [3]

Albiza tree and its relatives... F. *zygia*, F. *saman*, F. *gunnifer* and F. *procera*, are in many ways the best look-alikes for our mysterious canopied tree. This drawing does not do it justice. See the image on the next page for a more likely resemblance of our mystery tree.

The arrangement of their branches and foliage, the shape of the bole and primary limbs, and their height and crown shape, beg to be those from Oak Island. The tree became a very popular quick grower for timber production. It is a fast growing tree, reaching heights over 100 ft and aesthetically distinctive. [2] The Albizia seemed like an ideal species for reforestation planting early in the process of converting closed sugar plantations. Wanting to save the overburdened watershed where fields of sugar cane were no more, the Albizia was a perfect fix. Doubling as a light-timber tree, Albizia was planted throughout Hawaiian and other Pacific Islands. In addition, naturally spreading specimens have grown to 62" in diameter (DBH) and were firmly based in a large network of shallow roots. They've become a very invasive species! [3]

The downside to Albiza species is like anything which can grow 21 feet in its first year... has a short life and a weakness which makes it a dropout as a candidate. The *Falcataria moluccana* and hybrids do not fully develop their branches. They become brittle and weak and are prone to sudden limb shear. They have a shallow root system when by themselves and are susceptible to windthrow. Because of these two deformities, the Albiza tree which was once heralded as a great urban park standout, has now been known to be a killer. Falling branches and toppling trees have meant it is now aggressively being culled from urban and park settings throughout the Pacific Basin. Only if the trees are within a thick forested grove may they stay. [3] Like the dandelion – they will suddenly appear, release their bountiful seeds, and topple over dead.

Oak Island residency never happened. As a short-lived tree which is highly prone to windshear, windthrow and toppling, the Albizia would long ago have extirpated the area. [2] Finally, the Albiza Tree is in no way fond of the Nova Scotian climate. But wow, what a beautiful tree! Just don't stand under it.

Albizia Tree, *Falcataria moluccana*.
Courtesy: Mike Kane / Aurora Op/Aurora Photos [4]

Acacia

(*Vachellia tortilis)*
(A greggii)
(A abyssinica)
(A koa)
(A raddiana)

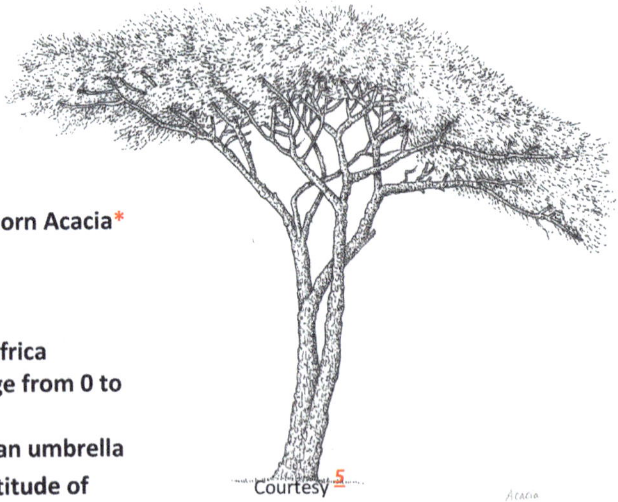

Common Name: **Umbrella Thorn Acacia***
Tree Type: **Deciduous**
Max Height: **24m (70 feet)**
Longevity: **Long-lived,**
Native Locale: **Middle East, Africa**
Hardiness: **Temperature range from 0 to 112 degrees.**
Description: **Tree resembles an umbrella With a very flat canopy, plentitude of Straight and hooked white thorns throughout the crown and upper branch structure. Very hard wood, good for charcoal, firewood. Grey-green leaves. The leaflets are very small. White flower clusters looking like puffballs, bloom in spring and summer. Hanging, coiled pod seeds. Gum from tree is edible, inner bark can be used to make rope. Tap root has been known to grow to depths of 170 ft., with lateral roots just under soil and expands out to twice the diameter of the crown. Requires full sun.**

Courtesy [5]

Source:
"The Living Wisdom of Trees: Introduction to Acacia," by Fred Hageneneder. Watkins Publishing.[5]

*There are many Acacia tree species which are often thought to be the Umbrella Thorn Acacia, have similar names, and grow with similarities – but have been reclassified into two different families. [6, 9] See Below:

- Flat-Top Acacia *(Vachellia abyssinica)*
- Australian Blackwood *(Acacia melanoxylon)*

Acacia is a very large genus of 1,300 species of shrubs and trees found throughout the subtropical and tropical regions, particularly of Africa and Australia (where they are known as wattles). [5] They are mainly shrubs, but several species reach tree size. The leaves are often bipinnate. The flowers are usually yellow and appear in small, rounded heads, mostly in winter or spring. The fruits are ovate to linear legumes.

The common acacia (A. *raddiana*) grows 16–26ft (5–8m) high, and its leaves divide bipinnately into small oblong to elliptical leaflets.[5]

A. *abyssinica* is native to Ethiopia and has 3–5in (7.5–12.5cm) long fruits.[5] The locust tree or false acacia (*Robinia pseudoacacia*) is not a species of this genus but, like the true acacias, a member of the pea family (*Fabaceae*).[5, 7] In the southwestern USA, the Cahuilla and the Pima tribes eat the pods or seeds of Catclaw Acacia (*A. greggii*) either raw, or ground and cooked in cakes.[6] In Hawaii, the wood of the Koa (*A. koa*) was used to make canoes.[6] The tribes of Israel made the Ark of the Covenant, the Tabernacle, the table, and altar from common acacia wood (*A. raddiana*).[5, 7] The *Acacia tortilis* is the iconic "Out of Africa" Acacia and the English common name of *Umbrella Thorn Acacia* refers to the trees overall shape, which often resembles an umbrella.[6] The Afrikaans name of "Haak en steek" meaning hook and stab, refers to the fact that there are often hooked thorns that can hook you, as well as long spines that can stab you.[8]

Since we started our review of the Acacia Tree the related genus Acacia has been completely overhauled, dismantled and re-identified.[9,10] Initially, genus Acacia comprised a group of plant species native to Africa, America and Australasia, but it has now been limited to contain only the Australasian species of that once large grouping.[8] This has led to the two Pan-Tropical lineages being renamed *Vachellia* and *Senegalia*, and the two endemic American lineages renamed *Acaciella* and *Mariosousa*. [8,9,10]

CLEAN UP ON ISLE ACACIA! Photo Courtesy of iStock.com.

Aleppo Pine (*Pinus halepenis*)

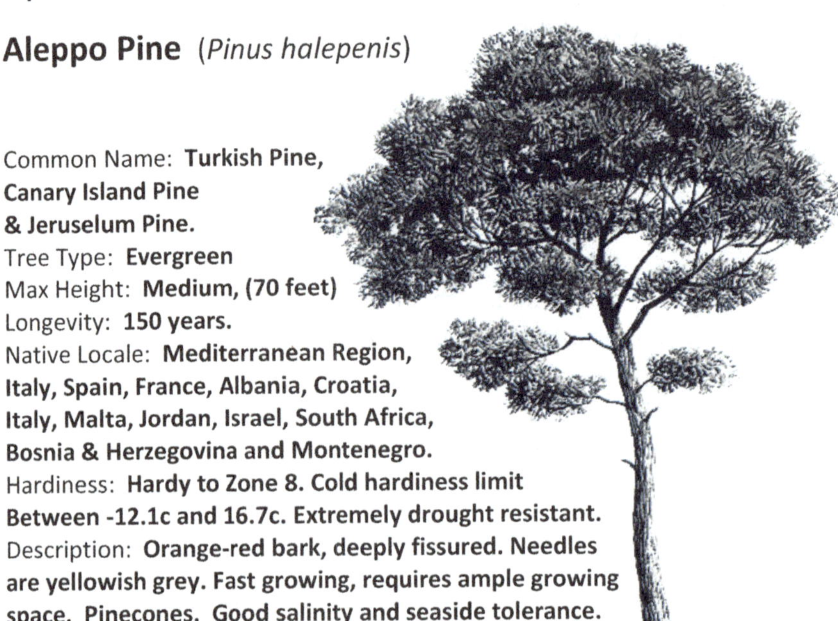

Common Name: **Turkish Pine, Canary Island Pine & Jeruselum Pine.**
Tree Type: **Evergreen**
Max Height: **Medium, (70 feet)**
Longevity: **150 years.**
Native Locale: **Mediterranean Region, Italy, Spain, France, Albania, Croatia, Italy, Malta, Jordan, Israel, South Africa, Bosnia & Herzegovina and Montenegro.**
Hardiness: **Hardy to Zone 8. Cold hardiness limit Between -12.1c and 16.7c. Extremely drought resistant.**
Description: **Orange-red bark, deeply fissured. Needles are yellowish grey. Fast growing, requires ample growing space. Pinecones. Good salinity and seaside tolerance. A true 'survivor' tree. Morphological characteristics stay constant over entire range and lifetime. Fine timber, hardiness and density. A Conical open-crowned shape tree.**[12]

Courtesy[11]

Aleppo Pine tree and its relatives... *P. sylvestris, P. maritima*, and *P. abasica.*

The Aleppo has a Single round trunk which is often divided to form in mature trees, a flat-topped or rounded crown with slender, irregular, and upturned branches. Its' crown form shaped by wind, especially near the sea. Needles rather sparsely arrayed along the branchlets. Pinecone scales shiny, yellow, or red brown, with no prickle. Used for resin and honey production and for livestock grazing.[12]

Image courtesy of Westend61/HKP [13]

Butternut Tree

(Juglans cinerea)

Common Name: **Butternut, White Walnut.**
Tree Type: **Deciduous**
Max Height: **82 feet max.**
Longevity: **Short-lived, rarely +75 yrs.**
Native Locale: **Native to Canada.**
Hardiness: **One of hardiest nut trees. Produces a chemical called juglone, which kills or stunts the growth of neighboring plants as it competes for sunlight and sources. Slow growing. Zone 3.**
Description: **Leaves arranged in an opposite, feather-like pattern, yellow or green in color. Bark has irregular, flat-topped ridges. Fruit is large, oval nut surrounded by green, hairy husk which is sticky. Similar in appearance to a Black Walnut. Sap can be made into syrup. Produces buttery-flavored nuts. The Butternut is intolerant to competition and will not survive if planted in shade. Must be overstory to survive. Subject to storm damage. Highly rot resistant.**[14]

Courtesy [14]

Courtesy; Treetopics.com/juglans_cinerea/gallery.[15]

Male and female flowers are borne separately on the same branch. As seen here, Male flowers grow in clusters which are called catkins, 2 to 5½" in length and pendulous. Flowers single in the leaf axils of 1 year old branchlets, flowers yellowish green with up to 15 stamens per flower.[15]

Stone Pine

(*Pinus pinea*)

Common Name: **Italian Stone Pine, Nut Pine, Umbrella Pine, Roman Pine, Parasol Pine, or Mediterranean Stone Pine.**
Tree Type: **Needled evergreen**
Max Height: **12-25m, (105ft max)**
Longevity: **60 years, (184 max)**
Native Locale: **Mediterranean region, Israel, Lebanon, Spain, Portugal, Cypress, Syria, Morocco, Algeria, Turkey, Sicily, Sardinia, Greece, Canary Islands, South Africa, North Africa, New South Wales. Prehistoric range: Sahara and Maghreb region. Known throughout Western Europe up To southern Scotland / New York.**

Courtesy[16]

Hardiness: **H4 through most of the UK. Zone 8 throughout US. Cold hardiness 10-20F. Prefers cool, Mediterranean temperate climate. No problem with cool or cold coastal temps.**
Description: **Broad flat crown over 26ft wide but Shallow in height. Trunk is sinuous and can be found short or long. Seldom straight. Bark Is thick, red, brown, or orangish, with gray patches and thick scaly irregular fissuring. Lower branches are died off. Long needles, mid-green in color. Non-flowering. Stem is not aromatic.**
Growth: **Young trees develop into bushy globes. Trees less than 5-10 years bear juvenile leaves very different than older trees. Cones take 3-4 years to mature. Most successfully propagate by seed. Many present-day stands are the result of historic planting some going back to Roman times. Congregatory. As adult, requires +6 hours full sun, grows in loam, silt, acidic, sandy, and chalky and acidic soils, or any area as long as it has good drainage and is moist. Resistant to drought. Quick growing to canopy dominance. Rarely attacked by pests and disease. Tree is heliophilous, xerophilous, and thermophilous.**
Uses: **Bark is used for tannins, resin used for multiple purposes. Cultivated worldwide for its seeds or pine nuts (pignolia) from within pinecones as a food and for making oil. Pinecone is edible. Planted in Cape of Good Hope, Africa, in 1700, by fleeing French Huguenot refugees from France. Used in shipbuilding for centuries, for curved framing.**[17]

"TheSpruce.com/Italian-stone-pine—growing-tips-3269335," by Vanessa Richins Myers. Updated 4-27-21. "Gymnosperm Database", by Christopher J. Earle. Updated 1-17-20.[17]

"Stone Pines often assume a shrubby, multi-stemmed shape when young, but as they grow upward, the multiple trunks usually merge into a single trunk, which then diverges into spreading branches high above the ground. Lower branches will naturally fall away as the tree grows upward and begins to assume its umbrella shape. Does not like climates with vast differences between winter and summer temperatures. Trees can be damaged by ice. Stone Pine needs no fertilization or pruning."[18]

Whatever you want to call them, the Stone Pine is a very distinct pine in which it is the only species. *Pinus pinaster* (Maritime Pine or Cluster Pine) has similar foliage but produce different pinecones.[19] The crown with a highly distinctive shape has a very flat, umbrella or parasol shape. Branches rise at 30 – 60 degrees above horizontal, branch tips upswept to vertical.[19] Their small cones resemble a children's comic idea of a hand-grenade, with delicious seeds (pine nuts) inside.

Over last 6000 years, considerable extension of the pine's native area was by man. It is assumed this pine originated in the Iberian Peninsula, as it is the only area away from ancient trade routes. Stone pine is abundant in S. Portugal and the adjoining Marismas area of the Guadalquivir River basin in S.W. Spain, where it forms extensive forests.[19]

"Stellar Pines over Estate." Photo courtesy of iStock.com[20]

The species in an archaeo-phyte *(unrecorded introductions by early man)* throughout the Mediterranean, and more recently has been naturalized in South Africa, California, Croatia, Italy, and Spain.[19] This pine prefers little temperature variation and is sensitive to environmental disturbance and difficult to regenerate. The first pine used and cultivated by man, its edible seeds have been harvested for perhaps half a million years or more.

Colin Wallace, in an unpublished manuscript, shows that written records document the economic and spiritual importance of this species in the Classical world:

> *"A Graeco-Roman papyrus of the second century AD records sixteen pine cones (stobeilon) among the multiples of items like cakes and palm-branches, supplied to a district governor for sacrifice to the river-god Nilos."*
>
> (Bowman 1986, 183/Sel Pap II no 403: source P Oxrhyncus 1211).

Maritime Pine *(Pinus pinaster)*

Common Name: **Cluster Pine, Turpentine Pine**
Tree Type: **Evergreen**
Max Height: **65-100ft, max. (115ft)**
Longevity: **30 years**
Native Locale:
Southern Europe, Spain, Portugal, Italy, Monaco, Gibraltar, Morocco, Algeria, France, North Africa, and Tunisia.
Hardiness: **H4, Hardy through most of the UK (-10c - -5c). USDA Zone 7**
Description: **Large conifer preferring marine coastal environs. Sensitive to frost. Wood is course grained and very resinous. Used for mining pit cribbing, fences, construction, and telephone poles. Planking for boat building. Distinct resinous odor when being worked. Low in decay density. Resin can be turned into turpentine and rosin.**[22]

Courtesy [21]

Maritime pine was originally highly prized as a source of timber and resins, but its attractive upswept branches and conical crown make it equally valuable as a landscape specimen. This species is well-suited to dry, sandy soil. It is also known as *cluster pine* or *French turpentine pine*. This species has two, or sometimes three, needles per bundle.[22]

Courtesy of iStock.com [23]

White Birch

(*Betula papyrifera*)

Common Name: **White Birch, Paper Birch, Canoe Birch.**
Tree Type: **Deciduous**
Max Height: **25 meters**
Longevity: **30-100 years**
Native Locale: **Canada, N. U.S.**
Hardiness: **Deciduous**
Bark: **White, thin, smooth bark Which peels off in large sheets.**
Foliage: **Pear-shaped leaves, turn Bright-yellow autumn colors.**
Description: **Prolifically produces catkins, Shade intolerant, with shallow root system, Lateral roots no deeper than 28 inches with No taproot. High winds likely to break trunk, with throwdowns common. Syrup derived from sap. Bark made for canoes. Vase-shaped crowns.** [25]

Courtesy [24]

Courtesy Skully/Alamy Stock Photo.[26]

White Birch Stand above highway at Corney Brook Park, NS, 1960's. Nova Scotia National Archives.[27]

Cork Oak *(Quercus suber)*

Common Name: **Cork Oak, Portuguese Cork**
Tree Type: **Evergreen**
Max Height: **15-20m, max. (25m)**
Longevity: **Oldest was 236 years old, at 46ft.**
Native Locale: **Southwest Europe, Northern Africa, Sardinia, Tunisia, Algeria, Morocco, France, Italy.**
Hardiness: **Best at 55-63f, can withstand temps down to 14f for short periods. Cannot tolerate freezing.**
Description: **Dense, asymmetrical crown, without branches until around 10ft up. Crown can be divided into several separate rounded partial crowns. Leathery leaves with 5-7 sharp teeth on both edges, upper side of leaf light green, underside is whitish and densely hairy. Thick longitudinal cracked cork layers of grayish brown on the trunk. Bark is characteristic of the Cork Oak. Cold winters can lead to complete defoliation. Acorns are ¾ to 1 ¾ inch in length and are shiny brownish red. Needs little light but cannot survive in dense populations. Very susceptible to gypsy moth which will eat entire crown bare.** [29]

Courtesy [28]

Courtesy of Roger Mechan, Feb. 2021. iStock.com [30]

The photograph above is in a Portugal orchard of Cork Oak trees stripped of bark from their lower half. Estimated height is less than thirty feet.

Wood Never Have Thought It

I believe – I KNOW - which tree is our 'Mystery Canopied-Tree' species which once graced Oak Island and gave the island its' name. Yes the look is dead-on identical but if it had not been growing in an almost identical environment, this match could never have been made. This tree was not native to the NEAF nor anywhere in the Western Hemisphere back then and wasn't brought to the continent until perhaps in 1804, but not officially until 1870.[31]

Reviewing the taxonomical characteristics of this species would not at all have brought it to our attention nor been given a second thought, as Its reputation as an enormous, robust broadleaf tree in both forest and stand-alone settings, simply would not qualify it. There is no reference in CABI (Commonwealth Agricultural Bureaux International), Kew Royal Botanic Gardens, nor other international plant indexes and references having any mention of tropisms or morphological effects on *this species* from exposure to constant ocean spray mist. Nor are there any botanical sources providing images of similar impacts. Therefore, it lay hidden in the indexes.

At this juncture in time and awaiting DNA and/or dendrological review for exact variation of the species and for the sake of historical record, our winning "World Contender" has been found. The trees you are about to be introduced to are alive as of June 2022; they are deciduous and have been botanist-certified as being *Acer pseudoplatanus L.*, commonly known as **the European Sycamore Tree** - *our Oak Island Mystery Canopied-tree match!*

So What does *Acer pseudoplatanus* (European Sycamore) look like you ask? The answer to that question is the entire reason we are including *A. pseudoplatanus* in our forensic investigation, as it bears little resemblance to those mystery canopied-trees on Oak Island, - *or does it not?*

European Sycamore

(*Acer pseudoplatanus L.*)

Common Name: **Sycamore Maple, Celtic Maple, Scottish Maple, Great Maple, Lock-and-Key-Tree, Plane Tree, False Plane Tree, English Harewood, Mock-Plane-Tree, Scottish Plane & Gray Harewood.**

Tree Type: **Deciduous**

Max Height: **35 m (115 ft)**

Longevity: **300-550 years +**

Native Locale: **Albania, Spain, Austria, Belgium, Bulgaria, Greece, Czech Republic, Georgia, Germany, Hungary, Italy, Lithuania, Poland, Romania, Switzerland, Southern Russia, Switzerland and former Yugoslavia.**

Courtesy[31]

Branches: **Form large, broad, rounded crown.**

Hardiness: **USDA Zone 3-4, RHS rated H7. Can grow and pollinate as far north as Torshavn, Faroe Islands; Reykjavik, Iceland; and Tromso, Norway.**

Bark: **Light gray, smooth bark when young and later flaking in irregular patches. When flaked off, exposes an interior bark which is smooth and appears pinkish to red in coloration. Provides considerable ecological tolerances to biodiversity, especially taxa such as lichens on its stem, more than many native tree species. This is why its barks sometimes seem mottled or spotty, most often by lichen growth.**

Buds: **Produced in opposite pairs, approximately oval in shape and pointed with the bud scales green, edged in dark brown with dark brown tips.**

Foliage: **Leaves are opposite, large 10 to 25 cm long and broad with five-pointed lobes that are toothed or serrated. They have a leathery texture with thick veins protruding on the underside. Dark green with a paler underside. Winged seeds (samaras) are released in spring. Autumn colors are described as dull, mild yellow, purplish to brown, insignificant. When leaves are shed they leave horseshoe-shaped marks called leaf scars on the stem.**

Description: **A tetraploid (each cell having four sets of chromosomes) unlike *Acer campestre* (Field Maple) and *Acer platanoides* (Norway**

Maple) which are diploid. Also, unlike the two mentioned, *A. pseudoplatanus* have 'V' shaped winged seeds, with the angle of the wings narrower. They grow flowers on hanging clusters called panicles and produce copious amounts of pollen and nectar attracting insects. Sycamores are very 'variable' across their wide range and have strategies to prevent self-pollination. Tolerant of a wide range of soil types and pH levels, except heavy clay. Highly wind tolerant, urban pollution tolerant, salt spray tolerant, and tolerant of low summer temperatures. Roots form highly specific beneficial associations with fungus promoting phosphorus uptake from the soil. Squirrels will strip the bark off branches, girdling the stem; as a result whole branches may die, leaving brown, wilted leaves and drop off. Coppiced stools grow rapidly to 4'3" within one year.

Above illustration and Taxonomic Characteristic Sources:[31, 32, 33, 34, 35]

Variations:

Several natural varieties such as macrocarpum Spach, microcarpum Spach, Tausch tomentosum, and forms such as erythrocarpum (Carriere) Pax, f. purpureum (Loudon) Rehder, and f. Sycamore may hybridize with *Acer heldreichii*, *Acer velutinum*, *Acer griseum*, and *Acer trifoliata*. Other recent varieties include *Acer pseudoplatanus Brilliantissimum* and *Acer pseudoplatanus pendulum* (1850).[32]

Continental authors note that Sycamore is favored by cold, moist conditions (Jones, 1945). Sycamore has evolved certain adaptations to exposed conditions and can produce a vigorous, luxuriant canopy even in areas of high wind and salt spray. However on particularly exposed sites there is considerable bud and shoot death, although new shoots are readily produced from dormant buds (Bingelli and Blackstock, 1997). This is a successful survival strategy but precludes such sites for the growing of sycamore as a timber tree (Bingelli and Blackstock, 1997).[35]

August 31st 2021, Arborist Don Pylant, was helping hunt for the species of those long-ago mystery canopied trees from Oak Island. He found and sent the initial tele-photo image from a photo catalog to fellow arborist(s) David Vaughan and Michael Nentwich, also involved in this forensic hunt. Seeing the same sinuous thin trunk with light-colored bark and the canopy opening up within the very top of the crown in an umbrella-spoke like fashion, with no lower branching seen, I knew these were looking like the same trees. Even the snags appeared similar in their wonky moribund state of death, here in the photo, as like on those from Oak Island.

Below is the image they forwarded to me, and here we are. Look carefully and what do we see?

Courtesy: Picxy.com/Rhysl

Do these trees resemble those canopied trees photographed between 1880-1945 on Oak Island? Look Closer....

Perhaps a closer view gives more to see what resembles that stand of Mystery Trees from Oak Island.

Courtesy: Picxy.com/Rhysl

And now - can you see the same sinuous thin trunk with light-colored bark, or no bark visible. Note the canopy opening up within the very top of the crown, in an umbrella spoke-like fashion, with no lower branching seen. Even the snags appear similar in their wonky moribund state of death, here as on Oak Island.

Courtesy: Picxy.com/Rhysl

On the following page is another current image (Dec. 2021) of this same stand of trees, taken by Botanist Dr. Stephen Bungard at the site itself. Clear proof these trees are deciduous and are neither coniferous nor evergreens.

Photograph by Botanist, Dr. Stephen Bungard, December 2021

Below photo, Courtesy Bowdin Expedition, Nova Scotia National Archives.

<u>Looks Can Be Deceiving</u>

Much of the reportage on European Sycamore was found within an excellent article by Dan Crowley (2020) titled, "*Acer pseudoplatanus*" from the website, <u>*Trees and Shrubs Online*,</u> Accessed 2022-01-29. (treesandshrubsonline.org/articles/acer-pseudoplatanus/). Some of the following images are also from that article.

Gstaad, Switzerland. Image MC de Laubarede

Yorkshire Wolds, UK. Image John Grimshaw

Yorkshire Arboretum, UK. Image John Grimshaw

Yorkshire Arboretum, UK. Image John Grimshaw

Isle of Raasay, Scotland Image Picxy.com/RhysL

Isle of Raasay, Scotland Image Ann Peters

Obviously the two photos above from the Isle of Raasay, do not at all look like the "*broad and massive European Sycamore used for windbreaks and shelter or would be a huge significance and importance in Britain's landscape*" as discussed and described. *Do they?*

Yet they match up with trees described in Footnote <u>***35***</u> on Page 17 and are further illustrated on the following page.

The image directly below was taken approximately 250 km from the Isle of Raasay and is a farming field on the outskirts of the hamlet of Portencross, Scotland, near North Ayrshire. This field is located on a windswept coastal peninsula where the Sycamore (*Acer pseudoplatanus*) were planted in a line acting as a windbreak for the farmers crops. The weather and salt spray tropism clearly show Sycamore, in such an environment, survives by growing distinctly different than other trees.

Photos courtesy of: Alamy

Or is there more to the story, as these Sycamore trees grew side-by-side as part of another row of trees offering windbreak, for a field not much farther inland from the same shore as those above.

Is it evident the trees which once grew on Oak Island, grow on the Isle of Raasay, and elsewhere in the British Isles, may be of a unique subspecies or variant? *Or is this all about blowing in the wind?*

Parts of the Acer pseudoplatanus Tree

Below is a comparison of images of leaf, buds, seed, and bark of the European Sycamore. This includes photographs taken by Botanist Dr. Stephen Bungard of a stand of *Acer pseudoplatanus* in Scotland.

Left column Images courtesy
Dr. Stephen Bungard

Collection of image sources include:
trees.standford.edu; Driverfordevice.blogspot.com; and iStock.com

In the greater United Kingdom, the Sycamore Tree has held its share of interesting positions throughout Great Britain history, further complicating when in fact they were brought from the mainland. Their fascinating biographical, botanical, and biblical history is presented in Chapter 6, *"Mirror Images."*

Below is a list of the variations/hybrids of *Acer pseudoplatanus*; yet none of their descriptors explain the morphology and traits we see in our mystery canopied trees. We await Dr. Bungard sending the specimens for absolute definitive identification of the Raasay Island canopy trees, which may help to determine the argument of heredity or morphology. If hereditary, then we can more exclusively identify from where the mystery canopied trees on Oak Island came from and their relationship with those on Raasay Island. If not, we are left with the morphological impacts of the shared environments of both stands of trees. Finding a third or fourth stand of species of trees or tree, and comparing their biome with the first two stands, will provide the proof in this specific discussion. Either way, European Sycamore (*Acer pseudoplatanus*) was not native to Oak Island or the Western Hemisphere in 1795. Nor was it native to the Greater British Isles, though the timing of its introduction is still very much being argued.

Someone brought them to Oak Island specifically and uniquely. Like the constructs within the island and the coconut coir fiber, and perhaps the red clover; these botanical oddities will provide the evidence to help identify the *WHEN*, and most assuredly, the *WHO* Of the Oak Island conundrum.

Additional Variations/Hybrids

Acer pseudoplatanus f. albertsii Schwer.
Acer pseudoplatanus f. albomarmoratum Pax
Acer pseudoplatanus f. albovariegatum (Hayne ex Loudon) Schwer.
Acer pseudoplatanus f. annae Schwer.
Acer pseudoplatanus f. atropurpureum Schwer.
Acer pseudoplatanus f. aucubifolium Schwer.
Acer pseudoplatanus f. aureovariegatum Schwer.
Acer pseudoplatanus f. bicolor Schwer.
Acer pseudoplatanus f. brevialatum Schwer.
Acer pseudoplatanus f. complicatum (H.Mort.) Schwer.
Acer pseudoplatanus f. concavum Schwer.
Acer pseudoplatanus f. costorphinense Schwer.
Acer pseudoplatanus f. cruciatum Schwer.
Acer pseudoplatanus f. cupreum Schwer.
Acer pseudoplatanus f. discolor Schwer.
Acer pseudoplatanus f. dittrichii (Ortm.) Schwer.
Acer pseudoplatanus f. erythrocarpum (Carrière) Schwer.
Acer pseudoplatanus f. euchlorum Späth ex Schwer.
Acer pseudoplatanus f. flavescens Schwer.
Acer pseudoplatanus f. grandicorne Borbás
Acer pseudoplatanus f. handjeryi (Späth ex Rehder) Geerinck
Acer pseudoplatanus f. handjeryi Schwer.
Acer pseudoplatanus f. insigne Schwer.
Acer pseudoplatanus f. laetum Schwer.
Acer pseudoplatanus f. latialatum (Pax) Pax
Acer pseudoplatanus f. leopoldii Schwer.
Acer pseudoplatanus f. luteovirescens Schwer.
Acer pseudoplatanus f. lutescens Pax
Acer pseudoplatanus f. metallicum Schwer.
Acer pseudoplatanus f. neglectum Schwer.
Acer pseudoplatanus f. nervosum Schwer.
Acer pseudoplatanus f. nizetii Schwer.
Acer pseudoplatanus f. opizii (Ortmann ex Opiz.) Schwer.
Acer pseudoplatanus f. palmatifidum Schwer.
Acer pseudoplatanus f. pseudonizetii Schwer.
Acer pseudoplatanus f. purpurascens Pax
Acer pseudoplatanus f. purpureum (Loudon) Rehder
Acer pseudoplatanus f. quadricolor Schwer.
Acer pseudoplatanus f. rubromaculatum Pax
Acer pseudoplatanus f. sanguineum Schwer.
Acer pseudoplatanus f. serotinum Schwer.
Acer pseudoplatanus f. serratum Schwer.
Acer pseudoplatanus f. siculum (Guss.) Borbás
Acer pseudoplatanus f. spaethii Schwer.
Acer pseudoplatanus f. subparallelum Borbás
Acer pseudoplatanus f. tricolor Schwer.
Acer pseudoplatanus f. trilobatum Schwer.
Acer pseudoplatanus f. variegatum (Weston) Rehder
Acer pseudoplatanus f. vitifolium (Tausch) Schwer.
Acer pseudoplatanus f. worleei Rosenthal ex Schwer.
Acer pseudoplatanus subsp. villosum (J.Presl & C.Presl) Parl.
Acer pseudoplatanus var. acuminatum Tausch
Acer pseudoplatanus var. albovariegatum Hayne ex Loudon
Acer pseudoplatanus var. anomalum Schwer.
Acer pseudoplatanus var. coloratum Pax
Acer pseudoplatanus var. complicatum H.Mort.
Acer pseudoplatanus var. crispum Schwer.
Acer pseudoplatanus var. erythrocarpum Carrière
Acer pseudoplatanus var. fieberi Pax
Acer pseudoplatanus var. flava-variegatum Loudon
Acer pseudoplatanus var. handjeryi Späth ex Rehder
Acer pseudoplatanus var. laciniatum Loudon
Acer pseudoplatanus var. latialatum Pax
Acer pseudoplatanus var. longifolium Loudon
Acer pseudoplatanus var. macrocarpum Spach
Acer pseudoplatanus var. medium Spach
Acer pseudoplatanus var. microcarpum Spach
Acer pseudoplatanus var. nebrodense Tineo ex Pax
Acer pseudoplatanus var. purpureum Loudon
Acer pseudoplatanus var. quinquelobum Schwer.
Acer pseudoplatanus var. siculum Guss.
Acer pseudoplatanus var. subintegrilobum Pax
Acer pseudoplatanus var. subobtusum DC.
Acer pseudoplatanus var. subtrilobum Schwer.
Acer pseudoplatanus var. subtruncatum Pax
Acer pseudoplatanus var. ternatum Schwer.
Acer pseudoplatanus var. tomentosum Tausch
Acer pseudoplatanus var. triangulare Schwer.
Acer pseudoplatanus var. vitifolium Tausch

Footnoted References

[1]. "*Silhouette of Albizia*." Published in the Hawaii Forest & Trail, Apr. 24, 2012. Hawaii Forest Blog, Flora & Fauna. https://hawaii-forest.com/albizia-moluccana/. (Accessed 04-12-22).

[2]. "*Understanding Albizia: Albizia "The Bad Boy of Trees*." Created by Wu Yewei, Dec. 2019. Wiki, Falcataria moluccana – Albizia. https://wiki.nus.edu.sg/display/TAX/Falcataria+moluccana+-+Albizia.

[3]. "*The Target: Albizia (Falcataria moluccana)*." Hawaii Invasive Species Council, Cabinet-level direction on invasive species issues. https://dlnr.hawaii.gov/hisc/info/biocontrol/latest-biocontrol/falcataria-moluccana/.

[4]. "*Albizia Tree on the Ranch*." Color photograph, courtesy Mike Kane/Aurora Ops/Aurora Photos. Moluccan Albizia trees line a plantation Road, Kauai, Hawaii. Jun. 19, 2010.

[5]. "*Silhouette of Acacia*." Published *in Living Wisdom of Trees: A Guide to the Natural History, Symbolism and Healing Power of Trees*." Section: "Acacia," by Lea Russell, Feb. 13, 2020. Compiled By Fred Hageneder. Watkins Publishing.

[6]. "*23 Species of Acacia Trees and Shrubs*." By Vanessa Richins Myers, Updated Apr. 5, 2022. Reviewed by Barbara Gillette. Published in The Spruce," online. https://www.thespruce.com/twenty-species-acacia-trees-and-shrubs-3269672.

[7]. "*Haak en Steek – Acacia*." https://proudplants.co.za/index.php/shop-online/haak-en-steek-vachellia-acacia-tortilis-detail?tmpl=component&format=pdf.

[8]. "*Ark of the Covenant*." By contributing writer Jenna Brooke Carlson, Aug. 24, 2021. Exodus 25:10. https://www.biblestudytools.com/bible-stories/ark-of-the-covenant.html.

[9]. "*Everything You Need to know about the Acacia Tree*." By Casey Hoffard, Dec. 10, 2018. https://www.plantsnap.com/blog/everything-acacia-trees/.

[10]. "*The Controversy over the Retypification of Acacia Mill. With an Australian Type: A pragmatic View*." By Kevin R. Thiele, et. al. Published in TAXON, 60(1), Feb. 2011. Pages 194-198.

[11]. "*Silhouette of Aleppo Pine*." By Jim Harter, Jan. 2013. *Plants: 2,400 Royalty-free Illustrations of Flowers, Trees, Fruits and Vegetables*, Dover Publications.

[12]. " *Pinus halepensis / Aleppo Pine*." Attribution from William Dallimore, Albert Bruce Jackson and S.G. Harrison's publication A Handbook of Coniferae and Ginkgoaceae, 4th Edition, 1967. Martin's Press, New York. The American

Conifer Society, online. https.//conifersociety.org/HAF000028/France-nice-view-of-aleppo-pine-tree.

13. "*France, Nice View of Aleppo Pine Tree, Image title*." Courtesy of Westend61/HKP, online Photo repository. (Accessed 04-15-22). https://www.westend61.de/en/imageView/HAF000028/france-nice-view-of-aleppo-pine-tree.

14. "*Silhouette of Butternut: A Landowner's Resource Guide*." Provided online by Museum of Dufferin Simcoe. Land Stewardship Network. (Accessed 04-15-2022). https://www.dufferinmuseum.com/forest/img/butternutlandownersguide.pdf.

15. "*Butternut Catkins Abloom*." http://www.treetopics.com/juglans_cinerea/gallery1.htm.

16. "*Silhouette of Stone Pine*." By Jim Harter, Jan. 2013. *Plants: 2,400 Royalty Trees From Illustrations of Flowers, Trees, Fruits and Vegetables*, Dover Publications. B/W drawing. Courtesy Gymnosperm Database," by Christopher J. Earle. Updated Jan. 17, 2020.

17. "*Italian Stone Pine – Growing Tips (3269335)*." By Vanessa Richins Myers. Updated Apr. 27, 2021. *Gymnosperm Database*, by Christopher J. Earle.

18. "*Pinus pinea in Europe: distribution, habitat, usage and threats*." By R. Abad Viñas, G. Caudullo, S. Oliveira, and D. de Rigo 2016. Published in European Atlas of Forest Tree Species. EU.

19. "*Mediterranean Pines and their History*." By Wilhelm Klaus, May 1987. Revised and edited by F. Ehrendorver. Published in Plant Systematics and Evolution, #162. Pages 133-163.

20. "*Stellar Pines Above Estate*." Stone Pines, a.k.a. Rome Pines, Italian Pines, etc., colored photograph. Courtesy of iStock.com.

21. "*Silhouette of Maritime Pine*." By Jim Harter, Jan. 2013. *Plants: 2,400 Royalty Trees From Illustrations of Flowers, Trees, Fruits and Vegetables*, Dover Publications.

22. "*Functional Genomics of Mediterranean Pines*." C. Avila, et. al., 2022. Published in De La Torre, A.R. (eds) The Pine Genomes – Compendium of Plant Genomes. Springer. https://doi.org/10.1007/978-3-030-93390-6_9. (Accessed 04-15-2022).

23. "*Cloudy Maritime Pine stand*," B/W photograph. Courtesy iStock.com.

[24]. "*Silhouette of White Birch, Betula papyrifera*." B/W drawing. Courtesy Natural Resources Canada. https://tidcf.nrcan.gc.ca/en/trees/factsheet/16.

[25]. "*White Birch, Betula papyrifera*." https://treecanada.ca/resources/trees-of-canada/white-birch-betula-papyrifera/.

[26]. "*Autumn Yellow Foliage of White Birch*." Color photograph. Courtesy of Skully/Alamy Stock Photo.

[27]. "*White Birch Stand above highway at Corney Brook Park, 1960's*." B/W photo. Courtesy Nova Scotia National Archives.

[28]. "*Silhouette of Cork Oak*." From Collection of Cork Oak Tree Vintage Illustrations by Ingk. Alamy Stock Images.

[29]. "*Quercus suber / Cork Oak*." https://en.wikipedia.org/wiki/Quercus_suber.

[30]. "*Portuguese orchard of Cork Oak Trees with bark removed*." Courtesy of Roger Mechan, Feb. 2021. iStock.com.

[31]. "*Silhouette of European Sycamore*." B/W drawing. Courtesy WikiMili, "*Acer pseudoplatanus*." Wikipedia, The Free Encyclopedia. Updated 11-10-21. www.wikimili.com/en/Acer_pseudoplatanus/Acer_pseudoplatanus_textura_del_tronco.jpg).

[32]. "*Acer pseudoplatanus L. from the website 'Trees and Shrubs Online*." By Dan Crowley (2020). Para. 6-8. (Accessed 01-29-22). https://www.treesandshrubsonline.org/articles/acer/acer-pseudoplatanus/.

[33]. "*A Review of Growth and Stand Dynamics of Acer pseudoplatanus L. in Europe: Implications for Silviculture.*" By Sebastian Hein, et. al., 2009. *Forestry*, Vol. 82, No. 4, 2009. DOI:10.1093/forestry/cpn043. Institute of Chartered Foresters, 2008 (Accessed 01-29-22).

[34]. "*Acer pseudoplatanus*," Wikipedia, The Free Encyclopedia. Updated 11-10-21. (Accessed 02-04-2022). wikimili.com/en/Acer_pseudoplatanus/Acer_pseudoplatanus_textura_del_tronco.jpg.

[35]. "*The Ecology and Biodiversity value of Sycamore (Acer pseudoplatanus) with Particular Reference to Great Britain*." By Andrew Dunbar Leslie, 2005. Published in *Scottish Forestry*, Vol 59. No 3. Pages 19-26.

Appendix H

DIRTY WORLD OF DETRITUS

After researching the information presented in Appendix A, "*Dissecting Dumbo Drumlin,*" I realized I did not have a future in geology like I dreamt while digging trenches and holes in my moms' garden as a kid. Not only was my math weak but the vocabulary would have "buried" me! So whether we are talking aggregate, boulders, breccia, clastics, clayey, cobbles, detritus, duff, erratics, evaporites, fill, gravel, pebbles, sand, sediments, silt, soil, tephra, or stony till, I have gotten down and dirty digging up some interesting factoids. So put on your hard hat, grab a trowel and gloves, and help me put this Oak Island operation in perspective.

First of all without a map from Zena Halpern, how did our ancient voyagers navigate through Mahone Bays' 365 drumlins? How long must it have taken them to find just the right island having three large oaks, one with a large branch reaching directly out over a hidden sinkhole? Was this island selected because they saw an island covered in Northern Red Oak? Maybe it was the brilliant red foliage of the Red Oak which initially caught their eye – *I say in jest!* But once they chose the island they hacked down all those oaks for construction material and being the conservationists they were, planted the unique mystery canopied trees later to be seen by other travelers. Did they bring a dozen sapling of those nonnative species along with them from where they came? Did they bring more of them and were they stored in and amongst the coconut fiber dunnage within their vessels hold? Did they use the coconut fiber as a planting medium; securing success when it came time to plant those canopied trees on the island? With 1.54 metric tons of coconut fiber onboard, is it possible they brought much more but used it on another islands as well?

There can be little doubt whomever came to Oak Island, had much work to perform and was very skilled in doing it.

Soil Solutions Settle

In Chapter 8, *"Planting Evidence,"* we discuss the Money Pit and the precise scientific equations which tell us how much time had elapsed since the Money Pit was filled in, from when it was located in 1795. This determination is made using a composite of no less than six separate geological notations and three organic notations from scientific analysis of conditions reportedly found within the Money Pit. Here I will outline several of the geologic conditions which will bear a scientific means to determine how much time had elapsed since the Money Pit was filled in.

The refilled soil in the depression is considered to have been "disturbed soil" (see glossary). In fact, it is more specifically 'disturbed clayey soil,' which is the soil type originally from the pit, later refilled back into the pit up to the top. Yet the first two feet of soil found atop the flagstone, known as the "O Horizon," was simply collected duff and forest floor debris.[1] As any long-time and growing depression would expressly collect, windblown dirt, leaves, twigs, seeds, acorns, frozen dead vegetation, and other assorted forest 'flotsam and jetsam' from the immediate biome; would fill the void over time.[1]

Now if you have ever dug a hole in your yard or garden, you know there seems to be more dirt dug out, then was in the pit originally. This is especially true after you try your darndest to put it all back into the hole. That 'excess dirt' is caused because the original "undisturbed soil" was compacted and lacked any oxygen molecules attached to its smallest of soil particles. Once dug up the soil aerates (oxygen attaches to each of those smallest of particles), giving it a swollen look which if handled, is easy to separate in your hands. Whereas the digging up of the original compacted soil required you to break it up into smaller chunks and pieces, as they were hard clods at best. It also dries out the soil when dug up. What moisture or water was attached to all those smallest of pieces, now fluffed with the shovel, has the air replace the water molecules attached to those particles. This is why you have what appears to be "left over" dirt that won't fit in the hole. Everything expanded except your hole! Over time there are at least three geologic events which affect the hole and the disturbed soil you put back in it. They are *Settlement* – the vertical movement of the soil, *Compaction* - the process of forcing air from the spaces between soil particles, and *Consolidation* - the process of forcing water from the spaces between soil particles. [2] Each one tells its own story, and combined, they tell us much more.

Had the dirt you dug up been put in a barrel or a large jar and the lid put on, the principal of settlement would work its thing and over time, the once-full jar will appear as if someone has been taking pinches of dirt out. But they haven't, it is just the soil has settled within its enclosure. Those particles of soil, once disturbed, now slowly move vertically down, and fill the voids and air between other soil particles.[2] As described within the Money Pit, the soil settled two feet below each log platform. When the searchers reached a sealed platform, removed some of the logs, they saw the ground below had settled over time, by two feet. Scientifically, we can figure out what "over time" actually means. This formulation repeats itself at each log platform providing us with redundant verification of the geological processes doing their thing.

This also happened at the top of the pit which we are calling the depression. However, the top ten feet of refilled disturbed clayey soil also had *compaction* and *consolidation* doing extra effort to shrink the pile of dirt. *What tells us this...*

The flagstones placed over the top of the pit of refilled dirt was done perhaps as a marker of where the dig had occurred for future visitors. Or maybe it was topped off with flagstone to protect an animal or human from becoming trapped within loose soil of the pit. As long as the plasticity of the soils was such, it could act like a bowl of quicksand. Meanwhile, over time the weight of the flagstone would put downward pressure on this refill and Squoosh the air out of the soil and speed up compaction.

Just like when you patted the top of your yard hole, or jumped on it with your foot to "get it all in."

Finally, we come to "consolidation." Consider consolidation as a combo attack on our disturbed pile of soil. Consolidation uses weather forces to help it "un-disturb" those smallest of particles of dirt. This is accomplished by repeatedly adding rain and snow which would obviously wet the dry soil. Replacing the oxygen attached to those smallest of pieces with water molecules, we get mud. Mud is wet soil with no more oxygen and becomes heavier in and of itself. The compaction forces on the wetted soil (mud) with the added weight squeezes out the water as the mud dries, and efforts itself into becoming less and less disturbed. Additionally, vibrations caused by wind, tree and root movements, animals, etc., will cause some or perhaps just the peripheral soils, to "shake" into their new hole home. We don't need an earthquake to do this, but movement causes settling to happen faster. Consolidation uses many factors to move the process of settlement along. Unlike the dirt in the jar sitting on a shelf, unaffected; consolidation puts the processes in our depression in overdrive.

Our depression is said to be below ground level, and saucer-shaped, with the center lower than the outside. This implies the entire 13 ft diameter of refilled disturbed soil, settled, or more likely, compacted under the weight of the flagstone. And then the further settling in the center, was most likely accelerated by moisture. As water pooled from rain and melting snow, or even by dew and frost melt, it would move across the flagstone and pour between the flagstone cracks in the center. Overtime, this repeated effect lets the water, through erosion principles, focus its' flow to the center of our depression. Every moisture event removes more spaces between those particles, but more so in the center where the water had pooled. And then the drying of that moisture adds to the consolidation of the soils into an undisturbed status.

But wait! There is much more. Remember McGinnis, Smith, and Vaughan had to dig down two feet of dirt before hitting the flagstone. This meant the ground had settled by almost four vertical feet in the top 10 foot above the first tier of the pit! The shape of the depression was two feet down in the center, and it had two feet of gathered duff below that, before you came to the flagstone. Since the flagstone was presumably on top of the filled-in pit, it is now almost four feet deeper within. So the combinations of soil settlement, compaction and consolidation depressed the refilled soil into a six foot contained area of "less" compacted soil, with two feet of duff atop it.

As already explained, the two feet of dirt our diggers could breeze through, came from the ever-changing life within the "O Horizon." You may have been in a forest which had a thick forest floor of pine needles. The volume of needles produced by trees within those stands, can create a carpet as deep as many feet. So this O Horizon, in and of itself, can tell us much about the time evolution of the area. As the settlement and compaction lowered the level of the flagstone-covered pit, the physics of a depression "collecting" things starts to happen. Over a period of time those top two feet of organics mix with windblow sands and leaves, etc., and create more dirt. This dirt would put more weight upon our flagstone cap of the ever-sinking depression.

Interestingly, no one talks about the material of the top two feet. No brushing aside fall foliage or raking away tens of thousands of acorn mast pieces, nor fighting the ever-expanding oak tree root system, which would have been enjoying that soft soil. *Huh?*

Each of these natural processes can be recreated into formulations. The produced calculation is the amount of time it took for these processes to work – such as leaving the soils settled down two feet and the decay of the logs to the degree with which witnesses sited. If the results for example, claim the process took 420 years for the soils to settle to that degree, then from the date of the find – 1795, we count backwards to determine the date the Money Pit was filled in. Now we more or less know the *WHEN* of our enigma.

Cornucopia of Calculations

The next few pages provide an assortment of answers to frequent questions of how much, how long, how big, and how come. These are relatively straight forward calculations based on what we believed happened on Oak Island from the telling of the tale. These calculations are best guestimates of what if would have taken to undertake this treasure task.

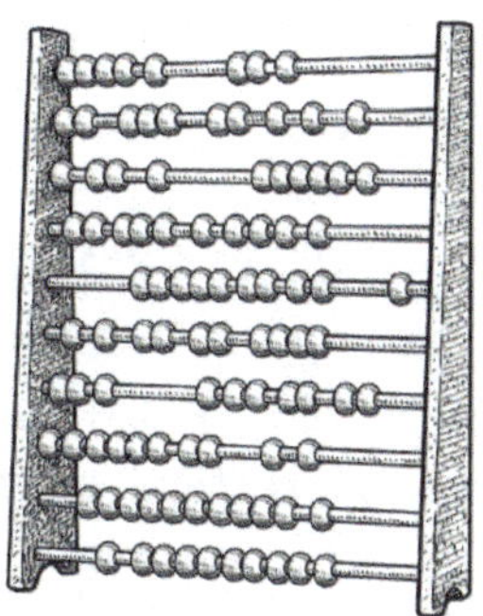

Courtesy: iStock.com

So our ancient voyagers arrived on scene and found a Mi`Kmaq welcoming party. Perhaps they inquired about vacant lots on nearby islands and the best places for finding oaks and flagstone. If instructed by the Mi`Kmaq they would find the best flagstone over in the Rocky River and the least inhabited island was Island #28, then our first ridiculous calculation is - how many canoe trips would our ancient voyagers need make to haul 1.69 metric tons (3724 lbs.) of flagstone?

In 1750 a Mi`kmaq bark canoe was delivered to Lord Anson and placed in the Boat House of the Chatham Dockyard where it was measured and examined.[3] It is presumed to be a war canoe, since it was a narrow, sharp-ended canoe, the bottom neither flat nor fully rounded, but a rounded V-shaped; this may indicate a canoe intended for coastal waters.[3] According to the traditions of the eastern Mi`kmaq and Malecite Indians, their war canoes were only large enough to carry three or four warriors and so must not have exceeded 18 feet in length.[4] Yet others describe Mi`kmaq canoes as 16' in length, while ocean-going canoes were from 20-28' long.[4] At 16' you can hold three adults.[3] The canoes were made of Birchbark, Cedar or Spruce framing and sewn together with rope made from Spruce roots (similar to coir fiber sewn boats) and caulked or sealed with Spruce gum.[4] With a two-mile row over to the island, I project they could have put approximately 200 lbs. of flagstone in each canoe if distributed correctly, and depending on the weighted canoes' draft. Not counting return trips, our prolific paddlers would need to make 19 trips to pilfer the prehistoric pavers. *Let's do some more math.*

FLAGSTONE PRESSURE Equation

The random flagstone at 2" thick, weighs 28 lbs. per square foot.[5] With 133 square feet making the 13' dia. Pit, this equates to 3,724 lbs. of vertical downward pressure or force placed on the soft disturbed soil fill. This is equivalent in weight to 4 gallons of water placed on every square foot across the area of the depression.

REFILL SOIL Equation

In addition to the flagstone, the vertical 10 ft of dry disturbed glacial clayey soil weighed 76 lb/ft^3.[6] The soil filling 10 ft height of the 13 ft diameter pit, would weigh approximately 45.9 metric tons per platform. This would equate to 760 lb/ft^2 downward pressure onto the oak platforms.

The Oak Island story discusses a wooden platform every ten feet, down to approximately 110 ft depth, or more. The description within the Money Pit clearly describes the 10 ft, 20 ft, 30 ft, 60 ft, 90 ft, 98 ft, and 103 ft platforms. The latter two being determined by borings through them. Otherwise, they use the term *marks, marker,* or tier for the 40 ft, 50 ft, 70 ft, 80 ft, and 110 ft platforms. Many people do not associate the descriptor of a "marker" as necessarily being an actual platform. Yet in mining of the day, a marker (marcher correct spelling) was a Scottish term to reference a platform or partial platform or landing.[7] It is hard to believe the "markers" *covered* in charcoal, or small inscribed stones, or puddled clay, or eelgrass and coconut fibers... were somehow just a 'mark covered' on the side of the pit walls or somehow suspended within the pile of the fill. Did someone lowered on a rope make a mark on the wall of the pit with these materials, or lay them on top of the soil at 10 ft of fill just so they could then dump another ten feet on top of that? Furthermore, without those platforms at those 10 ft 'marks,' what was supposed to hold up the dirt above? At 45.9 metric tons per ten-foot height of fill,[6] an oak log platform simply wedged into the side of the shaft could not hold more than the weight for two platforms, if at that. Other authors discuss further platforms or barriers going as far down as 171 ft. For now, 110 ft will do us.

ORIGINAL SOIL EXCAVATION Equation

The Money Pit was truly an impressive excavation. As the mining reports verified, the 13 ft diameter shaft maintained that shape down to a minimum of the 90 ft level. Assuming this continued to the 110 ft platform, the volume of dirt dug out of this shaft was more than 14,630 cubic feet, or 542 cubic yards! This 542 cubic yards of undisturbed (compact) glacial clayey soil would weigh 106 lb/ft^3, or approximately 703.4 metric tons[6] and comprised of up to 30-35% (32.5%) breccia of stones, boulders, and cobbles (see Appendix A, *"Dissecting Dumbo Drumlin"* page 6). Therefore, you are looking at needing as many as 54 tandem axle dump trucks[8] to move this load and there would be plenty of material for lengthy road construction.

"In my opinion, this is what the fabled '*serpent mound*' consisted of – rock refuse from the excavation."

David H. Neisen

Shape of Oak Islands' Serpent Mound

Courtesy: History Channel

Doug Crowell, Fellowship member on the TV Show, *"Curse of Oak Island,"* said he measured the 'serpent mound' and found it to be 4 ft high, and 134 ft long. Though he did not give a width measurement, the shows' video presents the serpent mound to be almost twice as wide as tall. The serpent mound is primarily made of larger rocks, boulders, and angular stones (breccia) which would be discarded having no use in road or filtration construction.

Yet the smaller boulders, stones, and cobbles could be used in road construction or as fill within the filtration system tunnel. For the most part these smaller boulders, stones, and cobbles were missing from the serpent mounds' TV appearance. The serpent mound with an estimated 8 ft wide base, equates to 4,288 ft^3 or 159 cubic yards, or 29.3% of the originally extracted volume from the Money Pit. Therefore the serpent mound represents approx. 90.2% of the breccia volume stratigraphy from the Money Pit. This is based on scientist estimates of the sinkhole being 30-35% breccia (*see Appendix A*). The illustration to the right, represents the proportional percent of breccia which would have been within the Money Pit, and the percent of that Money Pit breccia which made up the Serpent Mound.

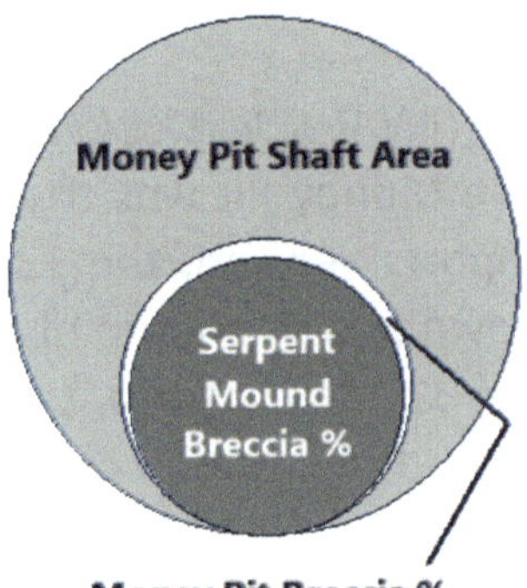

Courtesy Kyle Holden

EXCAVATION OF DEPRESSION Equation

The reason for the difference in weight, cubic yards, and metric tonnage original diggers excavated from the pit, from those in 1795 and 1804 when they re-dug the original pit, was primarily due to the condition of the glacial clayey soil. When those ancient voyagers started using pick axe and crowbar on Oak Island initially, the compacted soil weighed 106 lbs. per cubic foot.[6] Later when it was disturbed and aerated as it was re-excavated, the soft glacial clayey soil weighed only 76 lb/ft^3.[6] Furthermore the breccia of boulders, rocks, stones, and cobbles had essentially been removed from the soil before it was placed back into the pit. Additionally the soil was going to be compartmented and sequestered into 10 ft tall areas or 'containers' (between platforms). Since the original diggers were now just "re-filling" the equivalent of a 10 ft container, closing a platform and repeating the fill of each container up to the top of the pit; none of the downward loadbearing force from the tonnage of dirt was able to perform any compacting during the refill process. Even the thickness of each of the eleven oak log platforms (7") above the bottom, would have reduced the total vertical fill by 77 inches (almost 6.5 ft).

So with removal of the breccia calculated at approximately 32.5% of total excavated original volume, there was most likely excess soil remaining after the pit was refilled. Just like the hole in your yard! The primary cause of this was due to the change in soil condition, the lack of compaction due to compartmentalizing, and the loss of fill needed due to platform spacing - added to less fil to filler' up! I presume this excess dirt was that which we saw barely covering the serpent mound boulders.

Try to recall descriptions of the area around the depression when it was found by our Three Amigos. In Appendix C, *"On The Record,"* some commentators described the area as "having several tree stumps reflecting man's earlier presence" at the site. *Now that could be one heck of an understatement!*

The volume of lumber required to construct eleven oak timber platforms... one each at 10 ft increments, is astounding.

First, the generally agreed description of the oak logs tightly packed to form these platforms, were to have been 6-8 inches in diameter. Others described them with having the bark left on them. Everyone agreed they were tightly embedded into the surrounding hard clay walls of the pit. Some authors ascribe that to mean they were embedded, but perhaps only by six inches into the walls at either end. I contend they needed to be embedded by a good foot at both ends to ensure a fixed hold in consideration of a log warping, cracking, or splintering out from its embedment. So using the additional foot length of log on each end, the area necessary to construct each platform level would total a diameter of 15 ft. This allows the additional embedment of one foot at each end of the 13 ft diameter shaft. For ease of multiplication, lets also assume each log was 7 inches in diameter, as an 8 inch diameter log is quite a hefty piece of tree! 8 inches equates to a log of 25" circumference.

Finally, not all of a tree is used in this type of construction. Each tree provides a trunk or 'stem' as the timber to produce the lumber for construction. Yet part of that stem would have had branches removed. This is an inferior length or part of the stem due to issues of wood grain quality and direction and the amount of resin within that part of the stem. Therefore, when measuring a tree for its useful timber, the measurement of usable wood is referred to as the 'bole.' This would be the primary cutting mass of a tree for lumber. It is usually covered with bark and is from the trunk of the tree up through the first "branching" of the tree.[9] For the optimal section of construction-quality lumber, the mill would measure the bole of each tree below the first branching on the tree, down to the start of the roots; what is called the 'butt log.[10] This is where you get the needed length of the oak log, from end to end. However, since the length of each log in our platforms construction will vary in that 15' dia. pit, multiple length log sections could be cut from a single bole.

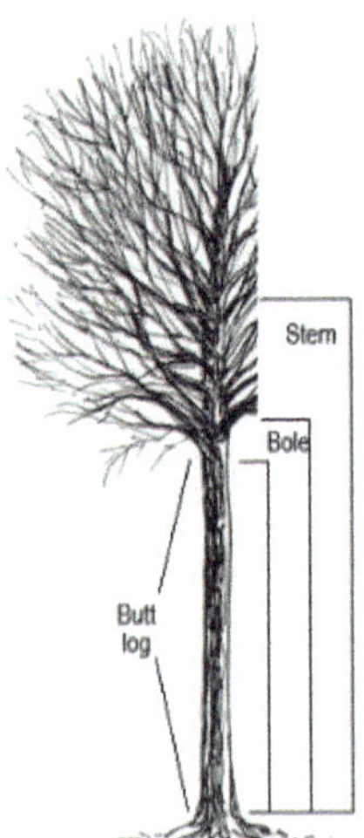

Created by David Neisen

One 15 ft bole for the center platform log is most likely a single tree. Whereas the same length of bole could produce three 5 ft length logs for the outer part of the platform, etc. *Capeesh?*

PLATFORM LOGS Equation

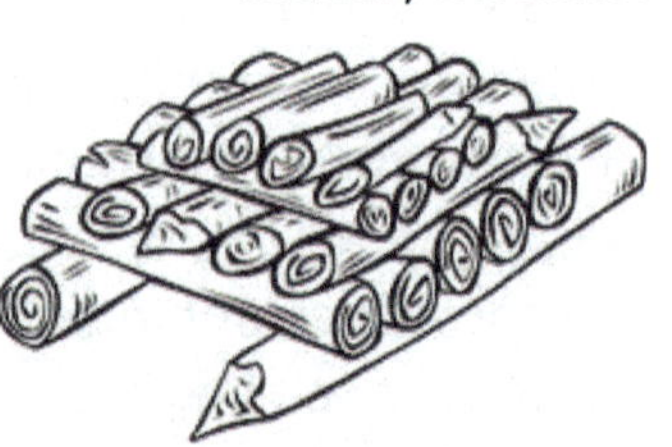
Courtesy iStock.com

To cover a 13 ft diameter area (19,114 in^2) across with 7 inch diameter logs, would take about 23 'widths' of logs, or 23 logs laid side by side to cover across the pit. The total linear length of 7 inch diameter logs to cover a 13 ft diameter area, with the inclusion of 1 ft lengths wedged into the pit walls on both ends, would require roughly 303 linear ft total.

This is 3,635 inches of log length. 303 linear feet of 7 inch diameter logs would suffice to cover a 15 ft diameter area, being 25,447 in^2.

Exactly how big of a tree is a 7 inch DBH (Diameter at Breast Height) Northern Red Oak tree (NRO)? Such a specimen would grow to be approximately 47 ft tall.[11] Or, more practically, how much linear feet of bole can be harvested from a tree of that diameter? Usually a tree with such a diameter is roughly 24-28 years old.[11] However, there is a tremendous difference in NRO tree structure when it grows in a forest, compared to growing out in the open with plenty of sun. This would definitely affect harvest productivity. Ironically, a forest grown NRO will yield more bole, or 'stem' log length.[12]

In a study done in Germany using Terrestrial Laser Scanning (TLS), the answer proved what may have seemed obvious. Titled, "*Intraspecific Competition Affects Crown and Stem Characteristics of Non-Native Quercus rubra L. Stands in Germany,*" the research showed NRO's in a high density forest canopy have less stem (bole) anomalies and branches (more usable bole length).[12] The tree, using tropisms, morphology, and branch-shedding abilities, kept their stems growing straight and tall, and severely limited the branching which affects stem length and quality, thus increases timber value.[12] Their report states,

> *"We examined the effect of competition intensity in tree and crown characteristics of Northern Red Oak. Crown dimensions decreased with increasing competition, but stem quality was, in general, better in denser stands. We conclude that increased competition was the main driver of enhanced stem quality and reduced crown size. To obtain higher timber quality, our results indicate that red oaks need, rather high stand densities to produce fewer external stem defects. External stem quality characteristics are strongly related to internal stem quality. With higher competition intensities, intended diameters of subject trees may be reached later, but stem qualities will be higher. Once the desired branch-free log lengths are reached, it is essential to release future crop trees from the competition in order to direct diameter increment primarily to these trees."*[12]

What this means is Northern Red Oak trees within a thick forest will grow taller, longer stems (boles), with less epicormic branching, and therefore, more wood to harvest for the task at hand. The maximum usable stem height, of a forest grown Northern Red Oak with a 7 inch DBH, at 24-28 years of age, is roughly 22 ft.[11] This is a piece of timber cut from the roots to the branching in the bole and again, is called a butt-log.

TOTAL LOGS Equation

It would take 303 linear ft of NRO stem or bole timber, with a DBH of 7", to construct a single log platform within the Money Pit. Therefore, building eleven such platforms would require 3,333 linear ft to complete all platforms. As everyone has been told, Oak Island was awash with towering NRO trees (*haha*), so our ancient voyagers would need to harvest a minimum of 152 of them! This assumes they could find oaks whose boles met the branchless stem height limit! In summation, 152 NRO trees with 7" DBH would need to be felled just for platform construction. Below is a photograph taken of what such an oak log platform found in the Money Pit may have looked like. There are 18 logs laid side-by-side in this image. Could this have been what our three explorers found as they reached the first 10 ft platform below the depression?

Photograph courtesy of oakislandtreasure.co.uk/photos

It is ironic, those whose comments are listed in Appendix C, "*On the Record,*" noted the lowest of platforms were neither oak wood nor of the diameter thickness as those upper platforms (see comments #6, #8, #11 and #16). I believe they said the 98 ft and 103 ft platforms were made of 6 inch diameter Spruce. Is it probable as they dug deeper and erected those platforms, the ancient voyagers simply ran out of oak logs? Or more logically, those two platforms were constructed of a smaller and different species of wood due to what was to lie between their surfaces. – *Something other than ten feet of dirt!*

***Red Clover, Red Clover,* Send *it* On Over!**

They knew a long time ago that ***It*** was the solution. But who listened to Varro, Cato, Theophrastrus, Columella, Palladius, or Virgil back then? Even in poetic form, Virgil in *"Georgics"* tried as he might to awaken them to the benefit of ***It***; yet they did not heed his warning![13] Eventually as cities grew larger and more densely populated such as London, Paris, Cologne, Milan, Florence, and Naples, as well as Cordoba, Seville, and Granada in crowded Arab Spain; people realized they had a problem on their hands, in the lands, and amongst their animals.[13] But they had forgotten the warnings of yore - ***It*** *was missing!*

There was a reprieve of the problem as The Black Death (1347-1352) halved the population of Europe and for a period of time people put the blame of famine only on that scourge.[13] They did not realize perhaps many of their countrymen fell to the Black Death because they were all suffering from being so weakened by the lack of ***It***.[13] Life was moribund and the world around them was fallow, atrophied, and without renewal.

Yet in the 16th century European populations had recovered and by the 1700's cities like Istanbul, London, and Paris were exceeding half a million inhabitants.[13] Others including Moscow, Berlin, Stockholm, and Copenhagen were growing even faster. The latter was the largest aggregation of people ever seen in that part of Europe by the middle of the 1800's.[13] Still, people remained ignorant from history's lessons of what ***It*** could do for them, and the delay was becoming a question of life or death.

Sometime back around 1000 AD, ***It*** was wild throughout Europe and readily available to those who remembered the scientific traditions. Those who knew of ***It*** and cultivated ***It*** and expressed the importance of ***It*** lived in Moorish Andalusia and in 1270 Albertus Magnus wrote about ***it***.[13] As the great Medieval scholar and Botanist, his words reached Christian Spain, which was itself dramatically rising in power and spreading influence. Others like agronomists Agostino Gallo and Camillo Tarello praised his words and the benefits he described to ***It***.[13] As Spanish territory increased so did the spread and use of ***It*** abound. By 1583 the domesticated ***It*** had reached France and with popularity growing, ***it*** was exported from the Netherlands to England in 1620.[13] Others like Sir Richard Weston who wrote a book called *"Discours of Husbandrie used in Brabant and Flanders"* created a sensation when published in 1644;[13] and suddenly ***It*** was back!

Throughout the British Isles, Europe, and Germanic cultures one could hear the loud chant of...

♬ Red Rover, Red Rover – ♬
*Send **Red Clover** on Over!*

Domesticated red clover was ***it***! It was the lost, legendary legume of the Pea Family which would nitrogenize, revitalize, and agronomize every pathetic pasture, every fallow farm, every groveling garden, and every lethargic livestock where it was sown! Whether in Denmark, Zealand, Sweden, Finland, or all those really hard to pronounce places across the continent, the introduction and mastering of the horticulture and implementation of the agronomy of red clover, vetch, lupins, broad beans, peas, and lentils saved Europe's bacon! In the 1780s and 1790s, farmers were planting 30-50% of their acreage in clover to feed the fields.[13] English Historian C.P.H. Chorley wrote the estimated increase in production in European agriculture between 1750 and 1880 was around 175% and he attributed two-thirds of that increase to the cultivation of these nitrogen-fixing legumes, particularly clover.[13]

Not only did red clover revitalize the land, but it is also an excellent and now abundant cattle fodder. Forage production increased dramatically and the critical disproportion between grazing and cultivated areas was finally reversed.[13] As we have discussed earlier, Nova Scotian Planters had to clear more land for feed crop cultivation for the livestock then to feed their family.

Deforestation and soil erosion was much abated with the introduction of clover. With clover it became possible to produce more on less land and in so doing, the agricultural production system could be stabilized.

With red clover growing in the barren, northern territories of Europe it had two dramatic effects. First, clover provided a suitable niche for the honeybee which therefore led to a dramatic increase in honey production.[13] Clover honey was a sweet improvement which furthered the wellbeing of the people. Second, it provided a fodder crop for cattle which was so desperately needed. Fatter cows caused herds to double and triple, providing more milk and therefore cheese.[13] Both became a critical nutritional base for those inhabitants as well as a new mercantile development. And still there was another, less realized benefit from clovers expansive use.

This would be the end to malaria which was a prominent disease in Europe. The malaria mosquito, *Anopheles atroparvus*, was big into biting cattle and other domestic animals yet would bite humans if nothing else was for lunch. With the dramatic rise of livestock due to clover improving feeds and being a fodder crop itself, it ironically improved the zoophilic mosquito's chances of finding animals to bite.[13] This proved fatal to the spread of malaria.[13] Cattle do not develop the disease, and the mosquitos life cycle was severed. In the 1770s, malaria was still one of the most common diseases in northern Europe, but in the 1860s it was practically eradicated, thanks to the green nitrogen revolution.[13]

The Agricultural Revolution of 1620-1850 throughout Europe, England, and the Colonies was basically a red clover-driven nitrogen revolution. Agronomist N.L. Taylor said, "*Clover has had a greater influence on civilization than the potato.*" For without clover there would have been no potatoes and without potatoes the tripling of the European population between 1750 and 1900 would not have been possible.[13]

Below is a map of Europe reflecting the migration timeline of red clover as it was introduced throughout the Agricultural Revolution.

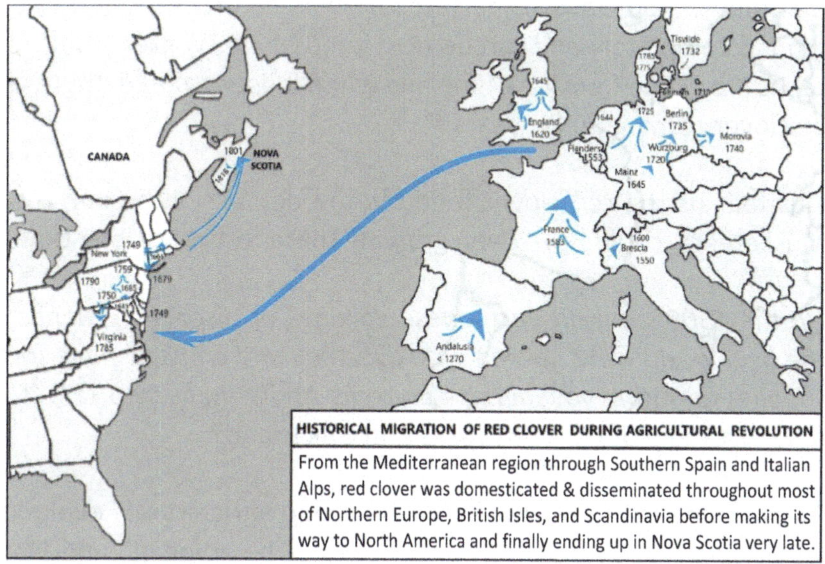

Created by David H. Neisen

As we reflect back to our area of interest, the farmers on Oak Island did grow Timothy Hay. Much later, alfalfa did most of what red clover had done. Alfalfa was not only a hit on SNL but became a standard provincial feed crop. Writer William Cronon, who wrote *"Changes in the Land, Indians, Colonists and the Ecology of New England,"* said,

> *"One thing that distinguished European [red] clover and timothy grass from other plants was precisely their ability to live on severely compacted soil containing little oxygen – the conditions found in cow pastures. Livestock grazing on newly cleared forest lands also aggravated soil erosion already taking place in these areas."* [14]

So how does red clover impact Nova Scotia and our treasure story?

Red clover *(Trifolium pratense)* is a short-lived perennial that overwinters in the Maritimes and grows 6 inches to 2 ft with a strong taproot and many branches. It becomes more quickly established than alfalfa, white clover, and other smallseeded clovers. It is the most aggressive perennial legume used in the Maritimes. Red clover is perfect for weed control as it covers the ground completely and can be frost-seeded into winter grains. Its seeds are viable for a long time and when it goes to seed, there will be clover coming up for years.[15]

This tells us the red clover found in the depression by our Three Musketeers, could have been growing there for a very long time.

"In the 1500's during Portuguese voyages of discovery, islands in the new world were seeded with livestock and crops to have fresh supplies for future voyagers." - Dr. Louis-Andre Vigneras 1972. Was red clover one of their "deposits" on Oak Island?

Meanwhile back to the past - the European Agricultural Revolution was slower if not downright rejected by the colonies, and Nova Scotia for all intents and purposes was treated as a colony. The colonies were made up of old-world Europeans who had long labored in more archaic and perfunctory approaches to the misery of farm life. The Scotch, Irish, French, Swiss, and Germans now cropping the colonies had left the continent before this revolution came common. They had been dealing with their own political revolution and breaking ties with Britain included not listening to their boasting of how to better the basics.

In German Pennsylvania, farmers began to hear of red clover as early as 1790. With reticence, German farmers slowly adopted the English practice of sowing upland fields in timothy hay and most importantly, red clover.[16] Also, with the adoption of upland field hay, those farmers who lacked meadows could raise winter fodder for livestock and no longer required letting fields lie fallow. [16] A hinderance to the new clover culture was both the poor quality of the seed imported from England, as well as the understanding of soil acidity which is not the alkaline soil preferred by most discerning of clover plants.[16]

The irony of ironies is the solution to this soil snag came from - *Nova Scotia!* New England colony farmers fixed their fields failings on plastering their plots with "land plaster."[16] So to please the pouting pratense, mined lime or gypsum from the *14th Colony* was imported to neutralize soil acidity, add calcium, and spread the love of alkaline.[16] The first gypsum coming into Philadelphia from Nova Scotia in the amount of 19,452 tons, arrived in 1816.[16] The land plaster did not need to be plastered on plenty, for as a few bushels was more than sufficient to convert an acre for our red-leafed clovers consumption.[16]

The Pennsylvania Dutch word for clover is "*Glee*," pronounced "glaa" (long a).[16] Curiously, the same word used as an adjective means small, which clover was as it did not grow tall (knee high at best) and had tiny seeds.[16] Appropriately, it only took a quart or two of seeds to sow an acre. Fagleysville, PA, blacksmith John Markley's 1805 Day Book often recorded selling *"ein quaed klaver saame,"- a quart of clover seed.* But I bet you had figured that out.

So what in darn nation was Nova Scotia's problem?

Remember, Nova Scotia was filled with people who for religious reasons wanted out of Europe. They had little or no experience farming and the entire vocation was really beneath their future plans. The pull was religious freedom, and the inducement was free land and the marketing by liars.

In attempts to "sell" Nova Scotia many wrote about the beautiful bounties awaiting those who moved to the new continent. People like T.F. Knight who in his essay *Nova Scotia and her Resources,* fibbed in flattery about *"a generous soil," "inexhaustible resources,"* and having every prospect of taking *"her place in the advance cart of the world's progress"* as *"the Great Britain of this new Continent."*[17] Or the exuberant Robert Grant Haliburton howling the *"agricultural capabilities of the province were unsurpassed."*[17] He falsifies in saying the long-productive Fundy marshlands were *"without a parallel in the history of agriculture."*[17]

And not to miss the band wagon, Abraham Gesner glamorizes the colony's in his musings *"The Industrial Resources of Nova Scotia,"* in saying *"always productive alluvial soils are equal to the Banks of the Nile."*[17] And not to be out bull-shitted, Sam Slick (no joke) slanders with *"Nova Scotians were either asleep or stone blind to the natural privileges of their country."*[17]

So they signed up and they came in waves. The first were the Planters. The one true statement about the Planters is the only thing they knew nothing about, was planting. Backwardness in agronomy and animal husbandry mixed with the myopic view of the bountiful splendor of old growth forests, with the maelstrom of hellish weather and warring heathens, Nova Scotia was going nowhere. Soon what developed experience there was of the land, was excised when both the Huguenots and the Acadians were forced out. Sporadic communities, cloistered in their own languages and beliefs, Nova Scotia would take one hundred years to finally figure the farming thing out.

Nova Scotian farmers were far from feeding family and their dwindling livestock, keeping food imports a retailers top priority. The consensus of mid-19th century opinion was in Nova Scotia *"The business of farming was in a backward state and comparatively unremunerative."* British agricultural chemist J.F.W. Johnston after visiting Halifax and Annapolis Royal in 1849, whined the province *"not made to yield half so much food as Great Britain, in proportion to the number of people employed in agriculture,"* and the reasons for this *"comparative deficiency of produce lay in a want either of skill or of preserving industry on the part of the cultivators."*[17]

The enlightenment spread slowly and unevenly because those farmers interested in the new methods were not in a position to adopt them. Red clover usage was tied to this obstacle. Yet these enlightened farmers were frustrated with the attitudes of their "incredulous countrymen" who needed to be convinced of the benefits they could reap. Others were frankly amazed to the apathy nor lack of positive indifference of the Plodholes around them.[17] Below is an early receipt for 12 lbs. of red clover.

Halifax Nova Scotia

Sable Isle

Courtesy: Nova Scotia National Archives, MG1 Vol. 950 #546.

The 1820s and 1830s saw several things begin to grow in the province, namely the issuance of the Agricola letters, establishment of the first wave of farming societies, and the distribution of red clover seed to new farm settlers. It would be another twenty years before the inertia of ignorance was imbued with intellectual impetus to overcome the impasse.

By 1847, the farming society of Pictou County went full hog on red clover. Clover became their first importance, and English red clover was clearly favored, although "American" and "yellow" varieties were tried. Known imports rarely exceeded 225 lbs. per year, which was sufficient to seed 20 or 25 acres when mixed with meadow grasses. Estimates for Pictou County peg red clover seed imports at one ton for the two mid-century decades.[15]

What in Gods Green Acres does this have to do with Oak Island?

As seen with this abbreviated history of red clover in Nova Scotia, there was no reason ***It*** should have been found on Oak Island. Up through 1820 at the earliest, the benefits of red clover would remain a foreign, nonnative vascular plant of no known import or attainability. It would be similar to you finding, acquiring, or trying to operate a 3-D printer just a decade ago. And still, it is not in your *Sharper Image* catalog today!

So the question remains; what was ***it*** doing singularly covering the depression in the forest on Oak Island – and why did ***it*** astonish our storytellers for being there? Several commentators describe the clover as foreign, unknown, and definitely out-of-place, as it grew in abundance in the depression! Yet they had no commentary regarding ***it*** having any treasure-related connection? No pirate-related conspiracy to imbue? In other words, what made ***red clover*** so odd to them to repeatedly make their point of it mysteriously being there? This item, which has no similarity to the embellishment of the block and tackle, therefore becomes a forensic fact to investigate.

Footnoted References:

1. "*Soils Profile*." BYJU Online Biology Program. Author Unknown. (Accessed 10-12-2021). https://byjus.com/biology/soil-profile/.

2. "*Soils and Settlements*." by Nick Gromicko, CMI and Kenton Shepard. InterNACH Online. https://www.nachi.org/soils-settlement.htm.

3. "*The Bark Canoes and Skin Boats of North America*." by Adney, Tappan, and Chapelle, 1964. Bulletin of the United States National Museum. Pages 1-242. https://doi.org/10.5479/si.03629236.230. Or https://www.google.com/books/edition/The_Bark_Canoes_and_Skin_Boats_of_North/BKZVCgAAQBAJ?hl=en&gbpv=1.

4. "*The Mi`kmaq: The Boat that Connected the Province*." Shubenacadie Canal Waterway. https://www.shubenacadiecanal.ca/the-mikmaq. Accessed 4-11-22.

5. "*Natural Slate – Flagstone*." Provided by Perry Hutts, Owner/Operator, Hutts Quarry, 3280 Hwy 202, East Gore, Hants County, Nova Scotia. https://www.huttsnaturalstone.com/about-us.

6. "*Unit Weight of Soils*." by Geo Technical Info. Career Development & Resources of Geotechnical Engineers. Chart 3 - Lindeburg, Civil Engineering Reference manual for the PE Exam, 8th Edition. Glacial Clay Soft, g(lb/ft^3). www.geotechnicalinfo.com/soil_unit_weight.html.

7. "*A Glossary of Scotch Mining Terms*." Compiled by James Barrowman, Mining Engineer and Secretary to the Mining Institute of Scotland, 1886. "March." Printed at the "*Advertiser*" Office, by W. Naismith, 1886. http://scottishmining.co.uk/Indexes/Barrowman.html.

8. "*Rigid-end, Tandem-axle Dump Truck*." 1-12 cu. Yards. 2021. www.earthhaulers.com. Dallas, Texas.

9. "*The Definition of Bole*." Online. https://www.vocabulary.com/dictionary/bole.

10. "*The Importance of a Tree's Butt*." by Steve Nix. ThoughtCo. (Accessed 04-20-2022). https://www.thoughtco.com/the-importance-of-a-trees-butt-1343234.

11. "*Crop Tree Release Improves Competitiveness of Northern Red Oak Growing in Association with Black Cherry*." by Thomas M. Sckuler. Northern Research Station, Timber and Watershed Laboratory, Parsons, WV. 26287.

12. "*Intraspecific Competition Affects Crown and Stem Characteristics of Non-Native Quercus rubra L. Stands in Germany*." by Katharina Burkardt, et. al., 2019. Article in *Forests*. Published Sep. 28, 2019. Silviculture and Forest Ecology of the Temperate Zones, Faculty Forest Sciences, University of Gottingen, DE.

13. "*A Plant that Changed the World: the Rise and Fall of Clover 1000-2000*." by Kjaergaard, Thorkild and translated by David Hohnen. https://thorkildkjaergaard.com/a-plant-that-changed-the-world-the- rise-0f-clover-1000-2000/.

14. "*Changes in the Land, Indians, Colonists and the Ecology of New England*." by William Cronon, 1983. Pg. 147.

15. "*Under Cover – A Guide to Using Cover Crops in the Maritimes*." by Janet Wallace and Jennifer Scott. Nova Scotia Organic Growers Association & Atlantic Canadian Organic Regional Network (ACORN). 2nd Edition. 2008.

16. "*Straw and Hay*." by Bob Wood. https://goschenhoppen.org/clover-part-1/.

17. "*Exciting a Spirit of Emulation Among 'Plodholes:' Agricultural Reform in Pre-Confederation Nova Scotia*." by Graeme Wynn. Seventh Atlantic Studies Conference, Edinburgh. 1988.

Appendix I

CUCKOO FOR COCONUTS

Such a finding and determination that fibrous organic material found within the Money Pit, Smith's Cove filtration system, and among other locations on Oak Island... was in fact coconut fiber - *was an astonishing artefact*! What of all things, was 'IT' doing here in Nova Scotia? Finding fibers here had no simple answers. Though at the time, It did legitimize and give credence to certain treasure-seeker theorists. They surmised of pirate bounty stolen from Spanish Galleons returning from looting South America, and now interred within the island. Yet it also had experts trying to proffer suggestions why such a need for so much coconut fiber!

So, when carbon-dating of the fibrous coconut material was dated as far back as **855 AD**[1]... a collective THUD was heard as everyone's jaw dropped to the ground!

As Gary Drayton could only say.... ***H O L Y S H A M O L Y !!!!***

Many of the other Oak Island Authors have websites which house treasure troves of documents like those referenced here. Their books do the lions' share of explaining every facet of the Oak Island legend. I urge you to check out both their books and websites to witness the original documents, letters, and reports! Each are truly ***BOBBYDAZZLERS***!

The coconut is the fruit from the Coconut Palm Tree (*Cocos nucifera*) which is of the tree family "*Arecaceae*" and is the only species of Palm Trees to produce coconuts.[2,3] The name 'coconut' is thought to have stemmed from a Spanish and Portuguese word 'coco' which translates to "head" or "skull".[2,3,4] A coconut has three visible indentations on it,[2,3] resembling eyes and a mouth – *hence* "coco." Just to be politically correct, the seed and tree have more than 250 different names, throughout the world and history.

The coconut palm is unsurpassable in its beauty and its utility because, on small islands where land-based natural resources are scarce, it provides almost all the necessities of life - food, drink, fuel, cooking oil, domestic utensils, medicine, timber and thatch for building houses, coir fiber for making ropes and mats, and many others.[2, 4, 6] In many tropical countries, coconut is an important part of the daily diet.[2, 4] Its main product is the oil extracted from the kernel. The residue is an important animal feed. The coconut water from the young nuts is a popular beverage. The jelly-like kernel of the young coconut is considered a delicacy. The shredded kernel is sold as desiccated coconut used in food and confectionary. The husk of the nut provides coir which is an important fiber that can be used for ropes, carpets, brushes, etc.[4, 5, 6, 7] It is more frequently used as a fuel source.[4, 6, 7] The shell of the nut is used for household utensils and the charcoal made from it is an excellent basic material for activated carbon.[6] Instead of being used for nut production, the inflorescences of the Coconut Palm can be tapped, yielding sap with high sugar content, from which sugar, alcoholic beverages and vinegar can be made.[6, 7] The leaves are used for roof thatching. The midribs of the leaves are used for brooms. Coconut wood is more and more being used for house building and other uses such as furniture or tool handles. [4, 5, 6, 7] All the parts of the coconut palm except the roots, are used in a peasant's household, so it is no wonder that this tree has also been called 'Tree of life.' [ALL]

There were two clearly differentiated, and distinct genetic subpopulations of the Coconut Palm prior to the 1900's.[5] This strongly suggest the palms were cultivated at two separate locations; one in the Pacific Ocean basin and the other in the Indian Ocean basin.[5] They are known by their Samoan names for traditional Polynesian varieties… ***niu kafa*** and ***niu vai***.[5]

The ***niu kafa*** coconut is shaped as a triangular, and oblong form with a large fibrous husk which is quite rigid.[5] Looks more like a football. The traditional belief is the ***niu kafa*** form of coconuts was the wild, ancestral form that did not reflect human selection; in part because it was better adapted to ocean dispersal.[5] "*Niu Kafa evolved by natural selection without human intervention*" (Harries). The ***niu kafa*** is considered a "tall" (as in tree form) classification from the Indian Ocean,[5] which is the predominant marketed fruit worldwide until the 20th Century. The kernel (meat) of these coconuts, called copra (KO-pra), is often pressed for oil, dried, and grounded for culinary purposes.[6] Their fibrous outer husks are most likely burned for fuel, or processed through "retting," which prepares them to be pounded, dried, and spun into rope, or "coir" (Kai-yer or 'care').

The ***niu vai*** coconut is a rounded shape with less outer husk and contains abundant sweet coconut water when unripe.[5] Quite often the ***niu vai*** fruit is brightly colored when they are unripe; either bright green, orange, or bright yellow.[5, 10] Sometimes they may be a beautiful gold with reddish tones, but always with a larger, yet thinner husk. They look more like a basketball.[5] The dwarf trees with ***niu vai*** fruits were "*domesticated by primitive man for the sweet uncontaminated water in the young fruit*" (Harries). As the domesticated hybrid form they had traits such as - the dwarf growing habit, self-pollination, and *niu vai* fruit variations.[5] Initially, ***niu vai*** only grew in the Pacific and then only in a small subset of harvested Pacific coconuts. The Coconut Palm tree hybrids bearing this fruit grew only several feet tall.[5]

Niu kafa **Coconut**

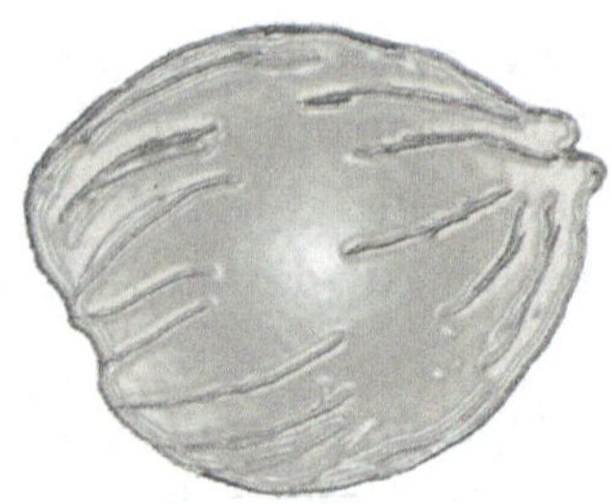

Courtesy of Artist, Miles Ballew.

In the Pacific Ocean, ***niu vai*** coconuts were likely first cultivated on islands in Southeast Asia, such as the Philippines, Malaysia, Indonesia, and perhaps the sub-continent as well.[5] Whereas, in the Indian Ocean, the likely center of cultivation of the ***niu kafa*** was the southern periphery of India, the Maldives & Laccadive islands, and later Sri Lanka (Ceylon).[5] Eventually, hybridization and silviculture by man, brought the two together in these biomes.

Niu kafa: 15–25% water, 27–36% shell, 46–52% meat
Niu vai: >35% water, >24% shell, <42% meat. P66 [8]

The Indian Ocean coconut was transported to the New World by Tamils, Arabs, then Muslims and finally, Europeans.[4,9] After visiting India, Portuguese explorer Vasco de Gama gathered the fruit at a stop in the East African port of Malindi, at the mouth of the Galana River in today's Kenya.[9] De Gama had become the first European to reach India by sea, circumnavigating Africa.[9] From this point he traveled back to Spain via the Cape Verde Islands and then the Azores; bringing home the impressive coconut in 1502.[9] He was the first to bring the coconut into the Atlantic Ocean Basin.[9] So, the coconuts found growing in Florida today, are largely the Indian ocean type, which is why they tend to be the tall, ***niu kafa*** form.[5]

In the past, the Coconut Palm Tree yielded its first nut (fruit) between 6-8 years of age.[8] The peak fruit production of the Coconut Palm Tree occurs after 15-25 years and can yield up to 100 nuts a year.[6]

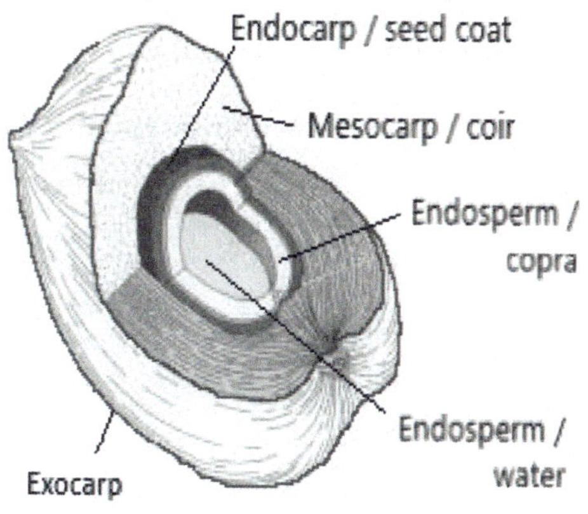

Courtesy: How Products are Made – Coir

A mature coconut can weigh 3.1 +lbs. Each is buoyant and is made up of an exocarp (the skin), and a thick fibrous Husk called the mesocarp Which is also generally called 'coir' (Kai-yer); and an endocarp (the nut shell), which inside has the meat/kernel/fruit known as 'copra' (Ko-pra).

Today, coconut hybrids are as varied as the locations where they are cultivated. Some of those varieties are known as; *Malaysian Yellow Dwarf, Dwarf Orange, Golden Malay, Maypan, King, Fiji Dwarf, Macapuno, East Coast Tall, and West Coast Tall.* The taste of the copra with hybridization has varied as well.[10]

The Coconut Palms' wide variety of uses amongst seafarers around the Equator, included; frond ribs as brooms, coir for cordage and caulking, and copra for sources of water, food, and medicinal use.[6] Coconut oil replaced whale oil for lamps aboard ships, coir provided stuffing for bedding, and woven into saltwater-resistant netting and mats. On shore, it is considered in many cultures as "The Tree of Life," as it can be used to make dozens of other products and is enjoyed around the world.[2, 6, 7] *Dunnage is not one of them!*

It is commonly thought coconuts spread around the world on ocean currents, until beaching and growing into life-sustaining grandeur. In some cases it was true. Coconuts did float from nearby island to island, yet that mode was limited as the coconut deteriorated over prolonged time in saltwater. Coconuts have been dispersed when tossed overboard or from shipwrecks with the drupes on board. Yet, it is man's intentional spread that has done the yeoman's job of distributing the coconut around the world.[5] The spread of the coconuts by seafarers can be seen below.

Initial Worldwide Distribution of Coconut Palm[5]

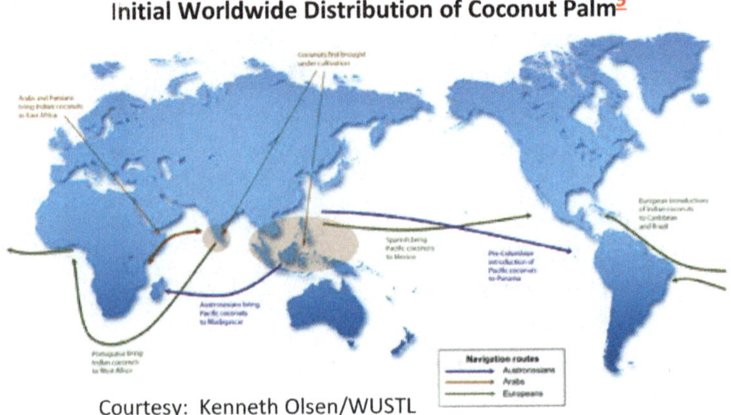

Courtesy: Kenneth Olsen/WUSTL

Independent Origins of Cultivated *Cocos nucifera* in the Old World Tropics

Geographical distributions of Indo-Atlantic and Pacific coconut subpopulations[11]

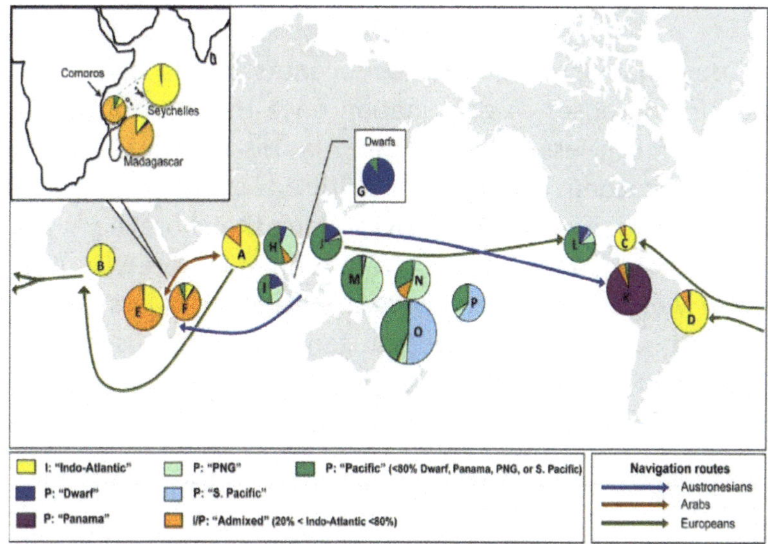

Courtesy: authors Bee F. Gunn, Luc Baudouin, Kenneth M. Olsen

Subpopulation designations correspond to assignments at Q$80% membership in Structure analyses at K = 5. 'I' and 'P' prefixes in the legend indicate 'Indo-Atlantic' and 'Pacific' population assignments at K = 2 assumed populations ($80% membership; see Fig. 1). Lines indicate proposed coconut dispersal routes by humans. Pie chart labels correspond to the following countries (ISO abbreviations) and sample sizes: A = IND, LKA, SEY (114); B = BEN, CIV, CMR, GHA (29); C = JAM, MEX (Atlantic) (13); D= BRA (72); E = KEN, MOZ, TZA (116); F = MAD, COM (65); G = Dwarf (54); H = CHN, KHM, MYS, THD, VNM (66); I = IDN (25); J = PHL (46); K = PAN (105); L = MEX (Pacific) (43); M= PNG (141); N = KIT, MHL, TUV (43); O= NCL, SLB, VUT (360); P = COK, FJI, PYF (30).[11]

Inset: subpopulation compositions for Madagascar, Comoros, and Seychelles. Pie chart composition is selected to reflect geographical population structure and does not correspond directly to GPC/CIRAD designations in Table 1. DOI:10.1371/journal.pone.0021143.g002 Origins of Coconut Domestication. PLoS ONE. www.plosone.org 4 June 2011 | Volume 6 | Issue 6 | e21143.

To clarify this image above, our ***niu kafa*** subpopulation is represented in yellow & orange, and our ***niu vai*** is represented in green & light green. Their crossbreeding and hybridization is reflected in the percentages of other colored coconut variations.

"Are you suggesting coconuts migrate?"

– Graham Chapman, **Monty Python**

Thor Heyerdahl proved floating coconuts in sea currents were ruined for purposes of germination once the nut bobbed in sea water for much less than 110 miles.[12] His experimental models proved the coconut could not have drifted across the Pacific Ocean unaided, to then grow into groves along the shoreline.[12] As the previous map shows, there were primarily three routes the coconut would have taken to reach ancient travelers heading to Oak Island. What is more, coconut genetics can tell us in each nut, the record of their prehistoric trade routes and of the colonization of the southern hemisphere and of the Americas![5, 11]

Courtesy: CARTOONSTOCK.COM.

"The Cocoanut Palm is nothing more than a huge feather duster turned upside down."

-Mark Twain[13]

Caring for Coconut Coir

When you look up into the Coconut Palm Tree, you see things much different than the coconut you buy at the grocery store. What we are familiar with is just the coconut nut or kernel. The coconut 'nut' or seed, grows within a larger protective sack. This is also why it is technically a drupe and not a nut. The nut is surrounded by a thick, fibrous, tough husk as the outer shell or sack. It is this much larger husk sack which we see up in the tall Coconut Palm Tree. This sack is very buoyant and can carry the seed to other shores so the seed within can successfully germinate. See Chapter 9, *"Foreign Fibers Found"*, Section 9c, *"Coconut Husk v Coconut Coir."*

Once you've convinced your little monkey friend to go up that +80ft tree and fetch some coconuts, it is time to harvest the seeds!

As they are neatly placed in a pile and awaiting your extended effort, you see all these coconuts housed in what appear to be ballistic bomb shelters - *protecting that nut from you*. So now it is time to de-husk. Harvesters separate the nut from the sack (exocarp) by slamming the husk sack upon a sharpened pole stuck upright in the ground.[6, 14] This punctures the husk sack without cracking the nut within. All this fibrous husk is biologically known as the mesocarp. This husk material is known generically, as the ***'coir'*** ("Kai-yer") of the coconut and protects the nut inside.

In many locales over most of the history of coconut cultivation, the husk sack is burned as a fuel source or used in local fertilizing.[14]

Today, with the consumer popularity of "going green," coconuts are back in a big way! The coconut by-products have generated billions of dollars from the dissection of these drupes. Coconut water, coconut oil, and Coconut copra (meat) top the list.[4] Yet the by-products from processing the husk sack or coir, is also generating big interest. So much interest in fact, coconut-growing countries are attempting to educate their growers of these potential value-added revenue streams.[4] What was once waste, is now sold around the world. From this husk (coir), harvesters use a process called "*retting*" to create those by-products.

The process of retting coconut husks started thousands of years ago.[all] This retting process has harvesters toss the removed coir sack (husk) into a saltwater-filled lagoon, pit, or pond, then let it soak for 10-12 long months.[6, 7] Frequently, they poke and prod the mass to 'baste' and marinate them. During this basting period, the anaerobic (bacterial) fermentation process does the work.[6, 7]

This process on mature coconuts, start a lignification transition which hardens, strengthens, and adds flexibility to the fibers within the husk.[6, 7] The lignin also colors the entire husk to a brown or dark brown color.[2, 6, 7] All that soaking in saltwater, swells, bloats, degrades, and dissolves the gelatinous pectic substances which hold the fibers together, which make up this husky sack.[6, 7] Once retted, the coir's loosened organic structure creates a manageable wad of fibers. Historically, at this point the villagers scoop out the coir husk and hackle, wash, and dry the loosened fibers.[6, 7] Once dry, workers beat it with.... Not a hammer, not a tennis racket nor an iron bar! They must use (back then) a wooden paddle. This tool allows the fibers to be paddled apart, but not become broken themselves.[6, 7] They paddle the wet wad of husk into finer fibrous fibers... which is similar to tenderizing a sloppy gelatinous soaked stuffed teddy bear until it falls completely apart. *Moving on.*

The broken up wad is left to dry on mats in the sun, raked periodically to fully dry and further separate the tangle.[6, 7] The husk, washed of its gelatinous glue and soluble membranes, is now a cleaner looking pile of thick hair. It's become a very useful and a valuable by-product called – coco coir or ***coir fiber***!

In the South of India and on Sri Lanka, where the best quality fibers are produced the average yield is 80-90 grams fiber per husk.[6, 14, 15, 16] Caribbean husks, by contrast, are relatively thick and may yield up to 150 grams of fibre.[15, 16]

They only recently started retting coconuts in the Caribbean. The other waste by-product generated from retting, is known as "*coir pith*" or "*coir peat*."[7, 14, 15, 16] This is actually the remnants of that gelatinous glue and soluble membranes which is now dry and lies like dust amongst the fibrous fur balls of coir on the mats. Husks are composed of 70% pith and 30% fiber on a dry weight basis.[6, 14, 15, 16] Up until twenty years ago, this by-product was stacked into communal waste mountains with no known purpose or use.[5, 7] Now with added ingredients and compacted into bricks, pith or peat is purchased as additional fertilizer for your gardens enjoyment.[5]

At this stage, the coir fibers, also known as "coco coir," are sorted, usually by length, and packed for further production use.[6, 16, 17] Many things can be made from it, like rope, twine, mats, planting medium, packing material, bedding material, brushes, netting, clothing, and on and on and on.[All] Europe initially imported bulk coir to make carpets, rugs, mats and brushes. It was too dangerous to transport in ships, so factories were built in India to make end products there. In our sphere of interest, coir was also used to caulk leaks in sailing ships, for cordage, netting – *and perhaps filtration!*

As mentioned, coconut coir fibers have gone green and are being introduced into many high tech products such as; fiberboard,[16, 17] soundproofing, construction materials, automotive products, and anything else that can be sold as a "biodegradable, earth-friendly, save-the-planet products, etc.[16, 17] Countries who had some familiarity with the Coconut Palm tree, are all scrambling to learn how to see the coconut anew, and 'ret' them some money from the current craze. This includes most of Oceana and Caribbean Sea.

Definitively, the answer to the question of *WHERE* did the coconut coir fibers originate, is clearly a Pre-Columbian answer. Appendix J, "*History Looks for Coir*" provides the reasons and answer to that question. Chapter 11, "*Harvesting the Truth*" walks you to the conclusions and solutions to this and other mysteries which make up the Oak Island legend.

Responding to 'New History'

At the very end of Appendix C, "*On the Record*," you may recall my email exchange with a Historian (#85) regarding numerous articles written on coconuts, especially during the medieval and colonial periods. After countering some initial statements with the historical facts as I had researched them, the respondent said,

> *"Unfortunately, it sounds like you've got a lot of old information there about coconut history – which is understandable, but there's much better history available now."*

A cold shiver ran down my back and a knot started to form in my stomach. Had I spent two years going cuckoo on coconuts learning 'old history' and will I make a fool of myself repeating nursery rhymes and old wives tales? Surely there must be some splitting of fibers to justify the statements made to me in this email as factual. And neither new nor old history will back up these claims. With a month or two before publishing, can I actually verify the veracity of these claims in time?

So I acquired the four articles the Historian had written; "*Gripping it by the Husk: The Medieval English Coconut*" (2017),[18] "*The Forgotten New England Coconut Dipper in the 19th-Century American Landscape*" (2019),[19] "*The Coconut Cup as Material and Media: Extended Ecologies*" (2021),[20] and "*Naming the Coconut and (de)Colonizing the Middle Ages*" (2022).[21]

Further, as suggested, I read the citations and bibliographic references in those articles with some relief. By now the knot had subsided and the angst was abating. But to make sure I was crossing the "T's" and dotting the "I's," I read one more book on coconuts. This was written by renowned coconut emeritus scientist, N. Madhavan Nayar, of the Tropical Botanic Garden and Research Institute, in Kerala, India. In 2021, he published a 424-page tome where he reviewed the research of others in the field of studying the Coconut Palm Tree (*Cocos nucifera*) and evaluated and consolidated their findings to date. This would become the current '*Bible*' on all things *Coconut* and is the comprehensive look at this field and its findings. The title is "*The Coconut: Phylogeny, Origins, and Spread*."[8]

The book reviewed the coconut research performed in the fields of history, prehistory, geology, archeology, botany, archaeobotany, paleobotany, palynology, paleopalynology, phylogeny, botanic phylogeny, genetics, molecular phylogeny, biogeography, paleo-magnetic stratigraphy, paleodistribution and entomology.
Wow - *Wanna play Scrabble?*

The book examined the following researchers and their findings:

> De Condolle (1886); Cook (1901, 1910); Beccari (1917); Hill, van Leeuwen (1933); Mayuranathan (1938); Bruman (1944, 1945); Heyerdahal (1950); Vavilov (1950); Merrill (1954); Massal, Barrau (1956); Wilson (1961); Fosberg (1962): Randhawa (1964); Corner (1966); Sauer (1967); Nayar, Riley, Kelley, Pennington, Rands (1971); Ward, Brookfield (1972); Moore (1973); Child (1974); Zeven, Zhukovsky (1975); Dransfield et al. (1984, 2008); Purseglove (1985); Bellwood (1987, 2004, 2013); Thaman (1992); Balick (1994, 2009); McKillop (1996); Gupta (1996); Possehl (1997); Kirch (2000); Thapar (2002); Gunn (2004); Prigge, Lagenberger, Martin (2005); King, Stansfield, Mulligan, (2006); Baudouin et al. (2006); Matisoo-Smith (2007); Baudouin, Lebron, Berger, Myrie, Been (2008); Singh (2009); Nayar, 2010; Johnson (2010); Storey, Quiroz, Matisso-Smith (2011); Kitalong et. al. (2011); Harries (1977, 2012); Bourdeix, Johnson, Tuia, Kape, Planes (2013); Abe, Ohtani (2013); Clement et al. (2013); Baker, Couvreur (2013); Camara-Leret, Paniague-Zambrana, Balsleve, Macia (2014); Baudouin, Gunn, Olsen (2014); Ahuja, Ahuja, Ahuja (2014); and Meerow et al. (2009, 2014).[8]

If you are looking for a deep read about this drupe and you frequently use the word 'extant' in your vocabulary, I recommend this is your source should you too become cuckoo for coconuts.

Obviously, I was trying to impress upon you the scope and relevance with which this book has currency with both *old* and *new* information on the topic of this subject. So now feeling confident in my research, let me address the 'new information' insights offered to me previously in Appendix C, "*On the Record.*"

> *"Of course, coconuts were introduced into the Caribbean by Columbus in 1492 – that's quite well known and has been confirmed through peer-reviewed genetic testing."*

Will "no" suffice?[8]

> *"Thanks to its water mills and ports, by the 18th century New England was a center of coconut processing and manufacture, believe it or not, and this industry is well recorded in newspapers of the period."*

The 18th century New England if I am not mistaken, represents the years 1700 to 1799. If that be true, then the above statement is off by more than half a century, as the Historians' references provided for verification of her statement above, they refer to factories in New Haven, CT., Waterbury, CT., and Providence, R.I. in 1856.[18] The latter location had two businesses employing 9 workers total, together turning out 110,000 coconut shell dippers in 1856, as stated in that reference.[18] Therefore they used about 55,000 coconuts, or roughly 525 coconuts a week in this '*center of coconut processing and manufacture*.' As was noted, this was not during the 18th century but the 19th century. Okay - *a typo?*

In addition, coconut shells were not to become a robust *product of manufacture* until the supply of the shells became more available, which happened around the time of the invention of desiccating the coconut meat (copra) and transforming it into coconut confectionery flakes. In 1895 the owner of Baker's Coconut Co., Franklin Baker of Philadelphia, received a cargo of fresh coconuts as payment from an exporter who was going bankrupt due to political unrest in Havana. Unable to sell the coconuts to Philly produce markets, he bought the machinery and developed a method for producing shredded coconut copra of uniform quality. A big hit with housewives and bakeries, within 2 years he sells his flour mill and established the Franklin Baker Co., dealing specifically in desiccated, shredded coconut flakes.[22]

Dare it be said; the growing supply of discarded desiccated drupe shells, definitely developed divergent dipper dynasties with or without water mills and ports. This byproduct dipped into a 19th century devoted Americana device.[23]

> *"Coir was widely used by Europeans throughout the colonial period, thanks to its durability and resistance to salt water. So there's actually no surprise in finding coir, even substantial amounts of it, in 18th century Nova Scotia."*

Not to be nit-picky, but timing is crucial to my research so let's clarify what the colonial period was. This was harder to do then I thought. Most go with the period of initial colonial settlement in Northern America, from 1607 with first settlers arriving in the British colony; until the issuance of the U.S. Constitution after the war of Independence, say 1780 – *hence no longer being a colony.* Being generous, let us widen the colonial period discussed, from 1600 – 1800, or the 17th through 18th centuries.

Oftentimes referred to as the 14th colony, Nova Scotia was trying to get its act together in settling the hostile and untamed lands. Failure after disaster after terrible weather and hostile Indians (Mi`kmaq), kept any resemblance of organized life a distant future. The population of Nova Scotia was a lonely 11,779 for the whole province in 1753.[24] In that year flax fiber and hemp fiber were primary crops, supplying all the twine and rope material the fledgling region could use.[24] Other than "sticks" for masts, nothing existed in substantial amounts in Nova Scotia, circa 1600-1800. Yet in 1876, D. Wyatt Aiken, editor and publisher of The Rural Carolinian stated, *"Coir cables, however, are not available in any except the warm latitudes, for cold weather makes them so brittle that they are liable to snap at any moment."*[13, 18] Lastly, when the Oak Island Treasure story was written in the mid-to-late 19th century, no one identified the bulk coconut fiber as the finished product known as coir and used in the making of cordage. To them - *it was simply dunnage.*

Holy Shamoly my dear researchers! Has history changed that much from last year to this year? Did Columbus "introduce' the coconut into the Caribbean after all? Was New England the center of coconut manufacture during the colonial period and recorded in all the newspapers I didn't read? And could it really be coconut coir fiber was widely used by Europeans throughout the colonial period and lots of it would be no Biggy in Nova Scotia? Is all this the "New History" along with that "new Math?"

Well it looks like it is time for some well-aged Tuba or a Toddy to finish my nut, shell, and husk research. *Oh by the way...* the coconut is not the largest nut in the world as she reports. The Seychelles' very own *Coco de Mer,* or *Seychelles Nut (Lodoicea maldivica) clocks in at 25 kg with a diameter of 1 meter.*[25] It is said to look like a woman's bottom. *Huh?* Finally, the Coconut Palm Tree produces drupes, not nuts. So a coconut is like a plum or a cherry – *a drupe*.

Courtesy: bennymarty/iStock.com

Courtesy: How Products are Made – Coir.

Split Coconut Husk after Seed Removed

Courtesy iStock.com

Footnoted References

1. "*Oak Island Hydrogeology, Hydrography and Nearshore Morphology, July – August 1995, Field Observations*." by David G. Aubrey, Wayne Spencer, Ben Guiterez, William Robertson, and David Gallo. Unpublished Draft Report. Woods Hole Oceanographic Institution, Woods Hole, Maine. April 8, 1996. 151 pages. https://www.oakislandtours.ca/les-macphie-research.html.

2. "*Coconut – History, Uses, and Folklore*." by Subhash Chanda Ahuja. CCS Haryana Agricultural University. Article in *Asian-History Journal*. 29 pages. January 2014.

3. "*Coconut: How the Shy Fruit Shaped our World*." by Robin Laurance. Brimscombe Port, UK. The History Press. 2019. Page 11.

4. "*Cracking Coconuts History*." by Ramin Ganeshram. AramcoWorld, Jan./Feb. 2017, Volume 68, No. 1.

5. "*Deep History of Coconuts Decoded*." by Diana Lutz. Washington University in St. Louis. *The Source* – Science and Technology. June 24, 2011.

6. "*Coir Process Technologies: Improvement of drying, softening, bleaching and dyeing coir fibre/yarn and Cellulose*." Agrotechnological Research Institute (ATO by), Wageningen, The Netherlands. No. 6. Common Fund Commodities. 2002.

7. "*Coir fiber process and opportunities-2*." by Akhila Rajan, at Govt. College Kozhinjampara. Published in The *Journal of Natural Fibers*, January 2008.

8. "*The Coconut Phylogeny, Origins, and Spread*." by N.M. Nayer, 2021. Academic Press is an imprint of Elsevier. 125 London Wall, London EC2Y 5AS, United Kingdom. P 66.

9. "*Vasco da Gama*." History.com Editors, Dec. 18, 2009. Last updated Aug. 21, 2018. https://www.history.com/topics/exploration/vasco-da-gama

10. "*Identification of Superior Dwarf Coconut (Cocos nucifera L.) Parental Cultivars for Hybrid Breeding*." By W.M. Mahayu, Taryono, Kumaunang, and Maskromo. Printed by SABRAO, *Journal of Breeding and Genetics*, 53 (2), Pages 278-289. 2021.

11. "*Independent Origins of Cultivated Coconut (Cocos nucifera) in The Old World Tropics*." by Bee F. Gunn, Luc Baudouini, Kenneth M. Olsen. 6 22-2011. PLoS ONE 6(6): e21143. DOI:10.1371/journal.pone.0021143.

[12]. "*Kon Tiki: Across the Pacific by Raft*." By Thor Heyerdahl, 1950. Mattituck: Amereon House. 240 Pages. https://infogalactic.com/info/Coconut#cite_note-Heyerdahl-31.

[13]. "*Coconuts*." By D. Wyatt Aiken, Editor/Publisher, Jan. 1876. Published in *The Rural Carolinian*, Vol. VII, Jan. 1876. Pages 573-575. https://babel.hathitrust.org/cgi/pt?id=nc01.ark:/13960/t7pn9fq2n&view=1up&seq=673&skin=2021.

[14]. "*Coconut Fibre: Its Structure, Properties and Applications*." by Leena Mishra and Gautam Basu. National Institute of Natural Fibre Engineering & Technologies Institute. Kolkata, West Bengal India. Section Yield of Coconut Fibre, Page 7, para. 10.2.1.3. Yield of Coconut Fibre. Researchgate. Pub. 339284598. February 2020. 27 Pages.

[15]."*Biofuels from Coconuts*." by Krishna Raghaven. 2010. 107 pages. Para. 1.1 Quantity and Energy Content of Parts of the Coconut Palm, Fig. 1 and Table 1. Biodegradability Section, P. 16. www.energypedia.info/f/f9/EN-biofuels_from_cocnuts-krishna_raghaven.pdf.

[16]."*Coir*." How Products are Made. Volume 6. 7 pages. www.madehow.com/Volume-6/coir.html.

[17]. "*Coir-The Natural Fiber from Coconut Husk*." by Line Cowley. Jun. 12, 2019. https://www.ecoworldonlone.com.

[18]. *"The Forgotten New England Coconut Dipper in the 19th-Century American Landscape." By Kathleen E. Kennedy, 2019.*

[19]."*Naming the Coconut and (de)Colonizing the Middle Ages*." By Kathleen E. Kennedy, 2022. Pages 61-85. Published in *Digital Philology: A Journal of Medieval Cultures*, Vol. II, No. 1, Spring 2020. Johns Hopkins University Press. P. 61-85. University of Bristol.

[20]. *"The Coconut Cup as Material and Media: Extended Ecologies." By Kathleen E. Kennedy, 2021. www.press.library.concordia.ca/projects/old-media-and-the-medieval-concept .*

[21]. *"Gripping it by the Husk: The Medieval English Coconut." By Kathleen E. Kenned, 2017. www.muse.jhu.edu/article/758503 "*

[22]. "*The Food Chronology: a food lover's compendium of events and anecdotes, from prehistory to the present*." by J. Trager, 1996. P. 346. See The Coconut Time Line: Mercantile, 1895, online. titled: Desiccated Coconut. at http://cocos.arecaceae.com/mercantile.html.

23. "*Did You Know Victorians Drank from Coconut Shells*?" by Eleanor Rose, May, 27, 2020. Article at online *Civil War Talk.* https://civilwartalk.com/threads/did-you-know-victorians-drank-from-coconut-shells.173257/.

24. "*History of the County of Lunenburg – 2nd Edition*." by Mather Byles DeBrisay, Judge of County Courts and Member of the Historical Society of Nova Scotia. Harvard College Library, Apr. 7,1896, Cambridge, Mass. Second Edition, 1895. Originally written at Bridgewater and La Have, February 1870 . Pgs. 301-306.

25. "*The Biggest Nuts in the World*." By Valery Skiba. Printed online In *The Magazine*. (Accessed 05-05-2022). https://tz.iiug2017.org/7496-the-biggest-nuts-in-the-world.html.

Appendix J

HISTORY LOOKS FOR COIR

So the hunt is on to find where our *modern* or *ancient* voyagers got the volume of coconut coir fiber to build their constructs on Oak Island. These fibers were clearly used for specific purposes in both the Money Pit and at Smith's Cove. We know the construct was built prior to 1795, and most arguably before 1700. The following are the **key factors** which shape our continued search through history for where these Oak Island fibers came.

The Age of Our Coconut Fibers

As repeated throughout this book, the radiocarbon-dated age of the five coconut coir fiber specimens we know of, range from **810** AD through **1330** AD. Logically, one would assume you would look for coconut coir fiber supplies from **1330** AD onward. It reasons, should you start your hunt in, say **900** AD, then you are looking for a source that hasn't even existed yet. Right? In addition, recent advances in radiocarbon dating would negate those specimens dated prior to 993 AD. Therefore those remaining specimens with ^{14}C dates focus our attention to the period of **1150** AD to **1400** AD or when exclusive of the ± ranges, then **1185** AD to **1330** AD. (See Chapter 10, "*Cracking the Nut*," subsection "*The Dating Game*" to review this period selection).

Or... is it possible these fibers were used long ago, but their age is disguising the age of those "ancient" voyagers?

There are many who believe the age of the fibers has nothing to do with this enigma. They contend those fibers could have been used by people not of the carbon-dated period. In other words, a "modern" voyager could well have taken those fibers – which may be very, very old, and used them on Oak Island in a more current period of time. Let's say, hundreds of years ago the treasure or whatever it was, had been protected in containers using coconut fibers. Then later in history, these items were moved by more modern day voyagers to Oak Island. Could we not therefore have both – modern voyagers and ancient coconut fibers?

That assumption does seem plausible at the moment. But to suggest the coconut coir fiber was merely crate stuffing, indicates our ancient voyagers hauled thousands of crates to the island to have amassed the volume of crate-stuffing fiber found. Was it not lucky those crates had just coincidentally been stuffed with the best medium in the world to build a very effective filtration system? What are the odds this was not intentional. Was this Oak Island construct long in the planning? Do we assume all of this coconut coir fiber was a subject of happenstance? *- So maybe not.*

<u>The Range of Cocos Nucifera</u>

The Coconut Palm growing region lies between 20° N and 20° S Latitudes on both sides of the equator. Though it is found beyond this range as far as 27° N and 27° S Latitudes, cultivation and nut production in these further regions has not been as successful and the palm does not fruit in cooler climates. The illustration below identifies zones of latitude for growth of The Coconut Palm Tree. These zones represent the growing regions for *Cocos nucifera:* with Zone #1, supporting high productivity potential; Zone #2, with medium levels of climatic benefit; and Zone #3, offering little or no potential for tree growth and fruit production.[1]

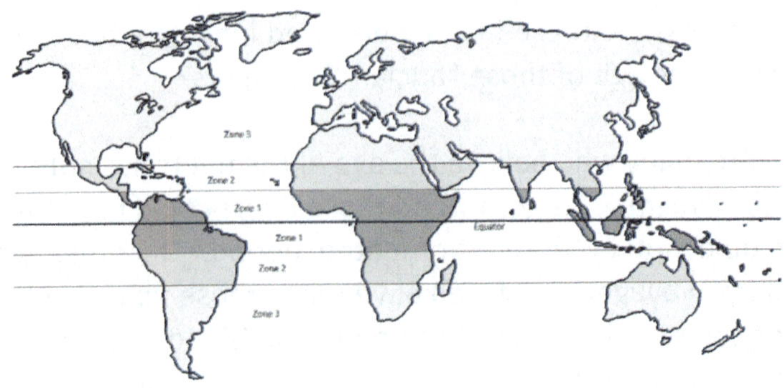

Source: Mike Foale, 2003.

Even when considering the historical changes in the environment, which have been significant, the studies of archeology, archeo-botany, paleobotany, and biography have well-defined the spread and cultivation of the *Cocos Nucifera*.[2, 3] *This palm* requires at least 70-80% humidity to fruit, abundant sunlight with minimum temperatures above 82°Fahrenheit, and annual rainfall of +50 inches.[4] We know of regions even within the grow zones, that never provided the Coconut Palm Tree a decent biome to home.

Quality of Coconut Fibers

We have also ascertained the fibers found on Oak Island were extracted from coconut husks through a process called retting. This uniquely treats, cleans, and enhances the fiber by making them stronger, more elastic, more absorbent, more buoyant, and more saltwater resistant.[5, 6, 7] The end-product is a fiber which can be as fine as human hair, light to dark brown in coloration from the lignification process, and which make coconut fibers almost non-biodegradable. It is the knowledge and application of this retting process which produce fibers for use as an excellent filtration medium, for cordage, and caulking. Instead of simply being organic material of the coconut husk, which would rot and decay like any fruit rind, husk, or skin; retting removes most all properties which would cause fermentation and chemical deterioration of the husks organic material. A Simple coconut husk laying on the ground would fully decompose in three to four years.[8] Yet the coconut fibers found on Oak Island and radiocarbon-dated, could be more than 7-800 years in age. Also, both Woods Hole Oceanographic Institute in 1996 and the lab used by Robert R. Dunfield in 1976, clearly identified the organic matter as coconut **coir** fiber.[9, 10]

Type of Coconuts Used

When our ancient voyagers were seeking coconut fiber there were two subgroups as previously discussed. They were the ***nui kafa***, which is often thought of as the 'tall coconuts,' considered by botanists as the wild, nonhybridized subgroup.[4, 11, 12] Conversely, the ***nui vai*** subgroup represented the smaller, dwarf tree variety which man had come to cultivate for food and water.[11, 12]

The ***nui kafa*** subgroup went westward into the Indian Ocean basin and the ***nui vai*** spread throughout the Pacific Ocean basin.[3, 11, 12] The ***nui kafa*** grew the 'football' shaped coconuts which had a much more fibrous husk, while the ***nui vai*** had the 'basketball' shape and its exocarp was thinner and its husk volume was less.[2, 12, 13] Though not determinative by itself, the ***nui kafa*** subgroup demonstrably represents the almost exclusive coconut variety historically used for coir production back in the day.[11] Whereas the ***nui vai*** dwarf variety was spread throughout oceans for its ample water, milk, and meat (copra).[4, 11, 12] In addition, those ***nui vai*** locales had access to superior plant fiber, such as sisal, abaca, hemp, rattan, and Date Palm for cordage and products not requiring the retting process.

With this knowledge and understanding we can eliminate the areas of China, South-East Asian coastal areas, and for a good portion of the Pacific Islands. For the most part, this excludes the three great archipelagos of Melanesia, Micronesia, Polynesia, and Australasia, known as *Oceania*. We can do so through confirmed genetic studies of Coconut Palm tree DNA, where hundreds of genotyped samples were identified with specific genetic markers. Each was uploaded into microsatellite regions and linked to form migration patterns.[11, 12]

So we are clear our *Cocos nucifera* – specifically ***nui kafa*** (the wild one), were grown in the Indian Ocean Basin and spread from there. Further, they were specifically found in the region of southern India, Sri Lanka, the Maldives & Laccadives archipelagos.[3, 4, 11] Historically, it is this region which engaged in retting coconut husks for both local and intra-ocean coir fiber commerce. The Coconut Palm tree hereditary dispersion can be seen in the graphic in Appendix I, "*Cuckoo for Coconuts,*" page 6.

<u>The Volume of Coconut Fibers</u>

Using forensic examinations, we have determined a conservative volume of coconut coir fiber found on Oak Island, with a minimum of total of 1.54 metric tons (See Chapter 10, "*Cracking the Nut*").

This is collaborated with historical reportage by those on scene at Oak Island and by residents nearby. To visualize this volume of coconut fiber, we have expressed how it would take up to 18,000 coconuts to produce enough coconut husks to make our coir fibers. These fibers would fill 2.5 40' shipping containers compacted on a 2:1 ratio. This understanding also helps us limit geographical regions throughout history which simply did not have the volume of trees to grow so much product, nor the societal knowledge and organization to produce the quantity found within Oak Island. *To note:* In a successful harvest a mature Coconut Palm Tree can produce up to 100 coconuts a year.[3, 12]

History shows before the Roman period, Indian traders and merchants sold exotic woods, cordage, and boats, as well as other more familiar exports, throughout the coastline ports of the greater Indian Ocean.[6] In a few trading locations, the growing of Coconut Palms and knowledge of retting their husks for coir fiber entered the culture of those communities. I can count two locations outside of the traditional region (India, Sri Lanka, & Lakshadweep) which the use coir for boat building today -Dhofar & Hormuz, is still practiced today. In most all other locations, either shifts in climate or disruption of trading routes by colonial powers, brought an end to such a practice. Others just never invested the time and energy needed for commercial aspects of such a process. In the 19th century, African communities had abandoned the lengthy work of retting. Whether this was part of the plantation revolt or they simply turned to other endemic plant fibers, I am not investigating here. However, As the British Empire spread in Africa, they again at the end of the century, attempted to generate plantation-style interest in coconuts and production of coir fiber .[14]

<u>*Purposes of the Coconut Coir Fibers*</u>

What should not be lost on this investigation is *WHY* coconut coir fiber was used on Oak Island. Coir fibers have been used by man for many products and purposes over centuries. It is now seeing its heyday in all things marketed as *green* and *biodegradable*! Yet the reader needs to acknowledge the fiber was used for a specific purpose in both the Money Pit and under the sands of Smith's Cove. Searchers did not find bales of coir rope, or stacks of coir mats or nets, nor sacks of coir fiber caulking. Nor have they found retted coconut coir fiber to be very biodegradable, either. As the WHOI researchers stated with their description of "**Pathway iv**" (*see Chapter 9*), our ancient voyagers "*brought and used the coconut coir fiber for flood tunnel purposes*." Exactly! WHOI researchers realized, in lieu of explaining away their presence by other reasons, the specific intent of that fiber was for the construction of a filtering system which would last over time.

In irony of all ironies, our popular theorems include Sir Francis Bacon of the mid late 1500's to the 1620's. Considered the '*Father of deductive reasoning*' and involved in the exploration of preserving documents using Quick Silver (mercury); many believe his involvement in Shakespearean Manuscript preservation finds his presence on Oak Island. So to inform you that the British scientist, author, and Rosicrucian was also one of the first to perform and record water filtration by attempting to purify saltwater, may not be noteworthy. However, his efforts using a sand filter method by experimenting with the digging of a hole on the ocean shore, allowing water to pass through to provide clean, potable water; is unmistakably a possible part of the filtration system operation on Oak Island.[15a]

If you exclude the possibility that Oak Island was perhaps a large laboratory for Bacon to operate freely, you may want to look again at how the Smith's Cove filtration system was constructed and how it operated effectively over so long a period, while under such violent attacks to its functionality. Allot of coincidences indeed.

Why couldn't those ancient voyagers simply have used more eelgrass in the filtration system construct, or applied algae, moss, wool, sponge, charcoal, peat, or alum to make it work? These were the mediums used in other attempts to filter water in that day and age. Or why not simply mix the blue putty puddled over the log platform within the Money Pit – with straw, grass, or hay to be sufficient and effective? Was the mixture of the coconut coir fiber to protect the putty from becoming saturated with water, causing it to become diluted enough to wash off the platform or destroy an airtight seal? Was the fiber applied to maintain the putty's usefulness whatever the reason it was applied? Once you wake up from the fallacy coconut fiber was simply stuffing or dunnage, and realize it was intentionally brought to the island – regardless of its age; you must consider *WHY*!

IF – you consider the proper construction of an efficient water filtration system is to provide relatively clean if not filtered water without clogging up a system with sand, debris, and algae, you start to see the immense benefits coconut coir fiber brought to that operation on Oak Island. As described elsewhere in this book, the retted coconut fiber provided both a semi-permeable membrane and an anchoring mesh net medium with which to secure the more fragile filtration membrane layer (eelgrass) profile below. Retted coconut fiber is the most resistant to chemical and microbial attack among all natural fibers! Eventually even in an anoxic environment, the eelgrass would deteriorate and decay. Whereas the coconut fibers found, were described as no-worse-for-wear under the sands, when it was raked up by those searchers. Strong tides frequently move volumes of sand back and forth and along any shoreline. The coconut fiber may have been used to affix or cover the top of the filtration system from being washed away as it provided a screen profile locking in some sand above and the eelgrass below.

The *Journal of Natural Fibers,* researched this type of functionality and is published in "Coir Fiber – Process and Opportunities;" saying...

> *"Coir netting with its tensile strength and the friction between coir and soil is appropriate to justify its application for use in slope stability. This would act as reinforcement for the earth fill and will not allow any shear surface to develop during failure. Coir geotextiles can be effectively used as reinforcement materials in soft soil stabilization."*[15a]

Furthermore, products such as "Coir Draining Blankets" are now used to consolidate clayey soils in a variety of sites worldwide.

Coir non-woven geo-textile is one of the materials, used as a horizontal blanket over vertical drains in the application of soil consolidation for geo textile applications.[15b]

Why were those retted husk fibers from the Coconut Palm tree selected for this trip? Of over 2,600 Palm Tree Species, what made this palm and this subgroup, both located so far away, worth the effort? As with all things done by man, it is often the easiest, cheapest, and most familiar that we turn to for our utilization. Here too, those who lived under the Coconut Palm, lived off the Coconut Palm. Those who lived in the Philippine archipelago, enjoyed abaca. Those from other parts of the world knew and exploited the materials around them, such as jute, hemp, sisal, agave, ramie, rattan, and many more. So for our ancient voyagers to have selected the retted husks from the Coconut Palm tree as their fiber of choice, means they had knowledge of its benefits and easy access to it. This question galvanizes the issue of coconut fiber and further refines the answer from *WHERE*.

Courtesy iStock.com

Reviewing our forensic investigation so far, we have deduced:

1) **We know the ^{14}C ages of coconut fiber specimens found on Oak Island. This gives us the chronological window to hone our investigation – 1150-1400 AD.**

2) **We know the geographical limitations with which the Coconut Palm Tree can grow and specifically produce coconuts within latitudinal zones. This is where coconut husks could be available.**

3) **We know coconut fibers on Oak Island were processed through husk retting, making into coir fibers, instead of simple husk debris. Retted coir is not very biodegradable. Use of coir fiber and the knowledge of the retting process should further define our area of interest.**

4) **We know which type of the two coconut sub-group genetic species were used, being the *nui kafa* variety. This tightly restricts the growing area and migration trail to this sub-group.**

5) **We know the volume of coir fiber used in the constructs on Oak Island. This should help identify sources capable of retting and producing that volume of coir fiber used.**

6) **We know how the coir fiber was used on Oak Island. This corresponds to why retted fiber was used and it also validates why these specific fibers were used where they were found. Knowing this helps understand why coir fiber and possibly from where it came.**

Incidental to these determinations but impactful to our search, we add the understanding, based on the science performed, the Money Pit could have been re-filled as long ago as 420+ years, bringing us to a similar date of 1375 AD. Coupled with the known migration history of domesticated red clover, these timelines reinforce that our ancient voyagers might have come from or visited the Iberian Peninsula. Let's move ahead and pick up more pieces of this puzzle.

Finding Foreign Fibers Afloat

As we move forward determining how our ancient voyagers acquired coconut coir fiber for their Oak Island operation, we separate two important aspects of this search at this point.

- *First*, can we identify *WHERE* on the planet this potential product could be acquired; and,
- *Second*, WHEN could it have been acquired from this location.

Later in this appendix we spend significant time examining the world's historical timeline to figure out where to p*in the fibers on the donkey*. However, we can speed up some of that analysis by starting with *"why did someone originally ret a coconut husk*?"

You do not need to ret a coconut husk if you are simply going to burn it as an energy source or use it as fertilizer, like 90% of the world used coconut husks for. You do not need to bother with the husk at all, if your intention is simply to acquire water, milk, honey, vinegar, fermented liquor, cooking oil, oil for candles/lamps, sweet meats, jaggery, or utensils made from the shell. So what is the primary purpose for working 10-12 months to soak, baste, steep, dry, beat, hackle, and separate all this fiber? Rattan, abaca, sisal and other plants produce fiber similarly used for sewing, thatching, lashing, and cordage products as well. Why not bring them along? What is unique about the retted coconut coir fiber that people worked so hard to have it? – *to sail the salt-watered seas!*

Coconut coir becomes almost indestructible from saltwater rot, as retting transforms the organic fiber into stuff which make any seagoing equatorial sailor secure in his vessels rigging and construction. Those retting coconut husks did so with the intent to sew or lash their logs, planks, and outriggers with fibers which can take their crafts out to sea for the challenge and survive.

Most ironically, it is the topic of sailing which links everything together!

We know our fibers arrived on Oak Island by way of oceanic travel. We learned about the creation of our island fiber and its migration throughout the seas of the world. We know ancient island peoples used such fiber to sew and stitch their boats together to expand their worlds. We also know of certain regions of the world who were renowned for their boatbuilding skills, fashioning unique woods with coir ropes, stitching and caulking to build highly desired ocean-going vessels. And we are romantically aware of past sailing ships which incorporated our island fiber into their daily use; *though dunnage be damned*. We have investigated every seaborne trade route for our fibers whereabouts. So it seems pretty clear the sailing vessel itself, will navigate our course to the hidden home of our island fibers. For what other primary endeavor back then, do we find for retted coconut coir fiber? Cordage – *check*. Caulking – *check*. Nets – *check*. Rigging – *check*. Lashing and sewing – *check, check!*

As we enter the ancient world where our ancient voyagers may have sought coir, it seems where the boats are, so floats our fibers. Therefore, let us look for what 'floats our boat,' by checking out the boats which used fiber to float, along the shores of ancient seas.

<u>*The Erythraen Sea*</u>

In the writings of *Periplus of the Erythraen Sea* we learn from an unknown mercantile sojourner who ventured up and down the coasts of East Africa, Saudi Arabia's southern coast, both coasts of India, and many places between them all. The period of the trip was estimated circa 50 AD. The names of locations are archaic at best, with many truly lost to historical records. Yet enough has been decoded in this travel log, to tell the story of coconut coir fiber usage; providing long-ago locations, users, and producers of coir. In this review, the important usage of coconut coir fibers were identified in the building of the boats commonly used. If the peoples of these visited locales had boats which were sewn together using coconut fiber, then the process of making those fibers were inherit within those populations – *or where to find them!* Pertinent excerpts are provided below, with commentary.

> Entry 15: Beyond Opone, "...*There are no wild beasts except the crocodiles; but there they do not attack men. In this place there are sewed boats, and canoes hollowed from single logs, which they use for fishing and catching tortoise. In this island they also catch them in a peculiar way, in wicker baskets, which they fasten across the channel opening between the breakers.*"[16]

This entry covers the travels from approximately present-day Mombasa, Kenya south along the coast past the Zanzibar archipelago on their left, past present-day Dar es Salaam, Tanzania, to Mafia Island, (Island of Menuthias). It is the mention of the "sewed boats" which attract our attention.

> Entry 16: *"Two days' sail beyond, there lies the very last market-town of the continent of Azania [Africa], which is called Rhapta; which has its name from the sewed boats (rhapton ploiarion) already mentioned; in which there is ivory in great quantity, and tortoise shell. Along the coast live men of piratical habits, very great in stature, and under separate chiefs for each place. The Mapharitic chief governs it under some ancient right that subjects it to the sovereignty of the state that has become the first in Arabia. The people of Muza now hold it under his authority, and send thither many large ships, using Arab captains and agents, who are familiar with the natives and intermarry with them, and who know the whole coast and understand the language."*[16]

Firmly in the ancient Swahili empire, the term *rhapton ploiarion* is the name for sewn boats, which in Swahili is *dows* (dhows). Rhapta was southern-most coastal Roman trading post, and mentioned by Diogenes, a seaman on the India Trade Route; and its location is believed to have been recently discovered under the shores of Mafia Island, just off the Tanzanian coast.[17]

> Entry 26: ..."*It was called Eudaemon, because in the early days of the city when the voyage was not yet made from India to Egypt, and when they did not dare to sail from Egypt to the ports across this ocean, but all came together at this place, it received the cargoes from both countries, just as Alexandria now receives the things brought both from*

> *abroad and from Egypt. But not long before our own time Charibael destroyed the place."*[16]

Eudaemon (Arabia Felix), was the southern coastal part of the Arabian peninsula, which includes todays' Yemen, Oman, and United Arab Emirates. It was also known as the Ancient Kingdom of Hadhramaut, the Capitol city was Saba (Sabbatha, later Salalah), which is mentioned later in this journal. The Yemini *Hadhrami people*, as well as Omanis, for centuries went to Beypore, in Kerala, India, to purchase their dhows.[18, 19] This was at a time when good timber (Teak, Black wood, Ebony) was available in the Kerala forests, and the availability of excellent coir rope and skilled shipwrights sheathed planks on dhow hulls sewn together with coir rope. Beypore dhows are known as 'uru' (also uri) in Malayalam, the local language in Kerala.[20] Long-ago settlers from Yemen, known as 'Baramis,' or 'Daramis' which could be derived from the word 'Hardamis,' were once active making uru's/uri's in Kerala.[20]

Across the Gulf of Aden, lies the Horn of Africa, the Cape of Spices, and present day Somalia. This entire area at the time of Periplus, used boats called *Beden*. Bedens were built in three types, 'Beden-seyed' for localized fishing, 'Beden-safar' for trading, and a larger version which were as big as 77 ft. in length and called "uwassiye." This larger Beden became the most common trading and voyaging vessel in the Arabian Sea.[21] All of these were boats sewn together with coconut coir fibers!

> Entry 36: ...*"To Ommana* [Pakistan] *frankincense is also brought from Cana, and from Ommana to Arabia boats sewed together after the fashion of the place; these are known as madarata. From each of these market-towns, there are exported to Barygaza and also to Arabia, many pearls, but inferior to those of India; purple, clothing after the fashion of the place, wine, a great quantity of dates, gold, and slaves."*[16]

Here again we find another coastal boat called "madarata's" constructed by their planks being sewn together. At that time, this technique is commonplace in the coastal town and region near the Iranian border. The Madarata comes from the Arab term "Muddarra'at" which means 'fastened with palm fiber' (Doum Palm & Date Palm).[16, 22]

> Entry 60: *"Among the market-towns of these countries, and the harbors where the ships put in from Damirica and from the north, the most important are, in order as they lie, first Camara, then Poduca, then Sopatma; in which there are ships of the country coasting along the*

> *shore as far as Damirica; and other very large vessels made of single logs bound together, called sangara: but those which make the voyage to Chryse and to the Ganges are called colandia, and are very large. There are imported into these places everything made in Damirica, and the greatest part of what is brought at any time from Egypt comes here, together with most kinds of all the things that are brought from Damirica and of those that are carried through Paralia."*[16]

Both the "Sangara" and the "Colandia" which is larger, are early vessels used by the Chola Dynasty (1st of 3 Tamil Kingdoms of South India). This was one of the longest running dynasties in the world's history.[23] These boats were used for voyages to the Ganges and Chryse. Later, these tied-log rafts were known under various Tamil names of 'kattu-maran' (= tide logs) [*sound familiar*], plus variants such as sangara, shangar, jangar, jangada, shangadam.[24, 25] In East Africa where the stories of the "Turturu of Tanzania" plus the "Thonga" of Mozambique/northeast South Africa, kept tales of sea-going rafts. 'Mozambique' may have resulted from the Indian term of musum-basa (= monsoon boat).[25]

Though *Periplus of The Erythraen Sea* was circa 1st Century AD, we realize sewn boats with palm fibers were used all along the eastern African coast from Mozambique to Eritrea, the coastal ports of the Arabian Sea, around the Gulf of Oman, and along the coast of western and eastern India, including Sri Lanka and most of the island archipelagos. The growing and cultivation of Coconut Palm trees is not the primary factor in our hunt, and they may not in fact inhabit all of those coastal regions. Most villagers of the eastern coastline of Africa sewed their vessels using other palm frond fibers, while specific regions at certain times, used coconut fibers. So as we examine geographical locations and what those existing cultures were sailing during *our timeline*, we also have to examine the types of fibers commonly used and their mercantile and trading history. Shipbuilding by Indian craftsman for customers along the shores of the Indian Ocean, dated back to before the Roman Empire.[26] Communities bought their boats and had no ready supply of coconut fiber, while others used locally produced Date Palm fibers instead. Still other locales may have engaged in retting coconuts only after Indian traders taught them how to maintain those boats with which Indian traders had sold them. Therefore, while looking for boats sewn with coconut fiber, we need to see if these geographically based boaters had a production base for our ancient voyagers to rake up.

Location! Location! Location!

Kenya / Mozambique / Tanzania

Zone One: The Malindi Kingdom of the Bantu-speaking people of the Swahili civilization appear to have been formed around the 9th century AD, and to have grown powerful in the century before Vasco de Gama ushered in Portuguese colonization of the region. From the pinnacle of their society in the 1400's the Malindi Kingdom began to deteriorate after European traders arrived. Territorially, the Malindi Kingdom included Madagascar, Mozambique, Tanzania, and Kenyan coastal zones.[27]

In an illiterate attempt to decipher and supply an abbreviated summary of the book *"From Dugouts to Double Outriggers – Lexical Insights into the Development of Swahili Nautical Technology,"* by Martin Walsh;[28] I will paraphrase the lexicology of the East African coast maritime development as it pertains to sewn boats.

> *"The indigenous innovation in adoption and adaptation of sewn boats is seen during the spectacular expansion of the early Swahili along the eastern African coast and across to its islands in the two hundred years or so following the emergence of Proto-Swahili sometime in the middle of the first millennium CE. This was a critical period in the development of Swahili maritime culture, which took place some centuries before the transition to the "fully maritime way of life" in the early part of the second millennium which archaeologists and historians have written about. As trade developed along coastal Africa the evidence of maritime development can be seen with the lexical evidence of the use of "loanwords" from the Persian Gulf and around the Arabian Sea, especially during the second half of the second millennium and with the era of European expansion. It is during this period when the versatile Swahili word 'dau' becomes the more commonly known word "dhow." This is the time when other Arabic loanwords for various kinds of larger seacraft enter the Swahili lexicon. The Bajuni region or northern Swahili 'mtepe,' the iconic sewn ship of the 19th and 20th centuries, was not the ancient boat it was*

assumed to be, though it included much older design features. The etymological connection of its name to the petioles and possibly other parts of the coconut palm suggest that it was named after some feature of its construction.

The Bantu word 'kyombo' "vessel, tool," and Standard Swahili 'chombo' "vessels" denote vessels, utensils, and watercraft. Another word was Proto-Sabaki 'Wato' "canoe." The general name for a canoe in Swahili 'mtumbwi' is a lexical innovation shared with and presumably borrowed by neighboring Seuta and Ruvu languages. Indeed, dictionary definitions and ethnographic descriptions refer primarily to dugouts made from a single tree trunk and emphasize that the name is never used to denote canoes with outriggers. They can reach more than six meters in length and the most seaworthy ones can be used for trolling as well as line fishing. The Arabic 'hūri' is described as the most common of primitive dug outs used in many parts of the Gulf, the Arabian Sea and the Red Sea and made of mango wood from the Malabar coast and imported from Bombay and Calicut (India) "ready hollowed." This is a loanword that might well have entered Swahili much more recently, along with most lexical transfers from around the Arabian Sea, nautical vocabulary included.

One of the most widely used Swahili names, with different types being named by a change of prefix – like diminutive 'kidau' (plural vidau), – or the addition of a qualifier, such as dau la mataruma, "with ribs," for the commonest kind of plank-built fishing-boat, and dau la msumari, "with nail," for the larger keeled dhows. These are proper sailing-craft which now carry large lateen sails, although this was not always the case: the 'dau la mtepe' carried a square sail of matting, and other kinds of sewn 'dau' might once have done so too. Unlike the 'mtumbwi' and other kinds of dugout canoe, the hull of the Swahili 'dau' is constructed solely of boards/planks and other pieces of cut and carved wood.

This form was probably also the source of the following records from the late 18th century: "In the 1780s, correspondence from the Mozambique captaincy evoked 'dallos' - boat belonging to Swahili merchants. A few French sources also mention local dalles." The earlier history of this name can be deduced from the existence of a cognate term, 'ndau,' recorded in Bajuni, 'Mvita,' and Standard Swahili dictionaries with the meaning "water-bailer," meaning a basket or ladle used to scoop up and dispose of excess water in the holds/bilges of boats and often made of coconut shells. If we reconstruct earlier 'ndalu,' it is apparent that 'ǰdalu' is its augmentative counterpart, and we can hypothesize that the larger vessel derived its name from the smaller one designed to keep it afloat. The use of water-bailers was critical in sewn boats, as different observers remarked about the leaky 'mtepe' observed that "two of the crew bale together, one man standing above the other in the hold, and pass to one another a kind of basket, known as ndao." The name of the bailer – 'ndau' and 'ndao.'

This etymology supports the conjecture that the original 'jdalu' was a sewn boat, surmised from the fact that nail-built boats were given their own name, 'dau la msumari.' It also provides us with an important insight into early Swahili history, suggesting that their spectacular expansion along the coast of eastern Africa was made possible by their ability to make and sail their own relatively sophisticated and robust sewn boats. Furthermore, it is likely the Swahili name was the source of Anglo-Indian "dhow" and the same must go for the series of related names, which include Arabic and Farsi 'dāw' "slave and trading vessel" and Indian counterparts like 'Gujarati ḍāu' and 'Marathi ḍāu,' which likewise appear to be loanwords. Much has been made in the literature of the sewn boats which survived into the twentieth century and are called 'mtepe' (plural mitepe) and described as a "sewn boat of up to 30 tons, double ended and with upright mast, hoisting a square matting sail." Some late examples were much larger than this, while a smaller, modified version known as the 'dau la mtepe' was also built. Ever since the mtepe was described as the "lineal descendant" of the sewn boats of Rhapta, researchers have waxed on.

Like most sewn boats in the Indian Ocean, the Bajuni 'mutepe' was sewn with coir, cord made from the fibre of the outer husk of coconuts. Crushed strips of coconut husk were also used to caulk the 'mutepe,' together with dried strips of the leafstalk of the Doum Palm (Hyphaene thebaica). Was cord made from the fibrous petioles of the Coconut Palm, "itepe," also used in the sewing or caulking of the mutepe? Was it used in some other way? Or was there a quite different connection between Coconut Palm petioles and the Bajuni boat? Interestingly, the association with coconut leaves is also present in Comorian cognates of mutepe: "Ngazidja mtseve," meaning - Coconut Palm leaves erected to make tight partitions, "Ndzuani mtseve," meaning - Coconut leaf with two rows of leaflets braided together on one side, and "Maore mutseve," meaning - Coconut leaf braided in a chevron, for making prayer mats and baskets." These definitions suggest the possibility that mutepe might originally have referred to an auxiliary structure such as a boat cabin, with its roof of matting and coconut leaf thatch.

It would be reasonable to assume that, in addition to dugout canoes 'mutumbwi' and sewn boats 'jdalu,' the early Swahili were also familiar with simpler watercraft, such as rafts. The sewing itself is quite different from the lashed-lug technique of traditional Austronesian boat construction. The cord used in Southeast Asian boatbuilding was also distinct. It was usually made from the fiber of the Kaong Palm (Arenga pinnata), called 'ijuk' in Malay. This is found in large handfuls about the bases of the petioles, though not of this palm only. When ijuk was not available, other plant fibers were used, including rattan fiber, which comes from the stems of different genera of climbing palms, but is not as strong as Sugar Palm fiber. While most of the sources refer to the Swahili 'sapa'/'shapa' as a raft made of logs, also describes its construction from the branches of the Raffia Palm (Raphia farinifera). As noted, there are similar boat names which are much older. The oldest of these is the Red Sea 'jalba' (plural jilāb or jalbāt), a sewn boat seen by Ibn Jubayr at the Red Sea port of Aydhab in 1183. [28, 29]

Also, see Malindi craft kamba ya miguu' meaning - "rope lashing, joining the outrigger boom to the connective," literally "cord of the legs." The cord or rope was properly twisted coir. From Arabic kanbār 'coir' + mguu 'leg'."[28]

When Vasco de Gama arrived in Malindi in April 1498, coconut coir fiber for maritime purposes was used along the coast.[4] So much so, de Gama had his ships re-rigged and re-caulked with coir fiber cordage and products during this trip. So perhaps it was the coast of East Africa which brought retted coconut coir fiber to the attention of Portugal when he returned to Lisbon in 1502.

Madagascar / Seychelles Islands

Zone Two: The ruins of fortifications built by Arab traders as far back as the 9th century underscore Madagascar's historical role as a destination for travelers from the Middle East, Asia, and Africa.[27] Islanders today use a single-tree trunk canoe in Madagascar called '*Lakanas*' (Malagasy). With outriggers, they are historically known as '*Piraga/o*' = French, or '*waka*' = proto-Malaya Polynesian.[30] In ancient times their dugout canoe of a single tree were known as '*mutumbwi*' and sewn boats as '*jdalu*.' Eventually this will be known as the frontrunner of the '*dhow.*'[28]

No sewing of coir, just lashing with Doum Palm fibers. Nor is there a history of coconut export or even regional trade in coconut by-products. Madagascar was once covered almost completely by forests, but the practice of 'slash-and-burn' to clear the land for dry rice cultivation has denuded most of the landscape, especially in the central highlands. Wood and charcoal from the forests are used to meet 80 percent of domestic fuel needs. Yet Madagascar represents an exception to the migration routes of coconut groups. Researchers find in Madagascar and the Comoros Islands just north, had a mixture of both the Indian Ocean type and the Pacific Ocean types (***nui kafa***, ***nui vai***) sub-groups.[4, 11, 13] Yet the mixture was not present in the Seychelles Islands just some six hundred miles northeast and outside of normal trading routes of the time.[11]

The Seychelles were home to Coco raisins (*perhaps Coker nuts*); nuts small and spherical, "resembling grapes." Therefore, they argue the Pacific Ocean basin sub-group was brought to Madagascar several thousand years earlier by ancient Austronesians originally there to establish trade routes with coastal East Africa from Southeast Asia.[11] This is supported by recent studies of rice varieties found cultivating in Madagascar. Both *japonica* (Southeast Asia) and *indica* (India) rice varieties there, reflect the mixing of horticulture.[26, 28] Finally, through DNA testing of the populace, the descendants of the people (ancient Austronesians) who brought both the coconuts and rice, are still living in Madagascar (Olsen).

Comoros Islands

Zone Two: The early occupation of the Comoros Islands is also generally dated to the 8th century, although it might have begun before. It is not entirely clear who the first occupants were. However, the strong archaeological signature of Southeast Asian crops suggests that Austronesians, possibly early Malagasy speakers, were there from the start (N. Boivin and A. Crowther 2018). There is no record of coir fiber being used to lash or construct boats. During our period of interest, trading in perfumes and slavery was big in the Comoros islands.[31]

Somalia / Djibouti / Eritrea

Zone One: Known as the Horn of Africa, this region is also known as the land of Punt, which then became the Kingdom of Aksum between 100-940 AD. Finally it was known as "Land of Barbaria." What it also is, is the home to the '*beden*,' a coconut coir sewn vessel, used throughout the Horn of Africa.[21]

Though technically in **Zone One,** this region of the eastern Coast of Africa, should have been a Coconut Palm delight. Unfortunately, unique weather patterns forbade it from happening. Eastern ports such as Cape Elephant (Cape Guardafui) and the city-states of Malao, Mosylium, Pano and Opone, suffered not having a beneficial growing climate due to the phenomena of a strong upwelling within the deep cold waters at their shores.[16, 32, 33] Additionally as the winds blew parallel to the coast, there was no high humidity pockets for the Coconut Palm to support growth as the colder waters cooled the air.[33] Therefore, the eastern coastline of this part of Africa receive less than 2" of rain fall annually.[32] On the northern coast of the Horn of Africa, monsoonal rains lose their moisture as they sweep from south to north across the interior of the Horn (Somaliland) before reaching the trading ports of Berbera, Djibouti, and Port Zeila.[32] Temperatures were extremely hot with little vegetation growing outside the shelter of the coastal strips where Date Palm populations overlook the shores of the Gulf of Aden.

So why all the vibrant trade which funded all of those kingdoms, dynasties, and Sultanates? Arabic and Muslim traders had learned long ago to "manage" the trade routes between the providers like India, China and the island archipelagos east of Java; by separating them from the end-users like the Romans, Greeks, Phoenicians, and other European and Mediterranean cultures. They injected themselves as middlemen, by actually restricting Chinese and Indian merchants and traders from sailing on to those customers.[16, 21, 34] The trading ports of Berbera, Djibouti, Zeila, Hormuz, Aden, and Opone, Mosylium, Malao and Pano were the end-of-the-line for the commerce going to Alexandria and beyond; and were the access points for camel-borne caravans bringing goods, metals, and slaves from the interior of the continent. In so doing, those city states, market controllers, and other middlemen would take hefty fees, taxes, and profits before allowing the goods to be sent on caravans to the Nile River Basin or headed up the Red Sea to Alexandria or through the Persian Gulf. This ploy was so effective, Roman archivist and writers named the Horn of Africa as the Cape of Spices, and thought it was the land where their cinnamon and other desired spices grew. As further stated.[21, 35]

> *"In the land of the African horn, washed by the salty water of Red sea and Indian ocean, there is an ancient civilization of traders, history of which could be traced up to the trade with an Ancient Egypt. It was the important trade partner of the Roman Empire and the source of*

> *cinnamon in there, gaining the name Regio Cinnamonifora. It didn't grow it though but sold cinnamon from India to the Mediterranean lands. At a certain time this civilization controlled the African Horn and the local trade."*[35]

Then again, perhaps the Romans understood but could not penetrate or interrupt this control of mercantile trade from the east. Procopius writes,

> *"Emperor Justinian had hoped via these routes to replace the Persians as intermediaries for the trade of silk from the east with his Aksumite allies, but it proved "impossible for the Ethiopians to buy silk from the Indians, for the Persian merchants always locate themselves at the very harbours where the Indian ships first put in (since they inhabit the adjoining country) and are accustomed to buy the whole cargoes."*[36]

Yet the cinnamon was from India, Ceylon, and ports east. Once the Portuguese arrived on scene and successfully took over these regions, those ancient trade routes were vulnerable and lost their profitability. This caused many of those commercial city-states to dry up and wither away. British explorer Richard Burton also fell for the con when he wrote;

> *"In the first place, Berberah is the true key of the Red Sea, the centre of East African traffic, and the only safe place for shipping upon the western Erythraean shore, from Suez to Guardafui. Backed by lands capable of cultivation, and by hills covered with pine and other valuable trees, enjoying a comparatively temperate climate, with a regular although thin monsoon, this harbour has been coveted by many a foreign conqueror. Circumstances have thrown it as it were into our arms, and, if we refuse the chance, another and a rival nation will not be so blind."*[34, 37, 38]

What about those 'Bedens' you ask? As Australasians, Tamils, and other cultures first set up these trading corridors, the receiving kingdoms and ports allowed businesses and shipwrights to maintain and repair those vessels which arrived with wares to trade. The Indian vessels were such a maritime improvement, those boats would become a lucrative export by Indian traders and shipwrights of their own accord. Therefore, the sewn and latched plank shipbuilding technology spread and was adopted with some of these trading port locations. In some cases this improved maritime technology stuck, and in the following location became their way of life as well.

Yemen / Oman

Zone Two: Coconuts were cultivated in Yemen's Al Mahrah and Hadramaut governorates and in Omani governates of Dhofar and the Sultanate of Oman.[4, 13] This land area is the eastern coastal shore of the Arabian Peninsula; from the end of the Red Sea, across the length of the Arabian Sea to the Strait of Hormuz in the Gulf of Oman. Since ancient times, this region of Oman and Hadramaut had longtime *dhow* trade relations with Burma, Malaysia, Indonesia, East Africa, and Zanzibar, as well as southern India and China.[4] The ancient coconut groves of Dhofar were mentioned by the medieval Moroccan traveler Ibn Battuta in his writings, known as *Al Rihla*.[13, 39] The annual rainy season known locally as Khareef, or monsoon, made Coconut Palm cultivation possible in this part of the Arabian east coast.[4] Coconut Palms only survived along the low-lying coastal shore where high saltwater humidity was boxed-in below the higher cliffs and escarpments of the interior. This humidity could keep them alive in combination with the rains of the Khareef and the necessary agronomy employed to attend to their upkeep and production. Yet coconuts were not cultivated in other environmentally suitable areas along this part of the Arabian Peninsula. The drought resistant Coconut Palm variety grown in these regions over the centuries, was the West Coast Tall (WCT) from India.[4] This is the wild, 'football-shaped,' thick-husked coconut which was the preferred coconut sub-group ***nui kafa*** which we have talked so much about. These other regions, kingdoms, or sultanates did not embrace the initial cultivation needed to support the Coconut Palm, supplying the raw materials for those type vessels; and built boats using other methods and materiel.

The singular coconut-producing area in the Middle East today, is the southernmost Dhofar region of Oman, bordering along Yemen which we just discussed.[13] Technically, Coconut Palms could be grown with initial cultivation in most places along the Persian Gulf, Arabian Sea, and Red Sea coasts, as these seas are tropical and supply enough humidity (through seawater evaporation) for coconut trees to grow.[4, 13] Salalah, where Taqah is located (in the Dhofar area), maintained large coconut plantations of the sub-group ***nui kafa***, similar to those found across the Arabian Sea in Kerala, India.[4, 13] Omani fishermen and traders needed the coir rope from the coconut fiber to stitch together their traditional high seas-going dhow vessels , which nails were never used.[4] The 'know how' of coconut cultivation and necessary soil fixation and irrigation is thought to have found its way into Omani, Hadrami, and Al-Mahrah culture by

Indian and local traders who returned from those overseas areas.[4, 13] Other ancient Omani boats sewn with coconut coir fiber, include the '*kambari*,' which is a more primitive boat used for lightering and for sardine fishing. It was entirely constructed by stitching coir fibers. The word kambari, derives from the Jabbali word for coconut fiber cordage, *kambar*. This name is regional, with '*kambari*' appearing to be the preferred name east of Mirbat (east of Taqah), while west of Mirbat the generic term '*sambuk*' is used. Unlike teak-built boats in most of Oman, the '*kambari*' is planked with mango wood. Its design is related to boats on the Somali coast called '*beden*' which are not related to the boats called '*badan*' in the Batinah coastal area of Oman (Vosmer).[28]

Hormuz (Ormus) / Julfar / Iran

Zone Three: The land on both sides of the Persian Gulf does have the humidity factor but is outside the needed growing zone for the Coconut Palm to grow and germinate nuts without much effort. Today, northern sections of Oman, UAE and countries of the Persian Gulf, grow non-native dwarf Coconut Palm cultivars imported from Florida, for decorative purposes only.[4] They provide the appearance of a tropical oasis without providing any coconuts. Furthermore, the coastline in the Persian Gulf has few port or anchorage places which would add protection to any *Cocos nucifera* interested in making a go at it. This is why when talking about palms in this area, we talk Date Palms. Julfar, found to be the original commercial center of ancient Kush, has a written record of being the most famed and prosperous trading town in the lower gulf. And it was home to the fertile Date Palm gardens of Shimal. **(x)** Yet since 700 BC. Indian traders have come to the port centers of Hormuz and Julfar.[36, 40] Both ports are located on the southern shore of the Persian Gulf, and on the western side of the Musandam Peninsula, located between the Persian Gulf and the Gulf of Oman. The skill of building or repairing boats using coir fiber is still practiced in this region today, but has primarily been replaced with modern shipwright technology, materials, and craftsmanship.

Another limiting factor to Coconut Palm tree agronomy in much of the Middle East's hot, dry climate, was that just such a climate favored the development of coconut mites. The mite causes immature seed dropping and can cause brownish-gray discoloration on the coconut's outer green fiber.[4, 13, 41]

Kuwait/Iraq

Zone Three: As you have read, boats fashioned this far up the Persian Gulf did not use the Coconut Palm tree and likely had no such source of those particular palms byproducts, as the dry climate was inhospitable to the *Cocos nucifera*. Also, as the Arabic and Muslim traders would not allow vessels from India and China to venture past the two ports mentioned above, there was no need for boat repair using coir fiber. However they did sail the *'huwayriyah,'* a reed-type craft used by Awazim fisherman. It was made from Date Palm boughs and bamboo lashed together from rope made by beaten-out Date Palm fruit stalks. Other reed and bundled-grass type craft were prevalent all along the Persian Gulf. As we look throughout the region, fishing boats and the means to "tie them together," were primarily based on the organic flora of the area. No local vessels sewn with coco coir here.

Indian States of Gujarat / Maharashtra & Connection to Land Trade

Zone Three: This region of India, Pakistan, and today's Iran, was home to an important trade route known as the 3rd Eurasian Land Bridge. This silk road commerce moved merchandise from Shenzhen to Rotterdam.[42, 43] Venetian traveler and merchant Marco Polo mentioned how goods were taken from Cambay (then Barygaza) in India to Aden (Yemen), and then 'those that go to Aden are carried thence to Alexandria (Egypt)'.[43] This allowed goods to be traded throughout most of the known world, from North Western Europe (South England, France, and Germany) to South East Asia (Sumatra, West Java, Malaysia, and Borneo and back).[43]
See the map below.

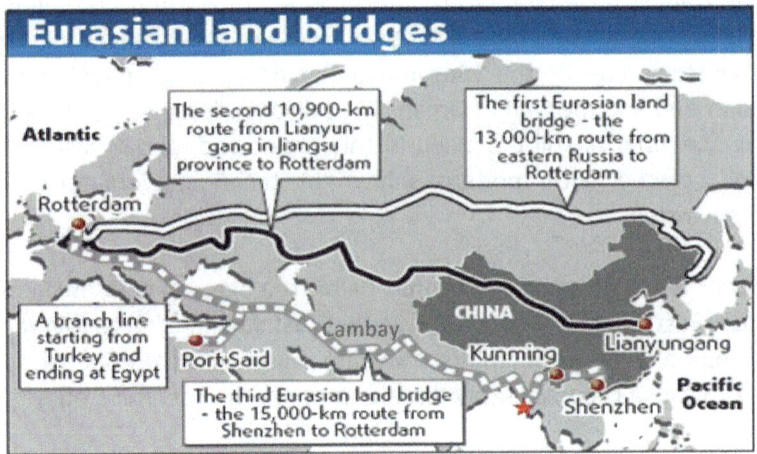

Graphic: Courtesy of Tian Chi.

This northwestern region of India and westward around the Arabian Sea was not a coconut producing region due to the weather and the prevailing winds.[13] Hot & dry, semi-arid and tropical dry, describes most of the landmass, even along the coastal regions of this area.[44, 45] This does not discount the use of boats sewn together with coconut fiber, but they would have been bought from or used by, boat builders further south along the Indian coast. Reed boats were plentiful for local commerce along the coast moving west toward Iran. Whether or not the trade route transported coconuts or more specifically, coir fiber as a cargo of trade, is highly doubtful.

The Mongol defeat of China in 1270 opened up and expanded trade with the west, which Genghis Khan supported.[43] This enabled the use of those land routes through southern Russia to West Asia, which had previously been too dangerous for regular trade caravans before the invasion. Under the Song dynasty, the Han Chinese were not allowed to leave the borders to engage in trade.[43] Europe became involved in the world economic system relatively late after the end of the Dark Ages, when trade was already well-established in the Middle East and Indian Ocean. Europe was only connected to the trade network through its contacts in the Mediterranean trading circle, which stretched from Genoa (North Italy) in the west to Cairo in the south-east and Caffa (on the Black Sea) in the north-east.[43] All three were large trading centers. Rotterdam was also a key link in the trade network, shown in the 3rd Eurasian Land Bridge on the previous page. This area was a busy trading area with trading caravans and ships coming and going from oasis in the desert and ports on the ocean; trading goods from China, India, Malaysia, Borneo, Arabia, Mongolia, the Mediterranean, Africa, and Europe.[43]

Land-based Trade Centers

Two of the three land-based trade routes culminated in ports where Venetian and Dutch merchants controlled the majority of the flow of commerce coming from the east.[43] However, in 1453 AD the Ottoman Turks captured Constantinople and created problems for European merchants by blocking the land route which passes through Afghanistan.[43] It also meant heavy taxation for merchant cargo passing from the Black Sea through Ottoman-controlled Constantinople, into the Aegean Sea and onto Venice and Genoa.[43] Additionally, the other Trade routes to India were problematic due to the Arab conquests in the 8th Century AD, and from the litany of Crusader wars plaguing the Levant region.[43] Suddenly every camel stop had a tax collector or another "middleman" requiring payoffs to let the payload pass. To add danger and violence to bulk carriage of coconut coir fiber, hoofing it along through some distant dusty dynasty; Chinese and Moghul Empires continued fighting on their turf too.

Warfare in the Middle East in the early 15-16th centuries made the land-leg of the silk trade just as dangerous.[43] Long-established Islamic routes which stretched from Middle Eastern cities like Cairo, Bagdad, Damascus across the Indian Ocean to India and beyond into South East Asia, were still functioning. Yet for European merchants, traders, and buyers, they had become more expensive and more problematic.

So technically, coconut coir fiber was a product possible to obtain through these historical trade routes. This collection of warring and weathering events resulted in Europe searching for new sea routes to India & China; bypassing all the drama afflicting their profitability.

But do we really envision a long and lengthy camel caravan of coconuts – *some 18,089 coconuts in fact!*

Whether using Dromedary camels in the Middle East or Bactrian camels in Central Asia, you are talking about a 229-camel caravan carrying over 20 metric tons of coconuts![46] Whereas, If the husks had been retted, the load of 1.5 metric tons of coir fiber would only take a caboose of 17 camels. This would still be an expensive operation replacing high-value silks, rugs, finished metals cargo, etc., for a product not worth much and considered as bedding for the camels.

As we recall, the fourth access Europe had with Afro-Eurasia commerce consisted of trade through sea routes via the Arabian Sea, the Persian Gulf, and the Red Sea. This route would lead traders to the best sources of coconut fiber our ancient voyagers could have found – *The Indian Ocean Basin*. So let's return to those places where coconuts, coir fiber sewn boats, and trade were combined.

Lakshadweep Archipelago

Zone One: Looking for isolation? How about 2-400 kilometers from the Indian mainland and southwest of Sri Lanka but spread out over 90,000 kilometers.[47] You too can live on one of 26 atolls, the remnants of a vast submerged mountain range in the Indian Ocean known as the Chagos-Laccadive Ridge.[48, 49] The other islands of the Maldivian Archipelago are lumped together with the Chagos Archipelago to become known as the Lakshadweep Archipelago;[48] and for this discussion it translates as *"1,000 islands."* I've also read it was *"100,000 islands!"*[47] Others report say it is less than 200 spits of sand which make up all these archipelagos. Regardless, this book is too long and I am not getting into that issue as well. But don't worry about nose bleeds as this bevy of mountain tops has an average ground-level elevation of 1.5 meters above sea level. The highest natural point is only 5.1 meters. It is the world's lowest-lying country.[50, 51] Climbing a ***nui kafa*** coconut palm will put you at a dizzying five times above the highest point of land!

We are discussing the Maldives, Laccadives, Aminidivi, Minicoy and Chagos Island groups – *are you keeping your islands organized?*

Jataka stories has mentioned these islands as They document the spread of Buddhism during 6th century BC. Islander stories suggest the arrival of Islam in 661 AD by Arabian merchants. Later, Cholas ruled the islands in 11th century, Portuguese in 16th century, Ali Rajahs in 17th century, Tipu Sultan in 18th century, and finally it was under British Raj control in the 19th century.[39]

Arab traveler *Ibn Batuta* talked about these islands in many of his stories. In 1030 AD, Al-Biruni (973-1048) divided the whole group of archipelago islands into the *'Diva Kuzah'* or Cowrie Islands (Maldives), and the *'Diva Kanbar'* or Coir Islands (Laccadives).[51, 52, 53] In so doing, the islanders settled on the name *'Lakshadweep'* or "One Thousand" ***or*** "One Hundred Thousand Isles" – *depending on which Coconut Palm tree you climb.*

The Moplas/Mappilla people (inhabitants of Maldives, Laccadives, Minicoy, and Amindivi islands) populate this Lakshadweep Archipelago spread throughout the Indian Ocean off the southwestern coast of India.[49, 54] Malayalam is the state language of Kerala, India and is the primary language spoken within the islands.[49, 54] Its written script has been significantly influenced by Arabic. The people of the islands migrated from the Kerala coast (Malabar) around the seventh century.[54] They came as Hindus, but later converted to Islam. Creating the Muslim communities from the union of Arab visitors and native women.[54] The Moplas/Mappilla were known for their remarkable shipbuilding and craftsmanship. *I can understand why!* Their ships, including the hulls, masts, ropes, stitches, sails, and other parts built entirely using different parts of the *Cocos nucifera* and coco-based materials.[53, 54] This too would be expected as there was no history of any indigenous forest in the entire archipelago region, at that time.[49] The Coconut Palms in Lakshadweep have been described by earlier researchers as mainly belonging to ***niu kafa*** subgroup type. [4, 39, 55, 56, 57]

The combined Lakshadweep archipelago was covered with these coconut trees. They, and cowry shells became the basis of island economies of the past.[49, 58] Today, those ***nui kafa*** Coconut Palms supply coir and copra which generates the main industry in the islands today.[49, 53, 59] Vinegar is also derived from coconut tree sap and is sold to the mainland. Breadfruit (an evergreen timber tree with edible fruits) runs a distant second to coconut in economic importance. Other foods that were raised include papayas, plantains (banana-like fruits), yams, sweet potatoes, maize, and beans.[54]

Though the French established coconut plantations in 1793 with slave labor,[60] It is more likely here in these *'1,000's of islands,'* that multiple types of coconut intermixed with island varieties and created hybrids of many unique Coconut Palms today.[4, 57, 61, 62, 63] Examples include the Laccadive Ordinary (LCT) which produce 127 small nuts a year per tree, and Laccadive Micro (LMT) producing 160+ very small coconuts per tree per year. These introduced hybrid variations have made it difficult to know which nut came here first.[39]

Courtesy iStock.com

Since most of the produced coir fiber from Lakshadweep island communities is boated back to Kerala for sale and included in export along with Keralan fiber, these sources of coir are tethered to Kerala, India as a single fiber source.

This previous image depicts individual islanders bringing their coir fiber production to the Island Monegar (leader), for his valuation of their fiber, and seeking inclusion for transport to the mainland for export sale.[64, 65]

Sri Lanka

Zone One: Known as *Lanka*, *Lankaderpa*, *Taprobane*, *Serendib*, and *Ceylon* - Sri Lankan history has early mention of the planting of coconuts discussed in the "*Mahavamsa*" during the reign of Agrabodhi II, around 589 AD.[39, 63] It is a large island off the south/southeastern-most tip of India and is separated by the Palk Strait. Almost 270 miles long and approaching 140 miles wide, the distinctive Sri Lankan civilization can be traced back to early 6th century BC.[66] Sri Lanka is home to "Theravada Buddhism," which has its literary traditions in the Pali language.[66] Hinduism and Islam have also shaped the history of this society.[66] It is also home to a sophisticated irrigation system which was created over 2,000 years ago for the drier parts of the island.[67]

Ceylon was also thought to be the ancient port of Tarshish (Thar Shih) of 'Ophir,' where King Solomon is said to have drawn ivory, peacocks, and other valuables.[68]

Ceylon was a major international trading center in gems, pearls, rice, elephants, jaggery from Date Palm, and cinnamon.[69] In 1400 BC, Ceylon was the worlds' largest exporter of cinnamon to Egypt and later, in 200 AD to the Roman Emperor Aurelian.[69] Merchant ships came from Middle East, Persia, Burma, China, Thailand, Malaysia, Indonesia, and Southeast Asia. The Moors dominated trade in both Sri Lanka and south India during the period of the Polonnaruwa Kings up through the early 1500's, with the advent of the Portuguese discovery.[66, 69] Yet through these mercantile periods, coconuts were a locally consumed product, primarily for the making tuba and of arrack, fermented drinks made from the sap of the *Cocos nucifera*.[70] Early Sinhalese kingdoms in Ceylon were Hindu enclaves and Hinduism is still practiced there today. The Coconut Palm and its nut were religiously so significant that the Hindus neither cut this tree nor do they use its wood for fuel. [39]

Sri Lankans did not produce coconut coir fiber as an export by-product until the arrival of Dutch control in the 1840's.[70] At that time, Dutch traders exported 2,380 tons of coir annually, for factories in Europe.[70]

This exportation ended as it became impractical to ship coconut coir fiber due to the high transportation costs involved (spontaneous fire hazard).[71] Europeans simply built factories in India and Ceylon to take advantage of the low labor costs and safely shipped final product from there. By 1861, Ceylon was populated with 20 million coconut palms in plantations; 5 million cultivated to produce toddy, 11.5 million to harvest 460 million nuts, and the remaining 3.5 million for other purposes.[4]

Yet more importantly, the primary indigenous sub-group of coconut palm tree on Sri Lanka, was the ***niu vai*** type. Known as *Rath Thembili*, the "King Coconut" was a semi-dwarf (shorter tree) which yielded a nut with much more liquid and remarkably sweeter due to higher sucrose content.[12, 13] Due to the carotenoid compounds in the King Coconut, it has a bright orange or brilliant yellow exocarp and has the familiar ***niu vai*** "basketball" shape.[12] Though Sri Lanka has had a strong involvement in coir production during Dutch control, it later became a second or third level by-product as the Island emphasized more export on milk, sap, copra, water and oil exports. The King Coconut ***niu vai*** variety was ripe for those markets and still is today.

Plant evolutionary biologists have been refining the grouping, sub-grouping, and genotypes of the *Cocos nucifera* in Sri Lanka since 1898, and as such, variations have become better understood, but more confusing. In 1958, The Coconut Research Institute of Ceylon, clarified the types of Coconut Palm trees on the island. They organized the cultivars of coconut types into three varieties; *"Variety typica," "Variety nana,"* and *"Variety aurantiaca."*[12] These three varieties come in a total of 13 forms. *Variety typica* has 8 forms, and primarily is our classic tall plantation coconut palm, producing the fibrous oblong (football shaped) coconut husk. The *Variety nana* has three forms and represent most island dwarf genotypes. The short trees produce a wide variation in exocarp coloration and endocarp consistency and flavor. They are the least hardy and have heritage in Philippines, Fiji Island, Vietnam, and Malaya. Finally, the native *Variety aurantiaca* has 2 forms and grow on mid-sized stems. The two forms are the *"King Coconut"* and the *"navasi-thembili."* The latter is of no commercial value as the water is insipid and the husk is thin and soft.[12]

The King Coconut on the other hand is the primary commercialized coco on the island due to its water flavor and volume today. What this shows is Sri Lanka would not have been our hotbed of coconut coir manufacturing during the time our ancient voyagers were seeking their fill of fiber. The island, regardless of what you called it when voyagers were visualizing their variety of materiel, would have found few ***nui kafa*** coconuts for harvesting. Nor would the indigenous Hindu population have treated the Coconut Palm tree for exploitation. The island did have both forests and Bambusa bamboo for which to build mighty vessels. So again, we find other products, like jute and bamboo, readily available which depressed coconut coir fiber assimilation into their constantly divided and bickering society.

Indian States of Kerala/Tamil Nadu/Karnataka

Zone One: The southwest coast of the Indian continent has had many names and different kingdom associations throughout history.[72a] I list here names of cities, ports, forts, and kingdoms which have been historically associated with the coconut coir harvesting from the land of Kerala, India. This incorporates the changing names of regions within the current Indian states of Kerala, Tamil Nadu, and Karnataka. All were at one time or another part of the Malabar coast.[72a] Much of what you have read from ancient history makes little sense when you haven't a clue where we are talking about. So with that in mind, take notes because the names through history get quite confusing.

When you think of coconut coir fiber from ***Kerala***, you are talking about the location recorded as: *Alleppey, Barace, Calicut, Cannanore, Cochin, Cranganore, Goa, Kannur, Kochi, Kollam, Kozhikode, Laccadives, Limyrike, Maldives, Male, Malayalam, Mangalore, Muziris, Naura, Nelcynda, biblical Ophir, Pallipuram, Pattanam, Ponani, Quilon, South Canara, Tanur, Tellicherry, Travancore, Tyndis, Venad, and all versions of Malabar*, to mention a few.[72, 72a, 73] Now add in the names of the archipelagos and you have a winning Scrabble list!

The people of South India were familiar with the coconut from antiquity and early Tamil (Sangam literature) has many references to it. The earliest of these poems, "*Tholkappiyam*" written by Tholkappier during 200 BC, refers to crop rotation and intercrops of ginger and turmeric for coconut and jackfruit plantations.[39] Remember our earlier discussion in other parts of this book, where we wondered if Samuel Ball planted red clover amongst his cabbage plants to add nitrogen to the soil and keep away harmful cabbage insects? That technique is called "*companion planting*" and is exactly what they were doing with planting ginger and turmeric amongst the coconut and jackfruit orchards! So roughly 2,000 years after planters tended to their coconut palm fields, a freed slave farmer may have relearned that ancient lesson in agronomy. You can see why reading about history is really reading about what mistakes man has already made and learning from them. Here is another reference representing the earliest of coconut comments from the Later Sangam (100 BC – 400 AD) literature.[72a, 74] *And moving on…*

Sandwiched between the Western Ghats mountains on the east and the Arabian Sea on the west, Kerala (also known as Malabar and Calicut) is one of the most beautiful States in India. A tropical paradise of waving coconut palms and wide sandy beaches, this strip of coastal territory slopes down from the Mountain Ghats in a cascade of lush green vegetation and varied forests.[72a] Primarily a lagoonal riverine estuary made up of backwater lakes, interconnected canals, and islets, the *Cocos nucifera* was almost the sole flora of the 900 kilometers of this Indian-style everglades.[74] It is the most commonly seen tropical tree in Kerala. In fact, even the name Kerala (Kerlam in Malayalam) is derived from this tree ('Kera' in Malayalam language means Coconut and 'Alam' means Land, so *Keralam* = Land of Coconut).[75, 39] Every aspect of Kerala's culture is evolved around the Coconut tree.[39, 75]

One can understand perhaps where ancient people discovered retting was a natural process. As the nuts ripened and fell from the palm tree forest, they rolled into the scads of ponds, pools, or lagoons - which make up this monsoonal landscape. Soon the fermenting nuts would have been bobbing and basting everywhere. People would find them in various stages of organic fermentation, finding these "dissolved husks" hairier than before. It would not take long for people to understand the benefits and use of these wet wasting husks.

In the upper elevations along the Ghats mountains were the exotic forests of Teakwood, Blackwood (Rosewood), Sandalwood, benteak and ebony wood.[23, 26] Today the various landscapes are known as the *Malabar Coast Forest* up to 250m elevation, then the *Nilgiri Hills Forest* from 250-1,000m, followed by the *Kerala Tamil Rain Forest* reaching elevations as high as 2,695m.[76] The combination of Teak wood and ample supply of retted coconut coir fiber generated the regions history of boatbuilding.

Little has changed in Kerala. Ropes and cordage made out of coconut fiber have been in use from ancient times. Indian navigators, who sailed the seas to Malaya, Java, China and to the Gulf of Arabia and East Africa centuries ago, had been using coir as their ship's cordage. Arab writers of the 11th Century referred to the extensive use of coir as ship's cables, stitching, fenders, and for rigging.[77] Today, this is the traditional area of coconut cultivation in India. Coconuts are big business in India and these Indian states represent the majority of the business: Kerala (45%), Tamil Nadu (27%), Karnataka (11%), Goa (8%), (larger Malabar area) and their represented percentage of coconut cultivation.[4] Here, which has the largest number of coconut trees, is famous for its coconut-based industries. Based on certain climatic and edaphic conditions, Kerala cultivates 95% of ***nui kafa*** sub-group *Cocos nucifera* trees.[78] These palms are specifically identified as the cultivar *West Coast Talls* (WCT). To confuse any sober reader, the WCT are further branded like wineries and vineyard locations. The nuts produced from WCT's within Kerala are known by the localities of their harvest, such as: *Annur*, *Bedakam*, *Kuttiyadi*, *Attingal*, and *Kanjira Pally*; and are therefore so named. We opted to not go that far in our identification of those Oak Island coconut fibers. *Perhaps next time!*

For those of you who do not want to read any more historical reasoning on *why not* coconut coir fiber could have been found in the Pacific Ocean basin or the Atlantic Ocean basin or the Caribbean Sea, we will conclude and announce our selection of where Oak Island coconut coir fiber originated. Doubters and naysayers should read on to fully understand why neither Spanish Galleons nor plundering pirates were the source of all that coconut coir fiber.

Of the three primary sources mentioned above, Ceylon (Sri Lanka) did not start an export level production of coir until the arrival of the Dutch in the latter-1800's. This venue for coir would postdate our time of interest. Even though Ceylon was the kingdom which initially introduced the benefits of husk byproducts to Indian

Kingdoms of the Malabar region and is today one of the primary sources of high quality processed coconut coir, Sri Lankans were neither producers nor providers of coconut coir fiber while our ancient voyagers were Googling for suppliers.

The Lakshadweep Archipelago including all "100,000 islands," was really an offshoot of the Keralan (Mappila Muslims) people and their wider trading activities. Lakshadweep was inclusive of the Maldives, Laccadives, Aminidivi, Minicoy, and Chagos Island groups, their sultanates, kingdoms and adherents.

Those island communities which were small and widely scattered, were tied to commercial operations out of Kerala and later, those operations in Alleppey and along the Malabar Coast. The French made a forceful effort to set up a coir factory during their colonialization attempts. The "amalgamation" of these distant archipelagos was directly due to French attempts to colonize and commercialize Lakshadweep coir producing potential. Even though Laccadive or Maldivian coconut coir is often talked up as superior to mainland quality coir, their products were combined – *intertwined even*, into the mats, rugs, ropes, brooms, brushes, and 'twine' sold to Europe, Africa, and the east from Kerala, India.

At the time of the death of our coconut coir fiber specimens which have been radiocarbon dated, the greater Lakshadweep island area was never organized, developed, or formed the cooperative necessary to provide 18,000 retted coconut husks on demand. Though this production capability changed with Portuguese, French, and Dutch colonization attempts, the acquisition of such volumetrics required coir customers to shop in Cannanore (Kerala).

Amongst the other regions of Oceana, those familiar with *Cocos nucifera* enjoyed it for other life-sustaining benefits or prospered commercially from other byproducts. This did not include retting the coconut husk. Some regions of China and Oceana – including parts of the Philippine Archipelago, and parts of Eastern and

Western Africa, were exposed to or practiced retting coconut husks. Commerce in quantities of coir were more often an import and not an export. And most all of these areas would eventually select other plant-based fibers – for creating cordage and for use in their maritime purposes. Other fibers like jute, hemp, sisal, rattan, cotton, bamboo, and fiber from Date, Doum, or Sugar Palms, were their selected materials. All of those other plant-based fibers were in many ways superior to coconut coir fiber for the purposes discussed in this book. Most importantly, they too were readily available and endemic in the lives of those other distant communities.

Based on ^{14}C datings of the coconut coir fiber specimens discussed in this book (1130-1400 AD), only **Kerala, India** could or did produce the volume of ***nui kafa*** retted husk fiber our ancient voyagers used on Oak Island.

For the reader who likes history or may want to continue following our forensic reasoning regarding why Kerala (under all of its names) India was our go-to supplier of coir, the chronologies outlined in the following pages demonstrate that discussion. To save thousands of pages of paraphrasing literature, we have attempted to condense the chronology of history which impacts the finding and acquisition of coconut coir fiber, our ancient voyagers needed for Oak Island.

The discussion is drawn upon research of the overall world during the demise of those carbon-dated drupes, and then turns to specific ocean basins to understand what coir was or was not doing to help or hinder our ancient voyagers in their search for coir.

HISTORY ANNEX

Trading and Timing in Turmoil

Not Satisfied? Still think Captain Kidd or other West Indies voyagers had the opportunity to corral some coir. For those of you who love history, I supply more evidence that my thesis is securely rooted. This review will further reveal where those ancient voyagers would not be able to find coir, and where they could have found coir. Let's review...

A Review Throughout the world

The vast amount of land between England in the west and China in the east, and Russia in the north and Java in the south is known as a whole as Afro-Eurasia.[79] Below is a list of impactful historical land-based milestones depicting the turmoil affecting the Afro-Eurasia trading network during our period of interest. Following this list, we see those milestones which impact coconuts within the different worlds' oceans.

835 AD: Beginning of invasion of Northern Europe by Vikings from Scandinavian Islands.

896 AD: Alfred the Great defeats Vikings, forcing them from England.

955 AD: Magyars defeated in Battle of Lechfeld, stopping Hungarians European advance.

1054 AD: Church is divided into Eastern Orthodoxy and Western Catholicism.

1066 AD: William the Conqueror defeats England after the Battle of Hastings.

1099 AD: First Crusades. Muslims are defeated and Jerusalem is retaken.

1119 AD: Order of Knights formed. Knights Templar founded.

1135 AD: England is submerged in The Anarchy.

1147 AD: The Second Crusades start.

1187 AD: Saladin recaptures Jerusalem.

1189 AD: Third Crusades begin.

1202 AD: Era of Fourth Crusade.

1206 AD: Genghis Khan elected and establishes the Mongol Empire.

1260-1270 AD: Mongols Conquer China.

1272 AD: Period of Ninth Crusade.

1299 AD: Ottoman Empire is formed.

1331 AD: Mongol conquest creates widespread famine, plague arriving killing 50%/

1337 AD: England & France begin *Hundreds Year's War* for European supremacy.

1341 AD: In India, the Great Periyar River flooded and changed its course, ending ports.

1347 AD: Black Death spreads throughout Europe killing 40% of the population.

1368 AD: Ming Rebellion led to fall of China's Mongol-led Yuan dynasty.

1368-1644 AD: China removes itself from global trade network. Decline of entire system.

1415 AD: Henry V defeats French at the Battle of Agincourt; new heir of France.

1453 AD: Ottoman Turks take over Constantinople, close access to Black Sea.

1453 AD: Hundred Years War ends.

1492 AD: Christopher Columbus lands in the Americas.

1499 AD: Vasco de Gama becomes first European to round-trip travel around Africa to India.

Furthermore, the Little Ice (LIA) started to wreak havoc throughout many northern areas of the world and combined with those hostilities above, made it inhospitable for the free flow of commerce. Though climatologist argue when the LIA was most impactful, the inclusive range was 1300-1850.[80] The typical human at that time had no problem identifying its start and its impact. The condition of European peasants during this period was little more than famine, hypothermia, bread riots, and despotic leaders. In the 13th century ice pack advanced southward in the North Atlantic and glaciers started to cover Greenland, which eventually was abandoned.[81, 82, 83] Cold snaps abruptly started in 1275 and 1300 followed by intensification from 1430 to 1455.[80, 81] The Baltic Sea froze in 1303 and 1306;.[80] while the "Glacial Maxima" was determined to have been from 1300-1850.[84] The Great European Famine of 1315-1317 was followed by smaller famines throughout Europe, Asia, and America.[80, 82, 85]

Crops failed all over the world. By the 1330s the global trading system was showing signs of imminent collapse.[43] Banks failed in Italy.[43] The ports in Genoa and Venice stopped expanding.[43] Labor difficulties in Flanders resulted in poorer quality cloth being produced and the number of local wars increased, as did 'protection' costs.[43] Greenland was largely cut off by ice from 1410 to 1720's.[80, 83, 83] The worldwide glacial expansion known as the "Grindelwald Fluctuation" began, lasting from 1560-1630.[80, 81]

Famines raged in France during 1693-94. Famines again In Norway 1695-96 and Sweden 1696-97.[80, 82] Both Estonia & Finland got their famines in 1696-97.[80, 82] The loss of population due to these famines is estimated at 10% for France, Norway, and Sweden, 20% for Estonia, and 30% for Finland.[80, 82, 83] The River Thames hosted Frost Fairs on the frozen river from 1608-1814.[80] This meant merchandize had to be rerouted or even sent to other markets. For Europeans - *things sucked!*

All this general misery of the populace was shown in the rise in all crimes and in scapegoating of combined their plight. Whether the witches brew or the misunderstanding of Jewish customs, these two groups received the brunt of the mobs and it did affect commerce.[43, 80, 85]

Perhaps being on a ship venturing to the ends of earth wasn't such a dangerous choice after all!

Atlantic Ocean Basin & Caribbean Sea Timeline

Those who yearn for a Caribbean coconut connection, or maybe a larger Atlantic Ocean involvement to our ancient voyagers efforts, are going to be disappointed. The window for coir fiber coming from this neck of the woods is non-existent until 1501. There were **NO** *Cocos nucifera* in the western hemisphere prior to that date.

Below is a compendium of some of the historical milestones depicting the spread of coconuts within the *Atlantic Ocean basin.* It is with the understanding of how the coconut found itself closer to Oak Island, that we can use to answer who may have brought them.

1342 AD: The Western Norse Settlements in Greenland seem to suddenly disappear.

1499 to **1549**: Cape Verde West Africa becomes initial coconut supply center for western hemisphere.

1501: Pedro Alvares Cabral writes King Ferdinand and Queen Isabella of Spain, of the benefits of coconuts, as he returns from India via Brazil.

1549: Diego Lorenzo, the Canon of Cape Verde, introduces coconuts to Puerto Rico, and possibly Veracruz, Mexico. These would be *Cocos* first stops in Caribbean.

1550: Sao Tome, a Portuguese island base near Cape Verde, start Coco Palm plantations; exposing Dutch, French & British mariners to coconuts, dispersing them within the Atlantic.

1553: Bahia region of Brazil gets Coconut Palms for cultivation, consumption, & export.

1577: Sir Francis Drake said, "*amongst other things we found here a kind of fruit called 'cocos,' which because it is not commonly known with us in England, I thought good to make some description of it, after leaving Cape Verde.*"

1592: England tasks sailors to 'appropriate' Spanish Ships from Africa & India & confiscate ebenwood, ivory, & coconuts; as was done to the *Madre de Dios*, in 1592.

1600's: European markets start receiving coconuts through the 'Maritime Silk Road.'

1610: Honduras reports a few young Coconut Palms growing at Port Trujillo.

1639: Island of Guanaja, Honduras east coast report Coconut Palms growing.

1644: Hollands' William Pizo reports Coconut Palms in Brazil.

1658: Honduran Islands of Roatan & Utila, next to Guanaja, report many Coconut Palms.

1673: Cape Verde's early plantation cultivation, sees first coconut harvest in 50 years.

1686: Cape Verde offers coconut refreshments to sailors & vessels, on outbound fleets.

1696: A few Coconut Palms are found in Jamaica.

1713: Fort Louisbourg, Cape Breton Nova Scotia, French military & settlers get coconuts.

1720: A few Coconut Palms are imported into Bilboa, Hispaniola.

1726: A shipwrecked sailor walked most of north coast of Honduras, noted seeing but one Coconut Palm during his 140-mile beach trek.

The very first time a coconut or any by-product of the *Cocos nucifera* entered into any lands or shores of the Atlantic Ocean Basin and the Caribbean Sea, was as Vasco de Gama sailed west around the Cape of Good Hope in 1499. He was the first explorer who in seeking a sea route to the markets of India and Arabia and beyond, went around the African continent and successfully came back. Many followed. And within one hundred years, the Dutch, German, Portuguese, and Spanish had made the same trip. Yet when de Gama made his first voyage bringing back coconuts and palms, he made a pit-stop in the Cape Verde Islands. There on the western coast of Africa, he introduced them to the coconut. It was a hit with locals who embraced it. Eventually, this region of Africa became a common resting stop for other maritime travelers, and as well, coconuts became a seafarers companion. Soon the 'spice trade' turned into the 'slave trade' which made the Cape Verde Islands so popular. Where the slaves went, so did the coconuts.

Brazil, Hispaniola, Puerto Rico, Vera Cruz, lesser Antilles, and South American coastal territories; now vacant of indigenous peoples who died from disease or enslaved for silver mining, got coconuts and eventually, coconut groves. Yet did anyone in the Atlantic Ocean basin know how to ret a coconut? Does anyone in the West Indies (Caribbean) or within those shores know how to ret coconuts and produce coir fiber? And those poor fellas in Western Africa and in the Cape Verde islands - did they learn how to ret those nuts before being enslaved? **No**.

None of these locations would know of the skills needed for retting – or even what the purpose was for. No one was stitching coir to keep their boats together in these waters, nor making ropes - already being made from local sisal, agave, or jute. Though Portuguese mariners did embrace using coir cordage for their ships as Afonso Albuquerque demanded, outside of Malindi in East Africa or along the Malabar Coast of India and islands of Lakshadweep, the knowledge of the retting process stayed with those sources.

Not only were coconuts new to the entire region, but they were also sparsely distributed amongst a wide array of islands, countries, cultures, and cuisines. It would have been akin to driving through a meatless vegan state, looking for a burger joint. They may have vegan burgers - *but are they the same?*

Getting or planting a coconut tree does not get you the masses of coconut fiber which were dug up on Oak Island. The trees themselves take 8-13 years before bearing fruit, and to reach peak production can take an added 20-25 years. A single tree found in such a fertile locale at peak production, can produce up to 100 nuts over a years' harvest. Even starting from the date of the first known growth of a coconut palm tree in the Caribbean (Puerto Rico in 1549), you would be looking around 1575 before you had enough Coconut Palm trees to gather enough coconuts for your Oak Island mission. Then someone would need to perform the retting process.

As discussed, coconuts in the Caribbean were new in 1549. As with 131 other palm species or sub-species which had been attributed to the genus *Cocos*; they were not the instant success we have imagined. With the death and disease brought by Spaniards, the Coconut Palm tree was not the "Tree of Life" in the minds of the diminished native inhabitants for quite some time. On slave ships, coconuts were most commonly a food stock, and controlled by the Captain. The husk waste or any uneaten nuts were not subjects of great interest or the zeal of local horticulturists. Those slaves were to tend to either cotton or sugarcane plantations – *not to Coconut agronomy*. Three hundred or more years would pass before coconuts become a plantation crop themselves within the Caribbean Sea.

Bermuda / Bahamas

Zone Three: For those of you who had hopes that perhaps Bermuda or the Bahamas were strongholds of the *Cocos nucifera*, you will be forever disappointed. Most of the tall mature coconut trees found in Bermuda were shipped to the island as seedlings on the decks of ships and needed constant care to survive. In more recent years, the importation of coconuts was prohibited, therefore a large proportion of the younger trees have been propagated from locally grown coconuts. In the winter months the growth rate of coconut trees declines due to cooler temperatures. Both Bahamans and Bermudians attest to reduced yield of nuts in comparison to tropical regions.[86, 86a] However, whilst cooler winter temperatures would be a factor in eliminating fruit harvests, the primary reason for the reduced yield is a lack of water.[86, 86a] Bermuda's soil is generally very shallow (1.5 to 3 feet) and much of a coconut tree's root mass is found in the porous limestone underneath the soil. Due to the porosity of the limestone, Bahama's and Bermuda's coconut trees do not generally have a sufficient supply of water with which they are able to support typical growth of fruit.[86, 86a] The rainwater quickly drains down through the limestone layer to the water table which is far too deep for a coconut's roots to reach.[86, 86a] No Coconut fiber here!

Pacific Ocean Basin Timeline

Below is a compendium of some of the similar historical milestones depicting the spread of coconuts within the Pacific Ocean basin. Is it possible the origin of our coconut coir fiber was from efforts within this area of the world? Do we indeed find coconuts closer to Oak Island from ancient voyagers traversing these waters?

1492: Discovery of the New World.

1501: King Manuel of Portugal writes letter to Ferdinand and Isabella of Spain extolling prime value of coconuts as drinking water & cordage for sailing ships.

1510: Ludovico di Varthema reported coconuts in Asia on his travels in 1501 and 1508.

1513: Vasco Nunez de Balboa crossed Isthmus of Panama discovering the Pacific Ocean. No mention of coconuts.

1519: Gaspar de Espinosa y Luna helped found Panama City and reported seeing "many beautiful large mameys *(Pouteria zapota)* and many palms with large coconuts."

1519: Stopping in Guam to restock, Venetian Antonio Pigafetta was greeted by natives wearing coconut shell masks and shaking coconut rattles.

1521: Ferdinand Magellan arrives in Cebu, and names the archipelago after King Philip 1 - now known as the Philippines.

1523: Gonzalo Fernandez de Oviedo y Valdes mistakenly claims he saw Coconut Palms on the Pacific coast of Panama.

1524: Francisco Pizarro Gonzalez led expedition to northern limits of Columbia, near the Cape of Corrientes, and reported seeing a large quantity of coconuts.

1526: Juan de Cabezas discovered Cocos Island off west coast of Costa Rica.

1527: Alvaro de Saavedra y Ceron explores Moluccas Islands, bringing coconuts in his ship to Colima, Mexico.

1538: Cortes opens the port of Acapulco to navigation; yet it is not populated until 1550.

1539: Alvaro de Guijo, resident of City of Panama sent two dozen coconuts to Hernan Cortes de Monroy y Pizarro (Conqueror of Mexico) with instruction on how to plant them.

1550: First introduction of coconut to the port of Veracruz on the eastern coast of Mexico. These originated from Cape Verde region of West Africa.

1565: First evidence of Coconut palms in Mexico from the Philippines via Spanish trade route, most probably from Manila Galleons.

1569: Alvaro de Mendana introduced coconuts from Solomon Islands to Colima, Mexico.

1571: Manila conquered, becomes New Spain's primary entrepôt in Pacific Ocean basin.

1580: Filipino sailors in Colima, Mexico tap the sap of coconut palms to produce tuba.

1602-1603: Commercial coconut groves in Spanish settlements on west coast of Mexico in the Diocese of Michoacan, on the beaches of Apasagualcos, and along the River Atoyac.

1612: 50 large coconut palm plantations in Colima, to produce coconut wine.

1631: Similar number of coconut palm plantations now in Diocese of Michoacan, for production of coconut wine commerce with mining operations in north & interior Mexico.

1720: Though coconut palms were ordered destroyed 104 years earlier, finally Juan de Acuna, Viceroy of New Spain, prohibited the production and trade of coconut wine. Though it took Viceroy, Duque de Alburquerque until the middle of the century before the abandonment of coconut wine production actually happened. No coir production known.

Our Pacific Ocean coconut connection offers few plausible avenues to obtain coconut coir Post-Columbus. The Pacific Ocean basin is home to one of the two major genetic subpopulations of coconuts (***nui vai***), and conveniently, it is next to the second subpopulation type of coconut, native to the Indian Ocean basin (***nui kava***).[1, 2, 4, 11, 39+] Therefore access and transport of coir is possible as coconuts were everywhere. The ongoing arguments of how or who transported the *first* coconuts across the Pacific shores from west to east, is not really germane. Especially if our ancient voyagers are pre-Columbian collectors of coir fiber. For finding coir fiber and transporting it any time prior to 1500 AD, directs us to a single area on the map of the world within another ocean. This is why none of the milestones for this ocean basin was highlighted in red.

When Francisco Hernandez in 1573-74 heralded the find of coconuts growing in plantation plots throughout Colima, Mexico (New Spain), his excited report said,

> *"The wide use of this plant to make vinegar, honey, sugar, wine and spirits, oil, milk, or butter. To use the fruit and seeds in the manufacture of cups decorated with gold and silver, fiber for making threads, wicks or fuses for gunpowder, cables and filling material used for sealing between planks in the construction of ships."*[87]

When and how and by whom exactly started growing coconuts in Colima and vicinity doesn't really matter either. What is important is that coconut coir fiber processing was not part of this new gig. In the Philippines, abaca (Manila Hemp) was Fiber King and coconut husks were simply burned as fuel or used as fertilizer.[89] So there was no known knowledge-transfer held by Filipinos of why anyone would want to process coconut husks into fiber. Their exclusive supply of manila hemp gave them the saltwater resistant, strongest fibers the world had ever known at that time![90]

But what the Filipinos did know, was impactful on our coconut story. Soon, everything centered on what was learned from the Filipino, Indio, and Chinese sailors "*Spain's Men of the Sea*"[90] who fled those galleons, once in New Spain.[88] They knew some about *growing Cocos nucifera* and allot about *fermentation!* Wine and brandy-like spirits became the entire embodiment of coconut silviculture in this small area where the Coconut Palm trees were growing in New Spain.[87, 88] The name of this new hot commodity was called 'tuba,' a Filipino (Tagalog) word.[87] Stills popped up next to every Coconut Palm tree.[88] The craze was based on "tapping" the sap of Coconut Palms like you would a Maple tree for its syrupy sap.[87] Yet sapping or tapping a coconut palm robs the palm from biologically producing seeds – *the coconut.*[88]

Therefore tapping for tuba, meant - *No coir for you!*

The indulgence in tuba depleted the churches monopoly on the sales of Spanish-sourced wine.[87, 88] The church complained, the government banned, and the locals rebelled by fermenting anything growing in the area.[88]

And yet no tithing for the church! Like marijuana in the United States today, the government realized it could tax marijuana (tuba equivalent) and locals would suspend the risky practice of fermenting other more dangerous crops.[87, 88] So tuba became an accepted vice and a profitable product even for the church.[88] Coco wine continues to be produced in Colima and vicinity to this day, and still, no one is retting any coconuts!

The bottom line to this little melodrama is knowing coconut coir fibers were never produced in New Spain.[87] Francisco Hernandez never saw the other potential by-products of *Cocos nucifera,* as he tempered his tantrum with a second round of tuba!

Coconuts only left Manila as coconuts, or very rarely, as a finished textile.[88] They were not used as dunnage on these ships, nor packing, not even as caulking in building the fleet of galleons in Manila.[90, 91, 92, 93] Coconuts traveled with Spain's Men of the Sea to provide a source of water and food – *nothing else.*[87, 88] Once the coconuts made landfall in New Spain, those few not eaten, were to become cultivated. Most importantly, the singular product from the Coconut Palm tree was for its sap; for the sole purpose of producing tuba, and coconut wine.[87, 88] As discussed earlier, these trees produced no coconuts and the fibrous husks they were born in. No coconut to harvest, no husk to de-husk, and no husk retted into coir!

One can clearly understand why retting coconut husks never entered anyone's mind. Moving bales of Nankin silks, Canton silks, Cambray linen, colored skeins of silk, raw silk, silk threads, white cotton, elephant cotton, Filipino cotton, damasks, satins, tapestries, drapes, blankets, towels, and other textiles - filled galleon after galleon, making Spain rich.[91, 92, 93] I've only touched on fibers and fabrics. Yet surviving records of Manila Galleon manifests, reflect no known consignments or listings on manifests of bails of abaca, hemp, jute, or coconut coir.[91, 92, 93] Nor was valuable cargo space given up to transport coconuts or their byproducts.[91, 92, 93] With all the fine silks and exotic fabrics flooding the area, none of these 'lesser' textiles would make the grade from this point forward.

The Indigenous peoples of New Spain used their own miracle plant fiber called "sisal." You can easily see why neither the Spaniards nor the locals would ever learn coconut retting techniques, nor look at the coconut and ponder its plethora of manufactured by-products. The historic record of coconut fiber production in any areas of New Spain or other colonized area says – *No!* And again... the Filipinos didn't make coir either - *they made charcoal and tuba.*

Finally, a much more direct scientific investigation has crossed all the "T's" and dotted all the "I's" on this subject. The morphometric analysis has been performed by archaeologists, ethnobotanists and paleobiolinguists, and strongly indicates the original introduction of the coconut into the Western Hemisphere.[2]

They find the coconut was most likely not introduced to Panama or South America via some ancient pre-Columbian ocean-going travelers across the great Pacific Ocean. Therefore, our ancient voyagers caravanning to Oak Island did not pick up their coir supplies from this region. Using genetic samplars, as well as mapped DNA analysis of modern coconut populations throughout the Caribbean, Central America, and South America; show the *Panama Tall* variety – thought first indigenous to the continent back then, is a very close relation to The Coconut Palm tree of the Philippines.[2, 4, 11, 39, 56] Both are also sub-group ***nui kafa***.

The Filipino coconut made its way via the Manila Galleon trade circuit to the Americas, circa 1540's. Some argue it came by man via the Solomon Islands to Colima. As for the New Spain east coast ports of colonial Campeche and Veracruz, those Coconuts heritage are from Cape Verde. The Coconut Palm tree genetic makeup in the Cape Verde Islands is from both East Africa as well as, India.[2, 4, 11, 39, 56]

So it was Vasco de Gama who spread the wild, football shaped WCT *Cocos nucifera* to the Caribbean Sea and Atlantic Ocean basin, furthering the home of the genetic sub-population of the WCT ***nui kafa***.

Therefore, the answer to the question - *could our ancient voyagers gathered up coconut coir fiber from the Pacific Ocean Basin?* can be summarized to a pretty definitive – ***No***.

Today the scene is somewhat different as coconut coir fiber have found new reasons for retting. But we are not talking about today – *are we*.

It is ironic the coconut found itself transported to Veracruz, Mexico (east coast New Spain) at almost identical time periods of those in Colima, on the west coast. As a harvested Colima coconut on the western coast of Mexico, the coconut traveled by land on pack-animals through Mexico City to Veracruz.[91, 92] Meanwhile, earlier plantings of coconuts by Vasco de Gama in a 1499 return stop In the Cape Verde Islands of Western Africa, meant they were ready for harvest for use with future slave ships traveling to the eastern coast of New Spain. Pack-animals brought coconuts to Veracruz in the late 1560's, while Cape Verde slaves landed in Puerto Rico and Veracruz in 1549 - *along with coconuts*.

There is no mention of coconut coir fiber in any of the historical literature involving the Manila-Acapulco maritime trade. Nor any literature or record of coconut coir from any country or island in Caribbean history! There are storytellers who argue whether coir fiber or abaca fiber was used in the construction of those Cebu-built Spanish galleon ships or for their caulking.[90, 91, 92] However, since abaca was a superior fiber to coir, both surviving well in saltwater, I have found no evidence within the general Filipino culture where retting was practiced at such a level to conceive coir industry had developed. This is not to say other Pacific Ocean Islanders, who frequently traded within the islands of the Philippine Archipelago, did not engage in coir commerce. As we have pointed to throughout this book, humans tend to use what they know and what is all around them. Even until WWII, Abaca (Manila Hemp) was an exclusive crop and sought-after product from the Philippines.[94]

The most telling of the Pacific Ocean basins' ***lack of involvement*** in coconut coir fiber production, comes from William S. Lyon, Director, Division of Plant Industry, Philippines. In his 1903 book entitled, "*The Coconut*," he writes,

> *"The fiber of the cocoanut husk, or coir, as it is commercially known, has never yet been utilized in this Archipelago, excepting occasionally for local consumption. Second in value only to the copra, this product has been allowed to go to waste. The rejected husks are thrown together in immense heaps, which are finally burned and the ashes, exceedingly rich in potash and phosphoric acid, are left to blow away. As the commercial value of the fiber is greater than the manurial value of the salts therein, it is economy to*

utilize the fiber and purchase potash and phosphoric acid when needed to enrich the soil… The greatest mine of horticultural wealth which is open to the shrewd planter lies in the heaps of waste and neglected husks that he can now procure from adjoining estates for the asking and cartage."[89]

Indian Ocean Basin Timeline

Below is a compendium of some of the similar historical milestones depicting the spread of coconuts and coir fiber production within the Indian Ocean basin. This compendium includes enough Pre-Columbian dates to imbue the longstanding involvement the coconut had around these waters. This is the true home to the Coconut Palm tree's coconut coir fiber industry. This is likely the region for the source of coconut coir fiber used by our ancient voyagers; either pre- or post-Columbus. This is an abridged listing from sources already cited.

850 AD: The Arab merchant Soleiman al-Tajir traveled to Guangzhou, China and recalled how residents used coir fiber and drank fermented coconut fluid called "toddy."

900 AD: In South Oman, traditional use of coconut fiber (*kambar*) to construct dhows and cordage is written about and persisted among local fishermen and transoceanic traders until recently.

1200's: Trade monopoly practices developed between Arabs and Venetians.

1254-1324: Marco Polo referred to the coconut as 'Pharaoh's Nut' when he ran across it in his travels to India, Sumatra, and the Nicobar Islands (in the Andaman Sea off the west coast of Malaysia).

1280: Marco Polo visited the Port of Hormuz and discovered seamen building ships without nails but sewing them together with coconut fiber. He was not a fan.

1280: Marco Polo In China, finds they had used coconut fiber for +500 years.

1300s: From Marco Polo's chronicles, Arab traders came from India, Sumatra, and Nicobar Islands to England before Portuguese sailors reached East Africa. These traders found the Maldives and Laccadives Archipelagos, who were known for their remarkable shipbuilding ability and craftsmanship. "*The ships, including the hulls, masts, ropes, stitches, sails, and other parts were built entirely using different parts of the coconut tree and various coconut-based materials.*"

1499: Vasco de Gama finds vessels built with coir in Malindi East Africa, and in all of his destinations in India.

1510: Portuguese Viceroy and Governor of Goa and Cananor, India - Afonso Albuquerque requires his entire fleet be refitted and rerigged with coconut coir cordage, as his ropes have rotted away during the previous monsoons.

1602: The Dutch East India Company started a new form of commercial capitalism, and in 1605, captured Indonesian islands once controlled by the Portuguese. This started the Dutch trade in many things to include coconuts.

1650's: Dutch fully replaced the Portuguese in both the maritime trade and the traditional overland caravans between the Indian Ocean and the Mediterranean Sea ports.

1858: First factory for manufacturing coir products opened in Alleppey, Kerala state of India, by Americans James Darragh and Henry Smail.

What have we figured out by looking back in time at the world? We know there were no coconuts husked in the Caribbean Sea or the Atlantic Ocean basin for our ancient voyagers to acquire. We know there was no transfer of the knowledge of the retting process from the Pacific Ocean basin through the west coast of New Spain, nor was it known in Western Africa when coconuts were introduced there from the Indian Ocean. We have current modern scientific DNA mapping of the spread of various *Cocos nucifera* cultivars and sub-group populations around the world. We have the historical evidence of those cultures who utilized coconut husks and coir fiber byproducts. And we have been told,

> *"In the Pacific, coconuts likely were first cultivated on islands in Southeast Asia, meaning the Philippines, Malaysia, Indonesia, and perhaps the continent as well. In the Indian Ocean, the likely center of cultivation was the southern periphery of India, including Sri Lanka, the Maldives and the Laccadives. The Indian Ocean coconut was transported to the New World by Europeans much later. The Portuguese carried coconuts from the Indian Ocean to the West Coast of Africa. So the coconuts that you find today in Florida are largely the Indian ocean type, Olsen says, which is why they tend to have the niu kafa form."* [11]

What we have yet to learn is the link between from where the coconuts were killed, retted, and distributed in Kerala, and how it was transported to the operations performed on Oak Island.

When Old Becomes Ancient

Someone made the decision to pack their vessel with a significant amount of coconut coir fiber, tree saplings, red clover seed, and their mystery treasure. What was their plan or their purpose? Was Oak Island their intended destination, or just a 'good place to park?' When did they get around to do this amazing feat? Unless Rick and Marty pull a rabbit out of the Money Pit with the next hammergrab, the only known scientific evidence with answers are the coconut fibers. And it tells us this was a very, very long time ago.

Yes, *I know*... many people like to link the coconut fibers to dunnage which in their minds tangentially links this entire endeavor to the West Indies, New World loot, and tropical Caribbean sands under a grove of Coconut Palms. - *Yet we know that dog don't hunt!*

Such fiber was not available to our ancient or modern voyagers if they were trying to scrounge them up in the Atlantic, Caribbean, or Pacific – *regardless of the fibers age.* They are notably old and notably not where they are supposed to be. Through our forensic investigation we have determined many attributes and distinction coir fiber encompasses. As WHOI researchers believed in their discussion of most likely pathways, we've demonstrated we may have to accept their hunch - *as the true Occam's Razor probability.*

Did our travelers go to where coconut coir fiber was or have it brought to them? That is truly a hard nut to crack, but we do know from where those coconuts and retted husks originated. The linkage of where the coir came from and who obtained it and when, and when was it placed on the island... is still an unanswered mystery. Did we get closer, yes. Are there further leads, yes.

Endnotes Referenced

1. "*The Coconut Odyssey – The bounteous possibilities of the Tree of Life*." By Mike Foale, 2003. Australian Centre for International Agricultural Research (ACIAR).

2. "*The Coconut Phylogeny, Origins, and Spread*." by N.M. Nayer, 2021. Academic Press is an imprint of Elsevier. 125 London Wall, London EC2Y 5AS, United Kingdom. P 66.

3. "*Coconuts in the Americas*." By Charles R. Clement, et. al. Instituto Nacional de Pesquisas da Amazonia, Brazil. The New York Botanical Garden. August 17, 2013. 28 pages. DOI 10.1007/s12229-013-9121-z.

4. "*Cocos nucifera L*." Source: FAOSTAT. Global Biodiversity Information Facility (GBIF), Copenhagen, Denmark. (Accessed 02-09-2021). https://www.gbif.org/species/113562924.

5. "*Coir*." How Products are Made. Volume 6. 7 pages. www.madehow.com/Volume-6/coir.html.

6. "*Coconut Fibre: Its Structure, Properties and Applications*." by Leena Mishra and Gautam Basu. National Institute of Natural Fibre Engineering & Technologies Institute. Kolkata, West Bengal India. Section Yield of Coconut Fibre, Page 7, para. 10.2.1.3. Yield of Coconut Fibre. Researchgate. Pub. 339284598. February 2020. 27 Pages

7. "*Coir fiber process and opportunities-2*." by Akhila Rajan, at Govt. College Kozhinjampara. Published in The *Journal of Natural Fibers*, January 2008.

8. "*Biofuels from Coconuts*." By Krishna Raghaven. 2010. 107 pages. Para. 1.1 Quantity and Energy Content of Parts of the Coconut Palm, Fig. 1 and Table 1. Biodegradability Section, P. 16. www.energypedia.info/f/f9/EN-biofuels_from_cocnuts-krishna_raghaven.pdf.

9. "*Oak Island Hydrogeology, Hydrography and Nearshore Morphology, July – August 1995, Field Observations*." by David G. Aubrey, Wayne Spencer, Ben Guiterez, William Robertson, and David Gallo. Unpublished Draft Report. Woods Hole Oceanographic Institution, Woods Hole, Maine. Apr. 8, 1996. 151 pages. https://www.oakislandtours.ca/les-macphie-research.html.

10. "*2 Page Letter from Robert R. Dunfield responding to questions*." By D'Arcy O'Connor. Oct. 21, 1976.

11. "*Deep History of Coconuts Decoded*." by Diana Lutz. Washington University in St. Louis. *The Source* – Science and Technology. June 24, 2011.

[12]. "*Taxonomy and intraspecific Classification*." By NM Nayar, University of Kerala. Dec. 2017. DOI: 10.1016/B978-0-12-809778-6.00003-6. 28 pages. https://www.researchgate.net/publication/312513113_Taxonomy_and_Intraspecific_Classification?enrichId=rgreq.

[13]. "*Coconut Palms on the Edge of the Desert: Genetic Diversity of Cocos nucifera L. in Oman*." By Lalith Perera, Luc Baudouin, et. al., 2011. Published in *Cord*, May 2012, 27 (1). ResearchGate.

[14]. "*Travels in the Coastlands of British East Africa and the islands of Zanzibar and Bemba: Their Agricultural Resources and General Characteristics*." By William Walter Augustine Fitzgerald, Fellow Royal Geographical Society, Fellow Royal Colonial Institute. London, England. Chapman and Hall, Ltd. 1898. Pages 620-635.

[15]. "*Sylva Sylvarum – Or a Natural History in Ten Centuries.*" By Sir Francis Bacon. Volume II. Reprinted by Kessinger Publishing Rare Reprints. Paragraphs 796, 881 & 882.

[15a]. "*Coir Fiber Process and Opportunities -2*." By Akhila Rajan & T. Emilia Abraham, PhD, 2007. Biochemical Aspects Sec. Published in *Journal of Natural Fibers*. 3:4, Pages 29-42.

[15b]. "*Coir Draining Blanket for Consolidation*." By M. Sudhakaran Pillai, 2001. Presented at International Seminar on Technical Textiles, 2001. Center Institute of Coir Technology. COIRBOARD, Bangalore, India.

[16]. "*The Periplus of the Erythraean Sea: Travel and Trade in the Indian Ocean By a Merchant of the First Century*." Translated from the Greek and Annotated By Wilfred H. Schoff, A.M., Secretary of the Commercial Museum, Philadelphia, PA. Published By Longmans, Green, and Co. New York, London, Bombay and Calcutta. 1912. *Pages annotated within the appendices of this book.*

[17]. "*2,000 Year Old Lost City of Rhapta May have been Found in Tanzania*." By Natalia Klimczak, Jul. 5, 2016. (Accessed on 04-22-2021) https://www.ancient-origins.net/news-history-archaeology/2000-year-old-lost-city-rhapta-may-have-been-found-tanzania-006234.

[18]. "*Indian Shipping: A History of the Sea-Borne Trade and Maritime Activity of the Indians From the Earliest Times*." By Radhakumud K. Mookerji. Pages 180-191.
https://ia800901.us.archive.org/33/items/indianshippinghi00mookrich/indianshippinghi00mookrich.

[19]. "*Indigenous Fishing Craft of Oman*." By Tom Vosmer, Western Australian Maritime Museum. Published in *The International Journal of Nautical Archaeology*, (1997) 26.3:2, Pages 17-235.

[20]. "*The Dhows of Beypore – URU*." Online Blog. Posted Apr, 27, 2012. https://uru-ship.blogspot.com/2012/04/dhows-of-beypore-uru-heritage-ship.html. (Accessed 02-21-2021).

[21]. "*History of Somalia*." Wikipedia Contributors (Online). Wikipedia, The Free Encyclopedia, Updated Jul. 16, 2022. (Accessed 07-16-2022) https://en.wikipedia.org/w/index.php?title=History_of_Somalia&oldid=1098534906.

[22]. *"The Seacraft of Prehistory."* By Paul Johnstone, 1980. Prepared online by Sean McGrail. See page 178. https://www.surfresearch.com.au/1980_Johnstone_Sea_Craft_Prehistory.html.

[23]. *"MIGRATION, TRADE AND PEOPLES, PART 1: ISSUES IN INDIAN OCEAN COMMERCE AND THE ARCHAEOLOGY OF WESTERN INDIA; Boats, Routes and Sailing Conditions of Indo-Roman Trade*," By Lucy Blue, Page 9. ISBN: 978-0-9553924-5-0.

[24]. "*From the Kattumaram to the Fibre-Teppa —Changes in Boatbuilding Traditions on India's East Coast*." By Henrik Pohl, Feb. 02, 2007. https://doi.org/10.1111/j.1095-9270.2006.00134.

[25]. "*Ancient India, West Africa & The Sea: Why It Could Not Be So*." By Harry Bourne. Published online at *Modern Ghana*. https://www.modernghana.com/news/829967/ancient-india-west-africa-the-sea-why-it-could-not-be-so.html.

[26]. "*The Archaeobiology of Indian Ocean Translocations: Current Outlines of Cultural Exchanges by Proto-historic Seafarers*." By Dorian Q. Fuller, Nicole Boivin, Cristinia C. Castillo, Tom Hoogervorst, and Robin G. Allaby, 2009. Sealinks Project, European Research Council. Delta Book World, New Delhi.

[27]. *"The Swahili Civilization in Eastern Africa."* By Elgidius B. Ichumbaki and Edward Pollard. Mar. 25, 2021. Oxford Research Encyclopedia. Published online. https://DOI.org/10.1093/acrefore/9780190854584.013.267.

[28]. "*From Dugouts to Double Outriggers – Lexical Insights into the Development of Swahili Nautical Technology*." By Martin Walsh. Published in Wacana, Vol. 22, No. 2, 2021.

[29]. "*In the Wake of the Dhow: The Arabian Gulf and Oman*." By Dionisius A. Agius, Jan. 2010. University of Exeter and King Abdulaziz University. ResearchGate.

[30]. "*Vezo People*." Wikipedia Contributors, Online. Wikipedia, The Free Encyclopedia. Updated Mar. 28, 2022. (Accessed 07-22-2022) https://en.wikipedia.org/w/index.php?title=Vezo_people&oldid=1079737869.

[31]. "*Comoros*." By Harriet J. and Martin Ottenheimer. Encyclopedia Britannica. Updated Mar. 9, 2022. (Accessed 07-15-2022) https://www.britannica.com/place/Comoros.

[32]. "*Horn of Africa*." Wikipedia Contributors, Wikipedia (Online). The Free Encyclopedia, Updated Jul. 1, 2022. (Accessed 07-15-2022). https://en.wikipedia.org/w/index.php?title=Horn_of_Africa&oldid=109589762.

[33]. "*Upwelling.*" Wikipedia Contributors, Wikipedia (Online). The Free Encyclopedia, Updated May, 14, 2022. (Accessed 07-15-2022) https://en.wikipedia.org/w/index.php?title=Upwelling&oldid=1087705093.

[34]. "*Maritime History of Somalia*." Wikipedia Contributors (Online). Wikipedia, The Free Encyclopedia. Updated May 29, 2022. (Accessed 06-28-2022). https://en.wikipedia.org/w/index.php?title=Maritime_history_of_Somalia&oldid=1090453646.

[35]. "*A long time ago in an Africa far, far away- 1836.*" *Blog* Geeska Suldaan: Majeerteen Somali PDM Victoria 2 AAR. Jun, 26, 2018. https://forum.paradoxplaza.com/forum/threads/geeska-suldaan-majeerteen-somali-pdm-victoria-2-aar.1107593/.

[36]. "*Peaches to Samarkand. Long Distance-Connectivity, Small Worlds and Sociocultural Dynamics Across Afro-Eurasia, 300-800 CE.*" By Johannes Preiser-Kapeller, Dec. 2014. Division for Byzantine Research, Institute for Medieval Research, Austrian Academy of Sciences.

[37]. "*First Footsteps in East Africa.*" By Sir Richard Francis Burton, Feb. 10, 1856. GoodPress, 2022. SCRIBD.

[38]. "*The Merchants' Magazine and Commercial Review*." By Freeman Hunt, 1856. Volume 34. P. 694.

[39]. "*Coconut – History, Uses, and Folklore*." By Subhash Chanda Ahuja, CCS Haryana Agricultural University. Article in Asian-History Journal. January 2014.

[40]. "*History of the Discovery and Appreciation of Pearls – The Organic Gem Perfected by Nature*." By Dr. Shihaan Larif, Nov. 25, 2021. Internetstones.com. https://internetstones.com/history-of-the-discovery-and-appreciation-of-pearls-the-organic-gem-perfected-by-nature-page-2/. (Accessed 04-05-2022).

41. "*17 Palm Tree Insects & Diseases and How to Treat Them*." Florida Palm Tree Association. www.Florida-palm-trees.com/palm-tree-insects-diseases/.

42. "*Advent of Europeans in India Upsc Notes: Portuguese, Dutch, English & French*." By Babu R. Pravin, Jun. 1, 2020. https://andedge.com/advent-of-the-europeans/.

43. "*The Afro-Eurasian Trading System in the 13th and 14th Centuries.*" Posted on h2g2: The Hitchhiker's Guide to the Galaxy. Posted online, May 4, 2006. https://h2g2.com/edited_entry/A10422181.

44. "*Climate of Pakistan*." (Accessed 07-18-2022) https://en.wikipedia.org/w/index.php?title=Climate_of_Pakistan&oldid=1098432766.

45. "*Makran.*" (Accessed 07-18-2022) https://en.wikipedia.org/w/index.php?title=Makran&oldid=1098415784.

46. "*Camel Train*." Wikipedia Contributors (Online). Wikipedia, The Free Encyclopedia, Jun. 11, 2022. (Accessed 02-21-2022) https://en.wikipedia.org/w/index.php?title=Camel_train&oldid=1092609372.

47. "*The Peopling of Lakshadweep Archipelago*." By M.S. Mustak, N Rai, M.R. Naveen, S. Prakash, et. al., 2019. Sci Rep. 2019 May 6;9(1):6968. doi: 10.1038/s41598-019-43384-3. PMID: 31061397; PMCID: PMC6502849.

48. "*Maldives–Lakshadweep–Chagos Archipelago tropical moist forests*." https://en.wikipedia.org/w/index.php?title=Maldives%E2%80%93Lakshadweep%E2%80%93Chagos_Archipelago_tropical_moist_forests&oldid=1041012558. (Accessed 07-12-2022).

49. "*Lakshadweep [Internet]*." Wikipedia, The Free Encyclopedia. (Accessed 07-12-2022). https://en.wikipedia.org/w/index.php?title=Lakshadweep&oldid=1096239113.

50. "*Maldives is the World's Lowest Country in the World*." By Deborah Byrd, Feb. 7, 2014. Online, EARTHSKY Communications.

51. "*Maldives [Internet]*." Wikipedia Contributors, The Free Encyclopedia; 2022 Jul 11, 17:16 UTC (Accessed 07-12-2022) https://en.wikipedia.org/w/index.php?title=Maldives&oldid=1097606631.

52. "*Laccadive Islands*." Published in the Encyclopedia Britannica 1911 and is available at https://theodora.com/encyclopedia/l/laccadive_islands.html. (Accessed 09-12-2022) [*a group of coral reefs and islands in the Indian Ocean, lying between 10° and 12° 20' N. and 71° 40' and 74° E. The name Laccadives (laksha dwipa, the "hundred thousand isles") is that given by the people of the Malabar coast and was probably meant to include the Maldives; they are called by the natives simply Divi, " islands," or Amendivi, from the chief island*] .

53. "*The Imperial Gazetteer of India, Vol. 8*." By William Wilson Hunter. Online https://www.ebooksread.com/authors-eng/william-wilson-hunter/the-imperial-gazetteer-of-india-volume-8-tnu/page-46-the-imperial-gazetteer-of-india-volume-8-tnu.shtml.

54. "*Mappila in India*." Online publication by the Joshua Project. Sponsored by the Bethany World Prayer Center. (Accessed 04-22-2022) https://joshuaproject.net/people_groups/17452/IN.

55. "*Comparisons of Laccadive Micro Tall (LMT) and Laccadive Ordinary Tall (LCT) in Cote d'Ivoire and India*." By Bourdeix R. Kumaran PM, et. al. Published in *Catalog of Conserved Coconut Germplasm – by country or origin – India*, and *The Indian Coconut Journal, 23.25*. (Accessed on 05-30-2022).

56. "*Microsatellite analysis of distinct coconut accessions from Agatti and Kavaratti Islands, Lakshadweep, India*." By D. Kishnamoorthy and P.M. Jacob, et. al., Jun. 2010. Published in *Journal Scientia Horticulturae,* 125 (3), Pages 309-315. DOI: 10.1016/j.scienta.2010.04.012.

57. "*Genetic and Phylogenetic Relationships of Coconut Populations from Amini and Kadmat Islands, Lakshadweep (India)*." By M.K. Rajesh, K. Samsudeen, B.A. Jerard, P. Rejusha and Anitha Karun, Mar. 19, 2014. Published online 09-11-2014.

58. "*Lakshadweep*". By William A. Noble for Encyclopedia Britannica, 12 Sep. 2021. https://www.britannica.com/place/Lakshadweep. (Accessed 07-12-2022)

59. "*The Indian Ocean Trade of Orissa in the Seventeenth Century*." By K.N. Sethi. Published in *Proceedings of the Indian History Congress*, 2004, Vol. 65, Pages 248-257.

the French established coconut plantations in 1793 with slave labor p28
60.

61. "*Laccadive Micro Tall (LMT) in Cote d'Ivoire.*" By R. Bourdeix, PM Kumaran, Rao EVV Bhaskara, and RV Pillai. Published in Catalog of Conserved Coconut Germplasm, India. 6 pages. (Accessed 07-1202022).

62. "*Origin and Evolution of Laccadive Micro Tall, a coconut cultivar from Lakshadweep Islands of India*." By K. Sarnsudeen, P.M. Jacobl, M.K. Rahesh, B.A. Jerard, and P.M. Kumaran. Published in Journal of Plantation Crops, 2000, 34 (3), Pages 220-225. ResearchGate. (Accessed 05-30-2022).

63. "*Coconut Strategy – 2018*." Part of A Global Strategy for the Conservation and Use of Coconut Genetic Resources, 2018-2028." Compiled by Roland Bourdex and Alexia Prades. CIPAD/CoGert.

64. "*Selections from the Records of the Collector or South Canara*." Report By G. L. Morris Esquire, Collector of South Canara on the Management of the Coir Monopoly on the Amindivi Islands. Aug. 1863. Mangalore. Printed at the Collectorate Press, South Canara. 1898. 33 pages. Administration of the coir monopoly employed a team of Monegars (village head man), Peons (workers) and Karani (clerks) per island or group of islands.

65. "*Selections from The Records of the Government of India, Revenue and Agricultural Department*." By George Watt, C.I.E, M.B., C.M. Vol. I, 1888-89. University of California at Los Angeles. Section. Coconuts and Coconut Products. Pages 197-214.

66. "*Sri Lanka – Encyclopedia Britannica.*" By Gerald Hubert Peiris and Sinnappah Arasaratnam. Encyclopedia Britannica. Updated Jul. 17, 2022. https://www.britannica.com/place/Sri-Lanka. Accessed 19 July 2022.

67. "*Sri Lanka – Wikipedia.*" Wikipedia Contributors (Online). Wikipedia, The Free Encyclopedia. Updated 07-17-2022. https://en.wikipedia.org/w/index.php?title=Sri_Lanka&oldid=1098773771. (Accessed 07-18-2022).

68. "*Seafaring in Ancient India*." Published in *A Tribute to Hinduism*, online. Sep. 7, 2005. (Accessed 05-11-2022).

69. "*Indian Ocean Trade before the European Conquest*." By James Hancock. World History Encyclopedia. Updated Jul. 20, 2021. https://www.worldhistory.org/article/1800/indian-ocean-trade-before-the-european-conquest/.

70. "*Ceylon and the Portuguese, 1505-1658*." By P.E. Pieris, Ceylon Civil Service. American Ceylon Mission. 1920. https://archive.org/stream/ceylonportuguese00pier/ceylonportuguese00pier_djvu.txt.

71. "*Coconut Fiber - Risk Factors and Cargo Loss Prevention Information, Self-Heating/Spontaneous Combustion*." Transport Information Service, German Marine Insurers GDV, Die Deutschen Versiche. https://www.tis-gdv.de/tis_e/ware/fasern/kokosfa/kokosfa-htm/.

72. "*History of Kerala, India*." Wikipedia Online. (Accessed 07-12-2022) https://en.wikipedia.org/w/index.php?title=History_of_Kerala&oldid=1094971844.

72a. "*A Survey of Kerala History*." By A. Sreedhara Menon, Aug. 2010. 1st eBook Edition. DC Books, Kerala State, India. www.DCBooks.com.

73. "*Malabar Coast*." Online source, Owl apps. (Accessed 05-11-2022) http://next.owlapps.net/owlapps_apps/article?id=30874446&lang=en.

74. "*Kerala Backwaters*." Wikipedia Online. (Accessed 07-12-2022). https://en.widipedia.org/w/index.php?title=Kerala_backwaters&oldid=109621.

75. "*State Symbols Of Kerala.*" PhilaIndia.info online. Posted Dec. 27, 1976. https://philaindia.info/state-symbols-of-kerala/.

76. "*South Western Ghats moist Deciduous Forests*." Wikipedia Contributors (Online). Wikipedia, the Free Encyclopedia. Updated Jul. 1, 2022. https://en.wikipedia.org/w/index.php?title=South_Western_Ghats_moist_deciduous_forests&oldid=1095898280.

77. "*Characterization of Annur and Bedakam Ecotypes of Coconut from Kerala State, India, Using Microsatellite Markers*." By M.K. Rajesh, et. al., Division of Crop Improvement, Central Plantation Crops Research. *International Journal of Biodiversity*, Vol. 2014, Article ID 260895, 7 pages. Hindawi Publishing Corporation. http://dx.doi.org/10.1155/2014/260895.

78. "*History of Coir – CCRI*." Coir Board Ministry of India, Alleppey, Kerala, India. Central Coir Research Institute. http://coirboard.gov.in/?page_id=6. (Accessed 09-15-2020).

79. "*Berkshire Encyclopedia of World History*." By William H. McNeill, publisher. 2nd Edition. Berkshire Publishing group. 2010. Current Online version, 2016. https://www.google.com/books/edition/Berkshire_Encyclopedia_of_World_History/ijNsPgAACAAJ?hl=en.

80. "*Little Ice Age*." Wikipedia Contributors, (Online. Wikipedia, The Free Encyclopedia. Updated 07-09-2022. https://en.wikipedia.org/w/index.php?title=Little_Ice_Age&oldid=1097211669.

81. "*Abrupt Onset of the Little Ice Age triggered by Volcanism and Sustained by Sea-ice/Ocean Feedbacks*." By Gifford H. Miller, et. al, Jan. 30, 2012. Published in Geophysical Research Letters, 39 (2). Bibcode:2012GeoRL..39.2708M. CiteSeerX 10.1.1.639.9076. doi:10.1029/2011 GL050168. S2CID 15313398. See also in #80 above.

82. "*Finding the Family in Medieval and Early Modern Scotland.*" By Elizbeth Ewanu and Janay Nugent, 2008. Ashgate. p. 153. ISBN 978-0-7546-6049-1.

83. "*The Lost Western Settlement of Greenland, 1342*." By Carol S. Francis, Mar. 9, 2012. Thesis, California State University, Sacramento.

84. "*Little Ice Age Geochronology*." By John P. Rafferty and Stephen T. Jackson, Mar. 18, 2016. Encyclopedia Britannica. https://www.britannica.com/science/Little-Ice-Age.

85. "*Black Death and Abrupt Earth Changes in the 14th Century. 1290-1350: Abrupt Earth Changes, Astronomical, Tectonic and Meteorological Events Leading up to and Culminating at the Black Death period at 1348*." by Sacha Dobler, Updated Version Jan. 2018. www.abruptearthchanges.com. 102 Pages.

86. "*Agriculture and Fisheries in the Bahamas*."(Accessed 07-20-2022) https://en.wikipedia.org/w/index.php?title=Agriculture_and_fisheries_in_the_Bahamas&oldid=1072570138.

86a. "*Field Notes: The Coconut*." Republished by Gordon R. Groves, Feb. 22, 2022. Originally published in *The Bermudian* on Feb. 1954. See online. https://www.thebermudian.com/home-a-garden/garden/field-notes-the-coconut/.

87. "*History of Coconut (Cocos Nucifera L.) in Mexico: 1539-1810*." By Daniel Zizumbo-Villarreal. Genetic Resources and Crop Evolution. 43: Netherlands. 1996. www.palms.org. Pages 505-515.

88. ""*Early Coconut Culture in Western Mexico*." By Henry J. Bruman, 1938-1939. The *Hispanic American Historical Review*. Institute of Social Anthropology, Smithsonian Institute. Pages 212 – 223. http://read.dukeupress.edu/hahr/article-pdf/25/2/212/749513/0250212.pdf.

89. "*The Cocoanut*," By William Lyons, 1903. Farmer's Bureau No. 8, Conclusion #8. Bureau of Agriculture. Bureau of Public Printing, Jun. 1, 1903.

90. "*Making the First Global Trade Route: The Southeast Asian Foundations of the Acapulco-Manila Galleon Trade. 1519 -1650*." By Andrew Christian Peterson, Aug. 2014.

91. "*The Manila Galleon and California*." By William Lytle Shurz. Published in *The Southwestern Historical Quarterly*, Vol. XXI, Oct. 1917. No. 2. 9 pages.

92. "*The Galleon Cargo: Accounts in the Colonial Archives*." By Cameron La Follette, Douglas Deur, Esther Gonzalez. 2018. *Oregon Historical Quarterly*, 119(2), Pages 250-281.

93. "*The Search for the Manila Galleon Log Books*." By Wayne V. Bert, 1990. Published in *Bulletin American Meteorological Society,* Vol. 71, No. 11. 1990.

94. "*Abaca (Manila hemp): The Fiber Monopoly of the Philippine Islands*." By G.S. Lee, 1920. Published in The Scientific Monthly, 11 (2), Pages 159-170. http://www.jstor.org/stable/6637.

Appendix K

FOLLOW THE COCONUT FLOTILLA

Many people theorize the impossible occurrence of very old coconut material on Oak Island was simply a byproduct of flotsam and jetsam. They contend that either all at once or over a long period of time, coconut fibers and husks fell from trees or man, and into the island waters of the Caribbean Sea, Atlantic Ocean, or other body of water. As the currents took the copious caravan of coconut components, they made their wandering way into the Gulf Stream north. Eventually, this flotilla of fibers floundered on the shores of an island along the coast of Nova Scotia. But only on one, in a bay brimming with hundreds of islands. Since the carbon-dating determinations of the coconut fibers found on Oak Island indicate a wide range of dates, the theorists herald the reoccurring frequency of many fibrous flotsams over an extended period of time.

A very long distance, but some say it's plausible. In nautical terms the distance from Puerto Rico to Mahone Bay, Nova Scotia, is 1,594 nautical miles away. However, this does not factor in the labyrinth of such tedious and problematic pathways with which the ocean currents would subject our floating fiber flotilla. Gyres, eddies, meanders, and cross currents all present problematic pathways north. Let us trace that path with the well-understood highway of ocean currents heading north.

Ocean current hydrography has been extensively studied and continues to be researched. Programs such as the Global Drifter Program, part of the Global Ocean Monitoring and Observing section of the National Oceanic & Atmospheric Administration (NOAA); is where you can link to GoMRI & CARTHE at the University of Miami Rosenthal School of Marine and Atmospheric Science.[1] Most of the information in this reportage is gathered from their 'surface currents' drifter website.[2] The International Surface

Velocity Program (SVP) monitors a myriad of marine ocean conditions and aspects.[2] The NOAA AOML Drifting Buoy Data Assembly (DAC) provides the information which informs us of how coconut fibers would have traveled from Puerto Rico to Nova Scotia, to include their speed.[2]

This appendix is built on the datasets gathered by near-surface buoys (drifters) between 1979 to 2003.[3] These are the datasets currently available online. The program receives approximately 31,200 transmissions from buoys, each day.[2] Ocean-current pathways and surface water speed have been averaged and correlated for seasonal variations. The distance reported at the end of this appendix is not the actual accumulated distance of drifters (buoys) on our ocean pathway, but an actual distance based on 71 GPS locations along the route(s) our flotilla would have taken. The speed of those archived datasets based on drifter data seen with Buoy ID# 09802862[4] (1999-2000) is used to project the duration of our flotillas journey. The imagery of this drifter data is shown in Fig. 6. This provides us a more realistic distance and speed for our coconut caravan, than variances which account for hurricanes and other weather or seasonal anomalies.

Courtesy: iStock.com

Like floating debris, the drifters never travel in a straight line. Shown at the end of this appendix are the "spaghetti plots" for each and every reporting drifter during this 24-year time sequence. These visualizations are provided so you can see the myriad of opportunities for our coconut fiber flotilla to get lost or meander forever. In addition, you can literally see the percentage of flotsam & jetsam which actually make it to Nova Scotia. These spaghetti plots are available for each leg of the journey and can be found at the websites cited in the Appendix Reference List.

Our waterborne travelers first begin their journey having entered the waters on the southern end of Puerto Rico, near Arroyo. This is where Coconut Palms were first sighted in the Caribbean, in 1549.[5] Part of the Greater Antilles, Puerto Rico is the eastern end island of the Cuban/Hispaniola/Puerto Rico Arc which separates the Caribbean Sea from the Atlantic Ocean. Fueled by strong upwelling regions offshore of northern South America and siphoned through the Lesser Antilles, the Caribbean Current is effectively divided into three main currents.[6] Depending on which side of Puerto Rico our coconut materials fall into the water, they either enter the north or central subcurrents. Most likely they would take a splash into the central Caribbean Current, which clocks at 60-65 cm s^{-1} (65 centimeters per second).[6] Drifter buoys, if not in the southern third of the current can languish in eddies and meanders created from underwater mountains and ridges. Our fibrous flotilla's first major obstacle is trying not to enter the Gulf of Mexico. This could doom our fibers to the eternal future of being trapped in a gyre's grip! The Caribbean Current transports relatively cool water from the Venezuelan coastal region into the interior of the Caribbean Sea where it is warmed.[6]

This Caribbean Current is a continuous flow throughout the Caribbean Sea. This brings the tropical waters northward to feed the Yucatan Current.[6] Figure 1, on the following page illustrates how floaters within these currents may enter the Gulf of Mexico's Loop Current, and never come out again.

Assuming the flotilla is still intact, it could be ejected from the Loop Current at speeds of 30-40 cm s^{-1}.[7] The average time, regardless of weather, would take our caravan about 160-180 days to clear this part of the journey.[4] See Figure 6. This is considered the "transport maximum" for the eastern Caribbean. Once past the Campeche Bank and in the Loop Current, our floaters enter into the Florida Current riding it around the Florida peninsula and up to North

Carolina.[7] This is a big "IF." Figure 1 below illustrates the Caribbean currents and their direction.

Courtesy: University of Miami Rosenthal School of Marine and Atmospheric Science, Florida.

Fig. 1

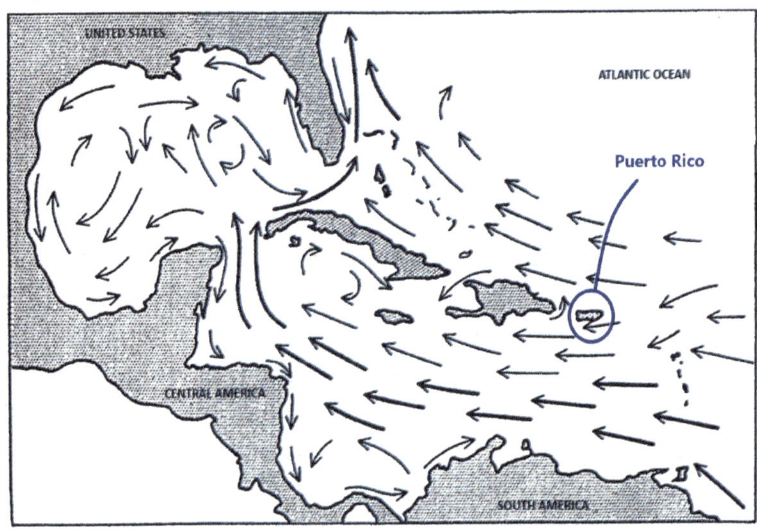

Caribbean Current to Yucatan Current Connecting to the Gulf Stream Current.

The Caribbean Current transports significant amounts of water northwestward through the Caribbean Sea and into the Gulf of Mexico, via the Yucatan Current. The source water from the Caribbean Current is from the equatorial Atlantic Ocean via the North Equatorial, North Brazil, and Guiana currents.[6]

Our hopes are the island of floating coconut fibers do not venture left into the Gulf of Mexico nor recycle back into the Caribbean Sea; this portends a total disaster for this theory to work. Thus, we are expecting for it to veer through the channel between Cuba and Florida, then hang a left and venture north up along the American Eastern Coastline. The above graphic illustrates the movement of the Florida Current out of the Caribbean Sea and up along the Eastern Seaboard coast of the United States.

This would be risky for any roaming raft of refuse!

With the Florida Current placing them officially in the Gulf Stream System, the coconut caravan heads due north along the U.S. shoreline to Cape Hatteras, North Carolina. Now traveling at 3 times the transport maximum of the Caribbean Current,[8] the wad of wet floaters attempts to "gun it" on the maritime highway! As expected on any highway, the Charleston Bump, a topographic irregularity at the 31°N, slows things down considerably.[8]

Fig. 2 Courtesy: LINC School, IFISC.

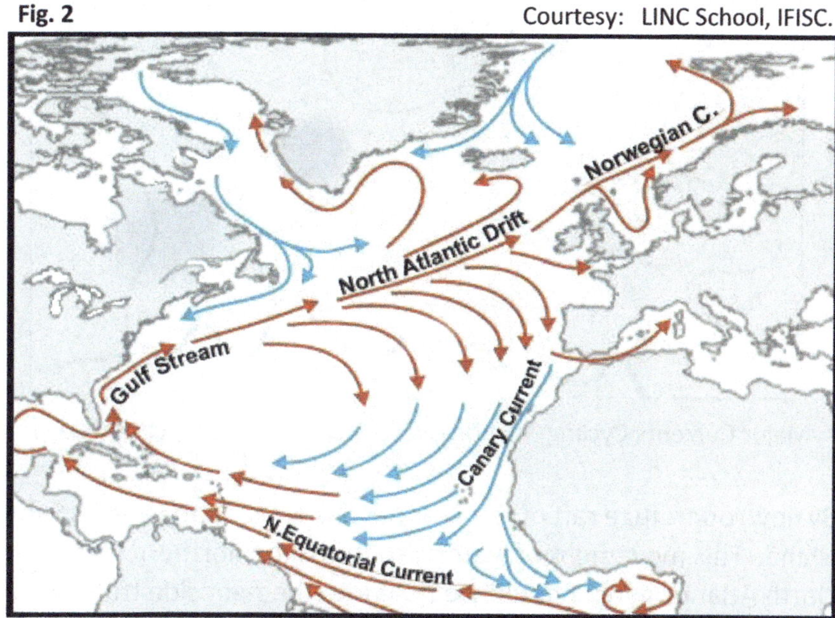

The Gulf Stream now takes over at Cape Hatteras, as the Florida Current ceases to follow the continental shelf. As the raft of refuse rides the Gulf Stream, the current itself changes from a single meandering front to multiple, branching fronts.[9] This is the most impactful aspect of our flotillas floating future.

The left branch curves north along the continental slope, eventually turning east between 50° and 52°N. This branch is called the North Atlantic Current. The right branch, however, flows southeastward towards the Mid-Atlantic Ridge and is called the Azores Current.[9]

To compound the importance for our floaters to get in the correct lane, are frequent highly dynamic mesoscale activities, along with rapid changes in the major surface currents.[9] Think of this as "riding the rapids" from the flows of the intersecting Labrador Current! See Figure 3 below.

Fig. 3 Courtesy: Nova Scotia Museum of Natural History.

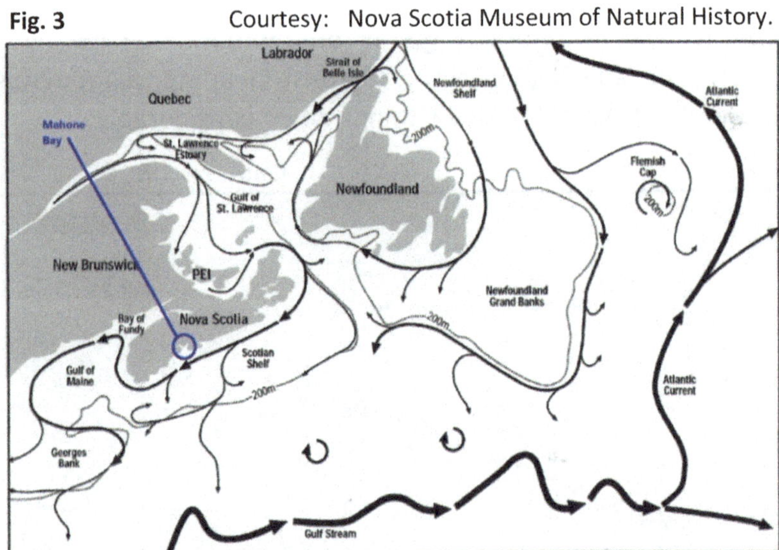

Major Currents Cycling offshore Nova Scotia in Atlantic Ocean Basin

By now, our refuge raft of refuse is passing Nova Scotia and its Sable Island. This movement of water also forms the northern half of the North Atlantic gyre. Should we float into the right side traffic lane, we have better odds of ending up on the shores of Puerto Rico than Nova Scotia.

Still, our coconut fibers face a formidable fork in the Atlantic Current. Should our floaters take the wrong path, their trip will be much, much longer. As the Gulf Stream evolves into the North Atlantic Current it heads to Europe bypassing Canada and Nova Scotia. In the above diagram, the thick black line at the bottom of the map shows the path of what was the Gulf Stream, which is now the North Atlantic Current, heading north around Newfoundland at cruising speed of 100 cm s^{-1}.[10] *Icebergs be damned!*

As the North Atlantic Current moves our coconut caravan poleward up past Newfoundland, the flow becomes the Irminger Current, which is the northward flowing component of the N. Atlantic subpolar gyre.[10] This in turn allows a U-turn for our floaters into the E. Greenland Current from the Artic Ocean, which then channels toward the coast. Moving less than 10-15 cm s^{-1} [6] along the Greenland continent south,[11] our water-weary wanderers are desperate for warmer climes!

Unfortunately, they may face even more disastrous perils caused by the low-density water within which they float.[11] With frequent vorticity, the breakup of our cozy coconut caravan is most assuredly in their future. This could ever eddy them along the Eastern Greenland continent if the Sea Goddess ***Ran***, is not waiving them onward. Hugging the shoreline and hoping for a slip into the West Greenland Current or the Labrador Current, our floating flotilla has shed more than just a few pounds! The fresh polar water cuts salinity which decreases the buoyancy of our frozen fibrous mass.[11] The reduction of salt leads to the buildup of sea ice exiting the northern end of Greenland. The East Greenland Current is estimated to carry upwards of 5,000 km^3 of ice equatorward annually.[11] Ninety percent of all of Artic Ocean ice is exported through the East Greenland Current![11] If not sinking, the coconut fiber floaters may be locked into sea ice forever! *Will they make it?*

Yet again, the coconut fibers which amassed in warm Puerto Rico are taken away from their intended destination and float helplessly north along the western coast of Greenland, in the West Greenland Current. Along with large icebergs the floating flotilla maneuvers towards Baffin Bay and suddenly they reverse direction as they close in on this large cul-de-sac bay.[12] *Hallelujah!* Finally a current they can like – the Labrador Current sends them towards their home destination. Riding high on the shelf, the caravan is going slower than everything else out in the Labrador Sea, speeding along at 100 cm s^{-1}. They however, pace themselves at their lower speed of 35 cm s^{-1}.[12]

But that means they are lucky, as deep fast waters would have looped them back again and again. *"Stay to the right," **Ran** regales!*

If only the coconuts could paddle to the right – *hug that shore!*

Mixed with the Baffin Island Current, the Labrador Current flows southeastward along the continental slope and divides into two branches at Hamilton Bank.[13] The smaller inshore branch carries about 15% of the water flow of the Labrador Current but is the only route plausible at this point for the fibers to make land.[13] Still, at 100 km wide and 150m deep, the inshore branch is split yet again around the Flemish Cap, reducing access to only 50 km wide.[13]

Do they stay on the slope and swing around the tail of the Grand Banks and onto the Scotian Shelf? Unfortunately, to date, NONE of the NOAA Drifting Buoy Datasets between 1979 and 2003 ever made it to this area of the Scotian Shelf.[6] A mass of several tons of needed coconut fibers floating to Oak Island have not given up hope yet.

Thinking all is lost, the coconut cruise finds themselves *(in a dream!)* entering into *The Slope Jet*, also known as the Slopewater Current. The literature on the Slope Jet is incomplete as most research in this area has focused mainly on the Gulf Stream dynamics, a few hundred kilometers to the south of the Scotian Shelf.[14] Though the hydrography is unknown, no drifting buoys have floated its water currents along the continent. This current travels in opposite but parallel currents with the Gulf Stream waters.[14]

Again, the plausibility is very low as winds come from the west off the continent.[13, 14] These headwinds only hinder the high hopes of the *floaton* trying to move against them and in close to the coastline.

Is it possible the coconut tidewrack made their way into the waterways around Newfoundland, then by the Gulf of St.

Lawrence, Northern New Brunswick, and Prince Edwards Island? Could they then segue onto the Scotian Shelf and around the eastern coast of Nova Scotia? Well, the water had to get there somehow, right?

But which island to select and fulfill its mission to become forever legend within the flotsam fantasies of floaters worldwide!

Can it be done? Did the weather not rip the organic raft apart or it sink within the waves along the route? Did birds not pick it apart for fibers or to eat castaway crustaceans? Would not fish nibble it to pieces, or a whale mistaken it for a pile of plankton?

Whether one coconut husk at a time or a crazy coco-caravan, this was a **12,904** Frequent Floater nautical miles trip at the minimum! This trip would have taken at the minimum, **4.5 years** to traverse while soaking in saltwater. Unfortunately this would have long exceeded the time for our coconuts to still maintain viability to germinate.[15] As the Thor Heyerdahl "Kon Tiki" Expedition clearly learned, the rumor of coconuts circumnavigating the world's oceans is just not true.[16] In addition, our retted raft would have biodegraded and disintegrated as the natural cellulose fibers and gelatinous pectin would have long-ago dissolved. Ocean action over such a long haul would have been similar to the beating, decortication, and the hackling process used to separate husk from seed.[17] Truly our fibrous flotilla was doomed from the beginning!

***Ran** cries for fibers.*

Close-up of Slope-Jet Current and lack of Drifter plots along the Nova Scotia Coastline.

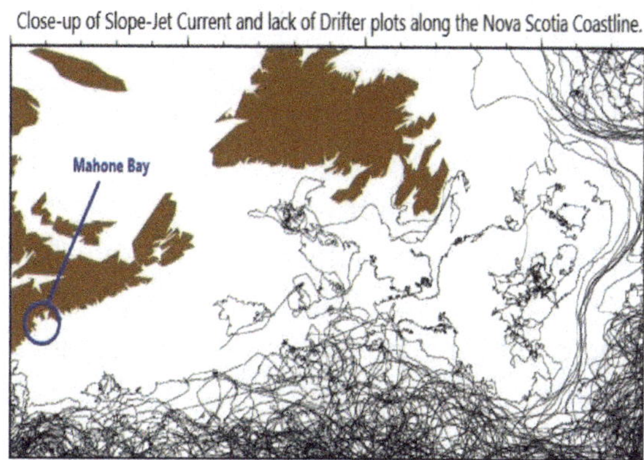

Fig. 4. See citation on the following pages.

Figure 5 below shows the travel our fibrous flotilla would have followed based on ocean and sea currents and flows. Starting from Puerto Rico, the Red Route flow reflects **10,515** nautical miles of lucky floating to the Scotian Shelf near Nova Scotia. Whereas the combination Red/Yellow Route flow reflects additional flotilla floating should they not catch the Irminger Current west of the British Isles. The total distance of this ocean current pathway is **12,904** nautical miles. These are direct travel miles and do not include buoy meandering. Neither pathway provide access to Mahone Bay unfortunately.

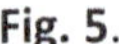
Fig. 5. Created by David H. Neisen

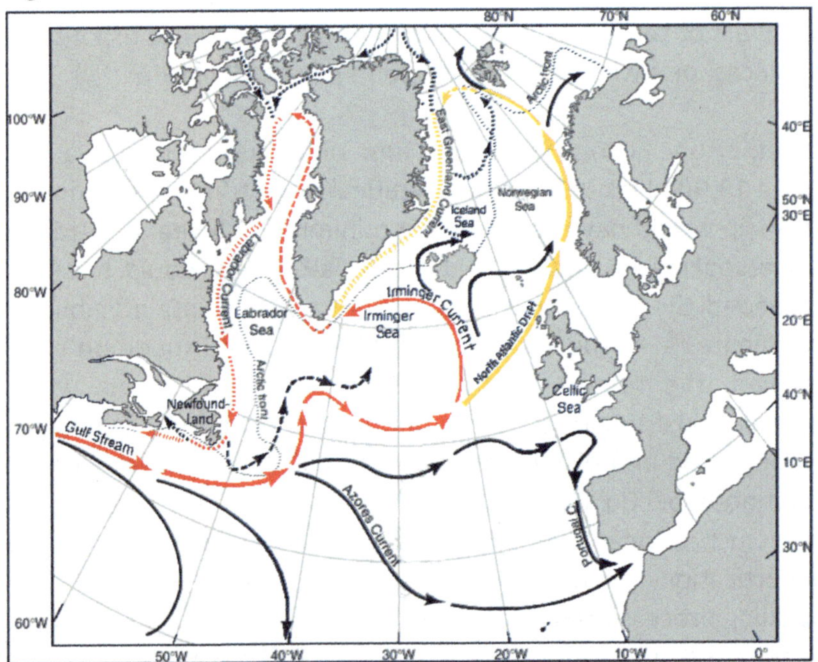

On the following page is a graphic illustration of the movement of a single Drifter buoy. Each dot along the travel line represents a satellite transmission report of its position, and the month of those reports is noted. This drifter buoy data is used in the "Formula" at the end of the appendix showing distance and duration of travel to Oak Island.

This specific Drifter (buoy ID# 09802862) was used to 'average' buoy travel experience. It is also provided to demonstrate the speed and indirect course which flotsam and jetsam is subject through various currents, gyres, eddies, and meanders.

Figure 6 is the spaghetti plot map for Buoy ID# 09802862 and is provided by NOAA AOML Drifting Buoy Data Assembly (DAC) Center.[4] Note the Start point and the End point on the map.

Fig. 6. *

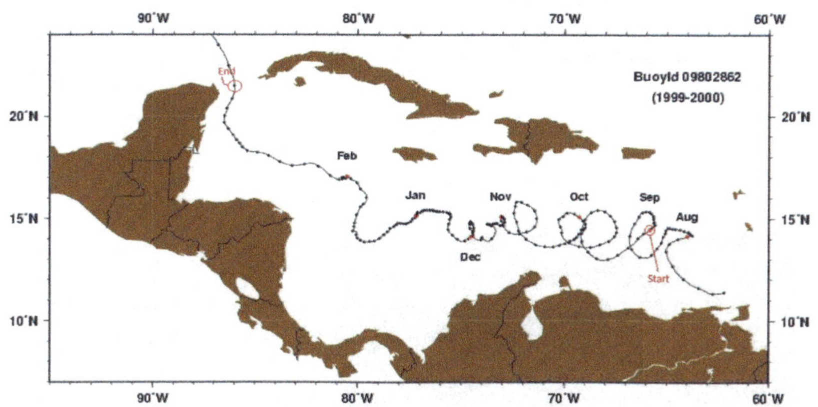

The spaghetti plot maps below displays the course taken by 24 years of ocean current research using drifter buoys and are courtesy of the University of Miami Rosenstiel School of Marine and Atmospheric Science, Florida.

SPAGHETTI PLOTS OF ARCHIVED DRIFTER BUOYS 1979 - 2003

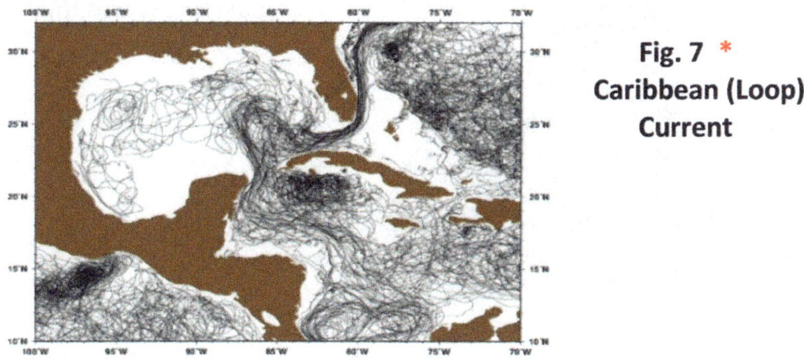

Fig. 7 *
Caribbean (Loop) Current

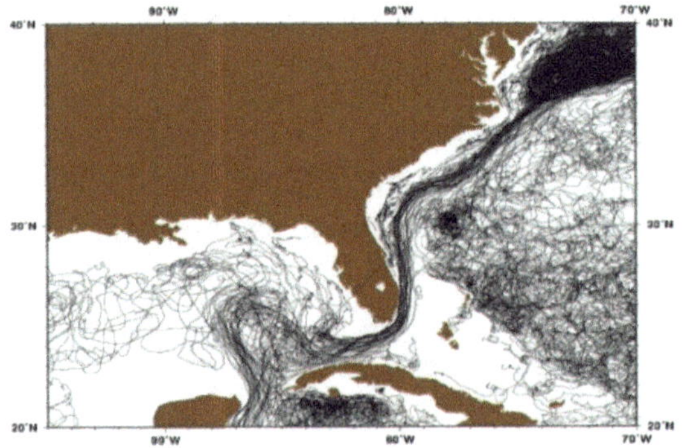

Fig. 8 *
Gulf Stream Current

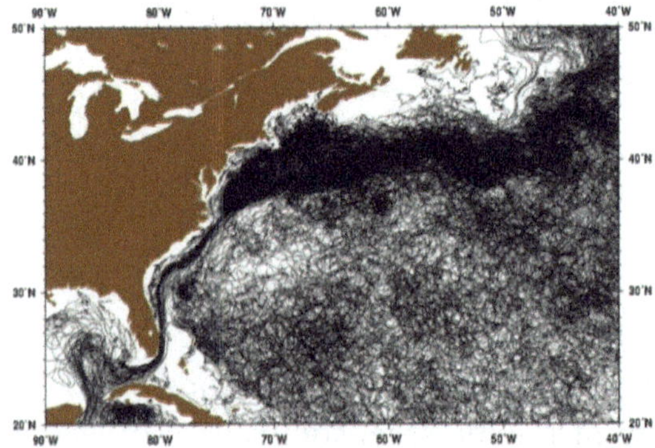

Fig. 9 *
North Atlantic Current

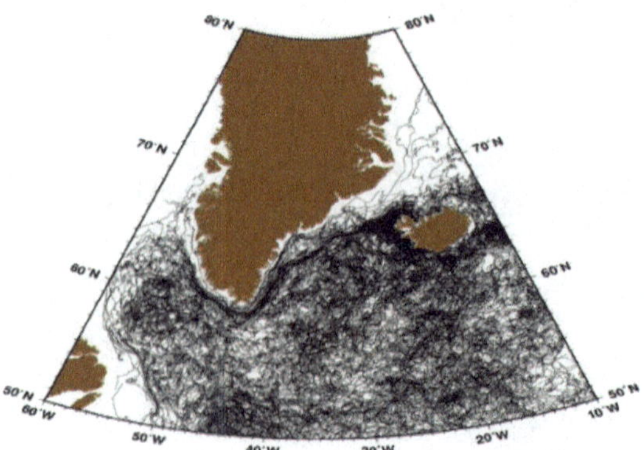

Fig. 10 *
East/West Greenland Current

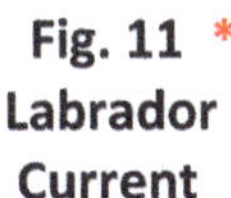

Fig. 11 *
Labrador Current

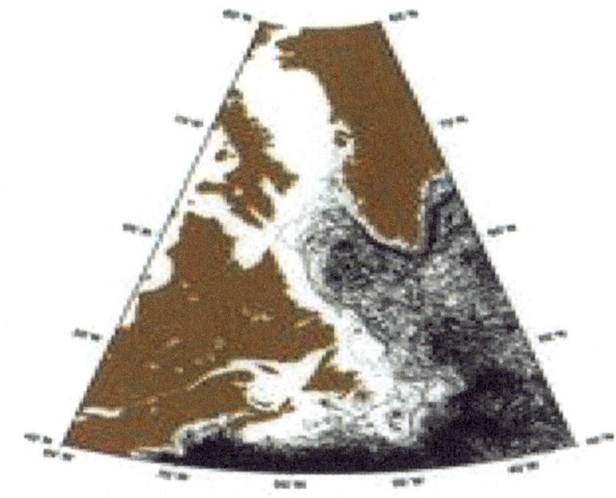

Fig. 12 *
Atlantic Ocean & Slope Jet Currents

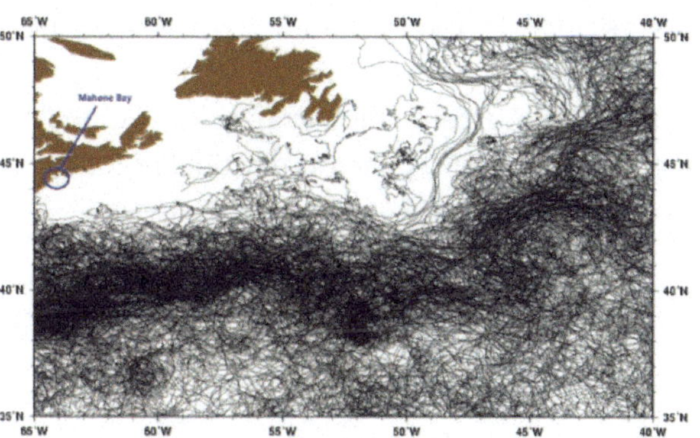

Fig. 13
Dinner Current
'Spaghetti al dente'

Spaghetti Clipart Transparent SeekPNG.com

**Images provided by NOAA AOML Drifting Buoy Data Assembly (DAC) Center and available at* https://oceancurrents.rsmas.miami.edu.html.

FORMULA

As discussed, our floating-coconut fiber flotilla traveled between 10,515 and 12,904 direct-route nautical miles to complete its journey from the southern tip of Puerto Rico to Mahone Bay, Nova Scotia, Canada. The duration of this travel took as little as 4.5 years.

How did we calculate that astonishing dataset?

As we discussed earlier, we first look at the various ocean and sea currents and flows which would dictate the travels of our fibrous flotilla. The map below shows the longer most likely route (Red/Yellow Route), and a shorter route (Red Route) should ***Ran*** have decided to lend a hand. The shorter Red Route could have been attainable perhaps. If the floaton was able to maneuver into the Irminger Current prior to passing Iceland, it would have saved a treacherous 2,500 charted nautical miles (yellow route).

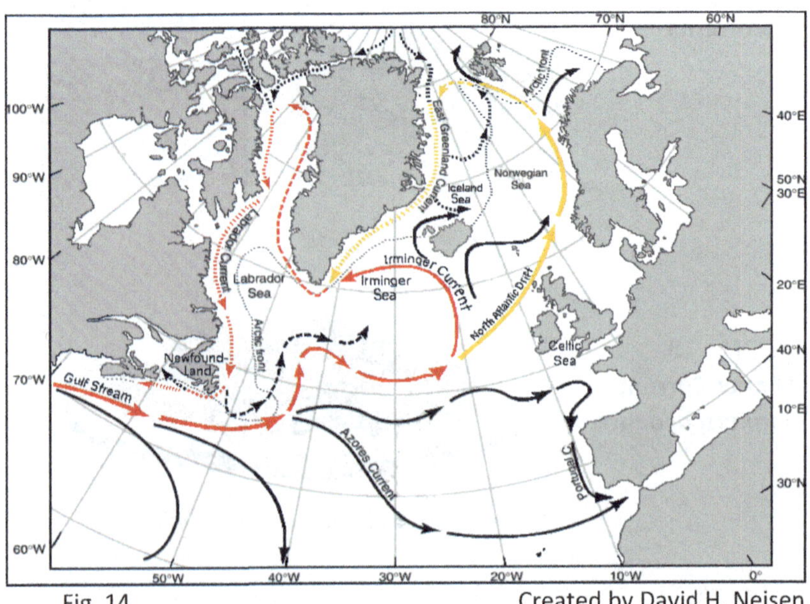

Fig. 14 Created by David H. Neisen

With this information we deploy 71 GPS markers along those routes dictated by the oceans currents and flows. This not only provides us with distance between GPS markers, but also the actual total nautical miles from the starting point in Puerto Rico, to our destination in Mahone Bay and on the shore of Smith's Cove, Oak Island. This also verifies the direct distance had the buoy floated directly from one marker to the next. This exercise can be duplicated at www.freemaptools.com/measure-distance.htm.

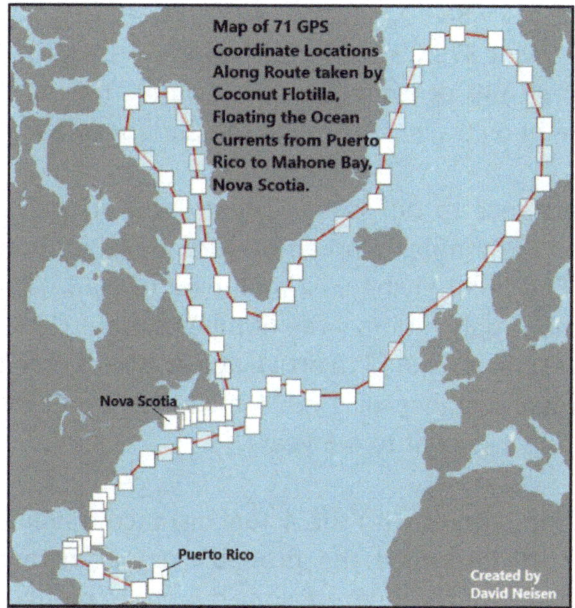

This mapping model can provide us the distances in nautical miles, kilometers, meters and centimeters. The centimeters given can allow us to directly compute the time to travel this route at the flow speed(s) discussed and notated earlier in this appendix.

Buoy ID# 09802862 travel through the Caribbean Sea was "time" plotted by the dates shown. For this buoy to travel from the Start Point to the End Point, as marked on Fig. 6, we can clearly note the duration of time to cover this distance was **173 days** (Sept. 1 thru Feb. 20). Though the actual flight distance from Start Point to End Point is 1,361 nautical miles, the drifter buoy actually traversed a plotted distance of **3,130.3 nautical miles**, or 230% the distance.

We can extrapolate the speed with which this particular drifter buoy traveled this distance by first converting the nautical miles into centimeters. 3,130.3 mi. x 185,200.1 cm = 579,731,873.03

centimeters. Then we take the number of days it took for the buoy to go from Start Point to End Point (173 days) and break that period down into seconds. 1 day = 86,400 seconds x 173 day = 14,947,200 seconds. Divide 579,731,873.03 centimeters into 14,947,200 seconds = 38.78 cm s^{-1} (39 centimeters per second). This is the speed with which the buoy traveled through the Caribbean Sea.

Knowing the total distance to our Nova Scotian location we can simply divide those 12,904 miles marked by GPS, by 1,361 miles from Start Point to End Point giving us a multiplier of 9.48. With this multiplier you can simply multiply the number of days (173) it took to go those 1,361 miles by 9.48 to arrive at a length of time to make the overall travel distance of 12,904 miles. [173 x 9.48 = 1,642.46 days]. This is equivalent to 4.5 years.

You can also use this multiplier with the actual distance traversed by the buoy drifter to determine the probable actual distance which the buoy traveled as it meandered along this entire pathway. Therefore, using the actual meandering distance of 3,130.3 nautical miles traveled from Start Point to End Point *by this one buoy*, multiplied by 9.48, equates to 29,675.24 actual nautical miles traversed by the buoy throughout the entirety of ocean currents pathway. So by making the same assumption our floating fibrous flotilla meandered and circled similarly to that which Buoy ID# 09802862 did, we can see parallels to the overall speed of the flotilla.

There are 185200.1 centimeters in a nautical mile. Multiplied by 29,675.24 nautical miles, the total number of centimeters in this distance is 5,495,854,448. Dividing this number by the number of days it took our floating fibrous flotilla to possibly reach Oak Island (1,642.5 days = 4.5 years), equates to 3,346,030.10533 centimeters covered per day in travel. Divided by the seconds in a day (86,400) means our floaton is averaging a speed of 38.72 cm s^{-1} (39 centimeters per second). A smidgen slower, but still making good time overall.

These are mental exercises and are basically useless except for telling us what a tremendous distance these floating fibers floundered within the seas of the world. Not only is it provable NO flotsam or jetsam from the Caribbean has ever made landfall on a Nova Scotian beach, but other jettisoned material from elsewhere in the Atlantic, would not have made it to the Scotian shelf; except perhaps, if launched from along the eastern Nova Scotian coastline itself. Furthermore, the travel distance and duration of travel would have thrashed apart, saturated, and sunk any wad of coconut fibers or other organic materials.

"EVEN IF A SHIP HEADING BACK FROM

THE CARIBBEAN OR SOUTH AMERICA WERE TO HAVE

TOSSED ITS LOAD OF COCONUT COIR FIBER,

BE IT ON THE SHIP AS A CARGO OR AS DUNNAGE – THE

FIBERS WOULD NEVER HAVE FLOATED TO OAK ISLAND

VIA THE OCEAN AND SEA CURRENTS."

David H. Neisen, 2022.

Footnoted References

[1]. "*Global Ocean Surface Velocities from Drifters: Mean, Variance, ENSO Response, and Seasonal Cycle*." by Rick Lumpkin and Gregory C. Johnson. Journal of Geophysical Research – Oceans. NOAA/Atlantic Oceanographic and Meteorological Laboratory, Miami, Fl. Apr. 19, 2013. 15 pages.

[2]. "*Ocean Currents Website*." University of Miami, Rosenthiel School of Marine and Atmospheric Science. https://oceancurrents.rsmas.miami.edu.

[3]. "*Global Drifter Program*." National Oceanic and Atmospheric Administration, Atlantic Oceanographic and Meteorological Laboratory, Physical Oceanography Division (PhOD). https://www.aoml.noaa.gov/phod/gdp/data_faq.php#metadata.

[4]. "*Buoy #09802862 Drifter Pathway Plotted*." Surface Currents of the Caribbean Sea, Example Plots from 4-D Current Experiment. Buoyid 09802862 (1999-2000). https://oceancurrents.rsmas.miami.edu/caribbean/img_aoml/caribbeanF3.html.

[5]. "*Coconut Time Line, The Nautical Period: 1499-1839*." Online repository of historical anecdotes about all things coconut. Updated Feb. 14, 2017. http://cocos.arecaceae.com/ancient.html.

[6]. "*The Caribbean Current*." by Joanna Gyory, Arthur J. Mariano, and Edward H. Ryan. *The Caribbean Current*. Surface Currents in the Caribbean Sea. Pages 1-8. https://oceancurrents.rsmas.miami.edu/caribbean/caribean.html.

[7]. "*The Loop Current*." by Joanna Gyory, Arthur J. Mariano, and Edward H. Ryan. *The Loop Current*. Surface Currents in the Caribbean Sea. https://oceancurrents.rsmas.miami.edu/atlantic/loop-current.html.

[8]. "*The Florida Current*." by Joanna Gyory, Elizabeth Rowe, Arthur J. Mariano, and Edward H. Ryan. *The Florida Current*. Surface Currents in the Atlantic Ocean. https://oceancurrents.rsmas.miami.edu/atlantic/florida.html.

[9]. "*The Gulf Stream*." by Joanna Gyory, Arthur J. Mariano, and Edward H. Ryan. *The Gulf Stream*. Surface Currents in the Atlantic Ocean. https://oceancurrents.rsmas.miami.edu/atlantic/gulf-stream.html.

[10]. "*The North Atlantic Current*." by Elizabeth Rowe, Arthur J. Mariano, Edward H. Ryan. *The North Atlantic Current*. Surface Currents in the Atlantic Ocean. https://oceancurrents.rsmas.miami.edu/atlantic/north-atlantic.html.

[11]. "*The East Greenland Current*." by Joanna Gyory, Arthur J. Mariano, Edward H. Ryan. *The East Greenland Current*. Surface Currents in the Atlantic Ocean. https://oceancurrents.rsmas.miami.edu/atlantic/east-greenland.html.

12. "*The West Greenland Current*." by Joanna Gyory, Arthur J. Mariano, Edward H. Ryan. *The West Greenland Current*. Surface Currents of the Atlantic Ocean. https://oceancurrents.rsmas.miami.edu/atlantic/west-greenland.html.

13. "*The Labrador Current*." by Joanna Gyory, Arthur J. Mariano, Edward H. Ryan. *The Labrador Current*. Surface Currents of the Atlantic Ocean. https://oceancurrents.rsmas.miami.edu/atlantic/labrador.html.

14. "*The Slope Jet Current*." by Angelique C. Haza, Barbie Bischof, Arthur J. Mariano. 2013. *The Slope Jet Current*. Surface Currents of the Atlantic Ocean. https://oceancurrents.rsmas.miami.edu/atlantic/slope-jet.html.

15. "*Biofuels from Coconuts*." by Krishna Raghaven. 2010. 107 pages. Annex 8, Recycling Husks, subsection Organic Manuring, p. 78. www.energypedia.info/f/f9/EN-biofuels_from_cocnuts-krishna_raghaven.pdf.

16. "*Kon Tiki: Across the Pacific by Raft*." by Thor Heyerdahl, 1950. Mattituck: Amereon House. 240 Pages. https://infogalactic.com/info/Coconut#cite_note-Heyerdahl-31.

17. "*History of Coir Industry*." Central Coir Research Institute of India. www.ccriindia.org/pdf/02Historyofcoirindustry.pdf.

Appendix L

DUNNAGE DONE – FLOATER A FOUL

There's a saying, *"A picture is worth a thousand words."* Perhaps it was that island depiction with the 1965 Readers Digest article that has lured so many into Oak Islands' intrigue. Those *mystery trees* in that image hooked me. I think conversely, it may have been those 'thousand words' of the article which did more to stir the imagination of the readers than just that one image. The Oak Island treasure story is fascinating because every word written of the lore, exponentially creates thousands of 'pictures' in your mind.

There is also a children's game *"Telephone,"* where a circle of kids pass along a short, whispered message. By the time the message has been 'passed' through the line of listening ears, the message has become so distorted, it becomes comedic. Often times participants swear that is what they heard! After review, they all realize they heard what they wanted to hear and told what they wanted to say.

In a way, this is what this book has been about – reversing the process by going from what we've heard involved characters have said about the facts; and trying to determine the original starting truth. Case in point – ***dunnage.***

To be clear and not to play word games, coir fiber was/can and still is, used to stuff boxes, crates, casks, or barrels being shipped as cargo. That is to say, *within* the crate an item is placed, and much coir fiber is placed around the item to prevent it from bouncing around within the crate and somewhat protect it in transport. This is similar to filling the box with Styrofoam peanuts, bubble wrap, kraft paper or air bubble sheets. *This is not what dunnage is.*

We've already acknowledged that the coconut coir fibers were not even the organic material Frederick Blair was referring to when he first uttered this narrative. But opinions die hard. And since those experts at Woods Hole Oceanographic Institute felt the issue of dunnage was elevated enough to earn a pathway of explanation – it deserves one last look at this myth. So with the thought of digging deeper into depths of dunnage, let us take it abit further.

Dunnage Done

Are you saying Coconut Fibers were Jetsam?

> **Dunnage:** *"the use of sufficient dunnage (pieces of wood etc.) is one of the principal precautions against damage to stowed cargo. Materials that are not affected by moisture are used as dunnage, such as: boards, matting, burlap, rattan. The dunnage is laid on the ceiling* ***and along the wooden cargo battens and all other*** *places where necessary. The object is to prevent or limit damage by crushing, chafing, shifting of cargo, sweat, moisture, or contact with hold pillars, etc."*[1]

Now try and consider you have just purchased a large, tall, and heavy ceramic pot at your local *Home Depot* construction store. The ceramic pot would not fit in your *Smart Car* and your wife's *Prius* was spending the weekend being charged. So you decide to simply rent a Box truck from *Home Depot*. Once you load this large, tall, and heavy ceramic pot in the cargo bed of the Box truck – *now what?* How do you protect it from jostling around in the back? Are you going to run back into the gardening section of the store to buy up all of the coir-fiber hanging pot mediums they may have? Still not enough stuffing to keep the pot from tipping over, right? If the *Home Depot* is out of coir.... Are you going to check out the packing department to buy all the bags of shipping peanuts to finish filling up the Box truck to protect your valuable? **Of course not!** Like in the cargo hold of a ship, you are going to place a mat or blanket around your new ceramic pot and tie it to the walls of the Box truck. You may even place a partition, board, or plywood up against the ceramic pot to keep your pot wedged into the corner of that truck. This would secure it from rolling around... as you travel the rough seas of the highway home. That piece of partition you used is called - *dunnage*.

> **Dunnage** – *"an expression used to describe timber boards which can be laid singularly or in double pattern under cargo parcels to keep the surface of the cargo off the deck plate. Its purpose is to provide air space around the cargo and so prevent 'cargo sweat'. Heavy-lift cargoes would normally employ heavy timber bearers to spread the load and dunnage would normally be used for lighter-load cargoes."* [2]

As you surmise, seafarers on a sailing ship are not themselves individually packaging the crated and cask'd cargo listed on the ships' manifest. They are not hammering away at wedging in the head of a 'firkin' or a 'hogshead.' Nor were they 'sheathing' a 'Frame crate.' They're jobs were to 'Yard and Stay!' Sailors were 'parbuckling' the barrels on board and preparing the 'tons burthen' on a 'Carrick' before they 'make for leeway.' Initially they were 'luffing' the 'derrick boom' and getting the parcels into the hold. When necessary, they were 'tomming off' the cargo with 'baulks' (beams) of timber and 'shoring' the cargo to minimize shifting, falling, or being damaged during the trip. The sailing crew would review the 'cargo plan' and assess the 'bale space capacity.' They used available boards, timbers, ballast stones, nets, ropes, blankets, and mats to both lockdown (tomming off) the cargo, balance the weight of the cargo throughout the ships stowage, and protect (shoring) the cargo items from each other, from getting wet, or catching on fire. This is a very important job and needs to be done properly – *back then and now!*

> **Dunnage**. *"Brushwood, scrapwood, or other loose material laid in the hold to protect the cargo from water damage or prevent it from shifting, or to protect the ceiling from abrasion."*[3]

Even today there are detailed international standard instructions on how to properly stow every type of cargo going shipbound. Bulk or baled coconut husks, coconut coir fiber, or coconut fiber-made products were a dangerous product, as you will read. No doubt it was one reason manufacturing of coconut coir fiber products were moved back to India. Quoting the *Maritime Transportation Information Service*, which says,

> *"In damp weather (rain, snow) the cargo must be protected from moisture since coconut fiber is strongly hygroscopic (hygroscopicity). It must be protected from sea, rain, and condensation water and also from high levels of relative humidity, if decay, staining, self-heating, mold, attack by microorganisms, and rusting of the steel strapping are to be avoided. Rusty strapping contaminates the coconut fiber and reduces its value. This cargo is to be secured in such a way that the bales/hanks or strapping are not damaged. Undamaged strapping is essential to maintaining compression of the bales during transport. If the strapping is broken, compression is diminished, which at the same time results in an increased supply of oxygen to the inside of the bales. This in turn increases the risk of combustion or feed a fire which has already started. Bursting or chafing of steel strapping may lead to sparking and external ignition. Coconut fiber must be stowed away from any heat sources. If the product is loaded for shipment in a dry state, it does not have any possible ventilation conditions. Problems arise if the product, packaging and/or ceiling/flooring are too damp. Since coconut fiber very readily absorbs oxygen, before anybody enters the hold, it must be ventilated and, if necessary, a gas measurement caried out, since a shortage of oxygen endangers life. Coconut fiber has an oil content of 2-5% (coconut oil). Coconut fiber is assigned to the Class of flammable solids. However, its specific characteristics and negative external influences may cause them to behave like a substance from Class of spontaneous combustion. Spontaneous combustion may occur as a result of exposure to moisture, animal and vegetable fats/oils, oil-bearing seeds/nuts, copra, and raw wool. This risk is further increased by the coconut oil present in coconut fiber. Coconut fiber is very highly susceptible to self-heating due to moisture. Firefighting is best performed using CO_2 or foam. It is very difficult to extinguish a fire because of the excess of oxygen in the coconut fiber, which maintains the fire from the inside. When fighting a fire, do not break the steel straps or open the*

> *bales, since relieving the compression increases the oxygen supply and makes it impossible to fight the fire effectively. Coconut fiber has a slight, unpleasant odor. A conspicuous musty odor indicates moisture damage inside the bale. Since coconut fiber may easily cause odor-tainting, it must not be stowed with odor-sensitive products (e.g. foodstuffs). Coconut fiber causes contamination due to the coconut oil it contains and must therefore be stowed away from easily stained products. Since coconut fiber is highly oxygen-absorbent, a life-threatening shortage of oxygen may arise in the hold or container."* [4]

Back during the golden age of sailing ships, having rain, snow, moisture, and humidity were daily conditions – *you are at sea!* Can you imagine the mess made by shoving bushels and bushels of coconut fiber as dunnage, between cargo casks, crates, and barrels, in an attempt to stop them from shifting in rough seas? Besides the absurdity of the physics of it all, now you have an absorbent material wadding up wet on and between the cargo you are attempting to keep dry and unstained! It is only a matter of time on a sailing ship before it migrates into the 'limber' and chokes up the 'limber holes' and causes a watery mess. Eventually it collects down in the bilge and clogs up the 'pump well.' Regardless of having a burr pump, a chain pump, or a suction pump, your use of these fibers are forcing a 'graving.' *Brilliant!*

Joseph Conrad wrote in his book "*Youth,*" the following account of days sailing.

> *"During a storm on our old wooden sailing ship with water was coming thru the hatches, through the planking seems, through the deck leaks and soaking the cargo... It was our fate to pump in that ship, to pump out of her, to pump into her; and after keeping water out of her to save ourselves from being drowned, we frantically pumped water into her to save ourselves from being burnt."* [5]

So coconut fibers were a problematic product for sailing ships to transport or use internally. That does not imply bales of it, or coir by-products were not shipped by sea. We know loose coconut coir fibers were shipped to factories in England as early as 1647; where they made twine, yarn, ropes, and carpets. Famous companies like Treloar and Sons in Ludgate Hill, Pierce Lesley & Co., William Goodacre & Sons Co., Madura Co., Coir Yarn Textiles Co., to name a few; imported coir fiber in the mid-1800s. Loose coir fibers were later used as a cheap wall insulation in residential buildings. K.R. Lawrence Bardoy, MBE of William Goodacre Operations in Alleppy, India, stated, *"Around the middle of the 20th Century, there was not a house in Europe that did not have some coir articles."* [6]

Thatched homes and buildings in Scotland used coir twine to lash down their roofs, anchoring the twine with rocks tied and hanging at the ends. Coir twine was widely used in planted hop fields for fielding the plants like grape production. But again, being part of the ship's cargo is a far cry from being their dunnage!

It would simply mean coconut fibers should or would never be used as maritime dunnage. Imagine those bales of exotic Nankin silks, Canton silks, Cambray linen, colored skeins of silk, raw silk, silk threads, white cotton, elephant cotton, Filipino cotton, damasks, satins, tapestries, drapes, and blankets[7]... all stinking, stained, infused, and sopping from those wads of fibrous coir material within those vessels? Or their spontaneous Combustion threat!

How can people have been so mistaken? Sometimes, even textual evidence is confusing or inaccurate...

Coker Nuts / Coquito Nuts

Coquito nuts are the fruits from the feather-leaved Palm (*Jubaea chilensis)*. Native to Chile, they have a thick trunk from which is obtained a sugary sap used for making wine and a syrup, and widely cultivated as an ornamental in warm dry regions (Spanish, diminutive of *coco*, "coco palm," from the Portuguese *côco*; see coconut). Coquito nuts look like miniature coconuts and have a very similar flavor to coconuts. They have a brown exterior and a white interior with a hollow center. They measure ½ to ¾ inch (1.3 to 1.9 cm) in diameter. They are completely edible (raw or cooked), and are crunchy, with an almond-like sweetness. Coquito nuts, also referred to as coker nuts, pygmy coconuts, or monkey's coconuts are the fruit of a Chilean palm tree.[10] The tree (*Jubaea chilensis*) takes up to fifty years to achieve maturity and is native to the coastal valleys of Chile. This palm grows in Mediterranean-type climates worldwide, including in the state of California.[8]

> *"**Dunnage** - Coker-nuts -- as they are now generally called, and indeed "entered" as such at the Customhouse, and so written by Mr. McCulloch, to distinguish them from cocoa, or the berries of the cacao, used for chocolate, etc. -- are brought from the West Indies, both British and Spanish, and Brazil. **They are used as dunnage in the sugar ships, being interposed between the hogsheads** [barrels]**, to steady them and prevent their being flung about**."* [9, 10]

Wow! Could the pygmy coconuts or the monkey's coconut or the Coker nuts or the Coquito nuts have been mistaken for small coconuts? Could the various names or misspellings have led some to believe this proves that the nuts from the Coconut Palm Tree (*Cocos nucifera*) are somehow related, and therefore the fiber of the latter is equivalent to the first? Were these 'nuts' (the size of grapes) truly confusing to the origins of coir fiber as dunnage and on Oak Island? This is not the sole source of confusion. In reading the next section, note how the descriptions have given confusion to understanding what is being said... similarly like the kids game "Telephone" we talked about earlier.

There is a source *on* dunnage which is like no other. Though the topic itself may not appear of interest, this 865-page bible on all things regarding stowage, was quite a fascinating read. It not only discusses dunnage and stowage with the sailors salty tongue, but the manuscript also told of stories of vessels in trouble, cultural nuances of ports around the world in the day and discusses the travels and travails of men of the sea. Appropriate quips, comments, and clauses are really too numerous to site. So I will limit the list of the litany of laws extolled in this 1878 version of "*On the Stowage of Ships and Their Cargos: With Information Regarding Freights, Charter-Parties, Etc., Etc.,*" by Robert White Stevens, Associate Member of the Institute of Naval Architects.[10] I have read two editions of this book and noticed the numbered index references have changed between the two. I assume editing and additional information were the reason. So I warn readers the numbers provided with each citation, may not be aligned with differing editions. The text is exact verbatim and reflects syntax and vocabulary of seafarers of the day.

> **182.** COFFEE, Coffee is sometimes shipped at Rio Janeiro in the same hold with hides, which are occasionally used for dunnage; the coffee often gets heated, and if the evil [water] is increased by deck leaks and putridity among the hides, the whole cargo will be damaged. In the West Indies it is shipped all the year round, but less during the hurricane months – from the beginning of August to the month of January. Coffee alone is dunnaged there with 8 or 10 inches of logwood, carefully covered with mats or old sails; in bags it should have staves or matting all up the sides. In the Common Pleas, 26th June 1866, *Palmer* sued *Lemon* for damage done to bags of coffee, shipped at Manilla, in the *Sepoy*. It was alleged that the coffee was strongly impregnated with the smell of rank Manilla oil which was stowed in the bottom of the hold. Verdict for plaintiff. At Ceylon, when cocoa-nut oil is stowed in the bottom, and **loose coir yarn is used for dunnage, to receive coffee, the yarn should be previously well covered with mats; the yarn should not come in contact with other cargo or the oil** (p. 145).
>
> **183.** COIR, a kind of yarn manufactured from the fibrous husk of cocoanuts; see rope. Bombay ton coir rope 10 cwt. Or 50 cubic feet (p. 146). **944.** ROPE: Coir, made from the fibrous covering of the cocoa nut, comes mostly from

Ceylon, Cochin, Bombay, etc. When confined in the hold it will soon rot if wet, or if water is allowed to drip on it, especially fresh water, which decreases its strength and causes injury from which, as with oil, it never recovers. Constant immersion in salt water is said to strengthen it. Coir junk [considered to be coconut husks for fuel, not retted] or yarn or fiber are often injured by stowage with oil at Ceylon, etc. When hanks [packages of coir yarn] have been stowed at Cochin, **between casks of oil**, spontaneous combustion has occurred; see oil. Coir rope weighs more than one-third, but not one-half as much as hemp rope (p. 528).

185. COKER or COCOA NUTS, a woody fruit covered with a fibrous husk, growing on a species of palm in most hot climates; they are shipped in the West Indies all the year round, as there are green nuts and ripe nuts on the same trees almost continuously; **they are generally used as dunnage, which should be stated on the bill of lading.** (p. 146). (see Coquito Nuts).

270. DUNNAGE, A quantity of loose wood, etc., laid in the bottom of a ship, either to raise heavy goods which might make her too stiff, or to keep the cargo sufficiently above the bottom to prevent its being damaged by water if she leaks. Sometimes it consists of loose articles of merchandize, permitted to be shipped for the convenience of stowing, securing, and filling up cargo. It is customary that all mats, wood, sticks, rattans, etc., necessary for dunnage, stowage, or the preservation of goods, should be free of freight. At Calcutta it is usual for rattans, etc., shipped as broken stowage, to pay a small freight; the words "to be used as broken stowage" are inserted in the bill of lading. **All cargo that is to be used for dunnage should be so stated in the bills of lading.**"(p. 184)

271. All perishable goods require dunnage; the quantity for different kinds will, in many cases, be found under their proper headings. The general rule is to have not less than six inches in the bottom and nine in the bilges, and to mat all the way up the sides with cargo in bags. The rule at Quebec is for "pot and pearl ashes, tobacco, bark, indigo, madders, gum, etc., whether in casks, cases, or bales, **to be dunnaged in the bottom and to the upper part of the bilges**, at least nine inches, and two and a half inches at the sides." As the whole of the water in the bilges cannot be removed when the ship careens [underway at sea], even with well-fitted bilge pumps, so the dunnage ought to be always deeper there, and especially in flat-floored ships, some of which require extra dunnage also at the bilges, with cargo in bulk, which naturally settles there when the ship is pressed with sail shortly after loading... To judge the thickness of brushwood [used as dunnage], stand on it and measure from under your feet. (p. 184)

274. Green or wet wood is totally unsuited for dunnage; it will damage both the cargo and the ship.... When sawing logwood do not let the dust remain in the hold, for if wetted it will discolour and damage sugar and other goods. (p. 185)

275. ...Apart from any local or specific regulations, the general rule is that the dunnage must be "sufficient" according to the nature and quality of the cargo. If a ship is not properly dunnaged, the master, unless there be any special circumstances to exonerate him, is liable to his owners for any properly ascertained loss accruing to them through his neglect. (p. 186)

279. DUNNAGE BATTENS, pieces of oak or fir, about two inches square, nailed athwart the orlop deck of ships-of-war, to prevent wet from damaging the cables, and to admit air; they are also used in sail rooms and magazines, to form a vacant space beneath the sails and powder barrels."(p. 187) [10]

If your re-read the underlined sections, it appears something is being used as dunnage, when in fact, it is instructing those products "to be dunnaged." As the book discusses repeatedly, not following proper stowage of cargo or usage of dunnage has caused many a shipper financial ruin or danger to the crew. Bad habits or practices out of certain ports in relation to certain cargos may have been commonplace initially. Eventually merchants, shippers, and insurers organized and produced and imposed standards, as in this 1878 volume shows.

As shown in Appendix C, "*On the Record*," several private National Archive Researchers with long histories in maritime research, were asked to find any connection with coconut fibers on vessels, used as dunnage. They have not found usage of coconut fibers in this manner. Their reports;

73. "Comments on Coconut Fiber as Dunnage," from J. Pennelope Goforth, Private National Archives Researcher. *Specialty:* Adventures in Alaska's Maritime History. 2021.

> *"I do a lot of research and writing on Alaska maritime history but never came across a reference to the use of coir (coconut fibers). I did a lot of poking around in the Alaska Commercial Company archives and the Alaska Steamship Company files but found nothing about their use as dunnage."*

74. "Comments on Coconut Fiber as Dunnage," from Mike Constandy, Westmoreland Research, Private National Archives Research Co. *Specialty:* Naval and maritime research, admiralty, ships logs and plans, sea lane and terrestrial UXO, 2021.

> *"I have read thousands of 19th Century maritime documents, manifests, bills of lading, etc., over the last thirty years, but I do not recall seeing any information relating to coconut fibers (coir) used as dunnage."*

For the sake of argument, let us assume a ship heading toward Europe from Ceylon. It had a coir fiber fire on board and stopped in Mahone Bay to put it out. In doing so and with the thought to eliminate the possibility the fire my rekindle, the ship removes ALL the coconut coir fibers from its hold and stowage areas. They simply bust open the bales, rake up the mess, and toss all overboard. Once assured the fire potential had been cleared they make way to their destination. Sounds pretty reasonable with the unknown fire risk under those circumstances. Unfortunately, this scenario does not answer two critically important questions.

> First: How did the ship acquire 400 hundred, 500 hundred, even 600 hundred-year old coconut coir fibers? *Special order?*
>
> Secondly: Why would these sailors bury all that coconut coir fiber under 3 ft of sand, spread out over 145 ft of the beach area? And did they dig the Money Pit to place the same coconut coir fiber onto the 60 ft. platform? *If you believe this is plausible, then aren't THEY our ancient voyagers?*

Yet if you think I was biased in my research, desperate to disprove dunnage as the definitive disclaimer on this drupes delivery to Oak Island, I will provide a few more sources here to allow you to fully understand what mariners thought dunnage was and was not.

Definitive Definitions of Dunnage

> DUNNAGE: "A term applied to loose wood or other material used in a ships hold for the protection of cargo." *Ports & Ships, Glossary of Maritime terms.* http://www.ports.co.za/maritime-terms.php.
>
> DUNNAGE: "Wood or other material used in stowing ship cargo to prevent its movement." *The American Association of Port Authorities, Glossary of Marine Terms.* https://www.aapa-ports.org/advocating/content.aspx?ItemNumber=21500.
>
> DUNNAGE: "Loose materials used to support and protect cargo in a ship's hold, also: padding in a shipping container." *Merriam-Webster Dictionary.* https://www.merriam-webster.com/dictionary/dunnage.
>
> DUNNAGE: "is defined as a material used between, beneath, at the sides of or on top of cargo stowed either in a ship's hold, or on deck or in a container with the aim of protecting the cargo from damage by chafing or wetness or to help stabilize a stow. If a shipowner does not use dunnage in the correct manner than he may be held liable for any resulting damage. Dunnage material comes in many forms, the most common being timber, plywood fibre board, hardboard, kraftpaper, plastic sheeting and bamboo. Timber dunnage can be of either hardwood or softwood and of differing thicknesses and widths. It is often unseasoned and roughly cut from logs unsuitable for other uses, still with the bark on and although cut to the same thickness, of uneven width and varying length." *Cargo Handbook.* https://cargohandbook.com/Dunnage .

DUNNAGE: "Material used in stowing cargo either for separation or the prevention of damage." *Port Tool Kit – Glossary*. https://ppiaf.org/sites/ppiaf.org/files/documents/toolkits/Portoolkit/Toolkit/pdf/modules/09_TOOLKIT_Glossary.pdf.

DUNNAGE: "Pieces of wood placed against the sides and bottom of the hold of a vessel, to preserve the cargo from the effect of leakage, according to its nature and quality. There is considerable resemblance between dunnage and ballast. The latter is used for trimming the ship and bringing it down to a draft of water proper and safe for sailing. Dunnage is placed under the cargo to keep it from being wetted by water getting into the hold, or between the different parcels to keep them from bruising and injuring each other. Padding in shipping container to prevent breakage." *Blacks Law*. https://blacks_law.en-academic.com/8684/dunnage.

DUNNAGE: "A term with a variety or related meanings. Typically dunnage is inexpensive or waste material used to protect and load securing cargo during transportation. Dunnage also refers to material used to support loads and prop tools and materials up." *Wikipedia*.

DUNNAGE: "Dun nage, n. [Cf. {Dun} a mound.] (Naut.) Fagots, boughs, or loose materials of any kind, laid on the bottom of the hold for the cargo to rest upon to prevent injury by water, or stowed among casks and other cargo to prevent their motion." *The Collaborative International Dictionary of English*.

DUNNAGE: " [dun'ij] n. [ML dennagium < ?] 1. a loose packing of any bulky material put around cargo for protection 2. personal baggage or belongings." *English World dictionary*.

DUNNAGE: "/dun ij/, n., v., dunnaged, dunnaging. n. 1. baggage or personal effects. 2. loose material laid beneath or wedged among objects carried by ship or rail to prevent injury from chafing or moisture, or to provide ventilation." *Universalium*.

DUNNAGE: "ˈdʌnɪdʒ/ (say dunij) noun. baggage or personal effects: *four trackers who would carry out the detective work and carry the dunnage and perhaps their masters as well when swamps and creeks were to be crossed." –Xavier Herbert, 1938. *Australian-English dictionary*.

DUNNAGE: "Pieces of wood placed against the sides and bottom of the hold of a vessel, to preserve the cargo from the effect of leakage, according to its nature and quality. There is considerable resemblance between dunnage and ballast. *Black's law dictionary*.

DUNNAGE: "(noun a) Loose material used to fill spaces to prevent items from shifting during shipment. The robot cameras and software direct the robots to unload the 40 pound parts from pallets (called dunnage) and place them on brackets fixed to a conveyor." *Wiktionary*.

DUNNAGE: "dun•nage [[t]ˈdʌn ɪdʒ[/t]] n. 1) baggage or personal effects 2) loose material laid beneath or wedged among objects carried by ship or rail to prevent injury from chafing or moisture or to provide ventilation • Etymology: 1615–25." *From formal English to slang*.

DUNNAGE: "auxiliary timber status Approved area forestry definition Non-commercial wood used to protect goods or as a support for transport. equivalents:

dunnage Russian: fastening wood. French: dunnage relationships: related term." *Lithuanian dictionary (lietuvių žodynas)*.

DUNNAGE: "noun Etymology: origin unknown Date: 15th century 1. loose materials used to support and protect cargo in a ship's hold; also padding in a shipping container 2. Baggage." *New Collegiate Dictionary*.

DUNNAGE: "A quantity of loose wood, &c. laid at the bottom of a ship to keep the goods from being damaged." *Glossary of Nautical Terms* (circa. 1814). https://woronorafire.org.au/maritime/Glossary.html.

DUNNAGE: "Materials of various types, often timber or matting, placed among the cargo for separation, and hence protection from damage, for ventilation and, in the case of certain cargoes, to provide space in which they tynes of a fork lift truck may be inserted." *Merkato Corp*. https://www.2merkato.com/articles/shipping/shipping-info/60-shipping-terms.

DUNNAGE: "Wood, etc., laid at the bottom of a ship, to keep the cargo dry." *Naval Marine Archive, The Canadian Collection*. http://www.navalmarinearchive.com/research/darcy_lever_glossary.html.

DUNNAGE: "means any material used for the purpose of protecting or holding in place cargo or freight during transportation by any carrier of property, and which is not an integral part of the carrier itself. Dunnage includes, but is not limited to, wood blocks, stakes, separating strips, timber, double decks, false floors, door shields, bulkheads, and other bracing. Dunnage generally does not remain with the cargo that is being transported and will not be delivered to the person who will ultimately receive the cargo. On the other hand, packing materials are generally part of the total package containing the cargo and are ultimately delivered to the customer as part of the cargo or merchandise. *Law Insider*. https://www.lawinsider.com/dictionary/dunnage.

DUNNAGE: " is a material used to protect cargo from damage due to friction between cargo and cargo or with the ship's hull, water, mixing of cargo, theft, and damage due to pressure from other objects. Dunnage is divided into two (2): Fixed Dunnage: Dunnage that has been permanently installed in the hold, including: cargo batten (dunnage mounted on the bottom or bottom of the hatch), wooden sleating (dunnage installed on the right and left of the hatch), wooden casing and botton calling. Unfixed Dunnage: Non-permanent dunnage is dunnage that is installed when needed or is needed, including: sasak from bamboo, sacks, tarpaulin, or plastic, block boards, plywood or playwood. Administering or ventilation: The purpose of the treatment is to remove moist air containing water vapor and replace it with fresh, clean and dry air from the outside. There are two types of shipbuilding, namely natural design and artificial or mechanical engineering. The implementation of air conditioning must always pay attention to and control the humidity of the air in the hold and it must be noted that what is meant here is not changing the air temperature in the hold, but to control the dew point in the hold by comparing the dew point of the outside air." *WuFushi Online Technology website*. https://www.wufushi.com/2021/10/principle-of-loading-on-ship.html.

DUNNAGE: "Loose wood, matting or similar material used to keep a cargo in position in a ship's hold. Effective bracing, blocking, and use of dunnage is essential. https://www.lexico.com/definition/dunnage.

I think we are done with dunnage gone jetsam. 

Floating a Foul

Are you saying Coconut Fibers were Flotsam?

As we have demonstrated in Appendix K, "*Follow the Coconut Flotilla,*" there is little chance our fibers found their way drifting to Oak Island. In *Floating a Foul*, we look into the reality of our oceanic mass surviving for such a length of time afloat.

Remember Thor Heyerdahl's Kon-Tiki expedition in 1947? He was seeking proof seafaring peoples could migrate across the Pacific Ocean basin from the west. On a balsa raft he and his adventurers traveled from near Lima, Peru, for 101 days and covered a distance of 4,340 nautical miles.[11] Other than running aground on Raroia Reef past Pukapuka (Danger Island) and then being towed to Tahiti; the adventurer had made his voyage. Heyerdahl did prove one thing – *coconuts don't swim for very long*. A popular belief was coconuts could surf the waves for up to 110 days and travel as much as 4,800 kilometers.[11] Once beached, the Coconut Palm Tree could germinate and populate along the coasts, providing sustenance for all humanity. Of the two hundred coconuts Heyerdahl did bring along, half were stowed on board and half floated within a submerged basket to let them float their way. None in the latter group survived very long and all went bad.[11] Bummer.

This brings up the question if Coconut fibers are able to float in the ocean for any distance at all. Coconuts themselves are not part of this investigation, as they have already been ruled unable to go the long haul.[11] Additionally, the presumption by those who postulate Oak Islands' fibers came from the Caribbean, were not of coconuts making the trek, but of retted coconut coir fiber making the float. Coconut coir fiber is light, buoyant, and highly water resistant. Its resistance to microbial action, saltwater, mechanical wear, and rot makes it unique in the fiber world.[12, 13] Yet before we rule it is indestructible, remember it too is biodegradable. Coir has a PH of

7-8, made up primarily of cellulose (43%) and lignin (45%).[14] Its cellulose does not dissolve in organic or acid solvents. [14] The fibers have a 10-12% porosity and can get waterlogged, as it can retain upwards of 7-8 times its' weight in water! [14]

So imagine this large volume of coconut fibers from Oak Island floating like an islet in the ocean itself. Is it a Fibrous Floaton or Sargassum Suds? Would this wad of organic macrophyte clumps and dissolved organic matter (DOM) corral and congeal into a coconut island, or be torn apart by the tides? It does have the basic chemistry to hang in there, but the ocean is a cruel place to learn you were wrong. Still, sargassum (gulf weed) is a known problem to many coastal dwellers and one cannot discount these floating islands do exist.[15] Any such journey would entice macroalgae to grow in and amongst the fibers as it meanders in the oceans epipelagic zone (first 200 meters of depth).[15] This is prime real estate most favored by those photo synthesizers like plankton, phytoplankton, zooplankton, and other seaweeds (algae).[15] It is shown that many a hitchhiker would take advantage of the ocean-going floater, to include larval and juvenile tuna, dolphin fish, wahoo, small shrimp and crabs, sea slugs, worms, and other microscopic and nearly-microscopic crustaceans.[15] Also amongst the tangle could be sardines, triggerfish, pompano, tripletail, billfish, flatback sea turtles, and even smaller filter-feeding animals called bryozoans.[15] The marine habitat throughout these floating fibers would be amazing. *Seasteading done right for sure!*

Yet success, breeds competition. Some definitely would look at this coconut caravan more as a seafaring smorgasbord. Bigger fish would love to dine on the life and dangling fibers of the float. Fish like Bluespine Unicornfish (*Naso unicornis*), Orangespine Surgeonfish (*Naso lituratus*), Bullet-headed Parrotfish (*Chlorurus spilurus*), and Rabbitfish (*Chimaera monstrosa*); as well as pelagic birds like sootys, manxs, skuas, petroles, jaegers, and phalaropes; would be frequent guests. [16] Would the fish eat the raft they rely on? Perhaps the birds would tend to pull out and take back the fibrous tendrils dangling on the top of the wad for nesting. Or simply a school of mackerel, spot, or cobia could tear apart our floater, digging in for those tiny morsels they seek.[17] The caravan would be shredded by these schools of Nova Scotian marauders. Worst of all, the coconut coir fiber float could be swallowed up hole by a baleen, humpback, or sei whale, in a single pass. It is more likely the fibers porosity would be the yoke around their necks. They would simply soak up too much water and lose their buoyancy over the trip and sink below. This, as explained in Appendix K, "*Follow the Coconut Flotilla*," would be the most likely scenario if it were to travel as far as the Arctic Ocean; as the salinity drops precariously. Whether they imbibed too much water or were shredded by sea life, this fibrous flotilla was doomed to dissolve into the deep – *or maybe not.*

Coconut fibers have shown amazing resistance to biodegrading anytime soon. Husks take 3-4 years to decompose lying on the soil.[18] In a study where various "biocontainers" were examined for their decomposition rates, coconut fiber-based eco-containers won the competition. Buried in the ground they out-sustained their competing container structures by fourteen weeks over other tested planting mediums.[19] Though they lost a significant portion of their tinsel strength, being made up of so much cellulose (80%) and lignin (18%) – both insoluble; coconut fiber-based containers lasted so long some worried about their classification as being labeled '*biodegradable*.'[19] Lignin has shown susceptibility to UV degradation. Though lignin is totally insoluble in most solvents and cannot be broken down into monomeric units, it could be damaged enough to lose its flexibility, strength, and structure.[19,20] Lignin also inhibits to a degree, the growth of bacteria that can degrade lignocellulose. Yet in aquatic systems, bacterial degradation can be quite extensive. Lignin is the most common aromatic organic compound found in the lignocellulose component of the plant cell wall.[21] Its characteristic ability to absorb UV (ultraviolet) radiation makes it susceptible to degradation on being exposed to sunlight.[21] So, exposed in the environment, lignin can be degraded by either biotically via bacteria or abiotically via photochemical alteration, and oftentimes the latter assists the former. Like in the retting process, coconut fibers floating in the ocean are also attacked aerobically and anaerobically.[22]

I can hear Gary Drayton exclaim, *"Yeah, Sunburn Baby!"*

Perhaps had the fibers still be conjoined with their husk chemical partners, their biodegradability could have carried them farther afloat, when considering the turbulent tides of the ocean. The phenolic substances present in the husk could have further checked the proliferation of microorganisms looking for a meal. The cold ocean water itself would dampen the damage caused by other bacteria. However, having been through the retting ringer, these fibers lost much of that repellant capability. Now stripped clean and alone, they realize the time in the lagoons, pools, and ponds; was nothing compared to the frenetic life at sea!

But alas, we cannot reject their hardiness and ability to survive! Having been buried under the fill within the Money Pit and the sands of Smith's Cove; coconut coir fibers were at the minimum, several centuries old when found. Unlike the eelgrass rotting away, and without too much discernability, our fibers were found fundamentally functionable and fresh. As fibrotic floaters, I think the verdict of "who dunnit" is still out. However, with obedience to the Viking Goddess ***Ran***, I will acquiesce to her strength and declare the ocean as the obvious victor over fiber - *in this challenge*.

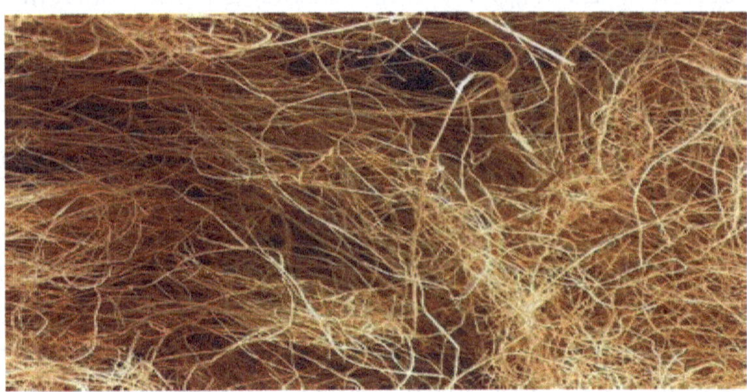

Courtesy: iStock.com

Footnoted References

1. "*The Maritime Industry Knowledge Centre*." Glossary. Maritime Industry Foundation. https://www.maritimeinfo.org/en/Glossary/.

2. "*Cargo Terms and Definitions*." by David J. House. www.maritimeconsultant.eu/cargo-terms-and-definitions. 8 Pages.

3. "*Oxford Handbook of Maritime Archeology*." by J. Richard Steffy, 2013. Illustrated Glossary of Ship and Boat Terms. https://www.oxfordhandbooks.com/view/10.1093/oxfordhb/9780199336005.001.0001/oxfordhb-9780199336005-e-48.

4. "*Coconut Fiber – Cargo Site Map*." Transport Information Service, Cargo Loss Prevention Information from German Marine Insurers. https://www.tis-gdv.de/tis_e/ware/fasern/kokosfa/kokosfa-htm/#transport.

5. "*Youth. A Narrative*." by Joseph Conrad, 1898. Project Gutenburg EBook. 30 Pages. https://www.gutenberg.org/files/525/525-h/525-h.htm.

6. "*History of Coir Industry*." Central Coir Research Institute of India. www.ccriindia.org/pdf/02Historyofcoirindustry.pdf.

7. "*Complete Cargo List for the 1701 San Francisco Xavier Spanish Galleon*." 2018. Manila to Acapulco. Published in the *Oregon Historical Quarterly*, Vol. 119, No. 2. Oregon Historical Society. 21 pages.

8. "*Coquito Nuts*." Nov. 15, 2019. https://en.wikipedia.org/wiki/Coquito_nuts.

9. "*1861, Coker Nuts – Dunnage*." by Henry Mayhew, 1861. London Labor Party. On the London Poor, Vol. 1. http://cocos.arecaceae.com/mercantile.html.

10. "*On the Stowage of Ships and Their Cargoes: with Information Regarding Freights, Charter-Parties, etc., etc*." by Robert White Stevens. 1878. Longmans, Green, Reader & Dyer. London. www.StevensonStowage1878.pdf. Pages 34-528.

11. "*Kon Tiki: Across the Pacific by Raft*." by Thor Heyerdahl, 1950. Mattituck: Amereon House. 240 Pages. https://infogalactic.com/info/Coconut#cite_note-Heyerdahl-31.

12. "*How Products Are Made – COIR*." Background section. www.madehow.com/Volume-6/Coir.html.

13. "*Coir Fiber Process and Opportunities -2*." by Akhila Rajan & T. Emilia Abraham, PhD, 2007. Biochemical Aspects Sec. Published in *Journal of Natural Fibers*. 3:4, Pages 29-42.

[14]. "*Coconut Fibre: Its Structure, Properties and Applications*." by Leena Mishra and Gautan Basu. Page 13, para. 10.2.1.3, "*Yield of Coconut Fibre Chemical Composition (in bone dry weight) and Fine Structure Parameters of Coconut Fibre and Jute*," Table 10.3; and para. 10.6.2, *Acid Treatments*." . ICAR – National Institute of Research on Jute and Allied Fibre Technology, Kolkata, West Bengal India.

[15]. "*Sargassum: Floating Nurseries*," by James Franks. Discovery Porthole. Northern Gulf Institute, University of Southern Mississippi, Ocean Springs, MS. 2 pages. National Oceanic and Atmospheric Administration (NOAA). 2010.

[16]. "*Pelagics – Atlantic & Gulf Coast USA*." Section, "Nova Scotia." https://www.surfbirds.com/Pelagic/ecoast.html.

[17]. "*Fishing Floaters*." by Todd Kuhn, Aug. 27, 2013. Published in *Saltwater Sportsman*. https://www.saltwatersportsman.com/blogs/short-strikes/fishing-floaters/.

[18]. "*Biofuels from Coconuts*." by Krishna Raghaven, Aug. 2010. 107 pages. Annex 8, The Coconut Palm; Recycling Husks, Organic Manures, P. 76. www.energypedia.info/f/f9/EN-biofuels_from_cocnuts-krishna_raghaven.pdf.

[19]. "*Comparing Strength and Biodegradability of Biocontainers*." by Matt Taylor, Michael Evans, Jeff Kuehny. Sep. 10,2010. Published in *Greenhouse Management*. www.Greanhousemag.com/article/gmpro-0910-biocontainers/.

[20]. "*Biodegradable Materials for Planting Pots – Chapter 4*." by B. Tomadoni, D. Merino, C. Casalongue, and V. Alvarez, Mar. 2020. Published in Advanced Applications of Bio-degradable Green Composites Materials Research Forum. Materials Research Foundations 68 (2020) 85-103. https://doi.org/10.21741/9781644900659-485.

[21]. "*Enzymatic Degradation of Lignin in Soil*." by Rahul Datta et. al., Jul. 3, 2017. Published in *Sustainability*, 2017, 9, 1163: doi:10.3390/su9071163. https://res.mdpi.com/sustainability/sustainability-09-01163/article_deploy/sustainability-09-01163-v2.pdf.

[22]. "*Coir Fiber Process and Opportunities -1*." by Akhila Rajan & T. Emilia Abraham, PhD, Jun. 27, 2012. Section Microbiology of Coir Retting, P. 32. Published in *Journal of Natural Fibers*. 3:4, 2006.

Appendix M

EXPERTS EXAMINE EVIDENCE

This Appendix is the repository for the reports on soils analysis and wood decay produced for this book, and the resume of Dr. Bryan G. Hopkins, Ph.D., CPSS, an expert in soil science and currently a Full Professor in the Plant and Wildlife Sciences Department at Brigham Young University. His academic teaching focuses on environmental chemistry and plant, soil, and water science and management. Professor Hopkins has multiple degrees in Horticulture and Agronomy and is currently the Coordinator for the North American Proficiency Testing (NAPT) program for the Soil Science Society of America (SSSA), which oversees data quality for approximately 150 analytical laboratories from around the world.

In addition, Professor Hopkins is the active managing owner of Hopkins Scientific LLC, in Provo, Utah. He and his staff of scientists and researchers were enlisted to perform an examination and modeling of a blind scenario, descriptive of the Oak Island setting. This scenario provided geology and atmospheric and weather conditions of the island and surrounding area. It also provided redacted witness statements, abridged written reports, affidavits, and descriptive writings of searcher activities when discussing rot of wood, settling of soil, and moisture conditions within the Money Pit.

They have submitted their initial draft report on the decay-based degradation of the logs within the pit, in an effort to attempt to determine an approximate window of time as to when the pit was refilled. This report is shown in this appendix and summarized in Chapter 8, *"Planting Evidence,"* & Chapter 11, *"Harvesting the Truth."*

First, below we provide the descriptive scenario, soils analysis, and weather evidence Dr. Hopkins was given to base his forensic examination report on.

<u>Authors Note</u>:

To create a blind study examination solely based on the forensic evidence provided in the descriptive scenario, which was gleamed from the written accounts of Oak Island searchers and storytellers; it was decided to *<u>not</u>* provide any detailed location information, time period, or other 'Oak Island Treasure Story - related details.' Therefore the descriptive scenario and additional forensic data provided, was disguised so as not to sound "familiar" or relatable to the Oak Island saga. The contract with Hopkins Scientific LLC, was also disguised to effectuate prevention of any bias or assumptions in examination of the evidence portrayed in the scenario, should any of the participants in the forensic examination know of or have heard of the Oak Island legend. All of the forensic evidence provided to Hopkins Scientific LLC, is directly based on the geologic reports by other scientist who have previously conducted research of the island. The weather information is also that of Mahone Bay for the year 2020. Witness statements, commentary and Oak Island records were used to collect those excised statements shown in the "Notes" section. The full contextual repository of those comments, statements and records can be found in Appendix C, *"On the Record."*

Once in receipt of the Draft Reports, Dr. Hopkins and his associates were informed of the true purpose of their contracted examination, and they agreed to continue their review of the evidence for a final report. I have also sent Hopkins Scientific LLC, additional scientific data reports conducted of the island over time by entities like Woods Hole Oceanographic Institute, Warnock-Hersey Intl., Golder Associates, Geological Survey of Canada, Nova Scotia Department of Mines and Energy, and others. Also provided were some of the witness statements and written descriptive accounts of Oak Island and the Money Pit, so they could review them in their full context.

The location used in this blind study was Machiasport Maine. Located 160 miles (257 km) as a crow flies from Oak Island. Machiasport is a quiet, seaport community of 962 inhabitants. Town is located at the head of Machias Bay & Little Kennebec Bay on the Gulf of Maine, part of the Atlantic Ocean.

SCENARIO
Wood Decay & Rot/Soil Settlement Timeline

A depression was discovered, which was found to be the top of a filled-in pit in a lightly forested area approximately 300 ft from the shoreline, extending out into a bay and exposed to the ocean. The elevation was estimated at 35 feet above sea level. The discovery was made by three local farmers examining their fields which may have yielded Timothy Hay. One of them stepped into a depression in a clearing amongst a mixed grove of softwoods and hardwoods consisting of Northern Red Oak, Hemlock, Spruce, Red and White Pine, Maple, Birch, and Aspen Trees. The depression itself was 18-24 inches deep in the center radiating out to a depth of 2-3 inches. The depression was unseen as a growth of red clover (*Trifolium pratense*) grew on top of the pit and around the depression, but not within the extended forest floor. **Note 1**

The three farmers began to dig into the depression; noticing the soil was soft and disturbed and could be dug with their hands and small shovels (See Soil attachment). They dug down 'two feet' and came upon a layer of flagstone. **Note 2** After removing all the dirt covering the flagstone, they found the depression was 13 feet in diameter and the flagstone was neatly placed and tightly fitted within this hollowed area and was then believed to be manmade. The flagstone was described as dark granite-looking with an olive green coloring. Witnesses said it seemed to have come from elsewhere.

It was decided the depression with the flagstone on top of it would be further investigated. The 2 inch thick flagstone pieces were removed. Eventually they were estimated to weigh a total of approximately 1.25 metric tons. Digging in the soft disturbed clayey soil down another estimated 6.5 feet (to 10 feet total depth), the men came to a platform which encompassed the entire 13 foot diameter pit area. The platform, at ten feet below the ground surface, was made of 6-8 inch diameter oak logs with bark left on them. They had been embedded into the hard clay walls of the pit and were tightly packed. Exposure of the pit walls revealed pickaxe/shovel marks from when the pit was initially created.

Workers found the oak logs were rotted and decayed at the position where these logs entered the pit walls (their pointed ends were approximately 1 foot into the walls at both ends). The decay was such, the oak logs could be broken from their hold near the pit walls with strong physical yank, push, or force upon them. **Note 3** When many of the oak timbers were removed from the platform, workers found more disturbed soil below. The top of the lower level of soil had impressions as though the oak logs had at one time been laying on top of that soil, which now appeared to have sunk 24 inches below the log platform. **Note 4**

With lighting lowered in the pit, workers dug down through this next level of soft, disturbed clayey soil, until again they came upon another log platform. No rocks or boulders had been encountered so far.

Now at 20 feet deep within the pit, a second platform of 6-8 inch diameter oak logs with their bark, was found to be embedded into the walls of the hard clay pit. Here again, rot and decay of the logs was significant enough to break them from the walls with force. **Note 3** Below this platform, was found more disturbed clay soil with a repeat of soil settlement approximately sunk 20-24 inches below. **Note 4**

Again, after more digging, approximately 30 feet down within the pit, workers digging in the disturbed soil found a third platform, ten feet below. This similar oak log with bark platform, had a layer of puddled clay or putty or moist clay, smeared on the top of the logs. This putty-like material covered the entire platform approximately 1-2 inches thick. **Note 5** The putty like clay was later to be determined to be palygorskite.

The logs at this level seemed less rotted and decayed, presumably because of the putty smeared on the top side. **Note 3** Removing this platform was more tedious as workers had to cut into the pit walls to extricate the oak logs. When this platform of oaks were removed, skeletal remains were found immediately below. All soils and bones from below this platform were carefully removed. The pit appeared to end at this depth as soils below the human bones, were undisturbed , dry, and very hard clay. This bottom depth was at 32 feet.

It is surmised, that at initial filling of the pit, the layer of flagstone was placed atop the refilled pit at forest floor level. The settling or compaction of the top 10 feet of disturbed fill within the pit, led to some consolidation by weathering and formed the depression. Over time, it is assumed, as this depression further settled, it filled in with forest floor materials, windblown soils, etc., atop the laid flagstone.

All pertinent case information regarding soils movement, combined with that for wood rot and decay, have been included in this "Scenario" description for your understanding and reference in your review. No other evidence or known facts which are believed helpful to you (field of study) in answering the following questions, exist. Any questions you may have regarding this Scenario should be sent by email and will be answered quickly. If you feel your question answers are conditional on knowing a particular fact, assumption, or detail; please include that in your comment section, but please try to answer the questions if possible.

Please make your expert assessment, experienced comments, or professional formulations, based on this evidence, or from scientific principals which address the following questions.

Any additional insight or references you may recommend regarding the principals of soil settlement, wood rot and decay or clay soil compaction, would be greatly appreciated. *Thank you for participating!*

Note #1. Depression at top of pit:

"A bowl-shaped depression... suggested that the soil had sunk where someone had buried something in the distant past."

"Beneath was a circular depression some 13 feet across and 18" deep in center."

Note #2. Layer of Flagstone:

"At a depth of two feet, they unearthed a tight layer of flagstones."

"Two feet from the surface, they uncovered a layer of flat flagstones which were roughly 2" thick."

Note #3. Decay Rot of Oak Logs:

"The outside of the logs were so rotten that they felt confident they must have been imbedded there for a great many years."

"The logs were rotten on the outside and at the ends where they were stuck into the walls of the hole."

"The logs were very much decayed on the outside and broke away."

"The logs were rotten and broken from the wall with a hard yank, suggesting that they had been buried for many years."

Note #4. Settlement of Soil Beneath Platforms:

"They dug a full ten feet down when they came across a tier of oak logs tightly attached to the sides, and the earth below the logs had settled nearly two feet."

"A two-foot gap was encountered below the oak log platform..."

"the earth below the logs had settled nearly two feet."

Note #5. Layer of Putty on Platform:

"There was so much of it [putty] that it was used by locals to putty windows."

DESCRIPTION OF SOILS PRESENT WITHIN THE PIT

Superficial soil = Glacial clayey till with silty sand.

Gravel - 11%
Sand – 35%
Clay & Silt – 54%

Windsor Grp = Limestone, Gypsum, Shale

<10' Dense brown glacial till. Matrix mainly clay, silt and sand.
>32' Hard glacial clay till.
>20' to 32' CL(unified) Plasticity 12% (low), liquid limit 20-25%

Comment = The soils are developed from materials deposited as glacial drift and they range in texture from sandy clay loam to course sandy loam. The maturely developed soils are Podzols. Under forest cover these soils have a gray ashy layer under the thin organic surface mat. This is underlain by a dark brown to yellowish brown horizon that grades into the parent material at a depth ranging from 16 to 26 inches. Leaching is more intense. No water or moisture was present or reported when the pit was re-opened.

O Horizon duff was not analyzed at that time. A patch of red clover (*Trifolium pratense*) was removed from site prior to excavation. Pit material excavated appeared to be disturbed clayey soil as described, and moderately easy to remove. No root material, rocks or boulders were said to be found within the disturbed fill pit.

Note to your Request:
We do not know when the pit was initially excavated, nor when it was refilled. We are confident the pit was filled with the soils extracted from the pit originally, minus breccia. The description of the soils at the site and in-situ, as best as we can ascertain is described above.
The hope is... we know when the pit was discovered. Can forensics using a "rate-of-time" elapsed to have created the observed soil settlement or the degree of rot of the wood as described, be able to create a timeline of when the pit was originally dug, or most likely – when refilled.

DESCRIPTION OF WEATHER/ATMOSPHERIC CONDITIONS ABOVE THE PIT

Note = This weather information has been gathered to provide you an understanding of recent annual weather indications and is only provided to help you understand weather of the location now, not at historical periods.

Temperature =
- Warm Season duration = 3.2 months
- Warm Season average = 66 degrees Fahrenheit
- Warm Season range = 60 to 74 degrees Fahrenheit

- Cold Season duration = 3.4 months
- Cold Season average = 40 degrees Fahrenheit
- Cold Season range = 18 to 42 degrees Fahrenheit

Clouds =
- Primarily clear skies = 4.5 months
- Primarily cloudy skies = 7.5 months

Precipitation =
- Wet = 10 months, 27% on average
- Dry = 1.7 months, 22% on average

Rainfall (includes snow conversion) =
- Most rainy = 3.9 inches (November highest)
- Least rainy = 1.8 inches (February least)

Snowfall =
- Most snowy = 5.2 months (.1 inches equivalent)
- Least snowy = 6.8 months (.0 inches equivalent)

Wind =
- Windier days = 6.6 months @ 7.5 mph on average
- Calmer days = 5.4 months @ 5.6 mph on average

Water temperatures = (nearby body of water – Atlantic Ocean)
- Warmer water = 3.1 months @ >56 degrees Fahrenheit
- Colder water = 4.2 months @ <39 degrees Fahrenheit

Humidity =
- Drier months = 5.0 months
- Muggier months = 5.1 months

Review of Rotting Red Oak - Machiasport Report

PROVIDED BY:

Professor Bryan G. Hopkins, Ph.D., CPSS
Hopkins Scientific, LLC

Our purpose in this report is to provide a liberal to conservative window of time that would reasonably result in the scenario you detailed in the appendix [scenario].

To restate the conditions, approximately 6-8 inch diameter N. Red Oak (*Quercus rubra*) log platforms were found buried at ~10, 20, and 30 feet deep into coastal Maine disturbed subsoil. The logs were inserted into the clay walls of the pit enough to suspend themselves and the soil above (the soil below within the pit settled approximately 2 feet). The logs generally held their shape when excavated but the outside and ends crumbled and broke when they were removed by giving a forced hard shake. The bottom [log] layer was covered in a clay putty that inhibited decomposition. The soil below was dry, likely due to the fact that the putty acted as moisture barrier. This observation leads us to believe that the logs were roughly 30 to 70% decomposed.

We created a quantitative model based on the findings of Schowalter (1998) in which they determined the rate of decay for the sapwood, inner, and outer bark to be approximately 16% per year. Similarly for the heartwood they found the rate of decay to be 1.2% annually. According to what was observed in Brown 2019, we estimated the percentage of the total diameter of the log of sapwood at 10% and heartwood at 90%. We used the assumed diameter provided by Mr. Neisen at 7.5" diameter, the 2 dimensional area of the log is calculated to be 139 cm2. With the assumed ratio, which comes to a heartwood area of 125 cm2 and a sapwood area of 14 cm2. With the previously stated rates of decay, and assuming that the sapwood would nearly completely decompose prior to the decomposition of the heartwood. Our conservative estimate to achieve a 95% decomposition of the red oak logs would be **270 years**. Akin to that estimate Tyrrell (1994) also found that it takes nearly 200 years for hemlock and hardwood logs to lose structural integrity and become partially incorporated into the soil. At >350 years, the two oldest hemlock–hardwood stands had accumulated volumes of logs >65 m3/ha distributed among all decay classes and appeared to be at a dead wood equilibrium in which rates of log production from mortality balance rates of wood loss by decay. Zhou (2007) found that hardwood snags or deadfalls suspended above the soil surface can take approximately 100 years to decay completely.

The liberal estimate of the rate of decay of the red oak logs is supported in part by the findings of Russell et al. (2014). They found that specifically for *Quercus rubra*, the residence time, or time to decay was between 49 and 73 years. This study was especially applicable to the scenario in question as it took place in eastern forests, including Maine. Similarly to previous findings, Mackensen (2003) found the decomposition rate of coarse woody debris, including larger diameter logs, to be between 49 and 92 years.

It is worth noting that all of the above mentioned studies examined the residence time or rate of decomposition of hardwood on or above the soil surface and not below it. Therefore, all these estimates are surely on the conservative side due to the following factors. The logs in this case were completely buried below the soil surface, Alban 1993 noted that logs in contact with the soil surface decay more quickly than those suspended above the soil surface. Likewise logs completely in contact with the soil surface will decay more rapidly than those partially in contact with the soil surface. Zhou 2007 found in their review of the impacts on decomposition of coarse woody debris that Fungi, other decomposing microorganisms and insects can't live if the humidity is below 30%. Their activities are improved with the increase of humidity, whereas also limited by a very high humidity. Some bacteria and fungi such as the soft rots fungi can survive in the high humidity of 240%. But only 30%–160% is the most optimal humidity for the growth of Basidiomycetes, a typical decomposer. According to the web soil survey, the typical depth to the water table ranges between 0 cm to >200 cm. Implying that the subsoil is typically humid, supporting adequate environments for microbial decomposers. Additionally the soil temperature consistently reads at approximately 55 degrees F which would further support subsoil decomposers. Compared to oak logs found on the surface that go through dry and cold winters, the sub soil logs are likely to decompose more quickly than a log sitting on top of the soil surface.

There are instances of timber mineshaft support beams lasting for over 150 years. However, according to Horner (1922), untreated timber in shafts on average only were useable for two years. Beyond 2 years, the untreated beams would rot and crumble. Most all of the timber beams that were used in mines were pressure treated as detailed in Horner (1922). Due to the special pre-treatment of these beams, this is not an accurate measure of hardwood decomposition.

Our initial findings supported by available scientific evidence indicate a reasonable window of time in which the 7.5" diameter red oak logs could have been placed within the coastal Maine subsoil. The limits of that window of time are 49 years at the liberal end and 270 years at the conservative end based on our model findings. However, this model is based on above soil surface rates of oak decomposition and requires adjustments for the dampening of the disease triangle influenced by the soil temperature.

For decomposition to occur the three points of the disease triangle must be present (Scholthof, 2006). This conceptual model shows the interactions between an environment favorable for disease development, a susceptible host, and a virulent pathogen. The concept of the disease triangle suggests to us that the red oak logs have not been preserved from decomposition over time. Some scenarios such as logs becoming submerged in peat bogs, or logs found in extreme arid regions have logs that survive hundreds if not thousands of years. Both of those scenarios, however, are missing at least one corner of the triangle, likely the proper environmental conditions. In the peat bogs, there is no oxygen found therefore no fungi are able to properly decompose it. Similarly in extreme arid regions such as logs found in ancient Egyptian ruins, there is virtually no water, yet again preventing the logs from decomposing. In this cold case [scenario], all three phases of the microbial triangle are present. Thus, this allows for decomposition.

Now we examine the conditions of the location the north red oak logs of this scenario are found.

> Host: This is the simplest of the three points simply because the host itself is the matter in question, the oak logs. This coarse woody material contains all the nutrients required for fungi decomposers to utilize (Schowalter, 1998).

Pathogen: The wood was found 10, 20, and 30 feet below the surface. Even supposing that there would be no fungi found at those depths, the logs themselves would be inoculated with spores prior to them being cut and buried. We know that fungi are the main decomposers of the world, therefore the presence of fungi spores would initiate the decomposition process below ground.

Environment: Most fungi are obligate aerobes, requiring oxygen to survive. They typically require a humid and dark environment and are known to prefer warm temperature but certainly can grow at nearly any temperature, even below freezing. They also require nutrients to be able to grow. We know that the soil conditions are not likely to be submerged in water, or anaerobic because the cavity where to skeletal remains were found was dry. And, the soil was reported as being relatively loose. Thus we can assume that the soil has sufficient oxygen to encourage fungi growth. The red oak logs would contain ample nutrients for the fungi. We also know that, with the exception of the "putty" covered logs at the deepest depth, the subsoil would have sufficient water to enable fungi growth. The weather in Machiasport Maine is typically wet with the most rainfall occurring in November with an average of 4.3 inches, the driest month is January with an average rainfall 2 inches. The soil temperature is not a measured variable on the web soil survey, however it is known that the temperature of the deep subsoil is typically the average of the air temperature for the year. The average air temperature in Machiasport is 44 degrees F, meaning the average sub soil temperature is 44 degrees F.

With the sub-soil temperature being consistently approximately 44 degrees F, the microbial decomposition would be inhibited (Gock 2003). This is high enough in temperature to still facilitate decomposition but low enough that the conditions are significantly below the optimal temperature for rapid degradation. It has been established that microbial growth is reduced at lower temperatures, but the reduced growth rate needs to be established. We communicated with a soil and plant pathology expert on what the observed rate of fungi growth would be under such refrigerated conditions (correspondence Brad Geary, Ph.D., Brigham Young University). Dr. Geary communicated to us that the expected rate of growth for fungi in our detailed description would be approximately 3-4 times slower than above soil, exposed growth.

In the scenario description, the logs are at a state that they can be pushed or pulled to break without completely disintegrating when handled. Prior to this we had assumed a 95% total decomposition ratio. However, with this description of the oak logs we believe that the actual ratio is closer to 30%-70% total decomposition. This is supported by the observation that the logs could be handled and required force to break but could still be broken apart.

The parameters of our model have now been sufficiently outlined that we can provide a reasonable window of time in which these red oak logs could have been buried in the soil. We have set the decomposition mass ration to between 30% and 70%, We know that the cooler subsoil temperature (44 degrees F) increases the microbial growth rate by a factor of 3-4, we have set it at 3.5 for this model. We also know that the rate of decay for the sapwood and outer bark is roughly 16% annually while the rate of decay for the heartwood is approximately 1% annually. The diameter of the red oak logs is 7.5 inches, the total 2 dimensional surface area is calculated at approximately 139 cm2. It's also established that the composition of red oak logs is typically 10% sapwood and 90% heartwood (Brown 2019). 10% of the total surface area is 13.9 cm2 and 90% of the of total surface area is 125.8 cm2. When all the outlined variables are input into this rate of decay model, we can then calculate a window.

Beginning with shorter end of the window, 70% original oak log mass remaining would take **175 years** to occur. For 50% of the original oak log mass to remain would take **273 years** to occur. For 30% of the original oak log mass to remain would take **420 years** to occur (Figure 1). While that range of 175 to 420 years is a significantly wide estimate of time, that is the best that can be derived given the information provided within the scenarios.

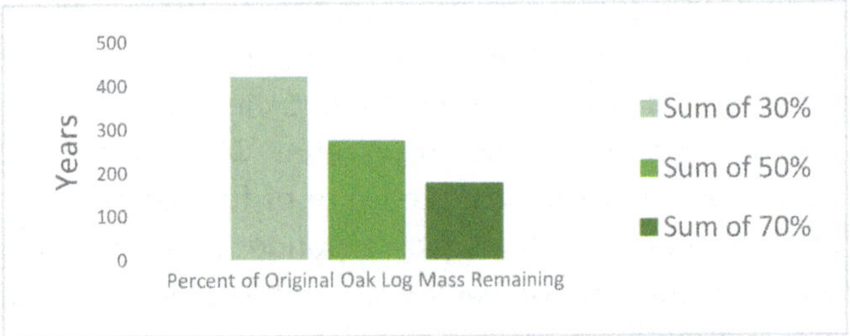

Figure 1: The amount of time it would take, given the inputs, to have a percentage of the original oak log mass remaining undecomposed. Created by Hopkins Scientific LLC.

Scenario: Rate of Decay of Red Oak Logs as Timeframe Indicator

Summary: In reference to your initial questions regarding the scenario you provided, we have listed our findings in relation to your request for elaboration.

Q. Can you ascertain the length of time it would take for newly felled, 7.5 inch diameter N. red oak logs with bark, having their ends embedded within hard clayey pit wall underground, with the described volume of disturbed clayey till soil placed on top of it; would rot or decay as described in this *Scenario*?

Q. Is there a formula or equation you used or is available, to determine the timeframes needed for level of decay/rot on oak logs, or other species of wood; and will you provide with your response, that formula/equation or reference?

Q. If the timelines of the rate of decay is different with other "hardwoods" or types of oak species (Northern red oak, Burr oak, etc.,), can you estimate or provide those timelines of decay for these specific oak species?

Q. Since this *Scenario* provides a subjective description of rot and decay: *"being able to use a person's physical pushing or pulling to break apart 7.5 inch diameter oak logs"*; is this description 'sufficient' or 'probable' to identify a date along the timeline of decay? Do you have any further thoughts or comments on this description in determining length of time of decay to this level?

Q. If you are using a formula or equation based on research of rot or decay of wood species; can you elaborate on the issue these logs were underground and subject to the *in situ* hard clay walls, and the disturbed, refilled clay soil placed upon them? Is there a study which you can reference which discusses rate of decay of wood underground versus above ground?

Q. Can you declare with any certitude that the degree of rot noted in this Scenario can accurately estimate an elapsed period of time, since the pit was filled in?

Q. Can you provide any worksheets, websites, or publications which a non-expert could read/review to better understand how to determine the rate of time it takes for (oak) wood to decay in similar conditions?

END REPORT//

Synergy of Soils Settlement - Report

We are about to enter the month of August and the completion of the book is at hand - *except for the Report on Soils Settlement*. Like life, things happen and not all of them are good. The soil expert working with me on this project has undergone brain surgery and is recouping as we speak. I know little of his status and can only pray he fully recovers and returns to his premier position within this field. Looking at his resume, a link is provided, you can see he has been a very hard scientist for a very long time. Perhaps it better he take some time to rest and spend with his grown sons. I do wish the best for Professor Hopkins.

To end this forensic analysis so close to its completion is not completely accurate. Perhaps the good Professor and his staff will be able someday to release his findings and we can post them on the website for all to read. Yet in the meantime we can surmise, like we have throughout this book, how the review of soil settlement, compaction, and consolidation at the Money Pit, can add additional timeline insight on what happened on this island. In fact, the timeline for rot and decay of oak logs within an environment such as the Money Pit, has already given us valuable windows with which to view the probabilities of *WHEN* certain activity happened on Oak Island.

Assumptions and general rates analysis of soils movement as described, can give calculated insight on a timeline, but with it not being specifically built on the geological conditions set out in Dr. Hopkin's research and report, the forensic review may ring hollow, even if accurate. There is no benefit in being given "general" assumptions when real forensic science can provide a distinct answer to our questions. A bit more patience is what is needed.

But with this marker on our timeline yet to be noted, we can still examine what we have collaboratively pieced together to get a much more informed view of the jigsaw puzzle before us.

On the bottom of this page is where a reader may go to read the resume of Dr. Hopkins to view his expertise in the matters of plant and soils science. He has unquestionable abilities to forensically analyze the Oak Island scenario in many unrealized ways. As we do not know all that we don't know or understand, his background warrants his invitation to meet with the Fellowship to discuss the scientific approaches heretofore unexplored and unappreciated in this investigation. In my limited understanding of the fields he has mastered, I can think of some questions which he may be able to shed light and help in reaping as many clues about Oak Island as possible. For example: can the soils of the Serpent Mound tell from where it came... piled up by Fred Nolan on a joy ride of his bulldozer, or from deep within the island? Can any additional information be garnered from his review of the spoils being washed and inspected for artefacts? Can he offer scientific insights regarding the reports of red clover said to be growing atop the depression, but nowhere else in the region? Can he proffer reasons for why the eelgrass and coconut coir fiber was part of the Smith's Cove 'filtration' system? Are there other applications of his skill set which could provide additional information to formulate answers to this mystery? Let us hope and pray we hear more from the good Professor in the future!

BRYAN GENE HOPKINS

RANK: Professor, Brigham Young University
DEPARTMENT: Plant and Wildlife Sciences
OFFICE LOCATION: 5117 LSB, Provo, UT 84602
OFFICE PHONE: 801-422-2185
EMAIL: hopkins@byu.edu
WEB: https://pws.byu.edu/directory/bryan-hopkins

CURRICULUM VITAE: https://pws.byu.edu/directory/bryan-hopkins

Appendix N

NOTORIOUS NETWORKS

This appendix refers specifically to Chapter 2, *"Fishy Business,"* and provides the referenced Figure 1, *"1752 Halifax Fisherman Census,"* and Figure 2, *"The Bounty of Mahone Bay."* The material provided below, like in Chapter 2, is the product of research by co-author Christopher L. Boze.

Figure 1. 1752 Halifax Fishermen Census

On Several Islands and Harbors, Employed in Fishery.				
Heads of Families.	Males above 16.	Females above 16.	Males under 16.	Females under 16.
On Cornwallis Island:				
Capt. Joseph Rouse	4	....	....	....
" Mauger	7	....	....	....
" Cook	5	....	....	....
—— Bradshaw	16	1	....	....
	32	1	....	....
At Ketch Harbour:				
John Grace	10	2	1	....
Capt. Gill	6	....	....	....
—— Brown	3	2	1	....
	19	4	2	....
At Sambro Island:				
Capt. Matterson	21	1	....	....
Thomas Youngston	1	1	1	1
	22	2	1	1
At St. Margaret's Bay:				
Benjamin Frog	10	1	2	....
James Ford	13	....	....	....
Adam Clown	1	1	....	1
—— Allen	5	....	....	....
	29	2	2	1

Courtesy: T.B. Akins, History of Halifax City, Nova Scotia Historical Society, 1895.

Figure 2. The Bounty of Mahone Bay

Halifax Gazette May 11th, 1754, part of a letter sent from a man in Halifax to his friend in New York. Courtesy of Google News Archive.

> *"I am informed that the sale of European goods is very dull with you, and the West Indies is glutted with your country produce, it being often sold there under prime cost. I think that if some of your trading men would come settle here and assist in carrying on the fishery, it would turn to their advantage... Our land from Cape Sanbrough to Cape Sables, is well timbered, and as good as any in the world, with as fine soft and fresh meadow as ever a scythe went into. Most of our rivers are navigable and abound with great plenty of salmon, and many convenient streams for mills. Our bays are full of islands, the land good and fit either for pasture or raising any kind of grains; and the great plenty of cod, herring and mackerel renders the place still more agreeable...*
>
> *We have only settled Halifax and Lunenburg as yet; but there is another town to be settled at Mahone Bay this spring, where there are many islands for the fishery, and many good harbors for shipping, it being between Halifax and Lunenburg: 400 barrels of mackerel have been caught there at one haul, and for want of barrels and salt many of them spoiled on the beach. Any people that will come to settle the islands or the Main, and has anything to carry on the fishery, will meet with all imaginable encouragement from the government without the least charge. New England, New York, and New Jersey were not settled for so little expense, neither have they such advantages as we have; for besides that the land produces everything as in Europe, by our fishery which in no place is so good, a great many poor people are employed. We hope in a few years; to be able to supply Oporto, Lisbon, and the Straights with fish, and make a sure remittance with oil, staves, ship plank & etc. to England, Ireland, and Scotland, and bring out a number of passengers to settle the country; anyone who goes upon this scheme, will have great encouragement, and make their fortunes in short time; and many who now defile this place, will be of another mind in a few years. We are daily making new discoveries on the Main and in our bays."*

Figure 3. "Joshua Mauger and The Halifax Party," By Christopher L. Boze.

Joshua Mauger was born on Jersey Island, off the north-west coast of France, in 1725. It is possible he spoke French as a second language and late in life he served as director of a French Hospital. If he did, this language would serve him well in Nova Scotia. Joshua got into the shipping trades with his uncle and became master of a ship at a very early age. In time he would marry his uncle's daughter, but Mauger would leave no surviving wife or children at his death in 1788. His assets were passed to various charities and his nieces and nephews.

It is unsure his path to Fortress Louisbourg, but in 1749 he is recorded as a victualer to the navy, during the fort's handover to the French. After a short trip to England to speak with the Board of Trade, he returned to Halifax as Victualer for the entire Royal Navy in Nova Scotia. He had also managed to secure a contract providing the entire rum supply. Overnight, Mauger had become one of North America's largest distillers. He would go on to parlay his position managing provisions into a commercial empire trading in rum, lumber, fish, vessels, and slaves.

One of Mauger's first duties was settling affairs and the transfer of wares from Fort Louisbourg to Halifax. However, while Governor Cornwallis had declared there was to be no trading with the French, technically - it was not against British law to do so. More than likely Mauger had established French suppliers for vegetables and the like, so it was only a matter of time before Cornwallis accused him of smuggling.

Cornwallis recommended the removal of Mauger to the Board of Trade, complaining that Mauger was trading with the enemy from his various "truck houses" at Pisiquid, Minas, Grande Pre, Annapalis Royal, and St. John River. Cornwallis also questioned how Mauger could negotiate with the Natives the payment of ransoms for the release of prisoners, when he could not.

Mauger defended himself to the Board of Trade, explaining that Cornwallis disrupted trade and was incapable of defending the citizens. He called Cornwallis incompetent and presented letters from "the real citizens of Halifax", signed by merchants and businessmen. The names give us a glimpse of merchants who supported and may have been in league with Mauger, and are form his "real citizens" in his letter:

> Joshua Mauger, S. Zouberbuhler, Samuel Sellon, Edward Buckleton, James Porter, Daniel Wood, Jonathan Gifford, William Schwartz, Edward Crawley, William Jeffray, Vere Rous, Francis Martin, John Brooks, Henry Wilkinson, William Nesbitt, John Woodin, James Ford, George Featherstone, Thos. Mattison, Joseph Antony, Alex. Kedy, James Fullon, William Murray, Louis Triquet, William Clapham, John Webb, Robert Catherwood, John Walker, Geo. Peter DeBreg, Richard Hollis, Henry Sibley, Edward O'Brien, Henry O'Brien, Thos. Wynne, John Grant, William Vauselson, Cheyne Brownjohn, Richard Tritton, Edward Lukey, Cyrus Jannin, John Willis, Roger Hill, Js. Deschamps, Robert Grant, William McGee, Joseph Rundel.

With the support of Halifax merchants, Mauger began to abuse Cornwallis. He ruined Cornwallis's credit with other suppliers by holding back payments, forcing Cornwallis to only buy from his shipping companies. Cornwallis flipped out and cried to the Board of Trade for Mauger's removal. But cry as he might to the Board of Trade - *Mauger was never replaced.* Seeing the writing on the walls, Cornwallis began complaining of his own health. He began writing to the Board of Trade, seeking a replacement governor.

The Halifax Party has also been accused of smuggling by Nova Scotian historian James S. MacDonald. In his work the *"Life and Administration of Governor Charles Lawrence, 1749-1760,"* MacDonald references Gifford, Murray, Mauger and Saul, each as *"a smuggler"* in his chapter index. It was MacDonald's belief that *"Gifford, Murrey and Saul, were agents of a smuggling fraternity from Boston that came to Halifax to take advantage of the general disorder of the young province."* However, it should be noted that proof of the Halifax Party's involvement in smuggling has never been proven.

Regardless, Governor Hopson replaced Cornwallis in 1752 and the Board of Trade allowed Joshua Meager to continue his services. Lunenburg is founded, and new opportunities are afforded to the merchants of Halifax in supplying the new settlement. Mauger becomes very powerful as a distributor between merchants. He opens new shipping companies with trusted partners, to bring in goods from New England and the West Indies. Sugar, rum, and slaves for Nova Scotian fish and lumber.

England and the lower colonies also expected to profit by suppling the new colony. Shipping companies received contracts for beads, blankets, clothing, shoes, vegetables, flour, and beef, whatever was needed. Land grants were given to soldiers, especially those who had participated in the 1745 "Siege of Fort Louisbourg." Many company start-ups gathered investors from both Old and New England with "get rich" schemes. Anyone that could, applied for land grants. It was a full-on land rush with the Mi'kmaq the lessor for it. Settlers quickly outnumbered the Mi`kmaq.

After Cornwallis's departure, replacement governors of Nova Scotia found that Mauger was easy to get along with - *when they gave him his way*. When unhappy, Mauger would complain to the Board of Trade and enlist his supporters to send complaints signed by at least 20 merchants. Distillers like Johnathan Gifford, William Murrey and Dr. Jonathan Prescott signed many of these letters as well as several other notables like Samuel McClure – *who operated the Halifax woodlot*. These men along with Thomas Saul, John Fillis, Michael Franklin, Jonathan Binney, John Butler, Ephraim Cook, Joseph Rundell, Thomas Kilby, the brothers Benjamin and Joseph Gerrish and Vere Rous, wife of Joseph Rous – *could form the core of what is known as the "Halifax Party."*

The Halifax Party was a trade network. But it was also the power and influence of the merchants (along with their connections) which gave credence to Mauger's complaints to the Board of Trade. This power would be used against any governor he had problems with - *and Mauger had problems with them all*. In fact, some his associates publicly bragged that Mauger was responsible for the recall of at least three governors, namely Belcher, Campbell and Legg. While this claim is impossible to prove, the fact remains Mauger and the Halifax Party, made life miserable for **any** governor who attempted to change the system. Those governors soon learned that Joshua Mauger not only had powerful partners in his business interests, but also powerful allies in the Board of Trade as well. Mauger's trading partners also influenced the Board of Trade. Men like Thomas and John Hancock, Charles Apthorp and Jonathan Trumbull from the lower colonies – *and possibly Brooks Watson in England*. Over time Mauger's protégés began filling government positions and the Mauger Machine was put into perpetual motion. In April 1762, the Nova Scotia House of Assembly, chose Mr. Joshua Mauger as the colony's agent in London. This was not too surprising since many of those elected to the House were business associates of his. In England, he could directly influence the Board of Trade. Mauger would also make his way to Parliament but would be accused of buying support by giving a town 1000 pounds for the use of public projects. Meanwhile back in Nova Scotia, his affairs would be managed by his agent John Butler and the many partners in his distilleries. After political retirement, Mauger would serve as a Nova Scotia "influencer" for the rest of his life.

But regardless of smuggling, fortunes were made and lost by merchants of the Halifax Party supplying the French and Indian War. As the war ended, many of the Halifax Party cashed out, again led by Mauger. After the second siege of Louisbourg in 1758, Mauger began liquidating his assets and settling his affairs in Nova Scotia. He sold his 27-ship fleet and installed John Butler as his agent to manage the businesses and land holdings he still held. Mauger had many partners to fulfill his rum contract to the military and jointly profited in the monopoly they held. Rum was his golden goose, and he would maintain this contract almost until his death.

In 1760, one of his last acts as a captain was to fill three ships with codfish. These ships were crewed by slaves he had personally trained in the art of sail and had made continual non-stop runs from Nova Scotia to the West Indies for years. Mauger made one last trip to the West Indies where he sold the cargos, the ships, and finally the crews. When Joshua Mauger left Nova Scotia, the power of the Halifax Party was handed over to his business partners – *or should I say, government*. One of Mauger's main adversaries, Governor Legg wrote to his cousin, Lord Dartmouth in 1775:

> *"The first assembly* [in 1758] *was composed of persons solely under the influence of Mauger... The means they adopted for securing power by squandering the money in the treasury and the money borrowed on useless works, bounties, &c., threatening the governor and members of council, many of them being officers of Government, with a refusal to vote their salaries, and, the members being traders, by keeping these members in debt; by granting to the distillers duties to exclude West Indian produce, and through the influence of Mauger to fill the council with their supporters so as to prevent any check on the assembly. They have so monopolized the trade, that the governor cannot introduce any measure for the public good, that is opposed to their interest, without complaint."*

It is fair to say that even with Joshua Mauger leaving the colony, elements of the Halifax Party continued to influence Nova Scotia for decades.

Bibliography

"*History of Halifax City*." by Thomas B. Akins. Nova Scotia Historical Society, 1895.

"*MAUGER, JOSHUA*: in *Dictionary of Canadian Biography*." by Donald F. Chard. vol. 4, University of Toronto/Université Laval, 2003–, accessed February 24, 2022. http://www.biographi.ca/en/bio/mauger_joshua_4E.html.

"*The 'Foreign Protestants' and the settlement of Nova Scotia: the history of a piece of arrested British colonial policy in the eighteenth century*." by Winthrop Bell. University of Toronto Press, 1961.

"*The Life and Administration of Governor Charles Lawrence 1749-1760*." by James S. MacDonald. Nova Scotia Historical Society, 1880.

"*The History of Parliament: the House of Commons 1754-1790*." by L. Namier and J. Brooke. edition 1964.

ATTACHMENT

The inclusion of the "Forming Tree" by Dr. Holdrege into "Oak Island Mystery Trees, and other Forensic Answers" is courtesy of The Nature Institute's reprint policy, found on their website. Nothing has been modified in this inclusion.

The Forming Tree

By Craig Holdrege

The trees you see below are in their winter habit. Without leaves, the form of the crown displays itself through the intricate branching pattern of the limbs. Each of these trees has a history behind it and the crown form reveals some of that history. But the history is no straightforward matter. It has different facets and in each particular tree is unique.

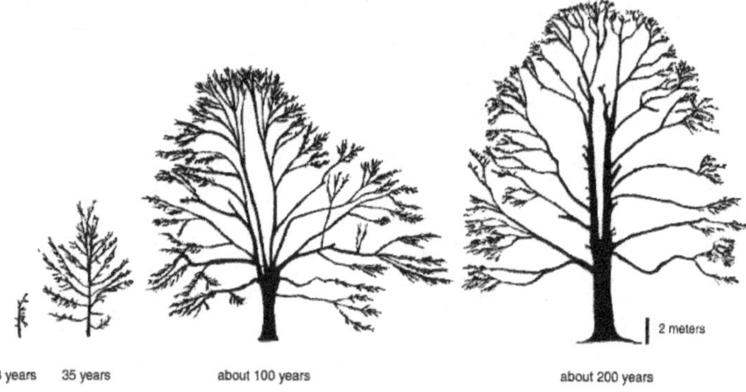

Figure 1. Schematic depiction of the growth of an individual tree, a European beech (Fagus sylvatica). (After Gleissner 2005, p. 66)

First, each tree belongs to a species. As a red oak or a white ash, a tree is part of a specific hereditary current that connects it with all other members of the species. Although a species has considerable plasticity and shows an often surprising variety of forms, it is nonetheless usually possible, with a bit of practice, to identify a tree species in the winter through its bark, branching pattern, buds, and so on.

The particular shape of the crown and the size of the trunk is relative to the crown in an individual tree express a different facet of the tree's history. A tree's crown develops over time and no broad-leafed tree maintains the same shape when it grows from a sapling to a 20- or 100-year-old tree (see Figure 1). While growing, the shape transforms. All the trees you see in the figure below had, as young trees, branches growing out of the trunk near to the ground. But all of these branches have since died off. As the trunk grew in diameter, the bark grew around the scar where the branch had separated from the trunk. The branchless lower stretches of the old trunk therefore no longer reveal outwardly the tree's growth history. The tracks are present, however, as knots deeper within the wood.

The trees in Figure 2 vary greatly in shape, and the crown of some trees is markedly asymmetrical. You might even call them misshapen. To understand these forms, you have to look not only at the growth process of the individual tree, but also at its growth in relation to the environment. Figure 3. Provides a partial solution to the riddle of these enigmatic forms – you no longer see each tree by itself but within a group of trees. Each tree can in reality only be understood when you see it as part of a larger whole.

Viewing the tree forms in isolation (Figure 2), you recognize that something isn't quite right, but then, seeing them in context, you realize – with an element of surprise, relief, and a sense of resolution – that everything is right. The individual trees fit together and form, as a group, one large crown.

Figure 2. (Below) A variety of tree forms. (Sketches by C. Holdrege)

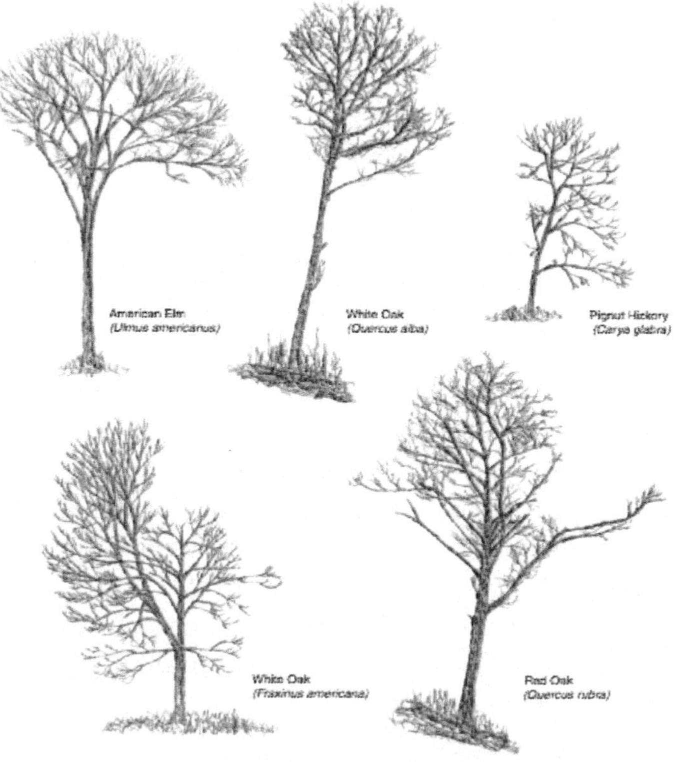

Figure 3. (Below) The five trees from Figure 2 depicted in context – as tree groups in which the trees together form a crown. Below: White ash, American Elm, and pignut hickory; red oak and white oak on a slope.

(Sketches by C. Holdrege)

Evidently, trees growing up in close proximity relate to one another. A tree does not have a predestined shape that it has to achieve. Rather, it develops in relation to a specific constellation of organisms and qualities (light, water, soil, exposure) constituting its environment. It is a remarkable phenomenon that different tree species can grow in concert to form an overriding crown of which each tree is apart.

When you study tree growth, you recognize that this co-development occurs largely in relation to light.

All plant growth is connected with light. In trees, the trunk brings the tree up into the light-filled atmosphere. But, as a rule, a tree trunk grows straight up; it is not directed toward the sun as a source of light, which in fact moves daily across the sky. This growth straight upward is known as negative geotropism since the trunk grows directly away from the center of the earth. The blossoms of numerous wildflowers, in contrast, follow the path of the sun during the day; they exemplify positive phototropism – growing toward the light source.

As the tree trunk grows straight upward, it send off side branches and, eventually, in most broad-leafed trees, the main trunk itself divides into smaller branches (unlike conifers such as spruce, fir, and hemlock, which usually maintain a central vertical trunk throughout their lives). Through this ongoing upward growth and branching, the tree form arises. Exactly how it arises depends on the particular context. (For more examples of how trees form within the context of their habitat see Buess 1992).

Figure 4. (Next page) depicts two white oaks with dramatically different forms. The broad-crowned oak grew as a free-standing tree at the edge of a pasture. It had, as a young tree, no neighbors growing close by. As is typical for a solitary tree, the crown gradually spread out broadly in all directions, attaining a relatively spherical shape. In general, branches grow outward and ramify into the space of greater brightness surround them.

Figure 4. Two different specimens of white oak (Quercus alba). The specimen on the left is a freestanding tree, while the tall, slender tree on the right grew in a forest.

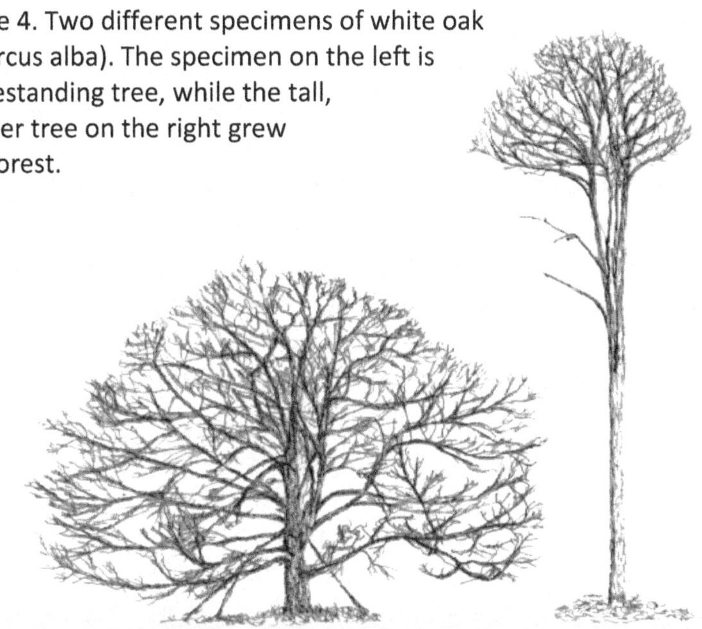

(Sketches by C. Holdrege)

The leaves and branches themselves create darkness so that the outward spreading is toward greater brightness. The crown as a whole is not growing toward the light source (the sun), but toward the brightness of the surrounding atmosphere. In our latitudes, the northern side of a tree will, in more or less subtle ways (leaf size and shape, for example), differ from the southern side, which is exposed to more brightness. Similarly, leaves that are at the outermost edges of the tree differ from leaves situated in the darker interior of the crown. By creating shade, a tree creates an environment for itself, influencing its own growth pattern. A tree is in part, its own context.

What about the small-crowned white oak with its long, upward-soaring trunk? This specimen grew in the woods. It partnered in growth with red oaks, sugar maples, and red maples. You have to imagine this single tree surrounded on all sides by other trees of similar height. All trees together form one large crown – the forest canopy. By growing up together, perhaps out of an abandoned pasture about 80 to 100 years ago, these trees began growing upward and unfolding. They produced shade for each other, and the dominant growth direction was upward into the light-filled space. The lower branches, which never grew to great size, died off in the increasingly shady environment of the upward-shooting trees. In this way, the long, branchless trunk developed, and we need to imagine the seemingly meager crown of the individual trees as part of the larger, dense, green canopy of the whole forest.

We can now better understand the tree groups in Figure 3. The group consisting of the white ash, American elm, and pignut hickory is a free-standing group In a pasture. The group forms one common crown that resembles that of a single free-standing tree. The common crown of the white oak and the red oak reveals a different context. This pair grows within a relatively bright oak-hickory forest at the edge of a small clearing in moderate light conditions, neither surrounded by brightness from all sides nor illuminated only from above. The common crown form reveals this intermediate situation: the trunks only divide at a considerable height, but then together branch out into a fuller crown than if they had grown in shadier woods.

Directing our gaze toward the form of trees leads us beyond the tree itself. It leads us to a web of relations of which the tree is part. Once you begin to see in such an organic form the tracks of its history and its relations to its surroundings, every meeting with a new tree is a source of excitement, a riddle waiting to be appreciated and deciphered.

Competition, Cooperation – or Neither?

In describing the trees in this article I have consciously avoided the terminology of competition often applied to biological phenomena. Virtually all contemporary ecological and evolutionary studies use competition as the central explanatory framework. On this view, a tree's genetic propensity is to capture as much light as possible, which maximizes its ability to do photosynthesis, grow, and produce fertile offspring that guarantee the survival of the species. Since every tree has this propensity, and growth creates shade that brings about death, each tree competes with its neighbors to maximize light uptake. Such competition is what brings about the "struggle for existence" that Charles Darwin placed at the heart of his evolutionary theory.

An opposing, much less common interpretation of the trees is that they are cooperating: each tree in a group survives and in so doing does not compete against its neighbors, but rather works together with them, adjusting its growth in relation to the others.

Both modes of interpretation are decidedly anthropocentric. Competition and cooperation are concepts drawn from human experience. Shouldn't we examine critically whether such concepts have any relevance to plants, which are such different creatures from ourselves? Imagine for a moment that we had no first-hand experience as ego-centered agents striving to secure and expand our own existence – the experience that underlies our concept of competition. Would the phenomena of tree growth I have described suggest our of themselves that we are dealing with competing agencies? I don't think so. Rather, the genetic propensity we ascribe to the plant to maximize light uptake as a survival strategy is a concept we project onto the plant, unaware that we are conceptually infusing its biology with an all-too human psychological characteristic. If we are interested in understanding the trees and not our own reflection in the trees, then we would do well to avoid such an interpretative framework.

Darwin noted that he was using the term "struggle for existence" (what we today call competition) in a "large and metaphorical sense." He writes in *Origin of Species:*

> *"A plant on the edge of the desert is said to struggle for life against the drought, though more properly it should be said to be dependent on the moisture."* Darwin, 1859

What a difference between these two ways of expressing the same phenomenon. The first projects competitive agency into the plant. The second simply states in a matter-of-fact way an essential quality of the plant in relation to its environment, namely its reliance on water. I would say, in agreement with Darwin, that the second formulation is undoubtedly more proper because it stays closer to the phenomena themselves and in so doing has the added virtue of leaving one open to further insights that may come with more study of the relations between plant, water, and desert. The idea of competition, by contrast, forces the phenomena into a closed frame shaped by our own, unrelated experience.

To avoid misunderstanding: I am not saying that Darwin or modern ecologists and evolutionary scientists believe plants are intelligent agents scheming to increase the survival of their species. In the barest terms, Darwinian competition is merely the result of the fact that all organisms produce more offspring than can survive. Individual organisms and species have to compete because there is no way all can survive with the limited resources a habitat, an ecosystem, or, in the end, the whole biosphere provides. But even this way of stating the relationships is more interpretive than you might think. It presupposes that you focus on the individual plants or species as things unto themselves that relate to each other as "others." As a consequence, species survival is assumed to be writ large in each genome, with competition a necessary outcome and therefore the dominant mode of species interaction. If you take this approach far enough, you end up with Richard Dawkins' "selfish genes," which become the competing atoms of biology (Dawkins 1990).

Charles Darwin writes,

> *"A plant which annually produces a thousand seeds, of which on average only one comes to maturity, may be more truly said to struggle with the plants of the same and other kinds which already clothe the ground."*
>
> (Darwin, 1859)

If Darwin hadn't been guided only by the metaphor of competition, he might just as well have emphasized that many seeds and seedlings provide nourishment for birds, soil, nematodes, slugs, woodchucks, and other creatures. The species does not exist merely "in and of itself;'" it is part of a larger whole. This is what we have seen in the development of tree forms. We may be tempted to say that the plants are sacrificing themselves for the greater whole. Do you recognize the strong anthropocentrism? It might be an uplifting thought that touches our feelings to thing of self-sacrifice in nature, but in may have little to do with the plants.

To employ concepts such as competition and cooperation is in one way easy and fulfilling. We know these qualities from the inside and we can wield them as a framework within which we place all the phenomena we encounter. If we could use the concept of competition in a free and playful manner, just to see what might show itself through this particular lens, and then shift to another point of view such as the one involving cooperation, we wouldn't need to worry much about the misuse of these concepts. Their limitations would be counterbalanced by the variety of perspectives, and we would gain through a dialectical process a richer understanding of the world.

But competition is the one reigning perspective used to interpret life. It has become a rarely questioned, unconscious habit of mind. People don't even notice they are using an interpretative framework and assume that competition is a fact of nature. A concept that is used habitually and unconsciously colors the world we see and limits our understanding. It no longer illuminates.

Appendix P (Bibliography)

IMAGE & RESOURCE REFERENCES

This Appendix has been by far, the hardest for me to complete and give it the care and respect I now know it deserves – *thank you Janet!*

Be that as it may, I have bastardized all the literary rules from the *MLA*, the *APA*, *Chicago*, and other writing realms of how to do a bibliography. Oh well, <u>don't buy my next book</u>!

I never understood why someone would think I would know the authors name of an article and in my couch potato frame of mind, the *"Title"* of the reference would or should be front and center. So that is how my books' bibliography will be handled - rightly or wrongly, properly or incorrectly, bigly or smally. Same attitude goes with the footnotes within the chapters and appendices. *Endnotes… footnotes… citations… references…* whatever you want to call all of that, I have inserted them for those who want to check my research or to have something to complain about. This is my technical writer *"swimming pool"* insertion, so you can find its fault and default easily.

The reason for the fancy footnotes embedded in the text with the bold and the underline and the italics; was simply so I could clearly see and find them within the text, as I am going blind. Nothing more complicated than that. If however you are as interested in what I wrote and discovered as you are with my misuse of literary guidelines, than I will be a happy camper.

Should I have mislabeled or miscited your literature, I do apologize and mean no copyright infringement, no libel or slander, nor infer less of the entity and sponsorship of the publisher in any way. I blame it all on my eyesight, typing skills and lack of a overpaying a publishing house.

This Bibliography Appendix is divided into two sections, the _Image References_ and the _Resource References_. The Image References identify the sources for each and every graphic, image, illustration, photo, and chart found within both volumes of "***Oak Island Mystery Trees and other Forensic Answers***," and is sorted By chapter/appendix and numbered By the order of their appearance within those sections.

The Resource References is a compilation of the sources used in researching the writing of these books and where citations were taken from other publications. They are listed alphabetically By the "Title" of the source researched and the format of their citation has been modified By the author. This Resource Reference Section separates out those citations of Land Deed property transactions tracked in Appendix D, "*Obscured Owners of Oak Island*," and is listed at the end of this appendix.

IMAGE REFERENCES

Inside Front of the Book

0-1. "Solomon's Island," B/W copy. By Robert W. Cook. 2021. www.bobcookartistry.com.
0-2. "Smith's Cove with rock," B/W photo. Courtesy W.R. Macaskill, Nova Scotia National Archives.

Chapter 1

1-1. "View of Oak Island from mainland," B/W photo. Courtesy of Nova Scotia National Archives.
1-2. "North American Continent," B/W graphic. Courtesy iStock.com.
1-3. "Old Nova Scotia Province," B/W map. Courtesy British Battles, www.BritishBattles.com/french-indian-war/general-braddocks-defeat-on-the-monongahela-in-1755-i/.
1-4. "Mahone Bay," B/W map. Created By David Neisen.
1-5. "Oak Island aerial-1994," B/W photo. Courtesy of Google Maps.
1-6. "Oak Island with lot parcels," B/W drawing. Created By David Neisen.
1-7. "Smith's Cove with boat," B/W painting. Watercolor By Robert W. Cook. 2018. www.bobcookartistry.com.

Chapter 2

2-1. "Foreign Protestants and the settlement of Nova Scotia," B/W map. Courtesy W. Bell.
2-2. "Sketch of Mauger Beach at Mouth of Halifax Harbor," B/W drawing. Courtesy of Nova Scotia National Archives.
2-3. "Magnified Map Section," B/W map. Courtesy of Crown Lands Record Centre, NS Dept. of Natural Resources.
2-4. "G Stone closeup," B/W photo. Courtesy of Nova Scotia National Archives.
2-5. "Halifax article newsprint, May 4, 1754," B/W image. Halifax Gazette, Courtesy Nova Scotia National Archives.
2-6. "Halifax article newsprint, arrival of Giffords & Smith," B/W image. Halifax Gazette, Courtesy Nova Scotia National Archives.
2-7. "Halifax announcement newsprint, August 13, 1754," B/W image. Halifax Gazette, Courtesy Nova Scotia National Archives.
2-8. "Halifax article newsprint, Letter from Barbados," B/W image. Halifax Gazette, Courtesy Nova Scotia National Archives.
2-9. "Halifax article newsprint, New York May 27," B/W image. Halifax Gazette, Courtesy Nova Scotia National Archives..

2-10. "John Giffords Will," B/W image. Courtesy of Ancestry.com.
2-11. "Map of Staten Island – 1780," B/W drawing. Courtesy of US Library of Congress.
2-12. "Great Kills Harbor," B/W photo. Courtesy of Marinas.com.
2-13. "Foreign Protestants and the settlement area map," B/W drawing. Courtesy of W. Bell.
2-14. "Halifax announcement newsprint, March 15," B/W image. Halifax Gazette, Courtesy Nova Scotia National Archives.
2-15. "Halifax article newsprint, January 19, 1754," B/W image. Halifax Gazette, Courtesy Nova Scotia National Archives.
2-16. "Portrait of Joshua Mauger," B/W drawing. Courtesy Nova Scotia National Archives.
2-17. "Audit Statement," B/W typography. Courtesy T. Akins, History of Halifax City, Parliamentary Budget of 1749.

Chapter 3

3-1. "Species Overlap and Range in NEAF chart." Courtesy Josh Noseworthy and Thomas M. Beckley. Borealization of the New England – Acadian Forest: a review of the evidence. *Environmental Reviews*. 28(3): 284-293. © Canadian Science Publishing or its licensors. https://doi.org/10.1139/er-2019-0068.
3-2. "Smith's Cove with boat," B/W painting. Watercolor By Robert W. Cook. 2018. www.bobcookartistry.com.
3-3. "Smith's Cove pit search," B/W photo. Dated 1897. Courtesy Nova Scotia National Archives.
3-4. "Boiler Arrives," B/W photo. Closeup image of material and trees. Bowdin Expedition, Nova Scotia National Archives.
3-5. "Field Observations Chart," Word table. Created By David H. Neisen.

Chapter 4

4-1. "Species Generic Tree," B/W illustration. Modified image from illustration at www.gradesix.mrpolsky.com.
4-2. "Limber Pine," Color manipulated B/W photo. US National Park Service - Public Domain.
4-3. "Quercus Alba set," B/W illustration. Created By Dr. Craig Holdrege, The Forming Tree.
4-4. "Tree Shapes," B/W vector images. Courtesy iStock.com.
4-5. "Smith's Cove w/ rock," B/W photo. Courtesy W.R. Macaskill, Nova Scotia National Archives.
4-6. "Trees on Bluff," B/W photo. Bowdin Expedition, Nova Scotia National Archives.
4-7. "Trees on Bluff enhanced," B/W photo. With triangle imprint on shrubs. Bowdin Expedition, NS National Archives.
4-8. "Aerial with Circled Trees," B/W photo. Seven circled trees. Courtesy of www.oakislandsociety.ca/.
4-9. "Corney Brook Park," B/W photo. Birch trees in background. Courtesy of Nova Scotia National Archives.
4-10. "Smith's Cove Canopied-Trees," B/W photo. Courtesy of Nova Scotia National Archives.
4-11. "Smith's Cove Canopied-Trees," B/W photo. Courtesy of Nova Scotia National Archives.
4-12. "Smith's Cove Canopied-Trees with branch markers," B/W photo. Courtesy Nova Scotia National Archives.
4-13. "Taxonomic Characteristics of Tree Species," B/W table. Created By David Neisen.
4-14. "Silhouette Burr Oak," B/W vector graphic. Courtesy of iStock.com.
4-15. "Burr Oak Root System," B/W illustration. Image found at, Burr Oak – Plant Fact Sheet. US. Dept. Agriculture.
4-16. "Exposed Old Burr Oak Tree," B/W photo. Courtesy of Missouri Division of Conservation.
4-17. "Silhouette Northern Red Oak," B/W vector graphic. Courtesy of iStock.com.
4-18. "Northern Red Oak," B/W photo. Courtesy Kids Encyclopedia, property of © American Forestry Institute. https://kids.britannica.com/students/assembly/view/126764 .
4-19. "1945 Aerial of OI western drumlin," B/W photo. Courtesy of Information Services Fond, NS National Archives.

4-20. "Quercus rubra," B/W illustration. Created By Dr. Craig Holdrege, The Forming Tree.
4-21. "Quercus virginiana," B/W vector graphic. Courtesy www.en.wikipedia.org/wiki/quercus_virginiana.
4-22. "Seaside Southern Live Oak," B/W photo. Courtesy of iStock.com.
4-23. "Old Northern Red Oak in Oak Centre," B/W photo. Courtesy Nova Scotia National Archives.

Chapter 5

5-1. "Glossary of the Craft," B/W photo. Courtesy of A.C.F. Jackson.
5-2. "Enoch's Vault," B/W illustration. Created By Robert W. Cook.
5-3. "Abiff's Meeting in Top Arc," B/W illustration. Created By Todd E. Creeson.
5-4. "Masonic Lodge with Two Pillars on cloth," B/W painting. Courtesy "*The Craft and its Symbols,"* p.11.
5-5. "Gold Bug," BW illustration. Cover of Allen Poe's Novel "Gold Bug" illustrated By Herpin Inv.
5-6. " Smith's Cove w/ rock," B/W photo. Courtesy W.R. Macaskill, Nova Scotia National Archives.
5-7. "The Light of Masonry," B/W photo, poster of masonic pillars and symbols. Courtesy www.masonicarts.com.
5-8. "Acacia Pin," B/W photo. Retail item for sale. Courtesy www.masonicarts.com.
5-9. "Acacia Tree," B/W photo. Photographed By G. Fader, P.Geo. 2021.
5-10. "Acacia Tree Branch," B/W photo. Photographed By G. Fader, P.Geo. 2021.
5-11. "Acacia Tree Leaves," B/W photo. Photographed By G. Fader, P.Geo. 2021.
5-12. "Acacia Tree Thorn," B/W photo. Photographed By G. Fader, P.Geo. 2021.
5-13. "Acacia Tree on Street," B/W photo. Photographed By G. Fader, P.Geo. 2021.

Chapter 6

6-1. "New Mystery Trees Found," B/W photo. Created from image By David H. Neisen. 2022.
6-2. "Smith's Cove w/ rock," B/W photo. Courtesy W.R. Macaskill, Nova Scotia National Archives.
6-3. "Smith's Cove Trees," B/W photo. Created By author James A. McQuiston FSA Scot. 2022.
6-4. "Mystery Stand of Trees," B/W photo. Photo taken By Picxy.com/Rhysl.
6-5. "Mystery Stand of Trees – Magnified," B/W photo. Photo taken By Picxy.com/Rhysl.
6-6. "Mystery Stand of Trees background #1," B/W photo. Courtesy Anne Peters, Your Adventure Wedding, 2018.
6-7. "Mystery Stand of Trees background #2," B/W photo. Courtesy Anne Peters, Your Adventure Wedding, 2018.
6-8. "Smith's Cove w/ boiler," B/W photo. Courtesy Bowdin Expedition, NS National Archives.
6-9. "Mystery Stand of Trees in Winter," B/W photo. Photographed By Dr. Stephen Bungard Ph.D. 12-2021.
6-10. "Satellite View of Tree Location," B/W photo. Courtesy Google Earth.
6-11. "*Acer pseudoplatanus* silhouette," B/W vector image. Courtesy iStock.com.
6-12. "*Acer pseudoplatanus* in Gstaad, Switzerland," B/W photo. Photographed By MC de Laubarede. "*Acer pseudoplatanus*," By Dan Crowley (2020), Trees and Shrubs Online, accessed 2022-01-19. www.treesandshrubsonline.org/articles/acer-pseudoplatanus/.
6-13. "*Acer pseudoplatanus* in Yorkshire Wolds, UK," B/W photo. Photographed By John Grimshaw. "*Acer pseudoplatanus*," By Dan Crowley (2020), Trees and Shrubs Online, accessed 2022-01-19. www.treesandshrubsonline.org/articles/acer-pseudoplatanus/.
6-14. "*Acer pseudoplatanus* in Gstaad, Yorkshire Arboretum, UK," B/W photo. Photographed By John Grimshaw. "*Acer pseudoplatanus*," By Dan Crowley (2020), Trees and Shrubs Online, accessed 2022-01-19. www.treesandshrubsonline.org/articles/acer-pseudoplatanus/.
6-15. "*Acer pseudoplatanus* in Raasay Isle, Scotland, UK angle #1," B/W photo. Photographed By Rhysl. Courtesy of iStock.com/Rhysl.
6-16. "*Acer pseudoplatanus* in Raasay Isle, Scotland, UK angle #2," B/W photo. Photographed By Ann Peters. Courtesy of Anne Peters, Your Adventure Wedding, 2018.

Chapter 7

7-1. "Field Observations," Word Table. Created By David H. Neisen. 2021.
7-2. "Oak Tree on Lot #5," B/W photo. Courtesy Robert Young, www.oakislandlotfive.ca .
7-3. "Stem of Oak Tree on Lot #5 (image 7-2)," B/W image. Modified By David H. Neisen. 2021.
7-4. "Stem Angle 1 of Oak Tree (image 7-2)," B/W image. Modified By David H. Neisen. 2021.
7-5. "Stem Angle 2 of Oak Tree (image 7-2)," B/W image. Modified By David H. Neisen. 2021.
7-6. "Northern Red Oak Bark," B/W photo. Courtesy of US National Park Service.
7-7. "Block and Tackle Basic Machines," B/W illustration. Courtesy NAVEDTRA 19037, 1994.
7-8. "Hoist Set-up," B/W illustration. Created By Anna Orel Designs. 2022.

Chapter 8

8-1. "Field Observations Part 2," Word Table. Created By David H. Neisen. 2021.
8-2. "Red Clover Drawing," B/W drawing. Created By Karen Arnold.
8-3. "Migration of Red Clover," B/W map. Created By David H. Neisen. 2022.
8-3. "Depression With Pit Below," B/W drawing. Created By Anna Orel Designs. 2022.
8-4. "Bell Pit – Coal Mining in N. Staffordshire," Courtesy of www.staffpastrack.org.uk.
8-5. "Optimum Platform Arrangement During Excavation." B/W drawing. Created By Anna Orel Designs. 2022.
8-6. "Buckets A, B, K," B/W illustration. Created By Georgius Agricola in "*De Re Metallica*." 1566. Courtesy Dover Publications.
8-7. "Buckets L," B/W illustration. Created By Georgius Agricola in "*De Re Metallica*." 1566. Courtesy Dover Publications.
8-8. "Water Buckets A, B," B/W illustration. Created By Georgius Agricola in "*De Re Metallica*." 1566. Courtesy Dover Publications.
8-9. "Wheelbarrows," B/W illustration. Created By Georgius Agricola in "*De Re Metallica*." 1566. Courtesy Dover Pubs. Publications.
8-10. "Vertical Windlass," B/W illustration. Created By Georgius Agricola in "*De Re Metallica*." 1566. Courtesy Dover Publications.
8-11. "3 Level Horse-drawn Windlass," B/W illustration. Created By Georgius Agricola in "*De Re Metallica*." 1566. Courtesy Dover Publications.
8-12. "Percent of Original Oak Log Mass Remaining," Word chart. Created By Hopkins Scientific, LLC. 2021.

Chapter 9

9-1. "Filtration System Side View," B/W illustration. 1895 Pamphlet graphic. Courtesy Les MacPhie Archives.
9-2. "Filtration System Overview," B/W Illustration. 1895 Pamphlet graphic. Courtesy Les MacPhie Archives.
9-3. "Coconut Island Cartoon," B/W drawing. Modified By David H. Neisen, courtesy www.CARTOONSTOCK.com.
9-4. "Hawser Coil," B/W photo. Courtesy www.en.wikipedia.org/wiki/hawser .
9-5. "Coconut Husks," B/W photo. Courtesy www.iStock.com.
9-6. "Coconut Coir Fiber," B/W photo. Courtesy www.iStock.com.
9-7. "Razor Blade," B/W vector graphic. Courtesy www.iStock.com.
9-8. "William of Occam Portrait," B/W portrait, uncited. Courtesy www.freemasonry.bcy.ca.

Chapter 10

10-1. "Farmer Raking Eelgrass," B/W photo from colored image. Courtesy David H. Neisen.

Chapter 11

11-1. "Those Trees," B/W photo. Courtesy of Rosemary Sheel.

Appendix A

A-1. "Surficial Geology," Colored illustration. Courtesy Steven Aitken, Ph.D., P.Geo. 2021.*
A-2. "Contour Map with Cross Section Lines," Colored illustration. Courtesy Steven Aitken, Ph.D., P.Geo. 2021.*
A-3. "Bedrock Geology & Structure Oak Island," Colored illustration. Courtesy Steven Aitken, Ph.D., P.Geo. 2021.*
A-4. "Sinkhole at Money Pit," Colored illustration. Courtesy Steven Aitken, Ph.D., P.Geo. 2021.*
A-5. "3D View of Sinkhole & Breccia Image," Colored illustration. Courtesy Steven Aitken, Ph.D., P.Geo. 2021.*
A-6. "Sea Level Change Chart," Colored illustration. Courtesy Steven Aitken, Ph.D., P.Geo. 2021.*

***Full attribution: Steven Aitken Ph.D., P.Geo. https://stevenaitken3.wixsite.com/scientific-facts.**

Appendix B

B-1. "Smith's Cove with rock," B/W photo. Courtesy W.R. Macaskill, Nova Scotia Archives.
B-2. "View From South Shore," B/W photo. Courtesy Bowdin Expedition, Nova Scotia Archives.
B-3. "NEAF Ecoregion Map," B/W illustration. Courtesy Josh Noseworthy and Thomas M. Beckley. Borealization of the New England – Acadian Forest: a review of the evidence. *Environmental Reviews*. 28(3): 284-293. © Canadian Science Publishing or its licensors. https://doi.org/10.1139/er-2019-0068.
B-4. "Species Overlap and Range in NEAF Chart," B/W chart. Courtesy Josh Noseworthy and Thomas M. Beckley. Borealization of the New England – Acadian Forest: a review of the evidence. *Environmental Reviews*. 28(3): 284-293. © Canadian Science Publishing or its licensors. https://doi.org/10.1139/er-2019-0068.
B-5. "Broad Arrow Mark," B/W vector graphic. Courtesy Historical Society of New England.
B-6. "Saw Mill and block house Fort Anne Creek," B/W photo of wood engraving. Courtesy Library of Congress.
B-7. "Major Nova Scotia Storms," B/W Word Table. Created By David H. Neisen. 2021.
B-8. "Aerial View of Oak Island – 1929," B/W photo. Courtesy Nova Scotia National Archives.
B-9. "Changes in Tree Species 1800-1993," B/W bar chart. Courtesy J. Loo and N. Ives. The Acadian Forest: Historical condition and human impacts[1]. *The Forestry Chronicle*. Vol. 79, No. 3, Page 462-474. May/Jun 2003.
B-10. "Range Map of Bur Oak," B/W chart. Courtesy Donnie A. McPhee and Jude A. Loo. Past and Present Distribution of New Brunswick Bur Oak Populations: A Case for Conservation. *Northeastern Naturalist*. **16**(1):85-100. 2009. Natural Resources Canada. Canadian Forestry Service – Atlantic Forestry Centre.
B-11. "Native Tree Species 1600-2021," Word Table. Created By David H. Neisen. 2021.

Appendix C

C-1. "Opining at Oak Island Determinations Board," B/W engraving. Courtesy www.iStock.com.

Appendix D

D-1. "Lot Ownership Chart," Word chart. Created By David Neisen and Chris Boze. 2022.

Appendix E

E-1a. "Jack Pine/*Pinus banksiana,*" photo. Courtesy www.srs.fs.usda.gov/pubs/misc/ag_654/volume1/pinus/banksiana.htm.
E-1b. "Jack Pine Silhouette," vector graphic. Courtesy https://tidcf.nrcan.gc.ca/en/trees/factsheet/43.
E-2a. "White Spruce/*Picea mariana,*" photo. Courtesy https://en.wikipedia.org/wiki/Picea_glauca.
E-2b. "White Spruce Silhouette," vector graphic. Courtesy https://plants.usda.gov/.
E-3a. "Black Spruce/*Picea mariana,*" photo. Courtesy https://en.wikipedia.org/wiki/Picea_mariana.

E-3b. "Black Spruce Silhouette," vector graphic. Courtesy https://sciencenotes.wordpress.com/2007/08/09/tree-silhouettes/.
E-4a. "Balsam poplar/*Populus balsamifera*," photo. Courtesy https://www.herbworld.com/learningherbs/POPLAR,%20BALSAM.pdf.
E-4b. "Balsam Poplar Silhouette," vector graphic. Courtesy https://www.calgary.ca/csps/parks/planning-and-operations/tree-management/top-tree species-for-calgary.html.
E-5a. "Tamarack/*Larix larcinia,"* photo. Courtesy www.confiersociety.org/conifers/larix-larcina/.
E-5b. "Tamarack Silhouette," vector graphic. Courtesy https://tidcf.nrcan.gc.ca/en/trees/factsheet/34.
E-6a. "*Balsam fir/Abies balsamea,"* photo. Courtesy https://www.plants.ces.ncsu.edu/plants/abies-balsamea/.
E-6b. "Balsam fir Silhouette," vector graphic. Courtesy https://tidcf.nrcan.gc.ca/en/trees/factsheet/80.
E-7a. "Trembling Aspen/*Populus tremuloides,"* photo. Courtesy https://www.fs.fed.us/database/feis/plants/tree/poptre/all.html.
E-7b. "Trembling Aspen Silhouette," vector graphic. Courtesy https://tidcf.nrcan.gc.ca/en/trees/factsheet/58.
E-8a. "Pin Cherry/*Prunus pensylvanica,"* photo. Courtesy www.srs.fs.usda.gov/pubs/misc/ag_654/volume_2/prunus/pensylvanica.htm.
E-8b. "Pin Cherry Silhouette," vector graphic. Courtesy https://tidcf.nrcan.gc.ca/en/trees/factsheet/59.
E-9a. "Red Cedar/*Juniperus virginiana,"* photo. Courtesy https://www.conifersociety.org/conifers/juniperus-virginiana/.
E-9b. "Red Cedar Silhouette," vector graphic. Courtesy https://tidcf.nrcan.gc.ca/en/trees/factsheet/133.
E-10a."Black Ash/*Fraxinus nigra,"* photo. Courtesy http://plants.classiclandscapes.com/11050016/Plant/157/Black_Ash.
E-10b. "Black Ash Silhouette," vector graphic. Courtesy https://tidcf.nrcan.gc.ca/en/trees/factsheet/27.
E-11a. "Red Pine/*Pinus resinosa,"* photo. Courtesy https://jsesposito.wordpress.com/2013/11/20/lessons-from-the-red-pine/.
E-11b. "Red Pine Silhouette," vector graphic. Courtesy https://tidcf.nrcan.gc.ca/en/trees/factsheet/49.
E-12a. "Eastern White Pine/*Pinus strobus,"* photo. Courtesy https://gobotany.newenglandwild.org/species/pinus/strobus/.
E-12b. "Eastern White Pine Silhouette," vector graphic. Courtesy https://tidcf.nrcan.gc.ca/en/trees/factsheet/50.
E-13a. "Largetooth Aspen/*Populus grandidentata* photo. Courtesy http://www.psn3.com/Peuplier,a,grandes,dents/fiche.html.
E-13b. "Largetooth Aspen Silhouette," vector graphic. Courtesy https://tidcf.nrcan.gc.ca/en/trees/factsheet/55.
E-14a. "White Elm/*Ulmus americana,"* photo. Courtesy https://kcarboretum.org/10-tree-list/127 ulmus-americana-disease-resistant-variety.
E-14b. "White Elm Silhouette," vector graphic. Courtesy https://tidcf.nrcan.gc.ca/en/trees/factsheet/76.
E-15a. "Yellow Birch/*Betula alleghaniensis,"* photo. Courtesy https://www.treeplantation.com/yellow-birch.html.
E-15b. "Yellow Birch Silhouette," vector graphic. Courtesy https://tidcf.nrcan.gc.ca/en/trees/factsheet/15.

E-16a. "Red Ash/*Fraxinus pennsylvanica,"* photo. Background removed for clarity of tree. Image taken By Richard Webb, Bugwood.org. Courtesy https://www.forestryimages.org/browse/detail.cfm?imgnum=1480634.
E-16b. "Red Ash Silhouette," vector graphic. Courtesy https://tidcf.nrcan.gc.ca/en/trees/factsheet/28.
E-17a. "Sugar Maple/*Acer saccharum,"* photo. Background removed for clarity of tree. Courtesy https://moonnurseries.com/product/acer-saccharum-commemoration/.
E-17b. "Sugar Maple Silhouette," vector graphic. Courtesy https://tidcf.nrcan.gc.ca/en/trees/factsheet/86.
E-18a. "Striped Maple/*Acer pensylvanicum,"* photo By Susan McDougall. Pittsfield, Mass. Courtesy https://northamericantrees.com/acer-pensylvanicum.html.
E-18b. "Striped Maple Silhouette," vector graphic. Courtesy https://tidcf.nrcan.gc.ca/en/trees/factsheet/83.
E-19a. "Red Maple/*Acer rubrum,* photo. Courtesy https://www.naturehills.com/red-maple.
E-19b. "Red Maple Silhouette," vector graphic. Courtesy https://tidcf.nrcan.gc.ca/en/trees/factsheet/84.
E-20a. "Red Spruce/*Picea rubens,"* photo. Courtesy https://treecanada.ca/resources/canadas arboreal-emblems/red-spruce/.
E-20b. "Red Spruce Silhouette," vector graphic. Courtesy https://tidcf.nrcan.gc.ca/en/trees/factsheet/41.
E-21a. "White Ash/*Fraxinus americana,"* photo. Courtesy https://www.srs.fs.usda.gov/pubs/misc/ag_654/volume_2/fraxinus/americana.htm.
E-21b. "White Ash Silhouette," vector graphic. Courtesy https://tidcf.nrcan.gc.ca/en/trees/factsheet/26.
E-22a. "Basswood/*Tilia americana,"* photo. Courtesy https://treemontgomery.org/wp content/uploads/2018/12/american-basswood-fall-color.png.
E-22b. "Basswood Silhouette," vector graphic. Courtesy https://kids.britannica.com/students/assembly/view/126778.
E-23a. "Eastern Hemlock/*Tsuga canadensis,"* photo. Courtesy https://www.coniferousforest.com/eastern-hemlock-canadian-hemlock.htm.
E-23b. "Eastern Hemlock Silhouette," vector graphic. Courtesy https://edis.ifas.ufl.edu/publication/ST646.
E-24a. "Silver Maple/*Acer saccharinum,"* photo. Courtesy https://treemontgomery.org/wp content/uploads/2018/12/silver-maple-fall.png.
E-24b. "Silver Maple Silhouette," vector graphic. Courtesy https://tidcf.nrcan.gc.ca/en/trees/factsheet/85.
E-25a. "Black Cherry/*Prunus serotina,"* photo. Courtesy https://www.ontario.ca/page/black-cherry.
E-25b. "Black Cherry Silhouette," vector graphic. Courtesy https://tidcf.nrcan.gc.ca/en/trees/factsheet/60.
E-26a. "American Beech/*Fafus grandifolia,"* photo. Courtesy https://www.kingnurseryil.com/product/american-beech-7-gal-18-42/.
E-26b. "American Beech Silhouette," vector graphic. Courtesy https://tidcf.nrcan.gc.ca/en/trees/factsheet/25.
E-27a. "Black Birch/*Betula Nigra,"* photo. Courtesy www.srs.fs.usda.gov/pubs/misc/ag_654/volume2/Betula/nigra.htm.
E-27b. "Black Birch Silhouette," vector graphic. Courtesy www.iStock.com.
E-28a. "Ironwood/*Ostrya virginiana,"* photo. Courtesy https://plants.jimwhitingnursery.com/Plant Name/Ostrya-virginiana-Hop-Hornbeam-or-Ironwood.
E-28b. "Ironwood Silhouette," vector graphic. Courtesy https://tidcf.nrcan.gc.ca/en/trees/factsheet/36.

Appendix F

F-1. "Smith's Cove with boat," B/W painting. Watercolor By Robert W. Cook. 2018. www.bobcookartistry.com.
F-2. "View of Oak Island from mainland," B/W photo. Courtesy of Nova Scotia National Archives.
F-3. "Aerial view of Eastern Drumlin," B/W photo. Circa 1933. Courtesy: Harold Reid, Nova Scotia National Archives.
F-4. "Aerial view of Eastern Drumlin 2," B/W photo. Circa 1933. Courtesy: Harold Reid, Nova Scotia National Archives.
F-5. "Isaac's Point Trees w Boat on beach," B/W photo. Circa 1909. Courtesy Bowdin Expedition, NS National Archives.
F-6. "Trees atop Crest with Frog Island," B/W photo. Circa 1909. Courtesy Bowdin Expedition, NS National Archives.
F-7. "Canopied Tree stand on bluff over Smiths Cove," B/W photo. Circa 1909. Courtesy Bowdin Expedition, Nova Scotia National Archives.
F-8. "Early Bowdin Camp at Smiths Cove," B/W photo. Circa 1909. Courtesy Bowdin Expedition, NS National Archives.
F-9. "Roosevelt Arrives at Camp," B/W photo. Circa 1910-12. Courtesy Bowdin Expedition, Nova Scotia National Archives.
F-10. "Bark," B/W photo. Magnified modification to Image F-9. Courtesy David H. Neisen.
F-11. "Leaves," B/W photo. Magnified modification to Image F-9. Courtesy David H. Neisen.
F-12. "Dead Snags of OI," B/W photo. Circa 1947. Courtesy NS Information Services, Nova Scotia National Archives.
F-13. "Dead Tree Osprey Nest," B/W photo. Courtesy Robert Young, owner www.oakislandlotfive.ca.
F-14. "Drilling Crew on Oak Island," B/W photo. Courtesy of Bowdin Expedition, Nova Scotia National Archives.
F-15. "Dodge Photo," Colored photo. Courtesy Robert Young Collection, Nova Scotia National Archives.
F-16. "Smith's Cove Image – Early Dig," B/W photo. Courtesy Bowdin Expedition, Nova Scotia National Archives.
F-17. "Smith's Cove Image – Logs," B/W photo. Courtesy Bowdin Expedition, Nova Scotia National Archives.
F-18. "Smith's Cove Image – Boiler," B/W photo. Courtesy Bowdin Expedition, Nova Scotia National Archives.
F-19. " Smith's Cove Image – Closeup," B/W photo. Courtesy Bowdin Expedition, Nova Scotia National Archives.
F-20. "Smith's Cove w/ Fence," B/W photo. Courtesy Nova Scotia National Archives.
F-21. "1945 Aerial of OI western drumlin," B/W photo. Courtesy of Information Services Fond, NS National Archives.
F-22. "View of Smith's Cove through the Trees," B/W photo. Courtesy of Clara Dennis Fond, NS National Archives.
F-23. "Balloon View of Oak Island," B/W photo. Modified By David Neisen. Courtesy Nova Scotia National Archives.
F-24. "View from South Shore," B/W photo. Courtesy Bowdin Expedition, Nova Scotia National Archives.
F-25. "View of Oak Island from mainland," B/W photo. Courtesy of Nova Scotia National Archives.
F-26. "View of Oak Island from Chester," Colored photo. Courtesy of www.tourismchester.ca.

Appendix G

G-1. "Silhouette of Albizia," B/W drawing. Courtesy Hawaii Forest & Trail, Apr. 2012. https://hawaii-fores.com/albizia-moluccana/.
G-2. "Albizia Tree on the Ranch." Colored photo. Courtesy Mike Kane/Aurora Op/Aurora Photos. Kauai, Hawaii. Jun. 19, 2020..

G-3. "Silhouette of Acacia," B/W drawing. Courtesy "The Living Wisdom of Trees: A Guide to the Natural History, Symbolism and Healing Power of Trees." Section – "Acacia," By Lea Russell, Feb. 13, 2020. By Fred Hageneneder. Watkins Publishing.
G-4. "Acacia Tree on African Plain," Color photo. Courtesy iStock.com.
G-5. "Silhouette of Aleppo Pine," B/W drawing. Courtesy Jim Harter, Jan, 2013. "Plants: 2,400 Royalty-free illustrations of Flowers, Trees, Fruits and Vegetables." Dover Publications.
G-6. "France, Nice View of Aleppo Pine Tree," color photo. Courtesy Westend61/HKP.
G-7. "Silhouette of Butternut," B/W drawing. Courtesy "Butternut: A Landowners Guide." Museum of Dufferin Simcoe. Land Stewardship Network.
G-8. "Butternut Catkins Bloom," color photo. Courtesy TreeTopics.com. http://www.treetopics.com/juglans_cinerea/gllery1.htm.
G-9. "Silhouette of Stone Pine," B/W drawing. Courtesy Jim Harter, Jan, 2013. "Plants: 2,400 Royalty-free illustrations of Flowers, Trees, Fruits and Vegetables." Dover Publications.
G-10. "Stellar Pines Above Estate," color photo. Courtesy iStock.com.
G-11. "Silhouette of Maritime Pine," B/W drawing. Courtesy Jim Harter, Jan, 2013. "Plants: 2,400 Royalty-free illustrations of Flowers, Trees, Fruits and Vegetables." Dover Publications.
G-12. "Cloudy Maritime Pine stand," B/W photo. Courtesy iStock.com.
G-13. "Silhouette of White Birch," B/W drawing. Courtesy Natural Resources Canada. https://tidcf.nrcan.gc.ca/en/trees/factsheet/16.
G-14. "Autumn Yellow Foliage of White Birch," color photo. Courtesy Skully/Alamy Stock Photo.
G-15. "White Birch Stand above highway at Corney Brook Park, 1960's," B/W photo. Courtesy Nova Scotia National Archives.
G-16. "Silhouette of Cork Oak, B/W drawing. Courtesy Cork Tree Collection, Alamy Stock Photo.
G-17. "Portuguese Orchard of Cork Oak Trees with bark removed," color photo. Courtesy Roger Mechan, Feb. 2021. iStock.com.
G-18. "Silhouette of European Sycamore," B/W drawing. Courtesy WikiMili, "*Acer pseudoplatanus*," Wikipedia, The Free Encyclopedia. Updated 11-10-21. www.wikimili.com/en/Acer_pseudoplatanus/Acer_pseudoplatanus_textura_del_tronco.jpg).
G-19. "Distant Stand of Mystery trees," color photo. Courtesy Picxy.com/Rhysl
G-20. "Closer look at Distant Stand of Mystery trees," Color photo. Courtesy Picxy.com/Rhysl.
G-21. "Very Close look at Distant Stand of Mystery trees," Color phot magnified. Courtesy Picxy.com/Rhysl.
G-22. "Daytime Wintry E. Sycamore," Color Photo. Courtesy Botanist Dr. Stephen Bungard. 2021.
G-23. "Winter - Acer. pseudoplatanus," B/W photo. Courtesy Botanist Dr. Stephen Bungard. 2021.
G-24. "1909 Closeup of Oak Island Trees," B/W photo. Courtesy Bowdin Expedition, Nova Scotia National Archives
G-25. "*A. pseudoplatanus* from Gstaad, Switzerland," Color photo. Courtesy MC de Laubarede.
G-26. "*A. pseudoplatanus* from Yorkshire Wolds, UK.," Color photo. Courtesy John Grimshaw.
G-27. "*A. pseudoplatanus* from Yorkshire Arboretum, UK.," Color photo. Courtesy John Grimshaw.
G-28. "A. pseudoplatanus from Yorkshire Arboretum, UK.," Color photo. Courtesy John Grimshaw.
G-29. "A. pseudoplatanus from Isle of Raasay, Scotland," Color photo. Courtesy Picxy.com/Rhysl.
G-30. "A. pseudoplatanus from Isle of Raasay, Scotland," Color photo. Courtesy Ann Peters.
G-31. "Farmer in the Field with Sycamores Background," Color photo. Courtesy Alamy Stock Photo.
G-32. "Two Lone Sycamore Trees Standing," Color photo. Courtesy Alamy Stock Photo.
G-33. "Collection of Sycamore Tree Parts, images within table," Color phots and B/W drawings. Courtesy sources include: trees.standford.edu, Driverfordevice.blogspot.com, & iStock.com.

Appendix H

H-1. "Abacas," B/W illustration. Courtesy iStock.com.
H-2. "Shape of Serpent Mound," B/W image. Created By David H. Neisen from image shown on History Channel show, COOI. 2022.

H-3. "Tree Dissection of Trunk," B/W drawing. Created By David H. Neisen. 2022.
H-4. "Stacked Logs," B/W vector graphics. Courtesy iStock.com.
H-5. "Photograph of Log Platform," color photograph. Courtesy Photograph courtesy of www.oakislandtreasure.co.uk/photos.
H-6. "Map of Red Clover Migration," Colored line art. Created By David H. Neisen, 2022.
H-7. "1807 Red Clover Bill of Sale," B/W photo. Courtesy Nova Scotia National Archives.

Appendix I

I-1. "Coconut Subgroup Types," B/W pencil art. Created By Miles Ballew. 2020.
I-2. "Coconut Dissection," B/W illustration. Courtesy How Products Are Made – Coir/History, P. 2. www.madehow.com/volume6/coir.html.
I-3. "Worldwide Coconut Subgroup Distribution," Colored illustration. Courtesy Kenneth Olsen/WUSTL.
I-4. "Independent Origins of Cultivated Coconut (*Cocos nucifera L.*) in the Old World Tropics," Colored Illustration. Courtesy of Bee F. Gunn, Luc Baudouin, Kenneth M. Olsen. *Origins of Coconut Domestication*. doi:10.1371/ journal.pone.0021143.g002. *PLoS ONE*, 06-04-11, Vol. 6, Issue 6, e21143. www.plosone.org.
I-5. "Coconut Island Cartoon," B/W drawing. Modified By David H. Neisen, courtesy www.CARTOONSTOCK.com.
I-6. "Coir – The Manufacturing Process," B/W illustration. Courtesy How Products Are Made, Coir/Harvesting and Husking, P. 4. www.madehow.com/volume6/coir.html.

Appendix J

J-1. "Coconut Growing zones Worldwide," B/W vector image. Courtesy of Mike Foale, 2003.
J-2. "The Erythraen Sea Map," Color vector image. Courtesy Wikipedia online.
J-3. "Eurasian Land Bridge Map," B/W vector image. Courtesy of Tian Chi.
J-4. "Islanders Checking in Coir production," B/W vector image. Courtesy of iStock.com.

Appendix K

K-1. "Oak Island Raft," B/W vector image. Courtesy iStock.com.
K-2. "Fig. 1, Caribbean Current Pathways map," B/W line drawing. Courtesy Joanna Gyory, Arthur J. Mariano, Edward H. Ryan. "The Caribbean Current." Ocean Surface Currents. https://oceancurrents.rsmas.miami.edu/caribbean/caribean.html.
K-3. "Fig. 2, Gulf Stream Current Atlantic Ocean Gyre Map," colored illustration. Courtesy https://ifisc.uib-csic.es/LINCschool/Sources/2-THC/from-EPS131/2 RAPID/gulf_stream.php.html.
K-4. "Fig. 3, North Atlantic Currents System map," B/W line drawing. T6.1 Ocean Currents. Vol 1, p 115. Courtesy Natural History of Nova Scotia.
K-5. "Fig. 4, Enlarged closeup of Fig. 12, Atlantic Ocean/Slope Jet Current Spaghetti Plots Map," colored image. NOAA AOML Drifting Buoy Data Assembly (DAC) Center. Courtesy Angelique C. Haza, Barbie Bischof, Arthur J. Mariano. "The Slope Jet Current." Ocean Surface Currents (2013). https://oceancurrents.rsmas.miami.edu/atlantic/slopejet.html.
K-6. "Fig. 5, Ocean and Sea Currents and their Pathways," colored image. Created By David H. Neisen.
K-7. "Fig. 6, Buoy #09802862 Drifter Pathway Plotted," colored image. Courtesy NOAA AOML Drifting Buoy Data Assembly (DAC) Center.
K-8. "Fig. 7, Caribbean (Loop) Current Spaghetti Plots Map," colored image. NOAA AOML Drifting Buoy Data Assembly (DAC) Center. Courtesy Joanna Gyory, Arthur J. Mariano, Edward H. Ryan. "The Caribbean Current." Ocean Surface Currents. https://oceancurrents.rsmas.miami.edu/caribbean/caribean.html.
K-9. "Fig. 8, Gulf Stream Current Spaghetti Plots Map," colored image. NOAA AOML Drifting Buoy Data Assembly (DAC) Center. Courtesy Joanna Gyory, Arthur J. Mariano, Edward H.

Ryan. "The Caribbean Current." Ocean Surface Currents. https://oceancurrents.rsmas.miami.edu/atlantic/gulf-stream.html.

K-10. "Fig. 9, Atlantic Ocean/N. Atlantic Current Spaghetti Plots Map," colored image. NOAA AOML Drifting Buoy Data Assembly (DAC) Center. Courtesy Elizabeth Rowe, Arthur J. Mariano, Edward H. Ryan. "The North Atlantic Current." Ocean Surface Currents. https://oceancurrents.rsmas.miami.edu/atlantic/north-atlantic.html.

K-11. "Fig. 10, East/West Greenland Current Spaghetti Plots Map," colored image. NOAA AOML Drifting Buoy Data Assembly (DAC) Center. Courtesy Joanna Gyory, Arthur J. Mariano, Edward H. Ryan. "East Greenland Current." Ocean Surface Currents. https://oceancurrents.rsmas.miami.edu/atlantic/east-greenland.html and "West Greenland Current." Ocean Surface Currents. https://oceancurrents.rsmas.miami.edu/atlantic/west greenland.html .

K-12. "Fig. 11, Labrador Current Spaghetti Plots Map," colored image. NOAA AOML Drifting Buoy Data Assembly (DAC) Center. Courtesy Joanna Gyory, Arthur J. Mariano, Edward H. Ryan. "The Labrador Current." Ocean Surface Currents. https://oceancurrents.rsmas.miami.edu/atlantic/labrador.html.

K-13. "Fig. 12, Atlantic Ocean/Slope Jet Current Spaghetti Plots Map," colored image. NOAA AOML Drifting Buoy Data Assembly (DAC) Center. Courtesy Angelique C. Haza, Barbie Bischof, Arthur J. Mariano. "The Slope Jet Current." Ocean Surface Currents (2013). https://oceancurrents.rsmas.miami.edu/atlantic/slopejet.html.

K-14. "Fig. 13, Dinner Current – Spaghetti Al Dente, B/W vector image. Courtesy iStock.com.

K-15. "Fig. 14, Fiber Flotilla Floating Route," colored drawing. Created By David H. Neisen w/map from https://instaar.colorado.edu/meetings/AW2012/abstract_details.php?abstract_id=54.

K-16. "GPS Markers of Currents," colored map. Created By David H. Neisen using www.freemaptools.com/measure-distance.htm.

Appendix L

L-1. "Coconut Coir fiber: retted & processed," Color photo. Courtesy iStock.com.

Appendix M

M-1. "Percent of Original Oak Log Mas Remaining," Colored bar chart. Created By Hopkins Scientific LLC.

Appendix N

N-1. "Typed Survey of Fishermen," B/W image. Courtesy T.B. Akins, History of Halifax City, Nova Scotia Historical Society, 1895.

Appendix O

All illustrations were created, produced, and compiled by the author Dr. Craig Holdrege and are subject to his copyright restrictions.

SOURCE REFERENCES

#

"*10X – Some Inconvenient Facts*." By John Wonnacott P.E. Published in *Blockhouse Blog*, Apr. 4, 2011. www.oakislandcompendium.ca. (Accessed 05-30-2022)

"*14th Colony to Confederation, 1749-1867.*" By Alex Boutilier. Governors, Placenames & Merchant Elites.

"*1691 Massachusetts Charter.*" The Federal and State Constitutions Colonial Charters, and Other Organic Laws of the States, Territories, and Colonies Now or Heretofore Forming the United States of America. Compiled and Edited Under the Act of Congress of June 30, 1906 By Francis Newton Thorpe. Washington, DC : Government Printing Office, 1909.

"*17 Palm Tree Insects & Diseases and How to Treat Them*." Florida Palm Tree Association. www.Florida-palm-trees.com/palm-tree-insects-diseases/.

"*1765 Land Grant Participants*." Includes: Jacques Boutilier, 1767. James Pernette, 1757. George Boehner. Casper Wollenhaupt (930 ac.), 1765. Joseph Pernette (810 ac.), 1765. George Boehner Sr. (160 ac.), 1765. John James Bissansa (445 ac.), 1765. John Smith (330 ac.), 1765. McKinnon, 1791. John Bearlson, 1897. Merton McLean, 1764. Ambrose Allen, 1785. William Hopkins, 1787. Jeremiah Rogers, 1778. Fred Patillo, 1791. James Sharp, 1776. John J. Beassion. James Becanson. Alexander Patillo. Robert Melvin. John Kinghorn. John Martin. Phillip Payzant. Jacob Shephard. Melvin Marshall. James Webber. Davie Crandall. Joseph Bazasar. NSNA.

"*1861, Coker Nuts – Dunnage*." By Henry Mayhew, 1861. London Labor Party. On the London Poor, Vol. 1. http://cocos.arecaceae.com/mercantile.html.

"*1945 Aerial of OI western drumlin*," B/W photo. Courtesy of Information Services Fond, Nova Scotia National Archives.

"*2 Page Letter from Robert R. Dunfield responding to questions*." By D'Arcy O'Connor. Oct. 21, 1976.

"*2,000 Year Old Lost City of Rhapta May have been Found in Tanzania*." By Natalia Klimczak, Jul. 5, 2016. (Accessed on 04-22-2021) https://www.ancient-origins.net/news-history-archaeology/2000-year-old-lost-city-rhapta-may-have-been-found-tanzania-006234.

"*23 Species of Acacia Trees and Shrubs*." By Vanessa Richins Myers, Updated Apr. 5, 2022. Reviewed By Barbara Gillette. Published in The Spruce," online. https://www.thespruce.com/twenty-species-acacia-trees-and-shrubs-3269672.

"*5 Worst Storms to Hit the East Coast*." By Paul Daly, Canadian Press, 2012. CBC News Posted: Sep. 11, 2012. Last Updated: Sep.11, 2012. https://www.cbc.ca/news/canada/5-worst storms-to-hit-the-east-coast-1.1138740.

A

"*Abaca (Manila Hemp) in the Philippines (Musa textilis)*." By M.M. SaleeBy, Chief, Fiber Division, Bureau of Agriculture. https://quod.lib.umich.edu/p/philamer/BBN0285.0001.001?rgn=main;view=fulltext.

"*Abaca (Manila hemp): The Fiber Monopoly of the Philippine Islands*." By G.S. Lee, 1920. Published in The Scientific Monthly, 11 (2), Pages 159-170. http://www.jstor.org/stable/6637.

"*About the Clan MacInnes*." Clan Macinnes Website. Pages 1-8. https://mcinnes.org/info.html. (accessed 12-12-21).

"*A Brief History of the Age of Exploration*." By Amanda Briney. Updated 01-24-2020. ThoughtCo. https://www.thoughtco.com/age-of exploration-1435006?print. (Accessed 09-28-21).

"*Abrupt Onset of the Little Ice Age triggered by Volcanism and Sustained by Sea-ice/Ocean Feedbacks*." By Gifford H. Miller, et. al, Jan. 30, 2012. Published in Geophysical Research Letters, 39 (2).Bibcode:2012GeoRL..39.2708M. CiteSeerX 10.1.1.639.9076. doi:10.1029/2011GL050168. S2CID 15313398. See also in #80 above.

"*Acadian Forest: History, Species, and Biodiversity.*" By Jamie Simpson, J. Loo & N. Ives. Woodland Woman. Mar. 4, 2021.

"*Account By James McNutt, Secretary of the Oak Island Eldorado Co*." Transcribed By Les MacPhee. Known as the Halifax Co. Diary of work carried out from Dec.1866/Jan.1867. Pages1-6.

"*Acer pseudoplatanus Datasheet.*" CABI – Commonwealth Agricultural Bureaux International. Sections 'Distribution & Distribution Table, and History of Introduction and Spread, para. 1-2. (Accessed on 01-26-22). https://www.cabi.org/isc/datasheet/2884todistribution.

"*Acer Pseudoplatanus L*." World Checklist of Selected Plant Families (WSCP). Royal Botanic Gardens, KEW. Retrieved 19 May 2016 – via The Plant List. (Accessed 02-03-22).

"*Acer pseudoplatanus L.*" From the website 'Trees and Shrubs Online," By Dan Crowley (2020). Paras. 1, 3, 4 and 6-8. (from 'Maples of the World, Van Gelderen 1994). (Accessed 01-29-22). https://www.treesandshrubsonline.org/articles/acer/acer-pseudoplatanus/.

"*Acer pseudoplatanus*." Wikipedia, The Free Encyclopedia. Sec. Distribution, Para. 1-2. Updated Nov. 10, 2021. www.wikimili.com/en/Acer_pseudoplatanus/Acer_pseudoplatanus_textura_del_tronco.jpg.

"*Acorn Production in Red Oak*." By Daniel C. Dey. Forest Research Information Paper No. 127. Ontario Forest Research Institute, Canada. 1995. 27 pages.

"*Advent of Europeans in India Upsc Notes: Portuguese, Dutch, English & French*." By Babu R. Pravin, Jun. 1, 2020. https://andedge.com/advent-of-the-europeans/.

"*Aerial photos show changes In Nova Scotia over the years*." By Len Wagg. 10-21-2019. *Local Lifestyles* – The Chronicle Herald. Pages 1-2. https://www.thechronicleherald.ca/lifestyles/local-lifestyles/aerial-photos-show-changes-in-nova-scotia-over-the-years-365363/. (Accessed 11 16-20).

"*Aerial view of Eastern Drumlin - 2*," Circa 1933. B/W photo. Courtesy Harold Reid, Nova Scotia National Archives.

"*Aerial view of Eastern Drumlin*," Circa 1933. B/W photo. Courtesy Harold Reid, Nova Scotia National Archives.

"*Affidavit from S.C. Fraser to A.S. Lowden*." copy By Frederick Blair. June 19, 1895.

"*Age Class, Longevity and Growth Rate Relationships: Protracted Growth Increases in Old Trees in the Eastern United States*." By Sarah E. Johnson and Marc D. Abrams. *Tree Physiology*. Oxford University Press. 2009. Pages 1317-1328.

"*A Glossary of Scotch Mining Terms*." Compiled By James Barrowman, Mining Engineer and Secretary to the Mining Institute of Scotland, 1886. "March." Printed at the "*Advertiser*" Office, By W. Naismith, 1886. http://scottishmining.co.uk/Indexes/Barrowman.html.

"*Agricultural Revolution in England: The transformation of Agrarian Economy 1500-1850.*" By Mark Overton. Cambridge University Press, 1996. www.BBC-History-British-History-in-Depth-Agricultural-Revolution-in-England-1500-1850. 4 pages. (Accessed 05-14-21).

"*Agriculture and Fisheries in the Bahamas*."(Accessed 07-20-2022) https://en.wikipedia.org/w/index.php?title=Agriculture_and_fisheries_in_the_Bahamas&oldid=1072570138.

"*A History of Chinese Maritime Activities*." Unknown. Copied from Geocities, October 2009. https://www.oocities.org/tokyo/harbor/3422/maritime.html.

"*A History of Indian Shipping and Maritime Activities from the Earliest Times*." By Radhakumud Mookerji, 1912. https://archive.org/details/HistoryOfIndianShippingAndMarytimeActivityFromTheEarliestTime.

"*A History of New England Fisheries: with maps*." By Raymond McFarland. D. Appleton & Co, 1911.

"*A History of Nova Scotia or Acadie*." By Murdoch Beamish. Vol. 1-111, Halifax, Nova Scotia National Archives. James Barnes 1866.

"*A Kindling of Ancient Memory – The Ainu/Anu People*." By Alice C. Linsley. Jan. 12, 2012. https://jandyongenesis.blogspot.com/2012/01/kindling-of-ancient-memory.html?fbclid=IwAR0bZsa77jQOcBAd2sn0z65u1vdjCjj1P5bDnnkYKmlYWGkulhKzQx4sNal.

"*A Kindling of Ancient Memory*." By Alice C. Linsley, Jan. 12, 2012. Jandy on Genesis Blog. 24 pages. (Accessed 04-11-20). Hhttps://jandyongenesisi.blogspot.com/2012/01/kindling-of-ancient memory.html?fbclid=Iwar067sa77jqocbad2sn0z65u1vdjcjj1p5bdnnkykmlywgkulhkzqx4snal.

"*Albert F. Hill Letter to Reginald V. Harris*." Dated Oct. 22, 1937. Research Assistant for Professor Fernald, Botanical Museum of Harvard University. MG1, Vol. 386. Nova Scotia National Archives.

"*Aleppo pine as a medium for tree-ring analysis.*" By J. Gindel. Tree-Ring Bulletin. 1944. 11(1), Pgs 6-8.

"*All Rounder – Exploring: Tamil Imperialism: (9th – 13th Centuries)*." October 2008. 7 pages. https://puravin.blogspot.com/2008/tamil imperialism-9th-13th-centuries,html. (Accessed 09-20-21).

"*Archeological History of the Voyages and Discoveries in the South Seas on Pacific Ocean II.*" P. 58-60.

"*A long time ago in an Africa far, far away- 1836.*" *Blog* Geeska Suldaan: Majeerteen Somali PDM Victoria 2 AAR. Jun, 26, 2018. https://forum.paradoxplaza.com/forum/threads/geeska-suldaan-majeerteen-somali-pdm-victoria-2-aar.1107593/.

"*American Beech Silhouette*." Natural Resources Canada. Last modified on 04-08-2015. https://tidcf.nrcan.gc.ca/en/trees/factsheet/25.

"*American Beech/Fafus grandifolia.*" By Jim King, King Nursery, Oswego, Illinois. https://www.kingnurseryil.com/product/american-beech-7-gal 18-42/.

"*American Canopy: Trees, Forests, and the Making of a Nation*." By Eric Rutkow, 2012. New York: Scribner, 2012. a Division of Simon & Schuster, Inc.

"*An Historical and Statistical Account of Nova Scotia*." By Thomas C. Haliburton. 1829. Joseph Howe.

"*An interpretation of multibeam bathymetry off eastern Oak Island, Mahone Bay, Nova Scotia*." By G.B.J. Fader and R.C. Courtney (1988). Geological Survey of Canada (Atlantic), Bedford Institute of Oceanography, April 1998. https://geoscan.nrcan.gc.ca/starweb/geoscan/servlet.starweb?path=geoscan/fulle.web&search1=R=209918.

"*Ancestry*." 1300 West Traverse Parkway Lehi, UT 84043.

"*Ancient Era, 5000 to 1000 BCE: Early Seafaring and Trade*. Indian Ocean History. *Ancient Era*, "Historical Overview." 2 pages. https://www.indianoceanhistory.org/assets/Site_18/files/Era%20Overviews/Ancient%20Era.pdf.

"*Ancient Figs of the Holy Land*." By W.P. Armstrong, Palomar College. *Figs of the Holy Land*. 16 pages. www.palomar.edu/users/warmstrong/ww0501.htm. (Accessed 02-12-22).

"*Ancient India, West Africa & The Sea: Why It Could Not Be So*." By Harry Bourne. Published online at *Modern Ghana*. https://www.modernghana.com/news/829967/ancient-india-west-africa-the-sea-why-it-could-not-be-so.html.

"*Ancient Sailing and Navigation*." Text copyright Canbooks, pictures By Marion Kaplan. https://nabataea.net/explore/navigation_and_sailing/. (Accessed 01-24-22).

"*Annals of Staten Island: From its discovery to the present time-1878*." By J.J. Clute. Heart of the Lakes Publishing, 1986.

"*Annotated List of the Mammals of Nova Scotia*." By Fred W. Scott and Andrew J. Hebda. (2004). Procedures. Nova Scotia Institute of Science. Vol. 42, Part 2, Pages 189-208. https://ojs.library.dal.ca/nsis/article/download/NSIS42-2scotthebda/3313. (Accessed 01-13-22).

"*A Nova Scotia Treasure Trove – Pt. 1*." By Charles Frederick Jamieson, 05-29-1926. Article in the *Lethbridge Herald*. 10 columns. www.reddit.com/r/oakisland/comments/efzj67/oakisland_newspaper_archives/. (Accessed 03-19-22).

"*A Nova Scotia Treasure Trove – Pt. 2*." By Charles Frederick Jamieson, 06-05-1926. Article in the *Lethbridge Herald*. 8 columns. www.reddit.com/r/oakisland/comments/efzj67/oakisland_newspaper_archives/. (Accessed 03-19-22).

"*Anthony Vaughan, 1751-1835*." The Free Family Tree @ www.wikitree.com/wiki/vaughan-4730.

"*A Plant that Changed the World: the Rise and Fall of Clover 1000-2000*." By Kjaergaard, Thorkild and translated By David Hohnen. https://thorkildkjaergaard.com/a-plant-that-changed-the-world-the- rise-0f-clover-1000-2000/. (Accessed 11-26-21).

"*Appalachian Glacier Complex in Maritime Canada*." By R.R. Stea (2011). In: Singh V.P., Singh P., Haritashya U.K. (eds) *Encyclopedia of Snow, Ice and Glaciers*. Encyclopedia of Earth Sciences Series. Springer, Dordrecht. https://doi.org/10.1007/978-90-481-2642-2_25.

"*A Review of Growth and Stand Dynamics of Acer pseudoplatanus L. in Europe: Implications for Silviculture.*" By Sebastian Hein, et. al., 2009. *Forestry*, Vol. 82, No. 4, 2009. DOI:10.1093/forestry/cpn043. Institute of Chartered Foresters, 2008. (Accessed 01-29-22).

"*Arrival of the Coconut in Mayaro.*" By Gerald A. Besson. May 2012. *The Caribbean History Archives.* Paria Publishing Co. LTD. Pages 1-2.

"*A Short History of Glemsford.*" By Rev. Kenneth W. Glass. Former Rector of St. May of the Virgin, Glemsford. *Chapter VI. 19th century industries – Silk, Horsehair, Matting.* 12 pages. http://www.foxearth.org.uk/glemsfordglass.html.

"*Assessment of Accuracy in determining Atterberg limits for four Iraqi Local Soil laboratories.*" By H.O. Abbas (2018). IOP Conference Series: Materials Science and Engineering. 433, Pages 12-30. https://iopscience.iop.org/article/10.1088/1757-899X/433/1/012030.

"*A Survey of Kerala History.*" By A. Sreedhara Menon, Aug. 2010. 1st eBook Edition. DC Books, Kerala State, India. www.DCBooks.com.

"*Atlantic Forage Guide.*" 2010. Forage and Corn Valley Evaluation Task Force, Atlantic Canada. http://www.gov.pe.ca/photos/original/ag_atlforaguide.pdf.

"*Atlantic Neptune.*" By I.W.F. Des Barres. 1789.

"*Attempted settlements at Port Royal and St. Croix.*" Encyclopedia Britannica, Vol. XVIII, p. 603.

"*A True Copy of, James J. Thompson, Provincial Land Surveyors List of First Settlers and their Lots.*" 1764 List is an earlier version than the 1784 List copied By Judge Debrisay's The History of Lunenburg County, 1st Edition. This 1764 Thompson List was fist included in the booklet, "*Some Historical Events of Chester, Nova Scotia,*" By Cottnam T. Smith, 1945. Publisher unknown

"*A View of a Saw Mill and Block House Upon Fort Anne Creek.*" By *W. Lane. Photograph. Retrieved from the Library of Congress.* www.loc.gov/item/2006691574/.

"*A voyage to the islands Madera, Barbados, Nieves, S. Christophers and Jamaica, : with the natural history of the herbs and trees, four-footed beasts, fishes, birds, insects, reptiles, &c. of the last of those islands; to which is prefix'd an introduction, wherein is an account of the inhabitants, air, waters, diseases, trade, &c. of that place, with some relations concerning the neighbouring continent, and islands of America.*" By Sir Hans Sloane, 1660-1753. Published 1707. https://archive.org/details/voyagetoislandsm02sloa/page/12/mode/2up?q=Quitagone.

B

"*Balsam fir Silhouette.*" Natural Resources Canada. Last modified 04-08-2015. https://tidcf.nrcan.gc.ca/en/trees/factsheet/80.

"*Balsam fir/Abies balsamea.*" North Carolina Extension Service Tool Box. https://plants.ces.ncsu.edu/plants/abies-balsamea/.

"*Balsam Poplar Silhouette.*" Top Tree Species for Calgary. Official web site of the City of Calgary, Alberta, Canada. https://www.calgary.ca/csps/parks/planning-and-operations/tree-management/top-tree-species-for-calgary.html.

"*Balsam poplar/Populus balsamifera*." Editor Maureen Rogers. HERBALPEDIA, The Herb Growing & Marketing Network, Silver Spring, PA. https://www.herbworld.com/learningherbs/POPLAR,%20BALSAM.pdf.

"*Barlow Comments on COOI*." By Scott Barlow, COOI Project manager." filmed on Curse of Oak Island, Season 7, Episode #21, By Prometheus Productions, 2019. On the History Channel or The Oak Island Encyclopedia, Vol. 2, p. 233.

"*Basswood Silhouette*." BritannicaKIDS. American Forestry Institute. https://kids.britannica.com/students/assembly/view/126778.

"*Basswood/Tilia americana*." By Dr. Jeff Kirwan, et. al. A program of Montgomery County, Maryland Government. 12-07-2018. Landowner Factsheets © 2004 Virginia Tech Forestry Department, all rights reserved. https://treemontgomery.org/wp-content/uploads/2018/12/american basswood-fall-color.png.

"*Bayer's Lake Mystery Walls*." By Scott Baltjes. Halifax, Nova Scotia.3 pages. https://www.atlasobscura.com/places/bayers-lake-mystery-walls. (Accessed 10-12-21).

"*Bell letter to R.V Harris*." By Hugh P. Bell, Head of Depart. Of Biology, Dalhousie University, July 22, 1937. Nova Scotia National Archives, MG1 Vol. 381, 1204.

"*Bell Pits of Street Gate (NZ210592)*." By Michael Southwick, Sep. 2013. Newcastle History blog & North-East History Tour blog. Alternately image from www.Staffpastrack.org.uk. Coal Mining in North Staffordshire. http://northeasthistorytour.blogspot.com/2013/09/bell-pits-of-street gate nz210592.html.

"*Bench Test of the Multi-Function Coconut Husk Processing Machine*." By Frederick Villa. Southern Luzon State University, Philippines. *Academy of Accounting and Financial Studies Journal*, Vol. 25, Spec. Issue 3. 2021. 3 pages.

"*Berkshire Encyclopedia of World History*." By William H. McNeill, publisher. 2nd Edition. Berkshire Publishing group. 2010. Current Online version, 2016. https://www.google.com/books/edition/Berkshire_Encyclopedia_of_World_History/ijNsPgAACAAJ?hl=en.

"*BETA Analytic Inc. Lab Report to Richard C. Nieman*." Dated Oct. 6, 1993. Beta Sample # 66584 - Organics. Radiocarbon dated, 1229AD. www.oakislandtreasure.co.uk.

"*BETA Analytic Inc. Lab Report on Dendro Adjustment to Richard C. Nieman*." Dated Nov. 18, 1994. Beta Sample #66584 – Organics. Radiocarbon dated, 1229AD. www.oakislandtreasure.co.uk.

"*BETA Analytic Inc. Lab Report on Beta Samples #66107 – wood, and Beta Sample #39897 – Fibers to Richard C. Nieman*." Radiocarbon dated, 1279AD. www.oakislandtreasure.co.uk.

"*Bias in Indian Historiography*." Edited By D.K. Devahuti, Publishers' Distribution. New Delhi. 1980. Page 90-100. Union Catalog of Thai Academic Libraries (UCTAL).

"*Bible Plants – Oriental Plane*." Old Dominion University. https://ww2.odu.edu/~lmusselm/plant/bible/planetree.php. (Accessed 02-12-22).

"*Big Storms of the Centuries in South-Western Nova Scotia*." Yarmouth Vanguard, 06-05-1990. Musee des Acadiens des Pubnicos. 3 pages. https://museeacadiens.ca/en/the-big-storms-of-the-centuries-in-south-western-nova-scotia/. (Accessed01-02-21).

"*Bilateral Trade Relations Between India and UAE – Historical Perspective*." By Dr. R. Thanga Prashath and K. Vinodkumar. Published in *Global Journal of Management and Business Studies*. Vol. 10, No. 1, Pages 1-7, 2020. https://dx.doi.org/10.37622/GJMBS/10.1.2020.1-7.

"*Bill of Sale – Red Clover*." Between the Eassons and the Hoyts and William Robertson & Co. 03-13-1797 and 07-29-1798. Nova Scotia National Archives. MG 1 Vol. 3478, B/166.

"*Bill of Sale – Sable Island*." Requested By Edward Wards. Oct. 1801. Nova Scotia National Archives. RG 31 Series 120 Vol. 2, #42.

"*Biodegradable Materials for Planting Pots – Chapter 4*." By B. Tomadoni, D. Merino, C. Casalongue, and V. Alvarez, Mar. 2020. Published in *Advanced Applications of Bio-degradable Green Composites Materials Research Forum*. Materials Research Foundations 68 (2020) 85-103. https://doi.org/10.21741/9781644900659-485.

"*Biofuels from Coconuts*." By Krishna Raghaven, Aug. 2010. 107 pages. Annex 8, The Coconut Palm; Recycling Husks, Organic Manures, P. 76. www.energypedia.info/f/f9/EN-biofuels_from_cocnuts-krishna_raghaven.pdf.

"*Biofuels from Coconuts*." By Krishna Raghaven. 2010. 107 pages. Para. 1.1 Quantity and Energy Content of Parts of the Coconut Palm, Fig. 1 and Table 1. Biodegradability Section, P. 16. www.energypedia.info/f/f9/EN-biofuels_from_cocnuts-krishna_raghaven.pdf.

"*Biotechnology in Coir Extraction and Waste Utilization*." By Dr. Anita Das Ravindranath, Senior Scientific Officer, CCRI. CORD, Vol XVII, No.2, 2001. Central Coir Research Institute, Kerala, India. 3 Pages. Coir Board Government of India. http://www.ccriindia.org/Bio_Tech_in_coir_extraction.html.

"*Black Ash Silhouette*." Natural Resources Canada. Last modified 04-08-2015. https://tidcf.nrcan.gc.ca/en/trees/factsheet/27.

"*Black Ash/Fraxinus nigra*." Classic Landscape Plant Finder. http://plants.classiclandscapes.com/11050016/Plant/157/Black_Ash.

"*Black Birch Silhouette*." www.iStock.com.

"*Black Birch/Betula nigra*." By H.E. Grelan. Southern Research Station, U.S. Department of Agriculture, Forest Service. https://www.srs.fs.usda.gov/pubs/misc/ag_654/volume_2/betula/nigra.htm.

"*Black Cherry Silhouette*." Natural Resources Canada. Last modified on 04-08-2015. https://tidcf.nrcan.gc.ca/en/trees/factsheet/60.

"*Black Cherry/Prunus serotina*." Ontario Ministry of Northern Development, Mines, Natural Resources and Forestry. Published 07-18-2019. Last modified 10-06-2021. https://www.ontario.ca/page/black-cherry.

"*Black Death*." By J.P. Byrne, 2012. P. 108.

"*Black Death and Abrupt Earth Changes in the 14th Century. 1290-1350: Abrupt Earth Changes, Astronomical, Tectonic and Meteorological Events Leading up to and Culminating at the Black Death period at 1348*." By Sacha Dobler, Updated Version Jan. 2018. www.abruptearthchanges.com. 102 Pages. PDF.

"*Black Death: An Intimate History*." By John Hatcher, 2010. Hachette, UK. P. 180.

"*Black Spruce – Aspen / Bracken – Sarsaparilla." Part I: Vegetation Types*." Baker Settlement, Lunenburg County, Nova Scotia. 2010. 2 pages.

"*Black Spruce Silhouette*." Monado. Science Notes. Last modified on 08-09-2007. https://sciencenotes.wordpress.com/2007/08/09/tree silhouettes/.

"*Black Spruce/Picea mariana*." Last modified on 02-23-2022. https://en.wikipedia.org/wiki/Picea_mariana.

"*Blair Letter to R.V. Harris*." By Fred L. Blair, Feb. 16, 1935. Discussion of lease of two 40 acre plots. Nova Scotia National Archives, MG1, Vol. 381, 769.

"*Blair Letter to R.V Harris*." By Fred L. Blair, Nov. 5, 1937. www.oakislandtreasure.co.uk.

"*Blair reply Letter to Mr. L. Elbert Smith of Dallas*." By Gordon Blair, Aug. 4, 1947. Traders Finance Corporation Limited, Saint John N.B.

"*Blankenship report of Digging in Smith's Cove*." By Daniel C. Blankenship, Nov. 1969.

"*Block and Tackle*." US Naval Training Manual, *Block and Tackle Basic Machines*, NAVEDTRA 14037, Chapter 2. Block and Tackle.1994. 6 pages.

"*Blue Carbon Stocks in Baltic Sea Eelgrass (Zostera marina) Meadows*." By Maria Emilia Rohr, et. al, Sep. 19, 2018. Published in *Journal Biogeosciences*, Apr. 27, 2016. ResearchGate. (Accessed 05-30-2022)

"*Blue Carbon Storage Capacity of Temperate Eelgrass (Zostera marina) Meadows*." By Maria Emilia Rohr, et. al, Sep. 19, 2018. Published in *Global Biogeochemical Cycles*, Vol 32, Issue 10, Pages 1457-1475. 18 pages. (Accessed 05-30-2022)

"*Boats, Routes and Sailing Conditions of Indo-Roman Trade*." By Lucy Blue. Part 1 of *Migration, Trade and Peoples*. Preface. Jul. 2005. The British Association for South Asian Studies. The British Academy, London.

"*Borealization of the New England Acadian Forest: a Review of the Evidence*." By Josh Noseworthy and Thomas M. Beckley. NRC Research Press. Global Conservation Solutions & Forestry and Environmental Management, University of New Brunswick. February 12, 2020. Environmental Reviews. 28(3): 284-293. https://doi.org/10.1139/er-2019-0068. © Canadian Science Publishing or its licensors. 12 pages.

"*Branch Shedding in Trees*." Jan. 2, 2016. https://arboriculture.wordpress.com/2016/01/02/branch-shedding-cladoptosis-trees/.

"*Bridgland Email Responses to David H. Neisen*." By James Bridgland, July 13, 2020. Park Ecologist, Cape Breton Highlands National Park, Ingonish Beach, Nova Scotia, Canada.

"British Battles of the French and Indian War." General Braddocks' Defeat on the Monongahela River, 1755. https://www.britishbattles.com/french-indian-war/general-braddocks-defeat-on-the-monongahela-in-1755-i/.

"British Intervention in the Baltic: 1800-1801." By Lt. Jason Lancastor, USNSWO, Apr. 2018. Australian Naval Institute. "Hemp for Cordage from the Baltic through end of 1790's," published in *Center for International Maritime Security*. www.navalinstitute.com.au/british-intervention-in-the-Baltic-1800-1801/.

"Brooster Telephonic Conversation with David H. Neisen." with Mr. Robert (Bob) Brooster of RENTOKIL, August 2020. Chester, Nova Scotia.

"Buoy #09802862 Drifter Pathway Plotted," Surface Currents of the Caribbean Sea, Example Plots from 4-D Current Experiment. Buoyid 09802862 (1999-2000). https://oceancurrents.rsmas.miami.edu/caribbean/img_aoml/caribbeanF3.html.

"Bur Oak – Plant Fact Sheet." Source: United States Department of Agriculture, Natural Resources Conservation Service.

"Bur Oak – Quercus macrocarpa." Prepared By Joseph D. Scianna, Research Hort. *Plant Fact Sheet*. United States Department of Agriculture, Natural Resources Conservation Service. 2009. 2 pages. http://plants.usda.gov. (Accessed 10-20-20)

"Bur Oak, Quercus macrocarpa." By A. Michaux. Massachusetts Division of Fisheries & Wildlife. Natural Heritage & Endangered Species Program. 2010. www.mass.gov/nhesp. 3 pages.

C

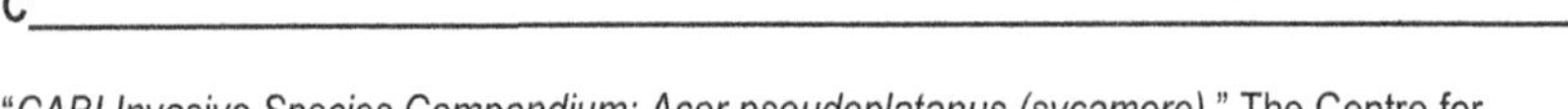

"CABI Invasive Species Compendium: Acer pseudoplatanus (sycamore)." The Centre for Agriculture and Bioscience International (CABI), Wallingford, UK. Retrieved 18 May 2016. (Accessed 02-03-22).

"Camel Train." Wikipedia Contributors (Online). Wikipedia, The Free Encyclopedia, Jun. 11, 2022. (Accessed 02-21-2022) https://en.wikipedia.org/w/index.php?title=Camel_train&oldid=1092609372.

"Canada before Confederation, A Study in Historical Geography." By Harris Cole and John Warkentin. 1974. Oxford, London, Oxford University Press.

"Canada's Plant Hardiness Zones." Natural Resources Canada. 2014. www.planthardiness.gc.ca.

"Canadian Forestry Chronical," By Sidney Perley, 1847. Pubs-dif-ifc.org. 6-25-2020. Pgs. 72, 120, 141, 201.

"Captain Anthony Vaughan interview." By Gilbert Hedden, dated 1939.

"Captain Kidd and Buried Treasure." By J.P. Forks. 1857.

"Carbon Sequestration in a Pacific Northwest Eelgrass (Zostera marina) Meadow." By Katrina L. Poppe and John M. Rybczyk. Published in Northwest Science, 92 (2), pages 80-91. http://www.bioone.org/doi/full/10.3955/046.092.0202.

"*Cargo Loss Prevention – Coconut Fiber*." Transport Information Service. German Marine Insurance Bd. 8 pages. https://www.tis gdv.de/tis_e/ware/fasern/kokosfa/kokosfa-htm/.

"*Cargo Terms and Definitions*." Compiled By David J. House. Maritime Consultancy & Marine Surveying. Capt. Reuben Lanfranco, BA (Crim), M. Jur (Int. Law), LL M (IMLI), Dip. Mar. Sur., AMRINA, FIFireE, MCILT, AFRIN, FNI MIM, RMS, RMC. Pages 1-8. www.maritimeconsultant.eu/cargo-terms-and-definitions. (Accessed 09-01-21).

"*Carpenter Ant, Prevention and Control*." Backyard Bud Brigade. Atlantic Provincial Environment Departments. PEI Department of Agriculture, Fisheries and Forestry, Agriculture and Agri-food Canada and Environment. Nova Scotia Department of Environment and Labor. April 2011. 2 pgs.

"Carpenter Ants in the House." By Destiny Malone, Adirondack.net 3-27-2013.

"*Case Studies on Application of Coir Geotextiles for Soil/Sand Stabilization*." By K.S. Beena, 2013. International Conference on Case Histories in Geotechnical Engineering. 7 https://scholarsmine.mst.edu/icchge/7icchge/session_06/7.

"*Catalogues of Historical Earthquakes in Italy*." Romano Camassi, 2004. Annals of Geophysics, Vol. 47.

"*Causes and Control of Wood Decay, Degradation & Stain*." By Todd Shupe, Ph.D., Stan Lebow, Ph.D. and Dennis Ring, Ph.D. Louisiana State University Agricultural Center, Research & Extension. Pub. 2703, Rev. 6/08. 26 Pages.

"*Cavities Under and Around Oak Island*." By Doug Crowell, the Blockhouse Blog. Jan, 6, 2017. www.oakislandcompendium.ca. 5 pages.

"CBD-III, Decay of Wood. " By M.C. Baker. MIT, National Research Council, Canada. 1969.

"Census." By Jacques De Meulles, Kt, Seigneur de La Source, Intendant of New France of Acadie. 1685-1686.

"*Ceylon and the Portuguese, 1505-1658*." By P.E. Pieris, Ceylon Civil Service. American Ceylon Mission. 1920.https://archive.org/stream/ceylonportuguese00pier/ceylonportuguese00pier_djvu.txt.

"*Challenges for the Boreal Forest Zone and IBFRA*." By S. Nilsson, 2000. IIASA 16 pages, @ http://forestportal.efi.int/view.php?id=1087&c=I1. See website International Boreal Forest Research Association. http://ibfra.org/about-boreal-forests/.

"*Changes in the Land: Indians, Colonists, and the Ecology of New England*." By William Cronon. 1983. (2010 current). See pg 147. Farrar, Strauss & Giroux publishers. 288 pages. (Accessed 02-09-22).

"*Chapter 10: Temperature Effects*." By J.M. Glime, 2017. In *Bryophyte Ecology*. Vol. 1. *Physiological Ecology*. Ebook sponsored By Michigan Technological University and the International Association of Bryologists. Updated 07-18-20. http://digitalcommons.mtu.edu/bryophyte/ecology/. (Accessed 10-10-21).

"*Characterization and Utilization of Coconut Fibers of the Caribbean*." By Nadira Mathura, et. al., Materials Research Society Symposium Proceedings, Vol 1611, 2014. DOI: 10.1557/opl.2014. 4.

"*Characterization of Annur and Bedakam Ecotypes of Coconut from Kerala State, India, Using Microsatellite Markers*." By M.K. Rajesh, et. al., Division of Crop Improvement, Central Plantation

Crops Research. *International Journal of Biodiversity*, Vol. 2014, Article ID 260895, 7 pages. Hindawi Publishing Corporation. http://dx.doi.org/10.1155/2014/260895

"*Characterizing Nitrogen Transfer from Red Clover populations to Companion Bluegrass under Field Conditions*." By R.M.M.S. Thilakarathna1, et. al.. 11-15-2012.. Article in *Canadian Journal of Plant Science*. Pages 1163-1173. Pubs.aic.ca. Dalhousie University. https://www.researchgate.net/publication/236325861. (Accessed 11-27-21).

"*Charles Darwin, Cats, Mice, Bumblebees and [Red] Clover*." By Norman Carreck NDB, Toby Beasley and Randal Keynes, 2009. 4 pages. Enhanced quotation By Thomas Henry Huxley's publication Collected Essays Volume 2: Darwinia. 1892. https://www.researchgate.net/publication/259358642_Charles_Darwin_cats_mice_bumble_bees_and_clover.

"*Charlotte Adams interview*." By D`Arcy O`Connor, Apr. 27, 1976.

"*Chester Branch W.I.N.S., History of Chester 1759-1767*." Progress-Enterprise Co. 1967. Zoe Valle Library, Chester, Nova Scotia. Women's Institute of Nova Scotia. 164 pages.

"*Chester Township Poll Tax Roll, 1791*." Chester/Lunenburg county – 1791. Nova Scotia National Archives, RG 1, Vol. 444. No. 4.

"*Chester Township Poll Tax Roll, 1793*." Chester/Lunenburg County – 1793. Nova Scotia National Archives, RG1, Vol. 444. No. 62.

"*Chester Township Poll Tax Roll, 1794*." Chester/Lunenburg County – 1794. Nova Scotia National Archives, RG1, Vol. 444½ No. 24.

"*Chester Township Poll Tax Roll, 1795*." Chester/Lunenburg County – 1795. Nova Scotia National Archives, RG1, Vol. 444½ No. 59.

"*Chester Township Records, 1762 – 1830*." Records kept By Town Clerk consisting of the "Publishments" of Births, Marriages and Deaths. Nova Scotia National Archives, MG9, B 9-3. See specific records cited.

"*Chronological Timeline of Canadian Historical Events*." Uploaded By Jessie Sun. SCRIBD. 5 pages. https://www.scribd.com/document/201362216/Chronological-Timeline-of-Key-Canadian-Historical-Events. (Accessed 10-02-20).

"*Civil Engineering Reference Manual for the PE Exam*." By Michael R. Lindeburg, P.E. 14th Edition. PDF ISBN: 978-1-59126-458-3. Library of Congress Control Number: 2014936761.

"*Cladoptosis: An Interesting phenomenon*." Plant Clinic, 2013. Texas A&M University. 2 pages. www.plantclinic.tamu.edu/2013/11/15/cladoptosis-an-interesting-phenomenon/. (Accessed 01-09-22).

"*Claude C. Chappel interview*." By D`Arcy O`Connor, Jul. 20, 1976.

"*Classifying Forestland from model-generated Tree Species habitat Suitability in the Western Ecoregion of Nova Scotia, Canada*." By Mark Baah-Acheamfour, Charles P.A. Bourque, Fan-Rui Meng, and D. Edwin Swift, Nov. 2012. **Published at www.nrcresearchpress.com/cjfr on 8 March 2013.**

"*Clay Soil Settlement: In-situ Experimentation and Analytical Approach*." By S. Bensallam et. al., 2014. *Soils and Foundations*, 54(2), p. 109 115. www.elsevier.com/locate/sandf. (Accessed 03-09-21).

"Climate, History and the Modern World." By Hubert H. Lamb. P. 332.

"Climate of Pakistan." (Accessed 07-18-2022) https://en.wikipedia.org/w/index.php?title=Climate_of_Pakistan&oldid=1098432766.

"Coastal Zone Soil Survey, Little Narragansett Bay – Connecticut & Rhode Island." Prepared by Deborah Surabien, Soil Scientist, USDA, Natural Resources Conservation Services. Apr. 2007. 74 Pages. (Accessed 05-30-2022)

"Coco Coir Fiber Production." By Dela Cruz, Pobre & Gabrido, 2002. Manual on Machinery and Equipment for Coconut By-product.

"Coconut Fiber - Risk Factors and Cargo Loss Prevention Information, Self-Heating/Spontaneous Combustion." Transport Information Service, German Marine Insurers GDV, Die Deutschen Versiche. https://www.tis-gdv.de/tis_e/ware/fasern/kokosfa/kokosfa-htm/.

"Coconut Fibre: Its Structure, Properties and Applications." By Leena Mishra and Gautam Basu. National Institute of Natural Fibre Engineering & Technologies Institute. Kolkata, West Bengal India. Section Yield of Coconut Fibre, Page 7, para. 10.2.1.3. Yield of Coconut Fibre. Researchgate. Pub. 339284598. February 2020. 27 Pages.

"Coconut – History, Uses, and Folklore." By Subhash Chanda Ahuja. CCS Haryana Agricultural University. Article in *Asian-History Journal*. 29 pages. January 2014.

"Coconut Palms on the Edge of the Desert: Genetic Diversity of Cocos nucifera L. in Oman." By Lalith Perera, Luc Baudouin, et. al., 2011. Published in *Cord*, May 2012, 27 (1). ResearchGate.

"Coconuts." By D. Wyatt Aiken, Editor/Publisher, Jan. 1876. Published in the Rural Carolinian, Vol. VII, Jan. 1876. Pgs 573-575. https://babel.hathitrust.org/cgi/pt?id=nc01.ark:/13960/t7pn9fq2n&view=1up&seq=673&skin=2021.

"Coconut Shell based activated carbon with no greenhouse gas emission." By Dr. P.A. Shankar, 04-27-2012. *Water Technology*. 12 pages. https://www.watertechonline.com/home/article/15538115/coconut-shell-based-activated-carbon-with-no-greenhouse-gas-emission. (Accessed 01-26-22).

"Coconut Strategy – 2018." Part of A Global Strategy for the Conservation and Use of Coconut Genetic Resources, 2018-2028." Compiled by Roland Bourdex and Alexia Prades. CIPAD/CoGert.

"Coconut Time Line, The Ancient Period: Before 1499." Online repository of historical anecdotes about all things coconut. Updated Feb. 14, 2017. http://cocos.arecaceae.com/ancient.html.

"Coconut Time Line, The Mercantile Period: 1840-1925." Online repository of historical anecdotes about all things coconut. Updated Feb. 14, 2017. http://cocos.arecaceae.com/ancient.html.

"Coconut Time Line, The Nautical Period: 1499 – 1839." Online repository of historical anecdotes about all things coconut. Updated Feb. 14, 2017. http://cocos.arecaceae.com/ancient.html. Updated March 9, 2015.

"Coconut: How the Shy Fruit Shaped our World." By Robin Laurance. Brimscombe Port, UK. The History Press. 2019. 219 pages.

"*Coconuts in the Americas*." By Charles R. Clement, et. al. Instituto Nacional de Pesquisas da Amazonia, Brazil. The New York Botanical Garden. August 17, 2013. 28 pages. DOI 10.1007/s12229-013-9121-z.

"*Cocos nucifera L*." Source: FAOSTAT. Global Biodiversity Information Facility (GBIF), Copenhagen, Denmark. (Accessed 02-09-2021). https://www.gbif.org/species/113562924.

"*Cocos nucifera L. – Production and Cultivation*." 2019. FAOSTAT, United Nations. 23 Pages. https://www.gbif.org/species/113562924.

"*Cohen Email Responses to David H. Neisen*." By Botanist Cynthia Cohen, July 6, 2020.

"*Coir*." How Products are Made. Volume 6. 7 pages. www.madehow.com/Volume-6/coir.html.

"*Coir Draining Blanket for Consolidation*." By M. Sudhakaran Pillai, 2001. Presented at International Seminar on Technical Textiles, 2001. Center Institute of Coir Technology. COIRBOARD, Bangalore, India.

"*Coir Fiber Bales for Sale*." https://www.alibaba.com/product-detail/coir-fiber-bales_50036094988.html.

"*Coir Fiber Process and Opportunities - 1*." By Emilia T. Abraham PhD and Akhila Rajan, 2007. *Journal of Natural Fibers*, Vol. 3(4), Pages 29- 41, and Microbiology of Coir Retting, Pages 31-15. January 2008. Researchgate, Pub. 216866706, or http://dx.doi.org/10.1300/J395v03n04_03. (Accessed 01-09-22).

"*Coir Fiber Process and Opportunities -2*." By Akhila Rajan & T. Emilia Abraham, PhD, 2007. Biochemical Aspects Sec. Published in *Journal of Natural Fibers*. 3:4, Pages 29-42.

"*Coir Processing Technologies: Improvement of drying, softening, bleaching and dyeing coir fibre/yarn and printing coir floor coverings*." By J.E.G. van Dam. Technical Paper No. 6, Pages 4-5, para. 2.2 Coir, and para. Coir Pitch. Dec. 1999. Common Fund Commodities. Department of Fibres and Cellulose Agrotechnological Research Institute. Wageningen, Netherlands. 61 pages.

"*Coir-The Natural Fiber from Coconut Husk.*" By Line Cowley. Jun. 12, 2019. https://www.ecoworldonlone.com.

"*Commercial and Industrial Cities of the United States: Coconut Dipper Manufacturers*." Published in Hunt's Merchants Magazine and Commercial Review, Jan. to Jun. 1856. Vol. XXXIV. Pages 672-678.

"*Comoros*." By Harriet J. and Martin Ottenheimer. Encyclopedia Britannica. Updated Mar. 9, 2022. (Accessed 07-15-2022) https://www.britannica.com/place/Comoros.

"*Comparing Strength and Biodegradability of Biocontainers*." By Matt Taylor, Michael Evans, Jeff Kuehny. Sep. 10, 2010. Published in *Greenhouse Management*. www.Greanhousemag.com/article/gmpro-0910-biocontainers/.

"*Comparisons of Laccadive Micro Tall (LMT) and Laccadive Ordinary Tall (LCT) in Cote d'Ivoire and India*." By Bourdeix R. Kumaran PM, et. al. Published in *Catalog of Conserved Coconut Germplasm – by country or origin – India*, and *The Indian Coconut Journal, 23.25.* (Accessed on 05-30-2022)

"*Complete Cargo List for the 1701 San Francisco Xavier Spanish Galleon*." 2018. Manila to Acapulco. Published in the *Oregon Historical Quarterly*, Vol. 119, No. 2. Oregon Historical Society. 21 pgs.

"*Complete List of Tree Species*." By Peman Pourmohammadi. Wood and Paper Science and Technology Report. 2002.

"*Conclusions on the Results of the Vegetation of Nova Scotia*." By Titus Smith. A paper delivered before the Halifax Mechanics Institute in January 1835 and printed the same years as his "The Natural History of Nova Scotia. Magazine of Natural History. London, England. December 1835. Pages 640-662. (PANS MG1, Box 1846, Folder 3).

"*Constandy Email Responses to David H. Neisen*." By Mike Constandy, 2021. Westmoreland Research, National Archives Research Co. *Specialty:* Naval and maritime research, admiralty, ships logs and plans, sea lane and terrestrial UXO.

"*Coquito Nuts*." Nov. 15, 2019. https://en.wikipedia.org/wiki/Coquito_nuts.

"*Cordage and Caulking – Excavations at Deptford on the Site of the East India Company Dockyards and the Trinity House Almshouses, London*." By Walton Rogers and D. Divers, 2004. Published in *Post-Medieval Archaeology*. 38/1, Pages 17 – 132.

"*Corney Brook Campsite, Cabot Trail Photographs*." 2020. Nova Scotia Information Service Nova Scotia Archives, No. NSIS 17047. Page 1. https://novascotia.ca/archives/nsis/archives.asp?ID=2057&language=. (Accessed 06-18-20).

"*Cotton Textiles and the Great Divergence: Lancashire, India and Shifting Competitive Advantage, 1600-1850*." By Stephen Broadberry and Bishnupriya Gupta, 2005. Department of Economics, University of Warwick, Coventry, United Kingdom. 44 pages.

"Cracking Coconuts History." By Ramin Ganeshram. July 2017. ARAMCOWORLD.

"*Craig Lorimer Telephonic Interview*." with D`Arcy O'Connor, Apr. 18, 1977. Forester with Harvard Forest, Harvard University, Petersham, Mass.

"CRC-Handbook-of-Biosolar-Resources." (USA). (1981) Vol. 2. P. 11-21, "Agricultural Revolution: Red Clover first cultivated in England in 1645, grown in Holland as a nutrient to plough back into field for crop production."

"*Crop Tree Release Improves Competitiveness of Northern Red Oak Growing in Association with Black Cherry*." By Thomas M. Sckuler. Northern Research Station, Timber and Watershed Laboratory, Parsons, WV. 26287-0404.

"Crown Permit." Blockhouse Blog, www.oakislandcompendium.ca.

"*Cynthia Cohen Email Responses to David H. Neisen*." By Botanist Cynthia Cohen, Jul. 6, 2020.

D

"*D`Arcy initial letter on 'oak trees' to Chief Botanist, James H. Soper*." By D`Arcy O`Connor, March 26, 1975. National Museums of Canada, Museum of Natural Sciences. Ottawa, Ontario K1A OM8 Canada.

"*Dan Blankenship report of Digging in Smith's Cove*." By Daniel C. Blankenship, Nov. 1969.

"*Daniel Vaughan, 1747-1808*." The Free Family Tree @ www.wikitree.com/wiki/vaughan-2098.

"*Das Pflanzenkleid der Mittelmeerländer.*" By Rikli, M.A. 1943. (cited in Mirov 1967).

"*David A. Crandal Land Grants*." Mi'Kmaq Holdings Resource Guide, Microfilm #15723, 1818. Nova Scotia Department of Lands and Forests, Nova Scotia Archives RG 20, Ser. A. 12 pages.

"*De Re Metallica*." By Georgius Agricola, 1556. Translated By Herbert Clark Hoover and Lou Henry Hoover, 1st Latin Edition. The Project Gutenberg eBook. Released date Nov. 14, 2011. https://www.gutenberg.org/files/38015//38015-h/38015-h.htm. (Accessed on 01-01-22).

"*Dead Snags of Oak Island*." Circa 1947. B/W photo. Courtesy NS Information Services No. 6219. Nova Scotia National Archives.

"*Dead Tree Osprey Nest*," B/W photo. Courtesy Robert Young, owner www.oakislandlotfive.ca.

"*Death Registrations: 1864-1877; 1908-1960*." Vital Statistics Division of Service Nova Scotia and Municipal Relations, Compiler. @ https;//www.novascotiagenealogy.com/Deaths.aspx.

"*Death Trap Defies Treasure Seekers for Two Centuries*." By Douglas Preston. 1988. *The Smithsonian Magazine*. Pages 53-65. Published By the Smithsonian Institution.

"*Decolonizing History: Technology and Culture in India, China and the West 1492 to the Present Day*." By Claude Alvares p. 94-95.https://archive.org/details/decolonizinghist0000alva/page/n9/mode/2up?q=dammer.

"*Decomposition and Nutrient Dynamics of Oak Quercus spp. Logs after five years of decomposition*." By T.D. Schowalter, Y.L. Zhang and T.E. Sabin, 1998. Ecography, 21: pages 3-10. Copenhagen, 1998.

"*Decomposition of Fallen Trees: Effects of Initial Conditions and Heterotroph Colonization Rates*." By T. Schowalter, et. al., 1992. KP Sing (eds) *Tropical Ecosystems: Ecology and Management*, Wiley Eastern Limited, New Delhi. Pages 373-383. Utah State University, Utah.

"*Decomposition Processes of Eelgrass, Zostera marina L*." By G.C. Pellikaan. Published in *Hydrobiological Bulletin*, 16, Pages 83-92, 1982. Springer Link. (Accessed 05-30-2022)

"*Deep History of Coconuts Decoded.*" By Diana Lutz. Washington University in St. Louis. The Source – Science and Technology. June 24, 2011.

"*Dendroclimatology of umbrella pine (Pinus pinea L.) in Istanbul, Turkey.*" By U. Akkemik. Published in Tree-Ring Bulletin 56:17-20.

"*Description and State of the New Settlements in Nova Scotia in 1761*." By Charles Morris. Report of the Canadian Archives, Appendix F. Sessional Paper 18, 1905. Nova Scotian National Archives.(PANS, V.32 Doc. 27). (Accessed 04-02-20).

"*Determining the Mechanical Properties of Hazel Forks By testing their Component Parts*." By Duncan Slater & Anthony Roland Ennos, Jan. 30, 2013. Springer-Verlag Berlin Heidelberg.

"*Development of a Coir Fibre Extracting Machine*," By Emmanuel Temidayo and Emmanuel Bayo Ayodele, Department of Wood Products and Engineering, University of Ibadan. International Research Journal of Engineering and Technology (IRJET) e-ISSN: 2395-0056 Volume: 07 Issue: 07 | July 2020 www.irjet.net p-ISSN: 2395-0072.

"*Dictionary of Canadian Biography: JOSHUA MAUGER*." By Donald F. Chard, Vol. 4, University of Toronto/Université Laval, 2003. (Accessed02-24-22). http://www.biographi.ca/en/bio/mauger_joshua_4E.html.

"*Did You Know Victorians Drank from Coconut Shells*?" By Eleanor Rose, May, 27, 2020. Article at online Civil War Talk._https://civilwartalk.com/threads/did-you-know-victorians-drank-from-coconut-shells.173257/.

"*Dig For Pirate Treasure.*" By Robert I. Nesmith. New York: Bonanza Books. Crown Publishers, Inc., 274 pages.

"Digging Deep – Environmental remains from Recent Excavations along Roman London's Walbrook Valley." By Karen Stewart. Acer pseudoplatanus writing tablet. MOLA Monograph No.37, London, UK. 2011.

"Distinguishing Red and White Oak." By Eric Meier. The Wood Database. 2021.

"Diton Coir Products Catalog." 1360 East Braymore Circle, Napersville, IL 60564. 2021. Product from Southern India. Products, Loose Coir/Coir Mis. (Accessed 09-13-21). www.diton.com/coirloose.html.

"*Dodge Photo*," Colored photo. Courtesy Robert Young Collection, Nova Scotia National Archives.

"*Drilling Crew on Oak Island*," Circa 1909-11. B/W photo. Courtesy Henry Livingston Bowdin Expedition, The Old Gold Salvage and Wrecking Company. Nova Scotia National Archives.

"*Dr. Stephen Bungard, Botanist, Email Responses*." With David H. Neisen, Dec. 12, 2021. Vice-County Recorder for the Botanical Society of Britain and Ireland.

E

"*Early Bowdin Camp at Smiths Cove*," Circa 1909. B/W photo. Courtesy Henry Livingston Bowdin Expedition, The Old Gold Salvage and Wrecking Company. Nova Scotia National Archives.

"*Early Coconut Culture in Western Mexico*." By Henry J. Bruman, 1938-1939. The *Hispanic American Historical Review*. Institute of Social Anthropology, Smithsonian Institute. Pages 212 – 223. http://read.dukeupress.edu/hahr/article-pdf/25/2/212/749513/0250212.pdf.

"*Early History of Mahone Bay Nova Scotia*." By Paul Wroclawski. NEARA Journal Vol. 44 No. 1, 2010.

"Early Settlement in Nova Scotia – A History to Refresh." By Leo J. Deveau, M.Ed. MLIS. Halifax Military Heritage Preservation Society (HMHPS), 3-26-2018.

"Early Survival and Growth of Planted Hardwoods in the Acadian Forest." By Xu MA. Nanjing Forestry University, Introduction Section. The University of New Brunswick. Jan. 2019. 48 pages.

"*Eastern Hemlock Silhouette*." (Tsuga Canadensis: Canadian Hemlock) By Edward F. Gilman and Dennis G. Watson. University of Florida IFAS Extension Service. Environmental Horticulture Department Document ENH-803, 1993. https://edis.ifas.ufl.edu/publication/ST646.

"*Eastern Hemlock/Tsuga canadensis."* Published By Supidpto Chakrabarti on 06-07-2016 in *Hemlock*. Coniferous Forest Online. Article was last reviewed on 26th December 2019. https://www.coniferousforest.com/eastern-hemlock-canadian-hemlock.htm.

"Eastern White Pine Silhouette." Natural Resources Canada. Last modified on 04-08-2015. https://tidcf.nrcan.gc.ca/en/trees/factsheet/50.

"Eastern White Pine/Pinus strobus." Native Plant Trust – Go Botany. https://gobotany.newenglandwild.org/species/pinus/strobus/.

"Eastern White Pine: Monarch of the Forest." By Sheereen Othman, Jan. 9, 2018 Edition, Arbor Day Foundation.

"Ecological Imperialism: The Biological Expansion of Europe, 900-1900." By Alfred W. Crosby, University of Texas, Austin. New Edition, Pages 152, 154-156 & 156-158. Cambridge University Press, 2006.

"Economic History of Kerala from 1800 to 1947 AD, Part II: TRAVANCORE, Change in Agriculture, Industry, Transport, Power and Education." By B.A. Prakash, Thiruvananthapuram Economic Studies Society. Nov. 2018. 85 pages.

"Economic Profile of Coir Workers in Kerala – A Case study of Cherhala Taluk in Alappuzha District." By J. Aswathy and Saranya A. Ajithkumar. Published in Shanlax International Journal of Arts, Science and Humanities. Vol. 5, No. 4. Apr. 2018. Pages 311-313. Apr. 28, 2018.

"EcoWorld Online" ecoworldonline.com/coir-the-natural-fiber-from-coconut-husk. Amazon LLC Associate Program.

"Ectomycorrhizal fungi of Pinus pinea L. in Northeastern Spain." By Ana Rincon, et.al. October 29, 1998.

"Eelgrass Insulation." Archipedia New England. www.archipedianewengland.org/eelgrass-insulation. (Accessed 10-22-21).

"Egypt after the Pharoahs." By A. Bowman. 1986. London: British Museum Publications.

"Encyclopedia of Packaging Technology." 3rd Edition. By Kit L.Yam. The Wiley Encyclopedia of Packaging.

"Encyclopedia of Plague and Pestilence: from Ancient Times to the Present." By George C. Kohn, 2008. Infobase Publishing. P. 31.

"Endemic Plants of Ethiopia: Preliminary working list to Contribute to National Plant Conservation Target." By Tesfaye Awas, Ph.D. Institute of Biodiversity Conservation. Addis Ababa, Ethiopia. 14 pgs.

"Enzymatic Degradation of Lignin in Soil." By Rahul Datta et. al., Jul. 3, 2017. Published in *Sustainability*, 2017, 9, 1163: 18 pages. doi:10.3390/su9071163. https://res.mdpi.com/sustainability/sustainability-09-01163/article_deploy/sustainability 09-01163-v2.pdf.

"Essays Upon Field Husbandry in New England and other Places, 1748-62." By Jared Eliot. Edited By Harry Carman and Rexford Tugwell.. New York. Columbia University Press. 1934. 261 pages. . https://openlibrary.org/books/OL6311129M/Essays_upon_field_husbandry_in_New_England_and_other_papers_1748-1762. (Accessed 10-17-21).

"Estimating Tree Stem & Branch Weight." By Dr. Kim D. Coder, Professor of Tree Biology & Health Care, Warnell School of Forestry & Natural Resources, University of Georgia. Publication WSFNR-17-33, Apr. 2017.

"*Evens Comments on COOI.*" By Dr. Rodger C. Evens, Dir. E.C. Smith Herbarium Biology Department and Plant Developmental Morphology & Systematics Laboratory at Acadia University." Filmed on *Curse of Oak Island, Season 7, Episode #21*, By Prometheus Productions, 2019. On the History Channel or The Oak Island Encyclopedia, Vol. 2, p.233.

"*Every Nook and Cranny, Placenames: Fact and Fiction, Eyre, Fearns and Clann Mhic Ruairidh, Book 3*." By Rebecca S. Mackay, M.A., FSA Scot. Published By Raasay Heritage Trust. 2015.

"*Every Nook and Cranny, Placenames: Fact and Fiction, Eyre, Fearns and Clann Mhic Ruairidh, Book 4*." By Rebecca S. Mackay, M.A., FSA Scot. Published By Raasay Heritage Trust. 2015.

"*Everything You Need to know about the Acacia Tree*." By Casey Hoffard, Dec. 10, 2018. https://www.plantsnap.com/blog/everything-acacia trees/.

"*Evidence for European Presence in the Americas in 1021 AD*." By Margot Kuitems, et. al., published Oct. 20, 2021. *Nature Magazine*. www.Nature.com.

"*Evidence Supporting the Theory that Vikings Walked on Oak Island: Now that Season Seven of The Curse of Oak Island has Ended*," By Dr. Doug Symons. May 2020. https://psychology.acadiau.ca/files/sites/psychology/resources/pdfs/Vikings%200ak%20island%20 Symons%20May%202020.pdf. (Accessed 06-03-20).

"*Example Plots from 4-D Current Experiment – Surface Currents in the Caribbean Sea*." Drifter Buoy ID 09802852. Rosenthal School of Marine and Atmospheric Science, University of Miami, Fl. Page 4. https://oceancurrents.rmas.miami.edu/caribbean/img_aoml/caribbeanf3.html. (Accessed 08-10-21).

"*Exciting a Spirit of Emulation Among the 'Plodholes': Agricultural Reform in Pre-confederation Nova Scotia*." By Graeme Wynn. *Acadiensis*, Vol. 20 No.1, Autumn, 1990. Pages 5-51. https://www.Journals.lib.unb.ca.

"*Expert Witness Report – Machiasport, Maine Cold Case*." By Bryan G. Hopkins, Ph.D. CPSS. 01-17-2022

F

"*Factors Affecting Strength and Stability of Wood Cribbing: Height, Configuration, and Horizontal Displacement*." By Thomas M. Barczak and Carol I. Tasillo. 1988. RI 9168. U.S. Department of the Interior, Bureau of Mines. 23 pages. (Accessed 05-24-21).

"*FamilySearch: Selwyn William Sellers, 1873-1949*." https://ancestors.familysearch.org/en/LTDN-XC3/selwyn-william-sellers-1873-1949.

"*Field Notes: The Coconut*." Republished by Gordon R. Groves, Feb. 22, 2022. Originally published in *The Bermudian* on Feb. 1954. See online. https://www.thebermudian.com/home-a-garden/garden/field-notes-the-coconut/.

"*Filter Media in Biofiltration Systems (Version 3.01) Guidelines*." Prepared by the Facility for Advancing Water Biofiltration (FAWB), Jun. 2009. 9 pages online. (Accessed 05-30-2022)

"*Find-a-Grave: Frederick Gerald Nolan*." https://www.findagrave.com/memorial/173079240/frederick-gerald-nolan.

"*Finding the Family in Medieval and Early Modern Scotland.*" By Elizbeth Ewanu and Janay Nugent, 2008. Ashgate. p. 153. ISBN 978-0-7546-6049-1.

"*Fires from Heaven. Comets and Diseases in circum-Mediterranean Disaster Myths*." By Dr. Amanda Laoupi. Centre for the Assessment of Natural Hazards & Proactive Planning – NTUA.

"*First Footsteps in East Africa.*" By Sir Richard Francis Burton, Feb. 10, 1856. GoodPress, 2022.

"*Fishing Floaters*." By Todd Kuhn, Aug. 27, 2013. Published in *Saltwater Sportsman*. https://www.saltwatersportsman.com/blogs/short strikes/fishing-floaters/.

"*Florence Eisenhauer Letter to M.R. Chappell*." Dated 10-12, 1955. MG1, Vol. 382, #1876. Nova Scotia National Archives.

"*Foreign Protestants & Settlements of Nova Scotia*." by Winthrop Bell.

"*Foreign Trade and Commerce in Ancient India*." By Prakash Charan Prasad. P. 203-212. Abhinan Publications 1977.

"*Forest Ecosystem Classification for Nova Scotia: Vegetation types*." (2010) Baker Settlement, Lunenburg County.

"*Forest Moss: Non-Timber Forest Products*." By Jerilynn E. Peck, Susan Moyle Studlar, Gary Kauffman and Patricia S. Muir, 2011. *Outreach*. 8 pages. College of Agricultural Sciences, Pennsylvanian State University. (Accessed 10-10-21).

"*Forests and Sea power. The Timber Problem of the Royal Navy 1652-1862.*" By Robert Green Halgh Albion. Cambridge, Mass. 1926. Appendix D. Pages 420-422.

"*Forests of Nova Scotia: A History.*" By Ralph S. Johnson, 1986. Nova Scotia Department of Lands and Forests. Four East Publications, Halifax, Nova Scotia. Chapter The 19th century 1801-1852, pages 60-73. https://archive.org/details/forestsofnovasco0000john/page/n7/mode/2up.

"*Forests of Nova Scotia: A History.*" Nova Scotia Department of Lands and Forests. Four East Publications, Halifax, Nova Scotia. P. 404-410.

"*Fraser letter to Mr. A.S. Lowden*," By S.C. Fraser, Jun. 19, 1895. From Briggs Corner, Queens, N.B. Pgs. 1-5.

"*Fred Blair letter to R.V Harris*." By Fred L. Blair, Nov. 5, 1937.

"*Frederick Joudrey, 1743-1812*." The Free Family Tree @ www.wikitree.com/wiki/joudrey-156.

"*Fred Nolan interview*." By D'Arcy O'Connor, May 18, 1975.

"*From Dugouts to Double Outriggers, Lexical insights into the Development of Swahili Nautical Technology*." By Martin Walsh, Faculty of Humanities, Universitas Indonesia.. *Wacana*, Vol. 22, No. 2 (2021): Pages 253-294. DOI: 10.17510/wacana.v22i2.954.

"*From Lisbon to Goa, 1500 – 1750*." By C.R. Boxer, 1984. Studies in Portuguese Maritime Enterprise. Variorum Reprints, London. (Accessed 05-30-2022)

"*From London to Land's End*." By Daniel Defoe and Two Letters from the :Journey through England By a Gentleman." 1888. Cassell & Company, Limited: London, Paris, New York & Melbourne.

"*From the Ground… The Story of Planting In Nova Scotia*," By Marjorie Major. 1981. Halifax: Petheric Press, P. 43.

"*From the Kattumaram to the Fibre-Teppa —Changes in Boatbuilding Traditions on India's East Coast*." By Henrik Pohl, Feb. 02, 2007. https://doi.org/10.1111/j.1095-9270.2006.00134.

"*Functional Genomics of Mediterranean Pines*." By C. Avila, et. al., 2022. Published in De La Torre, A.R. (eds) The Pine Genomes – Compendium of Plant Genomes. Springer. https://doi.org/10.1007/978-3-030-93390-6_9. (Accessed 04-15-2022).

G

"*Genesis of schlottenkarren on the Avon Peninsula of Nova Scotia (Canada) with implications for the geochronology of evaporite karsts and caves of Atlantic Canada*." By Max Moseley. *International Journal of Speleology*, 46 (2) Pages 267-276. Tampa, FL. May 2017. ISSN 0392-6672. https://doi.org/10.5038/1827-806X.46.2.2086, or www.scholarcommons.usf.edu/ijs. (Accessed 05-14-21).

"*Genetic and Phylogenetic relationships of coconut populations from Amini and Kadmat Islands, Lakshadweep (India)*." By M.K. Rajesh, K. Samsudeen, B.A. Jerard, P. Rejusha and Anitha Karun, Division of Crop Improvement, Central Plantation Crops Research Institute Kasaragod – 671124, Kerala, India. Article in *Plant Science*. DOI: 10.9755/ejfa.v26i10.18055. http://www.ejfa.info/. (Accessed 11-04-21).

"*Geographical Distributions of Indo-Atlantic and Pacific Coconut Subpopulation – graphic*." Origins of Coconut Domestication. June 2011. PLos ONE, Vol. 6, Issue 6, e21143. Page 4. www.plosone.org.

"*Geography as a Base for History*." By K.R.A. Narasiah. Tamil Heritage Foundation. Slideshow 36 pages.

"*George T. Bates interview*." By D'Arcy O'Connor. Aug. 16, 1976.

"*Genetic and Phylogenetic Relationships of Coconut Populations from Amini and Kadmat Islands, Lakshadweep (India)*." By M.K. Rajesh, K. Samsudeen, B.A. Jerard, P. Rejusha and Anitha Karun, Mar. 19, 2014. Published online 09-11-2014.

"*Gideon White letter*." By Nicholas Ogden. 03-25-1792, Shelbourne. "Bring clover seed when you come to Halifax. Nova Scotia National Archives. MG 1 Vol. 950, #546.

"*Glimpses of India: A Grand Photographic History of the Land of Antiquity, the Vast Empire of the Est, with 500 Superbly Reproduced Camera views of Her Cities, Temples, Towers, Public Buildings, Fortifications, Tombs, Mosques, Palaces, Waterfalls, Natural Beauty*," By J.H. Furneaux. Page 254. 1895. Published By C.B. Burrows, Bombay. 544 pages.

"*Global Drifter Program*." National Oceanic and Atmospheric Administration, Atlantic Oceanographic and Meteorological Laboratory, Physical Oceanography Division (PhOD). https://www.aoml.noaa.gov/phod/gdp/data_faq.php#metadata.

"*Global Meta-analysis of Wood Decomposition Rates: A Role for trait variation Among Tree Species?*" By James t. Weedon, et. al., 2009. Department of Systems Ecology, Institute of Ecological Science, Universiteit Amsterdam. *Ecology Letters*, 2009, 12: 45–56.

DOI: 10.1111/j.1461 0248.2008.01259.x. 12 pages. (Accessed 01-13-21).

"*Global Ocean Surface Velocities from Drifters: Mean, Variance, ENSO Response, and Seasonal Cycle*." By Rick Lumpkin and Gregory C. Johnson. *Journal of Geophysical Research – Oceans*. NOAA/Atlantic Oceanographic and Meteorological Laboratory, Miami, Fl. Apr. 19, 2013. Pgs. 1-15.

"*Glossary of Landform and Geologic Terms*." https://www.nrcs.usda.gov/wps/PA_NRCSConsumption/download/?cid=nrcs142p2_053182&ext=pdf. (accessed 10-17-21).

"*Goforth Email Responses to David H. Neisen*." By J. Pennelope Goforth, 2021. National Archives Researcher. Specialty Alaskan Maritime History.

"*Gordon Blair reply Letter to Mr. L. Elbert Smith of Dallas*." By Gordon Blair, Aug. 4, 1947. Traders Finance Corporation Limited, Saint John N.B.

"*Gravel barriers, headlands, and lagoons: an evolutionary model*." By R.W.G. Carter, J.D. Orford, D.L. Forbes, and R.B. Taylor (1987). Coastal Sediments '87, ASCE, New Orleans, LA, 1776-1792. https://www.jstor.org/stable/4298038?seq=1.

"*Grazing Livestock in Woodlands: Benefits, Detriments and Mgmt. Recommendations*." By David Mercker and Jason Smith. September 2019. UT Extension Institute of Agriculture, University of Tennessee.

"*Gripping it By the Husk: The Medieval English Coconut*." By Kathleen E. Kennedy. Published in The Medieval Globe, Vol. 3, Issue 1, 2017. See P. 7, Sec. The Coconut Cups of Late medieval England. Arc Humanities Press. https://muse.jhu.edu/article/758503. (Accessed 02-25 22).

"*Group Email Responses between Arborists Michael Nentwich, Don Pylant and David Vaughan*." with David H. Neisen, July 19, 2021.

"*Growing Guides – Companion Planting Clover*." Growing Guides of The United Kingdom, Apr. 26, 2019. https://growing_guides.co.uk/companion-planting-clover/. (Accessed 09-20-20).

"*Growing Guides – The History of Companion Planting*." Growing Guides of The United Kingdom, Sep. 28, 2016. https://growing_guides.co.uk/companion-planting-clover/. (Accessed 03-25-22).

"*Growth of Pinus Pinea and Pinus Halepensis as Affected By Dryness, Marine Spray and land use in a Mediterranean semi-arid Ecosystem.*" Published in *Dendrochronology 19* (2) 2001.

"*Guidelines for Filter Media in Biofiltration Systems, Version 3.01*." Prepared By the Facility for Advancing Water Biofiltration (FAWB), June 2009.

"*Guide to Different Tree Shapes for Your Yard*." By Danny Lipford. *Today's Homeowner*. Mar. 21, 2021. 4 pages. www.todayshomeowner.com/guide-to-different-tree-shapes- for-your-yard/. (Accessed 03-21-21).

"*Gymnosperm Database.*" By Christopher J. Earle. Updated Jan. 17, 2020. https://www.conifers.org/pi/Pinus_pinea.php.

H

"*H6, Introduction to Forests.*" Natural History of Nova Scotia, Vol. 1. Nova Scotia Museum of Natural History.

"*Hants County Nova Scotia Census – Daniel Vaughan*."

"*Harris Letter to George W. Grimm Jr*." By R.V. Harris, Aug. 22, 1936. Establishment of shell company. Nova Scotia National Archives, MG1 Vol.381, 960.

"*Harris letter to Dr. C.G. L. Friedlander*." By R. V. Harris, Aug. 19, 1966. Dalhousie University, Halifax, Nova Scotia. Nova Scotia National Archives, MG1 Vol. 385.

"*Harris letter to Gilbert D. Hedden - 2*." By R. V. Harris, Oct. 26, 1937. Reporting findings from Harvard Universities letter from A.F. Hill. Nova Scotia National Archives, MG1, Vol. 381, 1264.

"*Harris letter to Gilbert D. Hedden*." By R.V. Harris, Aug. 27, 1937.

"*Harris letter to Robert Dunfield*." By R. V. Harris, Jan. 31, 1966. reporting results from the Dept. of Obstetrics and Gynecology, The Albany Medical College of Union Univ., Albany, NY. Nova Scotia National Archives. MG1 Vol. 383.

"*Hatfield Telephonic Conversation with David H. Neisen*." By Ron E. Hatfield, Aug. 2021. BETA Analytic, Inc. President Ron E. Hatfield, Miami FL.

"*Hazard Analysis Critical Control Point (HACCP) Manual for the Coconut Industry*." Special Hazards and Preventative Measures Control. HACCP Training Manual #190304, Mar. 2019. 83 pages.

"*Helicopter Seeds: which trees do they come from.*" By Charlie Mellor, Woodland Trust Content Manager. May 30, 2019. https://www.woodlandtrust.org.uk/blog/2019/05/helicopter-seeds/.

"*Hidden behind Magdalena: Extreme Floods in Europe in 1342 and 1343*." By A. Kiss, et. al., 2015. Vienna Technical University. http://adsabs.harvard.edu/abs/2015EGUGA.1713985K.

"*Hill letter to R.V Harris*." By Albert F. Hill, Oct. 22, 1937. Research Assistant, Botanical Museum of Harvard University. Nova Scotia National Archives, MG1, Vol. 380.

"*Hindu Culture and The Modern Age*." By K.S. Bahadur Dewan. Ramaswami Shastri - Annamalai University. 1956 p. 74-75.

"*Historical and Statistical Account of Nova Scotia, Vol. 2*," By Thomas Chandler Haliburton. Published By Joseph Howe in 1829.

"*Historical Dictionary of Colonial America*." By William A, Pencak, Jul. 15, 2011. Section – Chronology. United Kingdom, Rowman & Littlefield Publishing Group. 8 pages. (Accessed 05-30-2022)

"*Historical Table: The Romance of Reality*." By C. Morris, 1893. Lippincott, Page 162f.

"*History and Construction of the Dhow*." Text copyright Canbooks, pictures By Marion Kaplan. https://nabataea.net/explore/navigation_and_sailing/. (Accessed 01-24-22).

"*History and Home of Coconut*." Sep. 1954. Indian Coconut Committee determination of coconut palm originated in Sri Lanka.

"*History in Numbers*." Copyright By Dave Fowler. www.historyinnumbers.com/events/black-death/facts/.

"*History of Chester 1759-1767*." W.I.NS. Chester Branch. Progress-Enterprise Co. 1967.

"*History of Coconut (Cocos Nucifera L.) in Mexico: 1539-1810*." By Daniel Zizumbo-Villarreal. Genetic Resources and Crop Evolution. 43: Netherlands. 1996. www.palms.org. Pages 505-515.

"*History of Coir Industry*." Central Coir Research Institute of India. www.ccriindia.org/pdf/02Historyofcoirindustry.pdf.

"*History of Coir – CCRI*." Coir Board Ministry of India, Alleppey, Kerala, India. Central Coir Research Institute. http://coirboard.gov.in/?page_id=6. (Accessed 09-15-2020).

"*History of Halifax City*." By Thomas B. Akins. Nova Scotia Historical Society, 1895.

"*History of India*." By Mountstuart Elphinstone. London. John Murray date of Publication, 1849. Volume 2. Page 166.

"*History of Kerala, India*." Wikipedia Online. (Accessed 07-12-2022) https://en.wikipedia.org/w/index.php?title=History_of_Kerala&oldid=1094971844.

"*History of Oak Island, Nova Scotia, and of the Work Done There at Different Time to Recover Buried Treasure*," By Frederick L. Blair. 1926. known as Exhibit B. Pgs. 4-5.

"*History of Somalia*." Wikipedia Contributors (Online). Wikipedia, The Free Encyclopedia, Updated Jul. 16, 2022. (Accessed 07-16-2022)https://en.wikipedia.org/w/index.php?title=History_of_Somalia&oldid=1098534906.

"*History of Tancook Island*." By Martha Farrar. 2021. 6 pages. www.sites.rootsweb.com/~tancook/page3.htm. (Accessed 01-03-21).

"*History of the County of Lunenburg – 1790*." By Mather Byles DesBrisay, Judge of County Courts, and member of the Historical Society of Nova Scotia, 1895. J. Huntington Wolccott Fund. Harvard College Library, Cambridge, Mass. Apr. 7, 1896. First Edition – 1870, Bridewater & LaHave.

"*History of the County of Lunenburg – 2nd Edition*." By Mather Byles DeBrisay, Judge of County Courts and Member of the Historical Society of Nova Scotia. Harvard College Library, Apr. 7,1896, Cambridge, Mass. Second Edition, 1895. Originally written at Bridgewater and La Have, February 1870 . Pgs. 301-306.

"*History of the Discovery and Appreciation of Pearls – The Organic Gem Perfected by Nature*." By Dr. Shihaan Larif, Nov. 25, 2021. Internetstones.com. (Accessed 04-05-2022) https://internetstones.com/history-of-the-discovery-and-appreciation-of-pearls-the-organic-gem-perfected-by-nature-page-2/.

"*History of the Oak Island Enterprise – Chapter I & II*." By James McNutt. Printed in *The Colonist* on Jan. 2, 1864, Truro, Nova Scotia. Pgs. 1-4.

"*History of the Phoenician Civilization*." By George Rawlinson. 2018.

"*History of Water Treatment*." By S.M. Enzler, MSc. https://www.lenntech.com/history-water-treatment.htm online. (Accessed 05-30-2022)

"HMS Victory 100-gun First Ship-of-the-Line." By JR Potts. AUS 173d AB, Oct. 16, 2020. Naval Warfare Ships. www.Militaryfactory.com.

"Hon. Edward Cornwallis: Founder of Halifax, Nova Scotia." By James S. MacDonald. Historical Society Vol. 12, 1905.

"*Horn of Africa*." Wikipedia Contributors, Wikipedia (Online). The Free Encyclopedia, Updated Jul. 1, 2022. (Accessed 07-15-2022). https://en.wikipedia.org/w/index.php?title=Horn_of_Africa&oldid=109589762.

"*Horse Whims*." By Tim Willoughby, Oct. 8, 2010. Aspen Times Weekly, Aspen, Co. Colorado. https://www.aspentimes.com/news/horse-whims/. (Accessed 10-22-21).

"*How Much Dirt Do I Need to fill a Hole*." DirtConnections, Sep. 27, 2009. https://www.dirtconnections.com/how-much-dirt-do-i-need-to-fill-a-hole/#:~:text=Sand%20tends%20to%20be%20prone,with%20several%20inches%20of%20topsoil. (Accessed 06-30-21).

"*How Products Are Made – COIR*." Page 1. Background. www.madehow.com/Volume 6/Coir.html.

"*How to Grow and Care for Bur Oak*." *The Spruce*. 4 pages. https://www.thespruce.com/growing-bur-oak-5091583. (Accessed 03-20-21).

"*Hugh P. Bell letter to R.V Harris*." By Hugh P. Bell, Head of Depart. Of Biology, Dalhousie University, Jul. 22, 1937. Nova Scotia National Archives, MG1 Vol. 381, 1204.

"Hurricanes and Tropical Storms." Environment and Climate Change, Canada.ca. Aug. 26, 2011. https://www.canada.ca/en/environment climate-change/services/weather-general-tools resources/hurricanes-tropical-storms.html.

"*Hydrating Coco Coir*." https://coir.com/growing-medium/hydrating-coco-coir/. (Accessed 03-23-22).

I

"*Identification of Superior Dwarf Coconut (Cocos nucifera L.) Parental Cultivars for Hybrid Breeding*." By W.M. Mahayu, Taryono, Kumaunang, and Maskromo. Printed By SABRAO, Journal of Breeding and Genetics, 53 (2), Pages 278-289. 2021.

"Illustrated Glossary of Ship and Boat Terms." By J. Richard Steffy. The Oxford Handbook of Maritime Archeology. Edited By Ben Ford, Donny L. Hamilton, and Alexis Catsambis. Dec. 2013. . Subject: Archaeology, Archaeological Methodology and Techniques Online Publication Date: 2012. https://www.oxfordhandbooks.com/view/10.1093/oxfordhb/9780199336005.001.0001/oxfordhb-9780199336005-e-48.

"*Impact of Solar Radiation on the Decomposition of Detrital Leaves of Eelgrass, Zostera marina*." By Anssi Vahatalo, et. al, Sep. 2019. Published in *Marine Ecology* – Progress Series. ResearchGate. 10 Pages. (Accessed 05-30-2022).

"Impact of the Holocene Transgression on the Atlantic Coastline of Nova Scotia." By John Shaw, Robert B. Taylor and Donald L. Forbes. Printed in the *Géographie physique et Quaternaire*, *47* (2), 221–238. https://doi.org/10.7202/032950ar.

"Independent Origins of Cultivated Coconut (Cocos nucifera) in The Old World Tropics." By Bee F. Gunn, Luc Baudouini, Kenneth M. Olsen. 6 22-2011. PLoS ONE 6(6): e21143. DOI:10.1371/journal.pone.0021143.

"India Through the Ages: History, Art Culture and Religion." By G. Kuppuram. Building Samanya and Visesa vessels. P. 527-531. https://www.google.com/books/edition/India_Through_the_Ages/AvggAAAAMAAJ?hl=en&gbpv=1&bsq=visesa.

"*Indian Ocean Five Island Countries*." Edited By Helen Chapin Metz. Aug. 1994, 3rd Edition. Federal Research Division, Library of Congress. Headquarters Department of the Army, DA Pam 550-154.

"*Indian Ocean Trade before the European Conquest*." By James Hancock. World History Encyclopedia. Updated Jul. 20, 2021. https://www.worldhistory.org/article/1800/indian-ocean-trade-before-the-european-conquest/.

"Indian Shipping: A History of the Sea-Borne Trade and Maritime Activity of the Indians From the Earliest Times." By Radhakumud K. Mookerji. Pages 162-191. https://ia800901.us.archive.org/33/items/indianshippinghi00mookrich/indianshippinghi00mookrich.

"*Indigenous Fishing Craft of Oman*." By Tom Vosmer, Western Australian Maritime Museum. Published in *The International Journal of Nautical Archaeology*, (1997) 26.3:2, Pages 17-235.

"*Insulation Effectiveness Comparison of Rice Hull, Coconut Fiber, and Crumb Rubber*." By Stephen Russell, et. al..2015. Department of Packaging and Materials Technology, Kasetsart University, Bangkok, Thailand. 5 Pages.

"*Inside Coconut Fibre: Its Structure, Properties and Applications*." By Leena Mishra and Gautan Basu. Page 13, para. 10.2.1.3, "*Yield of Coconut Fibre Chemical Composition (in bone dry weight) and Fine Structure Parameters of Coconut Fibre and Jute,*" Table 10.3; and para. 10.6.2, *Acid Treatments*." . ICAR – National Institute of Research on Jute and Allied Fibre Technology, Kolkata, West Bengal India.

"*Interview of Capt. Anthony Vaughan*." By Gilbert Hedden, dated 1939.

"*Interview of Charlotte Adams*." By D`Arcy O`Connor, Apr. 27, 1976.

"*Interview of Claude C. Chappel*." By D`Arcy O`Connor, Jul. 20, 1976.

"Interview of Fred Nolan, Owner of Lots, 5,9,10,11,12,13,14." By D'Arcy O'Connor, May 18, 1975.

"*Interview of George T. Bates*." By D'Arcy O'Connor. Aug. 16, 1976.

"*Interview of M.R. Chappell, owner of lots 6, 7, 8 , 15, 16, 17, 18, 19, 20, 23, 25, 26, 30, 31, 32*." By D`Arcy O`Connor, Jul. 20-21, 1976.

"*Interview of Mildred Restall*." By D'Arcy O'Connor. Aug. 10, 1976.

"*Interview of Peggy (Adams) Franklin*." By D`Arcy O`Connor. Apr. 28, 1976. Telephonically, Bridgewater, N.S. 1 Page.

"*Interview Questions/Written Responses to D`Arcy O`Connor*." By Robert Dunfield. Oct. 21, 1976.

"*Interview Responses of W. Lavern Johnson*." By D'Arcy O'Connor. Nov. 9, 1976.

"*In the Wake of the Dhow: The Arabian Gulf and Oman*." By Dionisius A. Agius, Jan. 2010. University of Exeter and King Abdulaziz University. ResearchGate.

"*Intraspecific Competition Affects Crown and Stem Characteristics of Non-Native Quercus rubra L. Stands in Germany*." By Katharina Burkardt, et. al., 2019. Article in Forests. Published Sep. 28, 2019. Silviculture and Forest Ecology of the Temperate Zones, Faculty of Forest Sciences, University of Gottingen, Germany.

"*Introduction to Forests. H6.1 Hardwood Forest. H6.2 Softwood Forest. H6.3 Mixed Forest*." Vol. I: Habitats, Natural History of Nova Scotia. 2010. 26 pages.

"*Ironwood Silhouette*." Natural Resources Canada. Last modified on 04-08-2015. https://tidcf.nrcan.gc.ca/en/trees/factsheet/36.

"*Ironwood/Ostrya virginiana*." Jim Whiting Nursery & Garden Center. Rochester, MN. https://plants.jimwhitingnursery.com/Plant-Name/Ostrya virginiana-Hop-Hornbeam-or-Ironwood.

"*Issues in Indian Ocean Commerce and the Archaeology of Western India*." Part 1 of *Migration, Trade and Peoples:* Edited By Roberta Tomber, Lucy Blue and Shinu Abraham. Preface. July 2005. The British Association for South Asian Studies. The British Academy, London.

"*Italian Stone Pine – Growing Tips (3269335)*." By Vanessa Richins Myers. Updated Apr. 27, 2021. *Gymnosperm Database*, By Christopher J. Earle.

J

"*Jack Pine Silhouette*." Natural Resources Canada. Last modified on 04-08-2015. https://tidcf.nrcan.gc.ca/en/trees/factsheet/43.

"*Jack Pine/Pinus banksiana L*." By T.D. Rudolph and P.R. Laidly. US Forest Service, US Dept. of Agriculture. *https://www.srs.fs.usda.gov/pubs/misc/ag_654/volume_1/pinus/banksiana.ht.*

"*Jamaica viewed with all the ports, harbours, and their several soundings, towns, and settlements thereunto belonging together, with the nature of its climate, fruitfulnesse of the soile, and its suitableness to English complexions. With several other collateral observations and reflexions upon the island*." By Edmund Hickeringill (1631-1708). https://quod.lib.umich.edu/e/eebo/A86321.0001.001?rgn=main;view=fulltext.

"*James Boswell: September 8th to 12th, 1773, Raasay Meeting with Flora McDonald*." A Vision of Britain Through Time. Extracts from *The Journal to the Hebrides with Samuel Johnson, L.L.D.* https://www.visionofbritain.org/.uk/travellers/Boswell/8. (Accessed 12-25-21).

"*James Bridgland Email Responses to David H. Neisen*." By James Bridgland, Jul. 13, 2020. Park Ecologist, Cape Breton Highlands National Park, Ingonish Beach, Nova Scotia, Canada.

"*James H. Soper Chief Botanist, initial Letter on Oak Trees*." By D`Arcy O`Connor, Mar. 26, 1975. National Museums of Canada, Museum of Natural Sciences. Ottawa, Ontario K1A OM8 Canada.

"James McNutt, Secretary of the Oak Island Eldorado Co. Account." Transcribed By Les MacPhie. Known as the Halifax Co. Diary of work carried out from Dec.1866 - Jan.1867. Pgs. 1-6

"John Brown Report on Boreholes I, II, and III." By John Brown, Walton Manganese Mines, Jan. 17, 1867. to the Directors of The Oak Island Co. and to W. J. Veith, J D Nash, and John Selnes. Transcript By Les MacPhie. Pg. 3.

"Joshua Mauger, Dictionary of Canadian Biography." By Donald F. Chard. Vol. 4, University of Toronto, 1979.

"Jotham Blanchard McCully Fonds, (2001-025)." 06-03-2016. Nova Scotia Archives, Halifax, Nova Scotia. 4 pages. https://memoryns.ca/index.php/jotham-blanchard-ccully-fonds. (Accessed 11-04-21).

"Journey Through the Upper Provinces of India, from Calcutta to Bombay 1824-1825." By Reginald Heber. 1829. Publishers Philadelphia, Carey, Lea & Carey. Vol. I and II p. 176).

"J.W. Andrews, C.E.M.E Consult Engineer, Sworn Affidavit." Brooklyn, NY. N.S. Archives, MG1 Vol.383. Part of F. Blair report.

K

"Kennedy Email Responses with David H. Neisen." By Kathleen E. Kennedy, Feb. 24-24, 2022. British Academy Global Professor, a.k.a. The Medieval Dr. K.

"Kerala Backwaters." Wikipedia Online. (Accessed 07-12-2022). https://en.widipedia.org/w/index.php?title=Kerala_backwaters&oldid=109621.

"Kon Tiki: Across the Pacific By Raft." By Thor Heyerdahl, 1950. Mattituck: Amereon House. 240 Pages. https://infogalactic.com/info/Coconut#cite_note-Heyerdahl-31.

"Kososflora Coir Fiber Bales." Kokos Flora Grow Naturally. https://kokosflora.com/coco_fiber/kokosflora-coir-fiber-bales/.

"Krysuvik-Trolladyngia Volcano Report." Global Volcanism Program, 2021. In: Sennert, S K (ed), Weekly Volcanic Activity Report, Jul.27, 2021. Smithsonian Institution and US Geological Survey. https://volcano.si.edu/showreport.cfm?doi=GVP.WVAR20210721-371030.

L

"Laccadive Islands." Published in the Encyclopedia Britannica 1911 and is available at https://theodora.com/encyclopedia/l/laccadive_islands.html. (Accessed 09-12-2022) [*a group of coral reefs and islands in the Indian Ocean, lying between 10° and 12° 20' N. and 71° 40' and 74° E. The name Laccadives (laksha dwipa, the "hundred thousand isles") is that given by the people of the Malabar coast and was probably meant to include the Maldives; they are called by the natives simply Divi, " islands," or Amendivi, from the chief island*].

"Laccadive Micro Tall (LMT) in Cote d'Ivoire." By R. Bourdeix, PM Kumaran, Rao EVV Bhaskara, and RV Pillai. Published in Catalog of Conserved Coconut Germplasm, India. 6 pages. (Accessed 07-12-2022).

"Lakshadweep [Internet]." Wikipedia, The Free Encyclopedia. (Accessed 07-12-2022). https://en.wikipedia.org/w/index.php?title=Lakshadweep&oldid=1096239113.

"*Lakshadweep*". By William A. Noble for *Encyclopedia Britannica*, 12 Sep. 2021. https://www.britannica.com/place/Lakshadweep. (Accessed 07-12-2022)

"*Land Grant and Transfer of Real Estate, seller Melbourne Chappell, TO buyer David C. Tobias, Recorded Jun. 29, 1977.*" Filed in Cape Breton, Nova Scotia. No. 582. Nova Scotia National Archives. All of the island except Lot 5 and Lot 23.

"*Largetooth Aspen Silhouette*." Natural Resources Canada. Last modified on Apr. 8, 2015. https://tidcf.nrcan.gc.ca/en/trees/factsheet/55.

"*Largetooth Aspen/Populus grandidentata.*" Plant Images. http://www.psn3.com/Peuplier,a,grandes,dents/fiche.html.

"*Last Will and Testament of Daniel McKinnon*." Extractions, Lunenburg County, Mf:0558683.

"*Late Quaternary geological history of Mahone Bay, Nova Scotia*." By N.E. Barnes, and D.J.W. Piper (1978). *Canadian Journal of Earth Sciences*, 15, Pages 586-593. https://www.nrcresearchpress.com/doi/pdfplus/10.1139/e78-063.

"*Leitir Fura*." Clan Macinnes Website. Pages 1-4. https://mcinnes.org/info.html. (accessed 12-12-21).

"*Les MacPhie Complete Archives from Doc. A00 to C10*." Created and Archived By Les MacPhie. Located at www.oakislandcompendium.ca.

"*Letter – Fire Devastated Crops*." Jun. 27,1792. Nova Scotia National Archives. MG 1 Vol. 950, #552.

"*Letter to James Soper*." Chester Municipal Heritage Society (MHS). National Museum of Canada. 1977.

"*Letter to Reginald V. Harris regarding Lots **1, 2, 3, 4, 5, 6, 7, 8, 9, 10, 11, 12, 13, 14** Oak Island*." By Fred L. Blair, dated 02-16-1035

"*Letter to Relatives, George Henry Monks Indian Accounts*." 1784, 1793-1799, 1807-1809. Microfilm 10912. Monk Family Fond, Nova Scotia Archives, MG 1.

"*List of Dutch East India Company Trading Posts and Settlements*." Wikipedia. Edited on Mar. 8, 2022. 5 pages. Retrieved from ttps://en.wikipedia.org/w/index.php?title=List_of_Dutch_East_ India_Company_trading_posts_and_settlements&oldid=1076007963.

"*List of Tree Species*." By Peyman Pourmohammadi. Sorted By hardwoods and softwoods. 15 pages. https://www.scribd.com/document/423893944/List-of-Tree-Species. (Accessed 10-22-20).

"*Little Ice Age*." Wikipedia Contributors, (Online. Wikipedia, The Free Encyclopedia. Updated 07-09-2022. https://en.wikipedia.org/w/index.php?title=Little_Ice_Age&oldid=1097211669.

"*Little Ice Age Geochronology*." By John P. Rafferty and Stephen T. Jackson, Mar. 18, 2016. Encyclopedia Britannica. https://www.britannica.com/science/Little-Ice-Age.

"*Log Weight Chart*." Provided By SherrillTree @ www.sherriltree.com. Information from the U.S. Department of the Interior, National Park Service sheet "*Rope, Knots and Climbing.*"

"*Lunenburg Census, 1784 – Timothy Zink*."

"*Lunenburg County Land Deeds: Index Vol. 1, 1759-1850; Vol. 2-13, 1775 -1849*." Lunenburg, Nova Scotia, Canada Record, Registrar of Deeds & FamilySearch. Image 8 of 540. htpps://www.familysearch.org/ark:/61903/3:1:3Q9M-CSV5G97C-P:may27,2022.

"*Lunenburg County Land Deeds: Index Vol. 1, 1759-1850; Vol. 6, P. 25, No. #52*." Recorded 08-25-1807.

"*Lycense Granted to Fell Pine Trees By Surveyor General of Woods, Jan. 25, 1788*." Issued By J.W. Wentworth, Surveyor General of all Woods of his Majesty in Nova Scotia, to Daniel Vaughan, Anthony Vaughan and James McCleod. Daniel Vaughan Records, Chester Township, #145.

M

"*Machiasport, Maine: Cold Case for David Neisen*." By Bryan G. Hopkins Ph.D., CPSS, Certified Professional Soils Scientist, 2021. Turfgrass Producers International. National Association of Landscape Professionals. Golf Course Superintendents Association of America. Professor, Brigham Young University, Department of Plant and Wildlife Sciences. Officer, Soil Science Society of America, North American Proficiency Testing. C.E.O. Hopkins Scientific, LLC. Expert Witness Report, Jan. 17, 2022. 8 pages.

"*Mahone Bay Island Names*." Compiled By Michael Ernst, Sidney Lang, Margaret MacDonald, Jim Rosbee, and Linda Wieser – MICA RD Committee. 2016. Mahone Islands Conservation Association. 9 pages. www.mahoneislands.ns.ca/islands/history/islandnames.php. (Accessed 11-20-20).

"*Mahone Bay*." By J.A. Bell, Halifax, NS. The New Dominion Monthly, Jul. 1870. Pages 17-26. www.reddit.com/r/oakisland/comments/efzj67/oakisland_newspaper_archive/. (accessed 03-19-21).

"*Mahone Harbor (#460) Tide Tables*." Government of Canada, Oceans and Fisheries Canada (2020). https://www.waterlevels.gc.ca/eng/data/table/2020/wlev_sec/460.

"*Making the First Global Trade Route: The Southeast Asian Foundations of the Acapulco-Manilla Galleon Trade – 1519-1650*." By Andrew Christian Peterson, Aug. 2014. University of Hawai'i at Manoa. 315 pages.

"*Makran.*" (Accessed 07-18-2022) https://en.wikipedia.org/w/index.php?title=Makran&oldid=1098415784.
"*Malabar Coast*." Online source, Owl apps. (Accessed 05-11-2022) http://next.owlapps.net/owlapps_apps/article?id=30874446&lang=en.

"*Maldives–Lakshadweep–Chagos Archipelago tropical moist forests*." https://en.wikipedia.org/w/index.php?title=Maldives%E2%80%93Lakshadweep%E2%80%93Chagos_Archipelago_tropical_moist_forests&oldid=1041012558. (Accessed 07-12-2022).

"*Maldives is the World's Lowest Country in the World*." By Deborah Byrd, Feb. 7, 2014. Online, EARTHSKY Communications.

"*Maldives [Internet]*." Wikipedia Contributors, The Free Encyclopedia; 2022 Jul 11, 17:16 UTC (Accessed 07-12-2022) https://en.wikipedia.org/w/index.php?title=Maldives&oldid=1097606631.

"*Malindi Kingdom*." Compiled by Global Security Online. See GlobalSecurity.org. 6 pages. www.globalsecurity.org/military/world/Africa/Malindi.htm. (Accessed 05-30-2022)

"*Manning Email Response to Stuart Niesen*." By Botanist Howard Manning, Jul. 3, 2020.

"*Manual on Machinery and Equipment For Coconut By-Product.*" By Dela Cruz, Pobre & Gabrido. 2002, http://pca.da.gov.ph/pdf/techno/coir_fiber.pdf.

"*Mappila in India*." Online publication by the Joshua Project. Sponsored by the Bethany World Prayer Center. (Accessed 04-22-2022) https://joshuaproject.net/people_groups/17452/IN.

"*Mapping Tree Root Systems with Ground-penetrating Radar*." By Jiri Hruska, Jan Cermak & Svatopluk Sustek, Jun. 6, 1997. Published in Tree Physiology, 19, pages 125-130. Heron Press.

"*Maritime History of Somalia*." Wikipedia Contributors (Online). Wikipedia, The Free Encyclopedia. Updated May 29, 2022. (Accessed 06-28-2022). https://en.wikipedia.org/w/index.php?title=Maritime_history_of_Somalia&oldid=1090453646.

"*Master Hudson's Third Voyage to Noua Zembla, 1609*." By Robert Juet, Transcribed By Brea Barthel for the New Netherland Museum and replica of the ship Half Moon. From the 1625 Edition of *Purchas His Pilgrimes*. Chapter 16. 30 pages.

"*McCallum letter to R. V. Harris*." By K.J. McCallum, Sep. 15, 1966. Professor of Chemistry, University of Saskatchewan, Saskatoon, Canada. Nova Scotia National Archives, MG1 Vol. 383, 2093M.

"*Mechanical Properties of Wood*." By David W. Green, Jerrold E. Winandy and David E. Kretschmann. Forest Products Laboratory. 1999. Wood Handbook – Wood as an Engineering Material. Gen. Tech. Rep. FPL–GTR–113. Madison, WI: U.S. Department of Agriculture, Forest Service, Forest Products Laboratory. 463 p.

"*Medieval Haywharf to 20th-century Brewery: Excavations at Watermark Place, City of London: Coir Cordage*." By Walton Rogers, L. Fowler, and A. Mackinder, 2014. MOLA Archaeology Studies Series 30.

"*Medieval Source Book: Ibn Baituta: Travels in Asia and Africa, 1325-1354*." P.43-46.

"*Medieval Trade in the Mediterranean World: Illustrative Documents*." By F. Lane, 1956. Translated By Robert S. Lopez and Irving W. Raymond. (Records of Civilization, Sources and Studies, Austin P. Evans, editor, Vol. LII.) 1965.Columbia University Press. New York. 2001.

"*Mediterranean Pines and Their History*." By Wilhelm-Klaus. Plant Systems and Evolution, By Springer-Verlag 1989. Revision, Dec. 11, 2010.

"*Men and Methods of the Early Days of Mining in Cape Breton*." Annual Meeting, Mining Society of Nova Scotia, Sydney, May 1922. Info: Henry C. Poole Esq. https://www.Mininghistory.ns.ca/cim/c1922001.htm.

"*Microsatellite analysis of distinct coconut accessions from Agatti and Kavaratti Islands, Lakshadweep, India*." By D. Kishnamoorthy and P.M. Jacob, et. al., Jun. 2010. Published in *Journal Scientia Horticulturae,* 125 (3), Pages 309-315. DOI: 10.1016/j.scienta.2010.04.012.

"*MIGRATION, TRADE AND PEOPLES, PART 1: ISSUES IN INDIAN OCEAN COMMERCE AND THE ARCHAEOLOGY OF WESTERN INDIA; Boats, Routes and Sailing Conditions of Indo-Roman Trade*," By Lucy Blue, Pages 3-13. ISBN: 978-0-9553924-5-0.

"MIGRATION, TRADE AND PEOPLES, PART 1: ISSUES IN INDIAN OCEAN COMMERCE AND THE ARCHAEOLOGY OF WESTERN INDIA; Strategies for Surface Documentation at the Early Historic Site of Pattanam, Kerala," By Shinu A. Abraham, Pages 14-28. ISBN: 978-0 9553924-5-0.

"MIGRATION, TRADE AND PEOPLES, PART 1: ISSUES IN INDIAN OCEAN COMMERCE AND THE ARCHAEOLOGY OF WESTERN INDIA; Archaeological Investigations at Pattanam, Kerala, New Evidence for the Location of Ancient Muziris," By V. Selvakumar, K.P. Shajan and Roberta Tomber, Pages 29-41. ISBN: 978-0-9553924-5-0.

"MIGRATION, TRADE AND PEOPLES, PART 1: ISSUES IN INDIAN OCEAN COMMERCE AND THE ARCHAEOLOGY OF WESTERN INDIA; Beyond Western India: The Evidence from Imported Amphorae," By Roberta Tomber, Pages 42-57. ISBN: 978-0-9553924-5-0.

"Mike Constandy Email Responses to David H. Neisen." By Mike Constandy, 2021. Westmoreland Research, National Archives Research Co. *Specialty:* Naval & maritime research, admiralty, ships logs & plans, sea lane & terrestrial UXO.

"Mining and Metallurgy to the Renaissance." By Matt Skinner, Lenny Frank, Michael Galvin, 1999. Project Number: 48-EMP-HGMW. Worcester Polytechnic Institute. Pages 29-76.

"Modern History: Or, The Present State of all Nations." By Thomas Salmon. Vol. XVII, Chapter X, Portugal. Pages 149-194. (Order of Christ, founded on the same account By Dionisius, son of Alphonsus III in 1319. Upon Abolition of the Knights Templar. P. 157.

"Morphological and Anatomical Studies of the Coconut." By E.H.D. Smith, Department of Botany, Agricultural University, Wageningen, The Netherlands. (Received 11-19-1970).

"Muster Roll – Neil McMullen, 1884." Nova Scotia National Archives, RG-8, C Series, Vol. 1884, P. 1-2.

"Mystery at Oak Island: Maps and Measurement." By D.J. Hanson, Director of the DeVere Foundation. May 15, 1997.

N

"Naming the Coconut and (de)Colonizing the Middle Ages." By Kathleen E. Kennedy, 2022. Pages 61-85. Published in Digital Philology: A Journal of Medieval Cultures, Vol. II, No. 1, Spring 2020. Johns Hopkins University Press. P. 61-85. University of Bristol.

"Natural Durability of Wood: A Worldwide Checklist of Species." By T.C. Scheffer and J.J. Morrell. Forest Research Laboratory, Oregon State University. Research Contribution 22. 58 pages. https://ir.library.oregonstate.edu/concern/technical_reports/dz010r37p. (Accessed 01-13-21).

"Natural History of Nova Scotia." By Derek S. Davis and Sue Browne. Nova Scotia Museum. QH106.2.N68N27 1997 508.716 C95-966009-7. 16 pages.

"Natural Slate – Flagstone." Provided By Perry Hutts, Owner/Operator, Hutts Quarry, 3280 Hwy 202, East Gore, Hants County, Nova Scotia. https://www.huttsnaturalstone.com/about-us.

"Neisen email Responses with Botanist Dr. Stephen Bungard." With David H. Neisen, Dec. 12, 2021. Vice-County Recorder for the Botanical Society of Britain and Ireland.

"*New England – Acadian Forest*." Prepared By M. Davis, L. Gratton, J. Adams, J. Goltz, C. Steward, S. Buttrick, N. Zinger, K. Kavanhagh, M. Sims and G. Mann. *World Wildlife Fund*. https://www.worldwildlife.org/ecoregions/na0410. (Accessed 03-18-20).

"*New England masts and the King's Broad Arrow*." By Samuel F. Manning, 1979. Greenwich, London: Trustees of the National Maritime Museum. Inclusive of the 1691 Massachusetts Bay Colony Charter Act: "*An Act for the Preservation of White and other Pine-Trees growing in Her Majesties Colonies of New-Hampshire, The Massachusetts-Bay, and Province of Main, Rhode Island, and Providence-Plantation, the Narraganset Country, or Kings-Province, and Connecticut in New-England, and New=York, and New-Jersey, in America, for the Masting her Majesties Navy*."

"*New Expedition to Oak Island Money Pit*." By Al Masters, SAGA Magazine. Vol. 43, No. 1, Pg. 27, Oct. 1971.

"*New Light on the 1497 Cabot Voyage to America*." By Dr. Louis-Andre Vigneras. Published in Hispanic-American Historical Review, 36 (1956). http://read.dukeupress.edu/hahr/article-pdf/36/4/503/783175/0360503.pdf

"*New Perspective on the Ecology of Tree Structure and Tree Communities through Terrestrial Laser Scanning*." By Yadvinder Malhi et. al., Dec. 12. 2017. Interface Focus 8: 20170052. http://dx.doi.org/10.1098/rsfs.2017.0052

"*Newport Township 1817 Census*."

"*Nieman letter to 'Oak Island Participants #1*." By Dick Neiman, Oct. 6, 1993. www.oakislandtreasure.co.uk.

"*Nieman letter to 'Oak Island Participants #2*." By Richard C. Nieman, Oct. 7, 1990. 3 Pages.

"*Noninvasive Measurements that Roughly Estimate the Age of a Tree*." By Steve Nix. Updated Oct. 8, 2019. https://www.treehugger.com/estimating-forest-trees-age-134332/.

"*Norse-Viking on Oak Island, 1007 A.D.?*" By Jack MacNab, May 19, 2022. Arranged By Hammerson Peters. 222 pages.

"*North Atlantic Subpolar Gyre Dynamics in The Absence of Major Freshwater Forcing*." By Ursula Quillimann, et. al., 2012. 42nd International Artic Conference – Winter Park, Colorado 2012. Pages 1-3, Fig. 2. https://instaar.colorado.edu/meetings/AW2012/abstract_details.php?abstract_id=54. (Accessed 01-16-22).

"*Northern Red Oak From Acorns to Acorns in 8 Years or Less*." By Stanley J. Zarnoch, et. al. Institute of Tree Root Biology, USDA Forest Service, Research Technician, University of Georgia, Athens, GA. 2002. Pages 555-558.

"*Northern Red Oak, Quercus rubra L., Fagaceae – Beach Family*." By Ivan L. Sander. *Silvics of North America*.1990. 7 pages. www.silvicsofnorthamerica1990.dendro.cnre.ut.edu.

"*Northern Red Oak*." Canadian Trees Tour, *The Tree Pages*. Pages 1-6. www.canadiantreetours.org/species-pages/Northern_red_oak.html. (Accessed 01-08-21).

"*Notes on the Triton/Nolan Pact & Lawsuit, RE Ownership of Oak Island Lots*." Unknown source. 3 Pgs. 1971. Lots *5, 9, 10, 11, 12, 13*, & *14*. Pursuant court case voids improperly registered Land deed transfers

"*Nova Scotia Archives and Record Management "Allotment*." Book, P. 137, Reel #13044; "Old Book" #1, P.44. Granted Gifford Is. #12, Young Is. #13, & Smith Is. #28, to establish a fishery.

"*Nova Scotia Commissioner of Crown Land Fonds*." Nov.19, 2019. Nova Scotia Archives, Halifax, Nova Scotia. 11 pages. https://memoryns.ca/index.php/nova-scotia-commissioner-of-crown-lands-fonds. (Accessed 11-04-21).

"*Nova Scotia Land Papers: 1795-1800, Green, James and others – 1784 – Lunenburg County*." 37,950 acres granted in Chester. Includes: License to Occupy, Memorial, Warrant to Survey, Surveyor's Report and Surveyor's Certificate. https://archives.novascotia.ca/land-papers/archives/?ID=313&Doc=document&Page=201101417.

"*Nova Scotian Biographies: Isaac Razilly*" 1587-1635." By Peter Landry 2012.

"*Nova Scotia National Archives, #201109808*."

"*Nova Scotia Supreme Court Final Order after Ruling*." Triton/Tobias v. F. Nolan. N.S. Supreme Court No. 0802, recorded 04-07-1986. Bridgewater, N.S.

O

"*Oak Island 1632*." By James A. McQuiston, FSA Scot. USA. 2017.

"*Oak Island and its Lost Treasure*." By Graham Harris and Les MacPhie. Halifax: Formac Publishing Company, Limited. 2019. Pages 26 & 27. 225 pages

"*Oak Island Connection*." By Kerrin Margiano. North Charleston, SC. Createspace Independent Publishing Platform. 2016. Chapters 1-7 & 15.

"*Oak Island Curses, Codes and Secret Societies*." By James A. McQuiston, FSA Scot. USA. 2022.

"*Oak Island Daily Work Diary from August 30 1862 – March 30 1863*." Owned By Paul Wroclawski, NS. Transcribed By Dennis J. King, 2014.

"*Oak Island Endgame*." By James A. McQuiston, FSA Scot. USA. 2021.

"*Oak Island Lot Ownership Map, 1781*." Created by William Nelson Dy Sr., Jul. 6, 1818. Old Plan No. 1046, Dept. of Lands and Fisheries. Beaton Institute, Cape Breton University. Also published in Joy Steel/Gordon Fader's *Oak Island Mystery Solved – Final Chapter*, P. 10, 2nd Edition, 2016.

"*Oak Island & New Ross*." By James A. McQuiston, FSA Scot. USA. 2021.

"*Oak Island - Nova Scotia*." By L. Macphie (2019). Oak Island Tours Incorporated. https://www.oakislandtours.ca/les-macphieresearch.html.

"*Oak Island Hydrogeology, Hydrography and Nearshore Morphology, July – August 1995, Field Observations*." By David G. Aubrey, Wayne Spencer, Ben Guiterez, William Robertson, and David Gallo. Unpublished Draft Report. Woods Hole Oceanographic Institution, Woods Hole, Maine. Apr. 8, 1996. 151 pages. https://www.oakislandtours.ca/les-macphie-research.html.

"*Oak Island Hydrology, Hydrography, and Near shore Morphology: Field Observations.*" MacPhie Archives. Jul-Aug 1995. Pages i–ii.

"*Oak Island & Western Shore Early Land Ownership Map*." Five Property Owners identified on Oak Island: *J. Mcinnes* (Northwest); *G. Mcinnes* (West Central); *T. Graves* (Isaacs Point); *J. Boutiller* (South Central).

"*Oak Island Lot Ownership Map, 1781*." Created By William Nelson Dy Sr., Jul. 6, 1818. Old Plan No. 1046, Dept. of Lands and Fisheries. Beaton Institute, Cape Breton University. Also published in Joy Steel/Gordon Fader's *Oak Island Mystery Solved – Final Chapter*, P. 10, 2nd Edition, 2016.

"*Oak Island Lot Ownership Map, Jul. 6, 1818*." Map from D.W. Crandal provided By Surveyor Nelson Dy Sr. Signed By Robert Smith and labeled "Old Plan." Nova Scotia National Archives.

"*Oak Island Lot Distribution Map, 2007*." Provided by MacPhie Archives. P. 5. Identifies Lots *1, 2, 3, 4, 6, 7, 8, 15, 16, 17, 18, 19, 20, 21, 22, 24, 26, 27, 28, 29, 30, 31, 32* - Oak Island Tours; Lot *5* – Robert S. Young; Lots *9, 10, 11, 12, 14* – Fred Nolan; Lot *13* – John Johnston; Lot *23* – Dan/Dave Blankenship; and Lot *25* – Alan Kostrzewe.

"*Oak Island Old Plan Map, 1818*." Only showing eastern end of Oak Island and provided By David W. Crandell and shows ownership of the following Lot *13* – Neal McMullen, Lot *14* – David Melvin, Lot *15* – David W. Crandell, Lot *16, 17, 18* – John Smith.

"*Oak Island Samuel Ball Lot Ownership Map – Lots 6, 7, 8, 24, 25, 26, 30, 31, 32, Hook Island, Mainland Farm, 2004*." Reflects Lot ownership changes between the years 1787 through 1812. Provided By Bee Stanton, 2004. www.creative@beestanton website.

"*Oak Island Lot Ownership Map, Change on Years 1787 through 1812*." Unknown source.

"*Oak Island Lot Ownership Map, undated*." Map signed By Robert Smith. Unknown source.

"*Oak Island Missing Links*." By James A. McQuiston, FSA Scot. USA. 2017.

"*Oak Island Money Pit New Expedition.*" By Al Masters, Oct. 1971. *SAGA Magazine*, Vol. 43, No. 1, pg. 2-7.

"*Oak Island Mystery: The Kempton Variant*," By Reverend A. J. Kempton, Summer 1909.

"*Oak Island Obsession: The Restall Story*." By Lee Lamb. Toronto: The Dundurn Group, 2006. 242 pgs.

"*Oak Island Plan of Property Owned by Sellyn Sellers, Sep. 5, 1935*." by Wildlife Artist, S. Edgar March (1870-1967). Registered Chester Township Land Deeds, Book 24, p. 368. Shows Lots *1, 2, 3, 4, 21, 22, 23, 27, 28, 29* - Archibald Dauphinee; Lots *6, 7, 8, 24, 25, 26, 30, 31, 32* – Sam Ball (Ingram & Francis Conrad); Lots *9, 10, 11, 12, 13, 14, 15, 16, 17, 18, 19, 20* – George W. Grimm Jr.(Sellyn Sellers).

"*Oak Island Plan of Pit Area Map*." By Robert K. Restall Jr. 1964. Copyright

"*Oak Island Tours & The Michigan Group (2005-present)*." Wikipedia, *Oak Island Mystery*. https://en.wikipedia.org/wiki/Oak_Island_mystery.

"*Oak Island Treasure Company's Public Share Offering.*" 1893. Capital $60,000.00 - $5 per share.

"*Oak Island Treasure: The Triumph of Hope of Reason*." By Peter Fortune, Ph.D. 2016. http://fortunearchive.com/Miscellaneous/Oak%20Island%20Treasure.pdf.

"Oak Island, The Reasons for Supposing Treasure is Buried There." By Paul Pry. For the *Yarmouth Herald*. Feb. 19, 1863. Pgs. 1-6.

"Oak Island." Published article By the Nova Scotia Bureau of Information, 1953. *Blockhouse Blog*, Apr. 29, 2016. Nova Scotia National Archives, MG1 Vol. 1228.

"Oak Islands Key Features and Landmarks." tab titled (Oak Trees), 2019. At www.oakislandmap.com/oak-islands-key-features-and-landmarks/ oak-trees-says.

"Oak Islands Mysterious Money Pit." By David MacDonald, Jan. 1965. *Readers Digest*, Jan.1965. Pages 136-140. Condensed from the Rotarian Publication. 1965.

"Obituary of Daniel Blankenship." https://www.echovita.com/ca/obituaries/ns/mahone-bay/daniel-christian-blankenship-8948996.

"Obituary of Frederick G. Nolan at Halifax Funeral Home." https://atlanticfuneralhomeshalifax.sharingmemories.ca/site/FrederickGNolan.html.

"Ocean Currents T6.1." *Natural History of Nova Scotia*, Vol. 1, Section T6.1. Nova Scotia Museum of Natural History. Pages 106-119.

"Ocean Currents Website." University of Miami, Rosenthiel School of Marine and Atmospheric Science. https://oceancurrents.rsmas.miami.edu.

"Ocean Sweet Spots: Seagrasses Release 32 billion Coke cans-worth of SUGAR into the soil – 80 times more than previously thought, study reveals." By Shivali Best, May 2, 2022. Published in *DailyMail.com*, May 30, 2022. 8 pages. (Accessed 05-30-2022)

"Ogden letter to Gideon White." By Nicholas Ogden. Mar. 25, 1792, Shelbourne. "Bring clover seed when you come to Halifax. Nova Scotia National Archives. MG 1 Vol. 950, #546.

"Old Church Map of Early Western Shore & Mahone Bay Island Owners." Unknown origin. Five Property Owners identified on Oak Island: *J. Mcinnes* (Northwest); *G. Mcinnes* (West Central); *T. Graves* (Isaacs Point); *J. Boutiller* (South Central).

"On some of the Vegetable Materials from which Cordage, Twine and Thread, are made." By James Mease, M.D.. The *American Journal of Science and Arts*, No. 1, Vol. XXI. 1807. Pgs. 9-17.

"On the Stowage of Ships and Their Cargoes: with Information Regarding Freights, Charter-Parties, etc., etc." By Robert White Stevens. 1878. Longmans, Green, Reader & Dyer. London. www.StevensonStowage1878.pdf. Pages 34-528..

"Open Social Media Comments." By Terry J. Deveau, 2021. Mi` kmaw Heritage Research and Restoration Association, Historian.

"Opening of Philippines Trade Route, 1566: Manilla Galleons."

"Origin and Evolution of Laccadive Micro Tall, a coconut cultivar from Lakshadweep Islands of India." By K. Sarnsudeen, P.M. Jacobl, M.K. Rahesh, B.A. Jerard, and P.M. Kumaran. Published in Journal of Plantation Crops, 2000, 34 (3), Pages 220-225. ResearchGate. (Accessed 05-30-2022).

"*Oxford Handbook of Maritime Archeology*." By J. Richard Steffy, 2013. Illustrated Glossary of Ship and Boat Terms. https://www.oxfordhandbooks.com/view/10.1093/oxfordhb/9780199336005.001.0001/oxfordhb-9780199336005-e 48.

P

"*Past and Present Distribution of New Brunswick Bur Oak Populations: A Case for Conservation*." By Donnie A. McPhee and J. Loo. Fredericton, Nova Scotia, Canada: *Northeastern Naturalist*, 16(I):85-100. Natural Resources Canada, Canadian Forest Service – Atlantic Forestry Center. 2009. 98 pages.

"*Past Nature: Public Accounts of Nova Scotia's Landscape, 1600-1900*." By Heather L. MacLeod, 1995. Saint Mary's University. Chapters 5 and 6 specifically. (Accessed 10-14-21).

"*Peaches to Samarkand. Long Distance-Connectivity, Small Worlds and Sociocultural Dynamics Across Afro-Eurasia, 300-800 CE*." By Johannes Preiser-Kapeller, Dec. 2014. Division for Byzantine Research, Institute for Medieval Research, Austrian Academy of Sciences.

"*Pelagics – Atlantic & Gulf Coast USA*." Section, "Nova Scotia." https://www.surfbirds.com/Pelagic/ecoast.html.

"*Periodic Reports on Oak Island Operations 1966 to 1994*." By Dan Blankenship. Compiled By Les MacPhie. Apr. 2019.

"*Pin Cherry/Prunus pensylvanica*." By G.W. Wendel. U.S. Department of Agriculture, Forest Service. www.srs.fs.usda.gov/pubs/misc/ag_654/volume_2/prunus/pensylvanica.htm.

"*Pin Cherry Silhouette*." Natural Resources Canada. Last modified Apr. 8, 2015. https://tidcf.nrcan.gc.ca/en/trees/factsheet/59.

"*Pine nuts as aphrodisiac*." By Johan Santesson. 2000. http://www.santesson.com/aphrodis/pine.htm, now defunct.

"*Pinus halepensis / Aleppo Pine*." Attribution from William Dallimore, Albert Bruce Jackson and S.G. Harrison's publication A Handbook of Coniferae and Ginkgoaceae, 4th Edition, 1967. Martin's Press, New York. The American Conifer Society. https://conifersociety.org/HAF000028/France-nice-view-of-aleppo-pine-tree.

"*Pinus pinea in Europe: distribution, habitat, usage and threats*." By R. Abad Viñas, G. Caudullo, S. Oliveira, and D. de Rigo, 2016. Published in *European Atlas of Forest Tree Species*. EU.

"*Plane Tree Symbolism*." Tree Spirit Wisdom website. Sec. Plane – Counsel, Genus: Platanus, para. 5-6. (Accessed 03-12-22). https://treespiritwisdom.com/tree-spirit-wisdom/plane-tree-symbolism/.

"*Plant Fact Sheet: Bur Oak Quercus macrocarpa Michx*." By Joseph D. Scianna. Natural Resources Conservation Service, U.S. Department of Agriculture. 2009. 8 pages.

"*Plant Resins: Chemistry, Evolution, Ecology and Ethnobotany*." By Jean H. Langenheim. Timber Press, Inc. 2003. Chapter 2 p. 54. 586 pages.

"*Plant use By Prehistoric Mediterranean Hunter-Gatherers – An Iberian perspective on Upper Paleolithic Plant Consumption*." By Jonathan Haws. University of Louisville. Pg. 51-54. Nov. 3, 2009.

"*Plantations, Slavery and Proto-Industrialism: Sugarcane in the Colonial British West Indies*." Llowell Williams. https://www.scribd.com/document/30458409/Plantations-Slavery-and-Proto-Industrialism-Sugarcane-in-the-Colonial-British-West-Indies.

"*Planting Improvement: The Rhetoric and Practice of Scientific Agriculture in Northern British America, 1670-1820*." By Anya Zilberstein Sept. 2008. History University of Massachusetts. Pages 235-239 and 246-247. https://docslib.org/doc/2318126/sep-09-28-i-archives.

"*Plants: 2,400 Royalty free Illustrations of flowers, trees, fruits and vegetables.*" By Jim Harter, p. 142-143. 1-16-2013. Dover Publications.

"*Platanus*." By Siusaidh NicNeill. The Sacred Sycamore. 2 pages. https://druidry.org/resources/the-sacred-sycamore. (Accessed 02-23-22).

"*Pleistocene geology and till geochemistry of central Nova Scotia*." By R.R. Stea and J.H. Fowler (1981). Nova Scotia Department of Mines and Energy, Map 81-1, Sheet 4, 1981. https://searchworks.stanford.edu/view/2488697.

"*Polderlands*." P. Wagret, 1968. London. Meuthen Publishers. P. 56.

"*Poplar, Balsam*." Editor Maureen Rogers. 2007. HERBALPEDIA. The Herb Growing & Marketing Network, Silver Spring, PA. (Accessed 10 15-21).

"*Portugal's Glory and Decay*." By Joam de Barros and Diego de Couto. Published in The North American Review, Vol. 83, No. 173 (Oct., 1856), Pages 456 to 476. University of Northern Iowa. https://www.jstor.org/stable/25104777.

"*Principal Features of Evaporite Karst in Canada*." By Derek C. Ford, 1997. *Karst Geomorphology*. Fourth International Conference on Geomorphology – Italy, 1997. This paper first appeared in *Carbonates and Evaporates*, 12 (IJ, 1997, Pages 15-23). (Accessed 12-04-20).

"Principals of Vegetation and Tillage." By John Young / Agricola. Halifax 1822. Citation in Dave Macintosh's *When The Work's all Done this Fall.* Pages 23-24. Corpo Forestale della Stato. 2004. Alberi Monumentali D'Italia. (Accessed 04-27-2019). http://www.corpoforestale.it/foreste&forestale/ricerca&progetti/alberi_m/index.htm.

"*Privateering and Piracy: The effects of New England Raiding upon Nova Scotia during the American Revolution, 1775-1783*." By John Dewar Faibisy, Jan. 1, 1972. University of Massachusetts, Amherst. 258 pages. Doctoral Dissertations 1896 - February 2014. 1320. https://scholarworks.umass.edu/dissertations_1/1320.

"Prized By Princes and Sea Farers." By Susan Hallett. Horizon Cook Book. Oct. 2017.

"*PROPERTYOnline, Lunenburg County, AAN #08219605*." Robert S. Young. Reported by FaceBook Social Group, "*Oak Island From the Other Side of the Causeway*," pub. 07-20-2022.

"*Pryor, William (1775-1859)*." By David A. Sutherland. 1985. Dictionary of Canadian Biography, Vol. 8. University of Toronto. http://www.biographi.ca/en/bio/pryor_william_1775_1859_8E.html. (Accessed 11-27-21).

"*Pursuing West: The Viking Expeditions of North America*." By Jody M. Bryant, 2015. Electronic Theses and Dissertations. Paper 2508. https://dc.etsu.edu/etd/2508

Q

"*Quercus rubra L. – Northern Red Oak*." By Ivan L. Sander, Research Forester, St. Paul, MN. *Silvics of North America*. 1990. Pages 727-733.

"*Quercus rubra*." Index of Species Information, Fire Effects Information System (FEIS), USDA. 25 Pages. https://www.fs.fed.us/databases/feis/plants/trees/querrub/all.html. (Accessed 12-09-21).

"*Quercus suber / Cork Oak*." https://en.wikipedia.org/wiki/Quercus_suber.

"*Quercus virginiana/Southern Live Oak*." https://en.wikipedia.org/wiki/Quercus_virginiana.

R

"*Radiocarbon Dating*." By Mike Christie, et. al.. *WikiJournal of Science*,1(1):6. 2018. Section – Use in Archaeology and elsewhere. 17 pages.

"*Radiocarbon Isotopic Evidence for Assimilation of Atmospheric CO2 by the Seagrass Zostera marina*." By Kent Watanabe and Tomohiro Kuwae, 2015. Published in *Biosciences*, 12, pages 6251-6258, 2015. Published by Copernicus Publications. (Accessed 05-30-2022)

"*Rambles Among the Bluenose*." By A.L. Spedon. 1863.

"*Red Ash Silhouette*." Natural Resources Canada. Last modified on Apr. 8, 2015. https://tidcf.nrcan.gc.ca/en/trees/factsheet/28.

"*Red Ash/Fraxinus pennsylvanica*," By Richard Webb, Bugwood.org. https://www.forestryimages.org/browse/detail.cfm?imgnum=1480634.

"*Red Cedar Silhouette*." Natural Resources Canada. Last modified Apr. 8, 2015. https://tidcf.nrcan.gc.ca/en/trees/factsheet/133.

"*Red Cedar/Juniperus virginiana*." By Sandra McLean Cutler, Author of "Dwarf & Unusual Conifers Coming of Age. https://www.conifersociety.org/conifers/juniperus-virginiana/.

"*Red Clover (Trifolium pratense)*." Atlantic Forage Guide. Red Clover – Page 13. 22 pages. http://www.gov.pe.ca/photos/original/ag_atlforaguide.pdf. (Accessed 10-17-21).

"*Red Clover (Trifolium pratense)*." By V. Heuze, G. Tran, S. Giger-Reverdin and F. Lebas, 2015. Feedipedia program By INRAE, CIRAD, AFZ and FAO. Updated 10-26-2015. https://www.feedipedia.org/node/246. Update By Tim Smith and Helene Thiollet (AFZ).

"*Red Clover Trifolium pratense*." By N.L. Taylor and R.P. Smith, 1981. Handbook for Biosolar Resources, Vol. II, p. 11-21. www.GaiaHerbs.com.

"*Red Clover*." *CRD Handbook of Biosolar Resources*." By Oskar R. Zaborsky. USA 1981. CRC Press. Vol 2, Pages 11-21. 608 pages. https://openlibrary.org/books/OL8260109M/CRC_Handbook_of_Biosolar_Resources. (Accessed 10-17-21).

"*Red Maple Silhouette*." Natural Resources Canada. Last modified on Apr. 8, 2015. https://tidcf.nrcan.gc.ca/en/trees/factsheet/84.

"*Red Maple/Acer rubrum.*" Nature Hills online Nursery. Plant photos. https://www.naturehills.com/red-maple.

"*Red Pine Silhouette*." Natural Resources Canada. Last modified Apr. 8, 2015. https://tidcf.nrcan.gc.ca/en/trees/factsheet/49.

"*Red Pine/Pinus resinosa - Lessons from the Red Pine,*" By J.S. Esposito, Nov. 20, 2013. https://jsesposito.wordpress.com/2013/11/20/lessons from-the-red-pine/.

"*Red Spruce Silhouette*." Natural Resources Canada. Last modified on Apr. 8, 2015. https://tidcf.nrcan.gc.ca/en/trees/factsheet/41.

"*Red Spruce/Picea rubens.*" Natural Resources Canada. Last modified on Apr. 8, 2015. https://treecanada.ca/resources/canadas-arboreal emblems/red-spruce/.

"*Relics of the Stone Age in Nova Scotia.*" By Harry Piers. 1896. From the Transactions of the Nova Scotian Institute of Science, Vol. IX, Session 1894-1895. https://electriccanadian.com/history/novascotia/relics.htm. (Accessed 10-12-21).

"*Report on ^{14}C on specimen "Beta-39897 to Richard C. Nieman*." By Drs. J.J. Stripp and M.A. Tamers, BETA Analytic Inc., Miami Florida. Sep. 28, 1990.

"*Report on ^{14}C on specimen "Beta-66584 to Richard C. Nieman*." By Drs. J.J. Stripp and M.A. Tamers, BETA Analytic Inc., Miami Florida. Oct. 6, 1993.

"*Report on ^{14}C on specimens Beta-66107 and Beta-39897 to Richard C. Nieman*." By BETA Analytic Inc., Miami Florida. Nov. 18, 1994.

"*Report on the Forest Trees of New Brunswick.*" By M. Perley. Simmonds' Colonial Magazine. Vol XI, No. 41. Toronto, Ontario. P. 129-428.

"*Report to Inspector of Mines for the Province, John Rutherford*," By Henry S. Poole, Esq. 1861. Printed By The Citizen Publishing Co. www.mininghistory.ns.ca.

"*Resins, Amber and Bitumen.*" By M. Serpico. *Ancient Egyptian Materials and Technology.* Cambridge. 2000. Pages 430-474.

"*Research Through Paul Wroclawski's website, Oakislandtheories.com*." Includes Oak Island Lot Ownership to 1795 and Lot Ownership research from Charles Morris through John Smith. Collected material as of Feb. 6, 2008.

"*Responding letter 'about oak trees' from Chief Botanist, James H. Soper*." to D`Arcy O`Connor, Apr. 4, 1977. National Museums of Canada, Museum of Natural Sciences. Ottawa, Ontario K1A OM8 Canada. #47.

"*Revealed: The Oak Island Treasure*." By Laverne Johnson. 1999. Benell-Atkins Printers, Vancouver. Available at www.freemasonry.bcy.ca/oakisland.

"*Reverend John Seccomb's Diary*." Nova Scotia National Archives, MG 1 Vol. 797C No. 5.

"*Richard Cunningham, 1748-1823.*" The Free Family Tree @ www.wikitree.com/wiki/cunningham-13844.

"*Rigid-end, Tandem-axle Dump Truck*." 1-12 cu. Yards. 2021. www.earthhaulers.com. Dallas, Tx.

"*Robert Brooster Telephonic Conversation with David H. Neisen*." with Mr. Robert (Bob) Brooster of RENTOKIL, Aug. 2020. Chester, Nova Scotia.

"*Robert R. Dunfield Written Question Responses to D`Arcy O`Connor*." By Robert R. Dunfield. Oct. 21,1976

"*Robert S. Young (1996-2020)*." en.wikipedia.org/wiki/Oak_Island.

"*Robert Young Email Responses to David H. Neisen #1*." By Robert S. Young, Jun. 18, 2020. Current owner of Lot #5, on Oak Island, Nova Scotia. www.Oakislandlotfive.com.

"*Robert Young Email Responses to David H. Neisen #2*." By Robert S. Young, Jun. 22, 2020. Current owner of Lot #5, on Oak Island, Nova Scotia. www.Oakislandlotfive.com.

"Roman London and the Walbrook Stream Crossing: Excavations at Poultry and vicinity, city of London." By Julian Hill and Peter Rowsome. MoLA Monograph. Series 37.

"*Roosevelt Arrives at Camp*," Circa 1910/12. B/W photo. PUBLIC DOMAIN / WIKIMEDIA COMMONS.

"*Rovertine letter to R. V. Harris*." By William A. Rovertine, Dec. 22, 1965. Dept. of Obstetrics and Gynecology, The Albany Medical College of Union University, Albany, NY. www.oakislandtreasure.co.uk.

S

"*Samuel Ball Last Will & Testament*." Last Will & Testament, Lunenburg Co. Registrar, Book 1, P. 37, Dated 10-01-1841, Probated 01-05-184.

"*Samuel Ball Will, Lunenburg, N.S*." Will Extracts www.occities.org/heartland/meadows/5699/lunwilla.html.

"*Sacred Trees of Norway and Sweden: A FRILUFTSLIV Quest*." By Douglas Forell Hulmes, Professor of Environmental Studies, Prescott College, Arizona, Sep. 14, 2009. 35 pages. (Accessed on 05-30-2022)

"*Sailing Vessels and Navigation in the Early Days*." By K.R.A. Narasiah. 37 page Presentation.

"*Sargassum: Floating Nurseries*," By James Franks. Discovery Porthole. Northern Gulf Institute, University of Southern Mississippi, Ocean Springs, MS. 2 pages. National Oceanic and Atmospheric Administration (NOAA). 2010.

"*S.C. Fraser Signed Affidavit to A.S. Lowden*." copy By Frederick Blair. Jun. 19, 1895.

"*Schofield letter to The Oak Island Exploration c/o Jon Ergin*." By C.H. Schofield, Oct. 7, 1970. National Research Council of Canada. www.oakislandtreasure.co.uk.

"*Scientific Rationalization of Indigenous Technology Knowledge on Nutrient Management in Lateritic Soils of Palakkad District in Kerala*." By P. Rajesh, F.M.H. Kaleel and V. Thulasi (2013). *Agriculture Update*. 8 (1&2): pages 26 to 30.

"*Scotland's 25 Best-loved Trees*." By Susan Swarbrick, Senior Feature Writer, *The Herald*. Nov. 10, 2018. https://www.heraldscotland.com/news/17212587.scotlands-25-best-loved-trees/. (Accessed 02-23-22).

"*Seafaring in Ancient India*." Published in *A Tribute to Hinduism*, online. Sep. 7, 2005. (Accessed 05-11-2022).

"*Seagrass Decomposition*." By Diana I. Walker, Gerard Pergent, and Stefano Fazzi, Dec. 2021. Chapter 16. ResearchGate. (Accessed 05-30-2022)

"*Sedimentary and tectonic setting of a mass transport slope deposit in the Halifax Group, Halifax Peninsula, Nova Scotia, Canada*." By J.W. Waldron, R.A. Jamieson, H.D. Pothier, and C.E. White (2015). *Atlantic Geology*, 51, Pages 84-104. https://DOI.org/10.4138/atlgeol.2015.004.

"*Selections from the Records of the Collector or South Canara*." Report By G. L. Morris Esquire, Collector of South Canara on the Management of the Coir Monopoly on the Amindivi Islands. Aug. 1863. Mangalore. Printed at the Collectorate Press, South Canara. 1898. 33 pages.

"*Selections from The Records of the Government of India, Revenue and Agricultural Department*." By George Watt, C.I.E, M.B., C.M. Vol. I, 1888-89. University of California at Los Angeles. Section. Coconuts and Coconut Products. Pages 197-214.

"*Shade and Flood Tolerance of Trees- SP656*." Sep. 2005. University of Tennessee Agricultural Extension Service. SP656-15M-9/05 R12-4910-051-001-06 06-0066. https://trace.tennessee.edu/utk_agexfores/60.

"*Shock Absorption of Crumb Rubber and Coconut Fiber*." By W. Alnashwan, et. al.. *International Journal of Advanced Packaging Technology*, 2014. 2(1) Pages 119-128.

"*Silver Maple Silhouette*." Natural Resources Canada. Last modified on Apr. 8, 2015. https://tidcf.nrcan.gc.ca/en/trees/factsheet/85.

"*Silver Maple/Acer saccharinum.*" By Dr. Jeff Kirwan, et. al. A program of Montgomery County, Maryland Government. Dec. 12, 2018. Landowner Factsheets © 2004 Virginia Tech Forestry Department, all rights reserved. https://treemontgomery.org/wp-content/uploads/2018/12/silver-maple-fall.png.

"*Size and estimated age of Genets in Eelgrass, Zostera marina, Assessed with Microsatellite Markers*." By T.B.H. Reusch, W.T. Stam, and J.L. Olsen, Sep. 15, 1998. Published in *Marine Biology*, 133: pages 519-525, 1998. Springer-Verlag. (Accessed 05-30-2022)

"*Smith's Cove Image – Boiler*," Circa 1909 B/W photo. Courtesy Henry Livingston Bowdin Expedition, The Old Gold Salvage and Wrecking Company. Nova Scotia National Archives.

"*Smith's Cove Image – Closeup*," Circa 1909. B/W photo. Courtesy Henry Livingston Bowdin Expedition, The Old Gold Salvage and Wrecking Company. Nova Scotia National Archives.

"*Smith's Cove Image – Early Dig*," Circa 1909-1911. B/W photo. Courtesy Henry Livingston Bowdin Expedition, The Old Gold Salvage and Wrecking Company. Nova Scotia National. Archives..

"*Smith's Cove Image - Fence*," B/W photo. Courtesy Nova Scotia National Archives.

"*Smith's Cove Image – Logs*," Circa 1909. B/W photo. Courtesy Henry Livingston Bowdin Expedition, The Old Gold Salvage and Wrecking Company. Nova Scotia National Archives.

"*Smith's Cove with boat watercolor*," By Robert W. Cook. 2018. www.bobcookartistry.com.

"*Soil Settlement Types, Calculations & Analysis – Settlement Limits*." By Haseeb Jamal, Aug. 25, 2017. GeoTechnical Engineering. https://www.aboutcivil.org/types-of-soil-settlement.html. (Accessed 03-09-21).

"*Soils Profile*." BYJU Online Biology Program. Author Unknown. (Accessed 10-12-2021). https://Byjus.com/biology/soil-profile/.

"*Soil Survey of Lunenburg County, Nova Scotia*." By D.B. Cann and J.D. Hilchey, 1958. Report No. 7 – *Nova Scotia Soil Survey*, Truro, Nova Scotia. Canada Department of Agriculture and Experimental Farms Service. 50 pages. Cat. No. A 52-2858.

"*Soil Type Unit Weight*." *Geotechnical.* www.Geotechnicalinfo.com/soil_unit_weight.html.

"*Soils and Foundation.*" The Japanese GeoTechnical Society. Oct. 2, 2013.

"*Soils and Settlement*." By Nick Gromicko, CMI and Kenton Shepard, InterNACHI's Director of Green Building. https://www.nachi.org/soils-settlement.htm. (Accessed 06-30-21),

"*Soils investigation, Oak Island, Nova Scotia. Report No. 530-110*." Warnock-Hersey International Limited (1969). Received By Carr and Donald and Associates, Toronto, Ontario, Jul. 31, 1969, and November 5, 1969. https://www.oakislandtours.ca/les-macphie-research.html.

"*Some Observations on the Early History of the Coconut in the New World*." By H.J. Bruman. 1944. Diego Lorenzo, Canon of Cape Verde, 1549. Acta americana 2: 220-243.

"*Songs, Poems, Stories and Prose emanating from the Rich Treasure of History and Traditions of Raasay, Fladda and Eilean Tighe*." By Rebecca S. Mackay, M.A., FSA Scot. Published By Raasay Heritage Trust. 2015.

"*South Western Ghats moist Deciduous Forests*." Wikipedia Contributors (Online). Wikipedia, the Free Encyclopedia. Updated Jul. 1, 2022. https://en.wikipedia.org/w/index.php?title=South_Western_Ghats_moist_deciduous_forests&oldid=1095898280

"*Species Profile of the Bur Oak*." By Mary Ann Riley. Kemptville College, University of Guelph, Canada. Apr. 3, 1997. www.songonline.ca/ecsong/essays/buroak.html.12 pages. (Accessed 03-23-21).

"*Sri Lanka – Encyclopedia Britannica.*" By Gerald Hubert Peiris and Sinnappah Arasaratnam. Encyclopedia Britannica. Updated Jul. 17, 2022. https://www.britannica.com/place/Sri-Lanka. (Accessed 19 July 2022).

"*Sri Lanka – Wikipedia.*" Wikipedia Contributors (Online). Wikipedia, The Free Encyclopedia. Updated 07-17-2022. https://en.wikipedia.org/w/index.php?title=Sri_Lanka&oldid=1098773771. (Accessed 07-18-2022).

"*State and Conditions of the Province of Nova Scotia together with some observations etc. 29th October 1763*." By Charles Morris. Bulletin of the Public Archives of Nova Scotia Annual Report. Appendix B, Pages 21-51. 1933. Nova Scotia National Archives.

"*Staten Island and its People: A History 1609-1929*." By William T. Leng, et. al. Historical Publishing Co. 1930.

"*State Symbols Of Kerala.*" Philalndia.info online. Posted Dec. 27, 1976. https://philaindia.info/state-symbols-of-kerala/.

"*Status and Conservation of Eelgrass (Zoestra marina) in Eastern Canada*." By Alan R. Hanson. Atlantic Region 2004, Canadian Wildlife Service. Technical Report, Series No. 412. Environmental Conservation Branch.

"*Steps in Coco Coir Fiber Decortication and Processing.*" By Dela Cruz, Pobre & Gabrido. 2002. https//www.pca.da.gov.ph/pdf/Techno/coir_fiber.pdf.

"*Stratigraphy of the Lower Paleozoic Goldenville and Halifax groups in the western part of southern Nova Scotia*." By C.E. White (2010). *Atlantic Geology*, 46, Pages 136-154. https://doi.org/10.4138/atlgeol.2010.008.

"*Straw and Hay*." By Bob Wood. https://goschenhoppen.org/clover-part-1/. (Accessed 11-29-21).

"*String: Unraveling the History of a Twisted Piece of Twine*." By Adam Hart-Davis. The Reader's Digest Association, Inc. Pleasantville, New York. 2009.

"*Striped Maple Silhouette*." Natural Resources Canada. Last modified on Apr. 8, 2015. https://tidcf.nrcan.gc.ca/en/trees/factsheet/83.

"*Striped Maple/Acer pensylvanicum,*" By Susan McDougall. The Trees of North America. https://northamericantrees.com/acer pensylvanicum.html.

"*Subsurface Investigation, The Oak Island Exploration, Oak Island, Nova Scotia: Draft Report No. 69126*." Golder Associates. Received By Triton Alliance Ltd., Montreal, Quebec, Apr. 28, 1971. https://www.oakislandtours.ca/les-macphieresearch.html.

"*Sugar Maple Silhouette*." Natural Resources Canada. Last modified on Apr. 8, 2015. https://tidcf.nrcan.gc.ca/en/trees/factsheet/86.

"*Sugar Maple, Striped Maple, Eastern Hemlock, Jack Pine, Ironwood Taxonomy*." www.machailwoods.org/nature-guides/trees/sugar-maple/. Apr. 2021.

"*Sugar Maple*." *Macphail Woods Ecological Forestry Project.* Tree Species Descriptions. 4 pages. https://macphailwoods.org/nature guides/trees/sugar-maple/. (Accessed 04-16-21).

"*Sugar Maple/Acer saccharum.*" Moon Nurseries Inc. Maryland. https://moonnurseries.com/product/acer-saccharum-commemoration/.

"*Summary of Documents and Results for Carbon Dating at Oak Island*." Compiled By Les MacPhie, Jul. 2006. 2 Pages. www.oakislandcompendium.ca.

"*Surficial geology, Halifax Harbour, Nova Scotia. Geological Survey of Canada*." By G.B.J. Fader, R.Q. Miller (2008). Bulletin 590; Natural Resources Canada; Geological Survey of Canada (Atlantic); Bedford Institute of Oceanography https://doi.org/10.4095/224797.

"*Sustainable Forestry in Nova Scotia*." By David Orton, Nov. 19, 2002. Published in The Northern Forest Forum, Winter Solstice, 2002, Vol. 9 No.4. http://home.ca.inter.net/~greenweb/'Sustainable'_Forestry_NS.html.

"*SW Nova Scotia Bedrock Map and Karst Risk Map (2020)*." Government of Nova Scotia, Department of Natural Resources, Geoscience and Mines Branch, Interactive Maps https://novascotia.ca/natr/meb/geoscience-online/maps-interactive.asp.

"*Sworn Affidavit of J.W. Andrews, C.E.M.E Consult Engineer*." Brooklyn, NY. N.S. Archives, MG1 Vol.383. Part of F. Blair report.

"*Sylva Sylvarum – Or a Natural History in Ten Centuries.*" By Sir Francis Bacon. Volume II. Reprinted by Kessinger Publishing Rare Reprints. Paragraphs 796, 881 & 882.

T

"*T12.1 Colonization By People*." Natural History of Nova Scotia, Vol. 1. Nova Scotia Museum of Natural History. 75 Pages.

"*T5.1 The Dynamics of Nova Scotia Climate*." Jun. 2005. 49 pages. National History of Nova Scotia, Vol. 1. Nova Scotia Museum of Natural History. (Accessed 05-30-2022)

"*T6.2, Ocean Currents*." Natural History of Nova Scotia, Vol. 1. NS Museum of Natural History.

"*Tamarack Silhouette*." Natural Resources Canada. Last modified Apr. 8, 2015. https://tidcf.nrcan.gc.ca/en/trees/factsheet/34

"*Tamarack/Larix larcinia*." American Conifer Society. *CONIFER Quality Magazine*.www.confiersociety.org/conifers/larix-larcina/.

"*Taxonomy and intraspecific Classification*." By NM Nayar, University of Kerala. Dec. 2017. DOI: 10.1016/B978-0-12-809778-6.00003-6. 28 pages. https://www.researchgate.net/publication/312513113_Taxonomy_and_Intraspecific_Classification?enrichId=rgreq.

"*Technical Information Kit – Pine Nuts*." Published By International Nut and Dried Fruit, #1572518550. Oct. 2019. www.nutfruit.org.

"*Technical Report*." compiled By Les MacPhie. Montreal, Quebec, Jan. 2008.

"*Telephonic interview with Craig Lorimer*." with D`Arcy O'Connor, Apr. 18, 1977. Forester with Harvard Forest, Harvard University, Petersham, Mass.

"*Terry J. Deveau Bio*." Senior Ocean-Acoustics Scientist, author, software engineer, Curse of Oak Island guest expert, Mi` Kmaw Heritage Research and Restoration Association. Herring Cove, NS.

"*Textiles and the Medieval Economy, Production, Trade and Consumption of Textiles – 8th to 16th Centuries*." Edited By Angela Ling Huang and Carsten Janke. Published in *Ancient Textiles Series*, Vol. 16, 256 pages. 2015. UK.

"*TH6, Red Oak – Yellow Birch / Striped Maple." Part I: Vegetation Types*." Baker Settlement, Lunenburg County, Nova Scotia. 2010. 2 pages.

"The 3:1 Pulley System." Ropebook BETA V2.2. Jul. 31, 2019.

"The Acadian forest: Historical condition and human impacts." By J. Loo and N. Ives, Paper presented at the "Old-growth Forests in Canada: A Science Perspective" Conference, Oct. 14-19, 2001, Sault Ste. Marie, ON. MAI/JUIN 2003, VOL. 79, NO. 3, THE FORESTRY CHRONICLE.

"The Acadian Forest: Historical Conditions and Human Impacts." - graphic: Change in Major Trees in NEAF from 1800-1993, J. Loo & N. Ives. 2003. The Forestry Chronicle – 2003.

"The Afro-Eurasian Trading System in the 13th and 14th Centuries." Posted on h2g2: The Hitchhiker's Guide to the Galaxy. Posted online, May 4, 2006. https://h2g2.com/edited_entry/A10422181.

"The Archaeobiology of Indian Ocean Translocations: Current Outlines of Cultural Exchanges by Proto-historic Seafarers." By Dorian Q. Fuller, Nicole Boivin, Cristinia C. Castillo, Tom Hoogervorst, and Robin G. Allaby, 2009. Sealinks Project, European Research Council. Delta Book World, New Delhi.

"The Archaeology of Roman London – The Upper Walbrook in the Roman Period." By Catharine Maloney with Dominique de Moulins. 1990. Volume 1 CBA Research Report 69.

"The Atlantic Advocate." By Jack Nickell. George Williams University, Montreal Library. Oct. 1965.

"The Bark Canoes and Skin Boats of North America." By Adney, Tappan, and Chapelle, 1964. Bulletin of the United States National Museum. Pages 1-242. https://doi.org/10.5479/si.03629236.230. Or https://www.google.com/books/edition/The_Bark_Canoes_and_Skin_Boats_of_North/BKZVCgAAQBAJ?hl=en&gbpv=1.

"The Biggest Nuts in the World." By Valery Skiba. Printed online In *The Magazine*. (Accessed 05-05-2022). https://tz.iiug2017.org/7496-the-biggest-nuts-in-the-world.html

"The Black Death, A Chronicle of the Plague." By Nohl Johannes, 1926. London, George Allen & Unwin Ltd. P. 56

"The Black Settlers of 'Treasure Oak Island' The Primary Generation – Samuel Ball." See,www.wsog.blogspot.com/2006/05/black-settlers-of-treasure-oak-island_07.html.

"The Blockhouse Blog Column Articles." By Doug Crowell. 2019. Blockhouse Investigations, at www.oakislandcompendium.ca.

"The Bones in the Pit – Who Built the Oak Island Money Pit and What's Hidden There." By Bill Thompson, Nov. 20, 2014. *Historical Prelude*. Pgs. 1-3. Ascendente Books Publishing. 2014. 491 pages.

"The Butuan Boats of the Philippines: Southeast Asia edge-joined and lashed-lug watercraft." By Ligaya Lacsina. National Museum of the Philippines. Researchgate. Pub. 339499336. Jan. 2015. *Bulletin of the Australasian Institute for Maritime Archaeology* (2015), 39: Pages 126 132.

"The Carboniferous evolution of Nova Scotia." By J.H. Calder (1998). Geological Society, London, Special Publications, 143, Pages 261-302. https://DOI.org/10.1144/GSL.SP.1998.143.01.19.

"*The Caribbean Current – Surface Currents in the Caribbean Sea*." By Joanna Gyory, Arthur J. Mariano and Edward H. Ryan. Rosenthal School of Marine and Atmospheric Science, University of Miami, Fl. Pages 1-8. https://oceancurrents.rmas.miami.edu/caribbean/caribbean.html. (Accessed 08-10-21).

"*The Chinese in Latin America and the Caribbean*," By Edward R. Slack Jr., Walton Look Lai, and Tan Chee Berg. 2010. *Chapter One, Sinifying New Spain: Cathay's Influence on Colonial Mexico via Nao De China*. Pages 5-31. Brill Publishing eBook. 237 pages.

"*The Cocoanut*," By William Lyons, 1903. Farmer's Bureau No. 8, Conclusion #8. Bureau of Agriculture. Bureau of Public Printing, Jun. 1, 1903.

"The Coconut Cup as Material and Media: Extended Ecologies." By Kathleen E. Kennedy, 2021. www.press.library.concordia.ca/projects/old-media-and-the-medieval-concept .

"*The Coconut in Micronesia*." By Leo Migvar. 1965. Division of Agriculture, Department of Resources and Development, Trust Territory of the Pacific Islands. Publication office, Saipan, Mariana Islands.

"*The Coconut Odyssey – The bounteous possibilities of the Tree of Life*." By Mike Foale, 2003. Australian Centre for International Agricultural Research (ACIAR).

"*The Coconut Phylogeny, Origins, and Spread*." By N.M. Nayer, 2021. Academic Press is an imprint of Elsevier. 125 London Wall, London EC2Y 5AS, United Kingdom.

"*The Coconut, How the Shy Fruit Shaped our World*," By Robin Laurance. 2019. The Pages 11-45. The History Press.

"The Colonial Journal." Published for Baldwin, Cradock, and Joy, Paternoster Row, et. al., 1816. Vol. I. January to Jul. 1816. Quarterly. GoogleBooks. 619. Pages.

"*The Complete Book on Coconut and Coconut Products (Cultivation and Processing)*." By NIIR Board of Consultants and Engineers, 2006. Accessed on 05-12-2022).

"*The Controversy over the Retypification of Acacia Mill. With an Australian Type: A pragmatic View*." By Kevin R. Thiele, et. al. Published in TAXON, 60(1), Feb. 2011. Pages 194-198.

"*The Cosmic Winter*." By B. Napier and V. Clube, 1990. Oxford Press. Page 43.

"*The Curse of Oak Island: The Story of the World's Longest Treasure Hunt*." By Randall Sullivan. New York: Grove Press. 2018. 2nd Edition. Introduction, p. 13-15. 410 pages.

"*The Decay Resistance of Oak Wood*." By Theodore C. Scheffer. Forest Pathology Special Release No. 13. Bureau of Plant Industry, Soils, and Agricultural Engineering, Division of Forest Pathology, Madison, Wisconsin. U.S. Department of Agriculture. Oct. 1943. 9 pages.

"*The Definition of Bole*." Online. https://www.vocabulary.com/dictionary/bole.

"*The Description and Natural History of the Coasts of North America*." By Nicolas Denys, 1632-1670. Pub. 1672, under title: "Description Geographique et Historique des Costes de L'Amerique Septentrionale: arec L'Histoire Naturelle du pais." Translated By William F. Ganong, Ph.D. Toronto: The Champlain Society. 1908. 605 pages.

"The Dhows of Beypore – URU." Online Blog. Posted Apr, 27, 2012. https://uru-ship.blogspot.com/2012/04/dhows-of-beypore-uru-heritage-ship.html. (Accessed 02-21-2021).

"The Dynamics of Nova Scotia's Climate, T5.1." Natural history of Nova Scotia, Volume 1. Pages 94-104. Nova Scotia Museum of Natural History. PDF. (Accessed 05-22-22).

"The Early Period of Sami History, from the Beginnings to the 16th Century." By Doug Simms. University of Texas, Austin, Texas. www.laits.utexas.edu/sami/dieda/hist/early.htm. (Accessed 09-24-21).

"The East Greenland Current – Surface Currents in the Atlantic Ocean." By Joanna Gyory, Arthur J. Mariano and Edward H. Ryan. Rosenthal School of Marine and Atmospheric Science, University of Miami, Fl. Pages 1-4. https://oceancurrents.rmas.miami.edu/atlantic/east greenland.html. (Accessed 08-10-21).

"The Ecology and Biodiversity value of Sycamore (Acer pseudoplatanus) with Particular Reference to Great Britain." By Andrew Dunbar Leslie, 2005. *Scottish Forestry*, Vol 59. No 3. Pages 19-26. https://www.researchgate.net/publication/246548466.

"The Enduring Journey of Samuel Ball, From Slavery to Freedom: Part One, 1761-1783." By Chipp Reid. 2020. Pages 15-21.

"The Epidemics of the Middle Ages." By J.F.C. Hecker. Translated By Benjamin Guy Babington, Dec. 16, 2020. Project Gutenberg eBook. https://gutenberg.org/files/63232/63232-h/63232-h.htm.

"The Evaluation of Constitutive Models in Prediction of Surface Settlements in Cohesive Soils – A case Study: Mashhad Metro Line 2." By Eslami Behnam, Golshani Aliakbar and Arefiazdeh M. Sina. ISSMGE *International Journal of Geoengineering*, Case Histories. Vol. 5, Issue 3, Pages. 182-198.

"The Extent of Indigenous-Norse Contact and Trade Prior to Columbus." By Donald E. Warden, Aug. 2016. Published in the Oglethorpe Journal of Undergraduate Research, Vol. 6, Issue I, Article 3. 26 pages.

"The Floating Sargassum (Phaeophyceae) of the South Atlantic Ocean – Likely Scenarios." By Marina Nasri Sissini, et. al., Mar. 10, 2017. Published in *Phycologia*, Volume 56 (3), 321–328.

"The Florida Current – Surface Currents in the Atlantic Ocean." By Joanna Gyory, Elizabeth Rowe, Arthur J. Mariano and Edward H. Ryan. Rosenthal School of Marine and Atmospheric Science, University of Miami, Fl. Pages 1-5. https://oceancurrents.rmas.miami.edu/atlantic/florida.html. (Accessed 08-10-21).

"The Food Chronology: a food lover's compendium of events and anecdotes, from prehistory to the present." By J. Trager, 1996. P. 346. See The Coconut Time Line: Mercantile, 1895, titled: Desiccated Coconut. at http://cocos.arecaceae.com/mercantile.html.

"The 'Foreign Protestants' and the settlement of Nova Scotia: the history of a piece of arrested British colonial policy in the eighteenth century." By Winthrop Bell. University of Toronto Press, 1961.

"The Forgotten New England Coconut Dipper in the 19th-Century American Landscape." By Kathleen E. Kennedy, 2019.

"The Forming Tree." By Craig Holdrege. *In Context*, No.14. Fall 2005. 5 pages.

"The Galleon Cargo: Accounts in the Colonial Archives." By Cameron La Follette, Douglas Deur, Esther Gonzalez. 2018. *Oregon Historical Quarterly*, 119(2), Pages 250-281.

"*The Gardener's Dictionary*." By P. Miller. Edition # 8. London. Pinus no. 8. 1768. Available: botanicus.org/title/b12066618. (Accessed 05-20-2011).

"*The Genus Pinus*." By George Russell Shaw. Publications of the Arnold Arboretum #5. Oct. 7, 2008. Pages 48-50.

"*The Ghost That Guards $30,000.00*." By Richard Barber and Peter Beamish, 1965. RV. Harris Papers (2608G), 9 pages, DRAFT. Nova Scotia National Archives, MG1 Vol. 390.

"*The Great Famine: Northern Europe in the Early Fourteenth Century*." By William Chester Jordan. P. 19.

"*The Gulf Stream – Surface Currents in the Atlantic Ocean*." By Joanna Gyory, Arthur J. Mariano and Edward H. Ryan. Rosenthal School of Marine and Atmospheric Science, University of Miami, Fl. Pages 1-6. https://oceancurrents.rmas.miami.edu/atlantic/gulf-stream.html. (Accessed 08-10-21).

"*The Halifax Gazette – 1754*." Goggle News Archive. news.google.com.

"*The Halifax Naval Yard and Mast Contractors, 1775 – 1815*." By Julian Gwyn. Public Record Office, ADM106/1653, Wentworth to Navy Board, Jun. 14, 1816. *The Northern Mariner/Le marin du nord,* XI, No. 4 & 7, Oct. 2001. Pages 1-25. www.scrn.org/northern_mariner/Vol.11.

"*The Hindu*." 2013. Wikipedia. https://en.wikipedia.org/wiki/1341#cite_note--2.

"The Historical Geography of Agriculture in Nova Scotia, 1851-1951." By Robert A. MacKinnon, 1991. University of British Columbia.

"The History of parliament: the House of Commons 1754-1790," By L. Namier and J. Brooke 1964 Ed.

"*The History of the CaribBy-Islands: viz. Barbados, St Christophers, St Vincents, Martinico, Dominico, Barbouthos, Monserrat, Mevis [sic], Antego, &c.*" By Charles de Rochefort (1605-16830, John Davies (1625-1693), Cesar de Rochefort (1690), Louis de Poincy (1660), Raymond Breton (1609-1679), and John Nicholas Brown (1900). Two books, XXVIII. The first containing the natural; the second, the moral history of those islands. Chapter VI, Book I, Pages 37-38.

"*The History of the European Commerce with India to which is subjoined A Review of the Arguments for and against The Trade with India, and The Management of it By a Chartered Company, with An Appendix of Authentic Accounts*." By David MacPherson, author of the Annals of Commerce. London, England. 1812. Pages 1-25.

"*The Imperial Gazetteer of India, Vol. 8*." By William Wilson Hunter. Online https://www.ebooksread.com/authors-eng/william-wilson-hunter/the-imperial-gazetteer-of-india-volume-8-tnu/page-46-the-imperial-gazetteer-of-india-volume-8-tnu.shtml.

"*The Irminger Current – Surface Currents in the Atlantic Ocean*." By Joanna Gyory, Arthur J. Mariano and Edward H. Ryan. Rosenthal School of Marine and Atmospheric Science, University of Miami, Fl. Pages 1-3. https://oceancurrents.rmas.miami.edu/atlantic/irminger.html. (Accessed 08-10-21).

"*The Importance of a Tree's Butt*." By Steve Nix. ThoughtCo. (Accessed 04-20-2022). https://www.thoughtco.com/the-importance-of-a-trees butt-1343234.

"*The Indian Ocean Trade of Orissa in the Seventeenth Century*." By K.N. Sethi. Published in *Proceedings of the Indian History Congress*, 2004, Vol. 65, Pages 248-257.

"*The Island of Raasay*." Raasay House Hotel. 2021. https://www.raasay-house.co.uk/about-the-isle-of-raasay/. (Accessed 12-12-21).

"*The Journal of a Tour to the Hebrides with Samuel Johnson, LL. D. (1785)*." By James Boswell. 1785. P. 142. (Accessed 1-4-22). https://archive.org/details/boswellsjournalo011419mbp/page/n167/mode/2up?q=Raasay+Island.

"*The King's Pines.*" Nov. 10, 2015, Edition, Mountain Top Arboretum.

"*The Knights Templar: A New History*." By Helen Nicholson, 2001. Stroud. Sutton Press. P.201. "The History of the Renaissance World: from the Rediscovery of Aristotle to the Conquest of Constantinople." By Susan Bauer Wise, 2013.

"*The La Formule Cipher Investigation*." By Doug Crowell. Feb. 11, 2017. www.oakislandcompendium.ca/blockhouse-blog/.

"*The Labrador Current – Surface Currents in the Atlantic Ocean*." By Joanna Gyory, Arthur J. Mariano and Edward H. Ryan. Rosenthal School of Marine and Atmospheric Science, University of Miami, Fl. Pages 1-4. https://oceancurrents.rmas.miami.edu/atlantic/labrador.html. (Accessed 08-10-21).

"*The Laki Fissure Eruption 1783-1784*." By Katrin Kleeman. Published *Encyclopedia of the Environment*, Jan. 14, 2020. https://www.encyclopedie-environnement.org/en/society/laki-fissure-eruption-1783-1784. (Accessed 10-12-21).

"*The Letters of Agricola on the Principles of Vegetation and Tillage.*" By John Young. Halifax, Holland & Co., 1822. Citation in Dave Macintosh's *When the Work's All Done This Fall.* Pages 23-24.

"*The Life and Administration of Governor Charles Lawrence 1749-1760*." By James. S. MacDonald. Nova Scotia Historical Society, 1880.

"*The Little Ice Age: How Climate Made History, 1300-1850*." By Brian Fagan. P. 31-33. "Early Years of the Little Ice Age in Northern Europe, 1300-1500." Shin Kim, 2007. Korean Minjok Leadership Academy International Program.

"*The Logistics of the Roman Army at War (264 B.C. – A.D. 235)*." By Jonathan R. Roth, 1999. Brill. Leiden, Boston, Koln. 422 pages.

"*The Lost Western Settlement of Greenland, 1342*." By Carol S. Francis, Mar. 9, 2012. Thesis, California State University, Sacramento.

"*The Loyalist Melvins of Charleston, Massachusetts, and Nova Scotia*." By Howard Storm Browne, UE. Williamsburg, Virginia. 18 pages.

"*The Maldives and Laccadive Islands in Ming Records*." By Roderich Ptak. Source: *Journal of the American Oriental Society*, Oct.-Dec. 1987, Vol. 107, No. 4. Pages 675-694. Published By *American Oriental Society*. https://www.jstor.org/stable/603307.

"*The Maldive Islands: An Account of The Physical Features, Climate, History, People, Productions and Trade*." By H.C.P. Bell, Ceylon Civil Service, 1882. Colombo: Frank Luker, Acting Government Printer, Ceylon, 1882.

"*The Manila Galleon and California*." By William Lytle Shurz. Published in *The Southwestern Historical Quarterly*, Vol. XXI, Oct. 1917. No. 2. Pages 117-126.

"*The Maritime Industry Knowledge Centre*." Glossary. Maritime Industry Foundation. https://www.maritimeinfo.org/en/Glossary/.

"*The Mechanics of Settling Dirt*." By Charlie D. Paige, Dec. 9, 2017. https://www.cohesivehomes.com/dirt-to-compact-and-settle. (Accessed 06-30-21).

"*The Merchants' Magazine and Commercial Review*." By Freeman Hunt, 1856. Volume 34. P. 694.
"*The Periplus of the Erythraean Sea: Travel and Trade in the Indian Ocean By a Merchant of the First Century*." Translated from the Greek and Annotated By Wilfred H. Schoff, A.M., Secretary of the Commercial Museum, Philadelphia, PA. Published By Longmans, Green, and Co. New York, London, Bombay and Calcutta. 1912. *Pages annotated within the appendices of this book.*

"*The Method*." By Thomas Higham. Radiocarbon Web Info. https://c14dating.com/. (Accessed 03-19-22).

"*The Micmac Indians: The Earliest Migrants' in Banked Fires*." By Harold McGee. Nova Scotia Archives – Library, Mi`kmaq Holdings. p. 28.

The Mi`kmaq: The Boat that Connected the Province." Shubenacadie Canal Waterway. https://www.shubenacadiecanal.ca/the-mikmaq. (Accessed 04-11-22).

"*The Money Pit: The Story of Oak Island and the World's Greatest Treasure Hunt*." By D`Arcy O`Connor. New York: Coward, McCann and Geohagen, 1978. 236 pages.

"*The Mystic Magic of the Sycamore Tree – Acer pseudoplatanus*." Blog By Jane Osborne. Ju. 11, 2018. (Accessed on 01-26-22).

"*The Natural History of Nova Scotia – Theme Regions*." By Derek S. Davis & Sue Browne. Co-published By the Nova Scotia Museum. Volume 2, Theme Regions. QH106.2.N68N27 1997 508.716 C95-966009-7

"*The North Atlantic Current – Surface Currents in the Atlantic Ocean*." By Elizabeth Rowe, Arthur J. Mariano and Edward H. Ryan. Rosenthal School of Marine and Atmospheric Science, University of Miami, Fl. P. 1-4. https://oceancurrents.rmas.miami.edu/atlantic/north atlantic.html. (Accessed 08-10-21).

"*The Norumbega Vinland Stone*." Posted Sep. 8, 2014. http://norumbegavinlandstone.wordpress.com. (Accessed 10-12-21).

"*The Oak Island Connection*." Kerrin Margiano. CreateSpace Independent Publishing Platform, North Charleston, SC.

"*The Oak Island Diggings*." By Jotham Blanchard McCully, Oct. 16, 1862. Published in *The Liverpool Transcript*. Pages 3 & 8.

"*The Oak Island Encyclopedia, Volume I*." By Hammerson Peters. 2019. From *Mysteries of Canada.com*, Pt 1, "The History" 1,120 pages. Pages 18-22.

"*The Oak Island Encyclopedia: Volume II*." By Hammerson Peters. Canada: Mysteries of Canada.com. 2020. 285 pages.

"*The Oak Island Enigma*." By Thomas P. Leary. Omaha, NA: Leary publications, 1953. Pgs 4-36.

"*The Oak Island Exploration: A Project of Triton Alliance Ltd.: Engineering and Operational Plans Including Cost Estimates*." Cox Underground Research, Limited. Westmount, Quebec. 1987.

"*The Oak Island Folly*." By 'Patrick,' 1861. Printed in *The Nova Scotian*, Sep. 30, 1861. Pgs. 1-4.

"The Oak Island Legend: The Masonic Angle." By Dennis J. King. 2010.

"The Oak Island Money Pit – Skeptoid." By Brian Dunning. Skeptoid podcast, Episode #129, Nov. 28, 2008. https//www.skeptoid.com/episodes/4129.

"*The Oak Island Mystery – The World's Greatest Treasure Hunt*." By Lionel & Patricia Fanthorpe. 2017. Chapter 1, Pages 18 & 32. 2nd Edition.

"*The Oak Island Mystery Solved: The Final Chapter.*" By Joy A. Steele and Gordon Fader, P. Geo. 2nd Edition. 2018. NIMBUS Publishing, Halifax, NS & Cape Breton University Press, Sydney, NS. 20 pgs. P. 2.

"*The Oak Island Mystery: The Secret of the World's Greatest Treasure Hunt*." By Lionel & Patricia Fanthorpe. Toronto: Hounslow Press, 1995. 221 pages.

"*The Oak Island Treasure*." By Charles B. Driscoll. *The North American Review*. Jun. 1929 Edition.

"*The Old Gold Salvage and Wrecking Company Archive*." Compiled By D'Arcy O'Connor. Oak Island Tours. Pages 1-9. https://www.oakislandtours.ca/the-old-gold-salvage-and-wrecking-company.html (Accessed 08-03-21).

"*The Open Database of the Corporate World. Oak Island Tours Inc*." Opencorporates, Company Number 2272393. Incorporated Date, 12-09-1987, Corporate Officers: Craig Tester, George Monroe, Martin Lagina, Richard Lagina, Dan Blankenship.

"*The Outriggers of Indonesian Canoes*." By A.C. Haddon. Published in the Royal Anthropological Institute of Great Britain and Ireland, Vol. L, Jan-Jun 1920. London.

"*The Overton Stone*." By Terry J. Deveau, Dec. 3, 2015. New England Antiquities Research Association (NEARA). http://neara.org/pdf/OvertonStone.pdf *or* https://vdocuments.mx/the-overton-stone-neara-the-overton-stone-terry-j-deveau-a-2015-12-03 the.html. (Accessed 10-12-21 and 02-13-22).

"*The Peopling of Lakshadweep Archipelago*." By M.S. Mustak, N Rai, M.R. Naveen, S. Prakash, et. al., 2019. Sci Rep. 2019 May 6;9(1):6968. doi: 10.1038/s41598-019-43384-3. PMID: 31061397; PMCID: PMC6502849.

"*The Periplus of the Erythraean Sea: Travel and Trade in the Indian Ocean By a Merchant of the First Century*." Translated from the Greek and Annotated By Wilfred H. Schoff, A.M., Secretary of the Commercial Museum, Philadelphia, PA. Published By Longmans, Green, and Co. New York, London, Bombay and Calcutta. 1912. *Pages annotated within the appendices of this book.*

"*The President and Council at Surat to the President and Council at Bantam.*" Dec. 1647.

"*The Raasay Mills*." By Rebecca S. Mackay, M.A., FSA Scot. Published By Raasay Heritage Trust. 2010.

"*The Region." Vol. 2.* The Natural History of Nova Scotia, NMBUS – The Nova Scotia Museum. Pgs 74 & 201

"*The Reluctant Treasure Hunter, Part One." Oak Island Obsession: The Restall Story*," By Lee Lamb. 2006. Excerpts of Mildred Restall's journal, 1955. Pages 44-45.

"*The Restall Story – Oak Island Obsession.*" By Lee Lamb. Dundurn Press, Toronto, Ontario, Canada. Chapter 10, p. 160.

"*The Sea-craft of Prehistory*." By Paul Johnstone. Published By Routledge & Kegan Paul. London. 1976.

"*The Search for the Manila Galleon Log Books*." By Wayne V. Bert. Published in *Bulletin American Meteorological Society*, Vol. 71, No. 11, Nov. 1990. (Accessed 08-18-21).

"*The Secret Treasure of Oak Island, The Amazing True Story of A Centuries-old Treasure Hunt*." By D`Arcy O'Connor. 2004. Guilford, Connecticut: The Lyons Press, 2004.

"*The Secret Treasure of Oak Island, The Amazing True Story of a Centuries-old Treasure Hunt*." By D`Arcy O`Connor. 2018. Updated Version. Published By Rowman & Littlefield Publishing Group.

"*The Settlement of Grasslands*." By Everett E. Edwards. Bureau of Agriculture Economics. Pages 16-25. https://naldc.nal.usda.gov/download/IND43894892/PDF. (Accessed 02-09-22).

"*The Ship-Building Assistant*." By William Sutherland. Royal Dockyard of Portsmouth & Depfor.

"*The Short Account of the Cocoa-nut Palm*." By Thomas Treloar, Cocoa Nut Fibre Warehouse, 42, Ludgate-hill, London. Free 15-page pamphlet distributed By Treloar & Sons, Carpets. 1852.

"*The Slope Jet Current – Surface Currents in the Atlantic Ocean*." By Angelique C. Haza, Barbie Bishof, Arthur J. Mariano. Rosenthal School of Marine and Atmospheric Science, University of Miami, Fl. https://oceancurrents.rmas.miami.edu/atlantic/slope-jet.html. Pages 1-3. (Accessed 08-10-21).

"*The Solution Caves of Nova Scotia: An Update*." By Max Moseley, 1988. Published in *The Canadian Cavers*, Fall 1988, 20, 2: Pages 38-41.

"*The Spice Trade in Medieval and Early Modern Europe*." Curated By Matthew A. McIntosh, Public Historian. Dec. 2, 2021. *The Brewminator*. 14 pages. https://brewminate.com/the-spice-trade-in-medieval-and-early-modern-europe/. (accessed 01-15-22).

"*The Sri Lankan Coconut Industry: Current Status and Future Prospects in a Changing Climate*." By P.M.E.K Pathiraja, G.R. Griffith, J.J. Farquharson and R. Faggian. 2015. *Australasian Agribusiness Perspectives*. Paper #106. Fig. 1 "Land under Coconut Cultivation in Sri Lanka, P. 5. ISSN: 1442-6951.

"*The Story of Oak Island – 1895*." By Frederick L. Blair. Included in *Buried Treasure*, part of Oak Island Treasure Company's Public Share Offering. "Additional" Information included section. Record Publishing Company. Stoughton, Mass. Pages 1-11. (accessed 03-19-21). www.reddit.com/r/oakisland/comments/efzj67/oakisland_newspaper_archive.

"*The Structures of English Wooden Ships: William Sutherland's Ship, circa 1710*." By Trevor Ketchington. Published in *The Northern Mariner/Le Main du nord*, III, No. 1 (Jan. 1993. 43 Pages.

"*The Swahili Civilization in Eastern Africa.*" By Elgidius B. Ichumbaki and Edward Pollard. Mar. 25, 2021. Oxford Research Encyclopedia. Published online. https://DOI.org/10.1093/acrefore/9780190854584.013.267.

"*The Target: Albizia (Falcataria moluccana)*." Hawaii Invasive Species Council, Cabinet-level direction on invasive species issues. https://dlnr.hawaii.gov/hisc/info/biocontrol/latest-biocontrol/falcataria-moluccana/.

"*The Toilers of the Isle*." Reprinted from the New York Times, Aug. 24, 1886. *Victoria Daily British Colonist*, Nov. 5, 1866. 4 Columns. www.reddit.com/r/oakisland/comments/efzj67/oakisland_newspaper_archive/. (accessed 03-19-21).

"*The Trading World of the Indian Ocean*." Online production by The World Economy, OECD. http://www.theworldeconomy.org/impact/The_Trading_World_of_the_Indian_Ocean.html. (Accessed 05-30-2022)

"*The Tree Species Pages: Northern Red Oak*." Canadian Tree Tours. The Tree Pages. www.canadiantreetours.org/species pages/Northern_red_oak.html. 2021.

"*The Trees at Keele - Sycamore*." Keele University, Staffordshire, UK. https://www.keele.ac.uk/arboretum/ourtrees/speciesaccounts/sycamore/. (Accessed 02-23-22).

"*The Trees of the Bible – List and Description*." By Thomson Dablemond. Sep. 18, 2018. Sec. 'Trees of the Bible,' p.1. (Accessed 01-26-22). https://weddingincana.com/the-trees-of-the-bible.

"*The True Story of Oak Island - DRAFT*." By M.R. Chappell. 1973. 83 pages sent to Dan Blankenship, Sep. 20, 1973.

"*The Unfriendly Soil: The Loyalist Experience in Nova Scotia, 1783-1791*." By Neil MacKinnon. Montreal. McGill-Queens University Press. 1988.

"*The West Greenland Current – Surface Currents in the Caribbean Sea*." By Joanna Gyory, Arthur J. Mariano and Edward H. Ryan. Rosenthal School of Marine and Atmospheric Science, University of Miami, Fl. Pages 1-4. https://oceancurrents.rmas.miami.edu/atlantic/west greenland.html. (Accessed 08-10-21).

"*The Windsor Group of the Mahone Bay area, Nova Scotia*." By P.S. Giles (1981). Nova Scotia Department of Mines and Energy. Paper Aug. 13, 1981. https://novascotia.ca/natr/meb/data/pubs/81paper03/81paper03.pdf. *And* https://novascotia.ca/natr/meb/pdf/81pap03.asp.

"*The World of Clover*." By Jared Eliot (1747 in Pieters 1926) Agronomy specialist in clovers.

"*Theme Regions – The Natural History of Nova Scotia.*" Vol. 2. Nimbus – The Nova Scotia Museum. Sections: #435, Eastern Shore Drumlins, Pages 74 & 83 and Bay of Islands, p. 201.

"*Thomas Embree, 1758-1820*." The Free Family Tree @ https://www.wikitree.com/wiki/Embree-897.

"*Timber Markets in New Brunswick and Nova Scotia and their Use in Assessing Stumpage Prices in other Canadian Provinces*." By Michael Stone, Bryce Macgregor and Susan Phelps, Sep. 10, 2004. Industry, Economics and Programs Branch, Canadian Forest Service. 48 Pages.

"*Timeline of the Hundred Year's War*." http://www.maisonstclaire.org.

"*To Nova Scotia: The Sunrise Province of Canada*." By T. Morris Longstreth. Chester, Nova Scotia. 1935. Published By D. Appleton-Century Company, New York. 290 pages. p. 26.

"*Tourist Guide – Oak Island Bicentennial Issue 1795-1995*." Produced By the Oak Island Exploration Company. www.oakislandtreasure.co.uk.

"*Traditional Mi`kmaq Birch Bark Canoe project underway at Kejimkujik National Park*." By Alexa MacLean, Aug. 2020. Global News. https://globalnews.ca/news/7258231/mikmaq-birch-bark-canoe-project kejimkujik-national-park/. (Accessed 04-18-2022).

"*Travels in the Coastlands of British East Africa and the islands of Zanzibar and Bemba: Their Agricultural Resources and General Characteristics*." By William Walter Augustine Fitzgerald, Fellow Royal Geographical Society, Fellow Royal Colonial Institute. London, England. Chapman and Hall, Ltd. 1898. Pages 620-635.

"*Tree Crowns Grow into Self-similar Shapes Controlled By Gravity and Light Sensing*." By Laurent Duchemin, Christophe Eloy, Eric Badel, and Bruno Moulia. Journal of the Royal Society Interface, the Royal Society, 15(142). 10.1098/rsif.2017.0976. hal-01829241. HAL archives ouvertes. Jul. 3, 2018. p. 2. https://hal.archives-ouvertes.fr/hal-01829241. (Accessed 10-22-20).

"*Tree Roots, Strongest and Deepest*." Rootwell, blog. 3 Pages. https://www.rootwell.com/blogs/tree-roots-strongest-and-deepest. (Accessed 10-03-21).

"Trees and Timber in the Ancient Mediterranean World." By Russell Meiggs. 1982. Oxford University Press. Pages 489, 490, 493.

"*Trees atop Crest with Frog Island in Back*," Circa 1909. B/W photo. Courtesy Henry Livingston Bowdin Expedition, The Old Gold Salvage and Wrecking Company. Nova Scotia National Archives.

"Trees of Acadian Forest 2." PDF. www.Parl.ns.ca/Woodenships.

"Trees of the Acadian Forest." Identification CD. Nova Scotia Province, Canada. Feb. 1, 2020.

"*Trees of the Bible: A Cultural History*." By Dr. Kim D. Coder, Professor of Tree Biology & Health Care, Warnell School of Forestry & Natural Resources, University of Georgia. Sections 'Confusion Trees' and 'Bible Trees,' Pages. 2-6. (Accessed 01-26-22). https://www.warnell.uga.edu/sites/default/files/publications/WSFNR-16-43%20Coder.pdf.

"Trees of the Sacred." By Christopher L.C.E. Witcombe. p.1. para. 4. From blog 'Sacred Places. https://www.bibliotecapleyade.net/mapas_sagrados/esp_mapassagrados_7.htm. (Accessed 01-26-22).

"Trees, Treaties and the Timing of Settlement: A Comparison of the Lumber Industry in Nova Scotia and New Brunswick 1784-1867." By Barbara Robertson. Nova Scotia Historical Review, Vol. 4, No. 1, Pages 37-55.

"Trees." By James Underwood Crockett. The Time-Life Encyclopedia of Gardening. Time-Life Books. 1967.

"*Trembling Aspen Silhouette*." Natural Resources Canada. Last modified Apr. 8, 2015. https://tidcf.nrcan.gc.ca/en/trees/factsheet/58.

"*Trembling Aspen/Populus tremuloides.*" By Janet L. Howard. 1996. Populus tremuloides. In: Fire Effects Information System, [Online]. U.S. Department of Agriculture, Forest Service, Rocky Mountain Research Station, Fire Sciences Laboratory (Producer). https://www.fs.fed.us/database/feis/plants/tree/poptre/all.html [04-04-2022].

"*Tropical Products Handbook* - Coconuts." By Brian M. McGregor, 1987. Tropical Products Transportation Handbook, No. 668. Pages 90-91. U.S. Department of Agriculture. https://naldc.nal.usda.gov/download/CAT89930509/PDF.

"Two Voyages to the New World." By John Josselyn, 1674.

U

"*Undercover – A Guide to using Cover Crops in the Maritimes*." By Janet Wallace and Jennifer Scott. Section, Clover. Nova Scotia Organic Growers Association. & Atlantic Canadian Organic Regional Network (ACORN). 2nd Edition. 2008.

"*Understanding Albizia: Albizia "The Bad Boy of Trees*." created By Wu Yewei, Dec. 2019. Wiki, Falcataria moluccana – Albizia. https://wiki.nus.edu.sg/display/TAX/Falcataria+moluccana+-+Albizia.

"Unit Weight of Soils." By Geo Technical Info. Career Development & Resources of Geotechnical Engineers. Chart 3 - Lindeburg, Civil Engineering Reference manual for the PE Exam, 8th Edition. Glacial Clay Soft, g(lb/ft^3). www.geotechnicalinfo.com/soil_unit_weight.html.

"*Upwelling.*" Wikipedia Contributors, Wikipedia (Online). The Free Encyclopedia, Updated May, 14, 2022. (Accessed 07-15-2022) https://en.wikipedia.org/w/index.php?title=Upwelling&oldid=1087705093.

V

"*Variation in drumlin orientation, form and stratigraphy relating to successive ice flows in southern and central Nova Scotia*." By R.R. Stea and Y. Brown (1989). *Sedimentary Geology*, 62, Pages 223-240. https://novascotia.ca/natr/meb/data/mg/map/pdf/map_1993-002_200_cln.pdf.

"*Varietal Classification of New Coconut (Cocos nucifera L.) Forms Identified from Southern Sri Lanka*." By G.K. Ekanayake, S.A.C.N. Perera, P.N. Dassanayake, and J.M.D.T. Everard. Published in *Cocos*, 2010. Pages 41-50. Printed in Sri Lanka.

"*Varieties and Forms of the Coconut Palm Grown in Ceylon*." By Dr. D.V. Liyanage, Botanist, Coconut Research Institute of Ceylon. 10 pages. https://core.ac.uk/download/pdf/52173386.pdf. (Accessed 11-03-21).

"*Vasco da Gama*." History.com Editors, Dec. 18, 2009. Last updated Aug. 21, 2018. https://www.history.com/topics/exploration/vasco-da-gama.

"*Vezo People*." Wikipedia Contributors, Online. Wikipedia, The Free Encyclopedia. Updated Mar. 28, 2022. (Accessed 07-22-2022) https://en.wikipedia.org/w/index.php?title=Vezo_people&oldid=1079737869.

"*View of Oak Island from Chester,*" Colored photo. Courtesy of www.tourismchester.ca.

"*View of Oak Island from mainland*," B/W photo. Courtesy Nova Scotia National Archives.

"View of Smith's Cove through the Trees," 1981. B/W photo. Courtesy of Clara Dennis Fond, 541 No. 96. Nova Scotia National Archives.

"Voyages." Hakluyt Society Ed. IX. Pages 326-337.

"Voyages and Travels Arranged in Systematic Order: Forming a Complete History of the Origin and Progress of Navigational Discovery and Commerce By Sea and Land., from the Earliest Ages to the Present Time." By Robert Kerr, F.R.S. & F.A.S. Edin. Illustrated By Maps and Charts. Volume XVII. William Blackwood, Edinburgh, and T. Cadell, London. 1816.

"Voyages of Samuel De Champlain, Vol. 2, 1604-1610." By Samuel De Champlain. Project Gutenburg eBook. Translated from French By Charles Pomeroy Otis, Ph.D. With historical illustrations By Rev. Edmund F. Slafter, A.M.

W

"Water Treatment in Ancient Scriptures and Writings – The History of Water Filtration." By Daniel, online. www.cleanwater.ie.

"Wealth and Prosperity in Nova Scotia Agriculture – 1851-1871." Uploaded By Kris Inwood on Apr. 8, 2015. *Canadian Historical Review*. Feb. 1993. Pages 240-275. https://www.researchgate.net/publication/5081893_Wealth_and_Prosperity_in_Nova_Scotia_Agriculture_1851-_1871. (Accessed 11-28-21).

"We – The Skythians: The Lie of the Land of Aegypt." By David Alan Ritchie. Dec. 12, 2012. eBook. (Accessed 02-13-22).

"What's Cooking? Food, Drink and the Pleasures of Eating in Old-Time Nova Scotia." A Short History of Food and Foodways in Nova Scotia. www.archives.novascotia.ca/cooking/history/. 2021. P.1-8.

"When a Tree Falls in a Forest." By Rebecca Heisman. Winter 2015. *Northern Woodlands*, Section Decay By the Numbers. (Accessed 07-01-21). https://northernwoodlands.org/knots_and_bolts/tree-falls-in-a-forest.

"When Maldives was Ruled By Catholic Kings Living all the way in Goa." By Ajay Kamalakaran, 2021.Fellow for History & Heritage Writings. Published in *Scroll.in.* https://scroll.in/magazine/1007554/when-maldives-was-ruled-By-catholic-kings-living-all-the-way-in-goa.

"When the Last Live-Oak Dies." By Doug Crowell, Mar. 13, 2016. *Blockhouse Blog*, Mar. 2016. Oak Island Mystery: Sub Section: Oak Island Mystery, 1934, By Frederick Griffin.

"White Ash/Fraxinus americana." By Richard C. Schlesinger. U.S. Department of Agriculture, Forest Service. https://www.srs.fs.usda.gov/pubs/misc/ag_654/volume_2/fraxinus/americana.

"White Ash Silhouette." Natural Resources Canada. Last modified on Apr. 8, 2015. https://tidcf.nrcan.gc.ca/en/trees/factsheet/26.

"White Birch, Betula papyrifera." https://treecanada.ca/resources/trees-of-canada/white-birch betula-papyrifera/.

"*White Elm Silhouette*." Natural Resources Canada. Last modified on Apr. 8, 2015. https://tidcf.nrcan.gc.ca/en/trees/factsheet/76.

"*White Elm/Ulmus americana.*" By Calvin F. Bey. U.S. Department of Agriculture, Forest Service. https://www.srs.fs.usda.gov/pubs/misc/ag_654/volume_2/ulmus/americana.

"*White Spruce/Picea mariana.*" Last modified on Feb. 23, 2022. https://en.wikipedia.org/wiki/Picea_glauca.

"*White Spruce Silhouette*." Plants Database, Natural Resources Conservation Services. US Department of Agriculture. https://plants.usda.gov/.

"*Who Was Samuel Ball*." Published by Deb Minter 07-06-2021. Facebook site, "*Oak Island: History not Myth*." Posted 06-23-2021.

"*Wildflowers: Plant of the Week – Robinia pseudoacacia*." U.S. Forestry Service. www.fs.fed.us/wildflowers/plant-of-the-week/robinia-pseudoacacia.shtml.

*"Wikipedia definition and description of **Acer pseudoplatanus.**" (*Accessed 01-26-22). https://en.wikipedia.org/wiki/Acer_pseudoplatanus.

*"Wikipedia definition and description of **Platanus.**" (*Accessed 01-26-22). https://en.wikipedia.org/wiki/Platanus.

"Windsor, Nova Scotia: A Journey in History." By L.S. Loomer, Jan. 1, 1996. West Hants Historical Society. 397 pages. (Accessed 10-12-21). https://www.werelate.org/wiki/Source:Loomer,_L._S._Windsor,_Nova_Scotia_:_A_Journey_in_History.

"Windthrow." Ontario Department of Lands and Forests. 1953. Forest tree planting. 2nd Edition. Bull. No. R 1. Toronto, Canada: Ontario Department of Lands and Forests, Division of Reforestation. p. 68.

"*W.I.NS., Chester Branch, History of Chester 1759-1767*." Progress-Enterprise Co. 1967.

"With Reference to Attempts Made at Various Times to Recover a Treasure Supposed to be Buried on Oak Island, Nova Scotia – DRAFT." By Frederick Blair. 1930. Public Archives of Nova Scotia, Halifax, NS. MG1 Vol. 383.

"*W. Lavern Johnson Interview Responses*." By D'Arcy O'Connor. Nov. 9, 1976.

"*Wood Decay / Forest Pathology*." By James J. Worrall. USDA Forest Service. kworrall@forestpathology.org. Online @ https://forestpathology.org/general/wood-decay/.

"*Wood: Strength and Stiffness*." Encyclopedia of Materials: Science and Technology. 2001 Elsevier Science Ltd. ISBN:0-08-0431526 pp. 9732-9736 5 pages.

"*Wood Strengths*." By Chris Messier-Messman, U.S. Forest Products Laboratory. *Woodwork Topics*. 10 pages. https://www.woodworkweb.com/woodwork-topics/wood/146-wood-strengths,html. (Accessed 10-03-21).

"*Woodlands Shaped By Past Hurricanes*." By David Dwyer, Forester. *Forest Times*. 1979. 4 pages. www.novascotia.ca/natr/forestry/programs/ecosystems/juan/HP-woodlandsBypast.asp. (Accessed 01-02-21).

"*World Trade in Medicinal Plants from Spanish America, 1715-1815*." By Stefanie Ganger. 2015. University of Cologne, Department of Iberian and Latin American History. *Medical History*, (2015), Vol. 59(1), Pages 44-62, DOI:10.1017/mdh.2014.70. Published By Cambridge University Press, 2015. (Accessed 09-06-21).

Y

"*Yellow Birch Silhouette*." Natural Resources Canada. Last modified on Apr. 8, 2015. https://tidcf.nrcan.gc.ca/en/trees/factsheet/15.

"*Yellow Birch/Betula alleghaniensis.*" Tree Plantation – Yellow Birch Trees. https://www.treeplantation.com/yellow-birch.html.

"*Young Email Responses to David H. Neisen #1*." By Robert S. Young, Jun. 18, 2020. Current owner of Lot #5, on Oak Island, Nova Scotia. www.Oakislandlotfive.com.

"*Young Email Responses to David H. Neisen #2*." By Robert S. Young, Jun. 22, 2020. Current owner of Lot #5, on Oak Island, Nova Scotia. www.Oakislandlotfive.com.

"*Youth. A Narrative*." By Joseph Conrad, 1898. Project Gutenburg EBook. 30 Pages. https://www.gutenberg.org/files/525/525-h/525-h.htm. https://jane-osborne.com/the-mystic-magic-of-the-sycamore-tree-acer-pseudoplatanus/.

Z

"*Zoysiagrass (Zoysia spp.) History, Utilization, and Improvement in the United States*." By Aaron J. Patton, Brian M. Schwartz and Kevin E. Kentworthy, Aug. 2017. Published in *Crop Science*, Volume 57, Issue S1, Pages S37-S72. https://acsess.onlinelibrary.wiley.com/doi/full/10.2135/cropsci2017.02.0074.

Below are the Land Deeds cited in Appendix D, *"Obscured Owners of Oak Island,"* verifying transfer of lot/parcel ownership on Oak Island, 1751-2020. The Light Blue **(number)** following a person or entity is the code assigned to them when tracking their ownership status throughout Appendix D.

Listing By Seller of Oak Island Property

"*Acadia Trust Company (10b), **TO** M. R. Chappell (10), Recorded – Lots **6, 7, 8, 15, 16, 17, 18, 19, 20, 25, 26, 30, 31, 32**, Apr. 20, 1957*." Filed with the Registry of Deeds at Bridgewater and Reg. of Probate, Book 26, P. 195, Quick Claim No. #374. NSNA. ***Lots 6, 7, 8, 15, 16, 17, 18, 19, 20, 25, 26, 30, 31 and 32.***

"*Alexander McNeil (37), **TO** Edward James (24) - Lot **20 & 21**, Jan. 19, 1791*." Lunenburg Co. Land Deeds, Vol. 3, P. 12, No. #16. **– Lot 20 & 21**

"*Alexander Pattillo (42), **TO** Donald McGinnis (32) – Lot **27**, May 3, 1791*." Lunenburg Co. Land Deeds, recorded 03-09-1807, Vol. 3, P. 730, No. #749. **Lot 27**

"*Alexander Pattillo (42), **TO** Donald McGinnis (32) – Lot **1**, Sep. 9, 1794*." Lunenburg Co. Land Deeds, Vol. 4, P. 192, No. #232. **Lot 1**

"*Ambrose Allen (01), **TO** John Monroe (39) – Lot **24**, Oct. 20, 1791*." Lunenburg Co. Land Deeds, Vol. 4, P. 39, No. #52. **Lot 24**

"*Anthony T. Graves (19), **TO** Edward Foras (68) – Lots **5, 9, 10, 11, 12, 13, 14**, Jan. 8, 1834*." Chester Township Land Deeds, recorded 02-12-1834, Vol. 10, P. 323, No. #425. **Lots 5, 9, 10, 11, 12,13, 14**

"*Anthony T. Graves (19), **TO** Frederick Zink (64) – Lots **5, 9, 10, 11, 12, 13, 14**, Feb. 14, 1839*." See Citation #2. **Lots 5, 9, 10, 11, 12, 13, 14**

"*Anthony T. Graves (19), **TO** John Strachan (54) – Lots **5, 9, 10, 11, 12, 13, 14**, Mar. 30, 1841*." Lunenburg Co. Land Deeds, recorded 04-07-1841, Vol. 12 P. 210, 378. Witnesses E. Pike & A. Primrose. **Lots 5, 9, 10, 11, 12, 13, 14**

"*Anthony Vaughan Sr. (57), **TO** Martin Marshall (30) – Lots **9 & 10**, Dec. 22, 1788*." See Citation #2. **Lot 9 & 10**

"*Anthony Vaughan Sr. (57), **TO** Thomas Embree (17) – Lot **4**, Jun 1, 1804*." Lunenburg Co. Land Deeds, Vol. 6, P. 730, No. #750. **Lot 4**

"*Anthony Vaughan Sr. (57), **TO** Nathaniel Melvin (38a) – Lot **17**, Jun. 25, 1790*." Lunenburg Co. Land Deeds, Vol. 3, 450. **Lot 17**

"*Archibald D. Dauphinee (15) et. al, **TO** Clarence James Beamish (04) – Lots and Parcels, Oct. 25, 1944*." Filed with the Dominion of Canada. No. 1142. Nova Scotia National Archives.

"*Archibald D. & Hannah Dauphinee (15), **TO** Gilbert Hedden (22) – Lots **6, 7, 8, 25, 26, 30, 31, 32**, Sep. 13, 1937*." Filed with the Dominion of Canada. Book No. 21, P. 402-403, No. #656. Originally in Book 8, P. 218-219, No. 132. Lots **6, 7, 8, 25, 26, 30, 31, 32**.

"*Archibald D. & Hannah Dauphinee (15) and Margaret Young (63), **TO** Clarence James Beamish (04) – Lot **23 and additional island acreage**, Sep. 28, 1944*." Filed with the Dominion of Canada. No. #1142. NSNA. See description of Lots and parcels. **Lot 23**

"*Burnell S. & Hazel R. Corkum et. al (13a), **TO** George W. Grimm Jr. (20) – Lots **15, 16, 17, 18, 19, 20**, Jul. 27, 1935*." Filed by Dominion of Canada. Book No. 21, P. 115-116, No. #175. Selling party includes: Hazel R. Corkum, Ruby E. Corkum, Wilfred & Audrey W. Corkum, Henry & Mary L. Corkum, and single adults Flora Corkum & Ross Corkum. NSNA. **Lots 15, 16, 17, 18, 19, 20.**

"*Burnell Corkum, Guardian of Andrew & Hope Gorkum (13a), **TO** George W. Grimm Jr. (20) – Lots **15, 16, 17, 18, 19, 20**, Jul. 27, 1935*." Filed with Supreme Court of Nova Scotia. SCONS File #3196. Book No. 21, P. 185-186, No. #297. NSNA. **Lots 15, 16, 17, 18, 19, 20.**

"*Casper Wollenhaupt (58), **TO** John Smith (51a) – Lot **18**, Jun. 26, 1795*." Lunenburg Co. Land Deeds, recorded 07-16-1795, Vol. 4, P. 101, No. #24. **Lot 18**

"*Crown (00), **TO** David Crandell (14) – Lot **15**, 1818*." **Lot 15**

"*Crown (00), **TO** Edward Smith (52) – Lot **2**, Aug. 20, 1766*." Drew Lot. **Lot 2**

"*Crown (00), **TO** Edward Smith (52) – Lot **19**, Aug. 20, 1766*." Drew Lot. **Lot 19**

"*Crown (00), **TO** James Sharp (49) – Lot **28**, 1784*." Granted by Gov. Parr. **Lot 28**

"*Crown (00), **TO** Mary Malay / Jesse White (29) – Lot **16**, 1768*." **Lot 16**

"*Crown (00), **TO** Moses Holt (67)* **– Lot 29**, *1765*." **Drew Lot. Lot 29**

"*Crown (00), **TO** Phillip Payant (43) – Lot **6**, Aug. 20, 1766*." **Lot 6**

"*Crown (00), **TO** Rev. John Secombe (48) – Lot **7**, 1767*." **Lot 7**

"*Crown (00), **TO** Richard Cunningham (66) – Lot **32**, 1784*." **Lot 32**

"*Crown (00), **TO** Samuel Ball (03) – Lot **32**, 1809*." **Lot 32**

"*Crown (00), **TO** Thomas Young (62) – Lot **31**, 1765*." **Lot 31**

"*Daniel Vaughn (57b), **TO** Neal McMullen Sr. (35) – Lot **11**, Oct. 6, 1789*." Lunenburg Co. Land Deeds, recorded 05-25-1797, Vol. 4, P. 230, No. #374. **Lot 11**

"*Daniel Vaughan (57b), **TO** Nathaniel Melvin (38a) – Lots **13 & 14**, Oct. 9, 1790*." Lunenburg Co. Land Deeds, Vol. 3, P. 447, No. #736. **Lots 13 & 14**

"*David Crandell (14), **TO** John Smith (51a) – Lot **15**, Jun. 10, 1819*." Lunenburg Co. Land Deeds, recorded 1820, Vol. 7, P. 413-414. **Lot 15**

"*David Ellis (16), **TO** Alexander Pattillo (42) – Lot **27**, Nov. 17, 1786*." See Citation #2. **Lot 27**

"*David Vaughan (57c), **TO** Anthony T. Graves (19) – Lot **5**, Sep. 19, 1832*." Lunenburg Co. Land Deeds, Vol. 10, #348. **Lot 5**

"*David Vaughan (57c), **TO** Daniel McEnnis (32a) – Lot **2 & 3**, Nov. 2, 1832*." Lunenburg Co. Land Deeds, Vol. 10, P. 491. **Lot 2 & 3**

"*David Vaughan (57c), **TO** John Smith (51a) – Lot **19**, Jul. 1827*." Lunenburg Co. Land Deeds, recorded 04-20-1827, Vol. 8, P. 514, No. #843. **Lot 19**

"*Dr. Jonathan Prescott (45), **TO** Robert Melvin Sr. (38) – Lot **8 & 22**, Jun. 16, 1784*." Lunenburg Co. Land Deeds, recorded 09-27-1790, Vol. 3, P. 429-30, No. #709. **Lot 8 & 22**

"*Duncan Smith (51), **TO** Allen Ambrose (01) – Lot **24**, Feb. 24, 1785*." Lunenburg Co. Land Deeds, recorded 02-28-1785, Vol. 3, P. 154, No. #248. **Lot 24**

"*Edward James (24), **TO** Joseph Bezanson (06c) - Lot **20**, Mar. 7, 1794*." Lunenburg Co. Land Deeds, Vol. 5, P. 140, No. #167. **Lot 20**

"*Edward Smith (52), **TO** Robert Melvin Sr. (38) – Lot **2**, Jun. 17, 1780*." Lunenburg Co. Land Deeds, recorded 08-08-1785, Vol. 3, P. 180-181, No. #295. **Lot 2**

"*Edward Smith (52),* ***TO*** *Timothy Linch/Zink (28/65) – Lot* ***19****, Mar. 28, 1768*." Recorded MG1, Vol. 384, NSNA. (originally Filed in Chester Township recorded on 08-25-1770, Book 1, No. #913, P. 347. **Lot 19.**

"*Erdie Powers (44) ,* ***TO*** *George W. Grimm Jr. (20) – Lots* ***15, 16, 17, 18, 19, 20****, Jul. 27, 1935*." Filed with Dominion of Canada. Book No. 21, P. 114-115, No. #174. Originally filed at Bridgewater, N.S., Book No. #16, P. 485. NSNA. **Lots 15, 16, 17, 18, 19, 20**

"*Francis Conrad et al. (12),* ***TO*** *Archibald D. Dauphinee (15) – Lots* ***6, 7, 8, 25, 26, 30, 31, 32****, Sep. 14, 1937*." Filed with the Dominion of Canada. Deed included joint ownership with Francis & Eva Gertrude Conrad (12) and Ingram & Quesetta May Conrad (12a). Book No. 8, P. 218-219, No. #132 Now No. 655. NSNA. **Lots 6, 7, 8, 25, 26, 30, 31, 32**

"*Frederick Zink (64),* ***TO*** *Anthony T. Graves (19), Lots* ***5, 9, 10, 11, 12, 13, 14****, Mar. 29, 1841*." Lunenburg Co. Land Deeds, recorded 03-29-1841, Vol. 12, P. 210, No. #377. **Lots 5, 9, 10, 11, 12, 13, 14**

"*Genevieve Walls et. al. (59),* ***TO*** *George W. Grimm Jr. (20) – Lots* ***15, 16, 17, 18, 19, 20****, Jul. 27,1935*." Filed with the Dominion of Canada, Book No. 21, P. 184, No. #295. Originally filed at Bridgewater, N.S., Book No. #16, P. 485. NSNA. **Lots 15, 16, 17, 18, 19, 20.**

"*George Bezanson (06b),* ***TO*** *Anthony Vaughan Jr. (57a) - Lot* ***4****, Apr. 19, 1807*." Lunenburg Co. Land Deeds, Vol. 5, P. 30, No. #64. **Lot 4**

"*Gilbert D. Hedden & Margarite C. Hedden (22),* ***TO*** *John Whitney Lewis (10a) – Lots* ***6, 7, 8, 15, 16, 17, 18, 19, 20, 25, 26, 30, 32*** *, May. 26, 1950*." Filed Dominion of Canada Book No. #693 NSNA. Originally in Book 8, P. 218-219, No #132; Book 16, P. 485; Book 21, P. 114, No. 173; Book 21, P. 114 115, No 174; Book 21, P. 115-116, No. 175; Book 21, P. 184, No. 295; Book 21, P. 185-186, No. 297. **Lots *6, 7, 8, 25, 26, 30, 32***, & **Lots *15, 16, 17, 18, 19, 20***. [Lot 31 missing]

"*Hector McLean (34),* ***TO*** *Donald McGinnis (32) – Lot* ***23****, May 4, 1790*." Lunenburg Co. Land Deeds, Vol. 3, P. 418-19; No. #690 & Vol. 3, P. 340, No. #555. **Lot 23**

"*Heirs of Mary Ellen Chapman (09) & Clarence James Beamish (04),* ***TO*** *M. R. Chappell (10) – Lot* ***23****, Jul. 25, 1955*." Filed by the Canada Permanent Trust Company on 02-22-1961, and Book 907, P. 605. On 02-02-1961, NSNA. Lot #23 is described as "*The George McGinnis Property*" as shown on Old Plan #1046, filed with the Department of Lands & Forests, based on survey taken by William Nelson Dy, Sr., dated 07-06-1818. This represents the final transfer of heir ownerships of Lot *23* to M.R. Chappell. **Lot 23**

"*Jacob Hatt (21),* ***TO*** *John J. Bezanson (06a) – Lot* ***31****, Jun. 28, 1797*." Lunenburg Co. Land Deeds, Vol. 5, P. 275-76, No. #377. **Lot 31**

"*Jacob Sheppard (50),* ***TO*** *Nathaniel Melvin (38a) – Lots* ***6 & 7****, Nov. 14, 1815*." Lunenburg Co. Land Deeds, Vol. 7, #188.83. **Lots 6 & 7**

"*Jacob Melvin (38c),* ***TO*** *Daniel McKinnon (32a) – Lot* ***22****, Mar. 14, 1795*." Lunenburg Co. Land Deeds, Vol. 4, P. 140, No. #170. **Lot 22**

"*James Columbus Vaughan (57d),* ***TO*** *David Vaughan (57c) – Lots* ***2, 5, 17****, Jun. 26, 1823*." Lunenburg Co. Land Deeds, Vols. 8, #513, P. 323, 343, 344, No. #513. **Lots 2, 5, 17**

"*James Anderson (02),* ***TO*** *Samuel Ball (03), Lot* ***26****, Nov. 10, 1788*." Lunenburg Co. Land Deeds, recorded 08-25-1807, Vol. 6, P. 25, No. #52. **Lot 26**

"*James Sharp (49) **TO** Donald MacGinnes (32) – Lot **28**, Mar. 3, 1788.*" Lunenburg Co. Land Deeds, Vol. 3, P. 419. No. #689. **Lot 28**

"*James Webber (60), **TO** Daniel Vaughan (57b) – Lots **14**, Oct. 8, 1781*." Lunenburg County Land Deeds, Vol. 2, P. 16, No. #25. **Lot 14**

"*Jeremiah Rogers (47), **TO** David Ellis (16) – Lot **29**, Apr. 2, 1778*." Lunenburg Co. Land Deeds, Vol. 2, P. 208, No. #301. **Lot 29**

"*Jerimiah Rogers (47), **TO** David Ellis (16), Lot **27**, 1778*." Crandall 1818 Survey, **Lot 27**

"*Jeremiah Rogers (47), **TO** J. Bexanson (06c) – Lot **27**, 1782*." See Citation #2. **Lot 27**

"*J.J. Beasanson (06a) Estate, **TO** Donald McGinnis (32) - Lot **29**, 1810*." Lunenburg Co. Land Deeds, recorded 1810, Vol. 6, P. 151, No. #335. **Lot 29**

"*John J. Bezanson (06a), **TO** Samuel Ball (03) – Lot **31**, Aug. 28, 1807*." Lunenburg Co. Land Deeds, Vol. 6, P. 26, No. #56. **Lot 31**

"*John Cochran (11), **TO** Alexander Pittillo (42) – Lot **1**, Feb. 19, 1785*." Lunenburg Co. Land Deeds, Vol. 3, P. 226. **Lot 1**

"*John Kinghorn (26), **TO** Alexander McNeil (37) - Lot **4**, Feb. 24, 1786*." Lunenburg Co. Land Deeds, Vol. 3, P. 355, No. #583. **Lot 4**

"*John Martin (31), **TO** Anthony Vaughan (57) – Lot **4**, Jul. 16, 1793*." Lunenburg Co. Land Deeds, Vol. 6, P. 64, No. #139. **Lot 4**

"*John Munroe (39), **TO** Robert Melvin Sr. (38) – Lot **12**, May 15, 1781*." Lunenburg Co. Land Deeds, recorded 08-10-1790, Vol. 3, P. 425, No. #702. **Lot 12**

"*John Monrow (39), **TO** John J. Bezanson (06a) – Lot **29**, Plumb & Marsh Islands, Nov. 16, 1796*." Lunenburg Co. Land Deeds, Vol. 5, P. 278, No. #330. **Lot 29**

"*John Monroe (39), **TO** Samuel Ball (03) – Lot **24**, Jul. 6, 1799*." Lunenburg Co, Land Deeds, recorded 10-11-1832. Vol. 6, P. 26, No. #55. **Lot 24**

"*John Pulsifer (46), **TO** Samuel Ball (03) – Lot **30**, Apr. 2, 1810*." Lunenburg Co. Land Deeds, recorded 09-20-1810, Vol. 6, P. 175, No. #389. **Lot 30**

"*John Whitney Lewis & Ann Lewis (10a), **TO** Acadia Trust Co. (10b) – Lots **6, 7, 8, 15, 16, 17, 18, 19, 20, 25, 30, 31, 32**, Dec. 5, 1950*." Filed with the Dominion of Canada, NSNA No. #880. (originally in Book 8, P. 218-219, No #132; Book 16, P. 485; Book 21, P. 114, No. #173; Book 21, P. 114-115, No #174; Book 21, P. 115-116, No. #175; Book 21, P. 184, No. #295; Book 21, P. 185-186, No. #297; Book 22, P. 493, No. #891; Book 21, P. 402-403, No. #656. **Lots *6, 7, 8, 15, 16, 17, 18, 19, 20, 25, 30, 31, and 32.*** [Lot 26 missing]

"*Joseph Bezanson (06c), **TO** John Smith (51a) – Lot **20**, Feb. 7, 1807*." Lunenburg Co. Land Deeds, recorded 03-02-1810, Vol. 6, P. 150-51, No. #333. **Lot 20**

"*Margaret M. Young (63), **TO** Archibald A. & Hannah Dauphinee (15) – Lots **23**, Oct. 1, 1931*." Filed with Commissioner of the Supreme Court of Nova Scotia. Book No. 368, Deeded on 09-22-1931. Originally Book No. 20, P.74, No. #69. NSNA. **Lot 23**

"*Martin Marshall (30), **TO** Neal McMullen (35) – Lots **9** & **10**, Jun. 17, 1793*." Lunenburg Co. Land Deeds, recorded 07-15-1795, Vol. 4, P. 99, No. #123. **Lot 9 & 10**

"*Mary Allen Chapman (09) & all heirs of Clarence J. Beamish (04), **TO** M. R. Chappell (10) – land parcels which make up Lots **6, 7, 8, 15, 16, 17, 18, 19, 20, 23, 25, 26, 30, 31, 32**, Jul. 20, 1961*." Filed Nova Scotia Supreme Court, Book 27, P. 339, No. #638. NSNA. Representing inheritance of shares for Kenneth Albert Chapman, Barbara Joan Chapman, Marjorie Ann Chapman, Judith Elizabeth Chapman, Carol Gladys Chapman, Robert Wayne Chapman, and Linda Fay Chapman in selling shares of ownership in the parcel of land lots on Oak Island known as "*south and west part of the island*," "*George McInnis Property*," and the "*James McInnis Property*," making up **Lots *6, 7, 8, 15, 16, 17, 18, 19, 20, 23, 25, 26, 30, 31, 32.***

"*Mary Malay (29), **TO** John Smith (51a) – Lot **16**, Jan. 20, 1798*." Lunenburg Co. Land Deeds, Vol.4, P. 369, No. #539. **Lot 16**

"*Mary Young & Margaret Wallace Young (62), **TO** Hannah Dauphinee & Archibald A. Dauphinee (15) – Lots **23 and additional acreage**, May 27, 1935*." Filed with the City & Co. of San Francisco, State of Calif. Book No. 21, P. 96, No. #148. NSNA. **Lot 23**

"*Melbourne R. Chappell (10), **TO** Dan Blankenship (07) – Lot **23**, Sep. 19, 1975*." Filed Quit Claim Deed in Chester Deed Office, recorded on 09-26-1975, Book 54, P. 161. **Lot 23**

"*Melbourne R. Chappell (10), **TO** David C. Tobias (55) – Lots **6, 7, 8, 15, 16, 17, 18, 19, 20, 25, 26, 30, 31, 32**, Jun. 15, 1977*." Filed in Halifax Co. Land Deeds, Nova Scotia, recorded on 06-29-1977, No. #582. **Lots *6, 7, 8, 15, 16, 17, 18, 19, 20, 25, 26, 30, 31, 32***

"*Nathaniel Melvin (38a), **TO** Neal McMullen Sr. (35) – Lots **13** & **14**, 1806*." Lunenburg Co. Land Deeds, recorded 07-15-1806, Vol. 6, P. 675, No. #690. **Lots 13 & 14**

"*Nathaniel Melvin (38a), **TO** Samuel Ball (03) – Lot **6**, Dec. 7, 1812*." Lunenburg Co. Land Deeds, Vol. 6 P.83, No. #189. **Lot 6**

"*Nathaniel Melvin (38a), **TO** John Smith (51a) – Lot **17**, Mar. 21, 1808*." Lunenburg Co. Land Deeds, recorded 03-21-1808, Vol. 6, P. 63-64, No. #138. **Lot 17**

"*Neil McMullen Smith (35a), **TO** Anthony T. Graves (19) – Lots **9, 10, 11, 12, 13, 14**, Jun. 18, 1832.*" Lunenburg Co. Land Deeds, Vol. 10, #76, P. 56. **Lot 9, 10, 11, 12, 13, 14**

"*Neal McMullen Sr. (35), **TO** Neal McMullen Smith (35a) – Lots **9, 10, 11, 12, 13, 14**, Dec. 21, 1827*." Lunenburg Co. Land Deeds, Vol. 9, P. 53. **Lots 9, 10, 11, 12, 13, 14**

"*Philip Payzant (43), **TO** Robert Melvin Sr. (38), – Lot **6**, Jun. 22, 1768*." Chester Township Public Notice of Will & Testament of land transfer of Lot 6, Oak Island, by Philip Paysant (43) to Robert Melvin (38). Witnessed by John Seecombe (48) and Thomas Floyd. 1 Page. See Citation #2. **Lot 6**

"*Rev. John Seccombe (48), **TO** Robert Melvin Sr. (38) – Lot **7**, Nov. 17, 1767*." Lunenburg Co. Land Deeds, Vol. 1, P. 1770, No. #336. **Lot 7**

"*Robert Melvin Jr. (38d), **TO** Samuel Ball (03) – Lot **8**, May 23, 1798*." See Palmer Papers, Loyalist Melvins-H., Browne/Chester Town Book, Citations, Vol. 6, P. 26, No. #51. **Lot 8**

"*Salome Esther McInnis (widow) (32), **TO** John McInnis (32) – Lot **1**, June 09, 1930*." Lunenburg Co. Land Deeds, Book 20, P. 74, No. #69. **Lot 1**

"*Selvin & Bessie Sellers (19b), **TO** George W. Grimm Jr. (20) – Lots **15, 16, 17, 18, 19, 20**, Jul. 27, 1935*." Filed with Dominion of Canada. Book No. #21, P. 114, No. #173. Originally filed at Bridgewater, N.S., Book No. #16, P. 485. NSNA. **Lots 15, 16, 17, 18, 19, 20**

"*Thomas Embree (17), **TO** George Beazanson (06b) – Lot **4**, Apr. 01, 1807*." Lunenburg Co. Land Deeds, Vol. 6, P. 64, No. #139. **Lot 4**

"*William Bowie, **TO** Hector McLean (34) – Lot **23**, Oct. 10, 1784*." Lunenburg Co. Land Deeds, Vol. 3, P. 340. No. #554. **Lot 23**

"*William Hopkins (23), **TO** Samuel Ball (03) – Lot **25**, Sep. 22, 1787*." Lunenburg Co. Land Deeds, Vol. 6, P. 24. No. #51. **Lot 25**

"*Unknown Source, **TO** Robert Melvin Sr. (38) – Lot **19**, 1784*." See Citation #2. **Lot 19**

END OF BIBLIOGRAPHY

Made in the USA
Coppell, TX
17 November 2022